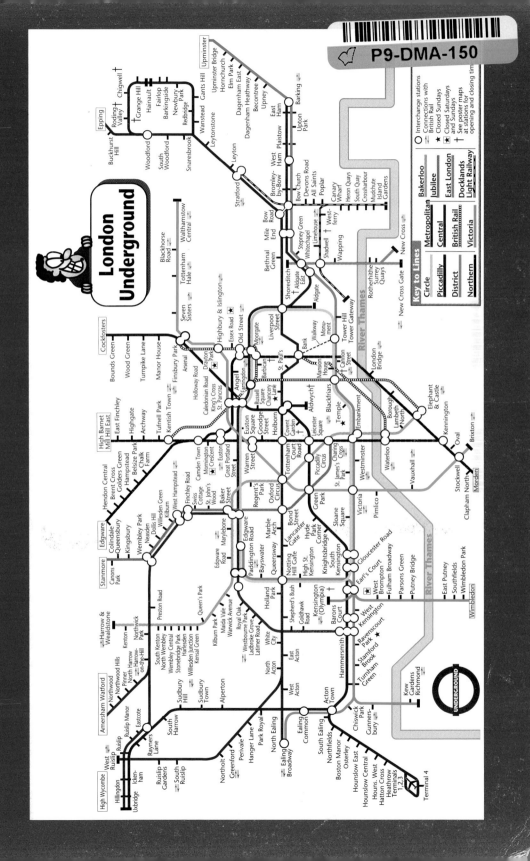

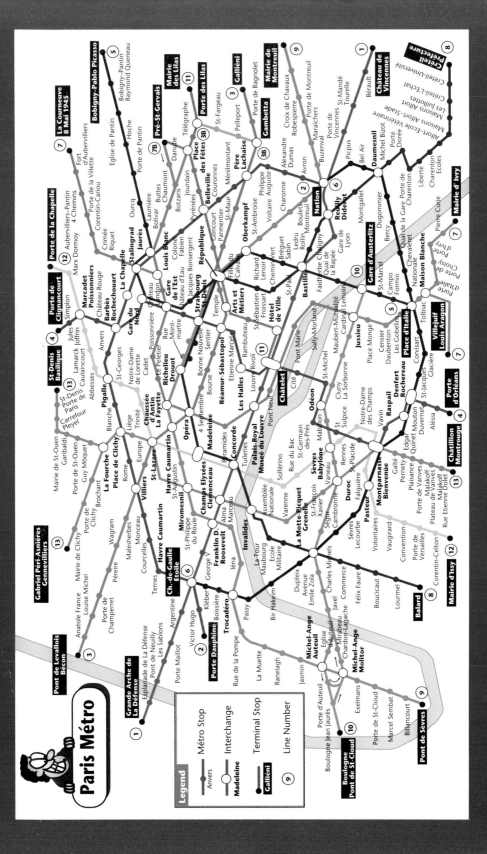

Paris Métro

Legend

— Métro Stop — Anvers
○ Interchange — Madeleine
● Terminal Stop — Galliéni
⑨ Line Number

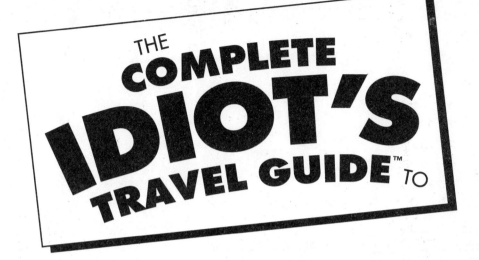

THE
COMPLETE
IDIOT'S
TRAVEL GUIDE™ TO

Planning
Your Trip to
Europe

by Reid Bramblett

Macmillan Travel   Alpha Books
Divisions of Macmillan Reference USA
A Simon & Schuster Macmillan Company
1633 Broadway, New York NY 10019-6785

ISBN 0-02862300-2
ISSN 1096-7672

Editor: Kelly Regan
Special thanks to Peter Bogaty and Ida McCall
Production Editor: Michael Thomas
Page layout: Jenaffer Brandt
Proofreader: Megan Wade
Photo Editor: Richard Fox
Design by designLab
Digital Cartography by Raffaele DeGennaro
Illustrations by Kevin Spear

Special Sales
Bulk purchases (10+ copies) of Frommer's and selected Macmillan travel guides are available to corporations, organizations, mail-order catalogs, institutions, and charities at special discounts and can be customized to suit individual needs. For more information, write to: Special Sales, Macmillan General Reference, 1633 Broadway, New York, NY 10019.

Manufactured in the United States of America

Contents

Part 4 The Heartland: Central Europe   243

16 Paris & Environs   245

17 Amsterdam & the Best of the Netherlands   276

18 Munich & Bavaria   299

Maps

About the Author

 An alumnus of Cornell University's anthropology department and of Macmillan Travel's editorial offices, **Reid Bramblett** has lived, traveled, and worked in Europe on and off over the past 15 years, taking notes all the while. After spending too much time hanging around bookstores dispensing travel advice, he started writing guidebooks; he is also the author of *Frommer's Tuscany and Umbria* and *Frommer's Memorable Walks in New York*. When not on the road researching the nooks and crannies of Europe or chained to his computer writing about them, Reid splits his time between Rome, Italy, and his native Philadelphia.

An Invitation to the Reader

In researching this book, we discovered many wonderful places—hotels, restaurants, shops, and more. We're sure you'll find others. Please tell us about them, so we can share the information with your fellow travelers in upcoming editions. If you were disappointed with a recommendation, we'd love to know that, too. Please write to:

The Complete Idiot's Travel Guide to Planning Your Trip to Europe
Macmillan Travel
1633 Broadway
New York, NY 10019

An Additional Note

Please be advised that travel information is subject to change at any time—and this is especially true of prices. We suggest that you write or call ahead for confirmation when making your travel plans. The author, editors, and publisher cannot be held responsible for the experiences of readers while traveling. Your safety is important to us, however, so we encourage you to stay alert and be aware of your surroundings. Keep a close eye on cameras, purses, and wallets, which are all favorite targets of thieves and pickpockets.

The following abbreviations are used for credit cards:

AE	American Express	EURO	Eurocard
CB	Carte Blanche	JCB	Japan Credit Bank
DC	Diners Club	MC	MasterCard
DISC	Discover	V	Visa
ER	enRoute		

Introduction

Congratulations! You've decided to go to Europe. Sure, you have a lot of decisions to make and details to nail down: where to go, how long to stay, and what to do once you're there—but that's no reason you should feel overwhelmed.

You've made the first smart move by buying *The Complete Idiot's Travel Guide to Planning Your Trip to Europe.* Step by step, I'll tell you how to design the European trip that's right for you. I'll help you get the best deal on everything from plane tickets to rail passes to rental cars. I'll steer you toward outstanding hotels and restaurants, give you my picks of the best sights and destinations, and teach you how to skirt the language barrier. Heck, I'll even help you pack!

This guide will also give you the lowdown on 15 of Europe's most popular destinations. It's all the scoop you need to conquer every city: historical background, local customs, out-of-the-way gems, and all. I'll show you how to barter in the street markets and recommend how much time to budget for seeing each major attraction. Most importantly, by the end of the book, you'll be privy to all the ways of traveling in Europe without breaking the bank.

One caution: So often people travel to Europe and treat it as just one giant museum of the past. Remember, there's a living, breathing, vital culture surounding you. Above all else, open yourself to new experiences, people, sights, and sounds. This guide will take you to Europe and back. The rest is up to you.

Now, here's what you'll find in *The Complete Idiot's Travel Guide to Planning Your Trip to Europe:*

Part 1, "Be Prepared: What You Need to Know Before You Go," walks you through every stage of planning your trip: how to choose which countries to visit; when to go; how to get there; whether to join a tour; how to get around once you're there; what to pack; and what it's all going to cost. Here you'll also find addresses, phone numbers, and Web sites where you can get more information.

Part 2, "European Survival Skills: A Primer," introduces you to life in Europe. You'll read about the finer points of finding that perfect hotel or restaurant. I'll show you how to save on overseas calls and where you can check your e-mail on the road and offer some tips to help you communicate in any language. I'll also speak frankly about everything from bargaining tactics and taking great photographs to dealing with museum overload and safety concerns.

Part 3, "Hail Britannia!: Welcome to the British Isles," begins the destination coverage, with a trio of info-packed chapters covering the best of the British Isles. There's London, from Westminster Abbey to the West End theaters, with excursions to Bath, Stonehenge, and Oxford. In Scotland, we'll wander Edinburgh's Royal Mile, take a gander at Victorian Glasgow, and look for the Loch Ness Monster. On our trip to Dublin, we'll savor a pint o' Guiness and strike out on a tour of the lush Irish countryside.

Part 4, "The Heartland: Central Europe," covers the heart of Europe. We'll start in the north with the great museums and cafes of Paris, the unofficial capital of Europe, before moving on to the canals of Amsterdam. Then we'll explore the Bavarian pleasures and palaces of Munich (with another driving tour thrown in for good measure). From there, it's off to Vienna, in all its 19th-century splendor, and the Swiss capital of Bern, gateway to the snowy Alps. We end our Central European tour in Prague, Eastern Europe's baroque, romantic gem.

Part 5, "Mediterranean Europe," belongs to—that's right—sunny Mediterranean Europe. Here you can time travel back to the ancient wonders of Athens, Delphi, and the Greek islands, as well as Rome and Pompeii. We'll visit Florence and Tuscany, the heartland of wine and the Rennaissance; float a gondola down the canals of Venice; explore Barcelona's Gothic Quarter; and discover the museums of Madrid in between day trips to the venerable cities of Toledo and Segovia.

Extras

The Complete Idiot's Travel Guide to Planning Your Trip to Europe is packed with special features that you won't find in other guidebooks. I've used them to make this guide as user-friendly as possible by highlighting the important information and useful tips to minimize your search for the info you want.

To help you plan your trip, I've included budget and flight information **worksheets**, as well as a train **chart** in chapter 4 that shows you the distance, ticket cost, and travel time between every major city in this book—it even tells you if you'll need to transfer and whether there's an overnight train available.

I've also sectioned off little tidbits of useful information in **sidebars,** which come in five types:

Dollars & Sense

Here you'll find tips on managing your money, especially how to cut costs without jeopardizing the quality of your experience. It's what you need to know to make your enjoyable trip more affordable.

Time-Savers

Look here for ways to avoid lines and hassles, the contact numbers for the local tourist office (a gold mine of information), strategies for getting that last hotel room before it's booked, and general advice on how to streamline the business of traveling.

Tourist Traps

These boxes steer you away from rip-offs, overrated sights, shady dealings, and pitfalls to be avoided; they also address things that are unabashedly touristy (but still fun). "Tourist Traps" also clues you in to the local quirks or unwritten rules that your American upbringing may not have prepared you for—hints will help minimize gaffes, breaches of etiquette, and punches in the nose.

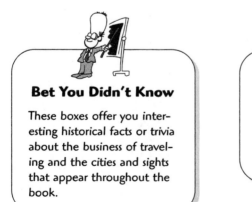

Bet You Didn't Know

These boxes offer you interesting historical facts or trivia about the business of traveling and the cities and sights that appear throughout the book.

Extra! Extra!

Check these boxes for handy hints, insider advice, interesting factoids, and off-the-beaten path sights.

I've awarded a **child icon** ( ) throughout the book to earmark hotels and restaurants that are especially suited to people traveling with children. For hotels, this could mean having a babysitter on call or simply having extra-large rooms and discounts for the kids. For restaurants, it implies a relaxed, family atmosphere and a menu featuring some simpler dishes that won't offend youthful palates and sensibilities—unlike *escargots* and other weird foods adults eat.

Appendices at the back of the book list important numbers and addresses covering every aspect of your trip, from tourist offices and airline 800-numbers to car rental Web sites. You'll also find phrase dictionaries of the survival basics to get your tongue off and running in the local lingos of the most popular European destinations, as well as a glossary of the art and architecture terms that appear most frequently throughout the book.

Acknowledgments

First off, no thanks are enough for my editor Kelly Regan, who shared with me the Herculean task of squeezing so much of Europe into so few pages. My gratitude also goes out to Monica Letzring, for providing London advice and office space. I am grateful for the continued support and encouragement from my parents Frank and Karen, who taught me how to travel. And finally, I thank Frances Sayers for her invaluable help at every step of the way— from planning the research trip and fielding the faxes to pre-editing the manuscript, unearthing all those fast facts, and putting up with my long hours at the computer.

Part 1

Be Prepared: What You Need to Know Before You Go

You've always wanted to go to Europe, but you're asking yourself, "Where to begin? So many countries, so little time!" Before you hop on that plane, you have to plan a trip that takes you to all the places you want to go without running you ragged or draining your pocketbook. This part will walk you through all the steps, guide you past the pitfalls, and arm you with the best insider's advice.

The next six chapters cover everything—from drawing up an itinerary, making a budget, and choosing guidebooks to shopping for plane tickets and choosing a tour operator. I'll also give you the lowdown on when to go, how to pack smart, where to get your passport, whether to get traveler's checks or use your ATM card, and how to get the most out of rail passes and rental cars. Follow my advice, and in no time you'll be winging your way across the Atlantic, itinerary in hand, armed with all the information you need to make this trip the European vacation of your dreams.

Chapter 1

Deciding Where to Go & What to See

This chapter is all about making a wish list and then making your wishes come true. I'll tell you straight off where to find the most famous sights of Europe, but I'll also point you toward many more that you may never have known existed. This chapter will get you thinking about how to make your dream vacation a reality. The chapter ends with some suggested itineraries and whirlwind tours that string together the best Europe has to offer. There are plenty of details you need to get started on a few months before you leave—things like passports (chapter 6), rail passes (chapter 4), plane tickets (chapter 3), and traveler's checks (chapter 5). But for now, just sit back and dream of the possibilities.

Sightseeing Cheat Sheets

How do you find out where to go to see the things in which you're most interested? These useful cheat sheets of the best and brightest among Europe's sights will get your imagination going and help your plans start to take shape. As you read along, highlight or star the sights and places that sound the most exciting. Later you can go back and pull these together into a "dream trip"—one that would most likely take six months to finish. After you make some tough choices, this list will form the basis of your actual itinerary.

Europe

0   160 Km

0   155 mi

North Atlantic Ocean

Norwegian Sea

Bergen

NORWAY

North Sea

DENMARK

GRAMPIAN
Aberdeen
TAYSIDE

Glasgow
Belfast
Edinburgh

IRELAND

DINGLE
PENINSULA
KERRY
COUNTY

Dublin

Liverpool

U. K.

Bath ● Oxford

STONEHENGE ■
Salisbury

London

THE
NETHERLANDS

Hamburg

Amsterdam

Bruges

GERMANY

BELGIUM

Brussels
Liege

Bonn

Frankfurt

English Channel

Le Havre

LUX.

Rothenburg
ob der Tauber

Paris

Strasbourg
Augsburg

LOIRE VALLEY

Munich
BAVARIAN ALPS

FRANCE

Bern
Innsbruck

Atlantic Ocean

Bay of Biscay

Bordeaux

SWITZERLAND
Geneva ●
BERNER
OBERLAND

LIECH.

Milan

Bilbao ●

Arles
Marseille

PROVENCE

Nice ■ **MONACO**

Florence

Porto ●

ANDORRA

Côte d'Azur

TUSCANY

PORTUGAL

Madrid

Barcelona

CORSICA

Lisbon ●

SPAIN

Córdoba

Valencia

ALGARVE

Seville ● ANDALUSIA
Granada
Malaga

SARDINIA

Cagliari

Costa del Sol

Mediterranean Sea

4

SWEDEN
Trondheim
Sundsvall
Gulf of Bothnia
FINLAND
•Tampere
Helsinki
St. Petersburg
Oslo
Gavle•
Stockholm
•Tallinn
ESTONIA
RUSSIA
Moscow •
•Göteborg
Baltic Sea
•Riga
LATVIA
LITHUANIA
Copenhagen
Vilnius •
KALININGRAD
•Minsk
Gdansk
BELARUS
Berlin
•Poznan
•Warsaw
POLAND
•Kiev
Karlovy Vary (Carlsbad)
•Prague
CZECH REPUBLIC
•Krakow
•Lvov
UKRAINE
Danube River
SLOVAKIA
Vienna
KITZBÜHEL ALPS
Bratislava
DANUBE VALLEY
Salzburg
MOLDOVA
Chisinau•
•Odessa
AUSTRIA
•Budapest
HUNGARY
•Cluj-Napoca
Ljubljana
Lake Balaton
SLOVENIA
Zagreb
CROATIA
ROMANIA
Constanta •
Venice
BOSNIA
Sarajevo
•Belgrade
Bucharest •
Black Sea
SERBIA
Varna •
Adriatic Sea
BULGARIA
ITALY
MONTENEGRO
•Sofia
Rome
Titograd
•Skopje
MACEDONIA
Istanbul•
Naples
•Tirana
•POMPEII
ALBANIA
TURKEY
Tyrrhenian Sea
GREECE
Aegean Sea
Ionian Sea
Delphi
Palermo
Athens
CYCLADES
SICILY
PELOPONNESE
CYPRUS
MALTA
CRETE

15 Highlights of Europe

These activities rank as some of the best in Europe (refer to the chapter noted in parentheses for more information):

- ➤ Craning your neck to stare at *God Creating Adam* on Michelangelo's **Sistine Chapel** ceiling in Rome (chapter 22)

- ➤ Wandering amidst the gargoyles atop **Notre Dame Cathedral** in Paris (chapter 16)

- ➤ Driving the **Ring of Kerry** on Ireland's southwest coast, which takes you past stunning coastline, colorful fishing villages, and prehistoric Celtic sites (chapter 15)

- ➤ Eating breakfast 10,000 feet up in the Alps, perched atop the **Schilthorn** and surrounded by snow-capped peaks and glacier-filled valleys unfurling at your feet (chapter 20)

- ➤ Spending a cozy evening ensconced in a **Bavarian beer hall** with a liter mug of Munich's best brew, a basket of warm pretzels in front of you, and an oompah band in the background (chapter 18)

- ➤ Attending a show in one of London's **West End theaters** (chapter 13)

- ➤ Doing a **tapas bar crawl** in Barcelona, sampling tasty tidbits all evening and strolling the people-packed streets (chapter 26)

- ➤ Attending a **classical concert under the stars** in the ruins of an ancient Roman theater above Florence (chapter 23)

- ➤ Clambering around the **ruins of Pompeii,** an ancient Roman city frozen in time by volcanic eruption (chapter 22)

- ➤ Cruising the **Grand Canal** of Venice past elegantly decaying palaces and sinking churches—all for the price of a bus ticket (chapter 24)

- ➤ Picnicking among the ruins of a **Mycenean city** hundreds of feet above the Mediterranean on the Greek island of Santoríni (chapter 27)

- ➤ Making a **pub crawl** through Dublin, draining creamy mugs of Guinness and clapping along to traditional Celtic music (chapter 15)

- ➤ Attending a heavenly performance of the **Vienna Boys' Choir,** who sing their hosannas at a church on the grounds of the lavish Hofburg Palace (chapter 19)

- ➤ Indulging your taste buds by splurging on a **five-star meal** in Paris, the holy city of haute cuisine (chapter 16)

- ➤ Wandering the fanciful and majestic landmarks of Prague—imposing, medieval **Prague Castle** and the romantic, statue-lined **Charles Bridge** (chapter 21)

Some Overlooked Gems

Avoid the tourists and visit these cool places:

➤ **Venetian Islands, Italy.** Venice can be one of Europe's most crowded cities if you just hang around the tourist sights, but just a water-bus ride away are several smaller islands in the Venetian lagoon where glass-blowing, fishing, and lace-making are still ways of life and the locals act as though you're the first stranger they've seen in weeks. There is a whole section on these islands at the end of chapter 24.

➤ **Dingle Peninsula, Ireland.** Dingle pennisula is one peninsula to the north of the Ring of Kerry and just as spectacular without the crowds (see chapter 15).

➤ **Spain.** Spain spent much of this century under a dictatorship, so it stayed off most tourist itineraries. But this country's rich history and amalgamated heritage of Celtic, Roman, Moorish, and Castillian influences make it one of the most diverse and culturally dense nations in Europe. Madrid is stuffed with museums, and Barcelona's an eminently livable city, but if you have to pick one region to explore, make it the southlands of Andalusia, full of Moorish palaces, Christian cathedrals, bullfighting, whitewashed villages, sherry, and flamenco dancing (see chapters 25 and 26).

➤ **Ostia Antica, Italy.** Why go all the way south of Naples to Pompeii when the abandoned ghost streets of Rome's ancient port lie just a metro ride outside the city and are much more romantically crumbling (see chapter 22)?

➤ **Arena Chapel, Padova, Italy.** Giotto was the father of modern art and the genius who kick-started the Renaissance back in the 14th century. Hordes visit his frescoes in Assisi each year, but only a trickle make it to this jewel of a chapel near Venice, almost every inch of which is covered with the master's vibrant painting. While the Assisi cycle recovers from 1997 earthquake damage, this remains the best site to appreciate Giotto and his art (see chapter 24).

➤ **Medieval hamlets and hill towns.** Europe is full of villages and small towns where the leisurely pace of life has helped keep the winding stone streets in a time capsule, places where only a few cars and telephone wires give the 20th century away. Most are just a short bus or train ride outside major cities.

The Most Overrated & Disappointing Sights

The following sights probably won't live up to your expectations:

➤ **Changing of the guard at Buckingham Palace.** Yawn.

➤ **Athens.** The Acropolis, Agora, and Archeological Museum are all musts, but the city itself is dirty, crowded, and boring. Plus it's a Herculean task to get there—if you don't fly, it's three days by train and ferry. Plan to spend more time exploring the fascinating interior of Greece and/or lazing about the islands.

➤ **The Leaning Tower of Pisa.** Don't get me wrong, that bell tower is beautiful to behold, and yes, it does lean off-kilter. The bad news is that you can't climb it because it's closed to the public for the foreseeable future. On the other hand, Pisa does house some less-known but fantastic Gothic sculpture and Romanesque architecture.

➤ **Tourist flamenco shows in Madrid.** Folk evenings set up for tourists are often poor quality and overpriced. I've recommended a few of the more authentic flamenco shows in chapter 25, but keep in mind that these are far from the real thing, which is a spontaneous nighttime ritual whose heartland is Andalusia, not Madrid.

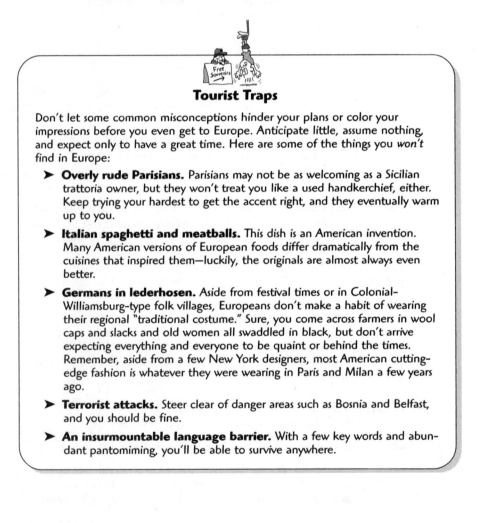

Tourist Traps

Don't let some common misconceptions hinder your plans or color your impressions before you even get to Europe. Anticipate little, assume nothing, and expect only to have a great time. Here are some of the things you *won't* find in Europe:

➤ **Overly rude Parisians.** Parisians may not be as welcoming as a Sicilian trattoria owner, but they won't treat you like a used handkerchief, either. Keep trying your hardest to get the accent right, and they eventually warm up to you.

➤ **Italian spaghetti and meatballs.** This dish is an American invention. Many American versions of European foods differ dramatically from the cuisines that inspired them—luckily, the originals are almost always even better.

➤ **Germans in lederhosen.** Aside from festival times or in Colonial-Williamsburg-type folk villages, Europeans don't make a habit of wearing their regional "traditional costume." Sure, you come across farmers in wool caps and slacks and old women all swaddled in black, but don't arrive expecting everything and everyone to be quaint or behind the times. Remember, aside from a few New York designers, most American cutting-edge fashion is whatever they were wearing in Paris and Milan a few years ago.

➤ **Terrorist attacks.** Steer clear of danger areas such as Bosnia and Belfast, and you should be fine.

➤ **An insurmountable language barrier.** With a few key words and abundant pantomiming, you'll be able to survive anywhere.

The Best Museums

British Museum, London
  (chapter 13)
National Gallery,
  London (chapter 13)
• Louvre, Paris (chapter 16)
Musée d'Orsay, Paris
  (chapter 16)
• Rijksmuseum, Amsterdam
  (chapter 17)
Alte Pinakothek,
  Munich (chapter 18)
Vatican Museums,
  Rome (chapter 22)
Uffizi, Florence
  (chapter 23)
Accademia, Florence
  (chapter 23)
Accademia, Venice
  (chapter 24)
Prado, Madrid (chapter 25)
Archaeological Museum,
  Athens (chapter 27)

The Best Ancient Sites

Stonehenge, England
  (chapter 13)
Newgrange, Ireland
  (chapter 15)
Roman Forum, Rome
  (chapter 22)
• Colosseum, Rome
  (chapter 22)
• Pantheon, Rome
  (chapter 22)
Ostia Antica, near Rome
  (chapter 22)
• Pompeii, near Naples
  (chapter 22)
The Acropolis, Athens
  (chapter 27)
The Ancient Agora,
  Athens (chapter 27)
Delphi, Greece
  (chapter 27)
Akrotiri, Santoríni,
  Greece (chapter 27)

The Best Churches & Cathedrals

Westminster Abbey,
  London (chapter 13)
Salisbury Cathedral,
  England (chapter 13)
• Notre Dame Cathedral,
  Paris (chapter 16)
Chartres Cathedral,
  France (chapter 16)
• St. Peter's, Rome
  (chapter 22)
Duomo, Florence
  (chapter 23)
St. Mark's, Venice
  (chapter 24)
Sagrada Familia, Barcelona
  (chapter 26)

The Best Medieval Castles

• Tower of London
  (chapter 13)
Edinburgh Castle
  (chapter 14)
Neuschwanstein, Germany
  (chapter 18)
Prague Castle (chapter 21)
Castel Sant'Angelo, Rome
  (chapter 22)

The Best Baroque Palaces

Versailles, Paris
(chapter 16)
Fontainebleau, Paris
(chapter 16)
Residenz, Munich
(chapter 18)
Schloss Nyphemburg,
Munich (chapter 18)
Hofburg, Vienna
(chapter 19)
Schönbrunn Palace,
Vienna (chapter 19)

The Best Small Towns

Bath, England
(chapter 13)
Rothenburg, Germany
(chapter 18)
Innsbruck, Austria
(chapter 19)
Siena, Italy (chapter 23)
San Gimignano, Italy
(chapter 23)
Toledo, Spain
(chapter 25)

How to Break Out of the Tourist Mold

Sometimes it pays to take the road less traveled. I always think of Michael Palin in *Around the World in 80 Days*; he cruised the canals of Venice in a garbage scow. When the sightseeing pressures and tourist crowds start eating at you, go off and do something different for a change. Not only will you recharge, but you'll also be rewarded with a unique experience that travelers who stick solely to the major sights miss out on. Be different and try the following:

➤ **Watch some local TV.** When you watch TV in Europe, you're not just being a couch potato, you're having a cultural experience!

➤ **Wander a residential neighborhood** to meet the locals, drink coffee with them, and play cards or backgammon.

➤ **Take a dip in Bern's Aare River.** How many capital cities do you know where the river's still clean enough to swim in (see chapter 20)?

➤ **Rent an apartment or villa** for a week or two instead of doing the hotel shuffle. Pick a city or region to explore and settle in and become a temporary native. Get to be a regular at the cafe on the corner and the little grocery store down the street.

➤ **Visit a small private museum** where some wealthy collector once lived and has left a dusty old mansion jumbled with valuable bric-a-brac ranging from Ming vases and Roman reliefs to medieval suits of armor and the odd painting by a Renaissance master.

➤ **If you're a jogger,** find out where the locals hoof it and join them for a morning's run. You'll clear your head, explore a city park, and perhaps make some new friends.

➤ **Hike in the countryside** for half a day, leaving the crowds of the big city behind.

The Best Romantic Escapes

Travel can accelerate and deepen any relationship. Here are a few ways to make your trip even more romantic:

➤ **Take a dinner cruise on the Seine.** The sights of Paris glide slowly past as you dine on fine French cuisine and float down the moon-dappled waters of the city's famed river (chapter 16).

➤ **View the sunset on the Greek Island of Santoríni.** With the deep green of the crescent caldera at your feet, you watch from the hotel room's private balcony as the fiery sun douses itself in the Mediterranean (chapter 27).

➤ **Picnic among the vineyards of Tuscany.** Buy some soft sheep's cheese, crusty bread, ripe fruit, perfect olives, savory salami, and a bottle of Chianti. Pull off on the side of the road and spread your blanket amid the landscape that inspired Michelangelo and da Vinci (chapter 23).

➤ **Spend an evening at the opera in Vienna.** Indulge in high culture at one of the world's greatest and most elegant opera houses (chapter 19).

➤ **Float along the moonlit canals of Venice on a gondola.** This particular brand of romance comes at a price, but you can't beat the setting (chapter 24).

➤ **Have a long, candlelit dinner anywhere.** European meals were meant for lingering, with multiple courses drawn out over hours, fine wine, and lots of atmosphere.

➤ **Stroll through the city in the evening.** After dinner, wander the streets of town without a guidebook in hand. Cross the Charles Bridge in Prague, climb the Gianicolo in Rome for a nighttime panorama of the city, explore the back streets or promenade down the Riva degli Schiavoni in Venice, or walk along the quays of the Seine or through Montmartre in Paris.

Experiences the Kids Will Love

Every kid has her own tastes, of course, but the following seldom fail to please:

➤ **Stonehenge, England.** Ancient ruins and sites are prime fuel for kids' fertile imaginations (chapter 13).

➤ **Brass rubbings in London.** A giant sheet of black paper, some over-sized gold and silver crayons, and a tomb relief of a knight in full shining armor to transfer occupies kids for an hour while you tour Westminster Abbey, and it gives them a souvenir, too (chapter 13).

➤ **Edinburgh Castle.** Actually, just about any castle is fun (chapter 14).

➤ **Disneyland Paris.** Here's the place to go for the kind of fun only an amusement park can provide (chapter 16).

11

- ➤ **Anne Frank House, Amsterdam.** A great learning experience that kids can relate to. It introduces children to the sobering message of the Holocaust through the eyes of one of their own, a young girl trying to grow up in a land that was against her. It's a tough lesson, but an important one (chapter 17).

- ➤ **Hoge Veluwe Park, Netherlands.** The kids can ride a bike through the greenery and climb around on some of the works in the outdoor sculpture garden of the museum (chapter 17).

- ➤ **Deutsches Museum, Munich.** This museum is one of the best hands-on science and technology museums in the world (chapter 18).

- ➤ **Rothenburg, Germany.** The children can play medieval soldier, patrolling the ramparts of the perimeter wall (chapter 18).

- ➤ **The Ice Palace, Jungfrau.** This place is fun to scramble around in, plus you ride a seemingly gravity-defying train to get up here (chapter 20).

- ➤ **Ski-lift gondolas in the Alps.** Riding a ski-lift gondola is a white-knuckle activity with jaw-dropping panoramas and the thrilling rush of gliding along hundreds of feet off the ground (chapter 20).

- ➤ **San Gimignano, Italy.** This place has it all: medieval ambiance, towers to climb, and a torture museum (chapter 23).

- ➤ **Picnics.** These are a money saver for you, and a break from the best-behavior rules and funny foreign dishes of restaurants for the kids.

- ➤ **Anywhere they can climb or crawl around in tunnels.** This means lots of castles, ancient ruins and tombs, catacombs, the sewers of Paris, town hall towers, cathedral domes and spires...but very few elevators.

Grand Tour: The Two-Week Vacation Edition

You now have an idea of what's out there to see. Before you start gathering information on specific destinations or looking for airfares, however, you'd probably like to know a bit more about the trip as a whole. What can you reasonably expect to do in a given amount of time? How long will it take you to see these famous cities you've always heard so much about? How can you link it all together? Once you know this information, you can approach your travel agent or look into package tours with an idea of what to expect (more on this in chapter 3). Then, you'll be able to hammer out the skeleton of the trip: your very own European itinerary.

All of the nitty-gritty details on just how to arrange the trip will be explained in the chapters to come, but for now, just read on and see how easy it is to take a European vacation. Picking all the places you want to visit is the easy part. Figuring out which of them you have time to see and how long to spend in each city is what takes some work.

Get Real! Five Ways to See It All Without Going Nuts

These few tips will help you whittle down your dream vacation into a feasible trip:

➤ **Delete duplicates.** Every sight in Europe is unique and worth seeing in its own right, but let's face it: After you see a few Greek temples, they all start looking the same. See Versailles or Fontainbleau, but not both. In the Alps, the Jungfrau sounds good, but so does the Shilthorn. Pick one and move on.

➤ **Stay centered.** Especially on a first trip, you may want to leave out some of the geographically peripheral areas—Spain and Portugal, Scandinavia, and especially Greece—because they take so long to get to. Use your limited time seeing as much of Europe as you can, rather than traveling days to get to a remote corner. I've kept this idea in mind when choosing the destinations you'll read about in parts 3 through 5.

➤ **Sidetrip selectively.** Day trips add variety, and I highly recommend them. But if you only have one day in Florence, don't try to fit in Pisa—you'll end up seeing neither. Pick your excursions wisely, and don't let them take away time from the main city you're visiting. Budget a full day to see any destination that's more than a city bus ride away.

➤ **Split up.** Are you planning six days in London because everyone in the family wants to see different things? Don't tour Europe as Siamese triplets. You can spend another few hours in the British Museum while your spouse visits Shakespeare's Globe Theatre and your teenager takes a bus tour out to Windsor Castle. What would take the whole clan a day and a half to see has just been conveniently reduced to a single afternoon.

➤ **You shall return.** Assume you'll be coming back. No matter how much you pack in, there will still be a lot left to see. Europe will wait.

How Will I Allocate My Time?

The following table gives you an idea of the minimum reasonable amount of time it takes to "do" Europe's major cities: to settle in, see the major sights, get a taste for the place, and maybe make one day trip. You can spend less time, but you'll be missing big chunks for sure. Also remember to add on at least an extra day for each major excursion or sidetrip you'd like to take, such as Bath or Stonehenge from London, Versailles from Paris, or Toledo from Madrid. Of course, you won't run out of things to do if you stay longer anywhere, and I highly recommend more days than this minimum for some cities in particular—Rome, Paris, and London come to mind. Most of these cities you couldn't exhaust in a lifetime of diligent sightseeing.

Table 1.1   How Much Time Should I Spend in Each City?

Amsterdam	2 to 3 days	Madrid	2 to 3 days
Athens	1 to 2 days	Munich	1 to 2 days
Barcelona	2 to 3 days	• Paris	3 to 4 days
Bern/Alps	1 to 3 days	Prague	2 to 3 days
• Florence	2 to 3 days	• Rome	3 to 4 days
Edinburgh	1 to 2 days	Venice	2 to 3 days
Dublin	1 to 2 days	Vienna	1 to 3 days
London	3 to 4 days		

Many travelers returning to Europe for the second or third time are discovering that there's so much to see outside of the major cities that they're forgoing trains and hotels for rented cars and villas. They go hill town-hopping and explore one tiny corner of Europe at a time, traveling at a leisurely pace away from the crowds and pressures of a rigorous sightseeing schedule in the big city. On a first visit, however, you'll probably want to pack in as many major cities and sights as possible, and there's nothing wrong with that.

The whirlwind tour still remains the best first-time visit. It gives you a sampling of everything, so you'll know which bits to come back and explore in more depth. It also gets all the "required" sights out of the way, so when you return (and you *will* come back), you can concentrate on discovering Europe's lesser-known sights and facets on your own. You won't exhaust Europe in one trip, and it's so easy to come back once you realize how effortless and enjoyable travel here is. I've been returning for 15 years and haven't even come close to seeing all I want to see.

Try This for Size: Itineraries That Work

Because most Americans get just two precious weeks of vacation, I've crafted most of these tours to fit that schedule. I've also included a three-week whirlwind extravaganza if you can carve out that much time for your trip. You'll notice that these itineraries include the two extra "freebie" days that the weekends snag for you when planning a vacation. Sure, you'll be exhausted at work on Monday, but boy will you have stories.

Keep in mind that open hours vary from season to season. Because summer is the most popular travel time, I arranged these itineraries assuming summer schedules. They may have to be tweaked if you're visiting in the off-season or if one of the days you happen to be in town falls on a Monday, Sunday, or another day when some sights may be closed. On occasion, I'll include specific train times and schedules, but bear in mind that this is just to get you thinking about how early to catch a train; rail timetables can and will change regularly, so always check the train times listed here against more current schedules (chapter 4 will show you how to do just that).

The "I Got Two Weeks & I Wanna See It All" Tour

Day 1   Your overnight plane lands in **London** (chapter 13) early. Head to Victoria Station and buy a Travelcard, book a Eurostar seat for moving on to Paris in a few days, and visit the tourist office for brochures on the Original London Sightseeing Tours (bus) and London Walks (walking tours). It'll be lunchtime by the time you check into your hotel, freshen up, and call the Globe Theatre to see whether a play is on for tomorrow at 2pm (if so, book tickets).

Time-Savers

Balance your itinerary with spontaneity, both in planning the whole trip and with the daily schedule. Although the two-week version here is whirlwind, leave some elbow room in the agenda if you're taking a longer trip. You need this both for relaxation en route—for at least every 10 to 15 days of rigorous sightseeing, plan on two days of doing little or nothing—and for changes of plans: fitting in unexpected opportunities such as a festival, taking day trips, or choosing to spend more or less time in a place once you get the feel of it.

Try to finish lunch by 2pm, and then head to the nearest stop on the map for the Original London Sightseeing Tours and take the 90-minute bus loop past the major sights of London. When you're good and oriented, plunge right into the sightseeing at the National Gallery, which will introduce you to many of the artists and eras you'll be seeing more of as the trip goes on. Have a traditional British dinner at Rules or Porters and try to get to bed early to start resetting your internal clock. You'll be getting up early in the morning.

Day 2   Today's the day for the London of the Middle Ages and Renaissance. Be at the Tower of London by 9:30am to get in on the first guided tour of this medieval bastion and its Crown Jewels. Afterward, visit St. Paul's cathedral and grab some lunch. Then head across the Thames River to tour the newly rebuilt Shakespeare's Globe Theatre and experience the open-air setting in which a play by the Bard was meant to be seen. If possible, see a play here (they start at 2pm). The tour itself only takes an hour; a play takes two to four hours.

After a particularly long play, you'll have to grab a quick dinner; if you just do the tour, you have the late afternoon to spend as you'd like. Either way, finish dinner by 6:30 or 7pm so you can join whichever historic pub walk London Walks is running that evening (they start at 7 or 7:30pm; the brochure will tell you where to meet). After your introduction to British ales and pub life, call it a night.

Day 3 Yesterday was medieval, but today you're going to stiffen your upper lip with some Victorian-era British traditions. Start out at 9am paying your respects to centuries of British heroes, poets, and kings buried at Westminster Abbey. Drop by the Victoria & Albert Museum for miles of the best in decorative arts and sculpture. Have a snack (not lunch) on your way to the world's grandest and most venerable department store, Harrod's. After a bit of high-class browsing inside, stop by the fourth floor's Georgian restaurant at 3pm sharp for a proper British high tea. Linger and enjoy it.

Head over to Big Ben and the buildings of Parliament around 5:30pm and, if government is in session (October through July), get in line to go inside and watch Parliament at work, vilifying one another in a colorfully entertaining way that makes the U.S. Congress seem like a morgue. Because you'll be out of there late, make sure you reserve a restaurant that specializes in late, after-theater meals (Chor Bizarre is a good choice).

Day 4 Spend the morning plunging into the British Museum, which catalogues human achievement across the world and throughout the ages. Take a quick lunch and embark on one of London Walks' historical tours at 2pm. It'll be done before 4pm, so you'll have just under 2 hours to head over to the Tate Gallery and indulge in some of the best art of the 19th and 20th centuries. Call it a night early so you can be up for the train to **Paris** tomorrow.

Day 5 Take the earliest Eurostar train through the Channel Tunnel to **Paris** (chapter 16). Get settled in your hotel and then have lunch. Afterwards, head to the Rodin Museum and then hustle on over to the Eiffel Tower before sunset to get your requisite picture and drink in the panorama of Paris. Treat yourself to a first-class dinner to celebrate your arrival in one of the world capitals of cuisine.

Day 6 Be at the cathedral of Notre Dame early (8am) to beat the crowds, and then clamber up the cathedral towers once they open to examine the famed gargoyles up close. Notre Dame affords a much more intimate view across Paris than the Eiffel gets you. When you get back to ground level, cross the square in front of the cathedral and descend into the Archaeological Crypt to puzzle out Paris's earliest origins.

Continue to the far end of the square for the jewelbox chapel of Sainte-Chapelle, hidden amidst the government buildings. Grab some lunch on your way to the Picasso Museum. Don't stay too long with the works of this 20th-century master (leave by no later than 2:30pm) because one of Paris's biggies lies ahead: the impressionist treasure trove of the Musée d'Orsay. Stay in there as long as they'll let you before heading off to dinner.

Day 7   It's day trip time. Catch the RER out to **Versailles** to spend a day exploring the palace to end all palaces, where a string of kings Louis held court in the powdered-wig exuberance of the 18th century. Take at least one guided tour, and save time to wander the acres of gardens. You should return to Paris in time for a pleasant stroll down the quays of the River Seine before dinner.

Day 8   Get up early and head to the Gare de Lyon train station to leave your bags and reserve a couchette for tonight's train to Venice. I hope yesterday's day trip helped you recharge because this morning it's off to the Louvre, which is French for "ridiculously huge museum." Pay your respects▸ to *Mona Lisa* and the *Venus de Milo* and have lunch in the cafeteria.

By midafternoon, give up on trying to see it all and take the Métro out to the original Bohemian quarter of Montmartre. Wander the streets, peek at windmills and vineyards, or people-watch and write postcards at a classic Parisian cafe, where you can rustle up an early dinner. Start back down to the Gare de Lyon by 7pm, so you won't be late for the 8pm overnight train to **Venice.**

Day 9   When you arrive in **Venice,** check out the next morning's schedule for trains on to Florence and leave your pack in the lockers; you can live out of the daypack for one night, and this trick lets you check into your hotel later in the day so you don't waste any time. Then dive into the city of canals (well, not literally). Head straight to one of Europe's prettiest squares, the canalside Piazza San Marco. Tour the glittering mosaic-filled cathedral and ride the elevator to the bell tower for sweeping views across the city and its canals.

Take the "Secret Itineraries" tour of the Doge's Palace at noon for a behind-the-scenes look at Venetian history and intrigue. Have a snack on your way to check into your hotel in the early afternoon, and then see the masterpieces of the Accademia in the midafternoon. Take a gondola ride before dinner and wander the quiet, romantic streets a while after your meal. Try to get to bed at a reasonable hour, because you'll have to get up early.

Day 10   Head to the train station at least 90 minutes before your train (this gives the slow water bus time to get there). Take the first morning train you can to **Florence,** call around for a room, and then drop your bags by the hotel. Have a lunch on the go so you don't waste time that's better spent seeing the Duomo (cathedral), climbing its ingenious and noble dome to get a city panorama, and marveling at the mosaics inside the adjacent baptistery. By 3pm, start heading a few blocks down to the world's premier museum of the Renaissance, the Uffizi Galleries. Spend the rest of the afternoon communing with Giotto, Botticelli, da Vinci, Michelangelo, Raphael, Caravaggio, and Titian until they boot you out the doors at 7:30pm. Have a Tuscan feast at Il Latini before bed.

Day 11   Be in line at the Accademia when it opens so you can see Michelangelo's *David* before the crowds arrive. If you don't linger too long, you can swing by Santa Maria Novella church before lunch for a look at its Renaissance frescoes (a young apprentice named Michelangelo helped out on the Ghirlandaio fresco cycle). Find a phone (this is important) and call ahead to Rome's Galleria Borghese to make an appointment "for tomorrow at 3pm" (a phrase which, in Italian, is pronounced "pair doh-*ma*-nee alle *queen*-dee-chee").

After lunch, while the city is shut down for the midday *riposo* (nap), make your way over to the Giotto frescoes in Santa Croce church, Florence's version of Westminster Abbey and the final resting place of Michelangelo, Galileo, and Machiavelli. On your way back to the heart of town, stop by Vivoli for the best *gelato* (ice cream) you'll probably ever have. Cross the jewelry shop-lined medieval bridge called Ponte Vecchio to get to Oltrarno, the artisan's quarter, and the Medici's grand Pitti Palace, whose painting galleries will keep you occupied until closing time at 7pm. Oltrarno is full of good, homey restaurants where you can kick back, toast your 36 hours in Florence, and vow a return.

Day 12   Get up extra early to catch the 7:30am train to **Rome.** You'll pull in around 9:15, which gives you plenty of time before lunch to check in, splash your face, and see the ancient Pantheon and the nearby church of Santa Maria Sopra Minerva, with its Michelangelo statue and Filippino Lippi frescoes. After a quick bite, head to Rome's prettiest square, Piazza Navona. Station yourself at Tre Scalini's outdoor cafe tables to enjoy their famous tartufo dessert while you watch children play soccer under the shadow of the fountains.

By 2:20pm, you should be waiting for the bus on Corso del Rinascimento. Grab the 116 minibus to the Porta Pinciana (you'll see a park). Enter the park and take the first path on your right (Viale di Museo Borghese) to get to the Galleria Borghese by 3pm. Tour its collections of Bernini sculptures and Raphael paintings until it closes at 5pm. Make your way to the top of the lively Spanish Steps, where you can mingle for a while before window-shopping down fashionable Via dei Condotti and the surrounding streets. By the time you get to the Corso, one of Rome's main drags, the evening *passeggiata* stroll will be in full swing, and you can strut your stuff with the Romans until it's time for a hearty and well-deserved dinner.

Day 13   Rome's all about Caesars, right? Start off your second day exploring the ruins of the Roman Forum, where orators once held forth, senators debated, and Julius Caesar strode through the streets. Unfortunately, little is left to see, but at least it will be easier to be out of there by 11:30 and on your way to see Michelangelo's *Moses* in the church of San Pietro in Vincoli before it closes at 12:30pm. After lunch, pay a visit to the Colosseum (you just look at it, take a peek inside at the floor plan, and you're done) and catch a bus back up Via de Fori Imperiali to Piazza Venezia.

Nearby is the elevated square Piazza del Campidoglio, where the Capitoline Museums will entertain you with ancient sculpture and Renaissance and baroque painting until 7pm. Make sure that before sunset, you go around the back right side of the central building on Piazza del Campidoglio where you're treated to a surprise panorama of the Forum from above, with the Palatine Hill and the Colosseum as a backdrop. Have dinner in the Old City tonight.

Day 14   You spend today on the other side of the river from the bulk of old Rome. Be up bright and early (I know, I never let you sleep in!) so that you beat the legions of tour buses to the Vatican Museums. Spend all morning there, drinking in such artistic wonders as Raphael's *Transfiguration,* Caravaggio's *Deposition,* the Raphael Rooms, and Michelangelo's incomparable Sistine Chapel ceiling. The Museums close at 1:45pm most of the year, so ◂ grab a snack on your way around the Vatican walls to visit the grandiose church of St. Peter's. See Michelangelo's *Pietà* and tour the tombs of popes • under the basilica before climbing its dome for a panoramic sweep of the city across the river. If you finish with St. Peter's quickly, you may want to head to the pope's nearby Renaissance fortress, the Castle Sant'Angelo on the river, which has a nifty museum on the castle's history and lots of medieval weapons and armor to please the kids. Either way, spend the evening in the medieval neighborhood of Trastevere, with its winding evocative streets, floodlit church facade mosaics, and hordes of excellent Roman restaurants.

Day 15   Spend your last full day in Europe outside the big city at Tivoli, a nearby hill town full of palaces, gardens, and the ruins of Emperor Hadrian's wildly eclectic villa. Return to Rome in time for dinner and afterward make your way to the famous Trevi Fountain. It's tradition to toss a few coins in, which ensures that one day you'll return to this Eternal City.

Day 16   Most flights from Rome back to the United States leave either in the morning or early afternoon. Either way, the day's a wash; you'll spend the morning getting to the airport and the day in the air.

The Grand Tour of Europe in Three Weeks

Days 1 through 8   The first week of this trip is the same as the "I Got Two Weeks..." trip—**London and Paris.** On the morning of day 8, go to the Gare de l'Est station, leave your bags, and reserve a couchette for the overnight train to **Frankfurt.** Because that train doesn't leave until after 10pm, you can spend a bit more time in the Louvre and in Montmartre on this tour than in the last one. Then it's off to Germany.

Day 9   In **Frankfurt,** pick up a rental car, which you booked before you left the United States, and drive **Bavaria's Romantic Road** (chapter 18). Drink velvety Franconian wine while you have your lunch amid the baroque palaces of Würzburg; visit the intricate, 1510 carved altarpiece at Crelingen; and spend the late afternoon in **Rothenberg,** Germany's perfect medieval town of half-timbered houses and cobblestone streets. The day trippers clear out in the evening, so you'll have Rothenburg's medieval charms all to yourself as you prepare to spend the night here.

Day 10   Walk the walls of **Rothenburg** in the morning and then drive the rest of the Romantic Road with stops in the cute village of Dinklesbühl and the noble Renaissance city of Augsburg. Arrive in **Munich** (chapter 18) in time to have dinner, toss back a few liter mugs of Bavarian brew in a wood-lined beer hall, and check into a hotel for the night.

Day 11 Drop off the rental car, put your pack in the train station lockers, and book an overnight couchette tonight for Venice. You don't have time to do all of Munich, so I recommend a high-speed tour through the baroque splendors of Residenz in the late morning. After lunch, visit the medieval collections of the Bavarian National Museum and the Renaissance master-pieces of the Altes Pinakothek, where you can stay until it closes (if you luck into town on a Tuesday or Thursday, that gives you until 8pm; otherwise, you have until 5pm). The overnight train to **Venice** leaves very late (around 11:30pm), so after a rib-sticking dinner, bide your remaining time in Munich in true Bavarian style at the Augustinerkeller beer hall, five long blocks past the train station.

Day 12 When you get to **Venice** (chapter 24), check into your hotel and then head to the center of town. See San Marco and take the "Secret Itineraries" tour of the Doge's Palace. After a light, late lunch, tour the Accademia, Venice's top painting gallery, and have a leisurely dinner. After dinner, call ahead to Florence and find a hotel room for tomorrow night because you'll be arriving in town late.

Day 13 In the morning, head over to the Scuola Grande di San Rocco for a festival of Tintoretto paintings, and then forget about sightseeing and spend the early afternoon lost in the alleyways of the city, discovering the local, small-town version of Venice off the well-worn and crowded tourist paths. Be on late-afternoon train to **Florence** (chapter 23), so you can arrive in time to check into your hotel and grab a late dinner.

Day 14 Be at the Accademia before it opens to beat the lines and crowds to Michelangelo's *David*. Then pop over to Santa Maria Novella and its early Renaissance frescoes. After lunch, hit the Duomo, clamber up inside its inge-nious dome for a Florence panorama, and visit the baptistery with its glitter-ing medieval mosaics.

Be at the Uffizi Galleries down the road by 2 or 3pm so you can get in a good four to five hours inside, drinking in the splendors of Renaissance painting though such works as Botticelli's *Birth of Venus* and da Vinci's *Annunciation*. After overloading on great art, treat yourself to a massive Florentine steak and powerful Tuscan red wine at dinner. You've earned it.

Day 15 In the morning, hit the Bargello sculpture museum to see Donatello and early Michelangelo statues. Then head off to more Michelangelo sculp-tures in the Medici Chapel. The Chapel is surrounded by the stalls of Florence's outdoor leather market, so wander a while, perhaps shop a little, and pop into the food and produce market in the middle for an ultra-fresh lunch on the go. *Don't forget*: Before lunch, stop by a pay phone and call ahead to Rome to reserve tickets at the Galleria Borghese for tomorrow at 3pm, as explained under day 11 of the two-week tour.

Spend the riposo hours in Santa Croce with its tombs of famous Florentines, frescoes by Giotto, and a leather school. Nearby is Vivoli, serving the best gelato the world has ever known. In the afternoon, head across the Ponte Vecchio to the Pitti Palace for its painting galleries. The Pitti's neighborhood, the Oltrarno, is full of excellent restaurants in which to spend your final hours in the city of the Renaissance.

Days 16 through 19　Starting with an early-morning train to **Rome** (chapter 22), spend days 16 through 19 exactly as days 12 through 15 on the "I Got Two Weeks..." itinerary, though be sure to fit in the Trevi Fountain on Day 17. On the morning of Day 19, take your bags to the train station to check them at the left-luggage office and to book a couchette for the overnight train to Bern before heading out to **Tivoli** for the day. Leave Tivoli by 4pm to get back to Rome by 5pm in order to pick up some picnic supplies for dinner on the train. The **Bern** train leaves around 7:50pm.

Day 20　This is a day of many train connections and spectacular, kiss-the-sky vistas. I'm including precise hours here because you need to keep a close eye on your watch to make all the train connections. Schedules may change, however, so double-check everything with your travel agent before you go. The train from Rome pulls into **Bern** (chapter 20) around 6:35am. You have about 45 minutes to exchange some Swiss francs, check your bags, grab a snack for breakfast, and reserve a couchette on tonight's Amsterdam-bound overnight train out of Bern.

Then catch the first train you can to **Interlaken.** Get off at the Interlaken Ost station and grab the first Jungfraujoch-bound train. You'll be 11,333 feet high by 11am, drinking in the views across snow-capped Alps and scrambling through the glacier-carved Ice Palace. To avoid cutting all these train connections too closely, take one last panoramic look into the majestic Alpine sweep and be on the 4pm train back down to Interlaken, where you'll catch a train back to Bern. Here you have about two hours to grab a *quick* dinner and then collect your bags before collapsing into your reserved bunk on the overnight train to **Amsterdam** (chapter 17), the final stop.

Day 21　You went to sleep in Europe's highest country and wake up in its lowest. What an adventure! You're probably worn out from all the running around, so start the day in Amsterdam relaxing with a canal cruise, ogling all those skinny, gabled 17th-century town houses. After lunch, take a tour through the infamous Red Light district, and then sober yourself up with a visit to the Anne Frank House across town, where the young Jewish diarist hid for years from Nazi occupiers. If you're tired, take an early dinner and hit the sack.

Day 22　Be at the Van Gogh Museum when it opens at 10am and spend the morning in the company of one of the 20th century's greatest masters. Recharge your batteries with a tour of the Heineken Brewery (summer only, take the 1pm tour), and then delve into the Rijksmuseum and spend the afternoon in the company of artists such as Rembrandt, Rubens, and Vermeer. In the evening, stroll the trendy Leidseplein district and feast like a king on an Indonesian *rijsttafel* at one of the neighborhood's many restaurants.

Day 23   As in the two-week tour, most flights from Amsterdam back to the United States leave in the morning or early afternoon, so you'll spend the morning getting to the airport and the day flying home.

Art Lovers' Europe

For this trip, you can work out the daily sightseeing schedules on your own, depending on what most floats your artistic boat. Most cities have 2½ full days of sightseeing time budgeted, which should be enough to give the major museums a good once-over.

Days 1 through 3: London   Your first order of business should definitely be the medieval, Renaissance, and baroque masterpieces of the National Gallery. The other great art collection is the Tate Gallery, which covers the British greats as well as international art of the 19th and 20th centuries from impressionism to contemporary works. You may also want to stop by the National Portrait Gallery; it exists more for the historical interest of the subjects, but it has some artistically fine portraits as well (especially by Holbein, Reynolds, and Warhol).

No museum buff should miss the Victoria & Albert Museum, which has London's best sculpture collection (Donatello, Giambologna, Bernini) and a fascinating exhibit on artistic fakes and forgeries, in addition to miles of decorative arts. If you're into Christopher Wren's brand of Renaissance architecture, the city's full of it; his greatest hit is St. Paul's. I can't imagine a trip to London without calling on the British Museum, at least briefly, where you can get the best overview of the ancient world's art forms (Greek, Roman, Egyptian, Assyrian, Asian, Indian, and Islamic). On the morning of **Day 4,** catch an early Eurostar train to Paris.

Days 4 through 6: Paris   You'll want to explore the treasures of the Louvre over a full day at least. Fans of impressionism and French art in general should devote at least two-thirds of a day to the Musée d'Orsay. Paris has so many smaller art museums it's hard to choose from among them and nearly impossible to squeeze them all in. Whole museums are devoted to single artists (Rodin, Picasso, Delacroix, Le Corbusier, Dalí), and others are devoted to eras—the medieval at Thermes de Cluny, the modern in the Pompidou. Two of my favorite, slightly lesser-known art treasures are the Delacroix murals in the church of St-Suplice and Monet's 360° *Waterlilies* in specially built basement rooms of the Orangerie, off Place de la Concorde. At the end of **Day 6,** hop on the overnight train to Florence.

Days 7 through 9: Florence   Reserve one entire day for the Uffizi galleries, a living textbook of Renaissance development. The Pitti Palace's Galleria Palantina covers the High Renaissance and baroque eras thoroughly. Michelangelo's *David* and his unfinished *Slaves* in the Accademia are a must, and Donatello reigns supreme at the Bargello sculpture museum. Fra' Angelico frescoed his brothers' cells at his monastery of San Marco, and they've set up a fine museum to him there. Florence's churches are so richly decorated I scarcely know where to begin: Giotto in Santa Croce; Ghirlandaio and Masaccio in Santa Maria Novella; Donatello and Michelangelo at San Lorenzo and again in the Museo dell'Opera dell Duomo. Then there's Brunelleschi's architecture from the Duomo to Santo Spirito to the Pazzi chapel at Santa Croce. Florence is one place where you'll run out of time before you run out of art.

Days 10 through 12: Rome   Take the morning train here from Florence on Day 10 and start in on the baroque period with Bernini's sculpture in Piazza Navona, Piazza Barberini, and the Galleria Borghese. The Vatican Museums (home to the Raphael Rooms, the Pinacoteca, and Michelangelo's Sistine Chapel) will take two-thirds of a day. The Capitoline Museums split their collections between ancient sculpture and mosaics and Renaissance and baroque painting. Some smaller museums include the Doria Pamphilij collections and the Galleria Nazionale d'Arte Antica at Palazzo Barberini.

Rome's churches are blanketed with art, from Filippino Lippi's frescoes in Santa Maria Sopra Minerva (where you'll also find Michelangelo's *Risen Christ*) to the Caravaggios in Santa Maria del Popolo and Michelangelo's *Moses* in San Pietro in Vincoli. Again, you're unlikely to run out of art to ogle in just three days here. On the evening of Day 12, get on the overnight train for the long haul to Barcelona.

Day 13: Barcelona   You should definitely take in the early works at the Picasso museum and make a survey of Gaudí's whimsical architecture in this Catalonian capital. On this tour, however, Barcelona's more of a way station and a one-day breather before we press on. At the end of the day, hop the overnight train to Madrid, where we'll plunge into its myriad museums.

Days 14 through 16: Madrid   Spain is the land of Picasso, Velàzquez, Goya, El Greco (by adoption), Murillo, and Ribera. You have a day to devote to the Prado and another day to split between the Reina Sofía museum (home of Picasso's *Guernica*), the Thyssen-Bornemisza Museum, and—if you can stand any more art at this point—the Museo Làzaro Galdiano. Day 16 is spent getting back home.

Castles, Palaces, & Moonlit Walks: Romantic Europe

As with the art tour, I'll leave much of the daily scheduling up to you in this tour—nothing kills a romantic mood more than being hurriedly shuttled from place to place.

Days 1 through 4: Paris   The mere mention of the City of Light conjures up romantic images, so it's a great place to start. See your fair share of Paris's famed museums—the Musée d'Orsay has both French Romantic-era painters and scads of those lovable impressionists, but take time to enjoy the finer points of Parisian life. Linger at cafe tables for hours, spend an evening strolling Montemartre, have long meals at fine restaurants and cozy bistros, explore Paris's parks, take a dinner cruise along the Seine river, and ascend the Montparnasse Tower one evening for a panorama of Paris that lives up to its nickname. To indulge in the romance of yesteryear, make at least one palatial day trip: either to Versailles, the palace to end all palaces; or to Fontainbleau, a royal retreat in the woods. On the evening of **Day 4,** board the overnight train to Frankfurt, where you'll pick up a car and tour the Romantic Road.

Day 5: Romantic Road   Spend this day in Franconia and Bavaria's prettiest countryside, visiting picture-perfect medieval towns and hamlets. With only one day, you only have time to hit Würzburg, Rothenburg, and one other, smaller stop (your pick) in order to end the day in Füssen, where you'll spend the night.

Days 6 and 7: Neuschwanstein and Munich   Spend the morning of Day 6 visiting Neuschwanstein, the fairy-tale castle of "Mad King" Ludwig II, a monarch who kinder souls might call "Hopelessly Romantic King" Ludwig II. Inspired by his friend Wagner's epic operas of love and drama, Ludwig decorated this 19th-century palace as a medieval fantasy land of how the "good old days" should have been. You'll have the car until the end of the day, so leave Neuschwanstein by noon to make the hour's drive up to Munich.

Stop at the ornate 17th-century Wittlesbach palace of Scholss Nymphenburg, just west of the city proper. Check into your hotel in Munich and drop off the car before spending a rousing evening in a Bavarian beer hall. The next day, spend some time exploring the Wittlesbach's city pad of the Residenz and take a walk in the beautiful Englisher Garten park, pausing in the leafy shade of an outdoor beer garden near the Chinese pagoda. If your romantic ideas run to the racy side of things, there's a museum of erotic art on Odeonsplatz. At the end of **Day 7,** take an overnight train to eastern Europe's drop-dead-gorgeous baroque capital, Prague.

Days 8 through 10: Prague   Prague is a city of baroque palaces and mighty fortresses, church concerts and powerful beers, hidden gardens and classical street musicians who play a mean Dvorak. Take a sunset stroll across the statue-lined Charles Bridge, and spend an afternoon delving into Prague's rich Jewish heritage at its synagogues and museums. Spend a day exploring Prague Castle, both for its soaring Gothic cathedral and to see how a fortress-city of the Middle Ages looked and worked. Make a day trip to Kunta Hora and catch the pulse of small-town Bohemia, and fit in as many evening concerts as you can in Prague. Take the overnight train to Vienna on **Day 10.**

Days 11 and 12: Vienna   Vienna recalls the glory days of the Austro-Hungarian empire, a city of 19th-century grandeur and a rich classical music heritage. The Hofburg palace complex doesn't quite hold up to Versailles, but it's a splendid specimen nonetheless—and you might get to hear the Vienna Boys' Choir sing. Other top palatial residences include the Belvedere Palace overlooking the city and the Hapsburgs' massive Schönbrunn Palace just outside it. Spend an afternoon at the brink of the Vienna Woods in a medieval village suburb doing a *heurigen* crawl from one fine wine tavern to the next.

The Viennese taught the French how to run a cafe, and you can while the hours away in many a *kaffehaus* amidst the trappings of the 19th-century and some of the finest coffee and pastries in Europe. Try to catch the Lippizaner horses practicing their equestrian ballet or take a cruise on the Danube if that's more your style. End Day 12 with a performance at the Staatsoper, one of the world's premier opera houses (I'd give it top billing for decor alone). On **Day 12,** take the overnight train to Venice.

Days 13 through 16: Venice *La Serenissima,* "The Most Serene" city of canals, palaces, Byzantine mosaics, and delicate blown glass, has made a romantic out of everyone, from Shakespeare and Thomas Mann to Casanova and Woody Allen. Venice has always been a haven of secrets, so I'll leave you to your own devices in exploring. Don't pass up a spin in a traditional gondola (despite the outrageous prices). Make sure you have a couple of long, drawn-out Italian feasts by candlelight, a cruise down the majestic sweep of the Grand Canal, and some moonlit strolls through the narrow, winding alleys and over countless tiny canals. Take one day to explore the smaller fishing, glass-blowing, and lace-making islands in the Venetian lagoon.

Chapter 2

How to Get Started

You have an idea of all the sights and cities of Europe that appeal to you, but what now? This chapter will help you start compiling detailed information on every destination by using tourist offices, guidebooks, the Internet, and agencies that cater to special interest groups (seniors, students, families, gays and lesbians, and travelers with disabilities). As you narrow down your choices of where to go and start figuring out what to do once you get there, you'll need to decide when to visit. If you plan carefully, you can catch spectacular cultural events or colorful festivals while you're on the road. The next four chapters will take you through planning the travel details (plane tickets, rail passes, packing, and so on), but while you're preparing the practical, you may also want to prepare mentally. Get in the mood by reading novels or watching movies set in your destination or even by brushing up on your history or language skills with books and classes.

Information, Please

You'll find no end of available information on Europe and its countries and cities. Sifting through it all and knowing which sources to trust and which to ignore takes some doing, however. Reading this book is a good start. In the next few sections, I'll cut through the sea of travel information out there and lead you straight to the best sources.

Milking the Tourist Office for All It's Worth

National tourist boards exist to help you plan a trip to their country. They'll gladly send you a big envelope stuffed with brochures and information packets just for making a phone call. Many of them are helpful enough that they'll address specific questions and concerns you might have. Even more useful, now that most of them are on-line, you can visit Web sites just loaded with country-specific info, as well as links to other sites. Appendix A lists each country's main national tourist board offices across the English-speaking world, along with phone numbers and Web sites.

That said, take any mailing from the tourist office with a grain of salt. Most of the material they send you is promotional and always puts the best spin possible on every aspect of the country—nowhere in it will you find the downside. They may send you a brochure of local restaurants, but this doesn't mean that these are the only, or even the best, dining possibilities in town. Most brochures are thinly veiled advertisements written by the properties themselves. The best joint in town may not belong to the promotional consortium that prints the pamphlet. Read between the lines and rely on a quality, impartial third-party guidebook for the real, opinionated scoop on the local scene.

Time-Savers

One of the most useful items a National Tourist Office can send you is a list of the **local tourist boards** in each city and province of the country. Be sure to request one. Local tourist boards have scads more information available, from sightseeing, hotel, and restaurant lists to events calendars, specialized tourism options, walking tour outfits, and so on. It pays to contact them directly.

Getting Information from the Internet

Yahoo! (**www.yahoo.com**), **Excite** (**www.excite.com**), **Lycos** (**www.lycos.com**), **Infoseek** (**www.infoseek.com**), and the other major Internet indexing sites all have subcategories for travel, country/regional information, and culture; click on all three to find information. One of the best hotlists for travel and destination information is Excite's **City.Net** (**www.city.net**).

Other good clearinghouse sites for information are Microsoft's **Expedia** (**expedia.msn.com**), **Travelocity** (**www.travelocity.com**), the **Internet Travel Network** (**www.itn.com**), **TravelWeb** (**www.travelweb.com**), and the **European Travel Commission** (**goeurope.com**). Of the many, many on-line travel magazines (the preceding sites will point you toward them), two of the best are **Condé Nast's Epicurious** (**www.epicurious.com**), based on articles from the glossy magazines *Condé Nast Traveler,* *Gourmet,* and *Bon Appetit,* and **Arthur Frommer's Outspoken**

Encyclopedia of Travel (**www.frommers.com**), written and updated by the guru of budget travel himself.

As often as possible throughout this book, I've included any establishment's Web site along with its phone number. (Remember to type **http://** before any address.) Keep in mind that the Internet is quite volatile, and sites come and go frequently. You may very well find a particular address out of date or a site moved elsewhere. Never fear, chances are that if there once was a Web site, it hasn't disappeared. Go to a site like Yahoo! and just search on the name of the site you're looking for. It'll usually pop up.

A Guide to the Guidebooks

Your guidebook is one of your closest travel allies, your pocket-sized friend with all the answers and the best insider's advice—and I felt this way even before I started writing them! It's the one item in your pack that can tell you which bus will go to the castle outside town, which hidden bistro has the best local food, and which hotels accept Visa or give discounts to families. It can provide the background on that fresco in the cathedral and instructions for using the local subway. It will direct you to the best shopping, the hottest disco, and the museums most worth your time and money. People who travel without guidebooks usually regret it and end up buying one on the road.

With so many series and specialty books, the travel shelf can be a confusing place; it's hard to tell which book may be right for you. Make sure you choose a guidebook that fits your personality, budget, and travel style. Guides that cover all of Europe, like this one, are great for planning and for whirlwind vacations, but for more focused trips you may also want a country, regional, or city guide.

The many **series** out there cater to specific audiences: middle-class adults and families (Frommer's, Cadogan, Birnbaum's), students (Let's Go, Berkeley), adult budget travelers (the famous Frommer's $-a-Day, Rough Guides, Rick Steves', Lonely Planet, Time Out), and upscale travelers (Travel & Leisure, Fielding, Fodor's, Access). Some focus on the sightseeing, art, and history (Baedeker's, Michelin Green guides, Blue Guides), others on hotels and/or restaurants (Karen Brown's, Cheap Sleeps/Cheap Eats, Michelin's Red guides, Food Lover's Companion). Some series go for glossy presentation and lots of pictures and diagrams at the expense of information (Eyewitness, Knopf Guides, Fodor's Exploring, Insight). Others focus on a style or means of travel: driving tours (Frommer's, Passport); walking tours (the "Memorable Walks" series from Frommer's, *[City]* Walks from Henry Holt); or shopping (Born to Shop). Many go for niche markets (the literary Companion Guides, the Sierra Club's outdoorsy Wild *[Country]*, Virago women's guides). Leaf through many; buy the ones you like.

I always get several guides to each destination, then ruthlessly rip them up and staple together related sections—say, every book's chapter on Paris—to make my own Frankenstein guide to each city. Stick this in your daypack to carry around town rather than lugging about several massive books. When you leave town, keep the sections as souvenirs, pass them along to a new arrival, or toss them onto the exchange bookshelf at the hotel.

Dollars & Sense

One mistake I see many people making in the bookstores—and I hang around the travel section a lot—is buying a guide based on **the cover price.** Chances are, you're banking a trip worth several thousand dollars and a lot of happiness on the information in two or three books, so you want to get the best advice possible. *Don't even look at the price when choosing a guide.* I'll tell you right now: the most expensive books are the $29.95 visually oriented books on glossy paper with lots of pictures. Most hover around $15 to $22—that's peanuts to your vacation expense account. Two or three high-quality guides are the best vacation investment you can make, and they will pay for themselves a hundred times over.

So, When Should I Go to Europe?

The usual answer is whenever you can get the vacation time. It may have to be summer, when the kids are out of school or your work schedule slows down. If you can hand-pick the dates for your European odyssey, however, consider these facts. Summer is usually high season when everything is up and running in Europe, but everything is crowded as well, and the temperature is often sweltering. There will be colorful folk festivals, but horrendous museum lines. On the other hand, Christmas in Paris can be lovely, but many people don't want to spend their vacations all bundled up against the cold. The best travel time? Mid spring (late April/early May). The worst? August, especially August 15 through 31 (see the following "Tourist Traps").

The Rain in Spain Falls Mainly in October: How's the Weather Over There?

The climate in Europe can vary dramatically from country to country, and even within a season. Although you may find the odd summer cold snap in Scotland or a balmy Sicilian day in December, Europe for the most part holds few seasonal surprises, with weather fairly similar to that of the northeastern United States. It (occasionally) snows on Greek islands in winter, and summer brings out the shorts in Scandinavia. On a similar note, it can broil beyond 100°F in southern Italy and Spain in August, and February means weeks of subzero temperatures in the northerly reaches of Great Britain and Finland.

When compared to the United States (disregarding the Pacific Northwest), Europe tends to be slightly wetter in spring, autumn, and winter and (if you don't count Arizona and New Mexico) drier in summer. Yes, it does tend to rain an awful lot in England, and the glacier-bound peaks of Switzerland never free themselves entirely from the snow. Basically, you should prepare for all possible vagaries of the weather. Bring a folding pocket umbrella, long underwear and clothes to layer, and lightweight togs for when it gets warm.

'Tis the Season for the Tourists

The most popular time to visit Europe is early summer, especially June and July. With the exception of ski resorts, this is the highest of **high season,** which means all of the services that cater to tourism throw open their doors and welcome in the droves. It also means that there *will* be droves. Despite the opportunity to hit some of Europe's best festivals, I try to avoid travel at this time of year. The continent teems with what seems like more foreigners than natives, temperatures can soar, hotels are perennially booked, prices are highest (especially for hotels and airlines), lines at the popular museums and sights can stretch for blocks, and the wait can last for hours.

Tourist Traps

Part or all of **August** is often considered part of the low season in many cities. Europeans go on vacation at this time, so the beaches are packed, but the cities are devoid of locals and crammed with tourists. Especially from August 15 to 31, most European cities either close down entirely (Rome is the most notorious) or go on severely shortened hours.

Of course, the dead of winter has its drawbacks, too. From mid or late November through Easter (except for Christmas week) is **low season** in most places. Although travel and hotel prices plummet and you can often have entire museums, churches, or even small towns to yourself, most local tourist industries take advantage of this calm period to freshen up. Hotels and restaurants close shop for a week or month; museums are shut for reorganization; monuments and churches are shrouded for cleaning or restoration; and shops, tourist offices, and local transportation go on shortened winter hours.

Some of the most touristed destinations, especially smaller cities, islands, spas, and places in the sun-drenched south, close up almost entirely. From a touring point of view, Greece in February is a waste of time. Bigger cosmopolitan cities such as London, Paris, or Rome should pose no problem. Keep in mind that it can get bitterly cold. You probably expect this weather in Scotland or Scandinavia, but winter does lash the entire continent. Although snow is probably not the first thing that comes to mind when you think of sunny Italy's Tuscany region, that's what I found there in spades in December.

You're left with the in-between **shoulder seasons,** the precise parameters of which depend on what airline you're talking to. They usually include spring (Easter through mid May) and fall (late October to mid or late November). Airlines offer reasonable rates, the majority of hotels, restaurants, and sights are open, and the weather tends to be pleasantly mild, if rather temperamental—prepare for rain, sudden heat waves, and/or cold spells. Savvy travelers often choose the shoulder season, when it might well be warm enough for a dip in the North Sea off of Ireland, but still cool enough for a ski run in the Alps. If you go then, you'll find Europe neither too crowded nor a ghost town.

Pagan Feasts & Keg Parties: Europe's Biggest Holidays & Festivals

Perhaps the harvest has come in, or the local saint's day has rolled around. Maybe all the regional orchestras are in town for one week, or boar-hunting season needs to be inaugurated. Or sometimes just because it's the second Tuesday in May again, Europeans will throw a festival. Arrive during one, and you'll encounter flower-strewn streets, military and religious processions, moonlit concerts in ancient theaters, mass blessings of sheep, jazz or Celtic music jams, violent Renaissance soccer, or raging bonfires. People dance in the town square; fountains spew wine; locals joust in medieval garb; and horses race through the streets. You never know what you'll be in for, but it's bound to be memorable.

Time-Savers

If you plan to be in town anywhere near a major festival or other cultural event, **book your hotel rooms as soon as possible.** Things fill up quickly at festival time, sometimes months in advance. For some of the big festivals in smaller places, such as the Palio in Siena, Italy, all the hotels within the town walls may be sold out over a year beforehand. Book a room in a neighboring town instead.

On most state and religious holidays throughout Europe, you'll find most everything closed or on reduced time schedules: sights, shops, banks, tourist and government offices, train and bus routes, and so on. Hotels and restaurants are either filled with revelers or closed for vacation. City public transportation may be cut back, but it is usually running.

I often plan entire vacations around a single big festival. All of the city's traditional sights may be closed (especially in smaller towns), but a visit is well worth it because it can become the most memorable time of your trip—a privileged glimpse into a slice of European life most tourists never get to witness. It's your chance to party down with the locals, shoot dozens of rolls of film, and take away some unforgettable memories. The following are the top 10 festivals in Europe; country guidebooks such as Frommer's have the room to list many, many more. Contact the local tourist offices for more information or specific dates.

➤ **Carnevale,** Venice, Italy (and just about everywhere else). Carnival is a true pagan holdover grafted onto the Christian pre-Lenten period. It's a feast of food and wine and a raucous celebration of spring where the world is turned upside down, allowing the lowliest to hobnob with the elite, and where everyone has a roaring good time. The whole Christian world celebrates this event (think Rio or New Orleans), but in Europe the most famous is Carnevale, the series of elegant-yet-drunken masked balls held in **Venice;** the holiday recalls the randy old days of Casanova's 18th century. Carnevale just about anywhere is a trip, from the satiric political floats in the port of Livorno, Italy; to the flower battles and bonfires in Nice, France; to the solemn burial of a sardine in Madrid, Spain (no, really!); to the chariot parades and wild bacchanal in the Greek city of Pátras. Carnival starts two or three weeks before Ash Wednesday (which usually means late February) and culminates in the final Tuesday—called "Fat Tuesday," which is *Mardi Gras* in French—before the sober period of Lent begins.

Tourist Traps

As in the United States, Christmas and New Year's Day in Europe, and to some extent the days in between, take on a holiday spirit and schedule. Most of Europe also takes off on Easter, May 1, and August 15. Europeans tend to celebrate more holidays on the church calendar than the United States does, especially in Catholic countries such as Italy, Spain, and, to a lesser extent, France.

➤ **Shakespeare season,** Stratford-upon-Avon, England. For fans of great theater, this a wonderful experience. The town where the Bard was born (and to which he retired) does a brisk business in the Shakespeare trade, and they'd never settle for anything less than the Royal Shakespeare Company performing its season here. You can get tickets through agents such as Keith Prowse (☎ **800/669-8687** in the United States); the season lasts from April through January.

➤ **Easter,** celebrated all across Europe. Celebrations vary widely between Good Friday and Easter Monday. In Florence, an ox-drawn cart laden with fireworks explodes in front of the cathedral; in Seville, Spain hooded processioners wail love songs to the Virgin; multicolored floats parade around Battersea Park in London. Easter falls around late March/early April.

➤ **Palio,** Siena, Italy. This bareback, breakneck, anything-goes horse race around the dirt-covered sloping main piazza of medieval Siena is one of the highlights of the Italian summer. Whips are used as much on the other riders as on the horses, and even a horse who's thrown its rider (far from uncommon) can take the prize. No matter who wins, the parties held before and afterward are street feasts to behold—and take part in. The people have so much fun, they have to do it twice: July 2 and August 16.

➤ **Running of the Bulls,** Pamplona, Spain. Surely one of the more dangerous festivals is that crazy week where people dressed in white with red kerchiefs let rampaging bulls chase them through the narrow streets of Pamplona. The mayhem lasts until the beasts, after trampling/goring a few of the slower runners and forcing most to jump the fences for safety, chase the last few right out into the harbor's waters. Much wine is consumed, fireworks are set off, and, of course, there are bullfights galore. You can enjoy it vicariously via Hemingway's *The Sun Also Rises* or see it yourself from July 6 to 14.

➤ **Bastille Day,** Paris, France. France celebrates its birth as a nation with parades, street fairs, feasts, and pageants. It starts with a procession along the Champs-Elysées and ends with fireworks over Montmartre. Bastille Day is July 14.

➤ **Edinburgh Festival,** Edinburgh, Scotland. One of Europe's premier cultural extravaganzas, this festival brings to town plays, film, music, dance, and art from some of the world's top performers and creative talents for three weeks every August. It's so big that it has spawned a **Fringe Festival,** which opens even more venues across town to smaller, more experimental acts. The highlight is the traditional bagpipes-and-kilt Military Tattoo at the castle. See chapter 14 for more details.

➤ **Bloemencorso,** Amsterdam, the Netherlands. This is one of the major flower festivals in a country obsessed with blooms. It starts as an inherently colorful parade of floral floats in the nearby flower market town of Aalmeer and ends in Amsterdam on the Dam Square. (Believe it or not, there are no tulips.) It takes place on the first Saturday in September.

➤ **Oktoberfest,** Munich, Germany. Picture tens of thousands of people sitting under giant tents draining liter-sized mugs of beer while whole oxen roast on spits and brass bands oompah in the background. Welcome to the world's biggest keg party (five million liters of beer all told). It actually starts two weeks before the end of September; the first weekend in October is the final flourish. See chapter 18 for details.

➤ **Christmas season,** also Europe-wide. It's a fun and festive time to be anywhere in Europe from a few weeks before the holiday until January 6 (the Epiphany). And luckily, in Europe, Christmas hasn't yet been completely commercialized. Be on the lookout for crèches (nativity scenes) in church chapels and public squares across the continent. Some are post-modern, some live, others are ultra-traditional. (My favorite is the one in Naples where the holy manger is an insignificant detail surrounded by a very Italian Bethlehem, complete with pizza parlors.) You can sing *Silent Night* on Christmas Eve in the town where it was written (Oberndorf, north of Salzburg, Austria), or watch the pope lean out his window in Rome at noon to give a mass blessing broadcast around the world on December 25.

Getting in the Mood: Books, Films, & Classes

Taking an extension course at the local university in European history, language, or art and reading up or watching movies on European cities and their cultures are by no means necessary. But a bit of steeping your brain in things European certainly doesn't hurt—and it stands to help you have a much richer, more rewarding vacation.

One of the most enjoyable and painless ways to soak up the past is reading novelizations of events or eras—perhaps not the most historically precise accounts, but much more fun than a textbook. Mary Renault brings ancient Greece to life in novels like *The King Must Die* (Vintage), *The Bull from the Sea,* and *The Persian Boy* (both Random House). Immerse yourself in Michelangelo and Renaissance Florence with Irving Stone's *The Agony and the Ecstasy* (Signet) or in the mythical heroes of Celtic Ireland and Gaul (in France) through Morgan Llywelyn's *Red Branch, Finn Mac Cool,* and *Druids* (Tor or Ivy Books). On a more somber note, you should definitely read the *Diary of Anne Frank* (Bantam Books) before visiting Amsterdam.

When you're ready for more heavy-duty background, Christopher Hibbert is the most readable historian I've ever come across, focusing mainly on anecdotes and character portraits to bring the past to life. His "Biography of a City" series (W. W. Norton) includes volumes on London, Rome, Venice, and Florence. Also look for his *The French Revolution, A Social History of the English, The Grand Tour,* and a passel of biographies on British and Italian notables and ruling families.

The travel section at your bookstore should carry both of the following series. *A Traveller's History of [Country]* (Interlink Books) covers most European countries, and a few cities, in pocket-sized paperbacks. *Culture Shock: [Country]* (Graphic Arts Center Publishing Co.) books are similarly accessible and easy-to-read guides that offer practical insight into the customs, social standards, and etiquette of European countries and cities.

Make It a Blockbuster Night

If you don't have the time or inclination to slough through a whole book, you probably have a couple of hours to sit down and watch a few movies. You don't have to run out and rent tourism videos or a stack of artsy foreign films with teensy subtitles (although that's fine, too—think of *Cinema Paradiso*). Keep it fun.

You needn't sit through all 12 hours of PBS's *I, Claudius* to get a handle on ancient Rome; Shakespeare's *Julius Caesar* (with John Gielgud in the title role) and even *A Funny Thing Happened on the Way to the Forum* are just as good. Even better, rent *Roman Holiday,* with Gregory Peck and Audrey Hepburn, and you can fall in love with a more modern version of Rome.

Kenneth Branagh's *Henry V* gives you a good feel for medieval battles and the vague idea that England and France were always fighting about something. Woody Allen's *Everybody Says I Love You* will put both Venice and Paris firmly on your itinerary, while the movie version of Hemingway's *The Sun Also Rises* takes you through the Paris of the Lost Generation and to Spain's Pamplona to watch the running of the bulls. *Rob Roy* and *Braveheart* will both teach you a bit of history and make you long to see the Scottish Highlands, while *A Room with a View* will fire up your imagination about Florence and romance under the Italian sun. See *The Sound of Music* before visiting Salzburg.

To mentally prepare for the entirety of your grand European tour, watch that fine documentary film *National Lampoon's European Vacation.* OK, so it's exceedingly silly, but the bungling misadventures of Chevy Chase and family are more true to life than any tourist brochure will let on. Traditionalists may prefer the dated but still relevant '60s classic *If It's Tuesday This Must Be Belgium,* which should be required viewing for anyone about to embark on an escorted tour.

A Family Affair: Traveling with Your Kids

Yes, you can travel with the children! Trips to Europe often have a much more profound impact on the children than the adults, opening their young eyes and minds to the diversity of the world's cultures and peoples. Be prepared to take things a bit more slowly; intersperse the heavy-duty cultural sights with some fun activities (which can be a welcome respite for everyone). You may want the hotel to find you a baby-sitter for a night here and there so you can go out for a romantic dinner, but on the whole, traveling as a family is far from impossible.

Europeans expect to see families together, because it's how they travel. You're likely to encounter entire clans, from grandmothers to babes in arms, caravaning around. In the Mediterranean countries especially, locals tend to love kids. You'll often find that a child guarantees you an even warmer reception from hotels and restaurants than you'd normally receive.

Most Europeans will coo over an infant or toddler, and an adolescent or teenager struggling to order her meal in the local lingo will receive loads of encouragement and attention. Ask waiters for a half-portion to fit the little one's appetite. With small children, three-star and four-star hotels may be your best bet; the higher cost will be more than offset by the baby-sitters on call and a better infrastructure for helping visitors access the city and its services. Still, even cheaper hotels can usually find you a sitter.

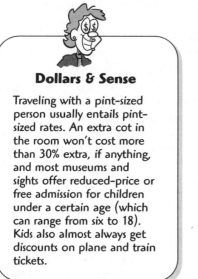

Dollars & Sense

Traveling with a pint-sized person usually entails pint-sized rates. An extra cot in the room won't cost more than 30% extra, if anything, and most museums and sights offer reduced-price or free admission for children under a certain age (which can range from six to 18). Kids also almost always get discounts on plane and train tickets.

There are many books full of hints and tips to help you travel with kids. Most concentrate on the United States, but two, *Family Travel* (Lanier Publishing International) and *How to Take Great Trips with Your Kids* (The Harvard Common Press), are full of good general advice that can apply to travel anywhere. Two reliable tomes with a worldwide focus are *Adventuring with Children* (Foghorn Press) and Lonely Planet's *Travel with Children*. Both are loaded with specific advice on dealing with everyday family situations, especially where infants are concerned, that become superhuman chores when they pop up on the road.

The University of New Hampshire runs **Familyhostel** (☎ **800/733-9753**), an intergenerational alternative to standard guided tours. You live on a European college campus for the two- or three-week program, attend lectures and seminars, go on lots of field trips, and do all the sightseeing—all of it guided by a team of experts and academics. It's designed for children (aged 8 to 15), parents, and grandparents.

Travel Tips for the Senior Set

People over the age of 60 are traveling more than ever before. Being a senior citizen entitles you to some terrific travel bargains. If you're not a member of **AARP (American Association of Retired Persons),** 601 E St. NW, Washington, DC 20049 (☎ **800/424-3410**), do yourself a favor and join. You'll get discounts on some car rentals and chain hotels. The big car rental agencies don't seem to want your European business because only National currently gives an AARP discount (10%), but the many rental dealers who specialize in Europe—Auto-Europe, Kemwell, Europe-by-Car—offer seniors rates 5% lower than average. See appendix B for contact information.

Mature Outlook, P.O. Box 9390, Des Moines, IA 50306-9519 (☎ **800/ 336-6330;** fax: 847/286-5024), offers discounts on car rentals and hotel stays at many Holiday Inns, Howard Johnsons, and Best Westerns. The $20 annual membership fee also gets you $100 in Sears coupons and a bimonthly magazine.

Most **major airlines** offer discount programs for senior travelers; be sure to ask whenever you book a flight. In most European cities, people over 60 or 65 get reduced admission at theaters, museums, and other attractions, and they can often get discount fares or cards on public transportation and national rail systems. Carrying identification with proof of age can pay off in all these situations.

Bet You Didn't Know

In an entirely unquantifiable benefit of travel in Europe, seniors are most often treated as respected elders and not marginalized, as they so often are in American society. In most of Europe, the older you get, the more vital a role you play in the community and the family. You'll routinely see three and four generations eating out together, and older people are viewed with dignity and respect. It's quite refreshing.

Grand Circle Travel (☎ 800/221-2610) publishes the free booklet "101 Tips for the Mature Traveler" and is one of the literally hundreds of **travel agencies** specializing in vacations for seniors. But beware: Many packages are of the tour-bus variety. Seniors seeking more independent travel should probably consult a regular travel agent. **SAGA International Holidays,** 222 Berkeley St., Boston, MA 02116 (☎ 800/343-0273), has 40 years of experience running all-inclusive tours and cruises for those 50 and older. They also sponsor the more substantial **Road Scholar Tours** (☎ 800/ 621-2151), which are fun-loving but with an educational bent.

If you want something more than the average vacation or guided tour, try **Interhostel** (☎ 800/733-9753) and **Elderhostel** (☎ 617/426-8056; **www.elderhostel.org**), both variations on the same theme: educational travel. Foreign universities host these tours, and the days are packed with seminars, lectures, many field trips, and sightseeing all led by academic experts. At around $2,000 to $3,500 a trip, this is the sort of affordable adventure to make the under-55 crowd green with envy. For Elderhostel, you must be over 55 (a spouse or companion of any age can accompany you), and they offer programs ranging from one to four weeks. Interhostel takes travelers 50 and over (any companion must be over 40), and it offers two- and three-week programs.

Although all the specialty books on the market are focused on the United States, three do provide good general advice and contacts for the savvy senior traveler. Thumb through *The 50+ Traveler's Guidebook* (St. Martin's Press), *The Seasoned Traveler* (Country Roads Press), or *Unbelievably Good Deals and Great Adventures That You Absolutely Can't Get Unless You're Over 50* (Contemporary Books). Also check out your newsstand for the quarterly magazine *Travel 50 & Beyond*.

Young at Heart: Travel Tips for Students

The best resource for students is the **Council on International Educational Exchange,** or CIEE (☎ 800/226-8624; **www.ciee.com**). It can set you up with an ID card, and its travel branch, **Council Travel**

Service (CTS), is the biggest student travel agency operation in the world. It can get you discounts on plane tickets, rail passes, and the like. Ask them for a list of CTS offices in major European cities, so you can keep the discounts flowing (and aid lines open) as you travel.

Dollars & Sense

On the road, whenever you have to pay for something, blurt out "Studente?" in a questioning voice with a smile and flash your ISIC. This is the international signal for "Hey, gimme a discount if there is one."

From CIEE, you can obtain the student traveler's best European friend, the $18 **International Student Identity Card (ISIC).** It's the only officially acceptable form of student identification, and it's good for cut rates on rail passes, plane tickets, and other discounts. It also provides you with basic health and life insurance and a 24-hour help line. If you're no longer a student but are still under 26, you can get a **GO 25 card** from the same people, which will get you the insurance and some of the discounts (but not student admission prices in museums).

Access Europe: Advice for Disabled Travelers

Although Europe won't win any medals for accessibility, the big cities have made an effort to accommodate people with disabilities in the past few years, and a disability shouldn't stop anybody from traveling. There exist no end of organizations to help you out with planning and provide specific advice before you go.

The **Moss Rehab Hospital** (☎ **215/456-9600**) has been providing phone advice and referrals to travelers with disabilities for years. The **American Foundation for the Blind,** 11 Penn Plaza, Suite 300, New York, NY 10001 (☎ **800/232-5463** or 212/502-7600) can fill you in on travel in general and how to get your seeing-eye dog into Europe with you.

You can join **The Society for the Advancement of Travel for the Handicapped (SATH),** 347 Fifth Ave. Suite 610, New York, NY 10016 (☎ **212/447-7284** fax: 212-725-8253), for $45 annually to gain access to their vast network of connections in the travel industry. They provide information sheets on travel destinations and referrals to tour operators that specialize in travelers with disabilities. Their quarterly magazine *Open World for Accessible Travel* is full of good information and resources. A year's subscription is $13 ($21 outside the United States).

Mobility International, P.O. Box 10767, Eugene, OR 97440 (☎ **541/ 343-1284** V/TDD, fax: 541/343-6812; **www.miusa.org**), is a worldwide organization promoting international disability rights, hosting international exchanges, and providing reference sheets on travel destinations for people with disabilities. Its *A World of Options* book has resources on everything from biking trips to scuba outfitters. Annual membership is $25; it costs $15 to receive just its quarterly *Over the Rainbow* newsletter. For more personal assistance, call the **Travel Information Service** at ☎ **215/456-9603** or 215/456-9602 (for TTY).

You might consider joining a **guided tour** that caters to travelers with disabilities. One of the best operators is **Flying Wheels Travel** (☎ **800/535-6790**). They offer various escorted tours and cruises, as well as private tours in minivans with lifts. Other reputable specialized tour operators include **Access Adventures** (☎ **716/889-9096**), **Accessible Journeys** (☎ **800/846-4537**), **Directions Unlimited** (☎ **800/533-5343**), and **Wheelchair Journeys** (☎ **206/885-2210**). In addition, the **Information Center for Individuals with Disabilities** (☎ **800/462-5015**) provides lists of travel agents who specialize in tours for travelers with disabilities.

Out & About: Tips for Gays & Lesbians

Much of Europe has grown to accept same-sex couples over the past few decades, and in most countries homosexual sex acts are legal. To be on the safe side, do a bit of research on the city or area you're planning to visit. As you might expect, smaller towns tend to be less accepting than cities. Gay centers include parts of London, Paris, Berlin, Milan, and Greece.

The **International Gay Travel Association (IGTA),** P.O. Box 4974, Key West, FL 33041 (☎ **800/448-8550** or 305/292-0217), is your best all-around resource. Members get a newsletter, advice on specialist travel agencies, and a membership directory. General gay and lesbian travel agencies include **Our Family Abroad** (☎ **212/459-1800;** gay and lesbian); **Above and Beyond Tours** (☎ **800/397-2681;** mainly gay men); **Islanders/Kennedy Travels** (☎ **212/242-3220;** gay and lesbian); and **Yellowbrick Road** (☎ **800/642-2488;** gay and lesbian).

There are also two good, biannual English-language gay guidebooks, both focused on gay men but including information for lesbians as well. You can get the *Spartacus International Gay Guide* or *Odysseus* from most gay and lesbian book stores, or order them from **Giovanni's Room** (☎ **215/923-2960**) or **A Different Light Bookstore** (☎ **800/343-4002** or 212/989-4850). The Ferrari Guides (**www.q-net.com**) is another very good series of gay and lesbian guidebooks.

Out and About, 8 W. 19th St. #401, New York, NY 10011 (☎ **800/929-2268** or 212/645-6922), is a monthly newsletter packed with good information on the global gay and lesbian scene. A year's subscription costs $49. *Our World,* 1104 North Nova Rd., Suite 251, Daytona Beach, FL 32117 (☎ **904/441-5367**), is a slicker monthly magazine promoting and highlighting travel bargains and opportunities. Annual subscription rates are $35 in the United States and $45 outside the United States.

How Will I Get There?

In This Chapter

➤ Picking a travel agent and knowing what to use one for

➤ To tour bus or not to tour bus: escorted versus package tours and who will be happiest on their own

➤ Taking a flight without getting taken to the cleaners: How to score the best airfares

You know where you want to go and what you want to see. You've brushed up on your background info, ordered all the brochures, bought your guidebooks, and are raring to cross the Big Pond. The pressing question now is, how do you get there?

Should you use a travel agent or call airlines on your own and surf the Web in search of deals? Would you prefer the comfort of a professional guide leading you around, or would you rather plunge into Europe with no safety net other than your wits, guidebooks, and sense of adventure? How do you get the best last-minute airline deals, find the tour best suited to you, and combat jet lag? This chapter will answer all that and more.

Travel Agent, Friend or Foe

A good travel agent is like a good mechanic or plumber: hard to locate, but invaluable once you've found the right person. The best way to find a good travel agent is the same way you find a good plumber or mechanic or doctor—by word of mouth. Because travel agents have access to more resources than the average person or the most complete travel Web site, they should be able to get you a better price than you could get on your own. They also can issue your tickets and vouchers right there in the office.

Any travel agent can help you find a bargain airfare, hotel, or rental car. A good one will stop you from ruining your vacation by trying to save a few dollars. The best ones can tell you how much time to budget for each destination, find you a cheap direct flight, arrange for a competitively priced rental car, get you a rail pass (see chapter 4), and even give recommendations on restaurants. Make sure you pick an agent who knows your destination. The reliable agent who books your company's business trips to Chicago or New York may be in over her head trying to arrange a vacation in Provence. Also make sure you check out any prospective agent with your local Better Business Bureau.

Dollars & Sense

Travel agents work on commission. The good news is that you don't pay the commission; the airlines, accommodations, and tour companies do. The bad news is that unscrupulous agents will try to persuade you to book the vacations that award them the biggest commissions. Some airlines have recently begun limiting or eliminating commissions altogether. The immediate result has been that travel agents don't bother booking these services unless the customer specifically requests them. Some travel analysts predict that if other businesses throughout the industry follow suit, travel agents may be forced to charge customers. When that day arrives, the best agents will be even harder to find.

To get the most out of your travel agent, do a little homework. Read about your destination (you've already made a sound decision by buying this book) and pick out some accommodations and attractions you think you like. If necessary, get a more comprehensive travel guide such as *Frommer's*. Check airline prices yourself in advance so you can do a little prodding in the office. Then take the information you've gathered to the travel agent and ask him to make all the arrangements for you.

I'd recommend using the travel agent primarily to book your transportation; save the hotel hunting to do yourself. Even the best agents cannot keep up with all the charming mom-and-pop accommodations in Europe. Because agents work mainly through chains, they may be able to get you a great price in a Florence hotel owned by Best Western, but the cheap

Time-Savers

Take your guidebooks to the travel agent. If the agent can't get you into the hotel of your choice, ask him or her to recommend an alternative. If you've brought your guidebooks, you can (hopefully) find an objective review of the agent's suggested replacement inn to read right there and then.

pension around the corner with mismatched antiques and homemade breakfasts probably isn't in their database. Travel agents tend to stick you in contemporary rooms with all the amenities of an American motel and all the
cookie-cutter lack of character as well.

Should I Travel Alone or Join a Tour?

Do you like to let your bus driver worry about traffic while you sit in comfort
and listen to a tour guide explain everything you see? Or do you prefer to
rent a car and follow your nose, even if you don't catch all the highlights?
Do you like to have lots of events planned for each day, or would you rather
improvise as you go along? Or do you like it somewhere in between, with
some of the travel details planned for you so you can devote your energies to
planning your daily sightseeing? The answers to these questions will determine whether you should choose a guided tour or a package tour or travel à
la carte under your own steam and ambition.

The Escorted Tour (Or, "If It's Tuesday, This Must Be Belgium")

Some people love escorted tours. They free you from figuring out complicated train schedules in a foreign language or spending lots of time behind
the wheel; they take care of all the details of booking hotels, (often) choosing
restaurants, and deciding where to go and how long to stay, and they walk
you through—or bus you past—every attraction with an accompanying
monologue on its history and importance. You know your costs up front,
and there aren't many surprises. Escorted
tours take you to the maximum number
of sights in the minimum amount of time
with the least amount of hassle.

Other people need more freedom and
spontaneity; they can't stand escorted
tours. They prefer to discover a destination by themselves, and don't mind getting caught in a thunderstorm without an
umbrella or finding that a recommended
restaurant in the guidebook is no longer
in business. For them, that's just the
adventure of travel. Escorted tours tend to
ride comfortably and unimaginatively in
the deepest ruts of the beaten path,
eschewing anything novel and treating
the bulk of Europe like so many living
postcards to be ogled from the tinted windows of an air-conditioned bus. Big bus
tours tend to write off even the most
interesting sights if a big parking lot is
not nearby.

Extra! Extra!

Even if you're on a fully
escorted tour with a live
guide, invest in a good
guidebook. It will give you
more background on and
insight into your sightseeing
beyond the pat infonuggets
dispensed by the tour guide.
Plus, it will serve as a trusted
companion for the time you
spend away from the group
and will help you discover
off-the-beaten-path sights,
go shopping, or pick a
restaurant.

Some Questions to Ask if You Want an Escorted Tour

Before you sign up for an escorted tour, you need to ask some questions.

1. **What is the cancellation policy?** Do you have to put a deposit down? Can the company cancel the trip if they don't get enough people? How late can you cancel if you are unable to go? When do you pay? Do you get a refund if you cancel? How about if they cancel?

2. **How jam-packed is the schedule?** Do they try to fit 25 hours' worth of activities into one day, or is there ample time for relaxing by the pool or shopping? If you don't enjoy getting up at 7am every day and not returning to your hotel until 6 or 7pm at night, certain whirlwind escorted tours may not be for you.

3. **How big is the group?** The smaller the group, the more flexible the schedule, and the less time you'll spend waiting for people to get on and off the bus. Also, the larger the group, the more some quaint little village will treat you like an invading barbarian horde to be fended off by throwing large amounts of over-priced souvenirs in your general direction. Tour operators may be evasive about group size until they know how many people have signed on, but they should be able to give you a rough estimate. Some tours have a minimum group size and may cancel the tour if they come up short.

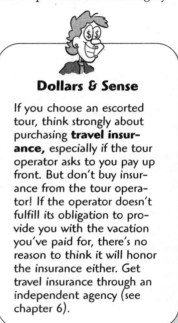

Dollars & Sense

If you choose an escorted tour, think strongly about purchasing **travel insurance,** especially if the tour operator asks to you pay up front. But don't buy insurance from the tour operator! If the operator doesn't fulfill its obligation to provide you with the vacation you've paid for, there's no reason to think it will honor the insurance either. Get travel insurance through an independent agency (see chapter 6).

4. **What is included?** Don't assume anything. You may have to pay to get yourself to and from the airport. A box lunch may be included in an excursion, but drinks might cost extra. Beer might be included but not wine. How much choice do you have? Can you opt out of certain activities, or are you committed for a full day? Are all your meals planned in advance? Can you choose your entree at dinner, or does everybody get the same chicken cutlet?

Hiking, Biking, Drinking, Digging: The Escorted Specialty Tour

Even if you're the most die-hard do-it-yourselfer, you might want to consider an **escorted specialty tour.** Although most people's image of the traditional guided tour is big bus stuffed with Americans in Bermuda shorts hitting only the major attractions in a conga line of snapshot-ready sightseeing, plenty of smaller, more focused tours are out there. Some specialize in art and history, others in opera or cooking. There are bike tours of Ireland, wine tours of France, and guided hikes through Sicily. You may ride across Tuscany on horseback, visit Greek ruins with an archeologist, or pay homage to the Shakespearean sights of England.

The best—and one of the most expensive—of the escorted cultural tour operators is **IST Cultural Tours** (☎ **800/833-2111; www.ist-tours.com**), whose tours are first-class all the way and are accompanied by a certified expert in whatever field the trip focuses on. If you missed out on study abroad in college, the brainy **Smithsonian Study Tours** (☎ **202/357-4700; www.si.edu/tsa/sst**) may be just the ticket, albeit a pricey one. The cheaper alternative is **Smithsonian Odyssey Tours** (☎ **800/258-5885**), run by Saga International Holidays (they save by staying in three- or four-star hotels rather than deluxe). Also contact your **alma mater** or **local university** to see whether they offer summer tours open to the public and guided by a professor.

One of the most reputable agencies running guided walks is **Country Walkers** (☎ **800/464-9255; www.countrywalkers.com**). There's no way I can list all the specialized tour agencies out there, but if you have Internet access, you should check out **Specialty Travel** (**www.specialty-travel.com**), which lists over 600 tour operators, often with links to their Web sites. For more traditional guided tours, contact any of the package tour operators listed at the end of the next section.

All Tied Up in a Neat Little Bow: The Package Tour

Package tours are not the same thing as escorted tours. They are simply a way of buying your airfare and accommodations at the same time and getting an excellent rate on both. Your trip is your own. In many cases, a package that includes airfare, hotel, and transportation to and from the airport will cost you less than the hotel alone if you had booked it yourself. That's because packages are sold in bulk to tour operators, who resell them to the public.

No two package tours are alike. Some offer a better class of hotels, others the same hotels for lower prices. Some offer flights on scheduled airlines while others book charters. In some packages, your choices of accommodations and travel days may be limited. One package may let you choose between escorted or independent vacations; another may allow you to add on just a few excursions or escorted day trips (also at prices lower than if you had arranged them yourself) without booking an entirely escorted tour.

Each destination usually has one or two packagers that offer better values than the rest because they buy them in bigger bulk. The time you spend shopping around will be well-rewarded. A word of warning to charm-seekers: like most escorted tour operators, packagers almost invariably stick you in a boringly modern and functional chain hotel, usually around the train station or edge of town, rather than a smaller and more intimate local inn. You may get all the comforts of home, but no native color or style.

The best place to start looking for a packager is the travel section of your local Sunday newspaper. Also check the ads in the back of national travel magazines like *Travel & Leisure, National Geographic Traveler,* and *Condé Nast Traveler.* **Central Holidays** (☎ 800/611-1139; www. centralholidays.com) is one of the best and most reputable packagers. **Liberty Travel** (many locations; check your local directory because there's not a central 800 number) is one of the biggest packagers in the Northeast and usually boasts a full-page ad in Sunday papers. **American Express Vacations** (☎ 800/241-1700; www.americanexpress.com/travel) and **Kemwell** (☎ 800/678-0678; www.kemwell.com) are two other reputable options.

Dollars & Sense

Another good packager resource are the major **airlines,** which often package flights together with accommodations. Another asset of the airline packages is that you can be pretty sure that the company will *still* be in business when your departure date arrives. Disreputable packagers are uncommon, but they do exist.

The Case for Being Your Own Tour Guide

The bulk of this book is designed to help you get a handle on going it alone and loving it. These first 12 chapters provide you with all the hints, tips, and tools you'll need to plan your own European odyssey and explain how to cope with any difficulties (think of them as adventures) you'll encounter along the way.

Travelers who take their entire trip into their own hands have to spend more time planning and troubleshooting, but they almost invariably have the most fun. They see exactly what they want to see, choose hotels and restaurants that fit their own tastes and budget, dally when they feel like it, or speed up the itinerary if necessary. Best of all, they get an entirely unique experience and take on Europe.

Time-Savers

When you plan your own trip, you need to **reserve** some things before you go. For peace of mind and ease of travel, I book the first and last night's hotel room and rooms in towns where I'll be arriving during a festival or event that draws visitors and fills up hotels. Also, I reserve rental cars and Eurostar tickets (that's the Channel Tunnel train between London and Paris) in advance. The rest can easily be done on the fly, leaving you the leeway to adjust your schedule as you go.

You could be encased in a climate-controlled bus, trundling from city to city in the company of 50 other Americans and learning more than you ever wanted to know about the hometown of the person sitting next to you. Or you could be learning about Paris in a second-class train couchette as you share your picnic lunch with a motley group of local young soldiers, middle-aged nuns, and ancient farmers. You have the freedom to say to blazes with the Medici Chapels or that flamenco show, and instead spend the day hiking in the countryside, shopping in boutiques, or whatever catches your fancy. You can spend the whole day inside the Louvre instead of being hustled through in two hours. Of course, when things go wrong, you're the one that has to fix them, and often you must do so in a foreign language. But treat every dilemma as an adventure, and memories about any crisis can prove to be the highlight of your trip—a humorous tale with which to regale your jealous friends back home.

Traveling on your own forces you to get in touch with the countries you're visiting and learn more about the locals and their culture. You go from being part of a tour bus crowd to being a single guy or gal, a little lost and in need of help. Smile wide, say "thank you" a lot in the local tongue, and rely on the kindness of strangers. It's the lone explorer and her family who are more likely to be invited into the cellar to sample a cup of the family's Chianti straight from the barrel or be let into the museum for a quick look around, even though it closes in half an hour.

Tourist Traps

Even if you're traveling in a group of two or perhaps with just a few friends and family members, you'll need **time apart** to keep from getting on each other's nerves. One more vast art museum may be heaven for you, but hell for your spouse. Split up on a regular basis, so Junior can watch the changing of the guard, Mom can dig into more Monets, and Dad can decompress at an out-door cafe table. My family's strategy is to part at the door of any museum so that everyone can go through at his or her own pace. On top of that, at least one day a week, we all go our separate ways to collect our own memories and travel experiences.

Happy Landings: Winning the Airfare Wars

Airfares are capitalism at its purest. Passengers within the same cabin on an airplane rarely pay the same fare. Rather, they pay what the market would bear whenever they bought their ticket. Business travelers who need the flexibility to purchase their tickets or change their itinerary at the last minute pay the premium rate, known as the full fare.

Passengers who can book their ticket long in advance, who plan to stay over Saturday night, or who are willing to travel on a Tuesday, Wednesday, or Thursday pay a fraction of the full fare. On most round-trip flights to Europe the full fare is $1,500 or more, but an **APEX fare** (advance purchase ticket, bought, depending on the airline, 7 to 21 days ahead of time) is usually $400 to $800. Obviously, it pays to plan ahead.

Airlines periodically hold **sales** on their most popular routes. These fares have APEX requirements and date restrictions, but you can't beat the price. Keep your eyes open for sales as you are planning your vacation, and then pounce on them. Most sales tend to take place in seasons of

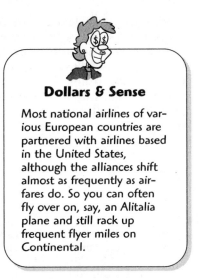

Dollars & Sense

Most national airlines of various European countries are partnered with airlines based in the United States, although the alliances shift almost as frequently as airfares do. So you can often fly over on, say, an Alitalia plane and still rack up frequent flyer miles on Continental.

low travel volume. You'll almost never see one around the peak summer vacation months of July and August or around Thanksgiving or Christmas, when people have to fly, regardless of what the fare is.

The national and country-affiliated airlines of European nations, such as Air France, Swissair, and British Airways, offer deals most frequently because their entire business in the United States is getting people to fly between the United States and their home country. With England already the cheapest country to fly into, competition between British Airways and Virgin Atlantic keeps a rousing chorus of sales and other great deals going all the time.

Wherefore Art Thou, Cheap Air Fare?

Consolidators, also known as **bucket shops,** are a good place to check for the lowest fares. Their prices are much better than the fares you could get yourself, usually 10 to 30% lower than published rates, and are often even lower than what your travel agent can get you. You see their ads in the small boxes at the bottom of the page in your Sunday travel section. They act as wholesalers, buying up blocks of unused seats direct from the airlines and reselling them to the public at cut rates.

Some of the most reliable consolidators include **1-800-FLY-4-LESS** or **1-800-FLY-CHEAP.** Another good choice, **Council Travel** (☎ 800/ 226-8624), caters especially to young travelers, but their bargain-basement prices are available to people of all ages. Bucket shops have a slim profit margin, and although most are honest, the low returns drive others to shady practices. You should check each out with the Better Business Bureau before you call and pay by credit card for the added insurance.

Another way to find the cheapest fare is by using the **Internet.** The number of virtual travel agents on the Internet has increased exponentially in recent

years. A few of the better-respected ones are **Travelocity** (**www.**
travelocity.com), which also advertises last-minute deals; **Microsoft**
Expedia (**www.expedia.com**), which will e-mail you weekly with the best
fares for a chosen destination; and **Yahoo!'s Flifo Global** (**travel.yahoo.**
com/travel), whose "Fare Beater" compares airlines to find the best going
rate. For most of these sites, just enter your dates and cities, and the computer looks for the lowest fares.

Time-Savers

Hunting on the Internet for great fares can be fruitful, but it can gobble up
hours of your time. Plus the system isn't quite where it should be yet, and you
often won't be able to get the lowest fare off the Web. If you're in a hurry
and have a trusted travel agent, it is usually quickest, easiest, and cheapest to
let her do all the research for you.

The Last-Minute Lowdown

Contrary to popular belief, waiting until the last minute to buy those
unfilled seats is *not* the cheapest way to get a ticket (except sometimes by e-
mail). Although these deals do exist, you run the chance of not finding any
seat, and the savings are often not much better than a regular APEX fare. If
you want to give it a try, call the **Last Minute Travel Club** (☎ **800/**
527-8646 or 617/267-9800).

Great last-minute deals are often available directly from the airlines through
a free **e-mail service.** Each week, the airline sends you a list of discounted
flights, usually leaving the upcoming Thursday through Saturday, and
returning the following Monday through Wednesday. Of course, this service
is mainly for the person who can drop everything and take a long weekend
in Paris. You can sign up for such services at any airline's Web site (see
Appendix B).

Does It Matter What Airport I Fly Into?

Flying into major cities is always the cheapest way to go. Almost without
fail, the lowest fares you'll find will be to London, so it makes the most economic sense to start or end your trip there. Plus, England is in many ways
the least "foreign" European country for Americans (the British do, after all,
speak English) and as such offers a way to ease into the cultural soup of
Europe more slowly. If England isn't in your plans, however, don't pay it a
visit just to get these low fares; the cost of crossing the Channel (at least $85

and at least four hours) usually offsets any savings.

Notice I say start *or* end in London. Take advantage of **open-jaw** plane tickets. Some airlines will let you fly, say, into London and out of Rome without a price hike (in other words, you pay half the round-trip fare to London, plus half the round-trip fare to Rome). This is wonderful for drawing up your itinerary. Because you're not restricted to making a big loop, you can draw a meandering line that connects the cities that catch your fancy, ending your trip in a remote corner such as Athens or Seville without then having to spend a day (or more) backtracking to your arrival point.

Time-Savers

Call your airline for a seat reservation rather than doing it at check-in if possible. That way, you have a better chance of getting the seat you want. Always call the day before and the morning of your flight to reconfirm everything and check for delays.

The Friendlier Skies: How to Make Your Flight More Pleasant

The bulkhead seats in the front row of each airplane cabin usually have the most **leg room,** but the lack of seat in front of you means your carry-ons have to go in the overhead bin. Plus, from here it's often hard to see the in-flight movie. Airlines sometimes put passengers with young children in the bulkhead row so the kids can sleep on the floor—terrific if you have kids, but not if you have a headache.

Emergency-exit row seats also have extra leg room. They are usually assigned at the airport on a first-come, first-serve basis, so ask for one when you check in. In the unlikely event of an emergency, you'll be expected to open the emergency exit door and help direct traffic.

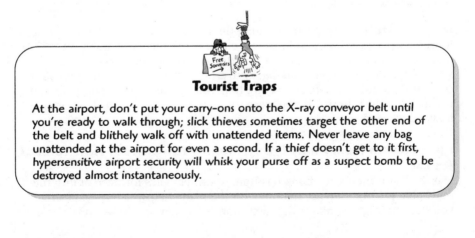

Tourist Traps

At the airport, don't put your carry-ons onto the X-ray conveyor belt until you're ready to walk through; slick thieves sometimes target the other end of the belt and blithely walk off with unattended items. Never leave any bag unattended at the airport for even a second. If a thief doesn't get to it first, hypersensitive airport security will whisk your purse off as a suspect bomb to be destroyed almost instantaneously.

If you have **special dietary needs,** be sure to order a special meal when booking your flight. Most airlines offer vegetarian, macrobiotic, kosher, lactose-free, and a variety of other meals. Even people without special needs opt for these meals anyway because they are made to order and, ostensibly, are better than the mass-produced dinners served to the rest of the passengers.

Wear casual but **comfortable clothes** and loosen them while on board. The days of getting dressed up in a coat and tie to ride an airplane went out with Nehru jackets and poodle skirts. Take off your shoes when on board. Also make sure to dress in layers; the supposedly controlled climate in airplane cabins is anything but predictable.

Flights to Europe are long no matter how you slice it. The shortest hop you can make is from the northeastern United States to Ireland's Shannon airport, a haul of 6½ hours; New York to Athens takes 10 hours. Get up and walk the aisles every couple of hours to work out the kinks and get your circulation going.

Extra! Extra!

If you're flying with **kids,** don't forget chewing gum to relieve ear pressure, a deck of cards, books, or favorite toys for entertainment, extra bottles, pacifiers, clothes, diapers, and the usual kit and caboodle.

There is an unfortunate trend toward pummeling you with video images for the entire flight. I was recently on a Rome to Philadelphia flight where they squeezed in two newsreels, a duty-free spiel, the video safety lecture, two episodes of *Frasier* and one of the British comedy *Keeping up Appearances,* and three full-length feature films. Not only is this insulting to your abilities to amuse yourself for a few hours, it also entices you to become a "seat potato" glued to the screen for the whole trip, when you should be sleeping to help fight jet lag. I bring a good book and try to ignore the flashing images before me.

Bring some **toiletries** aboard on long flights. Airplane cabins are notoriously dry places, so skin and lips will chap. Drink plenty of water on the plane to avoid dehydration, and don't drink alcohol, which will quicken your dehydration. If you're taking an overnight flight, pack a toothbrush to combat that end-of-the-flight feeling that you've been sucking on your seat cushion for seven hours. If you wear contacts, go for glasses instead or at least bring eye drops.

I Just Flew in from Philly & Boy, Are My Arms Tired! How to Beat Jet Lag

Everyone and their guidebook has homespun remedies for overcoming the inevitable **jet lag.** Staying hydrated on the plane helps, as does exposing your face to bright sunlight the next morning when you wake up in the new time zone. The best advice, though, is to get acclimated to local time as quickly as possible. Before you depart, begin rising and going to bed earlier than usual, and once you've crossed the Atlantic, go to bed according to the clocks of the country you're in. Wake up at a normal time the second day—even when your alarm beeps that it's 7am, but your tired body is telling you it's 1am.

Time-Savers

Most of Europe is six hours ahead of Eastern Standard Time. That means when it's 1pm in New York, it's 7pm in Paris. Britain is only five hours ahead (one hour behind the rest of Europe). Europeans usually use the 24-hour clock, also known here as military time. That means for noon, they write 12:00, and for 1pm, they write 13:00. The day ends at 24:00 (that's midnight). When speaking, Europeans might use either the 24-hour-clock number or a 12-hour-clock number (at 3pm, they may say "15 o'clock" or "3 in the afternoon," for example). It takes some getting used to. Remember: If the number is over 12, just subtract 12 and add a pm. For example, 20:00 would be 8pm.

Worksheet: Fare Game—Choosing an Airline

Arranging and booking flights is a complicated business—that's why a whole industry has grown up to handle it for you. If you're searching around for a deal, though, it helps to leave a trail of breadcrumbs through the maze so you can easily find your way to your destination and back. You can use the worksheets on the following pages to do just that.

There's a chance that you won't be able to get a direct flight, especially if you're looking to save money, so I've included space for you to map out any connections you'll have to make. If a connection is involved in the fares you're quoted, make sure to ask how much of a layover you'll have between flights. Nobody likes hanging around the airport for 8 to 10 hours. Be sure to mark the layover times in the appropriate spot on the worksheet, so you can compare them easily when you go back over everything to make a decision.

1   Schedule & Flight Information Worksheets

Travel Agency: _____ **Phone #:** _____

Agent's Name: _____ **Quoted Fare:** _____

Departure Schedule & Flight Information

Airline: _____ Airport: _____

Flight #: _____ Date: _____ Time: _____am/pm

Arrives in _____ Time: _____ am/pm

Connecting Flight (if any)

Amount of time between flights: _____ hours/mins.

Airline:_____ Flight #:_____ Time: _____am/pm

Arrives in _____ Time: _____ am/pm

Return Trip Schedule & Flight Information

Airline:_____ Airport: _____

Flight #: _____ Date: _____ Time: _____am/pm

Arrives in _____ Time: _____ am/pm

Connecting Flight (if any)

Amount of time between flights: _____ hours/mins.

Airline:_____ Flight #:_____ Time: _____am/pm

Arrives in _____ Time: _____ am/pm

2 Schedule & Flight Information Worksheets

Travel Agency: _____ **Phone #:** _____

Agent's Name: _____ **Quoted Fare:** _____

Departure Schedule & Flight Information

Airline: _____ Airport: _____

Flight #: _____ Date: _____ Time: _____am/pm

Arrives in _____ Time: _____ am/pm

Connecting Flight (if any)

Amount of time between flights: _____ hours/mins.

Airline:_____ Flight #:_____ Time: _____am/pm

Arrives in _____ Time: _____ am/pm

Return Trip Schedule & Flight Information

Airline:_____ Airport: _____

Flight #: _____ Date: _____ Time: _____am/pm

Arrives in _____ Time: _____ am/pm

Connecting Flight (if any)

Amount of time between flights: _____ hours/mins.

Airline:_____ Flight #:_____ Time: _____am/pm

Arrives in _____ Time: _____ am/pm

Planes, Trains, & Automobiles: How Will I Get Around Once I'm There?

In This Chapter

➤ How and when to fly on the cheap

➤ Mastering Europe's remarkable train system, from choosing the perfect rail pass to commandeering a sleeping berth

➤ When to rent a car

➤ How to get the best car-rental deal

Europe is nothing if not interconnected. Between planes, buses, rental cars, and especially trains, it's easier to move from country to country here using public transportation than it is to get from state to state back home. With the right rail pass, the ground rules for figuring out schedules, and a pocket-ful of helpful hints on how to get the best deal out of airlines, train stations, and rental car agencies, you can slash your travel time and budget in half. This chapter will give you the insider's scoop on how to do it all, and you'll be bopping all over Europe like a pro in no time.

The Pros & Cons of City-Hopping by Plane

Air travel within Europe makes sense only for covering very large distances in a limited amount of time, especially to get out to Spain, Portugal, Greece, Sicily, or Scandinavia. When is it worthwhile to fly instead of take the train? Weigh the extra money spent on a plane ticket versus the time—and on a Eurail pass, the rail days—you'd waste traveling by train. I choose wings over rails only when I'd otherwise have to spend close to a full day on the train.

There are four choices for air travel within Europe:

➤ **Regular flights on major European carriers.** This is the most expensive but surest option. You can arrange these flights at home through their 800 numbers (see appendix B) or through a travel agent or the airline's office in any European city.

➤ **Charter flights.** These flights are just like ones in the United States except that British charter flights tend to book whole planes, whereas U.S. charter companies usually just buy up sections of regular flights. Although these flights are generally reputable, they're occasionally prone to cancellation.

➤ **Consolidator tickets.** Often the cheapest way to fly, these tickets are available from bucket shops and budget travel agencies across Europe, especially in London and Athens. Although not definitively unreliable, this is the least safe way to go. Shady consolidators can go out of business overnight (pay by credit card for insurance), the rate of cancellation is higher, and many of the airlines (often Middle Eastern and Asian carriers) have lower safety rates than major U.S. and European carriers.

➤ **Small, no-frills airlines.** A recent development, these carriers offer bargain-basement rates, usually $50 to $250, for a limited set of routes, using secondary airports in major cities as hubs. They do this by taking a page from the U.S. regional airlines' book: cutting ticket costs along with the frills. This is your best bet for getting dirt-cheap, reliable tickets in Europe. Some companies are independent start-ups; others are baby branches of major airlines. The system is still evolving, but a few outfits that have emerged as dependable choices include **Easyjet** (in London ☎ **44-1582/700-0006**), **Debonair** (in London ☎ **44-541/500-300**), **Ryanair** (in Dublin ☎ **353-1/609-7800**), and **Virgin Express** (in Belgium ☎ **32-2/752-0505**).

Riding the Rails: Train Travel & Rail Passes

In Europe, the shortest (and cheapest) distance between two points is lined with railroad tracks. The train is the preferred mode of travel by everyone, from farmers and grannies to businesswomen and visitors. As a rule, European trains run on time, are clean and comfortable, and have a vast network that covers almost every minor city.

Many trains still have the old-fashioned couchette configuration. Each car has a corridor along one side; off of this corridor are 10 little couchettes, or compartments, which seat six to eight people (or, in first-class compartments, four to six people in slightly cushier chairs—but that's not worth the added expense). Sadly, most short-run trains are now switching over to the modern straight-through cars with seats running down both sides of an open aisle. These train always make me feel more like I'm at home commuting to work than traveling in Europe on a grand tour, but hey, that's progress for you.

The Need for Speed: Europe's High-Speed Trains

Europe has a rainbow of train classifications that range from local runs that stop at every tiny station to high-speed bullet trains such as France's TGV, which set the world's speed record for a national rail run (320 miles per hour, though it usually cruises at 130 miles per hour). These trains include specialized and expensive **high-speed trains** within nations (France's TGV, Italy's ETR/Pendolino, Spain's AVE), new international high-speed runs (Thalys from Paris to Brussels; Artesia from Paris to Torino and Milan in Italy), and the **Eurostar** Channel Tunnel train (see the "Dollars & Sense" sidebar concerning this). Beyond these, the fastest trains you'll usually take are **EC (Eurocity)** or **IC (Intercity).** The only difference between the two is that the Eurocity train crosses an international border (overnight versions are sometimes called **EN,** or **Euronight**).

Time-Savers

You can get much more information about train travel in Europe and receive automated schedule information by fax by contacting **Rail Europe** (☎ **800/438-7245; www.raileurope.com**). Until becoming a travel writer, I never found the need to purchase the rail schedule bible, the **Thomas Cook European Timetable** ($27.95 from travel specialty stores or order it at ☎ **800/FORSYTH**). Its 500 pages—updated monthly, but rumored to go quarterly soon—contain the daily schedules of all major European train and ferry routes. If you have Internet access, you can get to each country's national railway Web site, which include schedules and fare information, occasionally in English, via the handy links page maintained by **Mercurio** (**http://mercurio. iet.unipi.it/misc/timetabl.html**).

Many high-speed trains throughout Europe require that you pay a **supplement** of around $5 to $15 in addition to the regular ticket price. If you're buying point-to-point tickets, this supplement is included in the full price. With a pass such as Eurail, you may have to purchase this supplement separately. The train conductor will sell you one, but he also will assess you a small penalty fee. I always check at the ticket office to be sure and pay for it in advance.

In addition to supplements, **reservations** are required on some of the speediest of the high-speed runs, including Eurostar (the Channel Tunnel train), TGV in France, Pendolino in Italy, and long-distance trains in Spain. Any train marked with an *R* on a schedule needs to be reserved ahead of time for a fee ranging from $10 up beyond $50 (when a meal is included).

You can almost always reserve a seat within a few hours of the train's departure, but I play it safe by booking a few days in advance. You'll also need to reserve any sleeping couchette or sleeping berth.

Dollars & Sense

The **Eurostar** train connects London with Paris and London with Brussels through the Channel Tunnel; both trips take four hours. Because the ferry route takes all day and costs almost the same, Eurostar is a great deal. A one-way, first-class ticket including meal costs $199, second class (no meal) $139, and a leisure ticket only $99. If you have a rail pass (Eurail, Euro, BritRail, French, or Benelux), you can get a discount that brings the cheapest fare down to just $85. Your pass must be validated to get the discount, but on flexipasses (see "Ticketless Travel: Understanding Rail Passes" for an explanation), it doesn't use up a Eurail day.

Train Tickets: To Reserve or Not to Reserve?

There's no need to buy train tickets or make reservations through your travel agent before you leave the United States. Doing so will only lock you into a schedule that you may want to change once you're on the road. Plus, the travel agent will charge you a few extra bucks to take care of it. (Keep in mind, though, you will have to buy your rail pass before leaving the United States; see "Ticketless Travel: Understanding Rail Passes.")

I make only two exceptions to the no advance tickets rule. On the high-speed Artesia, you must buy a supplement, on which you can get a substantial discount if you have a rail pass—but only if you buy the supplement in the United States along

Tourist Traps

Most train schedules and signs use the **native names for cities,** not the English equivalent. Athens is Athinai, Cologne is Köln, Copenhagen is København, Florence is Firenze, Lisbon is Lisboa, Munich is München, Naples is Napoli, Pamplona may be Iruñea, Prague is Praha, Vienna is Wien, Venice is Venezia, and so on.

with the rail pass. The second exception comes from my experience: It's always a good idea to reserve a seat on the Eurostar. England's frequent "bank holidays" (three- or four-day weekends) book the train solid with Londoners taking short vacations to Paris.

Europe's Primary Train Routes

Tourist Traps

Make sure you get on the right *car*, not just the right train. Each car may very well be splitting off down the line and joining a train headed to a different destination. Getting on the right car is especially important when you're getting on a night train (if you have a reserved spot, you needn't worry). Each car has its own destination placard, which may also list major stops en route, and always check with the conductor.

The "Boxcar Willie" Plan: Taking Overnight Train Rides

Go to bed in Paris; wake up in Rome. How much more convenient can you get? Why waste a whole day watching the countryside (no matter how pretty) roll by between two cities when it's the cities themselves you came to see? On an overnight train, you not only get a cheap (if uncomfortable) bed for the night, you also get where you're going while you sleep. To maximize your time and money in Europe, make any trip over six hours an overnight ride.

You have four sleeping choices:

➤ **Sitting up.** This is a last resort; you won't get much sleep.

Tourist Traps

Don't drink the water on the trains, not even to rinse your mouth. It's for hand–washing only. Trains, especially overnight trains, dehydrate you quickly, so make sure you bring bottled water to sip throughout the night and to rinse your mouth and your toothbrush the next morning.

➤ **Fold-out seats.** In regular couchettes, you can usually pull facing seat bottoms out toward each other, collapsing the seat backs down. Do it to all the seats in the couchette, and you have a little padded romper room in which to nap, but usually no door lock. Privacy isn't guaranteed, so as soon as you find an unoccupied couchette, pull out all the seats, close all the curtains, turn out the lights, and lie down as if asleep—even if it's 5pm. Hopefully, potential roomies will pass your couchette by in search of a more inviting one.

➤ **Flip-down bunks.** This is always my first choice. Sleeping couchettes allow six to sleep in minor discomfort on narrow, flip-down, shelf-like bunks. Doors lock, the conductor keeps on eye on your car, and at around $20 for a reservation, it's one of the cheapest sleeping deals in

Europe. Unless you reserve an entire couchette, be prepared to share your room with strangers.

➤ **A berth in a sleeping car.** Usually this is only a first-class option, where you get a tiny room with two to three bunks and a private sink. It's more expensive and a smidgen comfier than a couchette. Strangers may populate the other bunk if you're alone.

In a couchette, you get a paper-thin **sleep sack** and a blanket. If you're **crossing an international border,** the conductor will take your passport when he comes around to cancel your ticket or pass. This is so the border patrol can sift through them all quickly when you cross at 3am, and you won't have to be woken up. Don't worry; you'll get everything back in the morning, and it's probably safer in the conductor's care overnight than it would be on your person. Speaking of which...

Time-Savers

Outside of each couchette is a little plastic window where bits of cardboard are inserted if someone at this stop or at one down the line has reserved a seat. Save yourself the trouble of getting booted out later in the trip by checking to make sure you're occupying an unreserved seat before you claim the couchette.

Train Safety: Getting Your Z's Without Getting Fleeced

Sleeping on the train is a relatively safe endeavor, but take a few sensible precautions. Couchette doors lock from the inside and can only be unlocked from the outside by a special key the conductor carries. **Always lock your door.** Feel free to underscore the importance of this to your fellow couchette buddies even if you have to pantomime it so that if they get up in the middle of the night to visit the bathroom down the corridor, they'll remember to lock up when they re-enter. Remember: You're sharing a room with up to five strangers, so don't flash anything valuable.

You should be fine. After 15 years and many, many overnight train rides, I witnessed my first robbery only two months ago. While we were both sleeping, the stranger who shared my couchette had his bag lifted from where it was hanging next to his head in the middle bunk. The door was unlocked when I awoke, but neither he nor I nor the conductor could figure out how it happened, unless the victim unlocked it in the middle of the night and had simply forgotten to relock it.

I, however, felt secure because I had reserved the top bunk, which gets much hotter than the lower bunks, but puts you out of all but the tallest thief's reach. It allows you to sleep with your head right next to your bags, which are stowed in a niche above the door. I had strapped my pack to the niche's guardrail, so that no one could simply tug it down and run off. Sure, I spent an extra minute the next morning extracting my bag from its cranny, but two of us walked out of that couchette, and only one of us still had his stuff.

Ticketless Travel: Understanding Rail Passes (Or, This Train Is My Rail, This Train Is Eurail)

The greatest value in European travel has always been the rail pass, a single ticket that allows you unlimited travel or a certain number of days within a set period of time. On trips where you cover countless kilometers on the rails, a pass will end up costing you considerably less than buying individual tickets. Plus, it gives you the freedom to hop on a train whenever you feel like it, making a day trip out of town easy and cheap. There's no waiting in ticket lines either.

The granddaddy of passes is the **Eurail** pass, which covers 17 countries (not including England); it's the whirlwind, pan-European tour's single best investment. It has recently been joined by its nephew, the **Europass,** which covers five countries, also not including England (though you can add up to seven more; more on that to come). The Europass is mainly for travelers who are going to stay within the heart of western Europe. Both Eurail and Europass have various **rail-and-drive** and **partner-pass** cousins (details on this also to follow).

All of these rail passes also often get you **discounts** on private rail lines (such as those in the Alps) and the Eurostar between London and Paris or Brussels (see the previous "Dollars & Sense" sidebar) and discounts or free travel for ferry crossings (Italy to Greece) and some boat rides on rivers (Rhine, Mosel) and lakes (especially Swiss ones). These bonuses can change from year to year, so check with the agency that issues you the pass and read the literature they send with it to see what extra goodies you may be getting.

Dollars & Sense

Rail passes are good all the way up to the borders of the countries they cover. So if you're traveling from a Eurail country to a non-Eurail country—say Vienna, Austria, to Prague, Czech Republic—you can go to the ticket window in Vienna and purchase a ticket for just the stretch from the Austrian/Czech border to Prague. Your pass will cover the Vienna-to-the-border segment.

How Does a Rail Pass Work?

From the date you buy the pass, you have six months to start using it. The day you want to begin using the pass, you have to have it **validated** at a European train station. Aside from reserving couchettes or buying supplements, this is the only time you'll have to wait in a ticket line. With consecutive-day, unlimited use Eurail passes, you just hop on trains at whim. The Europass and **flexipass** versions give you a certain number of days

(5 to 15) within a two-month window of travel. Printed on the flexipass are as many little boxes as you've bought days of travel. Every time you board a train, just write the date in the next free box (in ink). When the conductor comes around, he checks your ticket to make sure you've put down the right date.

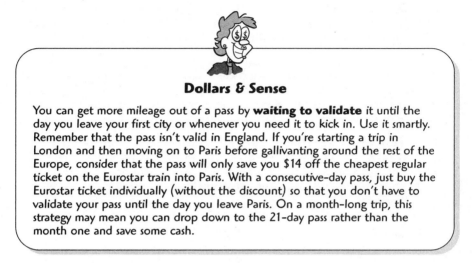

Dollars & Sense

You can get more mileage out of a pass by **waiting to validate** it until the day you leave your first city or whenever you need it to kick in. Use it smartly. Remember that the pass isn't valid in England. If you're starting a trip in London and then moving on to Paris before gallivanting around the rest of the Europe, consider that the pass will only save you $14 off the cheapest regular ticket on the Eurostar train into Paris. With a consecutive-day pass, just buy the Eurostar ticket individually (without the discount) so that you don't have to validate your pass until the day you leave Paris. On a month-long trip, this strategy may mean you can drop down to the 21-day pass rather than the month one and save some cash.

What about **overnight trains,** you say? No problem; a Eurail "day" starts at 7pm in the evening and runs 29 hours until the following midnight. In other words, when you board an overnight train after 7pm, write the next day's date in the box. You're clear for the overnight and any traveling you want to do all the next day.

What Kinds of Eurail Passes Are There?

If you're under age 26, you can opt to buy a regular first-class pass or a second-class **youth pass;** if you're 26 and over, you're stuck buying a first-class pass (except for sleeping cars, the class difference is negligible). Passes for kids 4 to 11 are half-price and children under 4 travel free. The prices listed here are for 1998, but keep in mind they'll rise each year:

➤ **Eurailpass.** Consecutive-day Eurail passes are best for those who are taking the train very frequently (every few days), covering a lot of ground, and making many short train hops. Eurail passes are good in 17 countries (see the following "Dollars & Sense" sidebar). They cost $538 for 15 days, $698 for 21 days, $864 for one month, $1,224 for two months, or $1,512 for three months.

➤ **Eurail Flexipass.** For folks who want to range far and wide, but plan on taking their time over a long trip and intend to stay in each city for a while, a flexipass is just the ticket. It's good for two months of travel, within which you can travel by train for 10 days (consecutive or not) at $634 or 15 days at $836.

➤ **Eurail Saverpass.** If you're traveling with buddies, you can all save big time (15% each) so long as you ride together. The saverpass for two to five travelers costs, *per person*, $458 for 15 days, $594 for 21 days, $734 for one month, $1,040 for two months, or $1,286 for three months.

➤ **Eurail Saver Flexipass.** This flexipass is for groups. You must travel together (two to five people), and you each pay $540 to travel by train for 10 days within two months, or $710 for 15 days within two months.

➤ **Eurail Youthpass.** The second-class ticket to Europe on the cheap, perfect for summer vacations and whirlwind tours. It costs $376 for 15 days, $489 for 21 days, $605 for one month, $857 for two months, or $1,059 for three months.

➤ **Eurail Youth Flexipass.** Are you on a study-abroad program? This may be the pass for you, because it allows 10 days of train travel within two months for $444 or 15 days in two months for $585—just right for long weekends and vacations between classes.

Dollars & Sense

Eurail countries: Austria, Belgium, Denmark, Finland, France, Germany, Greece, Hungary, Ireland, Italy, Luxembourg, the Netherlands, Norway, Portugal, Spain, Sweden, Switzerland.

Europass core countries: France, Germany, Switzerland, Italy, Spain.

Europass add–on "zones": Austria/Hungary; Belgium/Netherlands/Luxembourg; Greece (including the ferry from Brindisi, Italy); Portugal.

Note that Great Britain is not included in any pass.

➤ **Europass.** If your trip focuses on the core of western Europe (see preceding "Dollars & Sense" sidebar), then Eurail is wasteful spending. Go for the Europass to have two months in which you can take five days of train travel. The add-on "zones" let you expand the scope of your trip to other countries. The base pass costs $326, $386 with one zone added, $416 with two zones, $436 with three zones, or $446 with all four zones (notice the per-zone costs goes down the more you add). But, you ask, only five days of travel? You can add on up to 10 extra days (for 15 days total) at $42 per day (break out the calculator for this, because adding zones and days may bring your total up high enough that buying a Eurail makes more sense).

➤ **Europass Partner.** This isn't actually a different pass, but rather a way for one traveling companion to get a 40% discount on his own Europass. You must travel together, and because I assume you'll play nice and split the savings, you'll each pay 20% less than if you were going solo: $261 each for the basic pass, $309 with one zone, $333 with two zones, $349 with three zones, $357 with all four zones, and $34 each for each additional day.

➤ **Europass Youth.** This pass is the same deal as the Europass (no partner pass version, though), only in second class and for people under 26 only. The base pass costs $216, $261 with one zone, $286 with two zones, $301 with three zones, $309 with all four zones, and $29 for each additional day.

➤ **EurailDrive pass.** This pass is the best of both worlds, mixing train travel and rental cars (through Hertz or Avis) for less money than it would cost to do them separately. This is also one of the only ways to get around the obscenely high daily car rental rates in Europe that you pay when you rent for less than a week. With this pass, you get four rail days and three car days within a two-month period. Prices (for one adult/two adults each) vary with the class of the car: $435/$350 economy class, $495/$380 compact, $525/$395 mid-sized. You can add up to five extra rail and/or car days. Extra rail days are $55 each; car days cost $58 each for economy class, $78 compact, and $88 mid-sized. You have to reserve the first car day a week before leaving the United States, but you can make other reservations as you go (though it's always subject to availability). If there are more than two adults, the extra passengers get the car portion free but must buy the four-day rail pass for about $268.

➤ **Eurodrive pass.** This deal is similar to the EurailDrive pass, but it's for Europass countries only (and no add-on zones) and shorter trips. It's good for three rail days and two car days within a two-month period. Prices (one adult/two adults each) are $315/$265 economy class, $355/$280 compact, and $370/$290 mid-sized. You can add up to nine extra rail days at $42 a pop and unlimited extra car days for $55 to $85 a day, depending on the class of car.

Other Rail Passes

As if all the Eurail options weren't confusing enough, you can also buy **national passes** of various kinds: flexi, consecutive-day, rail-and-drive, rail-and-fly, kilometric (you buy a certain number of kilometers on the national rail system), and others. There are also **regional passes** such as **ScanRail** (for Scandinavian countries), **BritRail** (covering Great Britain, which is not a part of the Eurail gang), and the **European East Pass** (good in Austria, Czech Republic, Slovakia, Hungary, and Poland). Some types of national passes you have to buy in the United States, some you can get on either side of the Atlantic, and still others you must purchase in Europe itself. Remember that seniors, students, and youths can usually get discounts on

European trains—in some countries just by asking, in others by buying a discount card good for a fixed period. Rail Europe or your travel agent can fill you in on all the details.

Where Do I Buy My Rail Pass?

You have to buy passes for Eurail and its offshoots in the United States (they're also available from some major European train stations, but at more than 50% higher prices, so don't bother). You can buy rail passes from most travel agents, but the biggest supplier is **Rail Europe (☎ 800/438-7245; www.raileurope.com**). They also sell most national passes, except for a few minor British ones. My recommendation is to contact Rick Steve's **Europe Through The Back Door (☎ 425/771-8303; www.ricksteves.com**). He doesn't tack on the $10 handling fee all other agencies do, he sells all Europe-wide and all national rail passes, and he sends a free video and guide on how to use rail passes with every order. **BritRail (☎ 800/677-8585**) specializes in Great Britain, and **DER Tours (☎ 800/782-2424; www.dertravel.com**) is a Germany specialist that also sells other national passes (except French and British ones).

Crossing the Waters: Traveling by Ferry or Hydrofoil

You may occasionally find yourself crossing the waters in Europe, whether it be the traditional (pre–Channel Tunnel) English Channel crossing, en route to Greece from Italy, around Scandinavia, or just off to an island somewhere. **Ferry** travel can be scenic, but is invariably slow. For around double the money, you often have the option of taking a **hydrofoil** (sort of a ferry on steroids). It goes about twice as fast as the ferry, but you'll be stuck below deck for the entire trip. My advice: To get from England to France or Belgium, take the Eurostar train through the Channel Tunnel; the difference in fare is more than offset by the time you'll save and the aggravation and seasickness you'll avoid.

When *Don't* I Need a Rail Pass?

Nifty as they are, rail passes aren't the wisest investment for every trip. Eurail is primarily for people on an extended, whirlwind tour; Europass can be handier on short, more focused trips, but it still may be overkill if you only plan to take a few train rides over the course of your visit.

Will any pass be right for you? The answer will be different for every trip, so get ready to do some math. For example, you'd have to travel at least 22 days (24 days on the youth pass) on a two-month consecutive-day pass before it starts costing less per trip than the 15-days-within-two-months flexipass. Are the extra days worth it? It depends on your travel plans and how much liberty you want to be able to jump on trains at a whim. After you've drawn up an itinerary, estimate how much you think you'd spend on individual tickets using the "Train Travel Between European Cities" chart on page 68 (supplemented by quotes from Rail Europe, if you need to fill in any gaps). If a rail pass will save you dough and still do the job, then go for it.

Chart: Calculating Travel Times, Distances, & Costs

The "Train Travel Between European Cities" chart on page 68 is designed to give you a rough idea of how long and how much it will cost to travel by train to and from the major cities covered in this book. The numbers in the lower right of the chart are the distances between cities (in miles). The figures in the upper left of the chart represent approximate travel time and cost of a one-way, second-class ticket. Keep in mind the listed travel times have been rounded to the nearest half-hour on the shortest possible run (using the fastest trains and the quickest connections).

Use this chart just as you would a mileage chart in a road atlas—follow the columns up and across to hit upon the information you seek. (Note that the cities appear diagonally through the chart.) For example, to find out the distance from Florence to Paris, go to the Florence box and count four boxes to the right until you're under the Paris column—the answer is 745 miles. To find out the length of the trip and cost to get from Florence to Paris, go to the Florence box and count up four boxes until you get to the Paris row; you'll find that the trip takes $12\frac{1}{2}$ hours and costs $119. (An *N* within this box indicates that an overnight train is available; an asterisk indicates that a transfer of trains is required.)

A Station Is More Than the Sum of Its Trains

Like the trains themselves, European train stations tend to be clean and user-friendly, and the snack bars are better than you'd expect (in case you forget to pick up train picnic supplies in town). If you know how to use the train station for all it's worth, you can spend 20 minutes there when you first arrive in a city and come out of it well-oriented and fully armed for your visit.

Here's a useful battle plan upon arrival in a station:

1. Stop by the station's **ATM or bank** for a bit of local cash (not too much; a downtown branch will have better rates).

2. Hit the **tourist board** kiosk or desk and milk it for all the free info and handouts you can get.

3. Visit a **newsstand** to see whether the city maps for sale are better than the free one from the tourist office (usually the answer is yes, and the investment is worth it). Pick up a phone card (if you'll be in the country long enough to use it), grab a few city bus or metro tickets to get you started, and buy the local English-language information/events magazine.

Train Travel Between European Cities

Distance (in miles)

	Zurich	Vienna	Venice	Rome	Prague	Paris	Munich	Madrid	London	Florence	Barcelona	Athens	Amsterdam
Zurich	Zurich	N $103 9h	N $84 8.5h	N $106 10h	N $159 11h	$85 6.5h	$79 4h	N $220 *32h	N $170 *10h	N $87 8h	N $158 *13h	N $231 *40h	N $188 9h
Vienna	470	Vienna	N $60 9h	N $96 13h	N $40 5.5h	N $203 13.5h	N $68 5h	N $338 *23h	N $288 *19h	N $74 11h	N $302 *22h	N $221 *43h	N $219 *13h
Venice	325	380	Venice	N $49 5h	N $181 13.5h	N $140 12.5h	N $75 7h	N $184 *19h	N $225 *15h	$23 3h	N $133 *18h	N $174 *35h	N $251 *15h
Rome	526	666	355	Rome	N $170 *17.5h	N $123 14h	N $90 11h	N $192 *29h	N $208 *17h	$27 2.5h	N $142 *19h	N $125 *30h	N $282 *19.5h
Prague	418	177	527	779	Prague	N $170 15h	N $80 6.5h	N $320 *36h	N $287 *20h	N $148 15.5h	N $269 *27h	N $295 *47.5h	N $178 *13h
Paris	368	763	690	869	636	Paris	N $140 9h	N $135 13h	$85 3h	N $119 12.5h	N $99 11h	N $248 44h	N $68 5h
Munich	194	244	325	549	228	510	Munich	N $284 *22h	N $249 *14h	N $368 9h	N $234 *13h	N $215 *41h	N $176 8.5h
Madrid	1022	1481	960	1210	1430	790	1228	Madrid	N $220 *16h	N $170 *25.5h	N $50 8h	N $317 *59h	N $203 *17.5h
London	547	888	865	1057	744	249	660	1040	London	N $237 *15.5h	N $184 *15h	N $333 *47h	N $116 *6h
Florence	341	550	170	185	629	745	440	1110	935	Florence	N $120 17.5h	N $152 *32.5h	N $244 *17h
Barcelona	650	1108	825	838	1058	650	854	382	900	730	Barcelona	N $267 49h	N $167 *16.5h
Athens	1498	1154	780	1481	1335	1805	1279	2331	2016	1666	1916	Athens	N $407 49.5h
Amsterdam	498	711	740	1025	526	308	515	1099	297	775	962	1758	Amsterdam

Travel Time (in hours) **& Ticket Cost**

* = transfer required. N = overnight train available. Prices are for second-class, ticket only (overnight couchettes cost extra). Distance in miles. Length of ride is to the nearest half-hour on the shortest run (fastest trains/quickest connections). London figures are via the Chunnel and Paris or Brussels.

4. Now that you have some pocket change, you may want to dump your main bag in a **locker or left luggage office** for $2 to $10 a day and keep just your daypack. If you're just dropping by town for a half-day visit, the bags will stay there. If you're spending the night, go hotel hunting *without* your pack, and you'll have more stamina and bargaining leverage to get the best deal.

5. Head to the phones and call around for a hotel, or use the station's **hotel booking service** (see chapter 7 for more hotel advice).

Dollars & Sense

Although metros (subways) have turnstiles, most **public transportation** (buses, trams, funiculars) in European cities is on the honor system. You're expected to punch your ticket in a little box on the bus as soon as you board. Make sure you hold on to all tickets (metro, bus, or otherwise) for the duration of your ride, because spot inspectors board regularly or stop you in the metro tunnels. If they find you don't have a valid ticket, you can be fined on the spot for anything ranging from $20 to $300.

In smaller towns, the tiny station bar may double as the ticket office. Most stations, however, have banks of ticket windows. Try to figure out which window you need before getting in the invariably long lines. The bulk of windows will be for purchasing regular tickets; a few windows will be for people who just need reservations (if, for example, you have a Eurail pass but plan to take a reservations-required train or want to reserve a sleeping couchette). A few windows are for international or special high-speed trains only.

Before you exit the station, check out your train options for leaving town a few days down the line (as well as for any day trips you plan to make). That way, you can swing by a day or two before you leave to buy your tickets and reserve seats or couchettes rather than wait until the last minute when the lengthy ticket lines may thwart your precision-timed plans. The **rail information desk**—not to be confused with the city tourist board's desk,

Tourist Traps

Most train stations are fairly safe, but because they are central clearinghouses for bewildered tourists overwhelmed by a new city and probably not paying close attention to what's going on around them, pickpockets abound. Be careful, never abandon your bags, and don't be distracted by all the hotel touts who will swarm you offering rooms.

because the two won't answer each other's questions—usually has a long line, and the staff was born harried. Use the do-it-yourself information sources as much as possible. Modern stations in big cities often have **computerized rail information** kiosks and **automatic ticketing machines,** but both are often on the fritz.

Luckily, there's still the old-fashioned way. All stations have **schedule posters** that list the full timetables and regular track numbers for all trains that pass through. Usually, but not always, arrivals are on a white poster and departures are on a yellow one. These posters show how many trains a day go where you want to go, when precisely they leave, whether you need a reservation, and what the ultimate destination on that train may be (you may want to get from Paris to Pisa, but the train will be marked to Rome).

Track assignments may change on a daily basis. In larger stations, check those big electronically updated departure boards. Then seek out a conductor on the indicated platform and blurt out your destination in a questioning voice for reconfirmation before stepping on the waiting train. Once on board, I also triple-check with passengers who look like they take this train every day.

Another One Rides the Bus

Regional and long-haul bus service in Europe mirrors the trains in efficiency and the remarkable density of the network. If you can't get there by train in Europe, you almost certainly can by bus. Although buses cost about half as much as trains, they take two to four times as long and are five to ten times more uncomfortable. Avoid an overnight bus trip at all costs.

I only take buses when there is no train to where I'm going or if the bus makes a better connection. In some countries—especially Ireland, Greece, Turkey, Portugal, and parts of Spain and Scandinavia—the bus network is more vast and better connected than the train service. Otherwise, stick to the rails.

Hit the Road, Jacques: Renting a Car

The wind in your hair, the freedom to turn down any road, visiting vineyards, medieval hamlets, and crumbling castles with ease—as great as the trains are, sometimes a car is the best way to get footloose and fancy-free in Europe. You can be your own travel boss and get away from the structure of train schedules. It's the only way to explore any small region in depth.

Of course, you'll have to deal with aggressive drivers, navigate nerve-racking and confusing city traffic on occasion, and find and pay for parking whenever you stop. You aren't free to relax and do research on the trip between towns (you'll be driving, after all), and the gasoline prices will curl your toenails. Still, unless you walk or bike through Europe, there's no way to get closer to the land and have the true freedom to go where your travel dreams take you than to rent a car.

The Rules of the Road:
What You Need to Know to Drive in Europe

Except for driving on the left in Great Britain and Ireland (a confusing situation exacerbated by the presence of far too many roundabouts instead of intersections), **European road rules** are similar enough to American ones that you'll get by fine. There are, however, some important differences:

➤ Most European drivers are much more aggressive than American ones.

➤ *Do not ride* in the left lane on a four-lane highway; it is truly only for passing.

➤ If someone comes up from behind and flashes their lights at you, it's a signal for you to slow down and drive more on the shoulder so that they can pass you more easily (two-lane roads here routinely become three cars wide).

➤ Except for the German Autobahn, most highways do indeed have speed limits of around 60 to 80 miles per hour (100 to 135 kilometers per hour).

➤ Everything's measured in kilometers here (mileage and speed limits). For a rough conversion, one kilometer equals about .6 miles.

➤ That gas may look reasonably priced, but remember the price is per liter (3.8 liters equals one gallon, so multiply by four to guestimate the equivalent per-gallon price).

➤ Drive defensively and carefully, assume the other drivers have a better idea of what they're doing than you do, and take your hints from them.

So when should you rent a car? And which is better: renting a car or taking the train? If you want to cover lots of ground, concentrate on the cities, or go solo, then take the train. If you're exploring a single country or region, plan to hit lots of small towns, and are in a party of three or more, then rent a car (three people splitting one car rental is cheaper than three train tickets).

Do *not* rent a car just to get around a city. In fact, avoid having a car in town at all costs. I can think of no aspect of European travel less exciting or more stressful. Plus, parking fees gobble at your travel budget. Between hotel charges and garages and lots, expect to pay anywhere from $10 to $60 a day just to park the car. Save the vehicle for exploring the countryside. Arrange to pick up your rental car the morning you leave the first city on your planned drive and to drop it off as soon as you pull into the last city.

The best trips mix and match transportation a bit. For example, you can take the train to Florence, and then drive through the vineyards and hill towns of Tuscany to Rome. This is why rail-and-drive passes (see the previous section "What Kind of Rail Passes Are There?") can make a lot of sense. If you see

Bet You Didn't Know

Michelin maps are made for the visitor as well as the driver. They mark cities as uninteresting (as a tourist destination), interesting, worth a detour, or worth an entire journey. They also highlight in green particularly scenic stretches of road and have symbols pointing out scenic overlooks, ruins, and other sights along the way. Look for Michelin maps in the travel section of your local bookstore.

just the major cities of Europe, you're missing out on a big part of the continent, and I heartily recommend breaking up the metropolis itinerary with some jaunts through the countryside to smaller towns. It'll add spice and variety to your trip.

Oooh, Ahhh: Europe's Most Scenic Drives

Which portions of the trip are ripe for car rental? The open road beckons more in certain regions of Europe, and several well-established drives famously link towns of interest and/or take you through pretty countryside or spectacular scenery. These prescribed routes can be packed with travelers and the industries that cater to them in the summer months, but they tend to be worth it nonetheless. Here are some of the biggies that I include in this book:

➤ The **Ring of Kerry in Ireland** winds around a peninsula teeming with little fishing villages, prehistoric ruins, and grassy, sheep-dotted slopes (see chapter 15).

➤ The **Romantic Road in Bavaria, Germany** is full of small towns and cities that variously highlight the medieval, Renaissance, and baroque eras (see chapter 18).

➤ **Chiantigiana in Tuscany, Italy** takes you through the heart of the wine region between Florence and Siena (see chapter 23).

But you needn't stick merely to these well-trodden paths. Among the regions that just cry out to be explored by car are sun-drenched Provence in southern France, the Tuscany wine region of medieval and Renaissance hill towns in Italy, the dramatic Scottish Highlands, most of the lush Irish countryside, the mighty Alps (where the train system is fantastic but expensive), France's chateaux-filled Loire Valley, the villages of the Cotswolds in England, and Moorish-influenced southern Spain. Unfortunately, space constraints prevent me from discussing all these places in this book, but if the idea of a scenic drive appeals to you, by all means put the pedal to the metal.

Is My Drivers License Valid Over There or What?

If you do plan to drive in Europe, I recommend (although it's not required) getting an **International Driver's Permit** and carrying it in addition to your regular driver's license. It costs $10 from AAA (you don't have to be a member; call ☎ **407/444-4300** to find the office nearest you). If you are an

AAA member, ask for any free info and maps they can send you to cover the countries in which you'll be driving.

Dollars & Sense

Some countries, such as Austria and Switzerland, require that cars riding the national highways have special stickers in lieu of paying tolls (or as a supplement to cheap tolls). If you rent within that country, the car already has one, but if you're crossing a border, check at the crossing station to see whether you need to purchase a sticker on the spot for a nominal fee.

Rental Tips to Save You Time & Money
Follow these tips to get the best deal on a rental car:

➤ **Rent in the United States.** You'll get the best rates renting ahead of time directly through a U.S. company. If you're on the road and decide you want a car, contact someone back home and have them cut the deal, faxing the confirmation directly to your hotel—it's worth it. The numbers for the major rental com-panies, plus those that special-ize in European travel, are listed in appendix B.

Tourist Traps

Never leave anything visible in the car when you park it. When you check into a hotel, take all of your luggage in with you, even if you won't need it. This advice goes doubly in Italy and triply in Naples.

➤ **Shop around.** You'd think with such competition that the Big Three and other firms would offer similar rates. Nothing is further from the truth. For the same four-day weekend, you'll hear $49.95 from one company, and then the next will blithely say the best they can do is $129.99. Make sure when you ask what part of the quoted rate is the base rate, what's included (such as CDW), if taxes are included, whether you get unlimited mileage (which you definitely want), and any other restrictions.

➤ **Be flexible.** Sometimes if you pick up the car Thursday instead of Friday or at the downtown office rather than the airport, or keep it over the weekend, you'll save big bucks. When you give the rental firm your dates for pick up and delivery, let them know you're open to other dates as well if it means saving money. Also, for complicated reasons, it's sometimes cheaper to rent for a full week rather than two days.

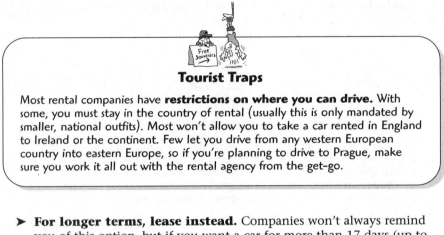

Tourist Traps

Most rental companies have **restrictions on where you can drive.** With some, you must stay in the country of rental (usually this is only mandated by smaller, national outfits). Most won't allow you to take a car rented in England to Ireland or the continent. Few let you drive from any western European country into eastern Europe, so if you're planning to drive to Prague, make sure you work it all out with the rental agency from the get-go.

➤ **For longer terms, lease instead.** Companies won't always remind you of this option, but if you want a car for more than 17 days (up to six months), tell them you want to short-term lease it.

➤ **Stick shift is cheaper than automatic.** A stick shift car can be up to 40% cheaper than an automatic shift. On Europe's many narrow, windy, hilly roads and tight streets in ancient cities, manual shifts give you better control as well.

Bet You Didn't Know

Leasing can also be a technical loophole for those too young to rent under official company policy. The minimum age for renting a car ranges from 18 to 27, but it's usually 21 to 25. Leasing, on the other hand, is often open to anyone over 18.

➤ **CDW is worth it.** If your regular insurance doesn't cover it, buy the collision damage wavier, or CDW, from the rental agency. This peace of mind comes at only $10 to $15 or so per day and basically allows you to total the car and not be held liable.

➤ **Remind them you've already paid.** Make sure you know exactly what you paid for when you arranged the car rental. For reasons I'll never understand, the pick-up office in Europe often somehow "overlooks" the fact that your credit card has already been charged for the rental cost, and they double-charge you. The hassle of working this out with the credit card people after you return isn't worth the trouble. Usually, you will get one charge on your card from the European office for the first full tank of gas it provides (which is almost never included in the original rental price).

➤ **Inspect the car before you drive away.** I know you want to jump in and get out on that Autobahn, but if the agency doesn't know something is wrong with the car when you drive it off, it will assume you broke it and charge you accordingly. If what's on the inspection form they want you to sign doesn't match the state of the car, point it out. Otherwise, once you drive it away, you are legally liable for its condition. Make sure all locks and doors work, check the various lights, and peruse the whole thing quickly for dents, scratches, and rips in the fabric.

➤ **Check for the repair and safety equipment.** Check the trunk for a jack, inflated spare, snow chains in winter, and a hazard triangle (most countries require you to hang this on the trunk if you're broken down by the side of the road). Check the glove compartment for a parking disc (ask the rental agency about this; they'll explain about the honor-system parking lots if the country has them).

➤ **Gas it up before you return it.** Take the car with a full tank so you don't have to worry about dealing with local gas stations just yet. Make sure you return the car with a full tank of gas as well. If you forget, the car rental agency will kindly fill it for you at obscenely jacked-up prices, just like in the United States. So save a bundle: just before you return the car, find a gas station and top off the tank.

Dollars & Sense

Your **credit card** may cover the CDW if you use it to pay for the rental, so always check with your company. However, Italy is the last hold-out—they won't accept credit card CDW. Instead, you must purchase it separately. Travel Guard (☎ **800/826-1300**) sells **independent CDW coverage** for a mere $5 a day.

Money Matters

Ah, yes. Money. The cost is usually the biggest hurdle, both psychologically and financially, when considering your European trip. Other guides gloss over questions such as, "Can I afford this?" and "What are the real expenses involved?" I'm here to give it to you straight: how much you can expect to spend on every major aspect of your trip and how to total it all into a reasonable budget. Then comes the bonus: over two dozen hints, tips, and secrets on how to slash that unwieldy budget down to a lean, mean vacation that you truly can afford.

A frugal attitude doesn't mean you can't have a good time. One of my cardinal rules of travel is that the less you spend, the closer you get to the real Europe, to the people and their culture. Realistically, you can't do Europe on $5 a day anymore; it's more like $60 to $90 plus transportation costs. Sure, excess money will buy you the luxurious extras and a greater degree of comfort. But travel in second class, stay in budget pensions and hotels where the European families lodge, eat heartily at local bistros, and you'll not only save money, you'll also meet Europeans and have a better, more fulfilling vacation for it.

After you hammer out your budget for paying for the trip, you have to decide how to carry and access your money: traveler's checks, credit cards, local currency, ATM cards, dollars, and so on. This chapter weighs the benefits and annoyances of each method and tells you how to get the most out of your dough. Finally, we'll enter the sometimes confusing realm of exchange rates, where one day you're thinking in terms of a few British pounds and the next calculating tens of thousands of Italian lire. I'll give you some advice about how to shop around for and secure the best rate.

OK, How Much Is This Going to Cost Me?

Two people could visit the same cities, spend the same amount of time in each, see all the same sights, and have expenditures that differ by thousands of dollars. This guide is designed to help you travel smart and stretch every dollar to the limit without scrimping on the quality of your trip.

Traveling frugally doesn't mean barely scraping by. It just means getting the best value for your travel dollar, knowing when to splurge, when to skimp, and how to be on the lookout for rip-offs. It's using museum cards and rail passes instead of buying individual tickets and dining on authentic home-cooked meals in local trattorias rather than on continental slop at overpriced tourist-oriented restaurants. It's looking for clean, comfortable, central, and safe hotels rather than those with minibars and massage services.

I'll get into specific tips on how to shave money off your costs in the next section, but first let's work out a rough trip budget. Estimating your trip costs isn't hard, but the totals will depend on your means and taste. Look through the listings in the second half of this book to figure out what price level of hotel and restaurant appeals to you. Come up with averages for these and plug those numbers into your expected daily expenses.

Budget **hotels** run around $60 per double, $80 for low-end moderate ones, and $100 to $150 for pricier pads. Local cuisine is as much a part of travel as sightseeing, so I'm generous with my meal budget. I take $12 as my average **lunch** allowance—I may spend more one day for a restaurant meal, considerably less the next day for a picnic. For **dinner,** I play it safe and assume a big meal every night with the works (appetizer, two courses, wine or beer, dessert, coffee) and expect to pay around $22 per dinner (that's per person based on dinner for two). I don't factor in **breakfast** because most hotels will give me a roll and coffee along with my room. If they don't, I can grab the same for $2 to $3 at any cafe and later scrape a few dollars off my lunch allowance that day to compensate. Museum hounds and **sightseeing** fanatics should be prepared for rising admission costs. Don't hold back here. I figure on an average of $5 per sight: $7 to $10 for biggies and $2 to $3 for smaller sights, which at four major sights per day is $20. If you're an inveterate **shopper,** budget extra for your purchases.

Take your estimates and make up something like the following table. Pad your total with some emergency cash by rounding up, and you'll have a good idea of your costs. Using just the information and suggested hotels contained in this book (plus one phone call to **Council Travel** to get an airfare and one Internet check at **www.raileurope.com** on the price of a train ticket from the Netherlands/Germany border to Amsterdam), I used the three-week grand tour from the end of chapter 1 as a sample and worked out a cost-per-person budget. The numbers are based on taking the trip with one companion (double rooms, shared meal costs, partner rail pass). The Euro-drive pass with an extra rail day makes sense for this trip, using the train pass only for the long overnight hauls—but validating it in time to get a discount on Eurostar—and paying separately for a few short Italian rail hops and the uncovered segment from the Netherlands/Germany border to Amsterdam. Always estimate high so you end the trip with some leftover cash, rather than a shortfall.

What If I'm Worried I Can't Afford It?

Don't worry. You can. A trip to Europe is a gift no one should deny them-selves. As you see in the following table, even a thrilling three weeks cover-ing most of Europe's greatest hits costs only around $3,183 per person. Too rich for your blood? Swallow a bit of pride, tighten your money belt, and try a little creative financing. There is some leeway in that budget.

You could sleep in unreserved compartments (the pull-out seat kind) instead of couchettes on overnight trains and cut out $80. A picnic only costs $7 per person or less; picnic all lunches and keep dinners down to $18 a piece—plenty for a full, hearty meal—and the dining total shrinks to $550. Make your photos your postcards and skip the souvenirs to bring the miscellaneous expense down to $4 a day. With these adjustments, your new grand total is now $2,773. Not peanuts, but a great value for what you're getting. If you travel smart and on a real tight budget, you could even take a two-week trip to Europe with around $1,000. The tips in the next section will help.

26 Money-Saving Tips

Of course, there are more ways to stretch that travel dollar than I could list here. Some of these tips highlight the best tips contained elsewhere in this book; most are new. This list is just to give you a taste for all the budget strategies out there. This book is loaded with lots more advice, hints, and tips on saving money—look especially for the "Dollars & Sense" sidebars in every chapter.

1. **Go in the off-season.** If you can travel at non-peak times (usually September through November or April through June), you'll find cheaper airfares and will be able to bargain more effectively for hotel rates. As an added plus, Europe is much less crowded than it is during the summer peak season (see chapter 2).

2. **Try a package tour.** For many destinations, you can book airfare, hotel, ground transportation, and even sightseeing just by making one call to a travel agent or packager for a lot less than if you tried to put the trip together yourself (see chapter 3).

The Three-Week Grand Tour Budget

Expense	Cost
Airfare (open-jaw NYC–London and Amsterdam–NYC)	$480
Eurodrive pass (per person basedon price for two adults, plus one extra rail day)	$322
Individual rail tickets (Eurostar $85; Venice–Florence $23; Florence–Rome $27; Jungfrau train $98; German border–Amsterdam $25)	$258
Two tanks of gas (that'll be all you need)	$70
Four nights in train couchettes ($20 each, because you can reserve a second-class couchette even on a first-class pass)	$80
18 nights in hotels ($30 per person per night, averaged from hotel prices in this book)	$540
44 meals (22 lunches at $12, plus 22 dinners at $22. Breakfast comes with hotel room; if not, grab a quick cafe breakfast and picnic for lunch to offset the cost)	$748
Sightseeing admissions ($20 a day for 18 days, leaving out Jungfrau day and Paris. For Paris, $32.60 covers the museums pass plus Eiffel tower admission)	$393
18 days of city transportation ($4 a day)	$72
Souvenirs, postcards, gelato, and miscellaneous stuff ($10 a day)	$220
TOTAL	$3,183

3. **Buy a rail pass.** Europe's greatest transportation asset is its train system, and its best value is the family of Eurail passes (see chapter 4).

4. **Sleep on overnight trains for $0 to $20.** With a rail pass, you can hop on an overnight train paying just $20 for a reserved bunk in a sleeping couchette, or take your chances on finding an empty sitting couchette where you slide down the seat backs to make a bed and sleep

for free. When you wake up, you've gotten where you're going plus saved yourself one night's hotel charges (see chapter 4).

5. **Forget private plumbing; take a room without bath.** Hotel rooms that share a bath down the hall rather than have their own private bath cost around two-thirds as much as rooms that are virtually identical but with their own plumbing (see chapter 7).

6. **Stay in Padova instead of Venice, Haarlem instead of Amsterdam.** In many places, hotels just outside the city, across the river, or in the next town over (20 to 30 minutes by train) may not be quite as conveniently located, but they are a great bargain. With the great transportation in most European cities, being away from the center of town doesn't necessarily put you out of the action.

7. **With kids, get a triple or cots, not two rooms.** Most European hotels let kids stay free in their parents' room or charge a nominal fee ($5 to $15) for the extra bed.

8. **Rent a room instead of staying at a hotel.** Even the cheapest B&B or pension can't beat the price (as low as $15 to $40) of a private room-for-rent. Plus, you often get to live in a real European's home—an experience no five-star hotel can give you (see chapter 7).

9. **Try the ultra-cheap accommodations.** You can sleep in Munich for $7 if you don't mind sleeping near 150 roommates, mostly students, on a wooden floor under a big tent. Europe abounds with budget options, from hostels where dorm bunks cost $8 to $20, campgrounds where you can sleep for as little as $4 to $15, and crash-ins like Munich's mega tent (I call it the Beery Big Top). (See chapter 7.)

10. **Get a double bed instead of two singles.** Fewer sheets to wash means savings for you. Even non-couple buddies can travel this way—although if you're an opposite-sex pair, I'd pretend you're married just to put traditionalist Europeans more at ease (see chapter 7).

11. **Never place a phone call from a hotel.** On long-distance calls, the markup is often 200%. They even charge for what should be free calls to the local AT&T, MCI, or Sprint calling card number. Always use a pay phone (see chapter 10).

12. **Do your own laundry.** Wash a few pieces in the sink each night, roll them in towels to sop up the dampness, and hang them on the radiator to dry—or even better, on the heated towel racks (a silly amenity even cheap places are installing). Doing the wash yourself is cheaper than going to a laundromat. Never pay the hotel to do it unless you enjoy being, ahem, taken to the cleaners (see chapter 7).

13. **If breakfast is included, stuff yourself.** If the room comes with it, don't be shy. Have three rolls and a big bowl of cereal. If there's a meat and cheese spread, load up. Trust me; you're paying for it all.

Stick an orange and another roll in your pocket for later, and you'll only have to have a light, inexpensive lunch.

14. **If you can get a room without breakfast for less money, take it.** Hotels charge around $10 for what is essentially a roll and jam with coffee or tea. If you can get around the breakfast charge, you can get the same thing at any cafe for $3 or less on your way out the door (see chapter 7).

15. **Try expensive restaurants at lunch instead of dinner.** This is a great way to sample top restaurants on a modest budget. Lunch tabs are usually a fraction of dinners at most pricey restaurants, and the menu often boasts many of the same specialties (see chapter 8).

16. **Lunch on pub grub in Britain and Ireland.** A sandwich and a sturdy pint of ale to wash it down with make a fine, cheap, quick, and very authentic meal in a British pub. Every country has its own options for sandwiches and snacking; see chapter 8 for more details and the "Quick Bites" box at the end of each destination chapter's dining section for places to try.

17. **Order from fixed-price and tourist menus.** Meals at a set price are almost always cheaper (up to 30%) than ordering the same dishes à la carte. The options are more limited than the main menu, but you can't beat the price (see chapter 8).

18. **Picnic.** You can dine like a king for well under $10 a person on a grassy patch in the city park, in your hotel room, or on the train (see chapter 8).

19. **Look before you tip.** Many restaurants include a service charge in your bill, so tipping another 15% is tossing your money out the window. Always ask if service is included. If not, tip 10 to 15% just like at home. If service is included, and you felt that your server did a good job, leave a bit extra on the table anyway (one of the currency's smallest bills per person—or in England, a pound coin each).

20. **The Paris Museum Pass.** The Paris Museum Pass is the single greatest example of a city doing right by its tourists. For a mere $23, you get unlimited entry for three full days to virtually all Parisian museums and sights (the Eiffel Tower is the only major one not on the list), plus you don't have to wait in any ticket lines! Some cities (Austrian and Scandinavian ones are great on this) have similar passes that also get you free travel on city buses and subways and other benefits.

21. **Visit the free or near-free sights.** London's British Museum is free, as are the Tate and National Gallery, Rome's Pantheon, most churches and cathedrals, lively piazzas, church services where choirs sing, medieval quarters, sidewalk performers and buskers, baroque fountains, city parks, and street markets across Europe. Capitalize on the free or near-free sights and experiences. For example, you can

witness first-hand Paris cafe culture for the price of a cup of coffee
($2) or cruise the Grand Canal in Venice for under $3 on the public
vaporetto.

Tourist Traps

Here are the top five ways *not* to try to save money.

1. **Never skimp on sightseeing.** Everything else aside, the sights are one of
   the main things you came all the way over here for. Occasionally, some
   touristy thing like a wax museum may be a waste, but anything of true cultural, artistic, or historical value invariably is worthwhile. Accept that the
   big sights cost $10 because they're worth it. Sure, $14 to see the Crown
   Jewels feels like a rip-off, but you wouldn't want to come away not having
   seen them, either. Let them have their profit; you're buying entertainment,
   enlightenment, and priceless memories.

2. **Don't save money at the expense of time.** Every hour counts and
   your time is your most valuable asset. Don't take the bus merely to save a
   smidgen over the train. Case in point: The Eurostar from London to Paris
   costs $99 and takes four hours. The train–ferry–train route is $86 and 10
   hours. That's a $13 savings, but wouldn't you pay $15 for an extra six hours
   in Paris?

3. **Don't travel with Dad's old army duffel.** Invest in a good pack that
   you can carry the distance and won't fall apart (I've watched the latter
   happen to inexperienced travelers more than once). This is a pay-off you
   never get to see, because a good pack won't fail you. In my closet is an old
   $200 pack that saw me through a year of study abroad, countless shorter
   trips around the United States, and six months on the road researching and
   writing my first travel guide before the zippers and seams started to go.

4. **Don't wear generic sneakers.** Also invest in a good pair of durable,
   lightweight walking shoes—something you can trudge around in on cobblestones for 12 hours a day, seven days a week. Rockport, Memphisto,
   and Ecco make some of the best. And for goodness' sake, leave the
   Birkenstocks at home.

5. **Don't pass on the CDW.** Some people will argue this one, but the collision damage waiver on rental cars truly is worth the peace of mind and
   insurance. Europeans drive aggressively, and the road signs are odd, so your
   chances of getting into an accident are considerably higher than they are in
   the United States. "Gold" credit cards often cover CDW, or to save $5 to
   $10, use Travel Guard's $5 coverage (see chapter 4).

22. **Take advantage of free or reduced-price museum days.** For
    example, the Vatican is free the last Sunday of the month. Many other
    museums have such policies (the Louvre picks the first Sunday of the
    month). The Louvre is also almost half-price after 3pm. Read your

guidebooks carefully and take advantage of the free days and hours of reduced admission. But keep in mind that the museums will also be the most crowded at these times.

23. **Walk a lot.** A good pair of walking shoes can save you a lot of money in taxis, buses, and metros. Paris, London, Madrid, and Berlin are the only places where you'll need to take public transport on occasion—how often depends on the amount of time and stamina you have. As a bonus, you'll get to know your destination more intimately on foot, exploring at a slower pace.

24. **Skip the souvenirs.** Your photographs, memories, and journal should be the best mementos of your trip. You can do without the "Roma!" T-shirts, Eiffel Tower key chains, Spanish matador hats, Bavarian cuckoo clocks, and other trinkets.

25. **Never pay in traveler's checks.** You'll get a bad exchange rate if you try to use them as cash; trade them in at the bank for local currency instead. Similarly, the exchange booth in the Eiffel Tower and anywhere else that's overrun with visitors gives the most miserable rates.

26. **Always ask for discounts.** You may be eligible for discounts on sights, transportation, hotels, you name it. Ask about everything; you could be pleasantly surprised. Members of AAA, trade unions, or AARP; frequent flyers; teachers; and members of other groups sometimes get discounted rates on car rentals, plane tickets, and some chain hotel rooms. Ask your company if it allows employees to use the corporate travel agent and corporate rates even for private vacations (you never know).

   Are you descended from an European immigrant group? Many ethnic travel agencies specialize in getting forgotten sons and daughters rock-bottom rates to return to the Old Country—check out the nearest ethnic neighborhood that fits your background. On the road, always ask if there are discounts for any demographic group to which you might belong. Are you over 60? Under 26? A student? A teacher or professor? A professional? How about a family discount, or at least one for just the kids? Work every angle to get the best price.

One-Stop Insurance for Your Travel Funds: The Pros & Cons of Traveler's Checks

A traveler's check is a pre-paid slip of paper worth $20, $50, or $100 (the other available denominations are not useful for European travel). You sign them once at the bank or issuing office when you buy them and again in the presence of the person who is accepting or cashing the check. Take them (along with your passport as identification) to any bank, American Express office, or exchange booth in Europe, and they will change the checks for the equivalent amount of local currency. (For more on shopping around for the best exchange place, see "Playing the Exchange Rate Game: Where to Get Some Local Cash.")

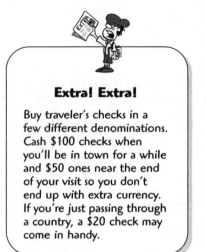

A traveler's check and the local American Express or Thomas Cooke office used to be your only means of getting some local currency abroad. Nowadays, traveler's checks are the dinosaurs of European travel. ATM cards and credit card cash advances are much cheaper and easier. The inconvenience of having to wait in line at banks or exchange booths, dig your passport out of the money belt, and get charged sometimes high commissions has led most frequent travelers to abandon traveler's checks in favor of the one-two-three trip to a street-corner ATM.

Extra! Extra!

Buy traveler's checks in a few different denominations. Cash $100 checks when you'll be in town for a while and $50 ones near the end of your visit so you don't end up with extra currency. If you're just passing through a country, a $20 check may come in handy.

So what make the checks still worthwhile? Insurance. They're theft- and computer-proof. Unlike hard currency, if you lose them you haven't lost your money—you can get replacements at no charge (be sure you keep a list of the check numbers in a safe place, separate from the checks themselves; otherwise, you can't get reimbursed). Sometimes you'll find the ATMs of an entire town evilly disposed to your bank card or Visa (perhaps a computer glitch or the phone connections to check your PIN are down). A handful of traveler's checks in your money belt can save the day, and they remain the safest way to carry your dollars.

Buy your traveler's checks in U.S. dollars, not some European currency; they're more widely accepted that way. Most banks issue checks under the names of **American Express** (☎ 800/221-7282), **Thomas Cook** (☎ **800/223-7373** in the United States and Canada, 44-1733-318-950 collect from anywhere in the world), **Visa** (☎ **800/227-6811** in the United States and Canada, or 44-1733-318-949 collect from anywhere in the world), or

Dollars & Sense

Most places charge you a 1% to 4% fee to buy traveler's checks. AAA members can buy American Express checks at no extra charge. Some banks also sell no-fee checks to account holders.

Citicorp (☎ **800/645-6556** in the United States and Canada, or 813/623-1709 collect from anywhere in the world). Also call these numbers if your checks are lost or stolen to get replacements as quickly as possible.

You'll have no problem getting these checks, especially the first three, accepted just about anywhere in Europe (discounting perhaps Angelo the town barber or the elderly couple with the five-table bistro). However, paying for a meal, purchase, or hotel room directly with a traveler's check is a good way to ensure you get the worst possible exchange rate. Use your checks to get local cash at a bank or the American Express office, not as currency.

Can I Use My ATM Card?

A decade ago, your bank card was, in Europe, just so much more useless plastic. These days you can saunter up to an ATM in virtually any city, and most small towns, and get local cash out the same as you would at home. This is the fastest, easiest, and least expensive way you can change money. You take advantage of the bank's bulk exchange rate (better than anything you'll get on the street) and, unless your home bank charges you for using a non-proprietary ATM, it's commission-free.

Time-Savers

Before you leave the States, buy some local currency, say $50 worth, for each country you'll visit. This primer cash will get you from the airport or train station to the better exchange rates of a downtown bank. Also, if you arrive in town late at night or on a bank holiday, the cash can tide you over until you get your hands on some more. Buy foreign currency in the United States at any bank (call ahead; not all branches carry the stuff). Shop around for the best rate, and ask the teller to give you small bills—whichever ones are worth around $10—because you'll need them primarily to buy inexpensive items like maps, bus tickets, and perhaps some lunch.

Both the **Cirrus** (☎ 800/424-7787; **www.mastercard.com/atm**) and **Plus** (☎ 800/843-7587; **www.visa. com/atms**) networks have automated ATM locators that list the banks in each country that will accept your card, or you can just search out any machine with your network's symbol emblazoned upon it. Europe is getting like the United States—there's a bank on virtually every corner, and most are globally networked. You can also get a **credit card cash advance** through Visa or MasterCard (contact the issuing bank to get a PIN). American Express card cash advances are usually only available from an American Express office.

Bet You Didn't Know

Unlike a regular charge, when you get an ATM cash advance on your credit card interest usually starts accruing immediately. On short trips, this interest is not a big deal. If you're gone for a while and not paying off your balance, however, it'll add up quickly.

Increased internationalism seems to have done away with the worry that your card's PIN needs to be specially enabled to work abroad, but it always pays to check with the issuing bank before you leave. Most European systems use four-digit PINs; six-digit ones often won't work. If at the ATM you get a weird message saying your card isn't valid for international transactions, most likely the bank just can't make the phone connection to check it (occasionally this epidemic can be citywide). Don't panic. Try another ATM, cash a traveler's check, or wait until tomorrow or until the next town.

Europe Takes Plastic: Using Your Credit Card

Visa and **MasterCard** are now almost universally accepted—and in many places preferred—at most European hotels, restaurants, and shops. The majority also accept **American Express. Diner's Club** is gaining some ground, especially in the cities and in more expensive establishments. Except in the poshest restaurants and hotels, most Europeans raise their eyebrows if you mention **Carte Blanche** and **Discover** has yet to provoke a reaction from anybody. Leave the gas station credit card at home. Never rely on credit cards alone. You'll sometimes find all your plastic useless at smaller, cheaper family-run businesses such as some inexpensive hotels and cheap trattorias, most rental rooms, and many neighborhood shops.

Dollars & Sense

Always carry some **emergency dollars.** On my first trip to Poland, I discovered that banks wouldn't change traveler's checks, and Krakow's American Express office was way outside town and rarely open. Luckily, my companion had $50 stashed away. We found an exchange booth in the train station that gladly gave us the worst exchange rate on the planet along with enough Polish zloty to tide us over until the American Express office opened.

You may want to let your card's issuing bank know that you're taking a trip. Most companies have a computerized watchdog that monitors your card's use, looking for radical changes in the frequency or location of charges. When it finds them, it freezes the account. Ideally, this system alerts them if someone steals your card and goes on a shopping spree, but it has the unfortunate side effect of leaving travelers in the lurch, because on a typical vacation you're charging more than usual and charging from strange places. In case of real **theft,** a whole section of chapter 11 is devoted to dealing with stolen wallets, lost credit cards and traveler's checks, and other travel mishaps.

Playing the Exchange Rate Game: Where to Get Some Local Cash

Always but *always* do some leg work before you change money, or you risk being ripped off. Exchange rates are the small-time financier's best way of milking inattentive tourists for all they can get (American exchange places do the same thing). **Exchange money in a bank** or at one of its ATMs if at all possible, but avoid patronizing the branch offices of banks you'll see in airports and train stations. To tap just that bit more out of the tourist trade, these outposts usually offer a rate inferior to that of the same bank's downtown office.

One Continent, One Currency? The Future of the Euro

Although this book deals with all prices in their local national currencies, know that the **Euro single European currency** looms large over continental money matters. The adoption of this single currency is a contentious move, and each country is fighting to get the best deal for itself as their economies merge. Germany and France both want the Euro—but each only if their countryman is in charge. Britain looks down its nose at the whole idea, and Spain and Italy are clamoring for the others to accept them as financially stable and "let them play," too. Plus, as European economies fluctuate, the national consensus in each country can swing from hearty support to fierce opposition of the Euro. You needn't worry about dealing with the Euro for a while. It's slated to take effect technically on Jan. 1, 1999; be issued as banknotes and coins in 2002; and replace national currencies on July 1, 2002.

Shop around for the best **exchange rate;** there can be a 40% difference between rates at banks right next door to each other. The business section of major newspapers lists the current rates for European currencies in two columns; for example, one column tells how many British pounds $1 will buy, and the other shows how many dollars a pound is worth. These published figures are prime rates; you won't find a street price quite as juicy, but they're a good guide.

At the beginning of each destination chapter in this book, I'll give you a ballpark estimate of the local exchange rate as of early 1998 (a period when the dollar was strong, which means it would buy you more foreign currency). All the dollar amounts in each chapter are calculated using that figure. Rates, however, can fluctuate wildly over even brief periods of time, although they tend to rise or fall slowly over the course of months. You have no control over this, but it will affect your trip.

Most banks display a chart of the current exchange rates they're offering either in an outside window or inside at the international teller's window. Make sure you're looking at the rate the bank is *buying,* not selling, U.S. dollars. When comparing bank to bank, look for the chart with the highest number in the "buying dollars" column. This will be the best rate.

When comparing rates, also factor in the **commission,** if any. The commission is a fee tacked on to the transaction; sometimes it's a flat fee equal to a couple of dollars, other times it's 2% to 10% of however much you're changing. Occasionally, a slightly less attractive exchange rate coupled with low or flat fee commission can cost you less in the long run (depending on how much you change) than a great-looking rate that's hiding a whopping commission in the fine print.

Time-Savers

Before you shop around, decide **how much money** you're going to exchange—this will help you figure out which rate-and-commission combo suits your needs best. I usually get enough to last a few days, because it saves the hassle of visiting the bank every day, and on a flat-fee commission it pays off. Stow most of this cash in your money belt and carry only enough for the day in your wallet.

You can also exchange money at commercial exchange booths (labeled multilingually as *change/cambio/wechsel*). The rates tend to be lousy and the commissions high, but they keep longer hours than the banks. Only use them as a last resort if all the banks are closed, and all the ATMs in town are for some reason not accepting your bank card. Multinational travel agencies such as American Express and Thomas Cook usually give good rates and will exchange their own traveler's checks at no commission. Hotels and shops offer abysmal rates.

Tourist Traps

On the rare occasion that someone approaches you on the street with a rate too good to be true, it is. That shyster's got **black market currency,** and if his bills aren't counterfeit, his sleight-of-hand method of counting them out certainly is. One other warning: You may see multinational **bill-to-bill changer machines** near some major attractions (you feed in dollar bills, it spits out the local currency). But the exchange rate is so bad that feeding your bills into these (perfectly legal) swindle machines is tantamount to flushing them down the toilet.

Chapter 6

Tying Up the Loose Ends

In This Chapter

➤ The fine print of travel: passports, customs, insurance, and other boring but important subjects

➤ Health concerns: pharmacies, medicine, hospitals, and when it's safe to drink the water

➤ The fine art of packing light: how to survive a month out of one bag

➤ From hairdryers to laptops: the lowdown on electronics and adapters

The trip is planned, and you're raring to go...but wasn't there something else to do? Ah yes, pack. What about all those other details: passports, visas, customs regulations, and health and trip insurance? Unexciting as these things are, they're an integral part of getting ready for a trip. This chapter will try to make handling these details as easy and painless as possible. At the end is a comprehensive section on precisely what you'll need to travel, so you can pack your entire world into one bag and have twice as much fun on the road as people who brought four times as much stuff. I finish the chapter off with a last-minute checklist to keep things in order as you count down your final days until that plane takes off and your European journey begins.

You Aren't Who You Say You Are Without a Passport

The only legal form of identification recognized around the world is a valid passport. You cannot cross an international border without it (land borders in Europe are notoriously lax, but the border patrol people definitely need to see it if you arrive by plane or ferry). Besides clothing, it is the only item you absolutely must have in order to travel. In the United States, you're used to your driver's license being the all-purpose identification card. Abroad, it only proves that some U.S. state lets you drive. Getting a passport is easy, but it takes some time to complete the process.

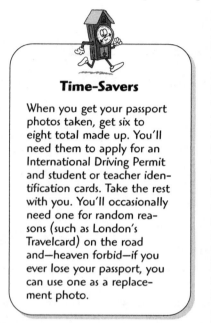

Time-Savers

When you get your passport photos taken, get six to eight total made up. You'll need them to apply for an International Driving Permit and student or teacher identification cards. Take the rest with you. You'll occasionally need one for random reasons (such as London's Travelcard) on the road and—heaven forbid—if you ever lose your passport, you can use one as a replacement photo.

If you're applying for a first-time passport or are under age 14, you need to do it in person at one of 13 passport offices throughout the United States, at many federal, state, or probate courts, or at major post offices (not all accept applications; call the number in the following paragraph to find the ones that do). You need to bring proof of citizenship, which means a certified birth certificate. It's wise to bring along your driver's license, state or military identification, Social Security card, and any other identifying documents. You'll also need two identical passport-sized photos (2"×2"). Get these taken at just about any corner photo shop; these places have a special camera to make them identical. You cannot use the strip photos from one of those photo vending machines.

For people over 15, a passport is valid for 10 years and costs $60 ($45 plus a $15 handling fee); for those 15 and under, it's valid for five years and costs $40 total. If you're over 15 and have a valid passport issued less than 12 years ago, you can renew it by mail by filling out the application, available at the places described earlier or over the Internet (see sidebar). When you apply by mail, you bypass the $15 handling fee, so the passport costs just $45.

Apply for your passport at least a month, preferably two, before you plan to leave on your trip. The processing takes three weeks on average, but it can run longer in busy periods (especially spring). It helps to speed things along if you write on the application a departure date within the next three weeks. To **expedite your passport**—in which case you'll get it in five business days—visit an agency directly (or go through the court or post office and have them overnight mail the application) and pay an additional $35 fee. For more information, and to find your regional passport office, call the **National Passport Information Center** (☎ **900/225-5674**) or get on the Web site (**travel.state.gov**; see following "Time-Savers" sidebar).

Keep your passport with you at all times securely in your money belt. The only times to give it up are at the bank for the tellers to photocopy when they change your traveler's checks, at borders for the guards to peruse (this includes giving it to the conductor on overnight train rides), when any police or military personnel ask for it, and *briefly* to the concierge when you're checking into your hotel (see sidebar).

Extra! Extra!

Hotel front desks, especially in southern Europe, will often want to **keep your passport overnight.** They have to register you with the police, and they like to pile all the passports in a drawer until the evening so they can do all the guests' slips at once. Smile and ask politely whether they can do their paperwork on the spot or at least let you come by in an hour or two to get it back. I always tell them I need it to go exchange money at the bank, whether I'm flush with cash or not.

A valid passport is the only documentation you'll need as an American to visit any European country. Your passport will be stamped wherever you enter Europe with a temporary tourist **visa** that's good for 90 days of travel within that country. If you plan to stay longer in any one country, contact any consulate of that country in the United States before you leave to get a specific visa or any U.S. consulate once you are abroad.

If you **lose your passport** on the road, go directly to the nearest U.S. consulate (do not pass go, do not collect $200). Bring all forms of identification you have, and they'll get started on generating you a new passport. This hassle should be avoided at all costs!

Time-Savers

The **U.S. State Department's Bureau of Consular Affairs** maintains a Web site (**travel.state.gov**) that gives you more than you ever wanted to know about passports (including a downloadable application), customs, and other aspects of travel in which the government has a say. It also has lots of scary-sounding travel warnings about health and terrorism on a country-by-country basis. Just remember when reading these warnings that well over half of the hazards they list, such as hepatitis, Lyme disease, or terrorist bombings, are threats you already face at home, so a place like France is not half as dangerous as these documents make it sound.

Well, I Do Declare! Getting Through Customs

Technically, there are no limits on how much loot you can bring back into the United States from a trip abroad, but the customs authority does put limits on how much you can bring back for free. This restriction is mainly to separate tourists with souvenirs from importers for taxation purposes.

You may bring home $400 worth of goods duty-free, providing you've been out of the country at least 48 hours and haven't used the exemption in the past 30 days. This limit includes not more than one liter of an alcoholic beverage (you must, of course, be over 21), 200 cigarettes, and 100 cigars.

Tourist Traps

Note that buying items at a **duty-free shop** before flying home does *not* exempt them from counting toward your U.S. customs limits (monetary or otherwise). The "duty" that you're avoiding in those shops is the local tax on the item (like state sales tax in the United States), not any import duty that may be assessed by the U.S. customs office. See chapter 12 for more details.

Antiques over 100 years old and works of art are exempt from the $400 limit, as is anything you mail home from abroad. You may mail up to $200 worth of goods to yourself (marked "for personal use") and up to $100 worth to others (marked "unsolicited gift") once each day, so long as the package does not include alcohol or tobacco products. You'll have to pay an import duty on anything over these limits. See chapter 12, "Shopping Strategies," for more rules on what you can and cannot bring home.

If you have further questions, look in your phone book under U.S. Government, Department of the Treasury, U.S. Customs Service to find the nearest customs office. Or check out the details on its Web site (**www.customs.ustreas. gov**). See chapter 12 for more on purchases abroad, everything from local taxes to size charts.

What About Travel Insurance?

Various trip and medical insurance packages (some all-inclusive, others mix-and-match for whichever facets you need) cover trip cancellation, lost luggage, medical costs, emergency evacuation, and other travel mishaps. Packages can cost as low as $40 to $60 per person for a vacation valued at $1,000, but they are usually 6% to 8% of the total value of your vacation. Never buy more than you need and always check first with the providers of your existing insurance policies (homeowner's, medical, credit card, and such) to see what they may cover.

Homeowner's policies may kick in for the loss of your clothing and personal items. Your health insurance provider may reimburse you for hospital costs incurred abroad (see the next section for details), and credit cards may cover airline accidents. Remember that the purchases you make with a credit card, including airline tickets, are often protected, but be sure to ask to what extent this coverage extends to items bought abroad and/or shipped home.

All of the following insurance providers are reputable:

Access America, 6600 West Broad St., 2nd Floor, Richmond, VA 23230 (☎ 800/284-8300)

Tele Trip Co. (Mutual of Omaha) Mutual of Omaha Plaza, Omaha, NE 68175 (☎ 800/228-9792)

Travel Guard International, 1145 Clark St., Stevens Point, WI 54481 (☎ 800/826-1300)

Aaaachooo! What If I Get Sick Away from Home?

I won't lie to you. Travel—especially the high-stress, never-stop, whirlwind variety—puts a strain on your system, leaving you vulnerable to illness. There are no exotic diseases to worry about in Europe, but occasionally there may be a different strain of flu going around that you might pick up more easily than a local would. That said, you probably won't get much sicker there than you would at home.

Yes, the **water** is almost always safe to drink. If it isn't, there will be a sign (*eau non potable, acqua non potabile, keine trinkwasser*) or a pictogram of a glass with one of those red slashed circles over it. Don't drink the water on the trains. Occasionally, the differing bacteria in European water fouls up American digestive systems used to their own bacteria, and you'll end up with the dreaded traveler's diarrhea. It shouldn't be a bad case though, and you won't be sick for long. At any rate, you'll be that much safer if you stick mainly to bottled water (fizzy mineral waters such as Perrier are one of Europe's everyday pleasures).

The change in diet and so many rich foods usually sidelines one person in five with **diarrhea** for a day or two—up to a week if you're particularly prone and traveling among the exotic spices of Turkey. It's just one of the many little joys of being a world traveler. The Pepto-Bismol people were thrilled a few years ago when someone discovered that, in addition to calming sour stomachs and indigestion, the pink stuff also cures diarrhea (not just treats the symptoms, but actually kills the bacteria). Carry the tablet kind, because the liquid presents spillage problems. Take it easy for a day, eat bland foods such as toast, bananas, rice, and tea for two days, and ride it out.

Take enough of your **prescription medication** to last your trip plus a week (just in case). Keep all pills in their original vials—that and an innocent smile will help prove to customs officials that they're prescription drugs, not narcotics. Bring along extra prescriptions written in each drug's generic, chemical name, not a brand name. This type of prescription will help customs officials approve it, and foreign druggists fill it. From the over-the-counter department, the only necessities are aspirin, Dramamine (trust me; European roads and bus drivers can test the iron of stomachs), Pepto-Bismol tablets (for indigestion and diarrhea), and decongestant (take it before your flight to cut down on ear-popping).

What You Need to Know About Drug Stores & Doctors

When Europeans feel sick, they don't call their doctor; they head to the local **pharmacy,** where the dying art of the skilled apothecary and knowledgeable druggist still lives on. Just walk in bravely, put your charade skills to work, and point to whatever hurts while moaning. I've entered Florentine apothecaries clutching my throat and left able to swallow again, stumbled in an exaggerated feverish delirium around a Toledo drug store, and on one memorable occasion did a Oscar-worthy pantomime of vomiting violently in a Greek pharmacy.

If you do need to visit the **hospital,** just find the nearest one and march right in. Doctors are an educated bunch, and most hospitals sport at least a handful who speak English. Much of Europe practices semi- or fully socialized medicine, so you may very well be taken care of swiftly, given a dose of medicine and a prescription for more, and sent on your way with a smile. At most, they'll bill you on the spot for $35 to $50. For added piece of mind, many big cities have **private hospitals with native English speakers.** Each destination chapter in this book lists the most convenient central hospital in town along with any hospitals that staff English-speaking physicians.

If you do end up paying for health care, especially if you have to be admitted for any reason, most **health insurance plans and HMOs** will cover, at least to some extent, out-of-country hospital visits and procedures. Most make you pay the bills up front at the time of care, however, and you'll get a refund after you've returned and filed all the paperwork. Members of **Blue Cross/Blue Shield** can use their cards at select hospitals in most major cities worldwide just as they would at home, which means lower out-of-pocket costs (☎ **800/810-BLUE** or **www.bluecares.com/blue/ bluecard/wwn** for a list of participating hospitals).

If you suffer from a **chronic illness,** talk to your doctor before taking the trip. For such conditions as epilepsy, diabetes, or a heart condition, wear a **Medic Alert Identification Tag** (☎ **800/825-3785**), which will immediately alert doctors to your condition and give them access to your records through Medic Alert's 24-hour hotline. Membership is $35, plus $15 annually.

For current tips on travel and health concerns in the countries you'll be visiting, plus lists of local English-speaking doctors, contact the **International Association for Medical Assistance to Travelers (IAMAT)** (☎ **716/ 754-4883** or 416/652-0137; **www.sentex.net/~iamat**). The **United States Centers for Disease Control and Prevention** (☎ **404/ 332-4559; www.cdc.gov**) provides up-to-date information on necessary vaccines and health hazards by region or country (by mail, their booklet is $20; on the Internet, it's free). When you're abroad, any local U.S. consulate can provide a list of area doctors who speak English.

Packing Light

Aside from a gung-ho, healthy attitude, the most important factor that will make or break your trip is your **luggage and how you pack it.** Will you pack for ultimate mobility, versatility, and necessity, or will you weigh your-self down with suitcases full of the kitchen sink and all related major appli-ances? When in doubt, leave it at home. The world is a small place; you can buy whatever it is, or some local equivalent, on the road if necessary.

Lay out everything you think you'll need to take and consider each item. If anything is not absolutely necessary, put it away. When you're done thin-ning the pile down, take whatever remains, pack half of it, and leave the other half at home—you won't need it. If it doesn't all fit in one pack and daypack, you're taking too much. If you can't easily lift the packed bag over your head, you've overpacked. Take a practice run: pack everything and then walk around the block two or three times. If you couldn't easily go another 15 turns, head back inside and lighten the load. Trust me, you'll be thankful later when you zip off to your hotel and the guy who sat next to you on the plane gets a hernia just trying to get his luggage out of the airport.

If an item you thought was necessary doesn't appear on the following pack-ing lists, ask yourself seriously whether it's truly indispensable. Most likely, you'll get by fine without it (or you can buy it over there) and that's one less item for you to lug around and waste your precious travel time dealing with. Make travel an exercise in simplifying your life.

I've Got the Whole World in My Pack

First of all, you must have the right luggage. My all-around choice is **a carry-on-sized backpack with a zip-off daypack.** Trust me; I live out of these things for six months at a time. Hard-backed suitcases are cumber-some and heavy, huge frame packs are for hikers, and both need to be checked on airlines, which is a wholly unnecessary hassle. Not only do you have to sit in the airport watching everyone else's luggage go in circles for an hour, but you're also trusting that your suitcase doesn't decide to holiday in Nepal while you're headed to London. With a carry-on size pack, you can cruise on and off the plane and sling your stuff on your back whenever you need to hoof it. Most importantly, it'll force you to pack light. Many models have straps and waist belts that tuck or zip away, converting the pack into a more respectable soft-sided suitcase for waltzing into your hotel lobby.

If you're not into carrying your world on your shoulders, so to speak, then your best bet is to purchase a piece of **flight attendant luggage.** Pilots and flight attendants have been whisking these compact, wheeled suitcases with long, retractable handles on and off of planes for years. They're now being manufactured for the mass market and come in a variety of shapes and styles. The long handles and large wheels make rolling it behind you a cinch, and you'd be amazed at just how much you can fit in one of the smaller models, which slide perfectly into the overhead compartment (the reason air-line employees have been using them all these years). Make sure you get a sturdy, well-made piece that can withstand the bumps and bruises of multi-country travel.

One note of warning (and a personal plea): airlines are (rightfully) cracking down on people who try to bring half the contents of their home onboard

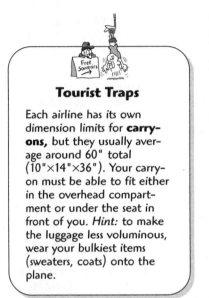

Tourist Traps

Each airline has its own dimension limits for **carry-ons,** but they usually average around 60" total (10"×14"×36"). Your carry-on must be able to fit either in the overhead compartment or under the seat in front of you. *Hint:* to make the luggage less voluminous, wear your bulkiest items (sweaters, coats) onto the plane.

with them. When the airlines say carry-on, *they mean it.* One bag of the dimensions listed in the Tourist Traps sidebar, plus one purse *or* tiny daypack, and that's it. Otherwise, they'll make you check your oversized carry-on at the gate, holding up the line and separating you from items (books, medicines, and so on) you expected to have available on the plane.

Whatever sort of pack or suitcase you choose, be sure to put a slip of paper with your name, home address, and destination inside each piece of luggage as well as attaching a sturdy **luggage tag with a concealed address window** to the outside (some criminals peruse visible luggage tags at the airport, collecting the addresses of people leaving on vacation).

Get as many **tiny travel locks** as you have zippered compartments on your pack and daypack and lock the dual zippers together. At first these locks are a little annoying to undo each time, but it becomes habit after a while, and it saves your valuables from all but the thieves who slash your bags open.

Keep clean clothes in one **nylon stuff-sack,** and dirty ones in another (of a different color). Roll your clothes so they look like so many sausages, and they'll take up less room than they would folded (and they fit in the stuff-sacks more neatly). Keep all toiletries in a waterproof **bathroom bag,** but carry your first-aid kit in your **daypack** (along with guidebook sections for the day, tissue packs, water bottle, journal, and umbrella). If you're traveling with others and plan to check your luggage, distribute everybody's stuff throughout all the bags, so no one is left in the lurch should any one bag disappear.

The Clothes Make the Traveler: What Exactly Should I Take?

Here are the four cardinal rules of traveling clothes:

1. Don't bring anything white.

2. Don't bring anything that wrinkles.

3. Bring clothes you can layer.

4. Don't bring too many!

That last rule is the hardest one for many people, but the equation is simple. Clothes take up the most room in your luggage, so be stingy with what you take. Believe me, it's easier to do a bit of laundry in your room every few nights than to bring a ton of stuff. Only your immediate traveling companions will know you're repeatedly wearing the same outfit. Socks, T-shirts, and underwear—the clothes most likely to, um, ripen quickly—are the easiest items to wash out and dry overnight. In truth, you can wear the same pair of jeans for quite a while before they begin walking around on their own in search of the laundromat.

Extra! Extra!

Leave space in your pack for accumulating **souvenirs.** If you find yourself running out of room, stop at any post office to ship home the personal items you've found you didn't need, or just before flying home, mail your dirty laundry to yourself. This way, you can carry your new purchases instead of entrusting them to the postal system.

One note on **dress norms** before the packing list. Most city-dwelling Europeans dress pretty snappy—not necessarily in the latest Armani suit, but well nonetheless. What most Americans would consider dolling themselves up for a special occasion or a nice meal out, Europeans put on as a matter of course for the daily evening stroll before dinner. Although you're certainly welcome to travel in whatever wardrobe makes you feel comfortable, you'll probably be happier trying to fit in, so save the Bermuda shorts and sleeveless T-shirt for that trip to Hawaii. If you bring just one smart, casual outfit, you'll feel less like a tourist and more ready to strut your stuff with the locals on the town's main drag.

Pack just the clothes on the following list:

- ☐ **Two pairs of pants.** One pair can be jeans, for durability, but take a pair of slacks for when you need some respectability.

- ☐ **One pair of shorts with pockets.** Although European adults don't often wear shorts, shorts are good for hiking and for use as a men's swimsuit (women: don't bring a swimsuit; buy it there if you need one).

Tourist Traps

If your camera fits into your pocket, so much the better. If you're carrying a bigger one, tote it in a purse or mild-mannered daypack, not a "steal-me" professional **camera bag.**

☐ **One long skirt or sundress.** The skimpiness at which your respectability will be questioned varies with the country, so hedge your bets with something long.

☐ **Four pairs of underwear.**

☐ **Three T-shirts.** Wear a T-shirt under long sleeves so the easily washed T-shirt will soak up the sweat.

☐ **Two long-sleeve shirts.** Turtlenecks layer great, but dry slowly. Button-down oxford-type shirts are dressier, but prone to wrinkles. It's your choice.

☐ **One dark sweater.** This item provides warmth, and you can use it to dress up.

☐ **Long underwear.** Bring this item only if you're visiting northern countries between late fall and early spring.

☐ **Four pairs of socks.**

☐ **One pair of good walking shoes.** Don't bring any dress shoes, heels, or anything you can't walk in all day for two weeks straight.

Tourist Traps

Some **cathedrals** in Catholic countries have a **strict dress code** of no shorts or skirts above the knee and no bare shoulders. St. Peter's will not let you in if enough of you isn't covered. Pack accordingly. Wear a shirt under sleeveless jumpers. Women can turn an oversized scarf (on sale cheap at nearby souvenir stands) into a makeshift skirt or shawl—as can men who are comfortable with their sexuality.

Keeping It Clean

The two bugaboos of traveling with toiletries are minimizing spillage disasters—store *everything* in resealable plastic baggies—and maximizing the tiny space inside a bathroom bag. Put all liquids, such as shampoo and detergent, into small, screw-top plastic bottles (available at most travel and luggage shops and some drugstores). Sample sizes of shaving cream and toothpaste, and a few tiny hotel soaps, are more than enough for several weeks. Keep toiletries and cosmetics to a minimum. I don't recommend taking perfume or cologne on the road; it's vain dead weight and a spill waiting to happen (imagine everything in your bag drenched with Chanel no. 5). For women, a touch of red lipstick is enough to turn any outfit formal. Here are the essential items:

- [ ] **Toothbrush and small tube of toothpaste.**

- [ ] **Comb.** Brushes are bulky; take one only if you truly need it.

- [ ] **Small soap bars and small shampoo.**

- [ ] **Razor and shaving cream.** Later in the chapter, I'll give you the skinny on electric razors.

- [ ] **Medicines.**

- [ ] **Extra glasses and contacts.** Count on losing them, and bring a hard glasses case. Also, bring enough saline solution to last you (parts of Europe sell it only in glass bottles).

- [ ] **First-aid kit.** Take at least a few adhesive bandages, antiseptic ointment, moleskin for the almost inevitable blisters, aspirin, Dramamine or those motion-sickness wristbands, hand lotion, lip balm (traveling promotes chapping), sunscreen, and a non-drowsy decongestant/ antihistamine.

- [ ] **Feminine hygiene products.** You could certainly buy tampons abroad, but take what you need with you, especially if you're brand-loyal.

- [ ] **Braided clothesline.** Available at travel stores, the nylon twists in this clothesline hold clothes without clothespins. Don't let hoteliers see you washing or drying clothes; most are inexplicably (but fanatically) against laundry in the room.

- [ ] **Laundry detergent.** Tubes of biodegradable handwashing solutions are available at any travel store.

- [ ] **Half a tennis ball.** This item is a good makeshift sink stopper.

- [ ] **Towel.** A small terrycloth towel is a lifesaver when you're confronted with the nonabsorbent, waffle-pressed towels of Europe.

- [ ] **Condoms.** U.S. brands are safer than most European ones.

- [ ] **Pocket-sized tissue packs.** These are invaluable for runny noses, substitute napkins, sudden spills, and bathroom emergencies.

Documents & Sundries

Carry all of your most important documents, such as your passport, plane tickets, rail passes, traveler's checks, driver's license, and credit cards, in a **money belt.** One of travel's necessary evils, these flat pouches that you wear under your clothes come in three main flavors: those that hang around the neck; those that are strapped around your waist, over your shirt tails but under your pants (larger and more safely concealed, but less comfortable and harder to access); and those that hang down your pants leg, attached to your belt by a loop (my personal choice, balancing both safety and ease of access—although occasionally awkward and embarrassing in that you have to reach down your pants to get at it). Leave at home all keys but your main house key as well as all unnecessary wallet items (library card, department store and gas station credit cards, and so on).

Dollars & Sense

Wear your money belt under your clothes as it was intended. I see countless travelers wearing the waist kind above their pants waist like some kind of flat fannypack or the neck kind bouncing on their belly like a tiny purse. Exposed like this, money belts make your most precious documents even less safe than they would be if you simply stuffed them in your pockets.

Here are the remaining items that you will need to carry:

- [ ] **Guidebooks and phrase books.**

- [ ] **Hard-backed journal and pens.** Bring these items and use them; you won't remember it all half as well as you imagine.

- [ ] **Camera.** You can get remarkably advanced pocket cameras these days to replace bulky, thief-tempting types. Bring extra batteries.

- [ ] **Film.** Film is very expensive in Europe, as is processing. Airport x-rays *will* fog the film (especially higher speed films), and those lead-lined bags just force the scanners to crank up the x-rays. Instead, stow all film in large, see-through baggies and have it hand-inspected.

- [ ] **Swiss Army knife.** The most useful features of this are the screwdriver/can opener, the blade, the corkscrew (for picnics), the tweezers, the scissors, and the file.

- [ ] **Battery-powered travel alarm clock.**

- [ ] **Small bottle of water.** Buy them as you go in Europe; they are exceedingly handy on long train trips.

- [ ] **Pocket sewing kit.**

- [ ] **Sunglasses.**

- [ ] **Address list.** Friends appreciate postcards at the time much more than a slide show afterward.

- [ ] **Tiny folding umbrella.**

- [ ] **Pocket flashlight.**

- [ ] **A novel.** This will entertain you during long plane and train trips. Many hotels have rotating bookshelves to trade it for a new one when you're done.

- [ ] **Passport.**

- [ ] **Money.** Bring traveler's checks, credit cards, an ATM bank card, and cash (European and dollars).

- [ ] **Driver's license and International Driver's Permit.** Bring these items only if you plan to drive, and always keep them in your money belt.

- [ ] **Airline tickets.**

- [ ] **Rail pass.**

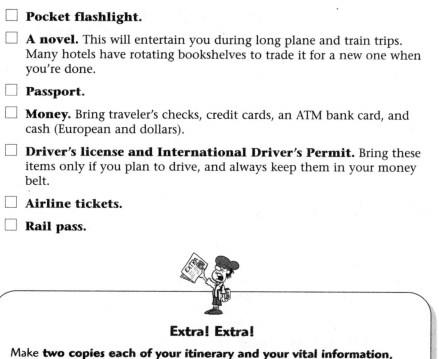

Extra! Extra!

Make **two copies each of your itinerary and your vital information,** the latter featuring the information page of your passport, your driver's license, and your student or teacher's identity card. Also include your traveler's check numbers, your credit card numbers (code them by writing them backwards), and the 800 numbers for the issuers of your bank cards, credit cards, and traveler's checks—if you lose any of these items on the road, you'll need to call it in immediately. Leave one copy of each with a neighbor or friend at home and carry the second copy with you in a safe place (separate from the originals) while you travel.

Europe Unplugged: Electronics *Not* to Bring

The only piece of electronic equipment I travel with that isn't battery-powered is my trusty Mac Powerbook—and I only need that because I have this strange job of writing travel guides. Electronics of any kind are just a big hassle that take up room in your luggage, waste time out of your schedule, and put hotel fuses out of commission. This hassle is five times worse with anything that has a cord. Take a small battery-operated alarm clock and one of those teensy flashlights for poking around ancient ruins and finding stuff in the dark. Beyond that, travel without electronics.

Still determined to lug around half a Radio Shack? Here's what you need to know. American current runs 110V, 60 cycles. Europe runs 210 to 220V and 50 cycles. You can't plug an American appliance into a European outlet without frying your appliance and/or blowing a fuse. You need a **currency converter or transformer** to bring the voltage down and the cycles up.

You can't plug an American appliance into a European wall even if you wanted to because American plug prongs are flat and parallel; much of Europe uses two round holes or some other configuration. You can get small **plug adapters** that make the switch, *but these are not currency converters.* You still need to go through a transformer to get the electrical current running properly.

Travel-sized versions of popular items such as hair dryers, irons, shavers, and so on come in "dual-voltage," which means they have built-in converters (usually you have to turn a switch to go back and forth). Most contemporary **laptop computers** automatically sense the current and adapt accordingly (check the manuals, bottom of the machine, or manufacturer first to make sure you won't burn the thing out). Plug adapters and converters are available at most travel, luggage, electronics, and hardware stores. Or call the **Franzus Corporation** (☎ **203/723-6664**) for a copy of its pamphlet "Foreign Electricity Is No Deep Dark Secret" (complete, of course, with a convenient order form for adapters and converters).

A **hair dryer,** even the teensy portable kind, is just another monkey on your back. The majority of European hotels from the moderate range up have built-in hair dryers in the baths. If you insist on lugging your own hot air over there, hear my plea and make sure that either it is dual-voltage or that you carry along a converter. Hotels black out on a regular basis when an American plugs in his 110V hairdryer and the appliance either explodes in an impressive shower of sparks or melts in his hands. This stunt has long since ceased to amuse hoteliers and other guests.

For shaving, I'd stick with Bic unless you have a battery-operated **electric shaver**—that way you won't have to bother with voltage problems. If not, however, most hotels have a special plug for low-wattage shavers *and shavers only.* Such outlets are usually identified by an icon of a half-shaven face. If you plug anything other than a shaver in there, you'll join the unpopular hair dryer-melting, fuse-blowing crowd.

If you're planning to bring along any other electronic device, ask yourself whether you really need it (*hint:* the answer is no). There is one exception. I often tote a **personal tape deck,** but not to listen to tunes—why shut your ears off from the audio portion of your vacation? I take one with a record button to capture the sounds and conversations of Europe and the occasional snippet of an audio journal.

Airlines will request that you don't have your computer, personal tape deck, CD player, or any other electronic device turned on during take-off and landing. On the off chance that the waves emitted by these items might foul up the computerized guidance systems, they're hedging their bets against your CD-ROM drive causing the plane to crash, and I for one am wholly on their side.

The Last-Minute Checklist: Did You Turn Off the Iron?

There are plenty of housekeeping details you need to take care of before you leave. Although most are fairly obvious, they are easy to overlook in the excitement of getting ready for a trip. It's best not to leave a house unattended; try at least to have a neighbor look in on your house from time to time to pick up the mail, feed the cats, water the plants, and generally make the place appear less abandoned. For longer trips, consider getting a full-time housesitter. Here are other household details you need to handle before you leave:

☐ Put a hold on your mail and newspaper deliveries.

☐ Get someone to look after your pets (or kennel them) and water the plants.

☐ Empty/defrost the refrigerator.

☐ Reconfirm your plane's seat reservation and hotel bookings.

☐ Put several lights in the house on timers (dining room at dinner time, TV room during prime time, and so on).

☐ Have a neighbor start your car once a week or so.

☐ Lock all windows and doors (don't forget the basement and garage).

☐ Arrange for a friend or car service to take you to the airport (in the end, this method is cheaper and better than leaving your car in the airport garage).

☐ Call the airline to double-check that your flight is on time.

☐ Get to the airport at least two hours before your flight.

☐ Sit back on the plane, take a deep breath, and tell yourself: "I'm on my way to Europe!" Bon voyage! Have a blast. Send me a postcard.

Part 2

European Survival Skills: A Primer

Whew! The worst of the planning work is over. From now on, it's all fun and learning to live, however temporarily, in Europe. The next six chapters are devoted to all the basic things you need to know: how to choose a hotel, what to look for in a restaurant, and how to construct a sightseeing schedule. I'll walk you through the finer points of communicating with the folks back home and teach you how to get around that pesky language barrier with the locals you'll meet along the way. You'll also get some frank advice on how to stay safe and healthy. Finally, get ready to shop with savvy—I'm here to steer you away from the ripoffs and clue you in to the bargains. Bienvenue! Wilkommen! Bienvenido! Benvenuto! Welcome to Europe!

Chapter 7

The Hotel Hunt & Additional Accommodations Advice

After transportation, your single biggest expense in Europe will be lodging, but lodging is also one of the easiest areas in which to save money. You can spend $300 to $700 on a posh palace in Paris, go to a simple, moderate hotel down the street for a $60 double, or check into a hostel for just $18 a night. The variety of accommodation options is astounding. With a little bit of leg-work, the hotel recommendations in this book, and the hotel hunting hints in this chapter, you'll never have to spend more than $80 to $100 a night for a perfectly nice, clean, centrally located double room—unless, of course, you want to.

Getting Acquainted with the European Hotel

Traditional European hotels tend to have fewer bells and whistles than American ones. For example, even the cheapest American chain motel has free cable. In Europe, however, few hotels below the moderate level even have in-room televisions. European hoteliers have different standards; their hotels tend to emphasize cleanliness and friendliness over amenities. Sure, they can be old-fashioned and somewhat worn around the edges, with either mismatched or aging 1960s functional furniture, but they're great deals.

Dollars & Sense

The **hotel listings in this book** use a ratings system from $ to $$$$$. These ratings do not reflect any official ranking system, but rather are my indication to you as to which hotels are the best value in that particular city. A ranking of $ indicates a budget gem, $$ or $$$ means a moderate hotel, $$$$ is applied to more upscale joints, and $$$$$ is for a recommended splurge. These ratings are applied on a city-by-city basis, meaning that a $ joint in an expensive city like London may cost about the same as a $$$$ hotel in a cheaper place like Athens. Check the hotel listing to find out what the range of rates is for the hotel you're interested in.

The cheaper, more traditional European hotels and pensions (smaller, family-run establishments) typically differ from American hotels in the following ways:

➤ The lobbies and rooms rarely jibe. Never judge a hotel by its entrance; expensive hotels almost always invest heavily in the lobby, often skimping on the rooms. Cheaper hotels may often have just a dingy desk in a hallway, but spotless, fine accommodations.

➤ Double beds are often two twin beds pushed together and made with a single top sheet and blanket (or two twin sheets made to overlap). Turn the mattress parts perpendicular to the springs and you won't suffer from separation anxiety (or end up slipping through the crack) in the middle of the night. Also, beware of lazy springs and mattresses that sag in the middle.

➤ Many hotels in old buildings don't have elevators. The few elevators that are available are so rickety and slow that they belong on the city's official register of historic relics.

➤ Floors are often covered with tile or linoleum instead of carpet.

➤ Bathrooms are radically different from the American norm (see the following section, "Rub-a-Dub-Dub, the Whole Floor Shares a Tub").

My advice is to treat the hotel room merely as a place to lay your head. Don't be too bothered if you didn't get chocolates on the pillow or complimentary bath salts. If you're there just to sleep, the room just needs to be safe, clean, and reasonably near to the sights. The money you save on lodging can go toward restaurant splurges, souvenirs, extra museum admissions, or the cost of transportation out of town for a day trip.

Rub-a-Dub-Dub, the Whole Floor Shares a Tub

So you think the cultural divide between Europe and America is best expressed in its languages, museums, architecture, or food? Nope, sorry. For an American traveling in Europe, nowhere is culture shock greater than in the bathroom. It all starts in your first cheap pension, when you discover that the only bathroom is down the hall, coed, and shared by everyone on the floor.

European hoteliers are a bit mystified as to why so many American travelers object to sharing a bath. Although more and more European hotels are installing bathrooms in every room, a bathroom in the room is by no means standard. If you won't accept the shared bath principle, you'll have to pay extra for a private bath in your room. **Important safety tip:** See the section on electricity in chapter 6 for details on what is not safe to plug in your bathroom outlets (here's a hint: everything).

The Early Bird Gets the Hot Shower

The European concept of a shower is to stick a nozzle in the bathroom wall and a drain in the floor. Curtains are optional. In some cramped private baths, you have to move the toilet paper outside the bathroom before turning on the shower and drenching the whole room. Another interesting bathroom fixture is the half-tub, in which there's only room to sit, rather than stretch out. The half-tub usually also sports a shower nozzle that has nowhere to hang—so your knees get very clean, and the floor gets very wet.

Hot water may be available only once a day and not on demand—this is especially true with shared baths. Heating water is costly, and many smaller hotels only do it once daily, in the morning. Once the hot water is used up, that luxury won't be available again until the next day. When you check in, ask "When hot water?" Take your shower quickly, soap up without water, and try to be first in line to avoid inadvertent freezing. In some countries, Britain in particular, you may have to turn on the hot water at a special mini-hot water heater either inside or just outside of the stall itself.

Bet You Didn't Know

The faucet marked *c* in romance-language countries (France, Italy, Spain) is for hot water; the cold-water faucet is marked *f*.

Before you go get showered up, keep in mind that traditional European towels are flat, waffle-textured and singularly unabsorbent. Follow the *Hitchhiker's Guide to the Galaxy's* advice—carry your own terry-cloth towel for just such an emergency (a hand towel is the least bulky).

Look Honey, Two Toilets!

That funny extra toilet that looks like a reclining urinal is called a **bidet.** The water jets that shoot up (and sometimes out) are intended to clean your, ahem, private parts and do a much more thorough job than toilet paper does. Do *not* use the bidet as an auxiliary toilet. Some travelers use it to wash out clothes or store fruit or beer. Personally, I just think about what it's truly used for and decide to do my laundry in the sink.

Hotel Hunting Strategies

I always reserve at least the first night's room before leaving the States, especially if I'm arriving on a weekend. Having a place to go straight away minimizes the stress and uncertainty upon arrival. Don't book the room for the whole first week, however. This way, you'll have the freedom to look elsewhere for lodging if your choice doesn't live up to expectations.

Reserving every night of the vacation ahead of time can crimp spontaneity and limit you to your first (and perhaps potentially bad) choices. Calling ahead from one city to the next to reserve at least the first night in a new town usually works out well. I have even gone so far as to simply search out a room by phoning from the train station upon arrival.

Time-Savers

If you call a hotel from home to reserve a room in advance, **always follow up with a confirmation fax.** Not only is it what most hotels prefer, but it is printed proof that you've booked a room. When **faxing hotels,** keep the language simple. State your name, number of people, what kind of room (make sure you say "double with one bed" or "double with two beds"), how many nights you want to stay, and the starting date for the first night. Write out the month longhand; Europeans numerically abbreviate dates day/month/year, not month/day/year as we do.

Of course, there are a few cases when such spontaneity can spell headaches. If you're traveling with young children, the last thing you want to do is loiter in the train station fumbling for coins as you try to simultaneously reserve a room and keep the kids from running off. Another detail that's crucial to know is whether you'll be arriving in town during a festival. If you are, you're probably in for the highlight of your trip, but if you haven't reserved a room far, far in advance (while still in the States), you could end up bunking down on a park bench.

Getting the Best Room at the Best Price, Even at the Last Minute

If you arrive in town without a hotel reservation, finding a hotel is much easier if you use either this book or a similar guidebook. Before you arrive in town (perhaps on the train ride in), read the reviews of hotels in this book thoroughly and figure out which ones best fit your taste and budget. Then prioritize your top choices by scribbling 1, 2, 3, and so on in the guide's margins. Ranking the hotels beforehand saves you the time and hassle of standing around in the train station with your companions saying, "Well, how does this one sound?" while other travelers snap up the vacant rooms.

When you get to the station, get some change or buy a phone card from a newsstand and begin calling hotels immediately to check for vacancies. This way, you get a leg up on the many people who march out of the station with their bags and walk to the nearest hotel to find a room. If you don't want to do the telephone work when you get to town yourself, the train station or tourist office usually runs a reservations service (see the "Using a Hotel Booking Service" section).

If you can't find a room this way, you can try wandering the streets checking each hotel you pass (the area around the train station is usually glutted with cheap hotels). Also try widening the scope of your search. Hotels outside the center of town often have more rooms available and are oftentimes cheaper than centrally located hotels. Hotels in the next town over may be even less expensive; if the hotel is anything more than a 30-minute commute by train, though, it won't be worth the hassle; use it only as a last resort.

> **Bet You Didn't Know**
>
> Smaller, cheaper hotels often **won't reserve far in advance** for short periods (fewer than three nights). This policy is to protect them from cancellations, and no assurance you offer to prove that you will show up seems to change it. Even when you have a reservation, these hotels will hold a room for you only if you call from the station and tell them you're on your way.

To get the best price on a room, follow these tips:

- ➤ **Ask to see different rooms.** When you get to the hotel, don't take the first room you're shown. Ask to see different ones. Open and close windows to see how well they shut out noise. Peek at the rates posted on the room door (usually there by law) to make sure they correspond with the rate you're quoted *and* the rate that's posted in the lobby. Ask about heating. Ask whether some rooms are cheaper than others.

- ➤ **Bargain.** Room prices are rarely set, especially in pensions and mom-and-pop joints. If you're staying one night in high season, you'll have to pay the going rate. But for stays in the off-season and for longer than three nights, ask for a discount. Many places offer weekend discounts. The more empty rooms a hotel has to fill for the night, the lower they'll go with the price. Keep in mind that double rooms are often cheaper with one large bed rather than two single beds. A triple with a cot for a family of four is much cheaper than two double rooms.

111

Dollars & Sense

Settle all hotel charges at the outset. You needn't pay in advance, but do agree on the rates, whether breakfast, taxes, and showers are included, what the phone rates are (never call long distance from the hotel), and so on. Also be sure that the price quoted to you is per room, *not per person.*

➤ **Check different hotels.** Many people don't want to bother with this method, but if you have an abundance of time and are counting the pennies, give it a try. Don't assume the first hotel you visit is the best. If you've called around and housing seems tight in town, take a room when you get it. But if rooms seem plentiful in the city, tell the first hotel you'll think about it and head to another one nearby. If you leave your luggage in a train station locker while you hunt for a hotel, you'll feel (and appear) more able to bargain and hunt effectively. Return to the hotel you liked best and ask for the best price they can offer. They'll often lower their rate if they think you have another option waiting around the corner.

➤ **Remember, rooms without baths are cheaper.** If you don't mind walking down the hall and sharing a bath, you'll often save considerably.

➤ **Ask for rates without breakfast.** You might shave $5 to $10 off the price of a room if you do without breakfast. Hotel breakfasts are always overpriced; they usually just consist of a roll and coffee or tea. You can get the same thing much more cheaply at any corner cafe or bar. The only hotel breakfasts that are worth keeping are the English breakfast feasts served in the B&Bs of Great Britain.

Extra! Extra!

Always take one of the hotel's cards after you check in. You'd be surprised by how easy it is to forget your hotel's name or precise location after a long day of sightseeing. Most cards have a little map on the back. If you're at a total loss, hop in a cab and show the driver the card. He'll get you home.

Using a Hotel Booking Service

When you arrive in town, a desk in either the train station or at the tourist office will act as a central reservations service for the city. Tell the people working there your price range, where you'd like to be in the city, and sometimes even the style of hotel, and they'll use a computer database to find you a room in town. In each city chapter in this book,

I've listed booking services in a "Time-Savers" sidebar under the accommodations section.

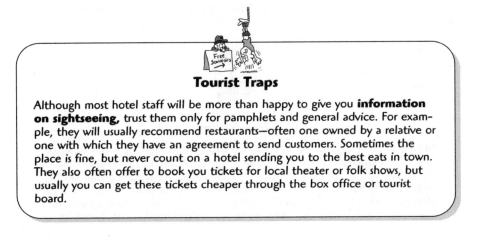

Tourist Traps

Although most hotel staff will be more than happy to give you **information on sightseeing,** trust them only for pamphlets and general advice. For example, they will usually recommend restaurants—often one owned by a relative or one with which they have an agreement to send customers. Sometimes the place is fine, but never count on a hotel sending you to the best eats in town. They also often offer to book you tickets for local theater or folk shows, but usually you can get these tickets cheaper through the box office or tourist board.

The plusses of using a service are the following:

☺ They do all the room-finding work for you. They speak English, whereas individual hoteliers may not, so they can act as interpreters in calling around on your behalf.

☺ When everything's booked up during a convention or festival, or perhaps just in high season, they can often find space for you in hotels that aren't listed in the guidebooks or other main sources.

☺ The best ones can match you with the perfect accommodations.

The minuses of using a service are the following:

☹ They usually charge a fee—a nominal one of $3 to $10, but a fee nonetheless. In many countries, hotels often charge higher rates to people booking through such a service; it's cheapest to contact hotels directly.

☹ At best, the tourist office booking desk will give you no opinion about the hotels; they'll just provide you with a list that perhaps includes amenities and prices, but little else.

☹ At worst, a booking agency, especially a private hotel booking agency (which is probably run by a consortium of hotels in town), will hardsell you places on their "push list." Rather than an honest evaluation, their "advice" is, more often than not, a biased sales pitch dictated by the hotel itself.

I've found wonderful little B&Bs in Ireland through the glossy promotional catalog the tourist office sent me. I've also had a Prague hotel agency stick me in what appeared to be a communist-era high school that took almost an hour (one metro and two tram rides) to reach from the city center. Once I got there, I discovered that the room made my college dorm room look like a suite at the Ritz. Read between the lines of promotional fluff and ask tough, pointed questions when you call around. If you don't like a room, you don't have to take it.

Time-Savers

Although having your hotel do your **laundry** is convenient, it is also expensive (and usually only an option at middle-range hotels and up). The most obvious alternative is to go to a coin-operated laundromat, but watching your clothes swish in circles for 90 minutes isn't exactly what you came to Europe for, is it? Most cities have laundry shops that will wash and dry your clothes based on weight (an average load costs $7)—poke around the local university district for them.

Not All Hotels Are Created Equal: The Truth Behind the Stars

In your information gathering, you may have run across terms such as "three-star hotel" or "four-star inn." What does the star thing mean exactly? Such hotel ratings systems vary widely from country to country and often from region to region. Most countries now use the star method (or a similar variant) to rate hotels, and most use a range of one to five stars. One star indicates a bottom-rung establishment; five stars usually means deluxe accommodations (although some countries confuse things further by having a deluxe category ranked above the fifth star). Stars are usually not directly tied to prices, but there's a pretty strong correlation. Most of the places you'll come across will be somewhere in the middle: two stars (budget), three stars (moderate), and four stars (upscale).

These ratings systems aren't perfect, especially at the top and bottom ends. Ratings are usually tied to amenities offered (and, less so, to rudimentary cleanliness) and rarely to the more subjective standards of overall pleasantness, quality of service, and friendliness of the innkeepers. Sometimes, an extra star can just mean the addition of a mini refrigerator with tiny bottles of vodka. As a result, a one-star hotel may just be a very simple but clean place, or it may be a roach-infested dump. In this guide, I have reviewed each hotel independently and honestly with no regard for the star rating. You may use the official ratings as a general guide, but always back it up by reading guidebook reviews and checking out the places on your own.

Beyond the Hotels: Other Types of Accommodations

This book reviews mainly standard hotels (along with a fair share of the more traditional and charming family-run pensions) because hotels tend to be larger and hence offer you the best chance of finding a room. Hotels aren't your only option, however. In fact, they're usually among the more expensive places to stay in town and are rarely the most fun or memorable. Even if your hotel room truly is just a place to lay your weary head, if you can get a bed that's both cheaper and in a more interesting setting, why not go for it?

Each country has its own hotel alternatives, from Alpine shacks to villas in Tuscany. There are far, far too many different accommodation options—some 36 by my last count—to cover them all here in depth. However, here's a quick rundown on the most popular variants on the standard hotel (for more information on each of these, it's best to check with the local tourist office):

➤ **B&Bs or pensions.** These places are usually small, family-run versions of hotels and are the places most Europeans stay on vacation. If the hotels in town charge $100 for a double, a pension will usually run only $40 to $60. They sometimes require that you pay for breakfast or half- or full board (meals included); private baths are rare (but getting less so); and the service is almost always friendly and personable. Never take the meal requirements unless there's no other option (as is often the case in resorty places like spas and beaches, especially in-season). Eating in a local restaurant is usually a better bet and offers more variety night-to-night.

➤ **Private room-for-rent.** Even the cheapest B&B can't beat the prices for renting a room in a private home, which can run as low as $15 to $40 for a double. It's a great option for singles because you don't pay the outrageous single-occupancy rate that hotel doubles charge. Rooms for rent are more hit-or-miss than a standard hotel, but at the absolute worst you're stuck in a tiny, characterless room. At best, you get comfortable digs, a very homey atmosphere, a huge home-cooked breakfast, and the chance to be an auxiliary member of a real European family for a few days. Find me the five-star hotel that offers *that*.

➤ **International chain hotels.** Usually bookable from the United States, these places are often enormous and impersonal and are usually located in the business or industrial districts at the fringe of town. They're expensive, but there's an assured level of amenities and services.

➤ **Motels.** Most travelers don't realize Europe has adopted this American form of modular innkeeping because motels hover around city peripheries at highway access points. If you're driving in and arriving late, these places are a great, cheap lodging option. They are utterly without

115

character, but they are often real bargains (some are even fully automated—it's like checking yourself into a slot at a giant vending machine for the night).

➤ **Converted castles and other historic spots.** Usually of high quality, these lodgings also range from the outrageously expensive to the state-run and surprisingly cheap. (Spain's *paradores* are the classic example of the latter.)

➤ **Apartment or villa rentals.** These accommodations are the best for long-term stays and to really feel like a temporary European. These are widely advertised in newspaper travel sections and magazines. They're easiest to arrange through a travel agent or villa rental consortium, but you'll sometimes find the best deals by contacting people privately in the destination itself (through local papers, English-language magazines, and the tourist board). Do a lot of shopping around, ask many questions, and look at lots of pictures. For particularly long stays, it pays for one member of the party to make a short reconnaissance trip to the country in question to check out the top options before you settle on one.

➤ **Farm stays.** These can be a great way to see a country's culture and people from the inside and on a personal basis. Quality varies widely, however; some are luxury country retreats; others are one step removed from sleeping in the barn with the family cow. You just have to take your chances.

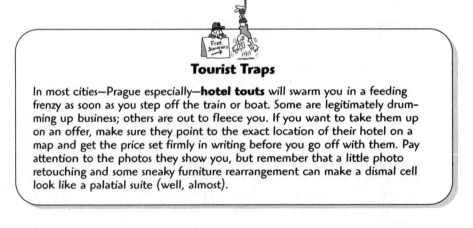

Tourist Traps

In most cities—Prague especially—**hotel touts** will swarm you in a feeding frenzy as soon as you step off the train or boat. Some are legitimately drumming up business; others are out to fleece you. If you want to take them up on an offer, make sure they point to the exact location of their hotel on a map and get the price set firmly in writing before you go off with them. Pay attention to the photos they show you, but remember that a little photo retouching and some sneaky furniture rearrangement can make a dismal cell look like a palatial suite (well, almost).

Hostels & Other Low-Budget Options

If you're really counting pennies, or if you're fond of fraternizing with primarily youthful backpackers, you might want to stay in a hostel. The only ones that are still officially "youth" hostels are in southern Germany, where the under 25 only rule is still applied. Most hostels are now open as cheap digs for anyone, with per-person rates ranging from $10 to $30 per night.

In a hostel, you stay in bunks in dorm-like shared rooms. Depending on the facility, there are anywhere from two or four beds per room to as many as 100 beds in a single gymnasium-like space; most hostels have a mix of smaller and larger rooms at differing prices. Many are sex-segregated by room or by floor. You always pay a per-person rate, and families can often find hostels with four-bunk rooms for semi-private housing. There are lockers for safekeeping your bags. Baths are always shared, breakfast is often included, and other meals are sometimes available.

Hostels tend to be far from the center of town, occasionally on the city outskirts, and they fill up with high school students in the summer. Hostels almost always impose evening curfews (usually between 10pm and midnight), midday lockout periods, and limits on how long you can stay (often no more than three days). You may only be able to reserve a day in advance, or not at all, so be sure to show up early.

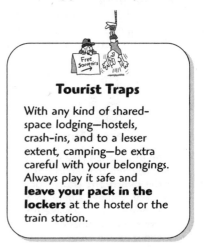

To stay in many hostels, you must be a card-carrying member of **Hostelling International** (☎ **202/783-6161**), or IYH as it's known abroad. Membership fees are $25 annually; for those under 18, it's $10, and for those over 54, it's $15. The card entitles you to a discount at official IYH/AIG hostels, but not at most private hostels (of which there are a few). You can also buy the card at many hostels abroad. Most hostels provide a blanket, but require that you use your own **sleep-sack,** which is basically two sheets sewn together. Buy one before you go (from Hostelling International) or make one if you plan to stay in hostels; some of them will sell you a sleep-sack on the spot, but a few will insist you rent one of theirs. For an independent Internet hostelling guide, try **www.hostels.com.**

Tourist Traps

With any kind of shared-space lodging—hostels, crash-ins, and to a lesser extent, camping—be extra careful with your belongings. Always play it safe and **leave your pack in the lockers** at the hostel or the train station.

In addition to hostels, you have several other options for inexpensive lodging:

➤ **Convents.** Especially in Catholic countries (Italy, Spain, and France), you can save big bucks and get an immaculately clean and safe room in a convent or other religious housing, no matter what your religious bent. Available in many major cities and pilgrimage sites, convents cost as little as $5 to as much as $50 per night (the occasional theology lesson is included). Don't expect your room to be any fancier than the cells the nuns or monks occupy. Many convents give preference to visitors of their own denominations and/or country of origin.

➤ **University housing.** Check with the tourist office or directly with local universities to see whether the colleges in town rent unused dorms rooms (at rates comparable to hostels). This option is usually only available during summer and over Christmas break when school is not in session.

➤ **Crash-ins.** Some cities (Munich, London, Paris, Venice, and Copenhagen) have what I call "crash-ins," open in the summer high season for the person on the extreme budget. In these hangar-like rooms or big-top tents, you'll get a floor mat, a blanket, over 100 room-mates, and a cup of tea in the morning; the cost ranges from $7 to $20. These giant slumber parties are mostly patronized by students, but they are open to all. Essentially, it's one step above rolling out your sleeping bag on a park bench (which, by the way, is highly unsafe, not recommended, and usually illegal).

➤ **Camping.** This is how my family used to travel around Europe; it can be a fun and cheap way to see the continent and meet Europeans. Most European camping is done in camper vans and caravans, not by tent. Camp only if you're driving (or biking or hiking); trying to combine train travel with camping is a time-consuming disaster. Rates usually run around $10 to $40 (this includes charges for each person, tent, vehicle, and so on). If you plan to camp, get the International Camping Carnet, a card that costs $30 from **Family Campers and RVers** (☎ **800/245-9755**). It's required at some campgrounds and gets you a discount at many more (plus, having the card prevents you from having to leave your passport with the front office). Most campgrounds are nifty little compact communities with showers, bars, restaurants, and grocery stores. Campgrounds are, however, usually at the edge of or just outside of town, so be prepared to commute for your sightseeing.

Dollars & Sense

One of Europe's greatest sleeping and travel bargains is the **overnight train.** For just $20, you get a bunk in a couchette, and you wake up in your next destination without having wasted a day getting there. (The main thing you'll be sacrificing is a sound sleep.) See chapter 4 for more details.

Chapter 8

Good Eats: What to Expect from a Restaurant

> ### In This Chapter
> ➤ The quirks and norms of typical European meals
> ➤ Pointers for finding the best local restaurants
> ➤ Deciphering the menu and ordering your meal
> ➤ The perfect picnic and fine fast food (McDonald's it ain't)

Sampling the local food is just as much a part of traveling as seeing all the sights, and finding the perfect restaurant can be as memorable as a day spent in the Louvre, maybe more so. You'll have the chance to savor interesting flavor combinations and to discover the joys of a three-hour dinner replete with multiple courses, good wine, and engaging conversation.

Many waiters, concerned that travelers' palates may reject some of the more interesting local dishes, may try to steer you clear from sheep's testicles and the like. Perhaps it's a service you're only too happy to let them perform, but take it from me—sheep's testicles aren't bad. Travel is an adventure; foreign dining doubly so. Bon Appetit!

European Dining Norms

Most European cultures have many different types of dining establishments, which go down in price—but rarely in quality or authenticity—as they get less fancy and formal. The top rung is called something that sounds like "restaurant" in almost every language. More casual restaurants abound, usually smaller and serving classic cooking like mama used to make, be it a French *bistro*, Italian *trattoria* or *osteria*, Austrian *beisel*, or German *bierhalle*. The establishments in this second category are the places to head on a nightly basis for filling, excellent, well-priced food and a homey, friendly atmosphere. Most cities also sport cafe-like places that serve hearty dishes; in Paris it's a *brassiere*, in Italy a *tavola calda*, in Spain a *tascas*.

The Marathon Dinner (or, "Waiter, Where's Our Food?")

The **main meal** of the day in Europe, which once was lunch but increasingly is becoming dinner, is often a long, drawn-out affair of three to five courses (plus wine, water, coffee, liqueur, and dessert) that can last two to four hours. In most of Europe, you're never rushed through a meal. Many Americans at first get annoyed in European restaurants because they think service is slow. It's not. The waiters are giving you time to savor every dish and the conversation at your table. After all, eating too quickly is bad for the digestion. When you get to Europe, remember how healthy you're being as you slowly spoon that creamy chocolate mousse into your mouth.

When exactly the **dinner hour** is, on the other hand, depends on where you are. As with so much else here, the trends vary as you move north or south on the continent. The Brits sit down to dinner between 5 and 6pm, the Italians start around 7:30 or 8pm. In Spain, restaurants don't even open until 9pm, and most customers don't arrive until 10pm. But don't worry that you'll be famished by dinnertime; in the countries where dinner starts late, there's usually a traditional evening stroll around 5pm during which you're expected to nibble on munchies (pizza in Italy, tapas in Spain, and so on).

Tourist Traps

Except in some of the top (and snootiest) restaurants in the big cities, you'll encounter stricter **dress codes** at cathedrals than at restaurants. Remember that Europeans tend to have a keen fashion sense and dress casually well any time they go out; you'll be fine in jeans, but I wouldn't dine in shorts and a T-shirt. If you're splurging on a top restaurant, call ahead to ask if jacket and tie are required for men.

Start the Day Off Right

Breakfast on the continent is, well, continental: a roll (or croissant) with butter or jam, plus coffee and/or orange juice. Your hotel will almost undoubtedly serve the same meal, but at ridiculously high prices ($7 to $15). Some hotels try to justify the price by laying out cheese, ham, and fruit as well, but you're still better off heading to the corner cafe or bar and grabbing a croissant and cappuccino alongside the locals on their way into work. It's the same grub as at the hotel, only less than half the price.

On the British Isles, though, you're in for a breakfast treat. At least once, if not more, indulge in a traditional English, Scottish, or Irish breakfast, which is a miniature smorgasbord of eggs, hams, cheese, oatmeal, sausages, "puddings," and jams. Speaking of smorgasbords, Scandinavian countries are the other exception to the continental breakfast rule, offering breakfast as well as dinner versions of their famous sampler feasts.

Lunch: More Than a Sandwich...Sometimes

Across Europe, **lunch** is a multicourse meal similar to dinner. As I've said before, lunch used to be the big meal of the day (especially in southern Europe), but modern work schedules have slowly squeezed out the big lunch and added those extra hours to dinner. It's just as well from a touring point of view, because you've got a lot of sightseeing to do during the day and probably won't want to spend more than an hour on lunch. Lunch is a good meal to grab on the run or to plan a picnic for, which will save you both sightseeing time and money for a splurge at dinner. The only remnant of the large lunch is **Sunday lunch,** which is often still the biggest meal of the week and a time in many countries for extended families to get together and have a massive meal that lasts for hours.

Culinary Stereotypes & Gastronomic Misconceptions

The American versions of European cuisines—whether brought over by immigrants years ago or recently imported by California chefs—usually take a number of liberties with their inspiration. For instance, several foods you *won't* find in Italy are spaghetti and meatballs, hoagies (grinders, subs, torpedoes, or whatever they call them where you live), Italian ices, and deep-dish pizzas (Italian ones are usually very thin and very crispy).

Dollars & Sense

The restaurants I'll be reviewing later in this book are rated from **$ to $$$$$.** These ratings merely reflect the average cost of a meal in each restaurant, from budget eats ($) through moderate meals ($$ to $$$$) and special-occasion splurges ($$$$$). Price rarely reflects quality in Europe, however, and you'll probably have some of your most outstanding dinners in $ or $$ places. As with hotels, these rankings are determined on a city-by-city basis—you'll notice that the $$$$$ restaurant in Athens (an inexpensive city) costs about the same as the $ joint in much pricier London.

The common stereotypes of European cuisines are often off the mark as well. For one thing, there's quite excellent British cuisine—yes, British! Not only is today's pub grub much better than its reputation, but many London restaurants now serve dishes excellent and complex enough to make the French across the Channel jealous.

Sure, you'll find a McDonald's in the heart of every city, and you'll probably find yourself ordering le Big Mac on occasion (Mickey D's almost always has great clean bathrooms), but I'd recommend sticking to local restaurants. Search out restaurants with the most authentic food and atmosphere. Be daring—order what you don't recognize on the menu, lubricate your meal with copious amounts of local wine or beer, and have a grand old time.

What's Different About a European Restaurant?

European restaurants differ from American restaurants in several ways:

➤ The interior design is not a good indication of food quality. Some of the very best restaurants can look much the worse for wear.

➤ Many have an unavoidable cover charge of $1 to $3 per person; you pay it simply for the privilege of sitting down to a basket of bread.

➤ Water does not come to your table automatically. When you order water, you get to choose between fizzy or non-fizzy bottled mineral water. (You can also order water from the tap, but the bottled stuff tastes better.)

➤ Europeans hardly ever use ice in their drinks, nor do they butter their bread (it tastes good enough on its own).

➤ Service is much more professional, but still very friendly. Waiters don't rush up to introduce themselves by first name and then interrupt every time your mouth is full; rather they appear when you need them and are very helpful.

➤ Portions are often smaller, but it's because you're expected to order more courses.

➤ In many countries, every dish ordered is served on a separate plate, so don't expect a little pile of vegetables to come automatically next to your steak.

➤ The salad comes at the end of the meal, before dessert (which makes a lot more sense, digestively).

➤ The tip (call it the "service") is often *included in the bill,* so always ask. If it's already included and the service was good, leave a bit more on the table anyway. If service isn't included, leave 10 to 15% of the bill.

Know Your Food Lingo

Here's a handy glossary of some food-related terms you may come across in Europe. The country with which each term is associated appears in parentheses at the end of each listing.

biergarten: An outdoor picnic area (though some are indoors) where you bring the food, and the establishment provides the beer. Some simple sandwiches, pretzels, and other noshes are sold as well (Germany).

bistro: A small, intimate, informal, usually moderately priced restaurant (France).

brasserie: A large, bustling, metropolitan restaurant that serves several daily specials along with an extensive selection of wines and beer (France).

heuriger: A rustic Austrian tavern where the specialty drink is wine (Austria).

kaffeehaus: A coffee house and social gathering place, almost identical to the traditional cafe (Austria).

konditorei: A pastry shop. Most such shops have expanded their menus and now often double as cafes (Austria, Germany).

mezédes: Small appetizers, dips in particular, served in Greek tavernas before dinner; similar to Spain's tapas (Greece).

osteria: See *trattoria* (Italy).

pane e coperto: In Italian restaurants, the unavoidable "bread and cover" charge of about 1,500L to 10,000L (90¢ to $6) added on to your bill (Italy).

prix fixe menu: A fixed-price meal of several courses (usually appetizer, entree, and dessert, plus wine and/or coffee) offered from a restaurant's menu; almost always an outstanding dining value (France).

pub grub: Simple food served in a pub for lunch or dinner; cheese sandwiches and steak-and-kidney pie are common examples (England, Scotland, Ireland).

tapas/tapeo: Savory appetizers served on small plates that are meant to tide one over until the late dinner hour; a *tapeo* is a walk that takes you from bar to bar, sampling tapas as you go (Spain).

tasca: A bar that serves tapas (Spain).

taverna: A homestyle bar/restaurant where both *mezédes* and larger, hearty meals are served (Greece).

tavola calda: A very informal (and sometimes self-serve) eatery where you usually choose from a pre-prepared selection of dishes. Good for a quick, light meal; also called a *rosticceria* (Italy).

trattoria: A traditional, family-run establishment that serves fresh pasta and other home-cooked food; similar to an *osteria* (Italy).

The Search for the Perfect Restaurant

Below are some helpful tips as you go about the business of choosing your daily eats:

➤ **Look for places that are crowded.** This is the simplest but most important rule. If people are staying away, there's a reason.

➤ **Look in your guidebooks.** Travel writers go to great trouble and indigestion to sample a wide range of local restaurants in search of the best and most interesting places (I should know). Read the restaurant reviews carefully and try a few that sound right up your gastronomic alley, but don't feel that you have to go to them. Poke around to find your own undiscovered gem of a bistro.

➤ **Get advice from your friends.** I've eaten some of my best meals on the advice of fellow travelers who've already scoped out a city. Word of mouth is a great way to find memorable meals.

➤ **Ask locals.** Taxi drivers, the person from whom you buy postcards, and anybody with whom you strike up an acquaintance are all good people to ask for advice on where to eat, but hotel concierges are not. Many often strike quid pro quo agreements with a nearby joint—it may indeed be a good restaurant, but there's no guarantee.

➤ **Look for places full of locals, not visitors.** If a trattoria seems to be entirely tourist-ridden, don't even bother. If the locals steer clear, there's usually a good reason. For years, a man has been standing across the street from the entrance to the Vatican Museums in Rome, waving a menu to attract tourists to his restaurant. The restaurant is usually crowded, but I've never seen an Italian in there—one look at the slop they're serving tells me why.

Tourist Traps

As I warn in the "scams" section of chapter 11, you have to be on your toes against **shady practices in restaurants.** Most places are honest, but all it takes is one rotten waiter. Scrutinize the bill carefully. Make sure the waiter didn't charge you for items you didn't order. Check that you're not being double-charged on the service. After you pay, make sure you're not short-changed.

➤ **Be wary of restaurants in popular sightseeing areas.** There may be perfectly fine restaurants and even great little bistros right near a major sight. But the parts of town most frequented by visitors also inevitably draw the largest proportion of low-quality joints—those that pander to out-of-towners by serving bland, uninventive versions of the local cuisine (like that place I mentioned across from the Vatican).

➤ **Case several places before choosing.** Look inside to gauge the clientele and read the menus posted outside to compare prices and offerings.

➤ **Look for the menus without English.** The sign "We Speak English" should read "We fleece tourists." Good restaurants don't have to play on visitors' fears of the language to drum up business. This is far from a hard and fast rule, but often the place with an untranslated menu will be better (or at least more authentic) than a place with each dish translated. Although those menu translations may be helpful (and can save you from having to furtively consult your phrase book), they are not necessary. In most European restaurants these days, at least one person speaks a smidgen of English. If not, in a pinch you can set aside pride and decorum and make do with barnyard noises. Point to a dish, raise your eyebrows, and cluck like a chicken. The waiter will usually catch on and say something like, "No, No. Baa-aa-aa-aa." Now at least you know that one's lamb.

➤ **Find the place with no sign, no menu.** Tiny, hole-in-the-wall restaurants with no menu at all or one on a chalkboard will often treat you to the greatest and most authentic food you'll ever find. It'll just be you, eight tables, mamma in the kitchen, a passel of neighborhood regulars watching the soccer match on television, wine from the family estate, and heaping portions of hearty, home-cooked, utterly incredible local food.

Decoding the Menu

Many guidebooks translate a limited list of local dishes and food names. Berlitz phrase guides have more and the pocket-sized Marling Menu-Masters (Altarinda Books) are particularly good resources for both ingredients and dish names. Alternately, you can take your English-Eurolingo dictionary and look up individual words on the menu. Again, most waiters speak enough English to at least tell you what plant or animal stars in a dish.

Have fun, sample the local chow, and be adventurous. Don't go through Europe leaving a trail of chicken cutlets in your wake. Ask what the specialty of the house is. Try the tripe or the squid. Let the waiter suggest his favorite dish—or trust him to put together the whole meal for you. The house wine is usually perfectly fine, if not excellent (plus, you can order quarter- and half-carafes rather than a full bottle), or let the waiter help pick out a wine to go with your meal. Go with the flow: In Bavaria, have beer and sausages; in Italy, wine and pasta. Be nosy, ask lots of questions. Look around the room and politely point and ask what other people are eating if it looks good.

For culinary variety, ask if there's a sampler plate of first courses. If you're friendly and show great interest in the food, waiters (and especially owners) love to show off their kitchen's talents to visitors. The more outgoing and curious you are, the better chance they'll bring out unexpected tidbits for you to try, invite you into the kitchen or down into the moldy ancient wine cellar, or join you at the table for an after-dinner drink on the house.

Dollars & Sense

Some people will tell you that a **fixed-price menu** is more expensive with more options than a stripped-down **tourist menu.** Whatever the restaurant calls them, meals at a set price are always cheaper (up to 30%) than ordering the same dishes à la carte. The tradeoff? Your options are more limited than if you ordered from the main menu. Shop around. Is your only choice four different pasta shapes in tomato sauce, or are there more inventive dishes available? Is beer or wine included, and how much—a glass or a half-liter? Is dessert or coffee included? *Prix-fisse, menu turistico, prezzo fisso, Gedeck*—it may not be the best meal you could have at that restaurant, but it's certainly the best budget option.

Picnicking & Street Food

A bottle of Chianti or Merlot, a crusty baguette, perhaps some fresh fruit, local cheeses and salamis, yogurt, and a pastry to top it all off makes a fabulous meal. Far from being a budget fall-back, picnicking in Europe can be as much fun and unforgettable as a meal in the finest Parisian restaurant. What with all the restaurants I eat in just to do my job, one of my most memorable European meals ever remains a late-night picnic in a hotel room in Italy.

European produce is usually always of high quality. Visit a few small **neighborhood grocery stores** or an **open-air market** and point to anything that looks like a local specialty; 100 grams is usually the perfect amount or one person. (Often if you just say "picnic," the workers will give you the appropriate portions.) You'll usually find **supermarkets** in the basements of large department stores. Stop at a half-dozen little neighborhood shops, and $6 to $10 per person later, you'll have a feast fit for a king.

Dollars & Sense

Try not to fall back on American fast-food chains if you're in a hungry pinch. The local specialties that make up the "fast food" of each European destination are almost invariably better—and much cheaper—than le Big Mac.

If you still crave a cooked meal, but don't want to pay for a full restaurant spread, each country has its own downscale version of snacking on delicacies or dining on prepared foods for not much more than the cost of the ingredients. In Britain and Ireland, the local pub will have stomach-filling grub and pints of ale to wash it down with. In Spain, head to tapas bars for appetizer portions with wine; in Italy, go to a tavola calda for steaming plates of spicy penne and herbed potato wedges. In France, you can get quiche to go at a *pâtisserie* (pastry shop) or *boulangerie* (bread bakery). In Vienna, try a *konditorei* for sandwiches and a slab of pastry or cake. The **"Quick Bites"** box at the end of each destination chapter's dining section will fill you in on the specifics, as well as offer a few suggestions for meals on the run.

Sightseeing Strategies

You've read the lists of top and lesser-known sights in chapter 1 and skimmed the destination chapters for more. You've got your trip all planned out and are getting a pretty good idea of what you want to see in Europe. But knowing where to go and knowing how to tackle the rigors of sightseeing are two different things entirely. This chapter will give you all the details you need to draw up fun, exciting, and doable daily itineraries and get the most out of your sightseeing, from walking tours to museums. I'll conclude with a few photography tips to help you capture those travel memories and experiences in shots the neighbors will *want* to come over and see.

Dealing with the Daily Tourist Grind

If you expect to see the best of Paris in just a few days, you'd better have a good game plan or the Eiffel Tower is going to slip through the cracks in your schedule, and you'll leave town without the joy of climbing the world's most famous TV antenna. Before you plan your daily agenda, you need to be aware of the quirks of European hours and days of operation.

Making the Most of Mondays & Mornings

Monday is the day that over half the museums in Europe are closed (although Paris prefers Tuesday). Also expect meager happenings on **Sunday,** the traditional day of rest for many businesses, including sights—although many sights may be open Sunday morning.

How do you deal with Sundays and Mondays? First, make sure the Monday rule applies to the cities and towns you want to visit by checking your guidebook for open hours and closed days. Next, when drawing up your trip itinerary, never plan to spend a Monday (or other closed day) in a small town. More importantly, be sure Monday is not one of your only two days in a city filled with museums. Plan to do about half as much on Sundays as you would on a weekday. Most importantly, find the sights in town that *are* open on Mondays or on Sunday afternoons and save them for those times when everything else will be closed.

After you've planned out how to deal with the Sunday and Monday situation, remember that the first rule of getting the most out of your daily sightseeing is to **get up early.** Be at the most popular sights when the doors open, and you'll beat the lines. I'm far from a morning person, but I routinely get up at 6:30am when traveling. Besides, especially in summer and in southern Europe, the sun can be broiling by midday, and you'll want to retreat to lunch and perhaps a nap to recharge your touring batteries.

Ahhhhhh, the Midday Siesta

You know how most people naturally get sleepy in the middle of the afternoon? Well, Mediterranean countries have always kept attuned to the biorhythms that American culture tries to ignore, and they've found a way to work around the body's internal clock. It's called the *siesta* (*riposo* in Italy).

Italy, Spain, Portugal, and Greece traditionally observe an early afternoon shutdown that begins at noon to 1:30pm and runs until 2:30 to 4pm. Museums, most churches, shops, businesses—just about everything except restaurants—lower the shutters and lock the doors so that proprietors can either go home (or head to a local trattoria) for a long lunch and perhaps a snooze during the day's hottest hours.

At first this break can be very annoying, especially if you're on a tight sightseeing schedule, but after a while you get used to it. Learn to take the siesta and revel in it. If your time is short, make sure you know which sights (often churches) will be open during siesta and save them to visit at that time. Sadly, the United States's economic influence is slowly forcing the rest of the world to live and work according to our hectic, stressful, non-stop schedule. Increasingly, businesses in larger cities are staying open through the middle of the day, and people are taking smaller, quicker lunches and bigger dinners (which any nutritionist will tell you is a trend in the wrong direction). It's good news for shoppers, but bad for the general quality of life.

Drawing Up a Daily Itinerary

You've been so careful planning every other aspect of your trip; don't leave the sightseeing to chance. I've seen too many people arrive at the doors of the museum or church that was to be the highlight of their trip only to find that it's closed today. And they're leaving tomorrow. You needn't micromanage your entire vacation, but it doesn't hurt to do a little advance planning to make sure you see what's important to you. After being shut out of my share of sights by not reading the fine print ahead of time, I've come up with a fail-safe method for creating daily agendas. I happily ignore my schedules as often as I follow them, but at least the process of drawing them up alerts me to the odd hours of special sights.

The following steps may seem like a chore, but they take less than 30 minutes on the train on your way into town (or in your hotel room on the night before you arrive). Some people prefer to go with the flow and see stuff as they come across it, and that's perfectly fine. But if missing the Pantheon will ruin your trip, this bit of advance paperwork can be a godsend.

Time-Savers

Although this section deals mainly with sights, don't forget to look for, and mark, any restaurant or activity that you want to be sure you hit. Virtually all restaurants close at least one day of the week; if you're in town for two days, make sure you're not going to miss that great-sounding trattoria. Other "extras" to check the hours on include day trips as well as cultural events (for example, does the opera perform every night? When are the soccer matches?).

1. Write all the sights you want to see down the left side of a piece of paper. Next to each, write the open hours, and then make a third column showing the day(s) each is closed. Underline any opening or closing hour that's exceptional (say, if something closes at 6pm instead of the town's usual 4 or 5pm; underline the "6pm" part). For outstanding exceptions (wow, it closes at 7:30pm), double-underline. Do the same for any unusual closed day. Mark places that stay open through siesta. If any sight has particularly restricted hours or days, put a box around it.

2. Below the list of sights, make a list of day trips and other activities you want to fit in (leather shopping in Florence, a tour of the sewers in Paris, a pub crawl in London).

3. Take a second piece of paper and make blank daily schedules for each day you'll be in town. Put in headings for Morning (leave five to six lines), Lunch (one line), Afternoon (five to six lines), Dinner (a line), and Evening (two to three lines).

4. Use the hours-at-a-glance sheet you made in step 1 to fill in your daily itinerary chart smartly. Stick the earliest-opening sights first thing in the morning, the late-closing ones at the end of the day, and open-nonstop sights into the siesta hours just after lunch (in Mediterranean Europe).

5. Fill in the later morning and earlier afternoon with the sights that keep more standard hours. Every attraction listed in this book tells you how long you can expect to spend there. Write on the schedule a time to arrive at each sight and when you need to leave in order to get to the next one. Schedule things that aren't as important to you in between things that are. That way, if you find yourself running short on time, you can cut sights out and still not miss the best stuff. Do this with a map in front of you, and budget time to get between sights. Don't pack the schedule too tightly, and don't forget to write in things like "*gelato* (ice cream) break."

6. Stuff the itinerary in your pocket when you go out for the day. Cross things off as you see them, and if you misjudged time and miss something, circle it so you can rearrange your afternoon or next day's schedule to fit it in. *Bonus:* These itineraries always help me later in writing my journal.

Nine Tricks to Enjoying Museums

Europe is just chock full of history and art. It has enjoyed quite the prodigious output over the past millennium, and by the time your vacation's over, you'll feel like you must have seen it all. Take these few hints in your back pocket to help get the most out of these grand halls o' great art without getting brain overload.

1. **Visit twice.** Some museums are just too big to attempt in a day. If you have the time and inclination, spread the visit over several days. Prime candidates for this strategy are the Prado, Louvre, British Museum, Vatican, National Gallery (London), and Uffizi.

2. **Split up.** Nothing is as subjective as taste in art, and there's no reason you and your companions need to stick together in museums. If you part ways at the front door and set a time to meet, you can each go through at your own pace and look at whatever darn well pleases you. This strategy also gives you some time apart (even the closest of friends and family get on one another's nerves after a while).

3. **Take the audio tour.** The later 1990s have brought a wonderful revolution to museum visits. Almost gone are the ancient, stilted cassette audio guides that march every visitor in lock step from one masterpiece to the next. Nowadays, most audio "tours" are digital, often little wands that you hold like an elongated cellular phone. The works on display have numbers next to them, which you just punch into the wand's keypad and it starts spewing out facts and background galore on the work, artist, era, and so on. When you tire of it, just hit stop and wander to the next painting. You go through at your own pace and hear only about what intrigues you.

4. **Take a guided tour.** You can learn a lot more than you would on your own if you're led through the collections by a certified expert, who will explain the significance and background of the most important works and answer all of your questions.

5. **Know your background.** Art is much more interesting and engaging when you have some idea what you're looking at. Just a little brushing up on European artists and movements, whether you just skim your guidebook for it or take a course in art history before you embark on the trip, will enrich any museum-going experience.

6. **Draw cartoon balloons.** Not on the paintings themselves—the guards might get miffed! I mean, put dialogue into the mouths of the figures on the canvas. Most of us get a little punchy after too many hours spent soberly contemplating creative genius. Feel free to make up stories to go with the scenes. Look for humorous details the artist painted in—any large canvas of a courtly scene or a banquet will feature things like a dog and monkey eyeing each other warily under the table, or two servants getting frisky with each other in the background.

7. **Know when the museum closes.** Museums empty out in the later hours, especially the biggies that routinely stay open until 7 or 8pm. If you plan to close the joint and are a fan of museum books and postcards, however, always check when the gift shop shuts its doors. Gift shops often close 30 minutes before the museum itself closes.

8. **Concentrate on the masterpieces.** You have to pace yourself, or even a moderate-sized museum will overwhelm you. Do not feel obligated to look at it all. On a first visit, or if you have limited time, just concentrate your energies on select paintings. Skip whole wings if you don't feel like going through. Many museums include on their floor plans a list of the masterpieces.

9. **Look at what you like.** In the end, art is supposed to be enjoyable, not a chore. There's something liberating about going through a museum and just *looking* at the paintings, pausing at the ones that you find most visually intriguing and studying them, and moving on without ever even glancing at the little placard that tells the artist, title, and background info.

Let an Expert Be Your Guide

Even solo travelers can get a lot of mileage out of sightseeing guides. Bus tours of the city, escorted day trips, walking tours around town, guided tours through museums or cathedrals—these are all what I call microtours (as opposed to the macrotours of fully escorted bus trips). Your guidebook and the tourist office can fill you in on the microtours available in each city.

Local guides who concentrate only on one city or sight are usually experts, not tour bus escorts who've merely memorized a canned spiel for each sight. By combining do-it-yourself planning and travel with microtours, you can get the best of both worlds. The best microtours are packed with more information (history, background, anecdotes, details, and explanations) than any guidebook has room to print.

➤ **The city bus tour.** This is great for city orientation and crossing the major architectural sights off your list. Almost every city has these city-run or private tours, which may last from 45 minutes to a full day, but usually average 60 to 90 minutes. There are three main flavors: the roundabout bus that trundles you past everything in one big loop; the hop-on, hop-off bus that makes a long circuit of the major city sights (you jump off whenever you feel like visiting a museum or whatever, then board a later bus when it swings by); and the mini guided tour, where everyone gets off the bus at certain stops and you're lead by a guide quickly through churches, museums, and other sights (these tend to last at least half a day). Most buses have either a live guide or a recorded spiel available in a dozen languages.

➤ **Guided specialty walking tours.** There's no better way to bring a city's culture and history to life than through a guide's anecdotes, character sketches, jokes, and tons of background details. It might be an Irish music pub crawl in Dublin, London's

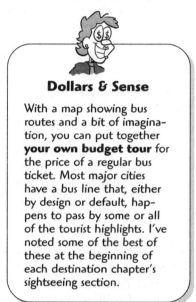

Dollars & Sense

With a map showing bus routes and a bit of imagination, you can put together **your own budget tour** for the price of a regular bus ticket. Most major cities have a bus line that, either by design or default, happens to pass by some or all of the tourist highlights. I've noted some of the best of these at the beginning of each destination chapter's sightseeing section.

Extra! Extra!

On walking tours, be a head-of-the-class nerd and **stick next to the guide.** Walking from stop to stop on the tour, you'll be able to chat on your own with her and ask questions, and you'll also get to hear her answers and explanations to everyone else's questions.

Shakespearean sights, the Rome of the Caesars, the hidden gardens of Paris, or Gaudi's buildings in Barcelona. For some walks, you must reserve in advance; for most, you just show up at a specified place and time and pay the guide a nominal fee ($4 to $7).

➤ **Guided tours of museums or cathedrals.** Whether led by learned volunteers, hired guides, a dusty professor, or a rotund old monk, a 30- to 120-minute tour of an individual sight can do the same thing for a cathedral or art gallery that walking tours do for a city. Guides can spin stories and give insightful commentaries on the meanings of every tiny detail of a sight or painting, conjuring up the past and enriching the experience of your visit tenfold.

➤ **Escorted daytrips.** If you don't want to hassle with figuring out the logistics of how to get out of the city and see some nearby sights and small towns, or you have limited time in which to do it, a local escorted bus tour can be just the ticket. It whizzes you out to the sights with a live guide who'll walk you through everything and returns you to town in time for lunch or dinner (most are either half- or full-day excursions). Using public transportation, for example, it's pretty much impossible to see both Siena and San Gimignano in a single day trip from Florence, but an escorted bus trip can do it no problem.

The Stendhal Syndrome: How to Deal with Cultural Overload

Stendhal, the French writer, collapsed one day while visiting Florence, overwhelmed by the aesthetic beauty of the Renaissance and exhausted by trying to see absolutely everything. Stendhal is an extreme case, perhaps, but he's not the last one to break down from too much Europe. You may not faint in the piazza, but you might catch a cold, become irritable and tired, or simply cease to care whether there's another Giotto fresco in that church. After a few days or weeks of full-steam-ahead sightseeing, believe me, you'll start wearing down. When the prospect of seeing the Louvre for the first time elicits from you merely a groan and a desire to take a nap, it's time to recharge your mental batteries. Here are some hints for working through the inevitable burnout:

➤ **Don't feel obligated to do or see anything just because it's famous.** Go see what interests you, and feel free to skip what doesn't float your boat. If you're going to wear yourself out, do so on the good stuff.

➤ **Pace yourself.** Soak up the kaleidoscope of Europe's cultural pleasures a little bit at a time. Schedule in rest periods. I've said this before, but it bears repeating: Don't pack too much into either your trip itinerary or your daily sightseeing agenda. Leave room to breathe, to picnic, to stop and smell the cappuccino.

➤ **Vary your sightseeing.** Try not to hit one big museum after another; visit a park, ruin, church, or chill out in a cafe in between. Give other areas of your brain a workout for a while. This way the whole trip doesn't blur into one large, colorful blob of old masters and Gothic cathedrals from which your memory can't distinguish where Paris left off and Prague began.

➤ **Take a siesta.** A nap in the middle of the day can do you a world of good, both mentally and physically. In Mediterranean countries, most everything is closed in the early afternoon anyway. Learn to take a *riposo* along with the Italians, and you'll not only appreciate their country more, but also get up the energy to finish the Florence sightseeing that did in good old Stendhal.

➤ **When it does start getting to you, take a break.** Go see a soccer match. Go shopping. Whatever it takes to bring your cultural appreciation back from the brink. If you sit down and write all those postcards you promised to send, chances are the act of describing to your friends back home the wonders you've seen and once-in-a-lifetime experiences you've had will make you psyched to get more of Europe under your belt. Next thing you know, you'll bop out of the post office raring to get back in the saddle and get on with the sights.

➤ **On occasion, take a vacation from your trip.** Stop racking up sightseeing points. Take a day to get off the beaten path.

Getting Off the Beaten Path

Spending time away from the big must-see attractions, going local at a corner bar, hitting the smaller towns, lazing on the beach, searching out minor, less traditional sights—all of this helps personalize your trip and make the whole experience more fulfilling. Everyone sees the Eiffel Tower, the Arc de Triomphe, the Louvre. Fall off the touristic bandwagon occasionally and forge a new, personal route through the wonders of Europe.

There are two lists in chapter 1: one of overlooked gems and the other of ways to break out of the tourist mold. Try some tactics from both of those or make up your own fun and find your own undiscovered places. Liberate yourself from your guidebook—yes! I really said it! Stow this and your other guides away once in a while and check out sights and restaurants without our advice. Wander into a church

Extra! Extra!

While reading this book, and certainly when visiting the sights themselves, you'll find a number of art and architecture terms thrown at you, like Byzantine, pediment, or Victorian. For those not fresh from an art history course—or if you just want to brush up—appendix C at the back of this book explains the most common terms, eras, schools, and styles in European art and architecture.

without even checking to see if it's listed in the book. Try a dish your menu translator doesn't cover. Enjoy the thrill of discovery.

Slide Shows Don't Have to Be Boring

Someone with a more sophisticated camera and lens than yours, who waited 365 days for the best light, and had a tripod and 36 exposures to get it right has taken a much better full-frame picture of that monument, church, or painting than you could ever hope to get. It's called a postcard. Accept this and buy a shot of Notre Dame or the *Mona Lisa* that was made by a professional. Of course you'll take a picture of it anyway, but don't waste more than one shot on an overall view. Instead, make your photos interesting, make them unique, and take home a lead-lined bag full of memories and great pictures, not just snapshots.

Before You Leave Home: Know Thy Camera

Unless you're a professional or a real heavy-duty amateur, the fanciest **camera-lens combo** you need is a basic 35mm Single Lens Reflex (SLR) with a 28 to 70mm lens. Get a lens cap with a little string to dangle it from the lens so you don't lose it. Of course, you can also get by perfectly well with a pocket **point-and-shoot** camera. They're getting more advanced every day, and some of the new Advanced Photo System (APS) cameras have a feature that allows you to switch film halfway through rolls (great for moving from outdoor shots that call for 100 ASA to dark cathedral interiors that want at least 400 ASA). Invest in at least a low-end pocket camera; don't bother with the disposable kind, which only take passable pictures under full, bright sunlight. The only useful disposable cameras are the panoramic, or, if you think you'll need one, the ones that work underwater.

Practice with your camera before you leave the States, especially if it's a new one and you're not sure how it behaves. Visit the sights of your home city, pretend you're in Europe, and snap away. Get to know the camera. Bracket your shots by shooting the same thing several times using different settings, with and without flash, and so on. Write down carefully exactly what you did or varied in each shot. Sure, you'll drop $20 to $40 to buy and develop several rolls of film, but it's better to know how the camera handles with different films and in different situations before you go off and shoot 20 rolls on vacation.

Don't Leave Home Without It: Buying Film

Buy all your **film** in the United States. It's cheaper, and you can be sure it hasn't been sitting on the shelf since 1982. Buy enough film to shoot at least one roll a day, more if you know you're the shutter-happy type. Bring more than you think you'll need. You can always use the extras after you get home, and it might save the day if you run into a festival and find yourself going through a roll an hour. Hold on to the plastic film canisters and store them in big, see-through plastic baggies so security people at the airport will pass it around the potentially harmful X rays (the higher the film speed, the more likely multiple exposures to X rays will fog the film). Bring several spare **batteries.** Use a **UV filter** on the lens to protect it from scratches (*not* a polarizing filter, which messes up more shots than it helps if you don't use it correctly).

Don't Be a Flasher

I have a good rule for the flash attachment: Don't use it. Flashes are the most overrated and least understood of camera features. If you don't know what you're doing, the flash effects cheapen most shots, so either read up on flash techniques in a photo book or consider using it rarely, if at all. Here are a few general guidelines:

Dollars & Sense

If you do have to buy photo supplies or film abroad, go to a camera shop or department store. Never buy film from a souvenir stand near a tourist sight; the markup is almost criminal.

1. If you take a flash photo of anything behind glass, you'll end up with a fuzzy image of the subject further obscured by a bright, white star-like image that covers a quarter of the picture. That's the flash reflecting off the glass; the camera usually auto-focuses on the glass, *not* the subject you're trying to capture.

2. Flashes always flatten a picture out, which 99% of the time is an effect you do not want.

3. *Do not take flash photos of artwork.* Flashes destroy paintings and frescoes, doing more damage than leaving a painting out under the sun for many days. Flash photos would make the *Mona Lisa* your grandchildren see a pale, faded image of itself.

Just about the only time I ever use a flash is if I'm trying to take a night shot, in which case I use the option most pocket cameras now have of a "night flash." This option basically exposes first the low light of the background by leaving the camera shutter open for a few seconds (you have to be very still), and then flashes so that the people or object in the foreground pops out of the image in a bright pool of light.

Say *Fromage*: Tips for Capturing Great Shots

The following are some guidelines for getting the pictures you want:

➤ **Shoot the details.** Any postcard stand can provide you with facade pictures, panoramas, and aerial shots. You're the only one who can concentrate on the minute details that enthrall you. Focus on the hideous devil in a *Last Judgment* mosaic, a rivet in the Eiffel Tower, laundry hanging from the Gothic windows of a Venetian palace, a single bunch of grapes on the vine in Provence, the intricate marble pattern of a Romanesque building, or a cat sleeping atop a broken ancient column.

137

Extra! Extra!

If you decide to bring a **camcorder,** make sure you can recharge the batteries on European current (see the section in chapter 6 on electricity). Make shots interesting, say starting with a minute detail and then pulling back or panning to show the entire structure. Just don't become a slave to the video camera, and try not to see all of Europe just through the viewfinder. I know you want to record and save your memories, but travel is much more fulfilling, intense, and rewarding when you live it instead of document it.

➤ **Frame the shot.** Make it interesting: Take the picture through an open window or archway or flanked by a pair of ancient columns on a Greek temple. Get an Alp reflected in a lake or a town hall reflected in a puddle. Snap a pub with racks of bicycles on either side. If you can't quite get the whole thing in a shot, give it up and zoom in for a detail instead.

➤ **Check your backgrounds.** Nothing spoils a medieval or bucolic scene like a TV antenna, telephone poles, or tourists milling in the background.

➤ **Grab the best light.** The light of early morning and late afternoon works magic on any scene, bringing out depth, deepening shadows, and warming up colors. The harsh noonday sun makes notoriously boring pictures.

➤ **Get the sun behind you.** Try to get any light source at your back or glancing in from the side if you're going for special shadow and light effects. The only time to let the light come right at you is to shoot a sun setting or rising directly behind a column on an ancient temple—a marvelous effect.

➤ **You know what the family looks like.** Explorers used to plant their county's flag to claim a new territory. These days we conquer by Kodak and plant the waving family. It's nice to take a picture of your husband in front of Big Ben—and something in the water makes it impossible to resist the urge to pose like you're holding up the Leaning Tower of Pisa—but you don't need to prove you were there at every single stop. Plus, it's more fun to get action shots of the family riding the train, going on a picnic, contemplating Rodin's *Thinker,* whatever. Show that you traveled in and interacted with Europe, not just that you knew how to smile and wave.

➤ **Look for the typical.** What sums up a country or culture? Half the things you'll remember most about any trip won't be the attractions but rather the sights and oddities of daily life over there. Go ahead, take pictures of old men playing cards, tiny Fiat cars, vegetable markets, double-decker buses, nuns on a scooter, or a sheep jam on a country road. Candid shots of people can be great, but may get some people mad. Be discreet and diplomatic.

➤ **Wait.** The perfect shot might not come out until the sun moves from behind that cloud or an unphotogenic tour bus pulls away. On the other hand, don't let a good opportunity slip away. If a shot is good but you think you should wait, take one picture immediately, and then stick around to see if it gets better.

➤ **Get close.** Unless you're shooting an Alp, try to get within 10 feet of most subjects. Fill up the frame. Keep shots dynamic.

➤ **Find a new angle.** Choose any angle that will get you a picture different from everybody's else's. You can turn that camera on its end; take some shots vertical, others horizontal. Eye-level is boring. Climb a tree, squat down, stand on a bench, hold the camera high above your head and point it in the general direction, or lie flat out on the ground. I do it all the time, and it makes for some great shots.

➤ **Keep track of your pictures.** You won't know which temple, church, or interior that was two months later at home. Writing down every frame is a bit excessive, but at least number each roll of film (use a Sharpie pen on the casing of the roll itself) and note in your journal when you change rolls. Then you should be able to reconstruct the photo album later.

Mastering Communication

How will you stay in touch with your loved ones, friends, and workplace while you're on the road? It depends on your preference and funds. Calling cards make phoning the States easy, but they're not cheap. The Internet explosion means home is just a mouse click away in a cybercafe. Some people prefer dashing off the old "Wish you were here!" postcard, and others practice the dying art of letter writing. This chapter will take you through the basics of them all. Then I'll tackle that myth known as the "language barrier" and give you a few simple keys to unlocking any foreign language and getting your message across no matter what the circumstance or local dialect.

Mamma Bell: Using Calling Cards

Calling overseas is expensive no matter how you do it, but there are different levels of expense. For instance, *never* make a transatlantic call from your hotel room, unless you're the kind of person who lights cigars with $100 bills. As I've pointed out elsewhere, phone charges are one of hotels' greatest legal scams. Surcharges tacked on to your hotel bill can be as high as a whopping 400% over what you'd pay were you to make the call from a public pay phone. They'll even overcharge for local calls. Just ignore your hotel room phone; look for one in a nearby bar or cafe instead.

The easiest and cheapest way to call home from abroad is with a **calling card.** It's like having a credit card strictly for phone calls. (Although now, some credit cards double as calling cards.) Before leaving home, set up a card account with MCI, AT&T, or Sprint. On the road, you just dial a local number—almost always free—and then punch in the number you're calling plus the calling-card number (usually your home phone number plus a four-digit PIN). If you're in a non touch-tone country like Italy, just wait for an American operator, who will put your call through. The card should come with a wallet-sized list of local access numbers in each country; if it doesn't, check the omnipresent ads in the *International Herald Tribune*. Incidentally, you can call any one of those companies' numbers to make a **collect call** as well; just dial it and wait for the operator.

Dollars & Sense

When you set up a calling card, say what you want it for, because each company offers a variety of cards and competitive programs tailored to all possible uses. Tell them you want the program and card best suited to making multiple calls from Europe to the United States.

When it comes to dialing direct, calling from the United States to Europe is much cheaper than the other way around, so whenever possible, have friends and family call you at your hotel rather than you calling them. When **calling Europe from the United States,** you have to dial the international access code (011), and then dial the country code (a number of one to three digits; each destination chapter in this book lists the country code under "Fast Facts"). Before the number itself, you have to dial a city code, which is like an area code in North America. Most of these codes begin with a zero (in Spain, with a 9), which you dial only if you're calling that city from another area within that country. To call that city from outside the country's borders, you drop the zero.

Each destination chapter also explains how to dial direct back **to the United States from Europe.** It works along similar lines: the international access code is often, but not always, 00; the country code of the United States is 1. After entering all those numbers, you punch in the area code and number.

Hey Mr. Telephone Man, How Does That Pay Phone Work?

European **pay phones** work basically like American ones, but with one major difference: phone cards. There are three types of phones in Europe, coin-operated, phone card-only, and the kind that takes both. Coin-operated phones are rapidly being supplanted by phone card units all over the continent (some of you may remember the old phone tokens of some countries, but those are a relic of the past).

Phone cards are pre-paid debit cards that you stick into the phone as if it were an ATM (in the United States, such pre-paid cards are often scams, but in Europe they're perfectly legal and respectable). Buy a phone card only if you're going to be in town for a while or if you plan to use it to make direct long-distance calls. If you're in town for only a few days and expect to make mainly local calls, just use pocket change. Often, a digital screen on the phone keeps track of how much money is left on your phone card. In most countries, you can feed cards to a phone one after the other as each gets used up, making phone cards and pay phones the cheapest combo for dialing direct to the States (although a good calling-card plan is always cheaper).

Dollars & Sense

Phone cards usually come in increments, say equivalent to $5, $8, $12, or $17. If you're buying them to make mainly local calls, get the least expensive kind possible (just in case you don't use it up; you can always buy more). For phoning home or making long-distance calls directly, the larger denominations are more useful.

Calling cards have made phoning the United States from Europe cheap and a snap from any pay phone, but some traditionalists still prefer heading to the **post office or international phone office** where you make your call on a phone with a meter and then pay when you're done. This method is no cheaper than direct dialing from a pay phone, but at least you don't need a bag full of change to do it (once phone cards caught on at public pay phones, these phone offices lost a lot of business).

Sending Mail: You'll Make It Home Before Your Postcards Do

Post offices work pretty much the same the world over. When you write the address, end it with a big *USA* under the city/state/zip code line so it will get routed correctly. Write *Par Avion* on any letter or postcard to ensure it goes air mail (that French term is used internationally). For writing letters, you can buy tissue paper-like stationery to cut down on weight (and hence cost) or get the nifty blue air-mail letter/envelopes, which you write on, fold up, lick, and seal—the letter itself becomes the envelope (these are widely available at stationery stores in the United States and abroad). Mail can take anywhere from a few days to a few months (the latter not uncommon for mail from Italy), but it usually finds its way across the ocean in two to six weeks.

Only mail larger packages to the States when absolutely necessary, because it's rather expensive. Only do so to make room in your pack or to send gifts home to get around the customs limits (see chapter 12). You can buy boxes at any post office, although you may have to shop elsewhere for the tape to seal them.

Time-Savers

Use a computer to pre-print **address labels.** This will not only save time and help you avoid carrying, and possibly losing, your address book, but it will also ensure you don't forget anyone.

Dollars & Sense

Save letters to mail from countries with low **postage rates.** Germany charges $2.15 for letters to the United States, but England charges only 67¢. Other expensive lands are the Netherlands and Austria. Cheapies include Greece, Ireland, and Spain. Italy's postal system is notoriously slow, but the Vatican's isn't, so when in Rome, mail everything from St. Peter's.

To **receive mail in Europe,** you have two options. The best is open only to American Express cardholders. Just have your mail addressed to: Your Name/Client Mail/Full Postal Address of the AmEx office in whatever city you'll be staying. The local AmEx office will hold it for 30 days after they receive it, and the service is free (again, it may take five days or six weeks for the letter to cross the ocean). Post offices offer the same service; just address the letter to: Your Name/Poste Restante/Address of the Post Office. Bring identification to the post office to claim your mail. The charge for picking up such held mail ranges from a few dimes to a few bucks. My advice is not to try to receive mail on the road unless absolutely necessary. With the unpredictable postal systems, you'll miss more letters than you receive. With cybercafes (see "Bet You Didn't Know"), you can communicate much more easily and quickly with the folks back home.

Breaking the So-Called Language Barrier

There is no language barrier; there's just a bit of a linguistic speed bump on the travelin' highway. Knowing a handful of key words and phrases, learning to count to two, and being able to pantomime will be enough to survive just

143

about anywhere. Plus, in most cities you'll find people who speak and understand enough English to get by in a pinch (more on when to use English in a minute). If you show you want to learn the lingo, locals will often be more than happy to teach you a bit.

Thank You (& Other Essential Phrases)

If you learn how to say nothing else in the local tongue, learn how to say **"thank you."** Especially if you don't speak the language, you will be relying on the kindness of strangers (waiters, clerks, guides, concierges, and anyone you stop to ask directions) to help guide you through their country. The least you should be able to do is thank them for it. It's polite, and it'll encourage them to help you further. After you learn "thank you," then move on to learning "yes," "no," "Where's the bathroom?" "please," "I would like," "Do you speak English?" and one, two, three. Listen to how locals pronounce things. Exaggerate accents. Speak volumes through your facial expressions. Copy gestures (but carefully—see the section on gestures).

The simple dictionary and **phrase guide** in appendix D gives you all the most essential words and phrases in French, Italian, German, and Spanish. In addition, bring along a more complete phrase guide and a pocket dictionary of English-French/French-English (or whatever language you'll need). Using these, you can ask any question, hopefully understand the answers, and decode most of what's on a given menu (if you can't find the full name of a dish translated, often you can at least find out that the second word is "chicken," which is usually enough to go on).

You can look up complex phrases and try to pronounce them properly, but in the interests of time and clarity, you'll often find it's much more expedient to resort to a combination of **charades** and **international pigdin.** Don't be shy about acting out what you mean. You don't need to know how to phrase a question properly, just how to add an audible question mark on any word by lilting up at the end of the word. Understand?

When trying to **read a foreign language,** don't be intimidated by the full sentence. Instead, look at all its parts. Examine words for things that ring a bell. Spanish and Italian are close enough when written down that you can often make out half of one if you have a good working knowledge of the other. English is an amalgam mainly of old High German and Latin, which have become modern German and the Romance languages: French, Italian, and Spanish. Look for words and word fragments you recognize and assume, within reason, that they mean what you think they mean. Make educated guesses, make your share of mistakes, but above all, make an effort to learn what you can and to communicate with Europeans on their terms. I enjoy collecting native ways to say "thank you" every bit as much as collecting postcards or museum books.

Bet You Didn't Know

Although I heartily encourage you to pick up as much of the local language as you can, here are some words that, pronounced "European-style," work in most countries: Alt (stop), auto, bank (pronounce it *bahn*-kah), beer (sometimes with an *a* at the end), bus (pronounce it *boos*), cafe, camping, ciao, couchette, English, hotel, information, kaput, moment (universal for wait), no, OK, pardon, photo, police, post (as in office), restaurant, student, taxi, telephone, toilet, and tourist (of course).

On the Polite Use of English

The old joke goes that if you speak three languages, you're trilingual; if you speak two, you're bilingual; and if you only speak one language, then you must be an American. Americans are notorious for barging through Europe demanding loudly that everyone speak English. When you're in a foreign country, never assume that the people there will, or expect that they should, speak English. Nothing is more arrogant. You are their guest; use their language. Prove the stereotypes wrong by learning the basics of the local lingo before you arrive in town and by being eager to pick up more from anyone who will teach you along the way. Still, on occasion, resorting to English is the best way to get your message across clearly. Just be polite about it, and *always* ask first "Do you speak English?" in the local language.

For the past 20 years, most European children have learned English in school or college, so chances are the majority of people under middle age, and many beyond it, will speak at least some English. Upon inquiry about their language skills, most will say "yes, a little English," and then prove to be surprisingly fluent. People involved in the tourist industry have learned all the English (and French, Japanese, German, and so on) they need to do their jobs. Hoteliers can book a room, waiters translate menu items, and people at admission booths can describe open hours and prices. When speaking English, choose only simple, direct words. Avoid idiomatic expressions or strange turns of phrase. Do not use extra words; do not use contractions. Speak slowly; enunciate clearly. Use short, simple sentences.

When "OK!" Is Not OK: Gestures

Be careful using any gestures. No single aspect of communication seems to have such diverse meanings and interpretations across different cultures. The V for victory symbol is fine palms out; if you make it with palms facing inward, you'll offend many Brits (it's their version of "giving someone the finger"). When holding up their fingers to count, Europeans start with the thumb for one. Holding up just the forefinger means "wait a sec" in most countries. You may be trying to order one cappuccino; they'll think you aren't ready yet.

Tourist Traps

Speaking of **body language,** be prepared that in northern Europe, especially England, people require a larger sphere of personal space than most Americans do and are very adverse to physical contact. When you get to Sicily, though, strangers will be throwing their arms around you and greeting you with a wet kiss on each cheek. The farther south you go, the more people touch. Manly, macho Mediterranean men walk arm-in-arm down the streets, and teenage boys will zoom up on their scooters and greet their pals with the double cheek peck so beloved of Hollywood types. Again, be observant and let the locals be your guide as to how to act and when to touch.

Never, ever hold out just your forefinger and pinkie raised to make "horns" (or the "I love you" gesture from sign language). Depending on how you hold your hand and where you are, you're either casting the Evil Eye, warding against it (which insults the people around you, implying that they are casting one), or calling someone a cuckold. The thumb-and-forefinger-circle that means "OK!" to you means "Up yours!" in some cultures.

A southern European gesturing "come here" looks like they're shooing you away; waving good-bye in Europe by opening and closing the hand, palm up, looks like an American "come here." Confused? You should be. There are whole books on this subject. Gestures are an integral part of communicating in Europe, especially the south, but until you learn the European body language, it might be best to keep your hands to yourself, so to speak.

Chapter 11

Crime & Safety

In This Chapter

➤ Fending off pickpockets, gypsies, thieves, and scams

➤ How to deal with theft or loss and still have a great trip

➤ Safety tips for the female traveler and pointed responses to pinched bottoms

➤ How the color of your skin may affect your travels and how to deal with potential prejudice

➤ Why you shouldn't be worried about terrorism or air safety

Random, violent crime rates are much lower in Europe than in the United States. Murder is rare, and terrorism is more a scary bluff than harsh reality. Be smart, be safe, and enjoy yourself. With your valuables in your money belt, the worst that might happen to you is that the day's spending money in your wallet gets stolen.

Reading this chapter might get a little scary, because all I'm concentrating on is the bad stuff. I know every time I read State Department travel advisories (**http://travel.state.gov**) and other safety statistics, they start making any place sound like a terrifying death trap. Take all this stuff with a few grains of salt. Other than taking some sensible precautions against theft, you shouldn't have to worry much about safety at all. I felt much less safe when I lived in Brooklyn than I ever have traveling or living anywhere in Europe.

City Savvy

European big cities are, on the whole, safer than U.S. ones. Your two biggest worries should be pickpockets and the crazy traffic—especially the kamikaze scooters that routinely go the wrong way up one-way streets and even drive on the sidewalks.

Peter Piper Picked a Pocket

Pickpockets target tourists, especially the American kind. The United States is a rich country, and they know that American tourists carry the best stuff and the most money in their wallets. Be especially careful anywhere that's crowded (buses, subways, train stations, street markets). Don't tempt thieves. Leave all your jewelry at home, and don't flash your wallet or valuables. When you aren't using your camera, keep it stowed in a plain bag (a camera bag is like carrying a big sign that says to thieves "Yo! Over here. Steal this camera."). Make yourself theft-proof by following this advice:

➤ **Keep everything valuable** (passport, credit cards, driver's license, plane tickets, rail passes, traveler's checks) **in your money belt** and wear it at all times (see the "Packing Light" section of chapter 6 for more on money belts). In your wallet, keep just a day's spending money.

➤ **Carry wallets in a buttoned back pocket** or, if you're in jeans, in your front pocket (no one's getting it out of there without your knowing it). Ride buses with one hand stuck nonchalantly in the front pocket with your wallet.

➤ **Sling your purse strap across your chest,** not just hanging off one shoulder where it can be easily snatched. If it has a flap, keep the flap and latch side against your body, not facing out where nimble fingers can open it. On the sidewalk, walk against the wall instead of by the curb, and keep your purse toward the wall. Beware of **Vespa thieves** who zip up on their scooters to snatch away purses.

➤ I travel in a trench coat (good for warmth, rain, a makeshift blanket, and fitting into European crowds). With **all my valuables in my inside coat or pants pockets** and the trench coat wrapped around me, I feel pretty pickpocket-proof. I always button up the coat before stepping on a bus, metro, or train.

The Kings of Thieves: Gypsies

Some gypsies take a different approach to separating you from your money. For many of these nomadic peoples, thievery is a way of life, and they're masterful at it. They are often easy to spot for their colorful but dirty and ragged clothes. They're most prevalent in southern Europe, but you'll find them everywhere—especially around major tourist attractions. Although the adults mainly beg—and are very pushy about it—the kids are the ones you have to look out for. They'll swarm you, babbling and sometimes holding up bits of cardboard with messages scrawled on them to distract you, and then rifle your pockets faster than you can say "Hey..." Near walls and in metro tunnels, they'll even be so bold as to pin you against the wall with the cardboard so as to fleece you more easily.

They aren't really physically dangerous, but they are very adept at taking your stuff, and they're tough to catch. The best defense is to be on the lookout. If a group of scruffy children approaches, yell "No!" forcefully, glare, and keep walking; if they persist, yell "Politz!" (close enough in any language). If they get near enough to touch you, push them violently away—don't hold back just because they're children. Act a little crazy; perhaps jump up, do a full spin, and come down in a karate stance with a primal shout. You may not win awards for your Bruce Lee impression, but you'll probably scare those kids away (they prefer befuddled, clueless-looking targets and steer clear of wackos).

Scams & How to Foil Them

Every con artist has his own tactics. Specific swindles to look out for are listed under "Safety" in each destination chapter's "Fast Facts" section. Here are a few common ones:

➤ Sometimes waiters will **pad bills with unordered items,** double the tax (15% for the state, and 15% for the waiter), or simply shortchange you.

➤ In countries that count pocket change in increments of hundreds, many unscrupulous types try to catch new arrivals by confusing them with all those zeros, **giving change for 5,000 lire when you paid with a 50,000 bill.** Until you get used to the money, examine each bill carefully before you hand it over and make a show of doing so.

➤ A stranger may offer to **help you change money** (alarm bells should go off immediately and you should say "No thank you") and then make friends with you and walk off with your wallet after hugging you good-bye.

➤ **Hotels may sneak in minibar, phone, or other charges** you shouldn't have to pay. Make sure you're paying the listed rate (or less, if you bargained them down) and have them explain the bill if it's any higher than the base rate (plus tax) times how many nights you stayed.

➤ This scam is perfectly legal: hotels charge **obscenely high telephone rates,** with markups anywhere from 150% to 400%, especially on long-distance calls. They'll often even charge you for the free local call to your calling card company! Pretend the hotel phone doesn't exist and use pay phones or the post office instead.

➤ When your friendly escort on a guided bus tour recommends the "best shop" for buying local crafts or souvenirs, 9 times out of 10 she's **getting a healthy kickback from that store** and the prices are heavily inflated. (In defense of tour guides, this is one of the only methods for them to eke out a living, as they are notoriously underpaid—in part because companies unofficially expect them to take advantage of this option as an unlisted perk.)

How Not to Get Railroaded: Train Safety Tips

I covered the rules for keeping your stuff safe and secure on an overnight train in chapter 4, but here's a recap:

➤ **Don't flash your valuables.** You're sharing a couchette with strangers.

➤ **Make sure the door is locked** and that everyone in the couchette understands the importance of keeping it locked (the conductor usually emphasizes this, but be a nerd and do it yourself, too).

➤ **Reserve the top bunk.** It's a hotter ride (heat rises), but it puts you above most thieves' easy reach, plus you can sleep with your head right next to your bags.

➤ **Stow your bags in the luggage niche above the door.** There's a little guardrail to keep them from sliding out; strap or lock your bags to this rail so a thief can't tug them down and run off. He won't work at it if he can't get them easily.

➤ **Wear your money belt while you sleep.** Do not take it off. After you've taken care of tickets and passports with the conductor, you may want to excuse yourself to the bathroom and strap that waistbelt around your upper thigh instead. This sounds creepy, but thieves with light touches do sometimes unzip your pants and deftly empty the money belt while it's still on your sleeping person—but if it's around your thigh, there's no way they can get to it without you noticing.

➤ You might want to **make a pillow out of your valuables.** It's not the most comfortable way to sleep, but if you wrap things in your sweater and poke it in a stuff sack, it may be soft enough to lay your head on.

➤ Be especially **careful sleeping in unreserved sitting couchettes,** where there are no locks on the doors.

Extra! Extra!

Any thief can tell a **rental car** by looking at the license plate. Don't tempt her. Do not leave *anything* in the car overnight, and when you're driving around by day, keep everything in the trunk so that when you get out, nothing is visible. Pack the trunk before you start out for the day, because putting stuff in the trunk when you park and then walking away is a clear invitation to any thief who happens to be watching.

Losing Things Without Losing Your Mind

Even when you take all the precautions and travel smart, that pickpocket may take you by surprise or you may simply get caught up with the excitement of travel and leave your wallet on an outdoor cafe table and blithely walk away. I once left mine at the gift shop of the cathedral in Krakow, Poland. When I returned half an hour later, huffing and puffing and looking around wildly, two Russian students came striding across the square toward me, holding out the wallet and saying "You lose?" I got lucky. Usually, if your wallet goes missing and it wasn't left in a restaurant or hotel, it's gone for good. If you heeded my advice and kept all your important stuff in your money belt, all you've lost is a day's spending money (and one wallet).

Above all, try not to let the loss of your wallet, money, credit cards, or other important documents ruin your trip. My father, a veteran of European travel and one of the most safety-savvy and cautious travelers I know, once had his pocket picked on the Madrid metro on his very first day in Spain. Although it certainly caused some problems, Dad had stowed all the really important stuff—including his cache of traveler's checks—in his money belt. Because of that foresight, aided in no small part by my mother's credit cards, he didn't have to trash the trip and went on to have one of the best two-week vacations of his life.

Time-Savers

If you lose your **passport,** go immediately to the nearest U.S. consulate. You are a nonentity without one. Bring along a photocopy of the information pages of your missing passport (that would be the two pages facing each other with your picture and vital information; don't bother photocopying the cover), those passport-sized photos you packed, and any other form of identification you still have with you.

What if I Lose My Credit Cards & Traveler's Checks?

On the photocopied sheet with your important documentation (see the box under "Packing Light" in chapter 6), include the U.S. phone numbers to report stolen or lost cards for all your credit and bank cards and write down the numbers of each of your traveler's checks. For obvious reasons, *make sure you keep this list separate from the cards and checks themselves.*

Should your cards or checks get lost or stolen, contact the issuing bank(s) immediately. In case you forgot to write down the emergency numbers, here's a cheat sheet: Citicorp Visa's emergency number is ☎ 800/645-6556. For American Express credit cards or traveler's checks, call ☎ 800/221-7282. MasterCard holders can call ☎ 800/307-7309. Unfortunately, you cannot make an 800 call toll-free from Europe, but you can still make one by using your calling card (you'll be billed the full rates as if it were a regular call).

Dollars & Sense

Write down the **identification number of each traveler's check** as you cash or use it. When you're in your hotel room each night, take out your master list of numbers and cross off the used ones. If the balance of checks get stolen at some point, you need to be able to report exactly which ones are gone in order to get them replaced. The check issuer will tell you where to pick up the new stash.

Of course, reporting cards as stolen means that if they turn up two hours later at the bottom of your bag, there's not much you can do about reactivating your accounts until after you get home. Although in the case of genuine card theft every second counts in reporting the loss in order to cut the thief off at the pass, I suggest finding a phone and quickly contacting the last hotel, restaurant, or other place you may have left your wallet or purse. If you have no luck, hang up, call the credit card company, and get ready to play Creative Vacation Financing as you continue your vacation without the aid of plastic.

Extra! Extra!

Most of this section deals with losing your monetary means and important documents. That's because these are the only things to be concerned about. The loss of any other item (clothing, toiletries, and so on) will be annoying, but not insurmountable. Look at it this way: If you lose all your luggage, you'll just have to come home looking like a European, having refit your wardrobe at flea markets, department stores, or fashion outlets.

Most credit card issuers delete your old account number and create a new one to transfer your account into, which means you need to get new cards. This is the time when, as American Express commercials waste no time trumpeting, carrying good old-fashioned **traveler's checks** can save the entire vacation. If you lose the traveler's checks and you remembered the all-important rule of writing down the check numbers in a safe place, you can get them rather speedily replaced in any big European city. You can also have a friend wire you money—most city and country guides list the local **Western Union** representative in every city.

Tourist Traps

Drugs and prostitution are illegal just about everywhere. It's just not a good idea to mess around with either in the first place. If you do get arrested, especially for carrying drugs (and *especially* if you do so across national borders), there's little the local U.S. consulate can do (or even wants to do) other than provide you with a list of lawyers. Your family or lawyer at home can only visit you in prison.

Hey, Bella American Woman!

European travel is as easy for women as it is for men. You may get complimented, whistled at, pinched, prodded, or propositioned, but you're probably physically safer than you are at home (Europeans see rape as even more repugnant than Americans do, and it is much less widely committed). All women should take precautions and play it safe, but even solo women should have few problems traveling alone, although it certainly helps and is safer to have a companion (of either gender). Women's lib notwithstanding, women seen without men are targeted more often by **thieves,** so be extra careful.

Most **European males,** especially those in southern European countries, act like peacocks around women, parading around to win admiration. When this behavior is not overly annoying, it can be quite comical. A single woman or a group made up of women only will get approached more often than a man or mixed group. This approach can be a great opportunity to make friends, get instant language lessons, or even flirt. Or it can be a darn nuisance. Just pick when you feel it's safe and you're in the mood to be friendly and when you should firmly ignore all those men falling over one another to be helpful, charming, and gallant. Dress modestly to avoid unwanted attention, and wear shades to avoid eye contact, an act which seems to translate as "come accost me" in some southern countries.

The farther south you move, the more ardent your suitors will become; in fact, the inverse is sometimes true—British men can be difficult to approach even if you *want* to. Yes, Italian (and other Mediterranean) men pinch bottoms and rub up against women, usually in crowded places, and make the most surprising and sometimes raunchy propositions. (Greek shopkeeps sometimes corner solo women and offer to show them some more "special merchandise" upstairs.) If you find yourself molested on a bus or other crowded place, tell the transgressor firmly "No!" and "Alt!" (international-ese for "stop") and proceed to pinch, scratch, elbow, kick, punch, and so forth to further discourage him. Or enlist the aid of a nearby local woman to noisily chastise the offending would-be Romeo and perhaps smack him with her purse.

Bet You Didn't Know

Europeans are much **less likely to hassle a married woman.** One trick that has worked wonders for solo women on the road is the fictional husband (he works even if you've got a spare one at home who's real). He's always just around the corner where you're going to meet him in five minutes, is the strong, jealous type, and best of all, he always leaves the toilet seat down. Even if you haven't tied the knot, you might want to wear a fake wedding band to ward off the more assiduous admirers.

Unfortunately, Hollywood films have provided Europeans with the impression that all American women are easy, and blonde American women doubly so. In many ways, Europe remains a rigid, formal, "traditional" society. The fact that American women are used to being more independent, straightforward, and openly friendly than their European counterparts has the unfortunate side effect of reinforcing that image. The practical upshot: American women are seen as fair and likely game. Take your hint from local women and stride confidently and purposefully down the street. Ignore any comments, catcalls, and wolf whistles, refuse to engage the harassers in so much as eye contact, and firmly fend off all courtiers.

On **buses and trains,** sit with other women or families (avoid empty train compartments because then your companions can choose you instead of the other way around; instead, find a couchette with five nuns and an empty seat and ask if you can join them). You should feel perfectly safe even in big cities and even at night. Many women report feeling much safer in Rome or Paris than they ever do at home and that they even feel fine walking through the deserted streets in the middle of the night all alone. Of course, it always pays to play it safe. Stick to populated streets after dark, and know where the bad neighborhoods are (each destination in this book has a "Fast Facts" section on safety that lists the less savory parts of town). The bottom line, though, is that physically you have much less to worry about in Europe than you do in most parts of the United States.

Racial Concerns

The material in this section ain't pretty, it just is, so I'm going to give it to you straight. The world is not yet color-blind, and Europe is no exception. Anyone not visibly of European descent is often treated at least as a cultural oddity in Europe. Rarely does it move beyond stares (though some African-American women do report a rather high incidence of impromptu marriage proposals in Italy). When racism does rear its ugly head in Europe, thankfully it's usually not in the form of physical violence.

Unfounded mistrust, however, can run rampant, and dark-skinned travelers often run into biased, infuriating treatment. You may be questioned longer at border crossings and on trains and get your baggage rifled through by officials much more often than the white folks do. At worst, a hotel may claim it's full for the night and then give a room to the next white guy who walks through the door. There's little you can do about all this, although—in one of travel's more unpleasant truisms—it helps to flash that American passport frequently and dress like a well-to-do tourist. If you are wronged because of your skin tone, strike a blow for social consciousness by lodging a complaint with the local police or special "tourist police" branch.

In general, **African Americans** won't run into any more racism, and usually less, than they would at home (I know that's not saying much). Cities like London and Paris have large local black populations, so you won't be treated as a standout. Be prepared to sometimes be treated with the double standards described previously and to be stared at, especially in smaller towns and in southern European countries. Europe has its share of skinheads, but neo-Nazis are more of a problem in the United States than they are in Germany.

People of **north African, Middle Eastern, Arabic, or Baltic** descent may run into more prejudice and hard feelings. The situation between many of these groups and the European majority parallels that between Mexican immigrants and the white majority in the United States. White Europeans are suspicious of people from the other side of the Mediterranean because many of them, fleeing poverty or political unrest, head to Europe (especially Italy, Germany, and France) for a "better life" of washing windows, selling trinkets, and doing similar work. Unfortunately, high unemployment, local public resentment, latent racism, and the rise of mafia-like immigrant employment syndicates conspire to keep these people in their marginalized and denigrated role. Do a bit of advance research to find out whether large immigrant groups have strained social tensions in certain areas (for example, Turks in Germany—which means anyone who looks Turkish or Greek—Albanians in Italy, Algerians in France).

So many tour buses blow through Europe full of Japanese and Chinese tourists on sightseeing tours/shopping sprees that **Asians** should find a pretty friendly reception here. You won't be the subject of nearly as many suspicions as other non-Europeans.

The Hollow Threat of Terrorism & Plane Crashes

What should you do about terrorism? Don't worry about it. The odds are astronomically against a terrorist smuggling a bomb onto your plane or lurking behind you on the Champs-Elysées. As the World Trade Center and Oklahoma City bombings have shown us, terrorism is a random act that can happen to anyone, anywhere—that's what makes it so scary—and it doesn't matter whether you're in the American heartland, Europe, or Tel Aviv. Frankly, I worry more about traffic and handgun fatalities at home than terrorism abroad.

155

You are over 54 times more likely to be murdered in a small American town than be killed by a terrorist abroad. The anti-American terrorism scares of the 1980s you have heard about have all but disappeared (at least in Europe). The statistics say that you are 2½ times as likely to be hit by lightning in the United States than you are to be killed in a terrorist attack either in the air or anywhere overseas. Just about the only thing you personally can do to ward off terrorism is to do your best not to stand out as a "rich American" (if you're anywhere above the poverty line, you're rich by world standards). We capitalists often make great targets for terrorists trying to make a political statement. Just steer clear of Belfast and Bosnia, and you should be fine.

As far as **air safety,** you've just seen the odds of terrorist bombs in general. There are, at worst, only one in three million airline fatalities per year—that includes bombs, mechanical failure, acts of God, and human error combined, and it includes the tiny private planes and marginal airlines that account for most crashes. If you limit the statistics to the major airlines and large passenger jets you'll be using, the risk numbers jump to something highly unlikely like one in six million (some reports peg it as high as one in 12 million). Statistically, you're much safer in the air and in Europe than you are driving to work. So don't sweat it; just fasten your seat belt, and enjoy the ride.

Chapter 12

Shopping Strategies

In This Chapter

➤ Europe's best buys: a list of each country's finest

➤ Bargain hunting and tips for the savvy shopper

➤ Getting what's coming to you: VAT taxes and refunds

➤ The Big Brother of merchandise: U.S. Customs and what they'll let you bring home

---

Some people come to Europe and make it one long shopping trip. Others just want to pick up a few souvenirs and the occasional hand-crafted product. Whatever your shopping style or inclinations, this chapter will fill you in on what you need to know to be a smart shopper in Europe, from best buys and size charts to VAT refunds and customs limits.

It's a Buyer's Market

The following list points out some of the top buys in Europe (items on which a country really shines are in **bold**). Because taste in shopping varies, I've included all the sorts of special-to-that-country merchandise. If you want my advice on what to buy, though, stick with the hand-crafted and the unique. Now "hand-crafted" can apply as much to a fine wine, hand-tatted lace, or crystalware as to a Bavarian carved wood Nutcracker, Irish wool sweater, or painted Italian ceramic plate—so long as it's something you couldn't find anywhere else and something that to you helps define the local culture in some way. If you have the money, Europe's a great source for art, antiques, and high fashion. The rest of us can have fun haggling for semi-antiques and leather jackets at street markets.

➤ **Austria: Antiques** (especially 19th-century Biedermeir); gold, silver, and enamel jewelry; **petit point embroidery;** porcelain (Wiener Augarten); wool products (Loden)

➤ **Czech Republic: Antiquarian books and prints, antiques, Bohemian crystal,** handicrafts, jewelry, Soviet-era kitschy trinkets (watches and so on with the hammer and sickle)

➤ **England:** Antiques (Chippendale), aromatherapy (The Body Shop is British), **ceramics** (Wedgwood, Spode, bone china), Royal Family memorabilia, **raincoats** (Barbour, Burberrys), "tapestry" (needlepoint kits), tweeds

➤ **France:** Antiques, **cosmetics,** crystal and glass (Baccarat, Lalique, Saint-Louis), Faience ceramics, fine foods (pâtés, truffles, Dijon mustard), **Hermés scarves** and ties, **high fashion,** lace, lingerie, **perfume, wine and champagne**

➤ **Germany:** Beer steins, cutlery (WMF), **handicrafts and wood carving** (cuckoo clocks, nutcracker soldiers, toys)

➤ **Greece:** Antiques, ceramics and cookware, crafts, **embroidered clothing** (vests, blouses), **jewelry** (especially silver), **leather** (more sturdy products, like bags and sandals, than supple items like clothing), *flokati* woven wool rugs

➤ **Ireland:** Crafts, **hand-knit sweaters** (especially from the Aran Islands), **lace, linen,** recordings of traditional Irish music, **Waterford crystal, woolens and tweeds** (especially from Donegal)

➤ **Italy:** Antiques, **art, ceramics** (folk and fine; Faenza near Bologna, Deruta and Gubbio in Umbria, Amalfi Coast), **glass** (Venice), **fashion** (Milan, Florence), **industrial design** (coffeepots, lamps, and so on), jewelry (gold and silver), **lace** (Venice), **leather** (Florence), religious objects (Rome), **shoes**

➤ **Netherlands: Antiques, cheese,** chocolates, **crystal** (from Leerdam or Maastricht), **Delftware ceramics, diamonds, flower bulbs** (check with U.S. customs about which kinds you can take home), pewter (from Tiel)

➤ **Scotland: Plaids and tartans, Scotch,** sheepskins, silver jewelry, tweeds, wool sweaters

➤ **Spain: Ceramics and tiles,** lace, leather (Barcelona), **sherry**

➤ **Switzerland:** Cheese, **chocolate, music boxes,** tin- and copperware, toys, **watches and clocks,** wood carvings

Tips for Shopping Wisely

Smart shoppers follow these guidelines:

➤ **Check out American prices** on items you think you may want to buy before you leave home. This way, you'll know whether you're getting a bargain by buying it abroad.

➤ The **main shopping drag** in any city offers some of the best window shopping, but be prepared to drop a huge chunk of change if you want to purchase anything. You may find the same item in another shop on a lower-rent street for less.

➤ **Shop in street markets** for the best prices, most open haggling, and most fun. The quality of the merchandise is iffier than that of shops, but you can get great deals on everything from designer knockoffs to bootleg tapes.

➤ **Shop around.** Prices vary dramatically from shop to shop, stall to market stall, and they usually vary inversely with their distance from any major tourist sight. Let the store owners know you're comparing prices, and the asking rate may go down on the spot.

➤ **Designer clothing** is not any cheaper in Paris or Florence boutiques than it is in Big City, USA. There are bargain-basement fashion outlets in European fashion capitals, of course, but they usually offer no better deals than you'll find in the United States. Of course, there's always that cachet of having bought those shoes in Florence or that dress in Paris.

➤ **Shop selectively.** Don't gobble up every trinket you see. Go for the items that truly bring out a country's spirit, style, or culture. It may be a beautiful museum book, chunky Irish sweater, or a kitschy British Beefeater guard doll to hang on the Christmas tree. Just make sure it's memorable to you.

➤ Everything becomes **cheaper as you move south.** You could buy four times as much in Greece as you could in Paris or Oslo for the same money.

➤ Make sure any **videotapes** you purchase are in U.S. format, because you can't view European tapes on a U.S. machine (most videos at tourist sights are available in many formats).

➤ If it's at all expected in a given situation, always **haggle** (more on that in a few minutes).

➤ On most **escorted tours,** the guide will take or direct you to shops that offer "special prices" to people on your tour. Ninety percent of the time, the shop is feeding the guide a **kickback.** (Guides are so scandalously underpaid, this is often the only way they can scrape by.) Usually, the store passes this percentage along to you by jacking up the prices. Although some guides do give honest recommendations, and even some of those kickback arrangements don't adversely affect you via markups, it's impossible to know when a recommendation is on the level. I'd take the cynical route and ignore any guides' suggestions.

➤ **Scrutinize labels, kick the proverbial tires,** and otherwise show that (or look like) you know what you're doing. Shopkeepers who see a savvy customer are less likely to try to pull the wool over your eyes— even when you're trying on sweaters.

➤ **Dress respectably, but not too well.** You want merchants to know you're a paying customer and not tourist riffraff who's just window shopping, but you don't want to give them the idea that you're loaded. Prices will go up on the spot if they think you're capable of paying them, especially in markets but even in stores.

➤ **Know the VAT refund minimum** for the country you're in, and if your budget and plans are going to allow you to spend near or over that amount, try to do all your shopping in one store so you can get that refund—it's like getting an automatic 20% (or so) discount.

➤ **Count your change, and make sure the receipt is complete and accurate.** Don't be rude about it, but make sure you haven't gotten a rotten shopkeeper who's trying to scam or shortchange you. The receipt is important because you will need it for any VAT refund, plus in some countries, you must carry your receipts for any purchase (even a cup of coffee) away from the store with you (it has to do with the local government trying to foil tax cheats, but the laws affect you as well).

Time-Savers

You can save yourself time and hassle should something go wrong with a purchase being shipped home if you **snap a photo** of it before it's wrapped up. This photo makes excellent proof of purchase when it comes to insurance claims.

➤ **Ship breakables home.** It may cost a bit more, but the longer you keep your more fragile purchases with you bouncing down the road of your trip, the greater the chances that your Waterford crystal will end up Waterford shards.

➤ If you find that you're running out of room in your luggage, ship those fragile items home first, then **mail home your personal stuff you don't need, like dirty laundry,** rather than entrusting all your purchases to the postal system.

Clothing Size Charts

The United States, Britain, and continental Europe all use different systems for measurements. The following charts should only be used as guides to steer you towards a near fit. As anyone who's ever shopped knows, clothing size is much more subjective than it should be (especially for women), and sizes vary among manufacturers and from store to store.

Women's Coats and Dresses

United States	4	6	8	10	12	14	16	18
Europe	34	36	38	40	42	44	46	48
Great Britain	6	8	10	12	14	16	18	20

Women's Shoes

United States	5	6	7	8	9	10
Europe	36	37	38	39	40	41
Great Britain	4	5	6	7	8	9

Men's Suits

United States	34	36	38	40	42	44	46	48
Europe	44	46	48	50	52	54	56	58
Great Britain	34	36	38	40	42	44	46	48

Men's Shirts

United States	14	$14\frac{1}{2}$	15	$15\frac{1}{2}$	16	$16\frac{1}{2}$	17	$17\frac{1}{2}$
Europe	36	37	38	39	41	42	43	44
Great Britain	14	$14\frac{1}{2}$	15	$15\frac{1}{2}$	16	$16\frac{1}{2}$	17	$17\frac{1}{2}$

Men's Shoes

United States	7	8	9	10	11	12
Europe	39	41	43	44	45	46
Great Britain	6	7	8	9	10	11

Market Culture & Bargaining

For the most fun shopping anywhere in Europe, head to an outdoor market. It may be the fruit and vegetable market open each morning, the daily leather market stalls of Florence, the weekly antique and flea markets of London's Portobello Road, or the monthly antiques extravaganza in Arezzo.

Even non-shoppers will have fun exploring street markets. Shoppers will find great bargains.

Market stalls are where you'll find the most colorful characters (among merchants and shoppers alike), the best deals, the widest variety of goods (from fine art to used plumbing supplies), and the best chances to haggle. They're also where you'll find the most attempts to fleece the unsuspecting tourist, the most cunningly disguised Gucci or Hermés knockoffs (although, if all you want to buy is an imitation, this is perfect), and the potentially shoddiest merchandise. Aside from commerce, markets are also great for taking pictures, soaking up local character, decompressing from too many museums, and getting cleaned out by pickpockets in the crowd. Have fun, be careful.

Dollars & Sense

Definitely **haggle** in any street market across Europe—in some, it's insulting (and economically unsound) not to. When it comes to shops, bargaining may not be appropriate and, at any rate, is always more low-key. Bargain harder as you move south. Shops in London never haggle (and will be offended if you try). Those in Greece almost always do. Read your guidebooks to find out which countries honor this ancient art in the shops as well as on the streets.

Marketplaces are bastions of bargaining, havens for hagglers, and here's how to do it:

1. Never start out appearing **too interested.**

2. Fix in your head **what you think the item is worth** to you, and don't let the bargaining end up much above this figure.

3. **Let the stall owner make the first offer.** Look shocked.

4. **Counteroffer** with at least half as much (more if his price seems outrageous), at which point he will act extremely offended. Don't be fooled or frightened away no matter what his reaction. That's his role. He will grumble and complain and look like he's mad if you end up getting to the right price, but that's how he's supposed to act. Trust me, he won't sell you an item for less than he's willing to get for it. He's the pro; if anyone's going to get a raw deal, it'll be you if you don't bargain stridently. Any price he ends up agreeing upon is fine with him, no matter how wounded he acts.

5. Now begins **the back and forth,** a ping-pong match of prices that draws closer to some median as you go. This median depends on the place, the merchant, and the item. The thing may only be worth as

little as 25% or as high as 75% of his original asking price. This back and forth is a way to feel each other out and decide where the price should be. It's supply and demand on a person-to-person basis. At the beginning, however much he comes down in price, you go up by, at most, half that much. For example, if he knocks off 60 francs, you add 30 francs to your next counteroffer.

Bet You Didn't Know

Take your time throughout the haggle process. Get to know the shopkeeper. Especially in Greece, Turkey, and as you get closer to the Middle East or North Africa where haggling is an art, you may spend an hour with the owner on big items, drinking tea, showing each other pictures of the family, getting friendly. This is all part of the ritual. Hurried hagglers overpay and may truly offend the merchant.

6. **Consider each counteroffer** you make theatrically and carefully. Re-examine the item as you ponder. Find flaws in it, maybe the price will come down (don't harp on this one or you *will* eventually insult the merchant, plus co-opt your own position; if it's so shoddy, why would you want it?). The higher you're forced to go, the less enthused you should appear.

7. **Play good cop/bad cop.** Your companion who's standing next to you has the job of appearing completely uninterested in the item and trying increasingly to drag you away. She's tired and wants to leave, or thinks the thing is outrageously overpriced, or doesn't like it. If you're at the stall alone, make up a spouse back at the hotel and invoke him or her as the reason you can't spend too much.

8. If you truly can't budge the merchant quite as low as you want, **try walking away.** Don't do it until you're getting close to the right price, and do it slowly so he has time to call you back with a better offer! This offer will usually be the right price (or at least his final offer), and the haggle is over. Sometimes this strategy backfires, and he'll let you leave. If you truly still want the item, swing by the stall later on, after having comparison-shopped (whether you did or not). Appear only marginally still interested, and drop your offer down from the last price you were offering (say to two-thirds of the offer) to prove you'll only take it now if it's a true bargain. Often, the shopkeeper will spit out a figure closer to the original median you two were working toward, and that's it. The deal's sealed.

9. **Once you agree on a price, you must buy.** If you can't get the merchant down to a fair price, don't buy it. Only pay what you're willing to pay (but be willing to pay fairly; don't expect a leather jacket for $10).

Taxing Matters: VAT & How to Get a Refund

Most purchases in Europe have a built-in **Value Added Tax (VAT)** of around 17% to 33%, depending on the country (Switzerland doesn't do it). This tax is the European version of a state sales tax, only it's already embedded in the price rather than being tacked on at the register. Non-European Union (EU) citizens are entitled to have some or all of this tax refunded if they spend more than a certain amount at any one store. This amount ranges from as low as $80 in England (although some stores, like Harrod's, require as much as $150) to $200 in France or Italy (always *before* tax).

Dollars & Sense

You can also avoid the VAT by having your purchases **shipped** directly from the store, but this may get extremely pricey.

Request a VAT refund invoice from the cashier when you make your purchases and bring this invoice to the customs office at the airport of the last EU country you'll be in to have it stamped before you leave Europe. In other words, if you're flying home from England, bring all your slips from Italy, France, Germany, and so on to the airport in London. Once back home, and within 90 days of the purchase, mail all stamped invoices back to the stores, and they will send you a refund check. This process usually takes a few weeks or months; the longest I've waited was 18 months.

Many shops are now part of the **Tax Free for Tourists** network (look for a sticker in the store window). These shops issue a check along with your invoice which, after you have the invoice stamped at customs, you can redeem for cash directly at the Tax Free booth in the airport (usually near customs or the duty-free shop), or you can mail it back to the store in the envelope provided within 60 days for your refund.

Bring It on Home

What and how much you can bring into the United States is controlled by the U.S. Customs office. **Customs (www.customs.ustreas.gov)** basically views you as a small-time importer/exporter, and importers have to pay a governmental duty (tax) on any foreign-made item they bring into the country. Within certain limits, however, they won't impose an import tax. They realize that the majority of travelers are merely bringing home items as souvenirs or gifts or for their personal use. They magnanimously allow you to bring in a few drops of that Italian wine for free.

Tourist Traps

In **duty-free shops,** the duty you're avoiding at airport shops and onboard planes and ships is the local VAT tax you would otherwise be charged on an object. It's like getting your VAT refund before you buy. Duty-free shops are *not* a "get out of U.S. Customs limits free" card as many people believe. Lately, duty-free shops have gotten greedy and are charging the same, if not higher, prices than the shops downtown, which means they are ripping you off because they're pocketing that hidden 15 to 25% extra that would be the state tax. Know what the going rate and the VAT are so you can tell if an item at the duty-free shop truly is a bargain.

As long as you've been out of the country at least 48 hours and haven't "imported" anything in the past 30 days, you may bring home **up to $400 worth of goods** per person tax-free (that means a family of four has a combined limit of $1,200). There are also limits imposed on certain items. You may only bring into the United States: one liter of alcohol (you must be over 21), 200 cigarettes, and 100 cigars. Antiques over 100 years old and works of art are exempt from the $400 limit, as is anything you mail home (see sidebar). The first $1,000 worth of goods over $400 you pay a flat 10% duty on. Beyond that, the duty is assessed on an item-by-item basis.

Dollars & Sense

Once per day, you can **mail yourself** $200 worth of goods duty-free; mark them "for personal use." You can also mail up to $100 worth of goods per day to someone else (if you have lots of friends, you can mail $100 worth to each), labeled "unsolicited gift." Any package must state on the exterior a description of the contents and their values. I get over my moral compunctions by sending items that *are* actual gifts home this way. You cannot mail alcohol, perfume (it contains alcohol), or tobacco products.

To prevent the spread of diseases, **you cannot bring into the United States** any plants, fruits, vegetables, meats, or other foodstuffs (Dutch elm disease, hoof-in-mouth disease, and the Mediterranean fruit fly epidemic were all brought into the United States by unscreened travelers). This restriction includes even cured meats like salami (no matter what the shopkeeper in Europe says, the U.S. customs folks won't let it pass). You may bring in the following: bakery goods, all but the softest cheeses (the rule is vague, but if the cheese is at all spreadable, don't risk confiscation), candies, roasted coffee beans and dried tea, fish (packaged salmon is OK), seeds for veggies and flowers (but not for trees), and mushrooms. Check out the USDA's Web site (**www.aphis.usda.gov/oa/travel.html**) for more information.

Part 3

Hail Britannia!: Welcome to the British Isles

The British Isles make an excellent first stop on your European tour for one main reason: They speak English there—although if you've ever heard a true Scottish brogue, you'll know I use the term "English" broadly. Starting here allows you to adjust to some of the quirks of traveling in Europe without having to deal with a foreign tongue right off the bat. For some people, Britain feels somewhat more familiar than other parts of Europe. So although England may seem exotic when you arrive, if you've first spend time in Sicily, Bavaria, and Budapest, London may seem tame and ordinary by comparison. But keep in mind, you will have to drive on the "wrong" side of the road.

OK, so you're convinced: you'll start your trip in Great Britain and Ireland. But what can you do there? You can go kilt-shopping on Edinburgh's Royal Mile, take a musical pub crawl through Dublin, or join a London walking tour on the trail of Jack the Ripper. London is a metropolis with world-class museums and a vigorous street life and an arts capital with a sightseeing list that could keep you busy for months. If you can't find the Loch Ness monster in Scotland, make friends instead with Fungi, the playful dolphin that lives in Ireland's Dingle Bay. Drink Guinness from its Dublin source, browse through Harrods in London, and get funky at Edinburgh's Fringe Festival. Whether you take high tea in Bath or hike the highlands of Scotland, the British Isles will be a memorable part of any European vacation.

Chapter 13

London & the Best of England

In This Chapter

➤ Navigating the city by Tube

➤ The poshest hotels and most welcoming pubs

➤ Attractions not to miss, from Big Ben to the British Museum

➤ The lowdown on London's theater scene

➤ Excursions to Bath, Stonehenge, and Oxford

London. Home to Big Ben and the British Museum, bobbies and Beefeaters, punk hairdos and the stiff upper lip, fish 'n' chips and the royal family, giant black taxicabs and double-decker buses, time-traveling phone booths and tea-time at Harrods, Sherlock Holmes and the Crown Jewels. You can break out the opera glasses for an evening of West End theater, dance in cutting-edge clubs, and drink in the pubs where Shakespeare got sloshed. And oh yes, there is a London Bridge, but despite reports to the contrary, it *isn't* falling down. London also has some of the world's foremost museums, including exhaustive collections of everything from paintings, antiquities, and historical artifacts to decorative arts, wax models, and film memorabilia.

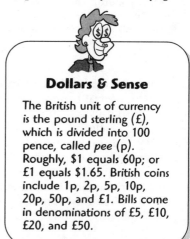

Dollars & Sense

The British unit of currency is the pound sterling (£), which is divided into 100 pence, called *pee* (p). Roughly, $1 equals 60p; or £1 equals $1.65. British coins include 1p, 2p, 5p, 10p, 20p, 50p, and £1. Bills come in denominations of £5, £10, £20, and £50.

Anything less than three days spent here is folly; four or five days is more reasonable. I know that kind of thinking is tough on a tight schedule, but if you're flying into London, remember that upon arrival in Europe it's wise to plan one day of officially doing nothing to recover from jet lag—so giving London five days in your itinerary won't be so hard.

Getting Your Bearings

London is huge, and it sprawls. Its 625 square miles consist of many small towns and villages that have slowly been gobbled up in a centuries-long urban expansion. Officially, London is divided into 33 boroughs, but most of its seven million residents still use traditional neighborhood names, and I'll do so as well. The following map is labeled with the main districts and thoroughfares of London, and the following section provides an overview of the character of each district.

Time-Savers

The **Tourist Information Centre** in Victoria Station is always incredibly crowded, but the people who work there are as helpful as a harried staff can be. Much better is the **British Travel Centre,** at 4–12 Lower Regent St., half a block from Piccadilly Circus. It has scads of information on all of Britain, plus a nifty travel bookshop, BritRail ticket window, and both travel and theater ticket agencies. You also can find information desks at Heathrow Airport and Liverpool Street station. Frustratingly, no office will answer phone inquiries. To find other tourist office locations and their open hours, call ☎ **0171/730-3450.** For recorded tourist information call ☎ **0839/123456** (cost is 42p per minute). The best way to find out what's going on around town, from shows to restaurants to events, is to buy a copy of *Time Out* magazine, published every Tuesday and available at newsstands.

London's Neighborhoods in Brief

The bulk of central London lies north of the Thames (west of it when the river turns southward) and is more or less bounded by the two loops of the District and Circle Tube (subway) lines. Central London can be divided into **The City** and the **West End.** Today on the eastern edge of London's center, **The City** is the ancient square mile where the Romans founded the original *Londinium.* It's now home to world financial institutions, St. Paul's, the Tower of London, and the one-time center of newspaper publishing, Fleet Street. The **West End** is much, much larger and more amorphous, comprising many neighborhoods whose names you'll get used to as you trundle about this lively center of London's restaurant, shopping, nightlife, and museum scene.

Among the major neighborhoods within the West End is **Holborn,** which abuts The City and is another old district today filled with the offices of lawyers and other professionals. North of this district is the academic **Bloomsbury,** home to the British Museum and the University of London. West of Bloomsbury, **Fitzrovia** is an old writer's hangout with shops and pubs that fades into **Soho** to the south. Farther to the west, the bland residential grid of **Marylebone**'s streets draws visitors to Madame Tussaud's and the haunts of the fictional Sherlock Holmes.

Below Bloomsbury things get livelier. **Covent Garden** and **the Strand** comprise an upscale restaurant, entertainment, and funky shopping quarter. To the west, **Soho,** once a seedy red-light district, is these days scrubbed more-or-less clean to house numerous budget eateries and London's Chinatown. To the south is **Piccadilly Circus/Leicester Square,** party central with the bulk of London's theaters; lots of crowded pubs, bars, and commercial clubs; the biggest movie houses; and Piccadilly Circus, a bustling square of traffic and tacky neon.

Southwest of Piccadilly Circus are the posh old residential streets of **St. James** (picture a gentlemen's club and expand it several blocks in each direction). Northwest of this (west of Soho) neighborhood is fashionable and tony **Mayfair,** which is full of pricey hotels. **Westminster,** running along the western bank of the Thames' north-south stretch, is the heart and soul of political Britain, home to Parliament and the Royal Family's Buckingham Palace. Westminster flows into **Victoria** to the south. Centered upon Victoria train station, this neighborhood remains genteel and residential, not rundown like station neighborhoods in most cities. Northwest of Victoria and west of Westminster is **Belgravia,** an old aristocratic zone full of stylish townhouses that's just beyond the West End.

Dollars & Sense

If you'll be exploring London to any extent, one of your most useful purchases will be **London A to Z,** one of the world's greatest street-by-street maps. It's the only publication that lists every tiny alley and dead-end lane of the maze that is London's infrastructure. You can buy one at any bookstore and most newsstands.

Culture Shock

Know your lingo: In London, the subway system is called the Underground, or Tube for short. Don't call it the subway; over here, a Subway sign indicates a pedestrian tunnel that goes under a busy street. In other words, you can take the subway to get to the Tube, but you can't take a ride on the subway. Got it?

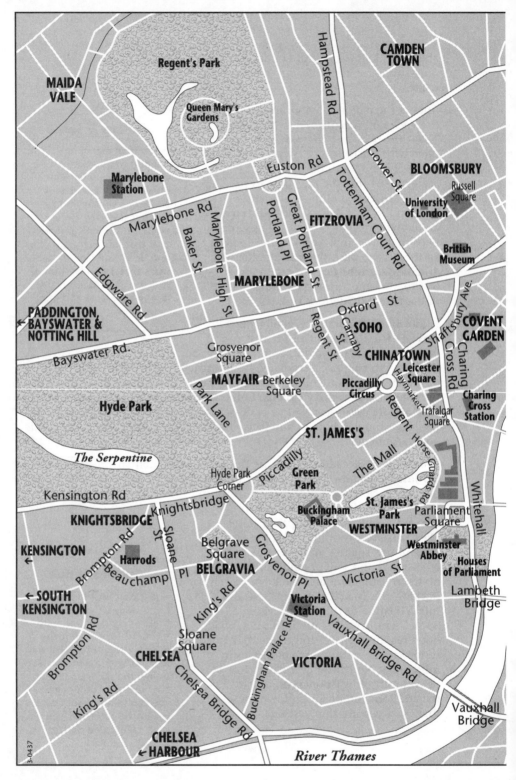

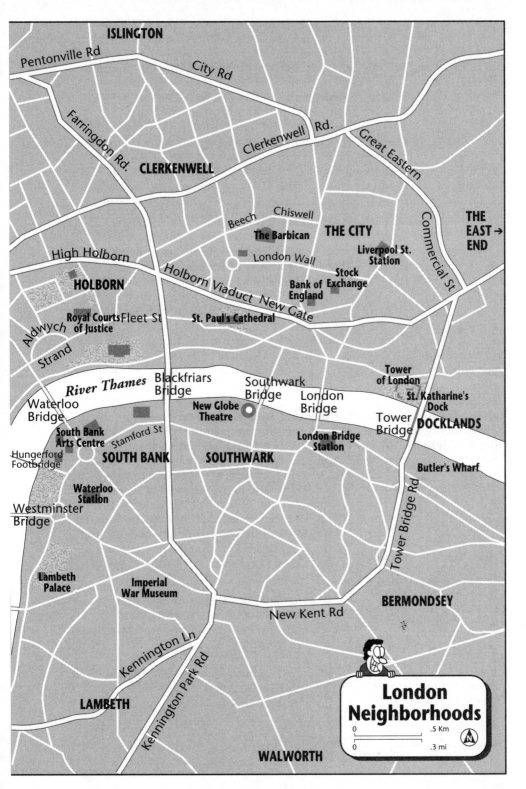

ISLINGTON

Pentonville Rd

City Rd

Farringdon Rd.

Clerkenwell Rd.

Great Eastern

CLERKENWELL

THE
EAST →
END

Beech   Chiswell

The Barbican

THE CITY

High Holborn

London Wall

Liverpool St.
Station

Commercial St

Holborn Viaduct

Stock
Exchange

HOLBORN

New Gate

Bank of
England

Royal Courts Fleet St
of Justice

St. Paul's Cathedral

Aldwych

Strand

River Thames

Blackfriars
Bridge

Southwark
Bridge

London
Bridge

Tower
of London

St. Katharine's
Dock

Waterloo
Bridge

New Globe
Theatre

Tower
Bridge

DOCKLANDS

South Bank
Arts Centre

Stamford St

London Bridge
Station

Hungerford
Footbridge

SOUTH BANK

SOUTHWARK

Butler's Wharf

Westminster
Bridge

Waterloo
Station

Tower Bridge Rd

Lambeth
Palace

Imperial
War Museum

BERMONDSEY

New Kent Rd

Kennington Ln

LAMBETH

Kennington Park Rd

London
Neighborhoods

0   .5 Km

0   .3 mi

WALWORTH

West of the West End, the neighborhoods are divided north-south by enormous **Hyde Park.** South of it stretch the uniformly fashionable residential zones of **Knightsbridge, Kensington,** and **South Kensington,** which are also home to London's grandest shopping streets (Harrod's is in Knightsbridge). South of Belgravia and South Kensington is the artists' and writers' quarter of **Chelsea,** which manages to keep hip with the changing times (it introduced miniskirts in the 1960s and punk in the 1970s). North of Hyde Park are the more middle-income residential neighborhoods of **Paddington, Bayswater,** and **Notting Hill,** popular among budget travelers for their plethora of B&Bs and inexpensive hotels. Nearby **Notting Hill Gate** is similar and is becoming a rather hip fashion and dining center in its own right.

On a first-time or quick visit, you probably won't venture too far beyond this huge area of central London, but here are a few of the outlying districts. East of The City you'll run into the revitalized **Docklands,** home to many businesses and grand upscale housing developments of the 1980s. Also out this end of the city is the **East End,** ever an economically depressed area—part of the real London of the working class and many recent immigrants. On the other side of the Thames are **Southbank** and, just across the river from The City, **Southwark.** Both are arts and cultural centers, especially the former, which contains London's premiere performance halls as well as the National Theatre.

Planes, Trains, & the Tube: Getting Into & Around Town

Trains coming from Dover (where ferries from the continent land) arrive at either **Victoria Station** or **Charing Cross Station,** both in the center of town (10½ hours total travel time from Paris via the ferry route). The direct Eurostar trains that arrive from Paris (a trip of 2 to 2½ hours) and Brussels (a trip of 2 hours, 10 minutes) via the Channel Tunnel pull into **Waterloo Station** in Southbank. If you're coming from Edinburgh, you'll arrive at **King's Cross Station** in the northern part of London.

Transatlantic **flights** usually land at **Heathrow Airport,** a 50-minute underground ride west of the city center (the Picadilly Line is the one that runs out to the airport). A soon-to-be inaugurated service called **Heathrow Express/Fastlink** will provide a high-speed rail link from Heathrow Airport to Paddington Station. Details were not finalized as this book went to press, but the trip into town is expected to take 15 minutes, and cost £5 ($7.50).

Bet You Didn't Know

Britain is actively trying to make over its image into something more progressive. Sadly for traditionalists, this transformation includes doing away with such things as double-decker buses, the bobbies' tall helmets, and those great bright-red telephone booths that sci-fi hero Dr. Who used to travel through time.

If your charter flight or plane from the continent lands at **Gatwick Airport,** which is 25 miles south of London, or **London Stansted Airport,** which is 50 miles northeast of town, you'll have to take one of the express trains into town. Some flights from Britain and northern Europe land at **London City Airport,** at the east end of town, where shuttle buses take you to various nearby Tube stops.

London is so big you really can't cover it on foot. The city has an extensive network of those famous red double-decker **buses,** which are slowly disappearing in favor of new buses that look more modern. But the fastest and most popular way to zip around town is the **underground (subway),** known affectionately as the **Tube.** You can use the Tube and its many transfer stations to tunnel your way just about anywhere in London—but I suggest taking the bus a few times (not during rush hour) because you get a much better feel for the city layout when you travel above ground. Bus stop signs with a red slashed circle on white are compulsory stops; if the slashed circle is white on red, it's a request stop, and you have to wave down the bus. The "Travelling in London" pamphlet available at all Tube stops and tourist centers outlines the major bus routes, and it includes a copy of the ubiquitous Tube map, which is helpfully tacked on to just about any brochure, sign, or other tourist-related thing in London (including T-shirts).

Dollars & Sense

The traveler's ticket to London's buses, Tube, and light rail systems is the **Travelcard** (valid only after 9:30am, and not on night buses or airport lines). You'll need a passport-sized photo—there are instant-photo booths in most underground stations near the ticket offices where you buy the pass. **One-day Travelcards** are valid in zones 1 and 2 and cost £3.20 ($5.30) for adults and £1.70 ($1.65) for kids 5–15. **Weekly Travelcards** for zone 1 cost £13 ($21.65) for adults and £4.80 ($8) for kids; for zones 1 and 2, the cost is £15.70 ($26.15) for adults and £5.30 ($8.80) for kids. **Zone 1** covers all of central London—plenty for the average visit; zone 2 is the next concentric ring out, getting in most of the outlying attractions. For **longer trips or single tickets,** there are machines in Tube stations. Families should ask about the Family Travelcard. If you need to travel before 9:30am, either buy a single ticket or look into the one-day, unlimited-time LT Card.

Your other travel option is to hail one of those giant black taxi cabs that prowl the London streets like overweight panthers. The highly trained, experienced drivers are veritable fonts of London information. They know every tiny alley of this city and most of its history—in fact, many people use them as auxiliary city guides, pumping them for information as they ride. Prices, however, are far from a bargain (see the "Fast Facts" entry on Taxis).

Fast Facts: London

American Express   The main American Express office, 6 Haymarket, SW1 Y4BS (☎ 0171/930-4411), near Piccadilly Circus, is open Monday to Friday 9am to 5:30pm and Saturday 9am to 4pm. The currency exchange desk is open Monday to Saturday 9am to 5:30pm and Sunday 10am to 4pm.

Doctors/hospitals   Ask the concierge if your hotel keeps a doctor on call. Otherwise, try **Doctor's Call** (☎ 0700/037-2255). **Medical Express** (☎ 0171/499-1991) at 117A Harley St., W1, is a privately run clinic. It's open Monday to Friday 9am to 6pm and Saturday 9:30am to 2:30pm. For 24-hour emergency care, go to the **Royal Free Hospital,** Pond Street, NW3 (☎ 0171/794-0500) or the **University College Hospital,** Grafton Way, WC1 (☎ 0171/387-9300).

Embassy   The U.S. Embassy (☎ 0171/499-9000) is located at 24 Gros-venor Sq., W1A 1AE. For passport and visa information, contact the **US Passport & Citizenship Unit,** 55-56 Upper Brook St., W1 (☎ 0171/499-9000, extension 2563 or 2564).

Emergency   Dial ☎ 999 to call the police, report a fire, or call an ambulance.

Pharmacies   Try **Bliss the Chemist,** 5 Marble Arch, W1 (☎ 0171/723-6116), open daily 9am to midnight, or **Boots,** 75 Queensway, W2 (☎ 0171/229-1183), open Monday to Saturday 9am to 10pm and Sunday noon to 5pm. Police stations keep a list of chemists (pharmacies) open late hours. Just dial ☎ 0 and ask for the local police.

Safety   London is friendly to its visitors, and in heavily touristed areas, you may feel safer than you do in your own hometown. Areas where you may be more uneasy—Tottenham, South London, and Hackney—lie far beyond central London. Still, it is a big city, so it's wise to take general precautions to prevent being targeted by thieves or pickpockets. I'd be a little wary in Soho as well; although it's not nearly as dicey as it was in the 1970s and 1980s, it still has pockets of seediness.

Taxis   London's Tube and buses should get you around town nicely, but for longer distances, travel at night, or just the novelty of riding in one of those fabled London cabs, you may opt for a taxi instead. Hail a taxi on the street or find one at a taxi *rank* (stand). Keep in mind that you'll pay for your fun: London's taxi fares are steep. The initial charge for a lone passenger is £1.40 ($2.30), then 20p (30¢) for every third of a mile thereafter. Additional passengers raise the fare 40p (25¢) each, and luggage adds 10p (15¢) per piece to the final fare. Expect to pay surcharges for travel after 8pm, on the weekend, and on holidays. To call for a taxi, dial ☎ 0171/272-0272 or 0171/253-5000, but note that *the meter begins running when the driver picks up the call.*

Minicabs are meterless taxis that operate out of offices rather than cruise for fares. These taxis are more useful at night when the Tube stops running and few regular taxis are available. Negotiate the fare before you get in. You'll find minicab stands in popular spots like Leicester Square; or try Abbey Cars

(☎ **0171/727-2637**) in west London; Greater London Hire (☎ **0181/ 340-2450**) in north London; London Cabs Ltd. (☎ **0181/778-3000**) in east London; or Newname Minicars (☎ **0181/472-0400**) in south London.

Telephone   You'll see three kinds of pay phones in London: one that accepts only coins; the Cardphone, which takes only Phonecards; and one that accepts both Phonecards and credit cards. The minimum charge for a local call is 10p (15¢) for the first two minutes. Stick to small coins at coin-operated phones because they don't make change. Phonecards are sold at newsstands and post offices for £2 ($3.30), £4 ($6.65), £10 ($16.65), or £20 ($33.30). Credit card pay phones accept the usual credit cards—Visa, MasterCard, American Express—and hang around in packs at the airports and train stations.

The country code for the United Kingdom is **44**. London has two city codes: **0171** and **0181**, but if you're calling from outside the UK, drop the initial zero. To call London from the United States, dial **011-44-171** or 011-44-181, and then the local number. To call the United States direct from London, dial **001** followed by the area code and phone number. To charge a call to your calling card, or make a collect call home, dial **AT&T** (☎ **0800/890-011**), **MCI** (☎ **0800/890-222**), or **Sprint** (☎ **0800/890-877** or 0500/890-877).

Transit Info   Call ☎ **0171/922-8844**.

London's Hotel Scene (or, The Changing of the Sheets)

People complain about Paris, but in my book London is by far the more expensive town, especially when it comes to hotels. Usually your best bet on a budget here is to find a B&B, pension, or small hotel offering low rates. You won't sleep in style, but you'll be able to afford the rest of your trip.

Time-Savers

The two best-connected hotel room booking services are the **Victoria Station Hotel Reservation Service** (☎ **0171/828-4646**) in Victoria train station and the **Hotel Booking Service** (☎ **0171/932-2020**) of the official tourist board, also in the station. Both charge a £5 ($8.30) booking fee. Specializing in **B&Bs** is **Uptown Reservations** (☎ **0171/351-3445**) at 50 Christchurch Rd., or before you leave, try contacting **Bed & Breakfast** (☎ **800/367-4668** in the United States).

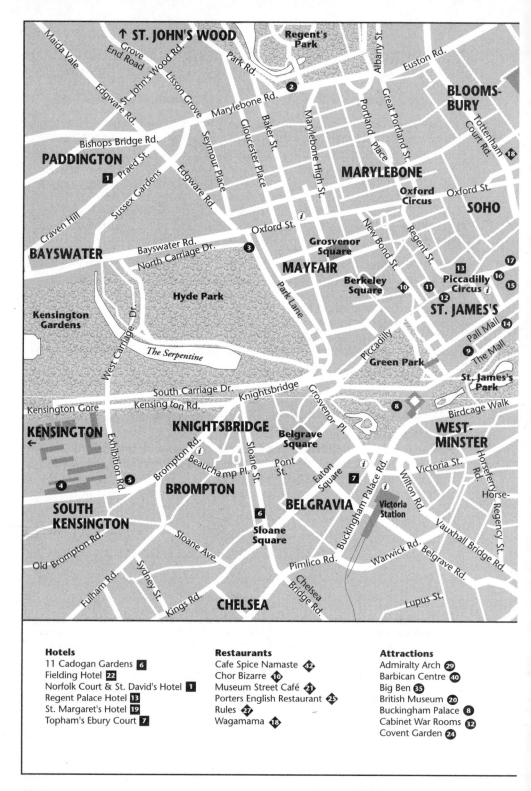

Hotels
11 Cadogan Gardens **6**
Fielding Hotel **22**
Norfolk Court & St. David's Hotel **1**
Regent Palace Hotel **13**
St. Margaret's Hotel **19**
Topham's Ebury Court **7**

Restaurants
Cafe Spice Namaste **42**
Chor Bizarre **10**
Museum Street Café **21**
Porters English Restaurant **25**
Rules **27**
Wagamama **18**

Attractions
Admiralty Arch **29**
Barbican Centre **40**
Big Ben **35**
British Museum **20**
Buckingham Palace **8**
Cabinet War Rooms **32**
Covent Garden **24**

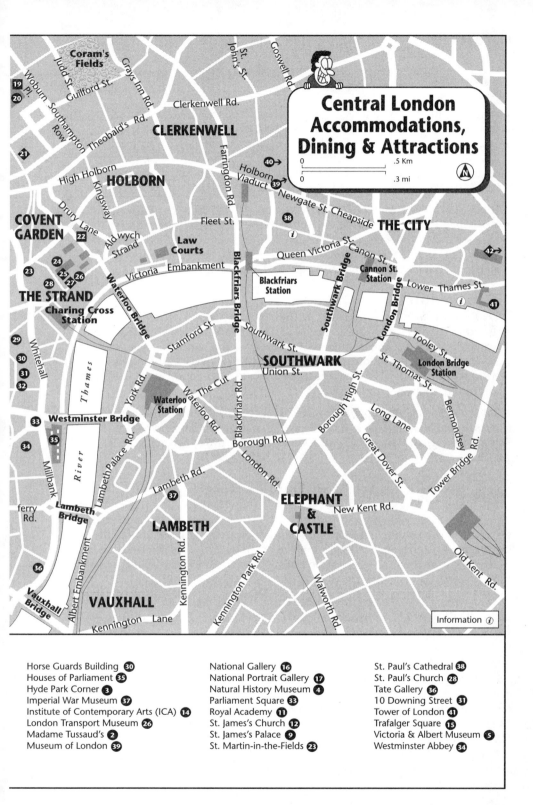

Central London Accommodations, Dining & Attractions

0 ___ .5 Km
0 ___ .3 mi

Map labels:

Coram's Fields, Judd St., Grays Inn Rd., St. John's St., Goswell Rd., Woburn Pl., Guilford St., Southampton Row, Clerkenwell Rd., CLERKENWELL, THE CITY, HOLBORN, High Holborn, Theobald's Rd., Farringdon Rd., Holborn Viaduct, Newgate St., Cheapside, Fleet St., Queen Victoria St., Canon St., Cannon St. Station, Lower Thames St., COVENT GARDEN, Drury Lane, Kingsway, Aldwych, Strand, Law Courts, Victoria Embankment, Blackfriars Bridge, Blackfriars Station, Southwark Bridge, London Bridge, THE STRAND, Waterloo Bridge, Charing Cross Station, Stamford St., Southwark St., SOUTHWARK, Union St., Tooley St., London Bridge Station, St. Thomas St., Whitehall, Thames, York Rd., Waterloo Station, The Cut, Waterloo Rd., Blackfriars Rd., Borough High St., Long Lane, Bermondsey Rd., Westminster Bridge, Borough Rd., Great Dover St., River, Lambeth Palace Rd., Lambeth Rd., London Rd., ELEPHANT & CASTLE, New Kent Rd., Tower Bridge Rd., Millbank, Lambeth Bridge, ferry Rd., LAMBETH, Kennington Rd., Kennington Park Rd., Old Kent Rd., Albert Embankment, VAUXHALL, Vauxhall Bridge, Kennington Lane, Walworth Rd.

Information ⓘ

Horse Guards Building 30	National Gallery 16	St. Paul's Cathedral 38
Houses of Parliament 35	National Portrait Gallery 17	St. Paul's Church 28
Hyde Park Corner 3	Natural History Museum 4	Tate Gallery 36
Imperial War Museum 37	Parliament Square 33	10 Downing Street 31
Institute of Contemporary Arts (ICA) 14	Royal Academy 11	Tower of London 41
London Transport Museum 26	St. James's Church 12	Trafalger Square 15
Madame Tussaud's 2	St. James's Palace 9	Victoria & Albert Museum 5
Museum of London 39	St. Martin-in-the-Fields 23	Westminster Abbey 34

11 Cadogan Gardens
$$$$$. Chelsea.

This refined hotel of yesteryear in a posh neighborhood provides a cozy private home feel and discreet comfort in a 19th-century building. Victorian antiques and artwork are placed throughout the hotel, which also has a restaurant and a small gym. Rooms overlooking the private garden are the most sought after. Finding this place is tricky—there are four Cadogan Gardens streets that all intersect. See the following directions.

11 Cadogan Gardens. ☎ **0171/730-7000.** *Fax: 0171/730-5217.* **Tube:** *Sloane Square; from the Tube stop, walk the long way across the square, and turn right (north) out the far corner onto Pavilion Rd.; take an immediate left onto Cadogan Gardens, then your first right onto another Cadogan Gardens. The unheralded hotel is on the right.* **Rates:** *From £161 ($268.65) double. AE, DC, MC, V.*

Fielding Hotel
$$$. Covent Garden.

This old-fashioned hotel sports tiny, worn, but comfy rooms and traditional charms. It's in one of the best parts of town, on a gas lamp-lit street across from the Royal Opera House and near the bustling Covent Garden piazza. Few inns in this central, restaurant-filled area are such good values, and none is as quirkily friendly and familiar.

4 Broad Ct., Bow St. ☎ **0171/836-8305.** *Fax: 0171/497-0064.* **Tube:** *Covent Garden, and then walk 1 block down James St., turning left onto Floral St. Cross Bow St., and opposite Floral is Broad Ct.* **Rates:** *£88–£98 ($146.60–$163.27). AE, DC, MC, V.*

Norfolk Court & St. David's Hotel
$. Paddington.

Things aren't fancy at this comfortable old B&B (only six rooms have showers), but it's been doing something right to draw a constant stream of clients since the 19th century. The furniture is mismatched, but the atmosphere is welcoming and the price great at one of the best B&Bs in a neighborhood full of them.

16-20 Norfolk Sq. ☎ **0171/723-4963.** *Fax: 0171/723-3856.* **Tube:** *Paddington, then exit onto Praed St.; catercorner to Paddington Station is Norfolk Sq.* **Rates:** *£44–£54 ($73.30–$90) double. MC, V.*

Regent Palace Hotel
$$$. Piccadilly Circus.

This massive (908 rooms), institutional hotel operates like a small city, with restaurants, bars, boutiques, and an after-hours pub. Rooms are as boring as can be, but the location is fantastic. First impressions lean toward a dorm or hostel, but the clientele is a mix of students, businesspeople, families looking for value, and seniors in town for two weeks of theater. Longer stays and rooms without baths come with lower rates.

Piccadilly Circus (between Glasshouse and Sherwood sts.); take exit 1 from the tube station, and the hotel is opposite where you emerge. ☎ ***0171/734-0716*** *or 0171/734-7000.* ***Fax:*** *0171/734-6435.* ***Tube:*** *Piccadilly Circus.* ***Rates:*** *£78–£103 ($130–$171.65). AE, DC, MC, V.*

St. Margaret's Hotel
$$. Bloomsbury.
Cleanliness and comfort are the watchwords at this old hotel, the best on a quiet street lined with cheap accommodations. The rooms are carpeted and have worn but cared-for furniture; those on the back side of the hotel are nicest. Service is friendly, and the breakfast is large. Best of all, the British Museum is right around the corner.

26 Bedford Place. ☎ ***0171/636-4277.*** ***Fax:*** *0171/323-3066.* ***Tube:*** *Holborn; walk 2 blocks north on Southampton Row, turn left on Great Russell St., go 1 block, and turn right on Bedford Place.* ***Rates:*** *£70 ($116.62) with bath, £52.50–£54.50 ($87.50–$90.80) without bath. No credit cards.*

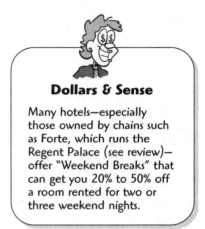

Dollars & Sense

Many hotels—especially those owned by chains such as Forte, which runs the Regent Palace (see review)—offer "Weekend Breaks" that can get you 20% to 50% off a room rented for two or three weekend nights.

Topham's Ebury Court
$$$$. Belgravia.
In its third generation of family management, the Ebury Court remains an excellent choice, near the station but in a fine residential area (Margaret Thatcher is a neighbor). The smaller rooms appear cozy rather than cramped; the owner is something of an interior decorator and has outfitted the rooms as an English country inn. It's all very Laura Ashley without crossing the line into frou-frou. Rates vary with plumbing and room size.

28 Ebury St. ☎ ***0171/730-8147.*** ***Fax:*** *0171/823-5966.* ***Tube:*** *Victoria; from Victoria Station walk 1 block west on Eccleston St. (which dead-ends at the station) and turn right on Ebury St.* ***Rates:*** *£115–£135 ($191.59–$225) double. AE, DC, MC, V.*

No, Really, the Food's Edible Now: London's Restaurant Scene
Part of an old joke about European stereotypes goes that in heaven the English are police, but in hell they're the cooks. Although you can still get pub grub lousy enough to curl your toenails, British cuisine has improved remarkably over the past decade. Not only have they started paying attention to the quality of old-fashioned dishes, but London's top chefs have also adopted and adapted numerous culinary techniques and ingredients from around the world and mixed them with a dash of time-honored tradition to

create **Modern British cuisine.** Add to this London's variety of ethnic restaurants—locals go out for **Indian** the way we go out for Chinese—and you won't ever have to touch steak and kidney pie unless you want to.

When you're not dining high on modern innovations, Britain still has a formidable array of time-tested dishes for you to try. The **ploughman's lunch** is a hunk of bread, a chunk of cheese, butter, pickle (relish), and chutney. The two most familiar of the many meat pies you'll run into are **Cornish pasty** (beef, potatoes, onions, and carrots baked in a pastry shell) and **shepherd's pie** (lamb and onions stewed under a lid of mashed potatoes—if they use beef, it's called **cottage pie**). The English are masters of **roast beef,** which is often served with **Yorkshire pudding** (a popover-like concoction cooked under the meat joint so the juices drip into it).

Then there are the truly oddly named British dishes, such as **bangers and mash** (sausages, of which the best are Cumberland, and mashed potatoes), **bubble-and-squeak** (which sounds like boiled mice but is actually fried cabbage and potatoes), or **toad in the hole,** what we call pigs-in-a-blanket (OK, so our name isn't much better). The Brits also do good game dishes, especially **pheasant** and **grouse.** Fans of **fresh fish** will enjoy London's cod, whitefish, haddock, herrings, and the mighty Dover sole. **Fish 'n' chips** (fried fish with french fries) is a greasy delight, and **oysters** from Colchester can also be fabulous. Intrepid travelers will try the Londoner's **kippers** (pickled herring) for breakfast.

Traditional **English breakfasts**—scarce in these days of the continental croissant-and-coffee—are tasty, but massive on the cholesterol counter: ham and/or sausage, fried eggs, and fried tomatoes alongside toast or scones with butter and jam. Even better is the **tea** ritual, detailed under "Other Fun Stuff to Do," later in the chapter.

If the Brits excel at anything edible, it's their **cheeses** and desserts. Of the former, blue-veined **Stilton** is the king, best enjoyed with a glass of port wine. Lots of regional delicacies pop up on the cheese board as well, one of the most famous being **cheddar.** If you prefer your meal to end with something sweet, English **puddings** are some of the best desserts around. **Trifle** is sponge cake soaked with brandy, smothered in fruit or jam, and topped with custard. Light cream whipped with fresh fruit is called a **fool,** and a **treacle pudding** is a steamed trifle without the sherry and with syrup instead of fruit.

Wash down your meal with a **pint of bitter**—but make sure it's a proper English ale and not a wimpy import or lager. A few of the most widely available are listed under the pub section of "Other Fun Stuff to Do."

Cafe Spice Namaste
$$$. The City. INDIAN/EASTERN.
The setting is boring—a huge space in a characterless, converted Victorian hall—but the Indian cuisine is some of the best in London. The owner, who

hails from the Indian island of Goa, has added specialties from his own land (try the three-alarm *sorpotel* pork), but you'll also taste Thai, Malay, Sri Lankan, and Singaporian influences. The daily specials are usually right on the mark, or try the complex chicken curry dish of *galinha xacutti*.

16 Prescott St. (between Mansell St. and Leman St.). ☎ *0171/488-9242. Reservations recommended.* **Tube:** *Tower Hill or Aldgate.* **Main courses:** *£5.50–£10.50 ($9.15–$17.50). AE, DC, MC, V.* **Open:** *Lunch Mon–Fri, dinner Mon–Sat.*

Chor Bizarre
$$$$. Mayfair. INDIAN.
The atmosphere is as pan-Indian as the cuisine at this London branch of an acclaimed New Delhi restaurant. The piecemeal decor is amalgamated from items picked up at Indian bazaars, and an eclectic menu represents the best of home-cooking from across the subcontinent. The best way to sample much of this bounty is to order a *maharaja thali,* which is many small bowls of house specialties.

16 Albemarle St. (between Piccadilly and Grafton St.). ☎ *0171/629-9802. Reservations highly recommended.* **Tube:** *Green Park or Piccadilly Circus; from Green Park, left onto Picadilly, then third on your left.* **Main courses:** *£4–£14 ($6.65–$23.30); set menus £19–£31 ($31.65–$51.65) among which is a four-course, pre-theater dinner that includes car ride to the theater for £21 ($35); kids eat free Sat lunch. AE, DC, MC, V.* **Open:** *Lunch, tea, and dinner Mon–Sat.*

Museum Street Café
$$. Bloomsbury. BRITISH.
This one-time kickabout caff (that's Brit for greasy spoon) is now a laid-back and popular restaurant with great prices and an even better cuisine. The chef puts a creative spin on British standards, using fresh ingredients and imagination. Anything charbroiled will be good; try the corn-fed chicken with pesto. There's no better place to decompress after a morning in the British Museum.

47 Museum St. (about 200 steps from the gates to the British Museum). ☎ *0171/ 405-3211. Reservations required.* **Tube:** *Tottenham Court Road, then walk up New Oxford Street and turn left onto Museum Street.* **Meals:** *Set price menus, £13–£16 ($21.65–$26.65) at lunch, £18–£22 ($30–$36.65) at dinner. AE, MC, V.* **Open:** *Lunch and dinner Mon–Fri.*

Time-Savers

Several of London's museums and sights have extremely good cafeterias or restaurants on the premises, so you don't have to leave them at lunchtime. You might want to plan on a meal in the Tate, National Gallery, or St. Martin-in-the-Fields church (where you get to eat in the crypt atop tomb slabs).

Kids **Porters English Restaurant**
$$$. Covent Garden. BRITISH.

London had so many pricey traditional restaurants, the Earl of Bradford decided there was room for reasonably priced, well-prepared British cuisine. He gambled right, and Porters became popular with people looking for the tastes they remember from boarding school and old-fashioned family dinners. The meat pies and puddings are particularly good; try the unusually flavored lamb and apricot pie with mint and Lady Bradford's famous banana and ginger steamed pudding.

17 Henrietta St. (half a block off the Covent Garden square). ☎ *0171/836-6466. Reservations highly recommended.* **Tube:** *Covent Garden.* **Main courses:** *£7.95–£10.95 ($13.25–$18.25); fixed-price menu £16.95 ($28.25) each for two people only. AE, DC, MC, V.* **Open:** *Lunch and dinner daily.*

Quick Bites

If you need an on-the-run snack, or if you're counting pennies and can't afford a fancy-schmancy sit-down meal, consider these snappy, affordable options. England's most famed street food is, of course, **fish 'n' chips,** which can range from flaky cod lightly fried with meaty chips (french fries) to unidentifiable, chewy fish-like substance fried with the scales still on until it's dripping with oil (let's not get into some of the horrible chips). To make sure you get quality, patronize **Johnnies Fish Bar** (☎ 0171/352-3876) at 494 King's Rd. or **North Sea Fish Bar** (☎ 0171/387-5892) at 7 Leigh St.—not the quickest of bites, but definitely the tastiest in its medium.

Pub grub takes a bit longer, but it's more atmospheric. Pub grub is no longer universally awful, but don't assume that it must be edible just because they serve it. The best can be had at fashionable **The Cow** (☎ 0171/221-0021) at 89 Westbourne Park Rd., posh **The Enterprise** (☎ 0171/584-3148) at 35 Walton St., and comfortably offbeat **Prince Bonaparte** (☎ 0171/229-5912) at 80 Chepstow Rd.

The most discriminating diners shop for their **picnic** delicacies in the gourmet food departments of **Harrods** at 87–135 Brompton Rd. or **Fortnum and Mason** at 181 Piccadilly. **Marks & Spencer,** at 458 Oxford St., has a cheaper grocery department for less fancy staples.

Rules
$$$$$. Covent Garden. BRITISH.

In a clubby, 19th-century setting, the oldest restaurant in London (1798) serves up game from its own preserve and some of the most staunchly British food in town, beloved of everyone from Dickens to Graham Greene.

You can't go wrong with the venison or wild fowl, or try the sea trout, mussels, or a delicious pie—just make sure you cap the meal off with one of Rules' famous puddings. This truly is a special place, well worth a splurge.

35 Maiden Lane (1 block off the Strand). ☎ *0171/836-5314. Reservations required.* **Tube:** *Charing Cross or Covent Garden.* **Main courses:** *£13.95– £15.95 ($23.25–$26.60); pre- and post-theater set-price dinner Mon–Fri £15.95 ($26.60); set-price lunch Sat–Sun £15.95 ($26.60). AE, DC, MC, V.* **Open:** *Lunch and dinner daily. Closed Dec 24–27.*

Wagamama
$. Bloomsbury. JAPANESE NOODLE HOUSE.

Still riding high on the trend charts, this popular basement noodle house offers great ramen, other Asian soups, and fried rice dishes in a minimalist decor and noisy, common-table seating. It's good for a break from the British Museum, but at lunchtime the crowd can get intense.

4 Streatham St. (off Coptic St., around the corner from the British Museum). ☎ *0171/323-9223. Reservations not accepted.* **Tube:** *Tottenham Court Road.* **Main courses:** *£3.80–£6.80 ($6.30–$11.30). No credit cards.* **Open:** *Lunch and dinner daily.*

Ready, Set, Go! Exploring London

You can get an excellent overview of the city's layout, and see many of the architectural sights at a snappy pace, from the top of a double-decker bus on **The Original London Sightseeing Tour** (☎ **0171/877-1722**). You'll find flyers all over the place outlining the different tours offered by this hop-on/hop-off bus with running live commentary. At £10 ($16.65)— £9 ($15) if you buy ahead at the tourist office—the "Original Tour" is the best all-around, spinning a 90-minute loop of the top sights with 6 minutes (15 in winter) between buses. Tickets are good all day—if bought after 2pm, all the next day as well.

Of the many walking tour outfits in this city, by far the biggest and best is **London Walks** (☎ **0171/624-3978**). I can think of no better London investment for fun, education, and entertainment. Just £4.50 ($7.50)—£1 off for seniors or students—buys you two hours with an expert guide on a variety of thematic walks: neighborhood jaunts, museums, pub crawls, or walks in the footsteps of Shakespeare, Churchill, Christopher Wren, or Jack the Ripper. On my last visit, I did eight of them (buy four at a time for a discount).

London Sights Not to Miss

The British Museum

The Brits have quite possibly the world's greatest archaeological collection, and even several days are not enough to explore every nook and historical cranny of this fascinating museum. My advice: Spend a couple of half-days here. Its treasures span history as well as the globe, from the Rosetta Stone—

185

Bet You Didn't Know

Talk about literary history! Documents at the British Museum truly span the ages, from a very yellowed copy of the *Magna Carta* (ca. 1215), to original Shakespeare folios, to manuscripts by the Brontës, to the first editions of children's classics, such as *Winnie the Pooh*. You'll also spy scribbled sheet music from those latter-day bards, Paul McCartney and John Lennon.

the key that cracked the code of Egyptian hieroglyphics—to the towering winged bull/men that guarded the gates to Assyrian palaces in 880 B.C. You can also see the 2,000-year-old Lindow Man, who was ritually strangled and drowned in a peat bog that preserved his shriveled body, and the famous Elgin Marbles, the grandest of the carved reliefs that once decorated Athens' Parthenon. Kids seem fascinated by room after room of Royal Egyptian mummies. You may have to pardon the dust for the next year or two, as the museum turns the central courtyard into a high-tech visitor's center and exhibition space. Guided tours of the museum's highlights costs £6 ($10) per person, but specialized "Eye Openers" tours of themed parts of the collections are free.

Great Russell St. (a block off of Oxford St.). ☎ *0171/636-1555. Tube: Holborn, Tottenham Court Road, or Russell Square; from Tottenham Court Rd., take exit 3 out of the station, then take the first right outside of the station.* **Admission:** *Free, but £2 ($3.30) donation greatly appreciated.* **Open:** *Mon–Sat 10am–5pm, Sun 2:30–6pm. Closed Dec. 24, 25, 26.*

The National Gallery

A huge neoclassical edifice houses some of the finest works the 13th to 20th centuries have to offer (start in the modern Sainsbury wing, way off to the left of the main entrance). The works include da Vinci's *Virgin of the Rocks,* one-third of Uccello's *Battle of San Romano,* Botticelli's erotic *Venus and Mars,* and Michelangelo's unfinished *Entombment.* El Greco's *Agony in the Garden* hangs alongside works by other Spanish greats Goya and Velázquez. Not to be left out, the northern European schools are represented by the likes of Rubens, Vermeer, and a pair of Rembrandt self-portraits.

The 19th-century Brits hold forth with Gainsborough, Constable, and Turner, but are outdone by impressionist masters Monet, Degas, Renoir, Seurat, and Cézanne. My favorite hidden treasures are da Vinci's huge drawing of the *Virgin and Child,* in an antechamber off the first room, and Hoogstraten's masterful optical illusion *Peepshow*. Free guided tours are available, but to set your own pace, donate £3 ($5) and carry along the informative digital audio tour. The on-site Brasserie restaurant is surprisingly excellent for museum chow.

Trafalgar Square (at the top of the square; you can't miss it). ☎ *0171/747-2885.* **Tube:** *Charing Cross.* **Admission:** *Free.* **Open:** *Mon–Tues and Thurs–Sat 10am–6pm, Wed 10am–8pm, Sun noon–6pm.*

Westminster Abbey

This grandiose early English Gothic abbey is one of Europe's major churches and a who's who of deceased Brits—one of the country's greatest honors is to be buried in this hallowed hall. Every English monarch from William the Conqueror in 1066 to Elizabeth II in 1953 was crowned here (save Edwards V and VIII), and most of them (up to 1760) are buried here as well, some in fantastic tombs. Many of the early 16th-century royal tombs were carved by Pietro Torrigiani, a Florentine who studied sculpture with—and bullied—the young Michelangelo.

The right transept is known as Poet's Corner, with memorials to Britain's greatest writers and creative types, plus the graves of Chaucer, Robert Browning, Rudyard Kipling, D. H. Lawrence, Dylan Thomas, Noel Coward, and Sir Laurence Olivier. Other notables who rest in peace inside the abbey include Sir Isaac Newton, Charles Darwin, Lord Baden-Powell (founder of the Boy Scouts), and composers Benjamin Britten and Handel. You can take an audio tour for an additional £2 ($3.30) or sign up for a £7 ($11.65) guided Super Tour. Although the Royal Chapels are closed on Sundays, you can explore the rest of the abbey unless a service is in progress. For information on times of services, call the Chapter Office (☎ **0171/222-5152**).

Broad Sanctuary. ☎ **0171/222-7110.** *Tube: Westminster or St. James Park; enter through the north transept.* **Admission:** *£5 ($8.25) adults, £3 ($4.95) students and seniors, £2 ($3.30) children 11–16.* **Open:** *Mon–Fri 9am–4:45pm, Sat 9am–2:45pm and sometimes 3:45–5:45pm; closed Sun, but you can attend services.*

Extra! Extra!

Here's something kids *and* adults can enjoy. Westminster's cloisters house a **Brass Rubbing Centre** (☎ **0171/222-2085**), where a few pounds will buy you time with a reproduction brass relief to transfer to black paper using metallic-hued crayons. Prices range from £3 ($5) for a small coat of arms up to over £30 ($50) for a full-sized knightly tomb relief. Rubbing images from tombs became a major pastime in the 19th century, but as zealous rubbers began to wear down the most popular and historic reliefs, replicas took their place. Junior can also relax at the rubbing center in the crypt/cafe of Trafalgar Square's St. Martin-in-the-Fields church—perhaps after a long morning trudging through the National Gallery next door.

Parliament & Big Ben

The debates of British Parliament rage inside this series of neo-Gothic 1840 buildings—a complex most famous for its 336-foot Victoria Tower, which is home to the world's most famous timepiece (still wound by hand) and is often referred to by the name of its chime's biggest bell, the 13.5-ton Big Ben. You can watch debates in either the House of Lords (more formal) or the House of Commons (much more colorful and controversial—you're likely to eavesdrop on shouting matches of often witty personal attacks and learned obscenities). Sessions can last until 11pm.

Bridge St. and Parliament Sq. (the line to get inside forms at the St. Stephen's entrance). ☎ *0171/219-4271; House of Lords 0171/219-3107.* **Tube:** *Westminster; Parliament is right across the street.* **Admission:** *Free.* **Open:** *Mid-Oct–July: House of Lords, Mon–Thurs and sometimes Fri from 3:30pm; House of Commons, Mon, Tues, and Thurs from 3:30pm, Wed and Fri from 9:30am.*

Tower of London

Come early to beat the crowds at London's best medieval attraction, a site of intrigue, murder, and executions galore. The hour-long tours guided by Beefeater guards are highly entertaining and informative (every half hour, 9:35am to 2:30pm, until 3:30pm in summer). They'll take you past the Bloody Tower (where Edward IV's two young sons were murdered and where Sir Walter Raleigh awaited execution for 13 years) through the 900-year-old White Tower (closed in 1998, but housing an armory of swords and plate mail, as well as a gruesome collection of torture instruments), and into Tower Green, where the heads rolled off Thomas Moore, Lady Jane Grey, and two of Henry VIII's wives (Anne Boleyn and Catherine Howard).

All the gore should be enough trade-off for the kids when you have to wait in line to be whisked past the Crown Jewels on a moving sidewalk. As you whoosh by, be sure to drool over the world's largest cut diamond, the 530-carat Star of Africa (set in the Sovereign's Sceptre), and drop your jaw at Queen Victoria's Imperial State Crown (still worn on occasion), studded with over 3,000 jewels. Say hello to the resident ravens, who are rather pampered because legend holds that the Tower will stand so long as they remain.

Tower Hill. ☎ *0171/709-0765.* **Tube:** *Tower Hill; head across Tower Hill Road to the Tower of London.* **Admission:** *£9 ($15) adults, £6.80 ($11.33) students and seniors, £5.90 ($9.83) kids.* **Open:** *Mar–Oct, Mon–Sat 9am–6pm, Sun 10am–6pm; Nov–Feb, Tues–Sat 9am–5pm, Sun–Mon 10am–5pm.*

Victoria & Albert Museum

I know you must be getting tired of all these superlatives, but the V&A is the greatest museum of decorative arts in the world—the definition of "fascinating" for some, of "a lesser circle of Hell" for others. While interior decorating aficionados are enjoying 14th-century embroidery, Chinese vases, Indian furnishings, and historic British candlesticks, less enthusiastic companions can amuse themselves with the largest collection of Renaissance sculpture outside Italy (featuring Donatello, Rossellino, and Bernini) and the "Fakes and Forgeries" gallery, cataloguing some of the best attempts at knocking off old masters. Chunks of the galleries will be closed on and off for refurbishment until 2001.

Cromwell Rd. ☎ *0171/938-8500.* **Tube:** *South Kensington; the museum is directly across Cromwell Rd. from the station.* **Admission:** *£5 ($8.30) adults, £3 ($5) seniors, free for those under 18.* **Open:** *Mon noon–5:50pm, Tues–Sun 10am–5:50pm.*

Tourist Traps

Something between a still-life amusement ride and a serious gallery of historical likenesses, **Madame Tussaud's** (☎ **0171/935-6861**) is more than just a wax museum, but less than the must-see sight it's made out to be. Madame herself took death masks from the likes of Marie Antoinette (which was easy, what with her head already detached and all), and Ben Franklin (while very much alive) personally sat for her to mold a portrait. Many of the other waxy inhabitants of this gallery are also true to life, and some of the historical dioramas are interesting—although whether they're £8.95 ($14.90) worth of interesting I'll leave up to you to decide. The museum is open daily from 10am to 5:30pm.

Tate Gallery

You never get to see the same Tate twice, because the only way to display the enormous collections is to rotate all the works every year. There are two main collections. The official "national collections of British art" (15th century to today) means room after room filled by Gainsborough, Reynolds, Stubbs, Blake, Constable, and especially Hogarth and J. M. W. Turner. The international modern art collection encompasses everything from the impressionists on—from Rodin's *The Kiss* and dozens by Picasso, Matisse, and van Gogh to Dalí, Giacometti, and Modigliani, and later works by Mark Rothko, Jasper Johns, Henry Moore, Julian Schnabel, Frank Stella, Anselm Keifer, and a host of other contemporary-era artists. The Tate also has an excellent cafe and numerous high-quality special exhibitions. The Tate is in the process of renovating a huge former power station on Bankside to house the modern art collection.

Millbank. ☎ *0171/887-8000.* **Tube:** *Pimlico, then walk to Vauxhall Bridge Road and turn right (walking toward the river). Make a left onto John Islip Street. The Tate Gallery is on your right.* **Admission:** *Free (a charge for special exhibitions).* **Open:** *Daily 10am–5:50pm.*

St. Paul's

Christopher Wren's architectural Renaissance masterpiece stood alone during Nazi air raids, (virtually) untouched by the bombings and fires that ravaged the city. Captured on newsreel footage, the image of the grand church's survival became a rallying point for Britain's pride and indomitable spirit during the darkest days of World War II. This embodiment of stiff British upper lip continues into the crypt, where national heroes such as the Duke of Wellington (who trounced Napoleon at Waterloo) and Lord Nelson are buried, alongside architect Wren, painters Constable and Turner, and adventurer/hero T. E. Lawrence (also known as Lawrence of Arabia). Less patriotic visitors will enjoy climbing the 365-foot-high dome that glitters with mosaics—or rather, they will enjoy the acoustic effects of the whispering gallery halfway up (murmur against the wall and someone 158 feet away on the opposite side can hear you) and the 360° panorama of London from the top (after 426 steps). Half-hour guided tours of the church cost £2.50 ($4.15) and get you into bits normally closed to the public.

St. Paul's Churchyard. ☎ *0171/236-4128.* ***Tube:*** *St. Paul's, then walk down New Change Street toward the large golden dome.* ***Admission:*** *Cathedral, £3.50 ($5.80) adults, £2 ($3.30) kids 6–16; Galleries £3 ($5) adults, £1.50 ($2.50) kids.* ***Open:*** *Mon–Sat 8:30am–4pm (galleries open at 9:30am).*

Tourist Traps

The **changing of the guard at Buckingham Palace** (☎ **0171/839-1377**), the Queen's London home, is one of Europe's most overrated attractions. It's like a bad halftime show by a over-drilled marching band. Come to the palace to make faces at the stoically unresponsive (and long-suffering) Beefeater guards if you must, but skip the 11:30am changing of the guard (daily Apr– Aug 7, then every second day). Contrary to popular belief, most kids won't get a kick out of it either. In August and September, you can take a spin through the palace if the Queen's not in (if the flag's a-waving, she's home).

Bet You Didn't Know

London tends to measure time by events of grand destruction. The Great Fire of 1666 destroyed almost every last inch of the medieval city (thatched roofs catch fire pretty quickly). Luckily, a Renaissance genius named Christopher Wren was on hand to rebuild the city, raising over 50 churches and countless other buildings. With World War II came the Blitz, German planes raining destruction again over the city. The result: the City of London is today an odd architectural mix of medieval houses, Renaissance churches, Victorian public buildings, and postmodern bank headquarters.

Other Fun Stuff to Do

➤ **From Kumquats to Wedgewood: Strolling Portobello Road Market.** London's most popular street market attracts antique collectors, bargain hunters, and lots of tourists (come early to beat the tour buses; it opens at 5:30am, but 9am will do fine). The outdoor fruit and veggie market runs all week, but on Saturdays the market balloons into an enormous flea and antiques mart. About 90 antique shops line the roads around here, so even during the week you can browse their dusty treasures (serious shoppers pick up the *Saturday Antique Market* guide). To get to the market, take the Tube to Notting Hill Gate.

➤ **Embarking on a London Pub Crawl.** Theater aside, the real traditional London evening out starts around 5:30pm at your favorite pub. From there, you move from pub to pub, sampling a quality hand-crafted ale at each, until you are figuratively (if not literally) doing a pub crawl. The city is bursting with these ale houses, but a few of the most historic and atmospheric are the sawdust-floored and rambling **Ye Olde Cheshire Cheese** at Wine Office Court (off Fleet Street, ☎ **0171/ 353-6170**); Dryden's old haunt the **Lamb & Flag** (known as "Bucket of Blood" from its rowdier days) at 33 Rose St. (☎ **0171/497-9504**); the Art Nouveau **Blackfriar** at 174 Queen Victoria St. (☎ **0171/236-5650**); and **The Anchor** at 34 Park St. (the present pub dates from 1757, but there's been a pub at this location for 800 years, with Dickens and Shakespeare as past patrons; ☎ **0171/407-1577**). Make sure you order some true English bitters, hand-pumped and served at room temperature. Try Wadworth, Tetley's, Flowers, and the London-brewed Young's and Fuller's.

Time-Savers

Schedule your drinking well. Keep in mind that most pubs are open Monday through Saturday from 11am to 11pm *only* and on Sunday from noon to 10:30pm.

➤ **Making a Shopping Pilgrimage to Harrods.** Harrods (87-135 Brompton Rd.) is the only store in the world that offers you anything and can back up its word. Legend holds that one prankster jokingly asked if the staff could procure him an elephant—then he got the bill. With 1,200,000 square feet and 300 departments, they carry just about everything—at prices not everyone can afford (on one day in 1986, they pulled in £6 million). The place is posh and snobbish (no shorts, no backpacks), but it's a worthwhile spectacle nonetheless. It started in 1849 as a grocer's, and their fabulous food halls are still the highlight of a visit—500 varieties of cheese, anyone? Call ☎ **0717/730-1234** for information.

➤ **Raising Your Pinky at a Proper High Tea.** Possibly the best British culinary invention was deciding to slip a refined, refreshing extra meal into the day. Between 3pm and 5:30pm, Brits the world over get an uncontrollable urge to sit down and take **tea,** the big steaming pot accompanied by a tiered platter of delicious finger sandwiches, slices of cake, and scones with jam and clotted cream. A full tea serving can run anywhere from £5 ($8.30) to £21 ($34.80). Two of London's classiest (and most expensive) afternoon teas are at the ultra-traditional **Brown's Hotel** (☎ 0171/493-6020) at 29-34 Albemarle St. and the Edwardian charm and splendor of **Goode's** (☎ 0171/409-7242) at 19 South Audley St., Mayfair Square. Less pricey but just as good are the teas at two of London's legendary department stores: **Fortnum & Mason's** street-level **Fountain Restaurant** (☎ 0171/734-8040) at 181 Piccadilly and the inimitable **Harrod's Georgian Restaurant** (☎ 0171/581-1656), up on the fourth floor at 87-135 Brompton Rd.

➤ **Taking in a Play at Shakespeare's Globe Theater.** Shakespeare was once part owner of, as well as performer in and main playwright for, a theater called The Globe at the Thames Bankside. Shakespeare's Globe Theatre is a recently built replica of the O-shaped building, with an open center and projecting stage, so for the first time since the Great Fire of 1666 burned all the old theaters down, you can listen to a Shakespearean-era performance in the sort of playhouse for which it was written. Performances are May to October; tickets for seats run £5 to £20 ($8.30 to $33.30). For only £5 ($8.30), you can be a groundling, standing in the open space right in front of the stage (not so easy on your feet—or your head, when it rains). Call ☎ 0171/928-6406 for more information. Even if you don't stop for a show, make some time during the day to come for a tour (☎ 0171/902-1500).

➤ **Club Hopping.** The city that gave the world punk, new wave, techno, and electronica still has one of the world's most trend-setting and ever-changing clublands. Raves are out (for now), replaced by organized mega-endeavors aimed at attracting thousands of people. The nature of the art means that any place I pen in this book will be out before the guide is, so pick up *Time Out* magazine to find out what's hottest this week. A few perennial faves include the once-fab-now-touristy-but-still-gloriously-tacky-in-neon **Hippodrome** (☎ 0171/437-4311) at Charing Cross Road and Cranbourne Street; the formerly massively hip, and still massively loud, garage and house beats of the **Ministry of Sound** (☎ 0171/378-6528), 103 Gaunt St.; the joyful sacrilege of dancing to house tunes in a converted church at **Limelight** (☎ 0171/434-0572), 136 Shaftesbury Ave.; and the slightly older (20-something on up) crowd kicking it to hip hop, R&B, swing, and soul at **Iceni** (☎ 0171/495-5333), 11 White Horse St.

➤ **Spending the Evening at the Theater.** London rivals New York for the biggest, most diverse theater scene. On any given night you can enjoy a range of entertainment from Homer to Stoppard, experimental one-acts to Andrew Lloyd Webber mega-productions, Shakespeare to

Kabuki. The West End has dozens of playhouses, but there are many other venues as well. The *Time Out* and *What's On* magazines list and often review the week's offerings, and the weekly pamphlet "Official London Theatre Guide" is stacked up virtually everywhere. You are best off going directly to the box office to get your tickets, which could cost anywhere from £15 to £50 ($25 to $83.30). But if you want to try to get last-minute tickets at a discount, the official booth is on Leicester Square. The tickets there are half-price (plus a £2 to £3.30 service fee) and sold on the day of the performance *only*. The seats are usually up in the rafters, and the service doesn't carry the big productions like *Phantom*.

➤ **Setting Your Watch: A Day in Greenwich.** London may set its watches by Big Ben, but Ben looks to the Old Royal Observatory at Greenwich for the time of day. This Thames port and shipping village keeps Greenwich Mean Time, by which the world winds its clock. Come here to straddle the Prime Meridian (0° longitude mark) and have one foot in each hemisphere, board that most famous of clipper ships the *Cutty Sark,* and, at the National Maritime Museum, immerse yourself in the history of the proud navy that won and maintained the British Empire for centuries. The **Tourist Centre (☎ 0181/ 858-6376**), at 46 Greenwich Church St., can give you more information, and it runs walking tours of this pretty town. Until the extension of the Jubilee Tube line (slated to have a stop in Greenwich) is finished, you can take a train here in 15 minutes from Charing Cross Station or the Docklands Light Railway from the Tower Hill Tube stop. But the classic route to Greenwich is an hour's float down the Thames in a ferry from Westminster or Charing Cross Piers.

Get Outta Town:
Day Trips & Excursions

Although there's enough to do in London to keep you busy for weeks, a day trip into the English countryside is an excellent way to escape the bustle of the city. Entire books have been written on this subject, but I've winnowed your choices down to three: Bath, with its ruins and stately 18th-century mansions; Salisbury, with its imposing Gothic cathedral (and the nearby ancient rock formation at Stonehenge); and Oxford, one of the world's first college towns.

Time-Savers

If you don't want the hassle of planning your day trips yourself, **Green Line (☎ 0181/668-7261**) in London offers guided bus trips. Bath, Stonehenge, the Cotswolds, and Avebury are grouped into a very full day; the cost is £24 ($40) for adults and £18 ($30) for those under age 15 or over 60. Oxford is a half-day trip; the cost is £6 ($10) for adults and £2.40 ($4) for those under 15 or over 60.

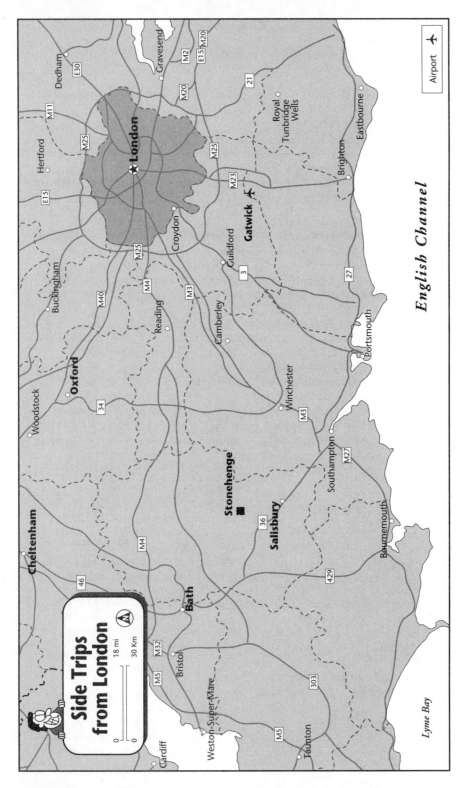

Side Trips from London

18 mi
30 Km

English Channel

Lyme Bay

Cardiff
Weston-Super-Mare
Bristol
Cheltenham
Bath
Taunton
Woodstock
Oxford
Buckingham
Reading
Camberley
Stonehenge
Salisbury
Winchester
Southampton
Bournemouth
Guildford
Gatwick
Croydon
London
Hertford
Dedham
Gravesend
Royal Tunbridge Wells
Brighton
Eastbourne
Portsmouth

M5
M32
M4
46
34
M40
M4
M5
303
429
36
M3
M27
3
27
21
M23
M25
M25
M25
M3
M3
E15
M20
M20
E15
M2
E30
M11

Airport ✈

Bath: Ancient Rome in Georgian Clothing

When Queen Anne relaxed at the natural hot springs here in 1702, she made the village of Bath fashionable again, but she wasn't exactly blazing new territory. The Romans built the first town here in A.D. 75, a small spa village centered around a temple to Sulis Minerva—only those wacky Romans would deify a spa experience, mixing the Latin goddess of knowledge Minerva with Sulis, the local Celtic water goddess. When the Georgians were laying out Britain's most unified cityscape in the 18th century with the help of architects John Wood Sr. and Jr., they also excavated Britain's best-preserved Roman ruins here.

Bath today is a genteel foray into the Georgian world. The highlights include having high tea in the 18th-century Pump Room, perusing Roman remains, and admiring the honey-colored stone architecture that drew in its heyday the likes of Dickens, Thackery, Nelson, Pitt, and Jane Austen. These luminaries enjoyed the fashionable pleasures of a city whose real leader was not a politician but rather the dandy impresario and socialite Beau Nash. Although doable as a day trip from London, Bath's charms really come out after the day-trippers leave, and savvy travelers plan to stay the night and next morning. **Trains to Bath** leave from London's Paddington Station at least every hour; the trip takes about 1½ hours.

Bath's top attractions are clustered together on the main square. A spin through the **Roman Baths Museum** (☎ 01225/477-785) with your digital audio guide in hand will give you an overview of the hot springs from their Celto-Roman inception (the head of Minerva is a highlight) to the 17th/18th-century spa built over them. You can't swim in the classically scenic and steaming main pool anymore, but you can drink a cup of its waters (taste: blech!) upstairs in the elegant **Pump Room** (☎ 01225/444-477). This cafe-restaurant offers one of England's classic afternoon tea services, but you can also get a good lunch here, all to the musical accompaniment of a live trio or solo pianist. Lunch is served from noon to 2:30pm, and tea is served from 2:30 to 4:30pm.

Time-Savers

The **Tourist Information Centre** (☎ 01225/477-761) is in the center of town in the Abbey Chambers, on a square off the lower flank of Bath Abbey. The best introduction to town is to take the **free guided walks** that leave from outside the Pump Room Monday through Friday at 10:30am and 2pm, Saturday at 10:30am, and Sunday at 10:30am and 2:30pm. From May through September there are also walks at 7pm on Tuesday, Friday, and Saturday.

While you're waiting for your seating in the Pump Room, head out to the square to examine **Bath Abbey** (☎ 01225/422-462), the focal point of Bath's medieval incarnation as a religious center. The 16th-century church is renowned both for the fantastic, scalloped fan vaulting of its ceilings and the odd, carved Jacob's ladders flanking the facade, which were inspired by a dream of the bishop who rebuilt this church on the site of an earlier one. Around to the right you can enter the **Heritage Vaults,** whose meager displays trace the history both of the abbey, which in some form dates back to the 6th century, and of the city itself.

Extra! Extra!

Aside from its major attractions, Bath in and of itself is a sight. Visit especially the architectural triumphs of **The Circus** and the **Royal Crescent,** both up on the north end of town. The latter has a highly recommended **Museum of Georgian Life** at no. 1 (☎ **01225/428-126**), where the guides will answer all your questions on life during Bath's glory days.

One of Bath's best restaurants is **The Hole in the Wall** (☎ **01225/425-242;** closed Sunday), 16 George St., where the quiet, elegant rooms are reminiscent of a country inn, and the food is a superb variant of Modern British cuisine. More touristy but better on a budget is the quaint **Sally Lunn's** (☎ **01225/ 461-634**), where the monstrous brioche-like Bath bun was invented in the 17th century. You'll find it at 4 North Parade Passage, reputedly the oldest house in Bath. It's closed Monday at dinner.

If you can swing the £160 to £235 ($266.65 to $391.65) per-double price tag, *the* place to stay in Bath is bang in the middle of one of the city's architectural triumphs at the **Royal Crescent Hotel** (16 Royal Crescent; ☎ in the United States **888/295-4710,** in the United Kingdom toll-free **0800/ 980-0987** or 01225/823-333; fax: 01225/339-401). For what are really reasonable prices, you get to live in that restrained Georgian splendor for a few days with a private boat and hot air balloon at your disposal. On a more modest budget, treat yourself to the hospitality and excellent meals (no dinner Sundays) offered by the Seymours in their B&B **Sommerset House** (35 Bathwick Hill; ☎ **01225/466-451;** fax: 01225/317-188). Rooms cost £20.50 to £32 ($34.15 to $53.30) per person, and dinner is £22 ($36.65).

Gothic Salisbury & Mysterious, Prehistoric Stonehenge
Many visitors hurrying out to see the famous Stonehenge are surprised to find that they stumble across one of Europe's greatest Gothic cathedrals along the way. Salisbury, gateway to South Wiltshire and its prehistoric remains, is a medieval market town that's a deserved attraction in its own right. Although you can come see the cathedral, scurry out to Stonehenge, and be back in London by nightfall, you'll be pushing it. There are about 18 daily **trains** making the 90-minute trip from London's Waterloo station to Salisbury. From here, you can grab a Wilts & Dorset bus for the half-hour leg out to Stonehenge, 12 miles north of the city at the junction of the A303 and A344/A360.

Salisbury's Tourist Information Centre (☎ 01722/334-956) is on Fish Row. The overpowering sight in town is the **Cathedral** (☎ 01722/328-726), whose spire dominates the landscape and whose construction started in 1220 and took a remarkably short 38 years. You can go halfway up the spire for a view of both the church architecture and the surrounding city and then visit the octagonal chapter house for a peek at some medieval manuscripts and one of the four surviving copies of the *Magna Carta*. Don't miss the peaceful cloisters or the brass rubbing center. History buffs will want to stop by the **Salisbury and South Wiltshire Museum** (☎ 01722/332-151) to get information about early humans and the remains of nearby prehistoric sites such as Stonehenge and Old Sarum. The tourist office can fill you in on the other Salisbury sights, mostly visitable 17th- and 18th-century homes, such as the **Mompesson House** (☎ 01722/335-659) on The Close.

Stonehenge (☎ 01980/624-715) itself is, in some ways, a bit of a letdown. Don't get me wrong—it's still one of the most incredible sights in Europe, highly conducive to contemplating the earliest dawn of human endeavor and terribly romantic when the sun sets behind it. But a rope barrier keeps you 50 feet away from the concentric circles of enormous standing stones; past visitors were fond of scratching their names into the venerable rocks.

Bet You Didn't Know

Although Stonehenge is associated in many people's minds with Druids, that Celtic religious sect was merely using an existing site. Stonehenge was a ancient mystery even to the 1st century B.C. Druids. It was begun by an unknown people before 3,000 B.C. and added to up until 1,500 B.C. All we know about Stonehenge is that it is a remarkable feat of engineering—some of the stones came from dozens of miles away—and acts like a huge astronomical calendar, aligned with the summer equinox and still keeping track of the seasons after more than 5,000 years.

Salisbury's finest dining is on the outskirts of town, but the city center does have **Salisbury Haunch of Venison,** 1 Minster St. (☎ 01722/322-024), a 1320 chophouse with tasty roasts and grilled meats. To stay the night, try a £102 to £130 ($170 to $216.65) double at **White Hart** (☎ 01722/327-476,** fax: 01722/412-761), with a Georgian old wing and a motel-like new one. A less pricey room can be had at **The New Inn & Old House** (☎ 01722/327-679), a B&B where the doubles range from £46 to £65 ($72 to $104).

Oxford: University Life 101

The City of Dreaming Spires, robed dons, budding intellectuals, and punting on the Cherwell is today surrounded by sprawling suburbs and clogged with the bustle of both a university town and a small industrial city. But don't let that keep you from making a pilgrimage to the school that has matriculated the likes of John Donne, Samuel Johnson, Christopher Wren, Edward Gibbon, William Penn, Charles Dodgson (Lewis Carroll), Graham Greene, and Percy Bysshe Shelley. Actually, Shelley never graduated; he was kicked out for helping write a pamphlet on atheism. (Now he has a memorial on Magpie Lane—go figure.) Oxford makes a comfortable day trip from London, but of course to really get to know it takes an overnight stay or two (or enrollment at the university). Regular **trains** from London's Paddington Station take just over an hour; Oxford Citylink **buses** from Grosvenor Gardens or Victoria Station take about 90 to 100 minutes and cost half as much. The **Tourist Information Centre** (☎ 01865/726-871) is opposite the bus station on Glouchester Green.

Time-Savers

Two-hour **guided walks** leaving from the tourist office give you a good feel for the place and stop at the major colleges and other city sights. If you've only got an hour, head to the train station, where **Guide Friday** (☎ 01865/790-522) will stick you on a bus with a guide who will rattle off commentary as you're whisked around the city.

Oxford University's "campus" is the city, spread over the town in a series of 36 colleges, each with its own long history and arcane traditions—like Christ Church College, whose Great Tom bell rings every evening at 9:05pm to signal the closing of the school gates, pealing 101 times in honor of the college's original 101 students. Many of the colleges incorporate architectural tidbits from their foundings in the 13th to 16th centuries. Because the primary business here is education, not tourism, fairly strict rules keep visits limited to certain areas at certain times and in small groups (six people maximum). Most colleges, when they are open, allow visitors to poke around discreetly from 2pm to 5pm (check the notice boards outside each college for specifics).

There's no room here to detail all of Oxford's colleges, but the top ones include **Christ Church,** dating from 1525 with the largest quadrangle in town and that big ol' bell (the top half of the bell tower was designed by Christopher Wren). The college chapel also happens to be the local cathedral, one of the tiniest in England. Try to fit in **Merton College,** the oldest (1264) with a library whose odd collections include Chaucer's astrolabe; **University College,** also ancient but whose present architecture is mainly 17th century; and perhaps the prettiest overall, **Magdalen College,** a 15th-century gem surrounded by a park and overlooking the Cherwell River. Call ☎ 01865/277-165 to ask about guided tours of the **Bodleian Library,** a bibliophile's dream (as a copyright deposit, it owns a copy of every book published in Britain) built and expanded from the 14th to 17th centuries and including a detached baroque rotunda of a reading room.

Oxford doesn't begin and end with the university, of course, and perhaps your first order of business in town should be to clamber up the academically unaffiliated **Carfax Tower** in the center of town armed with one of the aerial city maps they hand out at the bottom to get a bird's-eye handle on the city layout. If you only visit one museum in town, make it the **Ashmolean Museum** (☎ 01865/278-000), founded in 1683 and one of Britain's best. Beyond the musical instruments, antiquities, and international curios, the painting collection is most impressive, featuring works by Bellini, Raphael, Michelangelo, Rembrandt, and Picasso. Also make time to go **punting on the Cherwell,** which is poling a flat-bottomed boat along the placid river (visit Cherwell Boathouse at Bardwell Road, ☎ 01865/515-978).

Oxford's classic eatery is the **Cherwell Boathouse Restaurant** (☎ 01865/552-746), right on the river with a French cuisine of fresh ingredients and half-priced kids' meals. For pub grub, follow in the footsteps of Thomas Hardy, Elizabeth Taylor, and Bill Clinton (who studied at Oxford), all former regulars of **The Turf Tavern** (☎ 01865/243-235), a venerable 13th-century watering hole at 4 Bath Place. You can hole up for the night at the **Eastgate Hotel** (☎ 01865/248-244), 23 Merton St., The High. It's near the river, with modern £110 ($183.30) doubles in a country inn setting.

Chapter 14

Edinburgh & the Best of Scotland

In This Chapter

➤ Edinburgh's royal palaces and haunted hangouts

➤ Tips for scoring a kilt and sampling some scotch

➤ Demystifying haggis, Scotland's national dish

➤ It's a bird! It's a plane! Tracking Nessie in the Highlands

Dollars & Sense

The British unit of currency is the pound sterling (£), divided into 100 pence, called *pee* (p). Roughly, $1 equals 60p, or £1 equals $1.65. British coins include 1p, 2p, 5p, 10p, 20p, 50p, and £1. Bills come in denominations of £5, £10, £20, and £50. Scottish banks can print their own money, so you'll find three completely different designs for each note, plus the regular British pounds. They're all valid.

Hollywood would have you believe that Scotland is full of strapping lads (such as Mel Gibson or Liam Neeson) in tartan kilts hiking among high hills and through loch-filled glens dotted with woolly sheep while bagpipers play haunting Robert Burns tunes and stop every now and then for a bit of haggis. In some respects, these images *do* reflect the Scots' way of life, or at least history. This country is indeed proud of its heritage; local political parties are constantly striving for further autonomy from the Brits. On the other hand, Prince Charles is more likely to wear a kilt these days than the average Scotsman, and it's unclear whether anyone actually enjoys eating haggis, Scotland's answer to "mystery meat."

A clearer picture of Scotland emerges in the industrial and agricultural center of Glasgow and in Edinburgh, the gateway to the Highlands. Edinburgh is called the "Athens of the North," partly for its renowned university and intellectual life (Sir Walter Scott and Robert Burns lived here, and Robert Louis Stevenson is a native son) and partly because some neoclassical ruins top one of its hills. It's a town of fine arts and shopping, and some of the kickingest nightlife in Britain. The city is a cultural capital of Europe and hosts a performing arts blowout every August called the Edinburgh International Festival (see the following "Extra! Extra!"). I've done Edinburgh in a day before, but it deserves two or three—more if you can spare it.

Extra! Extra!

Since 1947, the **Edinburgh International Festival** has brought two to three weeks of theater, opera, arts, dance, music, poetry, prose, and even traditional culture (the bagpiping "Military Tattoo" parade uses the floodlit castle as a backdrop) to the city in August. The festival has also spawned multiple mini-festivals, including the famous Fringe Festival (also held in August, with many more acts, a lot more amateurs) and celebrations centered around jazz, film, television, and books. The main festival's headquarters (☎ **0131/226-5756**) are at 21 Market St.; those of the Fringe Festival (☎ **0131/226-5257**) are at 180 High St.

Getting Your Bearings

Edinburgh is a port town of sorts; its outskirts rest on the **Firth of Forth,** an inlet of the North Sea. The center of town is an ancient volcanic outcrop atop which glowers **Edinburgh Castle.** Due east of this is Waverley train station. Between the two runs **Princes Street Gardens** and the sunken train tracks. These gardens effectively divide the city between the **Old Town** to the south, and the gridlike **New Town** to the north.

Edinburgh's Neighborhoods in Brief

New Town, developed in the 18th century, is filled today with hotels and shops. The major east-west streets of **New Town** are **Princes Street,** bordering the gardens named after it, and **George Street,** which runs parallel to Princes Street two blocks north.

The main thoroughfare of the **Old Town,** spilling off the castle's mount and running downhill to the east, is called the **Royal Mile.** It's a single road, but

it carries several names: Lawnmarket, High Street, Canongate. Farther to the south is the **University District,** one of the hot spots for Edinburgh's famed nightlife.

Time-Savers

The **Edinburgh and Scotland Information Centre** (☎ **0131/ 557-1700**) is in the Waverley Shopping Centre at 3 Princes St., very near the train station. The Information Centre hands out free copies of the events magazine **What's On in Edinburgh.** A more in-depth version called **The List,** which has an excellent pub guide, costs £1.80 ($3). There's also an information desk at the airport.

Getting Around Town

Almost hourly **trains** from London (a five-hour ride) pull into **Waverley Station,** at the east end of Princes Street. **Buses** from London cost less, but take eight hours and arrive at the station on St. Andrew Square. Historic Edinburgh is not a big place, and you can walk most of it very easily. **City buses,** however, are cheap when you need 'em and offer speedy access to the residential districts that surround the city center—these districts are where you'll find the cheap hotels and B&Bs.

Dollars & Sense

On Edinburgh buses you **pay** by the mile, so tell the driver where you're get-ting off and drop exact change in the slot. Rides range from 40p (65¢) to £1.70 ($2.80). The **Edinburgh Free Ticket** costs £2 ($3.30) for a full day of unlimited rides. The **TouristCard** gets you the same, plus discounts at some sights and restaurants. You can get them for anywhere from 2 days (£4.80/$8) to 13 days (£20.20/$33.65). Purchase tickets and passes at the Waverly Bridge Transport Office (☎ **0131/554-4494**), right above the train station.

Fast Facts: Edinburgh

American Express Edinburgh's branch is at 139 Princes St., near Waverley Station (☎ **0131/225-7881**). It's open Monday to Friday 9am to 5:30pm and Saturday 9am to 4pm.

Consulate The U.S. Consulate is at 3 Regent Terrace (☎ **0131/556-8315**).

Doctors/hospitals Ask your hotel concierge to recommend a doctor or dentist, or, for a hospital, try the **Royal Infirmary,** 1 Lauriston Place (☎ **0131/536-1000**).

Emergency   Dial ☎ **999** in any emergency.

Pharmacies   There are no 24-hour pharmacies in Edinburgh, but **Boots** (48 Shandwick Place; ☎ **0131/225-6757**) is open Monday to Saturday 9am to 9pm and Sunday 10am to 5pm.

Safety   Violent crime is rare in Edinburgh, and you'll probably feel safe walking around the city day or night, but be aware that the city's drug problem has produced a few related muggings.

Taxis   Edinburgh's tourist sites are easily reached on foot, but a taxi may be more useful for longer distances. Hail a taxi or find one at a *rank* (stand), such as those at Hanover Street, Waverley Station, or Haymarket Station. To call a taxi, dial ☎ **0131/229-2468.** The initial charge is £1.20 ($2) for the first mile and 20p (30¢) for each mile thereafter. There is a surcharge of 60p ($1) between 6am and 6pm.

Telephone   A local call in Edinburgh costs 10p (15¢) for the first three minutes. Pay phones accept either coins or phone cards, which are sold at post offices or the tourist board in £1 ($1.60), £2 ($3.30), £4 ($6.65), £10 ($16.65), and £20 ($33.30) denominations.

The country code for the United Kingdom is **44.** Edinburgh's city code is **0131.** If you're calling Edinburgh from outside the United Kingdom, drop the zero. In other words, to call Edinburgh from the United States, dial **011-44-131** and the number. To call the United States direct from Edinburgh, dial **001** followed by the area code and phone number. To charge a call to your calling card, or make a collect call home, dial **AT&T** (☎ **0800/890-011**), **MCI** (☎ **0800/890-222**), or **Sprint** (☎ **0800/890-877** or 0500/890-877).

Transit Info   Call **Waverley Bridge Transport Office** (☎ **0131/554-4494**) or the **Lothian Region Transport Office** (☎ **0131/220-4111**).

A Place to Hang Your Kilt: Edinburgh's Hotel Scene

Time-Savers

The tourist office has a booklet listing local B&Bs and guest houses, and for £3 ($5) the staff will help you find room in one or space in a regular hotel.

Edinburgh hotels are not cheap. On top of this, all of them charge three different rates: off-season, high season, and Festival season. If you don't book well in advance for Festival time, you probably won't find a room—at least not anywhere near the city center. Even if you do book in advance, staying in the city center will cost more than double the off-season price. Luckily, Edinburgh has many pleasant suburbs no more than 20 minutes by bus from the center of town—neighborhoods where the rooms cost less year-round and where you'll find some of the only free space during the Festival. One

Hotels
Balmoral Hotel **16**
Bruntsfield Hotel **2**
Dalhousie Castle **26**
Ellersly Country House Hotel **1**
George Inter-Continental **14**

Restaurants
The Atrium **4**
Deacon Brodie's Tavern **11**
Indian Cavalry Club **1**
Pierre Victoire **7**
Witchery by the Castle **9**

Attractions
Burns Monument **23**
Calton Old Cemetery **25**
Edinburgh Castle **6**
Georgian House **5**
High Kirk of St. Giles **17**
John Knox's House **20**
Lothian House **3**
Museum of Childhood **21**
National Gallery of Scotland **12**
National Library **18**
National Portrait Gallery **15**
Nelson Monument **22**
Outlook Tower
  and Camera Obscura **8**
Holyroodhouse **24**
Royal Museum of Scotland **19**
Royal Scottish Academy **13**
Scotch Whiskey Heritage Center **10**

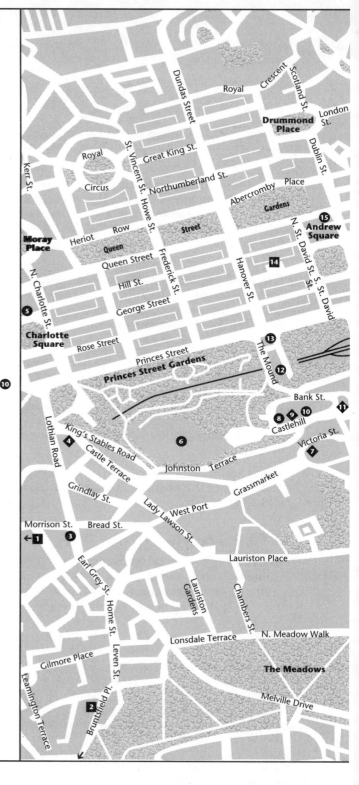

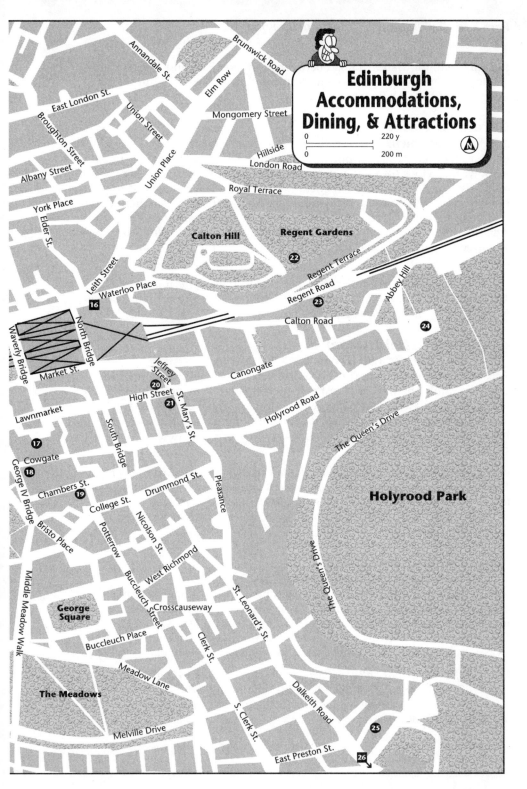

Edinburgh Accommodations, Dining, & Attractions

0   220 y

0   200 m

Brunswick Road

Elm Row

Mongomery Street

East London St.

Annandale St.

Union Street

Union Place

Broughton Street

Albany Street

Hillside

London Road

Royal Terrace

York Place

Elder St.

Leith Street

Calton Hill

Regent Gardens

22

Regent Terrace

Waterloo Place

Regent Road

23

Abbey Hill

16

Calton Road

24

North Bridge

Waverly Bridge

Market St.

Jeffrey Street

Canongate

20

High Street

St. Mary's St.

21

Lawnmarket

Holyrood Road

17

Cowgate

The Queen's Drive

18

George IV Bridge

South Bridge

Chambers St.

19

College St.

Drummond St.

Holyrood Park

Bristo Place

Nicolson St.

Pleasance

Potterrow

West Richmond

Buccleuch Street

George Square

Crosscauseway

St. Leonard's St.

The Queen's Drive

Middle Meadow Walk

Buccleuch Place

Clerk St.

Meadow Lane

The Meadows

Dalkeith Road

25

S. Clerk St.

Melville Drive

East Preston St.

26

such area, around Dalkeith Road between Holyrood Park and The Meadows, is filled with good, inexpensive guest houses that are just a 10-minute bus ride south of the Old Town.

Balmoral Hotel
$$$$$. New Town.

Edinburgh's premier luxury hotel perches atop Waverley Station, a city land-mark with its clock tower, kilted doormen, and bagpipers welcoming you to a slightly contrived Scottish experience. The Forte chain overhauled the hotel in the 1980s, and the large rooms are now outfitted in a reproduction-Georgian-meets-contemporary-comfort style, discreetly cushy and with full amenities. The Grill Room restaurant is highly recommended for Scottish and modern cuisine, as is N.B's pub for whisky, and the Palm Court for after-noon tea.

Princes St. (at the east end of the street, practically on top of the train station). ☎ **0131/556-2412. Fax:** *0131/557-8740.* **Bus:** *4, 15, 44 (but if you're arriving by train, you're already there).* **Rates:** *£165 ($275) double. AE, DC, MC, V.*

Kids Bruntsfield Hotel
$$. South of Old Town.

This 19th-century hotel near the Meadows is across from the Bruntsfield Links—possibly the world's oldest golf course. Behind the neo-Gothic facade lies a modern, pastel interior favored by businesspeople during the week and families on weekends. Good-sized rooms feature amenities such as trouser presses and in-house movies, and there's a restaurant and pub on the premises.

69-74 Bruntsfield Place. Take Lothian Rd. to Earl Grey St., and then go right onto Home St., which becomes Leven St. and then Bruntsfield Place; the hotel is on the left, across from the Bruntsfield Links. ☎ **800/528-1234** *from the U.S. or 0131/229-1393.* **Fax:** *0131/229-5634.* **Bus:** *11, 15, 16, 17, 23.* **Rates:** *£125 ($183.30) double. AE, DC, MC, V.*

Kids Dalhousie Castle
$$$. Bonnyrigg (8 miles southeast of Edinburgh).

Staying right in Edinburgh has its charms, but if you've come to Scotland for medieval romance, head outside town to this 15th-century castle over-looking a river. Once host to Henry IV, Sir Walter Scott, and Queen Victoria, Dalhousie has been renovated to provide luxurious modern comforts within a castle atmosphere. Don't miss a meal in the dungeon restaurant.

Bonnyrigg, Edinburgh (8 miles southeast of the city). ☎ **01875/820-153. Fax:** *01875/821-963. By car: Take the A7 8 miles southeast of Edinburgh toward Carlisle; the castle is just outside the village of Bonnyrigg.* **Rates:** *£125 ($208.30) double. AE, DC, MC, V.*

Ellersly Country House Hotel
$$$. In Murrayfield, west of town.
In an upscale residential district near Murrayfield rugby grounds, this Edwardian country house gives you the feeling you're staying at a posh private home. The rooms are recently renovated and well-sized (make sure to request one in the main house, not the boring annex). The Scottish and French meals can be worth the £23 ($38) extra, and it's only a five-minute ride from the center of town.

4 Ellersly Rd. 2.5 miles west of the city center on the A8; take Shandwick Place and veer right onto Corstorphine Rd. (A8). ☎ *0131/337-6888.* **Fax:** *0131/313-2543.* **Bus:** *12 or 24.* **Rates:** *£135 double ($224.91). AE, DC, MC, V.*

Extra! Extra!

Dalhousie Castle's sylvan setting beside a flowing stream should appeal both to romantic and outdoorsy types. The hotel organizes salmon and trout fishing, shooting, and horseback riding expeditions.

George Inter-Continental
$$$$. New Town.
The core of this hotel on tony George Street is a 1755 Georgian house. The oft-refurbished rooms feature all the amenities modern standards call for. You can enjoy the atmosphere of the original townhouse in the Scottish restaurant, but the new wing has the best rooms (fourth floor and above), which overlook the street.

19-21 George St. (steps away from St. Andrews Sq.). ☎ *800/327-0200 from the U.S. or 0131/225-1251.* **Fax:** *0131/226-5644.* **Bus:** *4, 15, 44.* **Rates:** *£175 ($291.55) double. AE, DC, MC, V.*

Greenside Hotel
$. New Town
This recently refurbished four-floor Georgian house dates back to 1786, and the antiques sprinkled throughout strike just the right note. All rooms come with private bath and open onto views of a private garden or the Firth of Forth. Drinks are served in the bar.

9 Royal Terrace. ☎ *and fax* **0131/557-0022.** **Bus:** *4, 15, or 44.* **Rates:** *£55 ($86.90) double. AE, DC, MC, V.*

Edinburgh Edibles: The Restaurant Scene
The Scots have traditionally started out the day with a bowl of surprisingly delicious **porridge.** Campbell's in a can doesn't know from genuine **scotch broth** soup (barley in a mutton-flavored stock). **Angus beef** makes both great steaks and roast beef; Scottish **lamb** is excellent, as are the many **game** dishes (rabbit, woodcock, red deer, and grouse).

Tourist Traps

Scotland's national "dish" is the infamous **haggis,** a fat, cantaloupe-size sausage made from sheep lungs, liver, and hearts mixed with spices, suet, oatmeal, and onions. It stinks to high heaven, and many are suspicious of whether the Scots themselves ever touch the stuff. Whether it's actually a national practical joke to be played on unsuspecting visitors or an earnest patriotic meal, you do have a cultural obligation to try it—if only once. Charles MacSween & Son, Dryden Road (☎ **0131/440-2555**), will be happy to inflict one upon you.

When it comes to fish, this country excels at preparing haddock, whitefish, herring (usually kippered and eaten for breakfast), and the mighty river salmon. At a Scottish high tea, you can sample freshly baked scones alongside some of the best fresh jams (especially raspberry), heather honeys, and marmalades in Europe. Also excellent are Scottish cheeses—look for cheddars, the creamy, oatmeal-coated Caboc, and cottage cheeses in particular.

The Atrium
$$$$. New Town. CONTEMPORARY MEDITERRANEAN.
This stylish and upscale nouvelle restaurant opened to acclaim in 1993. It has a weirdly moody ambiance of oil lamps and rusted metal set into the atrium of a modern office building. The dishes change with the trends and the chef's inspiration, but they are always tasty and primarily of Mediterranean ingredients, such as sun-dried tomatoes, couscous, and arugula. The well-presented dishes may center on anything from seared scallops to roast duck.

10 Cambridge St. (off Lothian Rd., beneath Saltire Ct.). ☎ *0131/228-8882. Reservations highly recommended.* **Bus:** *10, 11, 15, 16, 17.* **Main courses:** *£8.50–£11.50 ($14.15–$19.15) at lunch, £9.50–£16.50 ($15.80–$27.50) at dinner. AE, MC, V.* **Open:** *Lunch and dinner Mon–Sat. Closed Christmas week.*

Kids Deacon Brodie's Tavern
$. Old Town. SCOTTISH/PUB GRUB.
This 1806 pub is a favorite among locals and visitors drawn by the old tavern atmosphere, the good food, and the weird story of its namesake (see the following "Bet You Didn't Know"). Morbid history aside, the tavern serves passable pub grub on the ground floor, but head upstairs to the wood-lined restaurant, where the steak and ale pie (a variant on shepherd's pie) may have you scraping the plate for more.

435 Lawnmarket (the western spur of the Royal Mile, near St. Giles's church). ☎ *0131/225-6531. Reservations suggested.* **Bus:** *1, 6, 23, 27, 30, 34, 36.* **Meals:** *Start at around £5 ($8.30).* **Open:** *Lunch and dinner daily.*

Indian Cavalry Club

$$$. New Town. INDIAN.

This is the best of Edinburgh's Indian restaurants. Nepalese and Burmese dishes join the tandoori and other classic Indian cuisine found in Britain. The decor, with a different theme for each room, is reminiscent of the days when Britain's imperial flag flew over India. No one in town does curry better, and you can't go wrong with the fixed-price, five-course table d'hôte dinner that gives you a taste of the kitchen's best.

Bet You Didn't Know

Deacon Brodie was the real-life model for one of Edinburgh's most famous fictions. Brodie, a responsible, respectable city councilor and inventor by day, was by night a thief and murderer. In 1788 his dark side caught up with him, and after a trial he was hanged on a gibbet he himself helped perfect. The story inspired R. L. Stevenson to write *The Strange Case of Dr. Jekyll and Mr. Hyde.*

3 Atholl Place (off Shandwick Place). ☎ *0131/228-3282. Reservations required.* **Bus:** *3, 21, 23, 26.* **Main courses:** *£6–£10 ($10–$16.65); five-course dinner £16 ($26.65); two-course lunch buffet £6.95 ($11.60). AE, DC, MC, V.* **Open:** *Lunch and dinner daily.*

Pierre Victoire

$$. Old Town. FRENCH.

This crowded French bistro has become so popular for its great food at reasonable prices that a branch has sprung up across town. The original is still the best, though, so stop by for roast pheasant, grilled mussels in garlic, salmon with ginger, and other interesting riffs on French cuisine. A relaxed (if sometimes noisy) atmosphere, a bevy of local devotees, and a good selection of French wines add to the attraction.

10 Victoria St. (just off Grassmarket). ☎ *0131/225-1721. Reservations required.* **Bus:** *1, 6, 34, 35.* **Main courses:** *£5.80–£8.90 ($9.65–$14.80); fixed-price lunch £4.90 ($8.15). MC, V.* **Open:** *Lunch and dinner Mon–Sat (also Sun during the Festival).*

Witchery by the Castle

$$$$$. Old Town. SCOTTISH.

Admittedly a bit of a tourist magnet, this traditional restaurant touts itself as the oldest in town and is in the very building where the Hellfire Club met in the middle ages and where witches were once burned (one still haunts the place). The reception is warm, and the food is dyed-in-the-wool Scottish, with flavorful local dishes such as salmon from the Tay, Angus steak, and

Skye prawns. The wine list is impressively long, as is the roster of 40 malt whiskies.

Castlehill, Royal Mile (at the west end of the Mile, very near the Castle).
☎ *0131/225-5613. Reservations recommended.* **Bus:** *1, 34, 35.* **Main courses:**
£14–£21.50 ($23.30–$35.80); fixed-price two-course lunch £12.95 ($21.60).
AE, D, MC, V. **Open:** *Lunch and dinner daily.*

Quick Bites

The health-conscious and environmentally aware **Baked Potato Shop,**
56 Cockburn St. (☎ **0131/225-7572**), offers scrumptious stuffed potatoes,
Indian bhajias (curried dumplings), and (of all things) vegetarian haggis; the
single table seats only six. You can pick up a tasty donner kebab (spicy lamb
sandwich) and other middle-eastern take-out at the **Kebab Mahal,**
7 Nicholson Sq. (☎ **0131/667-5214**). There's no better one-stop shop
for picnic supplies than the basement supermarket of **Marks & Spencer**
(☎ **0131/225-2301**) at 53 Princes St.

A Bonnie Wee Bit o' Edinburgh Sightseeing

The LRT **Classic Tour Bus** runs circles around the major Edinburgh sights,
and a full-day ticket lets you hop on and off at any of its 15 stops. Buses run
about 15 minutes apart on the two-hour circuit and have guided commentary along the way; the upper deck of the bus is open in summer. You can
get tickets for the tour bus—£5 ($8.30) adults, £1.50 ($2.50) kids—at the
starting point, Waverley Station.

Edinburgh Sights Not to Miss

Edinburgh Castle

The castle rises sternly over Edinburgh and is deeply rooted in its volcanic
foundation as well as in the city's history. The core shelters the 12th-century,
Norman-style St. Margaret's Chapel from an earlier castle. In the Royal
Apartments, you get to gawk at the bedroom of Mary, Queen of Scots—the
very place she gave birth to James VI (later James I of England). The ostensi-
ble highlight is the Crown Chamber, where you learn all about the Scottish
Honours (the crown jewels) and more than you ever wanted to know about
the investiture of the Scottish king. But my favorite bit is creeping into the
prison cells to peer at the drawings scratched into the walls by early 19th-
century prisoners of the Napoleonic wars.

Castlehill. ☎ *0131/225-9846.* **Bus:** *1, 6.* **Admission:** *£6 ($10) adults, £1.50
($2.50) kids under 15.* **Open:** *Apr–Sept, daily 9:30am–5:15pm; Oct–Mar, daily
9:30am–4:15pm.*

National Gallery of Scotland

This honey-colored neoclassical temple houses one of the best mid-sized art museums in Europe, hung with a well-chosen selection of old masters and impressionist masterpieces. Spend a morning here in the company of Rembrandt, Rubens, Andrea del Sarto, Raphael, Titian, Velázquez, El Greco, Monet, Degas, Gainsborough, and van Gogh. You may find yourself pleasantly surprised by the many works of largely unknown Scottish artists.

2 The Mound (in the center of Princes Street Gardens, behind the train station). ☎ *0131/556-8921.* **Bus:** *3, 21, 26.* **Admission:** *Free.* **Open:** *Mon–Sat 10am–5pm, Sun 2–5pm (during the Festival, Mon–Sat 10am–6pm, Sun 11am–6pm).*

The Royal Mile

A stroll down the Royal Mile—the main drag of the old town that changes names from Lawnmarket to High Street to Canongate—takes you from Edinburgh Castle on the west end downhill to the Palace of Holyroodhouse on the east.

Dollars & Sense

The various small museums of the Royal Mile tend to be open Monday through Saturday, 10am to 5pm (a few stay open until 6pm in summer and are open on Sunday afternoons during the Festival). The Whisky Centre and Camera Obscura are open throughout the year, but Gladstone's Land is only open April to October. Most of the museums are free, but some (Whisky Centre, Camera Obscura, John Knox House, Gladstone's Land) charge a small admission of £1.30 to £3.80 ($2.15 to $6.30).

Start your tour immersed in the history, process, and lore surrounding single malts at the **Scottish Whisky Heritage Centre** (☎ **0131/220-0441**) at 354 Castelhill. Across the street is the **Outlook Tower and Camera Obscura** (☎ **0131/226-3709**), the top of which has retained the live image of Edinburgh-out-the-peephole, projected onto a white tabletop, that made it famous 150 years ago. It has also updated its exhibits to include modern advances in optics, such as laser holography. At 477B Lawnmarket, **Gladstone's Land** (☎ **0131/226-5856**) is a restored 17th-century home inside and out. A nearby alley leads to **Lady Stair's House** (☎ **0131/225-2425** extension **6593**), which celebrates the lives and works of Scotland's three great writers: Burns, Scott, and Stevenson.

Because it was (twice) briefly a cathedral, that honorary title is sometimes given to the **High Kirk of St. Giles** (☎ **0131/225-8442**). It's changed so much over the ages that today the main

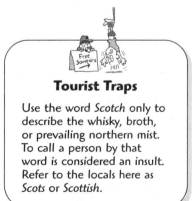

Tourist Traps

Use the word *Scotch* only to describe the whisky, broth, or prevailing northern mist. To call a person by that word is considered an insult. Refer to the locals here as *Scots* or *Scottish*.

draw is the **Thistle Chapel,** slapped onto the church's corner in 1911. The church's minister from 1559 to 1572 was the fiery John Knox, leader of the Scottish Reformation and perpetual antagonist to Mary, Queen of Scots. Tradition, if not the evidence, holds that he lived a few doors down at 43-45 High St. in the **John Knox House (☎ 0131/556-9579)**. This 16th-century building with projecting upper floors is the only remaining example of a building style that once lined both sides of the Royal Mile. Across the street at no. 42 is the **Museum of Childhood (☎ 0131/529-4142)**, a noisy place full of toys from Victorian to recent times.

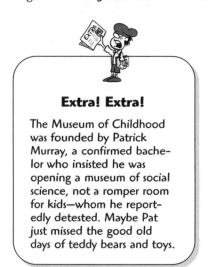

Extra! Extra!

The Museum of Childhood was founded by Patrick Murray, a confirmed bachelor who insisted he was opening a museum of social science, not a romper room for kids—whom he reportedly detested. Maybe Pat just missed the good old days of teddy bears and toys.

As the Royal Mile becomes Canongate, you'll pass at no. 142 **Huntly House (☎ 0131/629-4143)**, another restored 16th-century house filled with period rooms. Across the street is the clock-faced 1591 **Canongate Tollbooth,** a one-time council room, law court, and prison, now housing the **People's Story,** an exhibit on working life in Edinburgh from the 18th century to today.

Palace of Holyroodhouse

Scotland's sometime royal palace grew out of the guest house of a vanished 12th-century abbey (the nearby ruined nave is all that's left). Of James V's 16th-century palace, only the north tower—rich with memories of his daughter, the political pawn Mary, Queen of Scots—remains. There's a plaque where's Mary's court secretary Riccio was murdered by her dissolute husband and his cronies, and some of the queen's needlework is on display. Most of the palace is late 17th century. Although Bonnie Prince Charlie once held his roving court here, the palace was only recently restored after years of neglect.

Canongate (east end of the Royal Mile). ☎ *0131/556-1096. Bus: 1, 6.* ***Admission:*** *£5 ($8.30) adults, £3.50 ($5.80) seniors, £2.50 ($4.15) kids under 15.* ***Open:*** *Mon–Sat 9:30am–5:15pm, Sun 10:30am–4:40pm. Closed last 2 weeks in May, 3 weeks in late June/early July, and whenever the royal family is in residence.*

Calton Hill

Off Regent Road in eastern Edinburgh rises this odd Romantic paean to classical architecture. Besides a great view of the city and Edinburgh Castle (and behind you, to the Firth of Forth), the hill is scattered with a collection of 19th-century "instant ruins." These include a half-finished Parthenon (it ended up being no more than a colonnade). At the summit is the 100-foot Nelson Monument.

Bet You Didn't Know

Calton Hill's full-scale replica of the Parthenon in Athens was started in 1822 to honor Scottish soldiers killed in the Napoleonic wars. When funding ran out by 1829, the temple was left unfinished and was eventually dubbed "Scotland's Shame."

Other Fun Stuff to Do

➤ **Scaling Arthur's Seat.** Edinburgh's other great volcanic plug, Arthur's Seat, is, at 820 feet, just a hill in Holyrood Park. But it feels like a proper mountain as you make the 30-minute climb, and the summit rewards your efforts with a far-ranging view that sweeps across the city below and, in the distance, the Firth of Forth.

➤ **Men in Skirts: Sizing Yourself for that Kilt.** The Highlander's dress used to be a 16-foot-long plaid scarf wrapped around and around to make a skirt, with the excess thrown across the chest and up over the shoulder. After an 18th-century ban on the wearing of such traditional clan tartans, kilts became a fierce symbol of Scottish pride, and an industry was born. Today, a handmade kilt with all its accessories can run you upwards of £500 ($833.30), but even if a tartan scarf or tie is more your stripe, **John Morrison Ltd.,** 461 Lawnmarket (☎ **0131/225-8149**), or **Tartan Gift Shops,** 54 High St. (☎ **0131/ 558-3187**), can help you identify your clan (or one close enough) and match you to one of its traditional tartans.

➤ **Visiting a Few Old Edinburgh Haunts.** Although **Robin's Tours** are the best walking tours for hidden Edinburgh and history buffs (call ☎ **0131/661-0125** for times and meeting spots), the most entertaining walks around the city are led after dark by the deadbeats working for **Witchery Tours** (☎ **0131/225-6745**). Each guide is an officially deceased Edinburgher whose shade still reportedly inhabits this most haunted of cities. Your costumed spirit guide will lead you on a sometimes spooky, often goofy, and occasionally educational 90-minute tiptoe around the city's key historical and legendary spots in "Ghosts and Gore and Murder and Mayhem." Reserve a spot in advance for this tour.

➤ **Taking in a Penguin Parade at the Edinburgh Zoo.** From April to September, at 2pm daily, the zoo (☎ **0131/334-9171**) herds the largest penguin colony in Europe out of its enclosure to run a few laps around a grassy park. Don't miss the gorillas, either (or the great view that stretches to the Firth of Forth). The zoo's at 134 Corstorphine Rd; take bus 2, 26, 69, 85, or 86.

➤ **Sampling the City's Pubs & Nightlife.** Edinburgh is an unsung nightlife capital, with a lively performing arts and theater scene year-round. More nighttime fun can be had at **discos,** such as the always trendy **Buster Browns,** at 25 Market St., and the enormous **Century 2000,** at 31 Lothian Rd. The city is crawling with **pubs and bars,** especially in the Old Town around Grassmarket (**Black Bull,** no. 12), Candlemaker Row (**Greyfriars Bobby's Bar,** no. 34), Cowgate (**The Green Tree,** no. 182), and other University-area streets. In New Town, the slightly seedy Rose Street has a good string of pubs (try **Kenilworth** at no. 152). So toss back a pint of bitter or set up your own tasting marathon of wee drams of single-malt Scotch whiskys— the night is yours.

Extra! Extra!

For a more archetypal Scottish evening, you can either go with the hokey or the traditional. A bagpipe-playing, kilt-swirling "**Scottish Folk Evening**" is staged at big hotels such as the Carlton Highland or King James. A less forced *ceilidh* (pronounced *kay-lee,* a folk music jam session) happens nightly at the Tron Tavern on South Bridge or at any of the musical pubs listed in *The Gig* (50p/80¢ at newsstands and pubs).

Get Outta Town: Day Trips & Excursions

If you're looking to sample a bit more of Scotland, I recommend two excursions. Inverness serves as a good base for touring the craggy, romantic Highland countryside (don't forget to keep an eye peeled for the famous Loch Ness Monster). But if it's another taste of city life you seek, then head for nearby Glasgow, an art center that sports some amazing Victorian architecture.

On Nessie's Trail: Inverness & Loch Ness

Many first-time visitors to the Highlands on a tight schedule view Inverness—ancient seat of the Pictish kings who once ruled northern Scotland—merely as a stepping stone. Their quest is for that elusive glimpse of the monster said to inhabit the deep, still waters of Loch Ness, which stretches its long finger of water along a fault line southwest from Inverness. The largest volume of water in Scotland, the loch is more enormous than it looks. It's only a mile wide and 24 miles long, but at its murkiest depths, it plunges 700 to 800 feet to the bottom.

Truth be told, the Highlands hold more beautiful and rewarding spots, but no one can deny the draw of Loch Ness and its creature. Unless you take an organized bus trip (see sidebar) or drive on your own, you can't really do the Loch in a single day from Edinburgh. But you can take a late train to Inverness, spend the night, and tour the Loch quickly the next day before returning to Edinburgh. There are seven **trains** daily connecting the two cities and the trip is 3½ hours long. From Inverness, buses run regularly down the Loch to Drumnadrochit. Inverness's **tourist office** (☎ 01463/234-353), at Castle Wynd off Bridge Street, is more than used to teaching visitors the basics of Nessie-stalking and other Loch activities from lake cruises to monster-seeking trips below the surface in teensy yellow mini-subs (a rather obsessive £100/$166.65 splurge).

Although Inverness is one of the oldest settlements in Scotland, repeated burnings and wholesale destruction over the ages have left much of the city looking relatively modern—it was built in the last 150 years or so. So although the Castle is impressive enough, it only dates from 1834 to 1847. A smidge to the east of it, on Auld Castlehill of the Craig Phadrig, is the most ancient spot in town. This spot was the original site of the city castle, in which many historians believe Macbeth murdered King Duncan in 1040. (Shakespeare lifted many of his best plots straight from history.) Next to the modern castle sits the **Inverness Museum and Art Gallery** (☎ 01463/237-114), which gives you the lowdown on the life, history, and culture of the Highlands. To reach it, jog up Castle Wynd from Bridge Street. You can also learn about Gaelic language and culture from the **Highlands Association,** headquartered in the 16th-century Abertaff House on Church Street.

Across the river are the Victorian **St. Andrews Cathedral** on Ardoss Street (check out the Russian icons inside) and, on Huntly Street, the **Exhibition of Highland Music** (☎ 0463/715-757), with displays and instruments you can play. The **Loch Ness Show,** (☎ 01463/222-781) just across Ness Bridge on Huntly Street, offers a basic introduction to the Loch, its monster lore, and—what the heck—kilt-making. Farther west rises **Tomnahurich,** the "hill of the fairies," with a cemetery and panoramic views.

Time-Savers

If you just want a quick spin to Nessie's lair, **Lothian Regional Transport** (☎ 0131/554-4494), 27 Hanover St. in Edinburgh, offers an April to November bus tour of "Loch Ness and the Grampian Mountains" for £25 ($41.65) adults and £17 ($28.30) for children. (You'll have to provide your own suspension of disbelief.) In Inverness, **Highland Omnibus** (☎ 01463/ 233-371), at Farraline Park, offers Highlands bus tours and Loch cruises.

For **tooling around the lake,** you have to make a choice: the main A82 along the north shore, passing such monster haunts as Drumnadrochit and

Urquhart castle, or the more scenic southern shore route of natural attractions—pretty woodlands and the Foyers waterfalls. On a quick trip, the A82 gives you more to remember.

About halfway (14 miles) down the A82 from Inverness is the hamlet of **Dumnadrochit,** unofficial headquarters of Nessie lore. The **Loch Ness Monster Exhibition (☎ 01456/450-573)** will run down the legend of the monster for you with videos and disputed photographs, 6th-century legends, and sonar boat readings. Almost two miles farther down the road, **Urquhart Castle (☎ 01456/450-551)** crumbles on a spit of land jutting into the lake. Its grandly romantic ruins hold the record for the most Nessie sightings. The 1509 ramparts encompass what was once one of the largest fortresses in Scotland, blown up in 1692 to prevent it from falling into Jacobite hands.

Bet You Didn't Know

It all started in the 6th century when St. Colomba sent a monk swimming across the loch and a giant creature attacked. A few stern words from the saint, and the monster withdrew. The legend, however, has stuck. Is Nessie the Loch Ness Monster that emerged from the waters in the 16th century, knocking down trees and crushing three men with her tail? Or is she *Nessitera rhombopteryx,* a vestigial survivor from the age of the dinosaurs (her basic description sounds somewhat like that of a plesiosaur—then again, it also kind of matches some species of sea snake). One thing's for sure, monster legends and sightings have increased dramatically since the A82 road was blasted out of the lakeshore rock in 1933. Soon after, innkeeps Mr. and Mrs. Spicer thought they saw something break the surface of the waters one night, it was reported on a slow news day in the local paper, and the rumor spread like wildfire. In the end, the monster may be no more than the collective effect of faked photographs, water surface mirages brought on by too much whisky, a few unexplained lake phenomenon, and a string of Lochside villages whose economies are based on spinning tall tales to visitors. Sonar soundings and a host of keen-eyed watchers have not yet managed to prove, or disprove, Nessie's existence, and that is more than enough reason for 200,000 visitors annually to come, cameras and binoculars in hand, to search for the monster of Loch Ness.

The town of **Invermoriston** sits at the start of Glenmoriston, one of the prettiest valleys in the region, ideal for a short hike. At the head (southwest end) of Loch Ness stands the impressive **Fort Augustus,** an 18th-century fortress converted into a present-day Benedictine Abbey. From this "gateway to the Western Highlands" you can cruise Loch Ness or the 60 miles of the Caledonian Canal running from here to Fort William and the sea (22 miles are man-made locks, the rest are natural lochs).

One of the nicest inexpensive places to stay in Inverness is the **Glen Mhor Hotel** (☎ **01463/234-308;** fax: 01463/713-170), on the River Ness with great views for £59 to £94 ($98.30 to $156.65) per smallish double. Prices at **Dunain Park Restaurant** (☎ **01463/230-512**) are moderate to high, but the excellent Scottish cuisine is worth it. If you want to stay steeped in monster lore, shack up in Drumnadrochit at the **Polmaily House** Hotel (☎ **01456/450-343;** fax: 01456/450-813) for £46 to £105 ($76 to $175) per double, depending on the season.

Glasgow: A Victorian Industrial City Discovers Culture

Glasgow was an industrial revolution powerhouse, the "second city of the British Empire" from the 19th to early 20th centuries. With its wealth came a Victorian building boom, whose architecture is only beginning to be appreciated as the city comes off a decade-long publicity blitz. This civic and mental makeover of the 1980s has turned Glasgow from the depressed slum it had been for much of this century into a real contender for Edinburgh's title of cultural and tourist center of Scotland. With friendlier people and tonier shopping than the capital and a remarkable array of art museums, Glasgow has put itself firmly on the must-see map of Scotland. Spend at least one night, two if you can, to drink in its renewed splendors.

Half-hourly **trains** arrive in 50 minutes from Edinburgh, and the eight daily trains (four on Sunday) from London take almost six hours to arrive in Glasgow. The helpful **tourist board's office** (☎ **0141/204-4400**) is at 35-39 St. Vincent Place. The old part of Glasgow centers around the cathedral and train station. The shopping zone of **Merchant's City** is west of High Street. Glasgow grew westward, so the finest Victorian area of the city is the grid of streets known as the **West End.** All of these areas are north of the River Clyde. The city has a good **bus system** and an **underground** (subway) that swoops from the southwest in an arc back to the northwest. Rides on both are 60p ($1).

As far as sightseeing goes, it's art, art, and then some art for good measure. Luckily, admission to almost all of Glasgow's attractions is, ahem, scot-free. Make sure you fit in at least the **Glasgow Art Gallery and Museum** (☎ **0141/221-9600**), strong on Italian and Dutch old masters like Botticelli, Bellini, and Rembrandt, as well as the moderns—Monet, Picasso, van Gogh, Degas, Matisse, Whistler, and Ben Johnson. There's also a whole horde of Scottish artists represented, with works dating from the 17th century to the present. Most people breeze past the quite good collections of sculpture, ethnological artifacts, arms and armor, natural history, decorative arts, and relics of Scotland's Bronze Age.

The other great gallery of Glasgow is the **Burrell Collection** (☎ **0141/649-7151**), about four miles southwest of the city center in Pollok Country Park. The mind-boggling array of art and artifacts of this formerly private collection spans the globe, dating from the neolithic era to the modern day, with special attention to ancient Rome and Greece as well as paintings by Cézanne, Delacroix, and Cranach the Elder. Also in the park is the

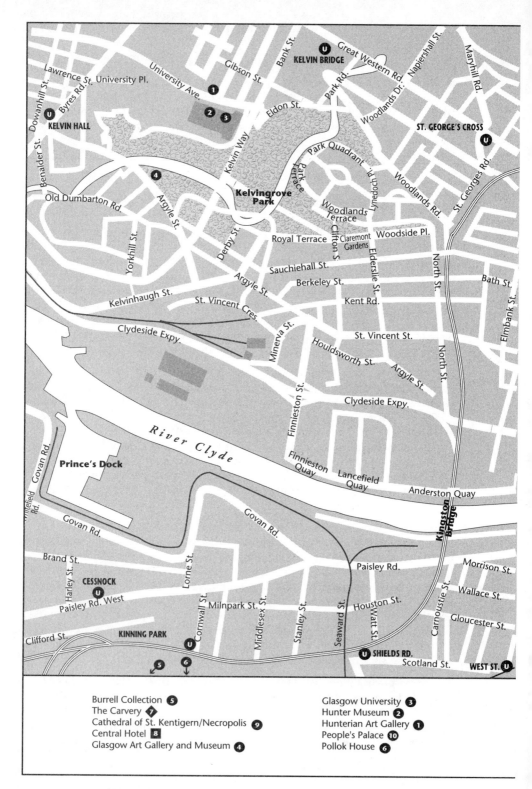

Burrell Collection ⑤
The Carvery ❼
Cathedral of St. Kentigern/Necropolis ⑨
Central Hotel 8
Glasgow Art Gallery and Museum ④

Glasgow University ❸
Hunter Museum ❷
Hunterian Art Gallery ❶
People's Palace ❿
Pollok House ⑥

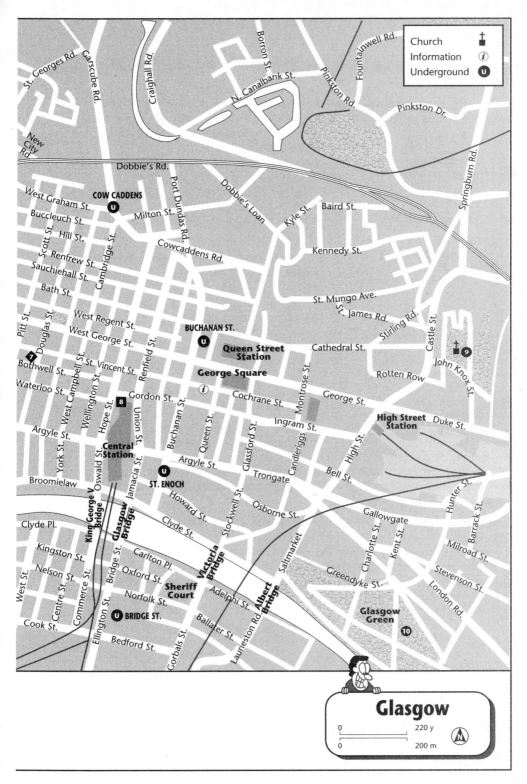

Church ✝
Information ⓘ
Underground Ⓤ

St. Georges Rd.
Carscube Rd.
Craighall Rd.
Borron St.
N. Canalbank St.
Pinkston Rd.
Fountainwell Rd.
Pinkston Dr.
Springburn Rd.

New City Rd.

Dobbie's Rd.

West Graham St.
COW CADDENS Ⓤ
Milton St.
Port Dundas Rd.
Dobbie's Loan
Kyle St.
Baird St.

Buccleuch St.
Hill St.
Scott St.
Renfrew St.
Cambridge St.
Cowcaddens Rd.
Kennedy St.

Sauchiehall St.
Bath St.

West Regent St.
Pitt St.
Douglas St.
West George St.
Renfield St.
BUCHANAN ST. Ⓤ
Queen Street Station
St. Mungo Ave.
St. James Rd.
Stirling Rd.
Castle St.
Cathedral St.
✝ 9

Bothwell St.
St. Vincent St.
St. Campbell St.
Wellington St.
Hope St.
Union St.
Buchanan St.
Queen St.
George Square ⓘ
Cochrane St.
Montrose St.
George St.
Rotten Row
John Knox St.
High Street Station
Duke St.

7

Waterloo St.
York St.
8
Gordon St.
Glassford St.
Ingram St.
Candleriggs
Bell St.
High St.
Hunter St.

Argyle St.
Central Station
Jamacia St.
Argyle St.
Trongate
Osborne St.
Gallowgate
Barrack St.
Milroad St.

Broomielaw
Oswald St.
Ⓤ **ST. ENOCH**
Howard St.
Stockwell St.
Saltmarket
Charlotte St.
Kent St.
Stevenson St.
London Rd.

Clyde Pl.
King/George V Bridge
Glasgow Bridge
Clyde St.
Victoria Bridge
Albert Bridge
Greendyke St.

Kingston St.
Nelson St.
West St.
Centre St.
Commerce St.
Bridge St.
Carlton Pl.
Oxford St.
Norfolk St.
Sheriff Court
Adelphi St.
Laurieston Rd.
Glasgow Green
10

Cook St.
Ellington St.
Ⓤ **BRIDGE ST.**
Bedford St.
Ballater St.
Gorbals St.

Glasgow

0 — 220 y
0 — 200 m

219

18th-century mansion **Pollok House** (☎ 0141/632-0274), with a fine series of Spanish paintings by El Greco, Goya, Velázquez, and others.

Next on the list is the **Hunterian Art Gallery** (☎ 0141/330-5431) at University Avenue, which controls the estate of the great artist James McNeill Whistler (born American, but proud to be of Scottish blood). Art Nouveau innovator Charles Rennie Mackintosh designed and built his own home, and though this architectural treasure was demolished in the 1960s, most of it has been painstakingly reconstructed here to house the gallery.

Extra! Extra!

Adjacent to the art gallery is the **Hunter Museum** (☎ 0141/339-8855), with a nifty collection of everything from archaeology (Roman and Viking) to paleontology and geology (dinosaur fossils). There's also an exhibit on the exploits of Captain Cook—in short, enough stuff to give naturalists and the kids a welcome break from all those paintings.

The kids—and certainly history buffs—might also get a kick out of the **People's Palace** (☎ 0141/554-0223) on Glasgow Green (Britain's first public park). Beyond a lush greenhouse filled with palms and a tea room, the museum contains a few drips and drabs of artifacts from the Middle Ages and Mary Queen of Scots, but the main collections bring to light the life of an average Victorian Glasgowian.

When you're all museumed out, rest in the pews of the **Cathedral of St. Kentigern,** an austerely but gorgeously Gothic 13th-century church with a 12th-century under-church of great pointy arches and web-like vaulting. Below the cathedral is the **Necropolis,** filled with fantastically diverse tombs in a jumble of architectural styles.

The huge **Central Hotel** (☎ 0141/221-9680; fax: 0141/226-3948), at 99 Gordon St. near the central station, has tatty turn-of-the-century charm for just £70 ($116.65) per double; barring that, the tourist office will help you book a room. Although revitalized Glasgow has plenty of refined international eateries these days, it's hard to beat the value of **The Carvery's** (☎ 0141/248-2656) hearty buffet of British specialties. It's in the Forte Crest Hotel, on Bothwell Street.

Chapter 15

Dublin & the Best of Ireland

In This Chapter

➤ On the trail of writers and rock stars in Dublin

➤ Hanging out in trendy Temple Bar

➤ Gaga for Guinness: where to sip an authentic pint

➤ Shopping for Arran sweaters and Waterford crystal

➤ Scenic drives and excursions to Celtic abbeys

The Emerald Isle is a lush land of deep history and broad smiles. Celts, Vikings, Normans, and the English have all trod this country's verdant slopes, leaving behind ancient ruins as well as a rich and varied heritage. Steeped in strong religious beliefs and scattered with the broken remains of vast medieval abbeys and monasteries, Ireland is home to literary giants, Guinness beer, and stupendous music. Although Dublin is alive with museums and some of Europe's greatest nightlife, a visit to Ireland is really about the rural landscape and the friendly welcome waiting in each small town. I say give Dublin a day or two tops and make sure you budget a few days for exploring the Irish countryside. Ireland is one country where renting a car makes a lot of sense.

Dollars & Sense

The Irish unit of currency is the Irish punt (often called pound and, like the British pound, denoted with a £), which is divided into 100 pence, called *pee* (p). Roughly, $1 equals 70p, or £1 equals $1.45. Irish coins include 1p, 5p, 10p, 20p, 50p, and £1. Bills come in denominations of £5, £10, £20, £50, and £100.

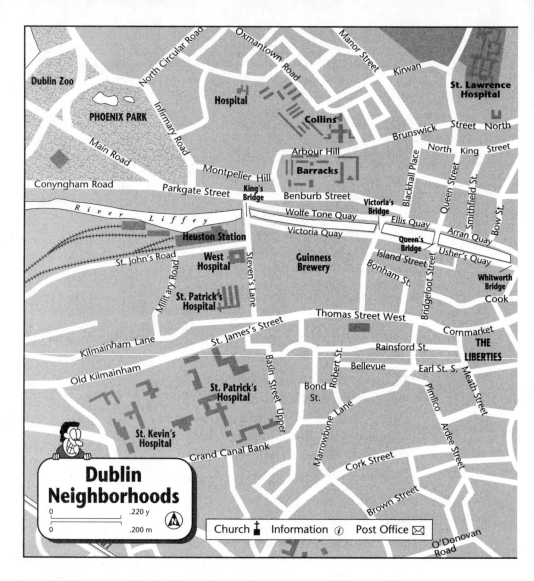

Getting Your Bearings

Dublin the city sprawls, but most of its sights are nicely compacted into a walkable area along the **River Liffey.** Most of what will interest you lies south of the Liffey, except some literary sights to the north around **Parnell Square.**

Dublin's Neighborhoods in Brief

North of the Liffey, the main drag of town is called **O'Connell Street.** O'Connell Street crosses a bridge of the same name to the south side, where it becomes a large traffic circle in front of **Trinity College.** It then narrows again into the pedestrian **Grafton Street.** Grafton Street continues south to spill into **St. Stephen's Green,** which is something between a square and a gorgeous city park. Off the northeast corner of this square is a complex of

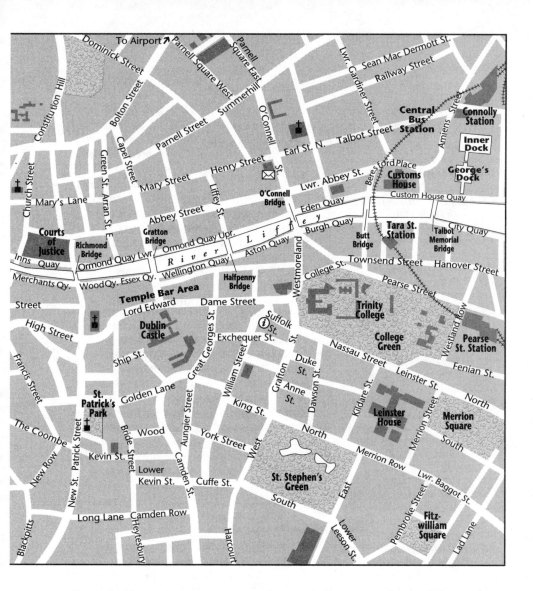

huge buildings that house the government and various national museums and libraries. To the east of the square lie several more verdant city spaces, such as **Merrion Square** and **Fitzwilliam Square.** Farther to the southeast is the fashionable embassy and hotel-filled 'hood **Ballsbridge.**

Back at that traffic circle in front of Trinity College, College Green leads due west past the impressive Bank of Ireland building and becomes **Dame Street. Temple Bar,** Dublin's always trendy, always fun, pub-, club-, and restaurant-filled district lies between Dame Street and the Liffey. (Temple Bar is connected to the north side of the Liffey by the slim photogenic span of the **Ha'penny Bridge.**) Dame Street changes names regularly as it moves west, passing Dublin Castle before reaching Christ Church Cathedral on the edge of the city center.

Time-Savers

The main **Dublin Tourism** office is in St. Andrew's Church (☎ **01/605-7700**), at Suffolk Street, a block west of Grafton Street. There are smaller branches at Baggot Street Bridge (near Fitzwilliam Square), 14 Upper O'Connell St., the airport, and Dun Laoghaire's ferry terminal. The **Temple Bar** neighborhood has its own info center at 18 Eustace St. (☎ **01/671-5717**). Newsstands carry the events mag *In Dublin*.

Getting Into & Around Town

Most trains (from the west, south, and southwest) arrive at **Heuston Station,** on the west end of town. Those from the north pull into the more central **Connolly Station. Buses** arrive at the **Busaras Central Bus Station** on Store Street near Connolly Station. This station is also where the two- to three-times hourly Airlink buses arrive from **Dublin International Airport,** which lies about seven miles (30 minutes) north of the city. These coaches cost £3 ($4.35). The 41 or 41A city bus will do the job a bit more slowly (and drop you off at O'Connell Street Bridge) for £1.10 ($1.60).

Dublin's green double-decker **buses** cover the city and suburbs pretty well, but as I said, Dublin's core is very walkable. To take a bus, hop on, say where you'll be getting off, and pay the driver (nothing bigger than a £5 note), who charges you according to the number of

Bet You Didn't Know

Although Ireland is part of the British Isles, and the people speak English, drive on the left, call their money pounds, and even eat fish 'n' chips, Ireland is *not* part of the United Kingdom. The Irish fought long and hard for their independence from the British crown (some 750 years) and have been an independent republic since 1921. A few counties in the north of Ireland, however, did not throw their lots in with this new country, and hence are still part of the United Kingdom.

Northern Ireland's decision to stay with the United Kingdom was far from unanimous. The pro-British residents (mostly Protestants of British descent) and pro-independence ones (mainly Catholics of older Irish lineage) are constantly at odds over the future of this corner of the Emerald Isle, fighting heated battles on both the political and paramilitary fronts. These "Troubles" have come to a head in numerous terrorist attacks, mainly centered on Belfast and other North Ireland cities (plus a few in London). Though it appears at press time that peace has finally been achieved, details must still be hammered out, and both sides must secure approval from their supporters. For now, Ireland remains a land divided.

stops. Up to about five stops is 60p (85¢); the most you'll ever be charged is £1.25 ($1.80)—except at night when the rate is a flat £2.50 ($3.60) fare.

The speedy electric train **DART** system is really for commuters, with only five stops you may need worry about: three in the city center (Connolly, Tara Street, and Pearse), the Lansdowne Road station in Ballsbridge, and the Dun Laoghaire station at the ferry docks. DART tickets cost 80p ($1.15). If you're arriving in Ireland by **ferry,** you can take DART into town (trains run from 7am to midnight). In the event your ferry arrives in the wee hours, bus 46A runs from the ferry docks to St. Stephens Green from 6am to 11:30pm.

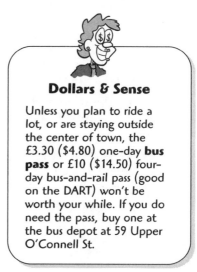

Dollars & Sense

Unless you plan to ride a lot, or are staying outside the center of town, the £3.30 ($4.80) one-day **bus pass** or £10 ($14.50) four-day bus-and-rail pass (good on the DART) won't be worth your while. If you do need the pass, buy one at the bus depot at 59 Upper O'Connell St.

Fast Facts: Dublin

American Express The office is at 116 Grafton St. (☎ **01/677-2874**), opposite Trinity College. It's open Monday to Saturday 9am to 5pm.

Doctors/hospitals In an emergency, ask your hotel to call a doctor for you. Otherwise, call the **Eastern Health Board Headquarters,** Dr. Steevens Hospital (☎ **01/679-0700**) or the **Irish Medical Organization,** 10 Fitzwilliam Place (☎ **01/676-7273**). For an emergency room, go to the **Mater Misericordiae Hospital,** 7 Eccles St. (☎ **01/830-1122**).

Embassy The U.S. Embassy (☎ **01/668-8777**) is at 42 Elgin Rd.

Emergency Dial ☎ **999** in any emergency.

Pharmacies **Leonard's Corner Pharmacy,** 106 S. Circular Rd. (☎ **01/453-4282**) is open daily 9am to 10pm. **Crowley's Pharmacy,** on Kilbarrack Road, is open late at night. Call ☎ **01/832-5332** for hours.

Safety Violent crime has been slow to come to Dublin, but with increased drug traffic, crime has risen. Although you may feel safer here than you do in your hometown, don't let yourself become careless.

Taxis Don't expect to hail a taxi as it drives by; Dublin taxis queue at *ranks* (stands) for their fares. You'll find ranks outside all the major hotels and transportation centers as well as on the busier streets, such as Upper O'Connell Street, College Green, and the north side of St. Stephen's Green. You can also call a taxi. Try **Access Taxis** (☎ **01/668-3333**), **Blue Cabs** (☎ **01/676-1111**), or **Co-op Taxis** (☎ **01/676-6666**). The minimum charge for one passenger is £1.80 ($2.50) for the first mile or the first nine minutes. Then the charge is 80p ($1.15) per mile. Each additional passenger or suitcase is 40p (55¢). Between 8pm and 8am and all day Sunday there is an extra charge of 40p (55¢).

Telephone A local call in Dublin costs 20p (30¢). Pay phones accept both coins and phone cards, which are sold at post offices. Ireland's country code is **353**. Dublin's city code is **01**. If you're calling from outside Ireland, drop the initial zero. To call Dublin from the United States, dial **011-353-1** followed by the number. To call the United States from Ireland directly, dial **001** followed by the area code and phone number. To charge a call to your calling card, or make a collect call home, dial **AT&T** (☎ **1-800-550-000**), **MCI** (☎ **1-800-551-001**), or **Sprint** (☎ **1-800-552-001**).

Transit Info The **Dublin Bus** number is ☎ **01/873-4222.** The number for **Dublin Area Rapid Transit** (DART) is ☎ **01/703-3504.**

Top o' the Mornin' to Ya: Dublin's Hotel Scene

Dublin's center has plenty of good, somewhat pricey, hotels, but you can find some great values if you look hard enough. Many of Dublin's largest hotels are characterless modern affairs, fine for laying down your weary head but utterly charmless. My advice is to seek out one of the number of hotels converted from historic Victorian and Georgian buildings. One of the nicest (and safest) neighborhoods is east of the city center in the embassy-filled residential zone of **Ballsbridge,** a short DART ride from downtown.

Time-Savers

Dublin also has a glut of B&Bs, which generally offer inexpensive accommodations in a friendly, small atmosphere. **Dublin Tourism** (☎ **01/605-7777,** fax: 01/605-7787) can help you find a B&B room for a £3 ($4.25) fee; they book rooms in traditional hotels as well. Another place to check is the **Central Reservation Service** at 1 Clarinda Park North in Dun Laoghaire, south of the city (☎ **01/ 284-1765,** fax 01/ 284-1751).

Ariel House
$$$. Ballsbridge.
In a posh residential suburb and just a block from the speedy DART train into town, Ariel House offers Victorian style, modern comfort, and timeless hospitality to a few lucky travelers (reserve early). The attention to refined detail is evident from the Waterford chandelier and carved cornices in the drawing room, to the period furniture, fine paintings, and Irish linens in the comfy rooms. Rates include a full Irish breakfast.

52 Lansdowne Rd. (east of the city center, beyond Merrion Square; from the DART station, turn left down Lansdowne Rd.). ☎ *01/668-5512.* **Fax:** *01/668-5845.* **DART:** *Lansdowne Rd.* **Bus:** *5, 7A, 8, 46, 63, 84.* **Rates:** *£79–£160 ($112.81–$228.48) double. MC, V.*

Kids Jurys Christ Church Inn
$. Old City.

One of Dublin's great central bargains, Jurys has rooms large enough to hold a family of four, but the price stays at just £59 ($84.25). Outside of its remarkable rates and great location to the west of Dublin's top sights, this modern inn holds few charms. But it is very clean and furnished with contemporary good taste and all your basic amenities.

Christ Church Place (across from Christ Church, where Werburgh St., Lord Edward St., and High St. meet). ☎ *800/448-8355 in the United States, or 01/475-0111 in Ireland.* **Fax:** *01/454-0012.* **Bus:** *21A, 50, 50A, 78, 78A, 78B.* **Rates:** *£59 ($84.25) double. AE, CB, DC, MC, V.*

Shelbourne
$$$$$. St. Stephen's Green.

An imposing red-and-white facade on Dublin's most stately square of greenery announces this historic hotel. Built in 1824, it has been host to actors, writers, and the signing of Ireland's constitution. Crackling fires and Waterford chandeliers greet you in the clubby entrance lounges, while guest rooms play out their varied-size comforts with modern conveniences and antique furnishings. Take afternoon tea in the Lord Mayor's Lounge.

27 St. Stephen's Green (right in the center of town, on the north side of the Green). ☎ *800/225-5843 in the United States or 01/676-6471 in Ireland.* **Fax:** *01/ 661-6006.* **DART:** *Pearse Station.* **Bus:** *10, 11A, 11B, 13, 20B.* **Rates:** *£190 ($271.32) double. AE, CB, DC, MC, V.*

Stauntons on the Green
$$. St. Stephen's Green.

A new hotel in a Georgian townhouse on Dublin's central square, Stauntons is one of the most historic-feeling hotels in the center of Dublin. The windows are tall, ceilings high, furnishings traditional, and fireplaces blazing in the public rooms. There's green every way you look, because the back rooms open onto Iveagh Gardens. The rates include breakfast.

83 St. Stephen's Green (on the south side of the Green). ☎ *01/478-2300.* **Fax:** *01/478-2263.* **DART:** *Pearse Station.* **Bus:** *14A, 62.* **Rates:** *£89 ($127.09) double. AE, DC, MC, V.*

Temple Bar Hotel
$$$$. Temple Bar.

There's no better place for being right in the heart of the action. Trendy Temple Bar got its own comfortable hotel in 1993, when over 100 rooms behind a Victorian facade were converted with traditional furnishings and modern amenities. There's a full Irish breakfast included in the price, plus a good pub, passable restaurant, and Dublin's liveliest neighborhood out the front door.

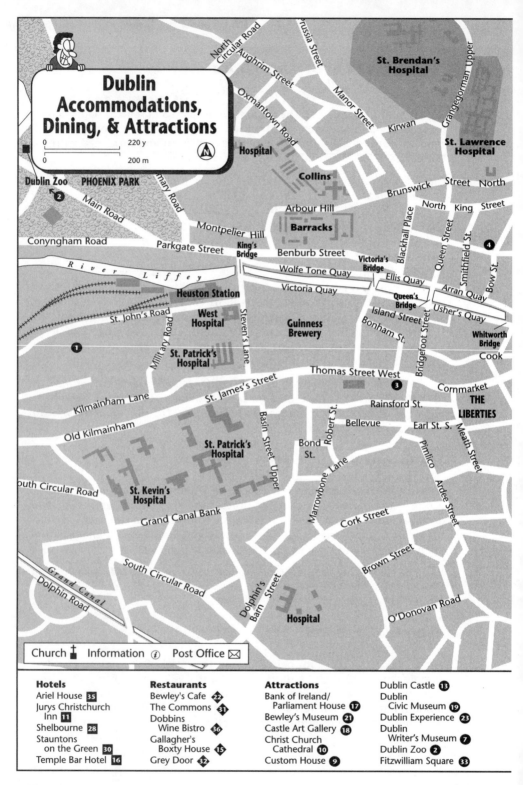

Dublin Accommodations, Dining, & Attractions

| 0 | 220 y |
| 0 | 200 m |

Phoenix Park
Dublin Zoo
Main Road
Conyngham Road
Parkgate Street
Montpelier Hill
King's Bridge
Benburb Street
Wolfe Tone Quay
Victoria Quay
Victoria's Bridge
Ellis Quay
Arran Quay
Queen's Bridge
Usher's Quay
Whitworth Bridge

North Circular Road
Aughrim Street
Oxmantown Road
Prussia Street
Manor Street
Kirwan
Grangegorman Upper

St. Brendan's Hospital
St. Lawrence Hospital
Hospital
Collins Barracks
Arbour Hill
Brunswick Street North
North King Street
Blackhall Place
Queen Street
Smithfield St.
Bow St.

River Liffey

Heuston Station
West Hospital
St. Patrick's Hospital
St. John's Road
Military Road
Steven's Lane
Guinness Brewery
Island Street
Bonham St.
Bridgefoot Street
Cook
Cornmarket
THE LIBERTIES

Thomas Street West
St. James's Street
Kilmainham Lane
Old Kilmainham
Basin Street Upper
Rainsford St.
Bellevue
Earl St. S.
Meath Street
Robert St.
Bond St.
Marrowbone Lane
Pimlico
Ardee Street

St. Patrick's Hospital
South Circular Road
St. Kevin's Hospital
Grand Canal Bank
South Circular Road
Cork Street
Brown Street
O'Donovan Road
Hospital

Grand Canal
Dolphin Road
Dolphin's Barn Street

| Church ✝ | Information ⓘ | Post Office ✉ |

Hotels
Ariel House **35**
Jurys Christchurch Inn **11**
Shelbourne **28**
Stauntons on the Green **30**
Temple Bar Hotel **16**

Restaurants
Bewley's Cafe **22**
The Commons **31**
Dobbins Wine Bistro **36**
Gallagher's Boxty House **15**
Grey Door **32**

Attractions
Bank of Ireland/ Parliament House **17**
Bewley's Museum **21**
Castle Art Gallery **18**
Christ Church Cathedral **10**
Custom House **9**

Dublin Castle **13**
Dublin Civic Museum **19**
Dublin Experience **23**
Dublin Writer's Museum **7**
Dublin Zoo **2**
Fitzwilliam Square **33**

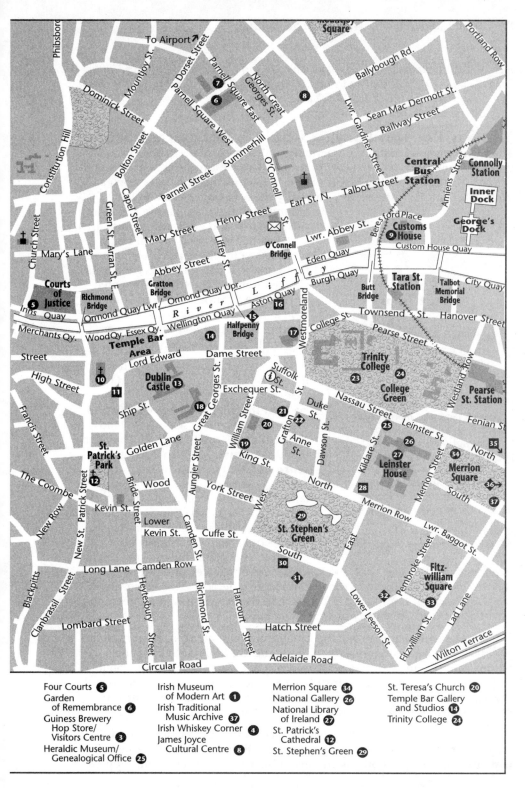

Fleet St. (off Westmoreland St., a block from the Liffey). ☎ **800/448-8355** in the United States or 01/677-333 in Ireland. **Fax:** 01/677-3088. **DART:** Tara St. **Bus:** 78A, 78B. **Rates:** £125 ($182.08) double. MC, V.

You Say Potato, I Say...: Dublin's Restaurant Scene

The Irish have a reputation, not entirely undeserved, of being a meat-and-potatoes—and nothing else—sort of people. This isn't really true, but even if it were, Irish **lamb** and **mutton** (you're in serious sheep country now) are quite excellent. So is the **steak,** especially the beef from central Ireland around Mullingar. You can trust me on this one; my Irish great-great-grandfather raised cattle there (and his son was a butcher). As for those **potatoes,** I never thought a root could taste so good until I visited Ireland. The Irish have managed to cultivate potatoes from a poor man's food almost into an art form; some varieties are so buttery and soft they need no condiments or accompaniment.

Tourist Traps

A traditional hearty **Irish breakfast** is a cholesterol convention you should indulge in at least once. A bowl of deliciously lumpy porridge, eggs, country bacon, scones with marvelous jams and marmalades, black and white puddings (scrumptious, especially if you don't think about what's in them), and a slice of tomato are all fried up—well, except for the scones and porridge—and served on a plate.

The other great food of Ireland, not nearly so well-known, is the **wild salmon** that swims in its rivers, especially in the mighty Shannon. This and other freshwater and sea fish (Ireland *is* an island, and Dublin Bay offers up wonderful **prawns**) give Irish chefs great **seafood** bounty with which to work. And work they do. Ireland is no longer a land of blackened meats and overcooked veggies. Its cooks have examined the French nouvelle and California eclectic schools of cooking and drawn from them techniques to apply to traditional ingredients and recipes. Irish food has made even greater strides toward refinement than British food has in the past two decades. Plus, in cosmopolitan Dublin, you'll find plenty of continental, French, Italian, and other ethnic restaurants to satisfy any hunger craving.

Other Irish foods that may grace your table are roast chicken, **boxty** (potato pancakes wrapped around meaty fillings), **coddle** (boiled bacon, sausages, onions, and potatoes), and lamb stew. Alongside almost every meal you'll find slabs of incredible, dense Irish **breads,** the best being brown bread and the dry soda bread. The most common pub snack is a **toasted ham and cheese sandwich,** which is just as basic as it sounds.

No survey of Irish cuisine would be complete without discussing the true main course of an Irish meal: beer. The Irish will tell you that imported **Guinness** in a can or bottle is another animal entirely from a pint properly pulled in an Irish pub—and they're absolutely right. Some purists insist on patronizing only the pub at the brewery itself (see the following section) in order to guzzle the rich, black, creamy, yeasty elixir straight from the proverbial vat. Guinness's lager is called Harp, and don't miss out on the Guinness rival from Cork, the dark **Murphy's.** Kilkenny's **Smithwicks** is tops when it comes to ales. For a break from the brew, quality **hard cider** is also on tap.

Extra! Extra!

The Irish invented **whiskey** (the legend pins it on a 6th century monk), and Old Bushmills (established in 1608) is the oldest distillery in the world. The "e" isn't the only difference between Irish *whiskey* and Scotch or English *whisky;* the unique Irish distillation process gives the stuff a cleaner, less smoky flavor. Other brands to sample include John Jameson, Powers, Paddy's, Tullamore Dew, Murphy, and Dunphy. The Irish drink their whiskey neat, and a few decades ago they started dumping it into coffee, mixing in sugar, topping it off with whipped cream, and serving it to arrivals at Shannon airport (this **Irish Coffee** may be touristy, but mm, mm, good).

Bewley's Cafe
$. Near St. Stephen's Green. IRISH.

This huge old-fashioned, high-ceilinged tea room on Dublin's main shopping promenade has been a favorite of Dubliners since 1840. You can get well-prepared light foods cafeteria-style, but Bewley's is most famous for its teas with scones and jams. There are other branches at 11-12 Westmoreland St. and 13 S. Great George St.

78-79 Grafton St. (on the main strolling drag in town). ☎ *01/677-6761. Reservations not required.* **Bus:** *15A, 15B, 15C, 46, 55, 63, 83.* **All foods:** *£1.65–£5 ($2.35–$7.15). AE, DC, MC, V.* **Open:** *Lunch and dinner daily (until 1am Mon–Wed, until 2am Thurs–Sat).*

The Commons
$$$$$. St. Stephen's Green. MODERN EUROPEAN.

Michelin has awarded one of its coveted stars to this refined eatery installed in a pair of 18th-century town houses. It continues to win accolades for its Georgian decor (spruced up with modern art) and its ever-changing and eclectic contemporary menu. The chef often features creations such as confit of duck on a beetroot boxty pancake or grilled shark with peppered carrot. In summer, be sure to take an aperitif in the stone-walled garden.

85-86 St. Stephen's Green (on the south side of the square). ☎ *01/475-2597. Reservations required.* **Bus:** *11, 13, 10, 46A.* **Fixed-price lunch:** *£18 ($25.70); fixed-price dinner £32 or £42 ($45.70 or $60). AE, DC, MC, V.* **Open:** *Lunch Mon–Fri, dinner Mon–Sat.*

Dobbins Wine Bistro
$$$. Near Merrion Square. IRISH/CONTINENTAL.
An intimate foodies' fave, Dobbins has seating in a cozy rustic interior or on a tropical patio. The chef uses many traditional Irish ingredients in his inventive dishes. The menu changes often, but may include roast herbed lamb; black sole stuffed with salmon, crab, and prawn; or duckling with orange and port sauce.

15 Stephen's Lane (between Upper and Lower Mount Streets, a block east of Merrion Sq.). ☎ *01/676-4679 or 01/676-4670. Reservations required.* **Bus:** *5, 7A, 8, 46, 84.* **Main courses:** *£12.95–£19.95 ($18.50–$28.50); fixed-price lunch £14.95 ($21.35). AE, DC, MC, V.* **Open:** *Lunch Mon–Fri, dinner Tues–Sat.*

Kids Gallagher's Boxty House
$$. Temple Bar. TRADITIONAL IRISH
Friendly, homey Gallagher's is a fixture both of Temple Bar and of traditional Irish cooking. Its specialties are the grilled potato pancakes called boxty, rolled around fillings of beef, lamb, chicken, or fish. Their open-faced lunchtime sandwiches are excellent, as is their salmon. The clientele is a mix of tourists seeking real Irish cooking and locals doing the same, trying to recapture that old "dinner at Grandma's" feeling.

20-21 Temple Bar (between Essex and Fleet Sts.). ☎ *01/677-2762. Reservations recommended, but not always accepted.* **Bus:** *21A, 46A, 46B, 51B, 51C, 68, 69, 86.* **Main courses:** *at lunch £2.95–£4.50 ($4.20–$6.45); at dinner £5.95–£9.95 ($8.50–$14.20). MC, V.* **Open:** *Lunch and dinner daily.*

Grey Door
$$$. Near St. Stephen's Green. RUSSIAN/SCANDINAVIAN.
The upper dining rooms in this Georgian town house are more elegant than the basement Pier 32 restaurant, which is more of an informal country inn (with traditional music some nights). At both you can get quality north-eastern European cuisine, such as *Kotley Kiev* (chicken Kiev stuffed with vodka butter) and *Galupsti Maskova* (cabbage stuffed with minced lamb).

23 Upper Pembroke St. (off Lower Lesson St. between St. Stephen's Green and Fitzwilliam Sq.). ☎ *01/676-3286. Reservations required.* **Bus:** *46A, 46B, 86.* **Main courses:** *£13–£21 ($18.60–$30); fixed-price lunch £15 ($21.45). AE, DC, MC, V.* **Open:** *Lunch Mon–Fri, dinner Mon–Sat.*

Things to Do Between Pints: Dublin Sightseeing
The two double-decker **bus tours** in Dublin are both very good for basic orientation and sweeping the sights with some commentary. The more formal guided bus tour is **Dublin Tour,** which starts at the Dublin Bus office at

59 Upper O'Connell St. Tickets are £8 ($11.60) for adults and £4 ($5.80) for kids under 16; tours leave daily at 10:15am and 2:15pm. For more flexibility, grab a £5 ($7.25) ticket (£2/$2.90 for kids under 16) for all-day access to the hop-on/hop-off **Dublin City Tour** buses, which run in circles from 9:30am to 4:30pm (April through September) and stop at all the major sights.

Quick Bites

Although you can get a quick meal at **Bewley's Cafe** (see previous review), the hands-down best "fast food" in Dublin comes from **Leo Burdock's** at 2 Werbaugh St., just around the corner from Christ Church cathedral (☎ 01/ 454-0306). It's a veritable temple of the fish and chip crowd, where you get some of the British Isles' greatest chips (french fries) along with your light and flaky fried cod or whiting fish. For picnic grub, Bewley's has takeout, or you can hit up the gourmet counters of the **Gallic Kitchen** at 49 Francis St. (☎ 01/454-4912), where you can put together a meal of salmon en croûte, quiche, and pastries to enjoy on a grassy spot in St. Stephen's Green (where summertime brings open-air concerts), Merrion Square, or Phoenix Park.

The tourist office has several map kits for **self-guided walking tours** on themes such as Old City, Cultural Heritage, or Rock 'n' Stroll (this is, after all, the country of U2, the Cranberries, Sinead O'Connor, and the Pogues, among many others). For a **guided hike** that covers the basic sights, try **Historical Walking Tours of Dublin** (☎ 01/845-0241), which leaves from Trinity College's front gate. Monday through Saturday in June through September, the tours start at 11am, noon, and 3pm; on Sunday, they start at 11am, noon, 2pm, and 3pm. From October through May, tours take place on Saturday and Sunday at noon only. You can also join several **thematic pub crawls,** which I'll get to later in the chapter.

Dublin Sights Not to Miss

Trinity College & the Book of Kells

In the middle of the city is an oasis of peace, green, and students scurrying with their books. Most visitors to the 18th- and 19th-century buildings of Trinity College

Bet You Didn't Know

Queen Elizabeth I founded Trinity in 1592 to enlighten and educate the Irish, or as she put it, "reform...the barbarism of this rude people." Trinity turned out more enlightened than its English counterparts Cambridge and Oxford, being the first to admit women (in 1903). Illustrious graduates include Jonathan Swift, Thomas Moore, Oscar Wilde, Bram Stoker, and Samuel Beckett.

head straight for the library, where there is a fine display on the medieval art of manuscript illumination—a craft at which the Irish excelled. The library is home to a precious trinity of illuminated manuscripts, including one of Ireland's most richly decorated, the 8th-century *Book of Kells*. Stolen from its monastery in 1007, the book was miraculously recovered from a bog three months later. Its gold-rich cover was missing, but the experience did little harm to the vibrant colors and remarkable detail in what is perhaps the most beautiful, important, and cherished illuminated manuscript in the world.

College Green (enter where Dame St. runs into Grafton St.). ☎ *01/677-2941.* **DART:** *Tara Street Station.* **Bus:** *5, 7A, 8, 15A, 15B, 15C, 46, 55, 62, 63, 83, 84.* **Admission:** *£3.50 ($5.10) adults, £3 ($4.35) students and seniors, kids under 11 free.* **Open:** *Mon–Sat 9:30am–5pm, Sun noon–4:30pm.*

National Museum

If you're into antiquities and Celtic civilization, make a beeline for Ireland's foremost archeological collection, which spans prehistory to the middle ages. Among its treasures are the 8th-century Tara Brooch, an intricately designed jewel of white bronze, and the famed Ardagh Chalice (also 8th century), a cup of beaten silver embellished with engravings, embossings, enamels, and gold filigree. You'll also see row after row of golden torcs, those thick yoke-shaped necklaces that were a symbol of royalty among Celtic peoples (and, if ancient Roman chroniclers are to be believed, the only article of clothing Celtic warriors wore into battle).

Kildare St. and Merrion Row. ☎ *01/677-7444.* **DART:** *Pearse Station.* **Bus:** *7, 7A, 8, 10, 11, 13.* **Admission:** *Free.* **Open:** *Tues–Sat 10am–5pm, Sun 2–5pm.*

Christ Church Cathedral

The remaining bits of the 12th-century Norman-style church erected here by Strongbow and his cohorts represent the oldest stone building in Dublin. Strongbow himself, who helped conquer Ireland for the Normans, supposedly rests in peace inside. Purists insist the sarcophagus was made about 170 years after Strongbow's death, and that the grave effigy is modeled after the Earl of Drogheda. Still others argue that no matter whence came the tomb, Strongbow's entrails at least are interred within, and a few hazard that the curious, small half-figure tomb right *next* to the main tomb is Strongbow's. (Myth lovers whisper that this smaller tomb is the tomb of Strongbow's son, sliced in half by his father when Strongbow suspected that junior lacked in the bravery department.) The church is mainly Gothic, largely rebuilt in the 1870s after being an indoor market. Visit the huge crypt underneath the church, once filled with taverns, which extends the length of the nave.

Kildare St. and Merrion Row. ☎ *01/661-8811.* **DART:** *Pearse Station.* **Bus:** *7, 7A, 8, 10, 11, 13.* **Admission:** *Free.* **Open:** *Tues–Sat 10am–5pm, Sun 2–5pm.*

National Gallery

As art galleries go, this one is not the tops in Europe. But it has a few important works by major old masters that make it a 30-minute must for art lovers.

The highlights are Caravaggio's tumultuous 1602 *Arrest of Christ,* Paolo Uccello's oddball 1440 *Virgin and Child,* and Vermeer's richly lit 1665 *Woman Writing a Letter.* The collections are fleshed out with works by Titian, van Dyck, Goya, Velázquez, Gainsborough, El Greco, and Degas.

Merrion Sq. W. ☎ *01/661-5133. **DART:** Pearse Station. **Bus:** 5, 7, 7A, 8, 10, 11, 44, 47, 48A, 62. **Admission:** Free. **Open:** Mon–Wed and Fri–Sat 10am–5:30pm, Thurs 10am–8:30pm, Sun 2–5pm.*

Extra! Extra!

A snit with Christ Church's bigwigs led Dublin's archbishop to promote the nearby church of **St. Patrick** to cathedraldom, effectively giving Dublin two cathedrals. Gothic St. Paddy's—supposedly founded on a site where St. Patrick baptized converts in A.D. 450—was raised in 1190 and rebuilt in the 14th century. Its main attraction is the simple floor tomb of its one-time dean, Jonathan Swift. Swift was the bitingly sarcastic author of *Gulliver's Travels* (a bit of social criticism that somehow found its way to the children's shelf) and *A Modest Proposal,* that famous essay about solving overpopulation and poverty by eating one's babies.

Dublin Castle

Dublin Castle sounds nice and medievally Irish, and indeed this was the site of the first earthen fort established by the Vikings. But the castle today is mainly 17th- and 18th-century state apartments and assembly rooms that served the ruling British government for 700 years. Of more ancient lineage, you do get to see the 13th-century Record Tower (Norman era) and, in the undercroft, the foundations of that Viking bunker and bits of medieval city wall.

Palace St. (off Dame St.). ☎ *01/679-3713. **Bus:** 54, 50, 50A, 56A. **Admission:** £2 ($2.90) adults, £1 ($1.45) students, seniors, and kids under 11. **Open:** Mon–Fri 10am–12:15pm and 2–5pm, Sat–Sun 2–5pm. Required 45-minute guided tours every 20-25 minutes.*

Bet You Didn't Know

The Vikings established most of Ireland's great cities—the Celts tended more toward loosely affiliated tribal clusters. In the 12th century, Viking invaders erected the earthen fortress that would become the modern capital at the spot where the rivers Liffey and Poddle ran together and formed a black pool (or, as they say in Irish, a *dubh linn*).

Dublin Writers Museum

Ireland's writers are legion; the short list includes Jonathan Swift, Oscar Wilde, James Joyce, Thomas Mann, Roddy Doyle, and Nobelists George Bernard Shaw, W. B. Yeats, and Samuel Beckett. This 18th-century house celebrates Ireland's famed scribes with first editions, letters, busts, and photos. It definitely could be more interesting—the audio tour spices it up a bit—so only bibliophiles and those keen on finding out more about Irish literature need apply.

18-19 Parnell Sq. N. ☎ *01/872-2077.* **DART:** *Conolly Station.* **Bus:** *10, 11, 11A, 11B, 12, 13, 14, 16, 19, 19A, 22, 22A, 36.* **Admission:** *£2.75 ($4) adults, £2.35 ($3.40) students and seniors, £1.15 ($1.65) kids under 11.* **Open:** *Daily 10am–5pm. Closed Mon Sept–May.*

Extra! Extra!

If the Writers Museum isn't enough, check out the definitive **James Joyce Cultural Centre** (☎ **01/878-8547**) at 33 N. Great George's St. and the **Abbey Theatre** (☎ **01/878-7222**), founded at Lower Abbey Street by W. B. Yeats and Lady Gregory in 1904 (plays are put on Monday through Saturday at 8pm). One of the most fun ways to visit the Dublin of books is to take the **Literary Pub Crawl,** a popular guided walking tour that meets at the Bailey Pub on Duke Street at noon and 7:30pm on Sundays year round and daily at 7:30pm May through September (also at 3pm June through August). Or try the **James Joyce Dublin Walking Tour,** a special treat you must book in advance through the Joyce Centre, because it is run by the Centre's curator—and Joyce's nephew—Ken Monaghan.

Guinness Brewery Hop Store

Alec Guinness refined his rich, black variant on stout in 1759, and by the mid-18th century his brewery was the biggest in the world. You can't get into the plant itself anymore, but there's an entertaining audio-visual display in the little Hop Store museum, with features on Guinness' long and clever advertising history and the lost art of the cooper (barrel-maker). The highlight, of course, is the pub, where you get a free half-pint of the famed brew.

Crane St. (off Thomas St.). ☎ *01/453-6700 ext. 5155.* **Bus:** *21A, 78, 78A.* **Admission:** *£2 ($2.90) adults, £1.50 ($2.15) students and seniors, 50p (70¢) kids under 11.* **Open:** *Mon–Fri 10am–4pm.*

Other Fun Stuff to Do
➤ **Spending an Evening in the Pubs & Clubs of Temple Bar.**
   Artsy, hopping Temple Bar is most people's favorite district of Dublin. It's a few streets along the Liffey packed with pubs, shops, bars, cafes,

galleries, entertainment venues, and fun. The neighborhood even has its own tourist office (see "Getting Your Bearings," earlier in the chapter), which publishes the worthwhile *Temple Bar Guide*. Wandering on your whims is the best way to visit Temple Bar, but a proper pub crawl here will include **Flannery's** (48 Temple Bar), **The Norseman** (Essex Street East), **Oliver St. John Gogarty** (57 Fleet St.), and its cater-corner neighbor **Auld Dubliner** (Temple Bar and Anglesea Streets.). Clubbers can dress to the nines and wait in line for **Club M** (in Blooms Hotel at Anglesea Street) or **The Kitchen** (6-8 Wellington Quay), a trendy new joint partly owned by U2. (Dublin's hottest disco, though, is **POD,** far from Temple Bar on Harcourt Street.)

Tourist Traps

Guinness Tricks & Etiquette: Guinness—like any other beer—is best "pulled" from a tapped keg. If you see the bartender fluidly cranking down the tap arm over and over, he's pulling a proper pint. When ordering Guinness, don't grab the glass when the barkeep first puts it down; he's letting the foam settle and will top it off after a minute or two. The famously thick head on a Guinness should stay intact until you get to the bottom of the glass. The old trick is to carve your initials, or a hokey shamrock, into the froth with a knife blade and watch as it remains undisturbed and intact all the way to the bottom.

➤ **Exploring Georgian Dublin.** All over town you'll see posters of colorful doorways surrounded by white columns and topped with a half-moon window. These are the Georgian Doorways of Dublin, part of an 18th-century neoclassical architectural style practiced across Britain during the reigns of Georges I to III. Dublin's great squares are lined with Georgian town houses, especially St. Stephan's Green and Merrion Square. On the latter, at **no. 29 Lower Fitzwilliam St.,** is a restored home you can enter and tour. The tourist office hands out a self-guided walking tour map of Georgian Dublin.

➤ **Tapping Your Feet on a Musical Pub Crawl.** If you have even the slightest interest in traditional Irish music—or if your only exposure to Celtic music is the New Wave stylings of Enya—take the Musical Pub Crawl, a touristy but fun guided walk of four Dublin pubs led by a pair of musicians. They'll introduce you to several traditional instruments, a couple of songs and styles, and give you plenty of time to introduce yourself to Ireland's beer as you go. After this primer, you'll be well-armed to check out pubs on your own to find less contrived "sessions" (impromptu traditional jams) going on. The tour begins in the upstairs room at Oliver St. John Gogarty's pub at the corner of Fleet and

Anglesea Streets in Temple Bar. Show up at 7:30pm Saturday through Thursday (from May through October).

➤ **Succumbing to a Hokey Audio-Visual "History o' Dublin" Experience.** Suspend your Swiftian sarcasm for a morning to make a clean sweep of several Disneyesque mixtures of rides, life-sized dioramas, audio tours, and earnestly bad acting that try, and sometimes succeed, to bring eras of Dublin's past to life. The "most like a tourist office booster video" award goes to Trinity College's 45-minute **Dublin Experience** (☎ **01/677-2941**) in the Davis Theater on Nassau Street. The cheesiest is **Dublinia** (☎ **01/679-4611**), at Christ Church Place off High Street, which tries to evoke medieval Dublin from the Norman era through the 1530s. Most fun is the imaginative **Dublin's Viking Adventure** (☎ **01/605-7777**), in Temple Bar off Essex Street, that gives you a simulated ride on a Viking ship and then a "tour" through a colonial Vikingsburg village peopled with costumed Dubliners. If you reserve ahead, you can top it all off (for £33.50/$48.60) with the "Viking Feast" at 7:30pm Wednesday through Monday.

Extra! Extra!

No self-respecting Dubliner would confine her pub-crawling just to Temple Bar. Make sure you also hit Dublin's oldest and greatest pub, the **Brazen Head** (west of Temple Bar at 20 Lower Bridge St.), as well as the Victorian **Doheny and Nesbitt** (5 Lower Bagot St.), the literary **Davy Byrnes** (21 Duke St.), and two musical bars **Kitty O'Shea's** (23–25 Upper Grand Canal St.) and **O'Donoghue's** (15 Merrion Row).

➤ **Digging for your Irish Roots.** No, not potatoes! If you're like me— and approximately 40 million other Americans out there—you've got some Irish in ya. Hundreds of Americans cross the Big Pond every year to search out their ancestors here, and the Irish are much obliged to help (for a modest fee). Many agencies specialize in lineage tracing, but your first stop should be the **Heraldic Museum/Genealogical Office** (☎ **01/661-8811**) at 2 Kildare St. Gawking at the museum's heraldry exhibit is free, but you've got to scrape up £20 ($29) to access its consultation service and start tracking down the Gaelic branch of your family tree.

➤ **I Don't Say This Often, But It's Time to Shop.** In the country that invented duty-free, you'll want to peruse some items of local craft and tradition, from tweeds and tin whistles to Waterford crystal, woolen sweaters, and whiskey. Dublin has several "everything Irish" stores (department store-sized gift shops, really) that cater exclusively to tourists, often by the busload. A few, though, have high quality control and are great if you're on a tight time schedule (all but one of the following are across from the south flank of Trinity College). Head for **House of Ireland** (☎ **01/671-4543**), at 37-38 Nassau St., or **The Kilkenny Shop** (☎ **01/677-7066**), nearby at 6-10 Nassau St. You needn't go all the way to the Arran Islands to pick up thick Irish woolen sweaters. Try the **Blarney Woolen Mills** (☎ 01/671-0068) at 21-23 Nassau St. or, even better, **Monaghan's** (☎ 01/677-0823) at 15-17 Grafton Arcade.

Get Outta Town: Day Trips & Excursions

Lovely as Dublin is, you really shouldn't come to Ireland without seeing a bit of its famed countryside. Scenic drives abound; and the excursions below will take you past ruined churches and impressive mansions, along rocky shorelines and stunning, verdant landscapes.

North of Dublin to Passage Tombs & Ruined Medieval Abbeys

Several sights just north of Dublin around the Boyne River Valley epitomize two of the greatest attractions of Ireland—prehistoric sites and ruined abbeys—in easily doable day trips. The most convenient base for the region is the town of Drogheda, which has regular **rail and bus links** with Dublin. Unfortunately, the **tourist office** (☎ 041/37-070) here is open June through August only, so for information you may have to visit the regional office (☎ 042/35-484) on Jocelyn Street in the city of Dundalk, farther up the road.

Top honors for sightseeing go to **Newgrange** (☎ 041/24-488), Ireland's most famous and most accessible passage tomb. This 36-foot-high mound of stones—some weighing up to 16 tons—was fitted together into a watertight engineering triumph well over 5000 years ago, before Stonehenge or the Pyramids were even contemplated. Guided visits down the 60-foot passage to the center are given daily 10am through 4:30pm from November through February, with evening hours lengthening as the season wears on (by June through September, it stays open until 7pm). While you wait for your tour, you can walk around the tomb, examin-ing the occasional carved Celtic swirl or decoration.

Located six miles northwest of Drogheda are the remains of the monastery **Monasterboice,** now represented mainly by its quiet, monumental cemetery. This graveyard is filled with Celtic high crosses, including the best preserved in Ireland, **Muiredeach's High Cross,** a 17-foot-tall example from A.D. 922 (look at the beauti-fully preserved "Taking of Christ" panel just above the base). Nearby are the ruins of **Mellifont Abbey,** a 12th-century reli-gious community of which little remains other than a stretch of colonnade and part of a pretty octagonal lavabo (ca. 1200).

You can stay in Drogheda at the modern **Westcourt Hotel** (☎ 041/30-965; fax: 041/309-7041) on West Street for £75

Extra! Extra!

For more Neolithic fun just a mile from Newgrange, visit the ongoing excavations at the much less–visited collection of grassy mound tombs known as **Knowth** (☎ 041/24-824), a site inhabited from roughly 3000 B.C. to A.D. 1200. Its hours are similar to those of Newgrange.

($100 to $128.60) per double. For food, check out the pub grub at **Weavers** (☎ 041/32-816) on Dominick Street; to sit down for a more complete meal, try the pricey French cuisine at the **Buttergate Restaurant** (☎ 041/ 37-407) on Millimount Square.

South of Dublin: Mansions & Monasteries in County Wicklow

The gardens and bogland of Country Wicklow begin within a surprisingly quick 15-minute drive south of downtown Dublin. You can easily visit the sights listed here in a day trip from Dublin and be back in time for dinner. Dublin's **tourist office** has information on County Wicklow; otherwise, you'd have to drive all the way through the region to Wicklow Town and the area tourism office (☎ 0404/69-117) on Fitzwilliam Square. This region is best seen by car, but if you're without wheels, **Gray Line Tours** (☎ 01/ 661-9666) takes busloads of tourists from Dublin to the major sights from May to September.

A few miles south of Dublin on the N11, just past the town of Enniskerry, lies **Powerscourt Gardens** (☎ 01/286-7676), 1,000 acres of late 18th-century gardens, grottoes, and fountains that make up one of the prime examples of "civilized naturalism" in Europe. The huge manor house was gutted by fire in 1974, but restorations are underway. About four miles on is the 400-foot **Powerscourt Waterfall,** tallest in Ireland (I wouldn't recommend walking it—the road is quite narrow).

The old Military Road (R115) slices through the wildest heights of the **Wicklow Mountains.** This eerie peatscape covered with heather and reddish scrub looks like it belongs somewhere on Mars, with only the Sally Gap pass and Glenmacnass waterfalls breaking up the moody boglands. At Laragh, detour west to visit one of the most secluded and magical (except when inundated by tour buses in summer) of Ireland's ruined monastic sites, **Glendalough** (☎ 0404/45-325), filled with high crosses, round towers, pretty lakes, and medieval stone buildings. All the sights listed here are open daily from about 9:30am to dusk.

Driving Rings Around County Kerry

County Kerry, although one of the most heavily touristed regions of Ireland, is also a true outpost of Celtic culture. Ancient Irish traditions flourish here, from music and storytelling to good pub *craic* (conversation) and some of the country's few remaining Gaelic-speaking pockets. The 110-mile Ring of Kerry, a scenic route circling the Inveragh Peninsula, is Ireland's most famous—and most tour bus-engulfed—drive. You can do the Ring in a day, but I'd give the area two or three in order to spend time in Killarney, tour the less-visited Dingle Peninsula, and see some of the other neglected sights off the Ring. There's frequent daily train service from Ireland's big cities into Killarney, the region's main town and tourist center. Killarney also houses the region's main **tourist office** (☎ 064/31-633) in the Town Hall off Main Street.

The thing to do in Country Kerry is **drive the Ring** (a well-signed stretch of route N70), visiting coastal villages, snapping pictures of inland lakes, and gawking at the mountainous heights of the Inveragh Peninsula along the

240

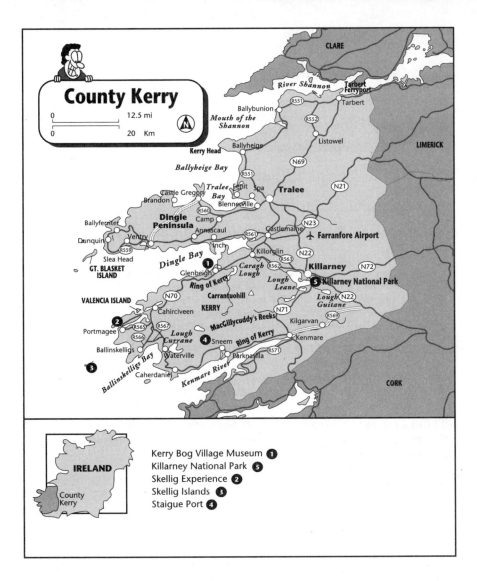

County Kerry

0 — 12.5 mi
0 — 20 Km

CLARE

River Shannon   Tarbert
                 Ferryport
R551   Tarbert
Ballybunion
Mouth of the   R552   Listowel   LIMERICK
Shannon
Ballyheige
Kerry Head
Ballyheige Bay   N69
R551
Tralee Fenit Spa   Tralee   N21
Castle Gregory Bay
Brandon   Blennerville
Dingle   Camp   N23
Ballyferriter Peninsula   Castlemaine   Farranfore Airport
Dunquin   Annascaul   R561
Ventry   R560
Inch   N22
R559   Killorglin
Slea Head   Killorglin R563
GT. BLASKET   Dingle Bay   ❶   Caragh R562   Killarney   N72
ISLAND   Glenbeigh   Lough   Lough ❺ Killarney National Park
Ring of Kerry   Leane
VALENCIA ISLAND   N70   Carrantuohill △   Lough   N22
Cahirciveen   KERRY   Guitane   N71
❷   R567   MacGillycuddy's Reeks   Kilgarvan   R569
Portmagee   R565 R566 Lough   Sneem Ring of Kerry   Kenmare
Ballinskelligs   Currane ❹   R571
❸   Waterville   Parknasilla
Caherdaniel   Kenmare River   CORK
Ballinskelligs Bay

IRELAND

County
Kerry

Kerry Bog Village Museum ❶
Killarney National Park ❺
Skellig Experience ❷
Skellig Islands ❸
Staigue Port ❹

way. Highlights include the **Kerry Bog Village** at Glenbeigh (thatched cottages recreated for us tourists), **Cahirciveen** (the main town), **Staigue Fort** (a well-preserved, Iron Age drystone fortress), and the towns of **Sneem** (cottages in festive colors) and **Kenmare** (stop for some lace). About halfway around the Ring, you can detour onto Valentia Island, connected to the mainland by a bridge and home to the **Skellig Island Experience.** This video and display center introduces you to the endangered natural habitats and medieval monastery of the dramatic Skellig Islands off the coast. This is as close as you can get to the interiors of these islets, because boats from Valencia out to the Skelligs themselves can only circle the islands. In order to preserve that precarious nature, no docking is allowed.

You can buck the crowds by driving a similar, much less touristed, and (in my opinion) even more scenic circle around the **Dingle Peninsula,** one inlet to the north of the Inveragh. Dingle is the main town, from which you can hire a boat to take you out to meet (if he's feeling playful) Fungi, the resident dolphin of Dingle Bay. Decompress from the white-knuckle driving on the Ring in the touristy city of **Killarney,** gateway to a beautiful National Park full of lakes; waterfalls; castles; woodlands; bogs; and the manor house, gardens, and romantically ruined abbey of Muckross.

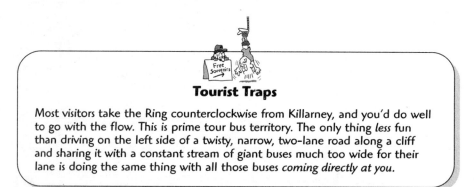

Tourist Traps

Most visitors take the Ring counterclockwise from Killarney, and you'd do well to go with the flow. This is prime tour bus territory. The only thing *less* fun than driving on the left side of a twisty, narrow, two-lane road along a cliff and sharing it with a constant stream of giant buses much too wide for their lane is doing the same thing with all those buses *coming directly at you.*

Three miles west of Killarney, near Fossa and right on the Lower Lake, sits the picturesque Victorian-era **Hotel Europe** (☎ **800/221-1074** in the United States, in Ireland 064/31-900; fax: 064/32-118), with doubles running £114 to £146 ($139.30 to $178.60). **Foley's** (☎ 064/31-217), in Killarney at 23 High St., serves excellent Irish food and seafood from Dingle Bay in a Georgian atmosphere.

Part 4

The Heartland: Central Europe

Welcome to the heart of Europe, where the destinations range from chic, sophisticated Paris—home to fine food, high fashion, and great art—to dreamy, baroque Prague, which burst out from behind Eastern Europe's tattered Iron Curtain to become a vigorous, growing capital. Come with me and we'll cruise the 17th-century canals of Amsterdam in search of Rembrandts and van Goghs, the Red Light District, and the house where Anne Frank hid from the Nazis. In Munich, we'll hoist a beer stein and discover how a city can harbor both the oompah-band cheeriness of Bavaria and the refinement of a cultural center financed by a cutting-edge industrial sector.

Join me in genteel Vienna of the Hapsburgs, and we'll explore the city that taught Paris how to do the cafe thing and the world how to build an opera house. In the Bernese Oberland of Switzerland, we'll scale the Alps to legendary heights on exhilarating gondola rides; tour ice palaces carved into glaciers; and take in the sky-scraping vistas from Europe's snowy summit.

Chapter 16

Paris &
Environs

In This Chapter

➤ The sightseeing skinny—scaling the Eiffel Tower and avoiding lines at the Louvre

➤ Great meals and fine wines in Europe's capital of cuisine

➤ Left Bank lounging: the best people-watching and poetry-writing cafes

➤ Excursions to sumptuous Versailles, Fontainebleau, and Chartres

Paris is the City of Light—the world capital of romance, birthplace of bohemians and impressionists, muse to Hemingway and the Lost Generation, and the high temple of haute cuisine. You can OD on art at the Louvre, cruise past 18th-century palaces on the Seine, write poetry at a sidewalk cafe table, dance in the colored glow of Notre Dame's stained glass, dine stupendously in a tiny bistro, or steal long kisses atop the Eiffel Tower. It's easy to romanticize this city—and just as easy to denigrate it. No doubt you've heard that the people are rude, the museums are crowded, the traffic is horrendous, the Champs-Elysées has become a McDonaldized strip mall, and everything is far, far too expensive.

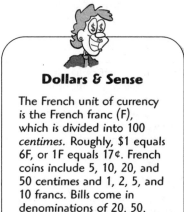

Dollars & Sense

The French unit of currency is the French franc (F), which is divided into 100 *centimes*. Roughly, $1 equals 6F, or 1F equals 17¢. French coins include 5, 10, 20, and 50 centimes and 1, 2, 5, and 10 francs. Bills come in denominations of 20, 50, 100, 200, 500, and 1,000 francs.

But these obstacles shouldn't stand in the way of a good time. So the people aren't as welcoming as those in the Sicilian countryside—if you don't expect them to be, you won't be disappointed. The museums are indeed popular, so go early to beat the crowds. As for the traffic, you don't need to drive—the Parisian Métro (subway) is fantastic. Sure, McDonald's and multiplexes have crept onto the Champs-Elysées, but you'll find plenty of elegant, authentic Paris elsewhere. Although Paris has the potential to be the biggest wallet drain of your entire trip, I also know of no city more chockablock with great values on everything from meals and hotels to shopping and museums. You've just got to be willing to search them out, and I'm here to help you do just that.

Although those positives and negatives are all true to some extent, they are by no means the sum of the city. Paris continues to strike a lively balance between the vibrant, modern metropolis of today and the majestic, historic city of yesterday. It's a town of hip nightclubs, cutting-edge cuisine, and the highest fashion, as well as one of venerable museums, cafe legends, and sweeping 18th- and 19th-century grandeur. It's this balance that keeps Paris intriguing, keeps it attractive, and keeps an army of visitors and faithful admirers coming back year after year.

Time-Savers

The main **tourist informa-tion office** (☎ 01-49-52-53-54) is at 127 Champs-Elysées, 8e. There are also offices in all the train stations (except Gare St-Lazare) and at every ter-minal of both Charles de Gaulle and Orly airports. The tourist office hands out *Paris Selection,* a monthly events magazine, but *Pariscope,* available at any newsstand, is much better and more in-depth.

Getting Your Bearings

The **Seine River** divides Paris between the **Right Bank** *(Rive Droite)* to the north and the **Left Bank** *(Rive Gauche)* to the south. Paris began on the **Ile de la Cité,** an island in the Seine that is still the center of the city and home to Notre Dame cathedral. It's also connected to the nearby posh residen-tial island of **Ile de Saint-Louis.** Traditionally, the Right Bank is consid-ered more upscale with Paris's main boulevards such as **Champs-Elysées** and museums such as the **Louvre.** The Left Bank is the old Bohemian half of Paris with the **Latin Quarter** around the university.

Paris Neighborhoods in Brief

Paris is divided into 20 districts called *arrondissements.* These districts start with the **first arrondissement** (which includes the Louvre neighbor-hood and the tip of the Ile de la Cité) and then spiral out from there. At the end of each address in this chapter, you'll see a number followed by an *e* (or in the case of 1, an *er*), such as 8e or 5e. Together they refer to the arrondisse-ment. Most of these districts also correspond with traditional, named neigh-borhoods. A Parisian address, spoken or written, isn't complete unless the neighborhood name or arrondissement is included. The last two digits of a zip code are the arrondissement, so an address listed as "Paris 75003" would be in the third arrondissement.

Among the major arrondissements on the Right Bank is the **3e.** Called **Le Marais,** this up-and-coming neighborhood manages to remain genuinely Parisian amid the swirl of tourism in the city center. The **4e** includes the Ile de la Cité, Ile St-Louis, the **Beaubourg** pedestrian zone, and the **Pompidou** modern art center. The **8e**—a natural extension westward of the 1er—is Paris's most posh area, consisting of ritzy hotels, fashion boutiques, fine restaurants, and upscale town houses. It centers along the grandest boulevard in a city famous for them: the **Champs-Elysées.** Although the sidewalks of this historic shopping promenade were recently cleaned up and widened, the Champs-Elysées has become merely a shadow of its former elegant self; it's no more than a string of international chain stores and movie theaters. The Champs-Elysées beelines east-west from the **Place de la Concorde**—an oval plaza at the western end of the Louvre complex where French royalty met the business end of a guillotine during the Revolution—to the **Arc de Triomphe.** The Arc is one of the world's greatest triumphal arches, a monument to France's unknown soldier and to the gods of car-insurance premiums (surrounding the Arc is a five-lane traffic circle where, it seems, anything goes). In the northerly reaches of the Right Bank lies **Montemarte,** still echoing with the ghosts of Bohemian Paris. The neighborhood is so distinct and charming it gets its own writeup under "Other Fun Stuff To Do" below.

The Left Bank arrondissements include the **5e,** the famous old **Latin Quarter,** named for the language spoken by the university students who gave it its once colorful, bohemian atmosphere. These days, it's another sad Parisian shadow of former glory, now replaced with gyro stands, souvenir shops, recent immigrants, and hordes of visitors wondering what all the fuss is about. The adjacent **6e** has been lucky enough to retain some of its counterculture charm. The students of Paris's Fine Arts School help liven up things here, especially in the **St-Germain-des-Prés** neighborhood of cafes, brasseries, and restaurants. The **7e,** tucked into a wide arc of the Seine, intrudes a bit on the St-Germain neighborhood, but its major features are the **Musée d'Orsay,** the **Eiffel Tower,** and the **Rodin Museum.**

Getting Into & Around Town

Paris has many **rail stations,** but most international trains arrive at one of the following three. The **Gare du Nord** serves the Netherlands, Belgium, Denmark, and northern Germany. Gare du Nord also serves all the trains coming from London—the destination for both the Eurostar direct train that comes through the Channel Tunnel (a dozen trains daily for a four-hour trip), as well as trains arriving on the last leg of the old-fashioned route: London–Dover by train; Dover–Calais by ferry; and Calais–Paris by train (four trains daily; 10.5 *long* hours for the trip). **Gare de Lyon** serves the south (Italy and parts of Switzerland), while **Gare de l'Est** handles trains from Switzerland, southern Germany, and Austria. Most **international flights** land at **Charles de Gaulle Airport (Roissy),** 14 miles northeast of the

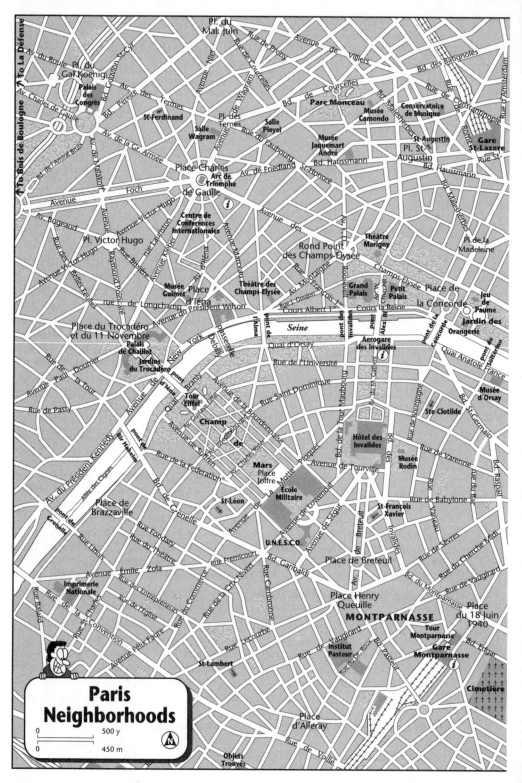

Paris
Neighborhoods

0 ____ 500 y
0 ____ 450 m

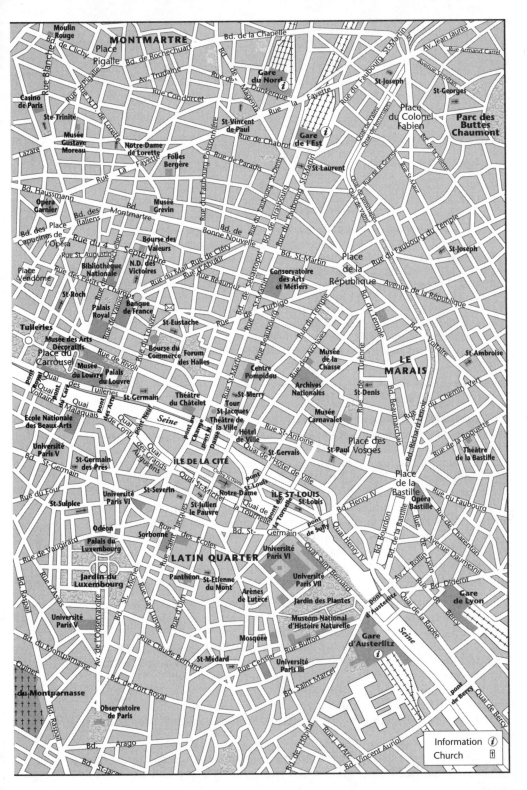

city. Some charter flights, as well as many national flights, land 8.5 miles south of town at **Orly Airport.** Both airports have shuttle buses that will take you to nearby RER (commuter train) stations, where you can catch trains into Paris.

Dollars & Sense

Paris transport **tickets** are good on the Métro, bus, and RER lines. Individual tickets cost 7.50F ($1.25), but a *carnet* (pack of 10) costs only 44F ($7.30). The **Paris Visite** card gets you unlimited travel on all forms of public transportation. The regular pass should be all you need, because it covers zones 1 through 3 (all of central Paris and many of its suburbs). It costs 50F ($8.30) for one day; 85F ($14.15) for two days, 120F ($20) for three days, and 170F ($28.30) for five days. Kids ages 4 to 11 pay half price. Passes covering zones 1 through 5 (*all* the 'burbs, including Disneyland Paris) cost twice as much, and passes for zones 1 through 8 (the entire Ile-de-France region) cost three times as much. You can buy tickets and passes at most Métro stations and tourist offices.

The Paris **Métro (subway)** is one of the best subways in Europe, a clean and efficient system so well interconnected that you'll never have to walk too far to find a stop. Using a Métro map, find which line you want to take and the name of the last station in the direction you want to take it. In the Métro tunnels, follow signs for that last station, and you'll get on the train going the right way. You might have to transfer to another line to get to your destination (though usually not more than once per trip). When transferring, follow the signs labeled *correspondance* toward the next line. Don't follow a *sortie* sign, unless you want to go to the station exit. You can make unlimited transfers on one ticket so long as you don't exit the system— although you will often find yourself walking what seems to be halfway to your destination in the long tunnels that connect some transfer stations.

You'll notice that most lines are numbered while others appear to be assigned letters. These lettered lines (A, B, C, and D) are technically not the Métro, but are part of the overlapping **RER** network. This high-speed commuter light-rail system services only major stops within the city, and it extends farther out into the suburbs. It uses the same tickets as the Métro (except when you're traveling way out into the 'burbs, for which you'll have to buy a separate ticket), and you can transfer freely between the two systems. Some RER lines are particularly useful; the C line, for instance, follows the left bank of the Seine closely (no Métro line does this) and also heads out to Versailles.

In all my trips to the City of Light, I've never found occasion to use the **bus** system, because the Métro works so well and is much faster than plodding through above-ground traffic. Plus, bus trips can get expensive. They use the same tickets as the Métro, but a single ticket is only good for two "sections," which may not get you to your destination. If you're traveling through three or more sections, you'll have to punch two tickets. Separate maps for each bus route are posted at bus stops, and each map has a blue-and-red bar running along the bottom. The stops that appear directly above the blue section of this bar are within the two-section limit. For stops over the red section(s) of the bar, you'll have to use two tickets. When the number of a bus route is written in black on a white circle, it means that the bus stops there daily; when it's written in white on a black circle, it means the bus doesn't stop there on Sundays or holidays.

Bet You Didn't Know

In most cities, subway car doors all open automatically when the train comes to a stop, but not in Paris. Here, whether you're boarding or getting off, you must either push a big button or, in older cars, turn a crank knob to open the door. This is surprisingly easy to forget. I can't count how many times I've stood on the train at my stop, staring stupidly at a closed door for a few seconds before sheepishly remembering to turn the knob.

Tourist Traps

Both ends of all RER lines split off like the frayed ends of a rope as they leave the city, so make sure the train you board is heading out to the numbered fork you want (for example, the C line has seven different end destinations, C1 through C7). Maps on the platforms show you the routes of each fork, and TV displays tell you when the next half dozen trains will be arriving and which number each one is.

Paris Fast Facts

American Express   The office at 11 rue Scribe (☎ **01-47-77-70-07**) is open Monday to Friday 9am to 6:30pm. The currency desk *only* is open Saturday 9am to 6:30pm.

Doctors/hospitals   **SOS Médicins** (☎ **01-47-07-77-77**) recommends physicians. **SOS Dentaire** (☎ **01-43-37-51-00**) will locate a dentist for you. The U.S. embassy will also provide a list of doctors. Both the **American**

251

Hospital of Paris, 63 bd. Victor-Hugo, Neuilly-sur-Seine (☎ 01-46-41-25-25), and the **British Hospital of Paris,** 3 rue Barbes Levallois-Perret (☎ 01-46-39-22-22), staff English-speaking physicians.

Embassy   The U.S. embassy is at 2 av. Gabriel, 8e (☎ 01-43-12-22-22).

Emergency   Dial ☎ **17** for the police. To report a fire, call ☎ **18.** If you need an ambulance, call ☎ **15** for **SAMU** (Service d'Aide Medicale d'Urgence), a private ambulance company, or call the fire department at ☎ **01-45-78-74-52;** you'll be rushed to the nearest emergency room.

Pharmacies   One pharmacy in each neighborhood remains open all night. One to try is the **Pharmacie Dhéry,** 84 av. des Champs-Elysées, 8e (☎ **01-45-62-02-41**), in the Galerie des Champs-Elysées shopping center. Or check the door of the nearest pharmacy; it will list the pharmacies open at night.

Safety   Paris is a relatively safe city with little violent crime, but there is plenty of theft. Around popular tourist sites, on the Métro, and in the station corridors lurk pickpockets—often children—who aren't afraid to gang up on you, distract you by holding or waving an item near your face, and then make off with your wallet. It only takes seconds, so hold on to your wallet or purse and yell at or push away your attackers—don't hold back because they're just children. Look out for thieves around the Eiffel Tower, the Louvre, Notre Dame, Montmartre, and other popular tourist sites.

Taxis   Although you can hail a taxi on the street, cabs in Paris are scarce, and it may be easier to hire one at a stand. Check the meter when you board to be sure you're not also paying the previous passenger's fare, and if your taxi lacks a meter, settle the cost of the trip before setting out. You can also call a cab to pick you up, but fares are higher because the meter begins running when the driver receives the assignment. Try ☎ **01-45-85-85-85,** 01-42-70-41-41, or 01-42-70-00-42.

The initial fare for up to three passengers is 13F ($2.15) and 3.36F (55¢) per kilometer. Between 7pm and 7am the per-kilometer charge rises to 5.45F (90¢). No surcharges apply if you have several small bags inside the taxi, but stowing larger bags in the trunk costs you 6 to 10F ($1 to $1.65) per bag.

Telephone   The minimum charge for a local call is 2F (30¢). Coin-operated phones take 1F, 2F, and 5F coins, but you're more likely to use a phone that requires a *télécarte* (phone card) sold at post offices and *tabacs* (newsstands/ tobacco shops) for 40F ($6.65) or 96F ($16). Just insert the télécarte and dial. For **directory assistance,** dial ☎ **12.**

France's country code is **33.** Calling anywhere within the country's borders requires dialing a 10-digit phone number (it already includes the city code) even if you are calling another number from within Paris. To call Paris from the United States, dial **011-33,** and then drop the initial zero of the French number and just dial the remaining nine digits. To charge your call to a calling card, dial **AT&T** at ☎ **0-800-99-0011, MCI** at ☎ **0-800-99-0019,** or **Sprint** at ☎ **0-800-19-0087.** To call the United States direct from Paris, dial **00** (wait for the dial tone), and then dial **1** followed by the area code and number.

Transit Info   For Métro information (in French), call ☎ 01-43-46-14-14.

The Paris Hotel Scene...or, Voulez–vous Coucher Avec Moi Ce Soir?

Paris has some 2,000 hotels, so surely you'll find a room. Finding a quality room in a desirable location and in your price bracket is the tricky part. This city is full of overblown, over-priced hotels and flea-bag dives even the scruffiest backpackers would turn up a nose at. Stick with me, though, and I'll help you find something that meets your needs, including some budget hideaways.

The general assumption, still holding true (but tenuously) these days, is that the Right Bank has more upscale hotels, while the bohemian Left Bank boasts more inexpensive options. On your first visit, you'll probably want to stay pretty close to the center of town, but don't fret if the only room you can find is out in le boondocks. The Paris Métro shortens distances dramatically; it will only take you a few minutes longer to get to the Louvre from the 16e than from the Latin Quarter. Besides, most repeat visitors to the city find themselves increasingly drawn away from the tourist center in favor of a more authentic Parisian neighborhood. Of course, you can also find that authenticity as close in as the Marais or St-Germain-des-Prés, but usually at a price.

In addition to the November-to-February low season, July and August are also slow in Paris. Many hotels shut down, and you can often bargain for good rates from the ones that stay open. Proprietors in Paris are notorious for charging varying rates for their rooms, so ask about cheaper digs if you feel the first room you're shown is too pricey. The cheapest rooms have no private bath, although inexpensive hotels here, as elsewhere in Europe, are slapping shower stalls into the corners of tiny rooms in order to raise the price. Good luck, and don't worry. I've had some of my best stays in Paris in small, fourth-floor walk-ups with unforgettable views across the rooftops.

Time-Savers

The tourist office will **book a room** for you, but only on the same day you plan to take it and for a fee ranging from 20F to 50F ($3.30 to $8.30), depending on the cost of the hotel. They also broker last-minute rooms that upper-class hotels are having a hard time moving, so you may luck into a deep discount on a posh pad.

Grande Hôtel Jeanne d'Arc
$$. The Marais (3e).
This place reminds me a bit of a floral-print motel relocated to Paris. Its rooms are larger—and certainly cleaner—than your standard French budget pension, and there are amenities galore, such as cable

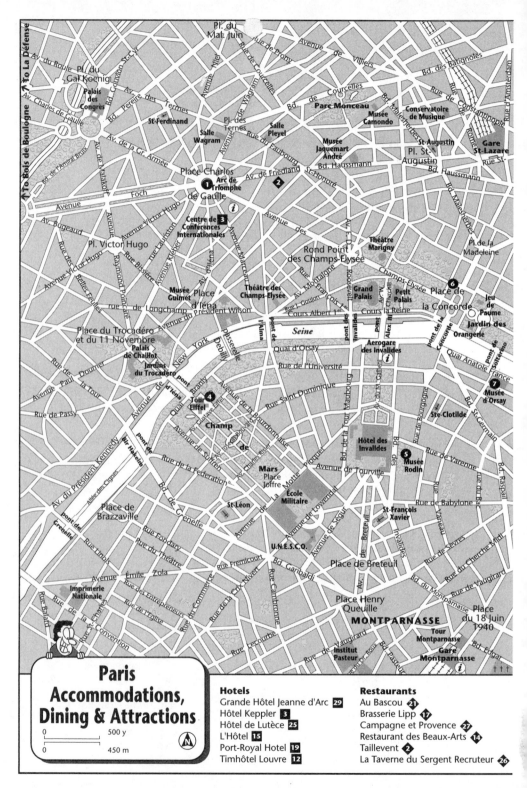

**Paris
Accommodations,
Dining & Attractions**

0 — 500 y
0 — 450 m

Hotels
Grande Hôtel Jeanne d'Arc **29**
Hôtel Keppler **3**
Hôtel de Lutèce **25**
L'Hôtel **15**
Port-Royal Hotel **19**
Timhôtel Louvre **12**

Restaurants
Au Bascou **21**
Brasserie Lipp **17**
Campagne et Provence **27**
Restaurant des Beaux-Arts **14**
Taillevent **2**
La Taverne du Sergent Recruteur **26**

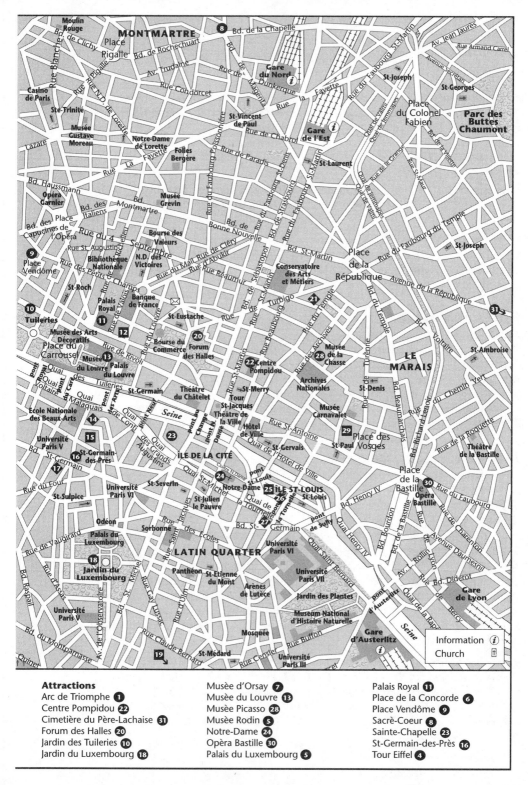

Attractions

Arc de Triomphe **1**	Musée d'Orsay **7**	Palais Royal **11**
Centre Pompidou **22**	Musée du Louvre **13**	Place de la Concorde **6**
Cimetière du Père-Lachaise **31**	Musée Picasso **28**	Place Vendôme **9**
Forum des Halles **20**	Musée Rodin **5**	Sacrè-Coeur **8**
Jardin des Tuileries **10**	Notre-Dame **24**	Sainte-Chapelle **23**
Jardin du Luxembourg **18**	Opèra Bastille **30**	St-Germain-des-Près **16**
	Palais du Luxembourg **5**	Tour Eiffel **4**

TV. It's right in the heart of the charming Marais district, so be sure to reserve ahead.

3 rue de Jarente (between rue de Sévigné and rue de Turenne, off rue St-Antoine). ☎ *01-48-87-62-11.* **Fax:** *01-48-87-37-31.* **Métro:** *St-Paul.* **Rates:** *300F–460F ($50–$76.65) double.*

Hôtel Keppler
$$. Trocadéro (16e).
This budget hotel looks much more upscale. It's in a quiet, untouristy, bourgeois neighborhood just a few blocks away from the Champs-Elysées. The Keppler is for frugal adults, not backpacking students, and the rooms are spacious and well-furnished.

12 rue Keppler (between av. Marceau and av. d'Iéna, south of the Arc de Triomphe). ☎ *01-47-20-65-05.* **Fax:** *01-47-23-02-29.* **Métro:** *Georges-V.* **Rates:** *460F ($76.65) double. AE, MC, V.*

Hôtel de Lutèce
$$$$. Ile Saint-Louis (4e).
The Lutèce occupies a converted 17th-century house accented with rustic details, such as wood-beam ceilings and terra-cotta floors. It's a refined hotel in a chic neighborhood with comfy rooms that are large for such a central location. It's on a street lined with restaurants and shops, just a five-minute stroll from Notre Dame. **Des Deux-Iles,** a sibling hotel, is a few doors down; between the two of them, there's a pretty good chance you'll get a room.

59 rue Saint-Louis-en-l'Ile (on the main drag of the island). ☎ *01-43-26-13-35.* **Fax:** *01-43-29-60-25.* **Métro:** *Pont-Marie.* **Rates:** *840F ($140) double. AE, MC, V.*

L'Hôtel
$$$$$. St-Germain-des-Prés (6e).
The flop house where Oscar Wilde died in 1900 is no more. (His parting words were "Either this wallpaper goes or I do.") Today, the French actor/owner of L'Hotel has arranged the whole thing as a kind of velvet and pink marble monument to curves. The funky, luxurious (but not large) rooms open onto a round central courtyard about 20 feet across, skylit, and with a fountain. Everything is done in good taste with furnishings from Louis XV and Empire styles to art nouveau. At the off-season rates, this hotel is definitely worth the money.

13 rue des Beaux-Arts (between rue Bonaparte and rue de Seine, one block from the Quai Malaquais). ☎ *01-44-41-99-00.* **Fax:** *01-43-25-64-81.* **Métro:** *St-Germain-des-Prés.* **Rates:** *May–July 12 and Sept–Oct, 1,000F–2,500F ($166.65–$416.65); Mar and Nov–Dec, 900F–2,200F ($150–$366.65); Jan–Feb and July 18–Aug, 600F–1,700F ($100–$283.35). All rates are for a double. AE, DC, MC, V. Closed July 13–17.*

Port-Royal Hotel
$. Latin Quarter (5e).
Although this hotel is on the far edge of the Latin Quarter, the Métro stop down the block keeps you just a few minutes from the city's center. These incredible rates come with surprisingly roomy, well-appointed accommodations. In short, it's a decent hotel at hostel prices.

8 bd. Port-Royal (near the intersection with av. des Gobelins). ☎ *01-43-31-70-06.* ***Fax:*** *01-43-31-33-67.* ***Métro:*** *Gobelins.* ***Rates:*** *208F–310F ($34.65–$51.65) double. No credit cards.*

Timhôtel Louvre
$$$. Louvre (1er).
The best thing about this place is that it's two blocks from the Louvre. It was once a writers' and artists' crash pad, but it has been relentlessly renovated into cookie-cutter blandness by a chain selling itself to the business set. However, the standardized comforts and low costs parlay into a great, central value for you.

4 rue Croix-des-Petits-Champs (off rue St-Honoré, 2 blocks east of the Palais Royal). ☎ *01-42-60-34-86.* ***Fax:*** *01-42-60-10-56.* ***Métro:*** *Palais-Royal.* ***Rates:*** *550F ($91.65) double. AE, DC, MC, V.*

Bon Appetit: The Paris Restaurant Scene
For the French, food is close to a religion, and they gladly worship at the altars of their award-winning celebrity chefs. Paris is perhaps *the* world capital of dining. Traditional haute cuisine—a delicate balance of flavors, sauces, and ingredients blended with a studied technique—includes such classics as *blanquette de veau* (veal in an eggy cream sauce), *pot-au-feu* (an excellent stew of fatty beef and vegetables), *coq au vin* (chicken braised in red wine with onions and mushrooms), *bouillabaisse* (seafood soup), and that hearty staple *boeuf bourguignon* (beef stew with red wine). But when people started thinking healthy a few decades back, buttery, creamy, saucy French cuisine quickly found itself on the "out" list of fatty, cholesterol-heightening foods. So the French invented *nouvelle cuisine,* which gave chefs an excuse to concoct new dishes—still French, mind you, but less fattening because they used fewer heavy creams and less butter and served only itty-bitty portions.

When the nouvelle trend lost steam, people began spinning off more healthful *(cuisine minceur)* and/or more creative *(cuisine moderne)* cooking styles. Add to these styles the capital's mix of French regional restaurants (Alsatian, Provençal, Basque, and others) and the many ethnic dining rooms, and you'll never want for variety. Dinner here is easier on your wallet these days. France's economic crisis has forced many restaurants to lower their astronomical prices, and some top chefs have opened up annexes dubbed "baby bistros," where they serve up culinary creations at relatively low prices.

French **cheese** is justifiably famous, with softies **Brie** and **Camembert** and blue-veined **Roquefort** topping the list. There's no way I can go fully into

French **wines** here, but your waiter or the restaurant's *sommelier* (wine steward) should be able to pair your meal with an appropriate vintage. But be careful—ordering wine by the bottle can jack up the cost of your meal in no time. Table wine by the liter carafe or *demi* (half a liter) is always cheaper and tastes almost as good as any fancy estate label. The top reds are produced in Bordeaux, Burgundy, Beaujolais, and the Loire and Rhone valleys. Great whites hail from Alsace, the Loire, Burgundy, and Bordeaux. Don't forget that sparkling white wine from the vineyards east of Paris called **Champagne.**

Some people may be intimidated by the idea of sitting down to what many— certainly the French themselves—consider the most refined food on the planet. Don't sweat it. The only people with a need to impress anyone are the chef and kitchen staff. Have your waiter suggest some dishes, and let the sommelier pick out a wine; then just sit back and enjoy the flavors.

Au Bascou
$$. Le Marais (3e). BASQUE.
In a simple and softly lit rustic interior, Jean-Guy Loustau serves up perhaps the best Basque dishes in the capital. (The Basque are a people from southern France/northern Spain known for their distinct dialect and excellent culinary skills.) Consider starting with a *piperade basquaise* (a light terrine of eggs, tomatoes, and spices) before moving on to roast wild duck or rabbit in a red wine sauce. The light, flavorful Basque wines are a perfect accompaniment. Service is snappy, so you might want to save this place for a night when you don't want to linger over dinner.

38 rue Réaumur (between rue du Temple and rue de Turbigo). ☎ *01-42-72-69-25. Reservations recommended.* **Métro:** *Artes et Metiers.* **Main courses:** *75F–90F ($12.50–$15). AE, MC, V.* **Open:** *Lunch and dinner Mon–Fri. Closed Dec 25– Jan 1; Aug.*

Brasserie Balzar
$$. Latin Quarter (5e). CAFE/BRASSERIE.
This worn, century-old restaurant is the place to come for French comfort food at reasonable prices. The welcoming waiters cheerfully dish up such hearty grub as *steak au poivre* (pepper steak), sauerkraut and ham, and fried calves' liver. It's no wonder Sartre, Camus, and James Thurber kept coming back for more.

49 rue des Ecoles (at rue d'Ulm). ☎ *01-43-54-13-67. Reservations strongly recommended.* **Métro:** *Odeon or Cluny-La Sorbonne.* **Main courses:** *90F–115F ($18–$23). AE, MC, V.* **Open:** *Lunch and dinner daily.*

Brassiere Lipp
$$. St-Germain-des-Prés (6e). CAFE/BRASSIERE.
Paris's most famous brassiere opened in 1880, although the delightful mirror-and-sepia-toned decor dates to 1914. Lipp's tradition and reputation as a writers' and intellectuals' hangout is almost as important as its food, which,

while rather expensive, is usually quite good. It's very popular with Parisian businesspeople at lunch, so come around noon to secure a table.

151 Bd. St-Germain (near the corner with rue de Rennes). ☎ *01-45-48-53-91. Reservations suggested, but not necessary.* **Métro:** *St-Germain-des-Prés.* **Main courses:** *88F–145F ($14.65–$24.15)* **Tourist menu:** *196F ($32.65, with wine). MC, V.* **Open:** *Lunch and dinner daily.*

Bet You Didn't Know

At Lipp's, you'll probably be seated upstairs, because the first floor is reserved mainly for regulars—the tables to the right of the door are for the Parisian intellectual elite. At lunch, you might run into renowned artists, writers, politicos, or American expatriates who try to relive the times Hemingway came to Lipp's to dream up stories.

Campagne et Provence
$$$$. Latin Quarter (5e). PROVENÇAL.

The Provençal smells emanating from the kitchen are enticing to the few customers lucky enough to secure a table in this small but ever-popular spot. The chef excels at both seafood (the garlicky crab cakes on a bed of crusted potatoes are especially good) and game (try the venison or roast fillet of duck) dishes. The wines are worthy, and, for cooking this classy, the price is a bargain.

25 Quai de la Tournelle (across from the Ile-St-Louis). ☎ *01-43-54-05-17. Reservations highly recommended (the day before, if possible).* **Métro:** *Maubert-Mutualité.* **Main courses:** *115F ($19.15).* **Lunch menu:** *120F ($20)* **Dinner menus:** *180F–215F ($30–$35.80). MC, V.* **Open:** *Lunch Tues–Fri, dinner Mon–Sat. Closed Aug (usually).*

Restaurant des Beaux-Arts
$. St-Germain-des-Prés (6e). FRENCH.

Across from the esteemed School of Fine Arts (which rejected Rodin three times) rises one of Paris's bastions of the budget diner, beloved by students and travelers alike. Hearty portions of family-style dishes at basement prices are what draw the crowds. It ain't fine cooking, but it'll do the trick and help you save a few francs to blow on that refined meal some other night.

11 rue Bonaparte (at the corner with rue des Beaux Arts, one block from the Seine's Quai Malaquais). ☎ *01-43-26-92-64. Reservations not accepted.* **Métro:** *St-Germain-des-Prés.* **Fixed-price menu:** *75F ($12.50, with wine). No credit cards.* **Open:** *Lunch and dinner daily.*

Taillevent
$$$$$. Champs-Elysées (8e). FRENCH.

Here's my splurge from the top four restaurants of Paris. It's named after France's first great chef and cookbook author (a 14th-century alchemist). The refined atmosphere is unobtrusive, so you can devote all your attentions to the creations of Jean-Claude Vrinat, who runs one of the foremost kitchens in town and is constantly incorporating the best of new trends into his art. Monsieur Vrinat was the restaurant's sommelier when his father was chef, and Taillevent's wine list is perhaps the best in Paris.

15 rue Lamennais (4 blocks form the Arc de Triomphe off av. de Friedland). ☎ *01-44-95-15-01. Reservations required weeks in advance, months if you can swing it. **Métro:** George-V. **Main courses:** 240F–380F ($40–$63.30). AE, DC, MC, V. **Open:** Lunch and dinner Mon–Fri. Closed Aug.*

La Taverne du Sergent Recruteur
$$$. Ile St-Louis (4e). FRENCH.
Supposedly, unscrupulous army sergeants would get potential young recruits drunk at this popular 17th-century eatery, and the saps would wake up in the barracks the next day as conscripts. These days the only danger is overeating because the fixed price menu gets you all you can eat from a huge basket of veggies and cured meats, bottomless glasses of wine, a selection of basic main dishes, and a cheese board.

41 rue St-Louis-en-l'Isle (on the main drag of the Ile St-Louis, just off rue des Deux Ponts). ☎ *01-43-54-75-42. Reservations recommended. **Métro:** Pont-Marie. **Set-price Menu:** 188F ($62.65, with wine). AE, MC, V. **Open:** Lunch Sun, dinner daily.*

Quick Bites
You can get fairly quick meals, even full ones, at many **brassieres** and **cafes,** and Paris doesn't lack for food on the go either. The French often make a snack out of a simple **baguette,** torn off in hunks as they walk. Paris's greatest street food is **crêpes,** sold at sidewalk stands and from store windows. They're best when cooked fresh on the spot for you, but in touristy areas, shopkeepers often make up stacks in advance and merely reheat them on the griddle when you approach. The cheapest, and in my opinion best, is *au beurre e sucre* (with butter and sugar), although you may prefer Nutella (a hazelnut-chocolate spread) and banana or ham and cheese. You can visit a supermarket or gourmet store for your **picnic** supplies, but it's more fun and Parisian to shop at the little local food stores and street markets (ask your hotel about the nearest one of those). Pick up a baguette at the *boulangerie* (bakery), cured meats and the like at a *charcuterie,* and other groceries at an *épicerie.* Top it all off with some fruit, pastries from a *pâtisserie* (the French excel at these), a bottle of wine, and you're set.

The Louvre & Then Some: Paris Sightseeing

For a quick overview of the major sights without getting off the bus,
Cityrama (☎ 01-44-55-60-00), 4 place des Pyramids, 1er, offers a two-hour
orientation tour on a big bus with big windows and tiny earphones that play
a canned commentary. This tour costs 150F ($25). The 260F ($43.30) tour
takes you inside the Louvre and Notre Dame, but it isn't worth it. You may
be interested in their summer night tour of illuminated Paris for 150F ($25),
though I'd vote for walking the moonlit streets on your own.

Shoestring travelers can just hop the **no. 95 city bus** and provide their own
commentary as they cruise past the Montparnasse Tower, St-Germain-des-
Prés, Louvre, Palais Royal, Opéra, and up to Montmartre—all in 50 minutes.
Sunday afternoons, the city runs an orange-and-white motorcoach called the
Balabus (**Bb** on the buses and bus stop signs) that crawls past Paris's visual
magnificence from the Gare de Lyon to the Grande Arche de la Défense
(three bus tickets to ride the whole route). It is also popular to **cruise the
Seine;** see the following "Other Fun Stuff to Do" section.

Dollars & Sense

By far Paris's best buy is the **Carte Musées et Monuments,** a pass that lets
you into most Parisian sights free (well, 65 of them; the only notable exceptions are the Eiffel and Montparnasse towers and the Marmottan museum). It
costs 70F ($11.65) for a one-day pass—if you use it just for the Louvre and
Musée d'Orsay, you've already saved 10 francs. You can also get three-day,
140F ($23.30), or five-day, 200F ($33.30), versions. The biggest benefit is that
you don't have to wait in line! You just saunter up to a separate window, and
they wave you through, like visiting royalty. You can buy the pass at any train
station, tourist office, or participating sight.

The Louvre

Anyone up for the greatest museum on Earth? The Grand Louvre—a
former royal palace opened to the public as an art gallery when the French
Revolution struck—has 195,000 square feet of galleries, five million visitors
annually, and over 30,000 works on display spanning three millennia.
Besides one of the world's top painting galleries, the Louvre also houses a
remarkable collection of antiquities from Greece, Etruria, Rome, Egypt, and
the Orient; a sculpture section that boasts two of Michelangelo's *Slaves;* and
a fine decorative arts division. A massive reorganization (which may keep
some sections closed until 1999) is busily opening up even more display
space than ever before. It would take about three days to properly scratch the
surface of all seven departments. Heck, it takes at least half a day merely to
walk through the halls to see da Vinci's enigmatically smiling *Mona Lisa,* that

261

armless beauty *Venus de Milo,* and the dramatic *Winged Victory of Samothrace*—just the three most famous of many instantly recognizable artistic icons that call the Louvre home.

The floor plans and information desks on site will help you get a handle on the basic layout and plan your visit, but the Louvre's problem is that there are too many masterpieces. To avoid aesthetic overload, and because you can only absorb so much, on a first visit you will probably have to ignore most of the works you're passing—pieces that might have been the pride of a lesser museum—in order to devote your art appreciation energies to the greatest hits. These include an incredible five more da Vinci paintings (the *Virgin of the Rocks* is stupendous), fragments from the Parthenon, Ingres's *The Turkish Bath,* Veronese's *Wedding Feast at Cana,* Vermeer's *Lacemaker,* self-portraits by Dürer and Rembrandt, Uccello's *Battle of San Romano,* Géricault's *Raft of the Medusa,* and David's *Coronation of Napoléon I.* If you have the time, try to take in the Louvre over several visits—in the long run, it's worth the multiple admissions.

You enter the Louvre through the glass pyramid in the Cour Napoléon courtyard, between the qaui du Louvre and rue de Rivoli. ☎ *01-40-20-50-50. Métro: Palais-Royal, Musée du Louvre.* **Admission:** *45F ($7.50) before 3pm, 26F ($4.30) after 3pm and on Sun. Free for those under 18. Free for everyone the first Sun of each month (but crowded).* **Open:** *Thurs–Sun 9am–6pm; Wed 9am–9:45pm; Mon 9am–6pm, plus main galleries until 9:45pm. The entrance/entresol, with its information desks, medieval Louvre exhibit, cafes, post office, and shops, stays open daily until 9:45pm.*

Notre Dame Cathedral

"Our Lady of Paris" is the heart and soul of the city, a monument to Paris's past slung in the cradle of its origins (see sidebar). The 12th- to 14th-century cathedral is a study in gothic beauty and gargoyles, at once solid with squat, square facade towers and graceful with flying buttresses around the sides. It's been remodeled, embellished, ransacked, and restored so often that it's a wonder it still has any architectural integrity at all (during the Revolution, it was even stripped of its religion and rechristened the Temple of Reason). The lines to get in are long (and Quasimodo's a no-show), but at least while you wait to get in you have time to admire the Bible stories played out in intricate stone relief around the three great portals on the facade. Much of the facade was (poorly) restored once in the 18th century and then again (as well as could be done) in the 19th. If you're keen to see some medieval originals, the upper tier of the central portal is ancient, and much of the sculpture on the right-hand portal has also survived from 1165 to 1175.

In the high, airy gothic interior, the choir section has a gorgeously carved and painted stone screen from the 14th century on its outer flanks and 18th-century wooden choir stalls along the inside. The main draw, though, are the three enormous rose windows, especially the 69-foot diameter north window, which has retained almost all of its original 13th-century stained glass. Save Notre Dame for a sunny day and the best light effects. No visit to Notre

Dame is complete without tackling the 387 steps up the north tower to examine those grotesque, amusing, or sometimes downright frightening gargoyles. From up here, you also get fine views of the city. One last thing you shouldn't forget to do is to walk around the building. Those famous flying buttresses at the very back, holding up the apse with 50-foot spans of stone strength, are particularly impressive. Cross the Seine to admire the entire effect from the quay on the Left Bank.

Place du Parvis de Notre-Dame. ☎ **01-44-32-16-70.** *Métro: Cité.* **Admission:** *Cathedral is free; towers are 27F ($4.50) adults, 18F ($3) ages 18–24 and 60+, 15F ($2.50) ages 12–17; the crypt is the same rates as the towers.* **Open:** *Cathedral, daily 8am–6:45pm (closed Sat 12:30–2pm). Towers, Apr–Sept 9:30am–6pm, Oct 9:30am–5:30pm, Nov and Feb–Mar 10am–5pm, Dec–Jan, 10am–4pm. Crypt, Apr–Sept 10am–6pm, Oct–Mar 10am–4:30pm.*

Extra! Extra!

At the opposite end of the square from the cathedral, a flight of steps leads down to the **Archeological Crypt** (☎ **01-43-29-83-51**), a 260-foot gallery extending under Notre Dame's square. This excavation includes the jumbled foundations, streets, and walls of a series of Parises, including the medieval and Roman cities. There's even a house from Lutèce—the town built by the Celtic Parisii tribe that flourished on the Ile de la Cité over 2,000 years ago.

Eiffel Tower

Looking like two sets of train tracks that crashed into each other, Gustave Alexandre Eiffel's tower rises 1,056 feet above the banks of the Seine in all its steel girder glory. The man who gave the Statue of Liberty a backbone designed this quintessential Parisian symbol merely as a temporary exhibit for the Exhibition of 1899 and managed to rivet together all 7,000 tons of it (with 2.5 million rivets) in under two years. Fortunately for the French postcard industry, the tower's usefulness as a transmitter of telegraph, and later, radio and TV signals saved it from demolition.

Critics of the day assailed its aesthetics, but no one could deny the feat of engineering. It remained the tallest manmade structure in the world until the Chrysler Building stole the title in 1930, and it paved the way for the soaring skyscraper architecture of the 20th century. The restaurants and bars on the first level are pricey, but not bad. The view from the second level is an intimate bird's eye view of Paris; from the fourth level, you can see the entire city spread out below and, on a good day, as far out as 42 miles. Visibility is usually best near sunset.

Champs-de-Mars, 7e. ☎ **01-44-11-23-23. Métro:** *Trocadéro, Ecole-Militaire, Bir-Hakeim.* **RER:** *Champ-de-Mars–Tour Eiffel.* **Admission:** *First landing, 20F ($3.30); second landing, 40F ($6.65); third landing, 56F ($9.30); stairs to second floor, 12F ($2).* **Open:** *July–Aug, daily 9am–midnight; Sept–June, daily 9:30am–11pm (in winter, stairs only open until 6:30pm).*

Musée d'Orsay

In 1986, Paris consolidated most of its collections of French art from 1848 to World War I in the most unlikely of spots: an old converted train station. Although the Orsay has earlier works by the likes of Ingres and Delacroix, its biggest draw is undoubtedly those crowd-pleasing impressionists. Many of the works here are so widely reproduced that you might wander through with an eerie feeling of déjà vu. Degas' ballet dancers and *l'Absinthe;* Monet's women in a poppy field, his Rouen cathedral painted under five different lighting conditions, and his giant *Blue Waterlilies;* van Gogh's *Restaurant de la Siréne,* self-portraits, peasants napping against a haystack, and his *Bedroom at Arles;* Whistler's *Mother;* Manet's groundbreaking *Picnic on the Grass* and *Olympia,* which together helped throw off the shackles of artistic conservatism and gave impressionism room to take root. Add in a generous helping of Cézanne, Gauguin, Rodin, Toulouse-Lautrec, Pissaro, and Seurat, and you could easily spend a full day exploring this museum.

1 rue Bellechasse or 62 rue de Lille. ☎ **01-40-49-48-41. Métro:** *Solférino.* **RER:** *Musée-d'Orsay.* **Admission:** *35F ($5.80) adults, 24F ($4) ages 18–24 and 60+.* **Open:** *Tues–Wed and Fri–Sat 10am–6pm, Thurs 10am–9:45pm, Sun 9am–6pm. June 20–Sept 20, it opens at 9am.*

Bet You Didn't Know

By the 1860s, French painting had become so rigid and formalized, not to mention bland, that the visible brush strokes and natural, everyday settings in works by Manet and Monet caused scandals when they were first exhibited. One critic referred to Monet's landscapes—made up of tiny daubs of bright paint with no sense of line at all—as "embryonic wallpaper." The artist explained that he was trying to capture the fleeting "impression" of light and color in the scenes, in the process often abandoning form and composition. Critical derision notwithstanding, Monet and his colleagues proceeded to buck artistic tradition and move art in more new directions than even the Renaissance had. Monet, Degas, Cézanne, Renoir, Sisley, Cassat, Signac, Gauguin, Pissaro, Seurat—these "impressionists" are now counted among the most beloved artists in the world.

Centre Georges Pompidou

The Pompidou is Paris's homage to 20th-century creativity. Aside from the gallery of modern art—featuring the works of Matisse, Chagall, Kadinsky, Bonnard, Ernst, Pollock, Calder, and Henry Moore—there are exhibits on industrial design, music research, photography, and the history of film. The cafeteria on the top floor has some fantastic views. Even if you don't want to go inside, come by to shake your head at the wildly colorful and controversial transparent inside-out architecture (it reminds me of the Habitrail network of plastic tubes my hamster used to scurry around in) and to enjoy Paris's best street performers on the sloping square out front.

Place Georges Pompidou. ☎ *01-44-78-12-33.* **Métro:** *Rambuteaux.* **Admission:** *Entire center, 70F ($11.65) adults, 45F ($7.50) ages 16–25 and 60+, free under 16; Museum of Modern Art only, 35F ($5.80) adults, 24F ($4) ages 16–24.* **Open:** *Mon and Wed–Fri noon–10pm, Sat–Sun 10am–10pm.*

Sainte-Chapelle

The interior of this tiny Gothic chapel, almost entirely hidden by the bulk of the Palace of Justice surrounding it, is a sculpture of light and color. The thin bits of stone that hold the tall stained-glass windows and brace the roof seem to dissolve in the diffuse and dappled brightness glowing through the 13th-century windows. The effect on a sunny day is, well, almost religious. The chapel was built in 1246 to house the Crown of Thorns.

4 bd. du Palais, 1er (in the Palais de Justice on the Ile de la Cité). ☎ *01-53-73-58-51.* **Métro:** *Cité.* **Admission:** *28F ($4.65) adults, 21F ($3.50) ages 18–25, 15F ($2.50) ages 12–17.* **Open:** *Apr–Sept, daily 9:30am–6:30pm; Oct–Mar, daily 10am–5pm.*

Rodin Museum

Once the critics stopped assailing Rodin's art, they realized he had been the greatest sculptor since Michelangelo, and the studio Rodin worked in from 1908 until his death in 1917 was opened as a museum to house some of the artist's greatest works. This place is one of my favorite small museums anywhere. In the rose gardens you'll find *The Thinker, The Gate of Hell, The Burghers of Calais,* and *Balzac.* Inside are collected many famed sculptures—*The Kiss, The Three Shades, The Hand of God, Iris*—along with some of Rodin's drawings and works by his friends and contemporaries.

77 rue de Varenne, 7e (in the Hôtel Biron). ☎ *01-44-18-61-10.* **Métro:** *Varenne.* **Admission:** *32F ($5.30) adults, 22F ($3.65) ages 18–26 and 60+. Free on Sun.* **Open:** *Tues–Sun, 9:30am–5:45pm (Oct–Mar to 4:45pm).*

Musée Picasso

Picasso left some $50 million in French inheritance taxes when he died. The state accepted instead 203 paintings, 177 sculptures, and thousands of sketches and engravings. The good news is that this collection is one of the most representative collections of Picasso's works in the world, spanning his entire career. The bad news is that the space is much smaller than the collection, and with the constant rotation of works, you never know whether you'll get to see masterpieces such as *Le Baiser, Pan Flute, Two Women Running Along the Beach, The Crucifixion,* or *Nude in a Red Armchair.*

5 rue de Thorigny, 3e (in the Hôtel Salé). ☎ **01-42-71-25-21. Métro:** *St-Paul or Filles du Calvaire.* **Admission:** *30F ($5) adults, 20F ($3.30) ages 18–25. Sun, 20F ($3.30) for everyone.* **Open:** *Wed–Mon 9:30am–6pm (Oct–Mar to 5:30pm).*

Other Fun Stuff to Do

➤ **While Away the Day in a Cafe.** Many European cultures have a third place, between home and work, where citizens play out their lives. In Paris, it's the cafe, a sort of public extension of the living room. In the cafe, intellectuals debate, executives make deals, politicians hold court, friends gather, and poets dream. You can sit all day over a single cup of coffee or order a light meal or a flute of champagne. Ensconce yourself indoors or stand at the bar, but most people choose to sit outside—in a glassed-in porch in winter or on the sidewalk in summer—because one of the cafe's biggest attractions is the people-watching. Many Parisian cafes are legendary, immortalized by historical circumstances and Hemingway novels.

Of the thousands of cafes from simple, tiny locals' joints to cavernous glittering belle époque bastions, here are some classics. **Les Deux Magots** (☎ **01-45-48-55-25**) 6 place St-Germain-des-Pres, established in 1885, was the haunt of Picasso, Hemingway, and Sartre. Sartre wrote a whole trilogy holed up at a table in **Café de Flore** (☎ **01-45-48-55-26**), 172 bd. St-Germain-des-Pres, a Left Bank cafe frequented by Camus and Picasso and featured in Gore Vidal novels. The Champs-Elysées may no longer be Paris's hot spot, but **Fouquet's** (☎ **01-47-23-70-60**) at no. 99 is still going strong based on its reputation, good food, and favorable reviews by Chaplin, Churchill, FDR, and Jackie Onassis. The American writer Henry Miller took his morning porridge at **La Couple** (☎ **01-43-20-14-20**), 102 bd. du Montparnasse, a brassiere that also hosted the likes of Josephine Baker, John Dos Passos, Dalí, and F. Scott Fitzgerald. Finally, you can make a pilgrimage to the art nouveau interiors of the new **La Rotonde** (☎ **01-43-26-68-84**), 105 bd. du Montparnasse, risen like a phoenix from the ashes of its namesake that once stood here. In *The Sun Also Rises,* Hemingway writes of the original, "No matter what cafe in Montparnasse you ask a taxi driver to bring you to...they always take you to the Rotonde."

➤ **Pay Homage to the Cultural Giants at Père Lachaise Cemetery.** Chopin, Gertrude Stein, Delacroix, Proust, Rossini, Oscar Wilde, Georges Bizet, Ingres, Isadora Duncan, Pissaro, Molière, Edith Piaf, Modigliani, and the Doors' Jim Morrison—you couldn't imagine most of these people getting together in life, but they fit well together in death. Pick up the map of the graves and spend a morning under the trees of this vast and romantic cemetery of rolling hills and historic tombs. People leave flowers at Chopin's monument; Marlboros, LSD-laced sugar cubes, and graffiti at Morrison's. In an era that shunned alternative lifestyles, Paris still buried lovers Gertrude Stein and Alice B. Toklas under the same tombstone (Toklas's name is on the back), and every day someone brings Stein a fresh rose (it was Stein who said, "A rose is a rose is a rose.") To get there, take the Métro to Père-Lachaise.

➤ **Bring in Da' Noise, Bring in Da' Tourists: Stroll through Montmartre, the Original Bohemian 'Hood.** One thing's for sure—*La Bohème* it ain't anymore. Although inundated by tourists these days, Monmartre, an old artists' neighborhood on Paris's northern edge (the 18e), still has an intriguing village flavor and remains one of the best Parisian areas to wander. Take the Métro to **Pigalle.** You're on the northwest edge of Paris's red light district here, which features hangers-on like the **Moulin Rouge** with its can-can shows (just down from the sex shop–lined boulevard de Clichy at place Blanche). Work your way uphill to the **Basilique du Sacré-Coeur,** a neo-Byzantine basilica built from 1876 to 1919 and towering over the city. Climb the dome for a vista that on clear days extends 35 miles.

Some of Montmartre's quirkiest sights include a pair of **windmills,** visible from rue Lepic and rue Girardon, and **Paris's only vineyard,** on rue des Saules. Next door to the latter, at rue Saint-Vincent 12, is the **Montemartre Museum** (☎ 01-46-06-61-11), dedicated to the neighborhood in a house that was at times occupied by van Gogh, Renoir, and Utrillo. Pay your respects to the writers Stendhal and Dumas, the composers Offenbach and Berlioz, and the painter Degas at their graves in the **Cimitère de Montemartre** on avenue Rachel. Finish the evening at 22 rue des Saules in **Au Lapin Agile** (☎ 01-46-06-85-87)—in Picasso and Utrillo's day called Café des Assassins—Paris's foremost spot for folk music.

➤ **Window-shop with the Best of Them.** Paris is a shopping capital, home to haute couture, fine perfumes, and gourmet foodstuffs. On boulevard Haussmann rise Paris's two flagships of shopping, the department stores **Au Printemps** and **Galeries Lafayette.** Au Printemps is a bit more modern and American-styled, and Galeries Lafayette is more Old World French, but both are very upscale and carry the ready-to-wear collections of all the major French designers and labels.

If you prefer to shop boutiques, the best concentrations of stores are in the adjoining 1er and 8e. No single street offers more shops than the long **rue du Faubourg St-Honoré/rue St-Honoré.** Even if you can't afford the prices, it's fun to have a look. Big houses like **Hermés** (no. 24) hawk ties and scarves, **Au Nain Blue** (no. 406) has one of the fanciest toy emporiums in the world, and the prices at **La Maison du Chocolat** (no. 225) are as rich as the confections. Window shop for leather at **Didler Lamarthe** (no. 219) or **Longchamp** (no. 390) or for cutting-edge fashion at **Hervé Léger** (no. 29) and **Lolita Lempicka** (no. 14). Just off the rue du Faubourg St-Honoré, at

35 av. Matignon, 8e, women will find **Anna Lowe** for runway samples and slightly worn creations of the big names at a discount. **Réciproque,** 89-123 rue de la Pompe, 16e, has slight bargains on a remarkably wide range of the big labels and top designers.

Some of the best **food shopping** is concentrated on place de la Madeleine, 8e, home to **Fauchon,** Paris's homage to the finest edibles money can buy (though it faces serious competition from neighbor **Hediard**). Don't forget your Paris outlet for caviar, truffles, foie gras, and other pâtés, **Maison de la Truffe. Jewels** glitter on place Vendôme, 1er, at **Cartier** (no. 7), **Chaumet** (no. 12), and **Van Cleef & Arpels** (no. 22). Stink like the best of them with discounts on **French perfumes** at **Parfumerie de la Madeleine,** 9 place de la Madeleine, 8e, or **Michel Swiss,** upstairs at 16 rue de la Paix, 2e.

A Flea Market Fling

If the prices at Cartier, Hermés, and the like set your head to spinning, you'll likely have more luck at the **Marché aux Puces de Clignancourt,** the city's most famous flea market. It's a group of several markets comprising almost 3,000 stalls, all along avenue de la Porte de Clignancourt. You'll find it all here: antiques, junk, vintage clothing, and just plain old cheap duds.

Usually Monday is the best day to get a bargain, because the crowds are fewer and vendors are anxious for the dough. Keep in mind, though, that you'll secure a far better price if you speak French and show you are serious about and respectful of the merchandise. Professional dealers often snatch up the best loot, but in the past, I've seen great buys on vintage French postcards, old buttons, and bistro ware.

Hours vary with the weather and the crowds, but stalls are usually up and running between 9am and 6pm. To get there, take the Métro to Porte de Clignancourt; from there, turn left and cross boulevard Ney, and then walk north on avenue de la Porte de Clignancourt.

➤ **Les Egouts de Paris: Tour the Sewers.** Take an hour to see Paris from a different point of view—that of a sewer rat. Over 1,300 miles of sewer tunnels share space with the Métro, electrical lines, catacombs, and reservoirs under the streets of Paris. From the **Sewer Museum** (yes, Paris has a whole museum for this, ☎ **01-47-05-10-29**), you can tour a few hundred feet of this intricate system and find out more than you ever wanted to know about the inner workings of a major city's circulatory system. It's open Saturday through Wednesday from 11am to 5pm at 93 quai d'Orsay (near the Eiffel Tower, not the Orsay museum, at the foot of the Alma bridge). Closed January 10 through 31.

➤ **Cruise the Seine.** The classic float down the Seine is offered by **Bateaux-Mouches** (☎ 01-42-25-96-10). Vessels depart every half hour (fewer in winter) from pont d'Alma on the Right Bank. Regular 90-minute trips with multilingual commentary cost 40F ($6.65). After dark, the boats sweep both banks with mega-powered floodlights— illuminating everything well, but sort of spoiling the romance. Luncheon and dinner cruises are considerably more expensive—500F to 600F ($83.30 to $100) for jacket-and-tie dinners, and the food is only so-so. A cheaper alternative to Bateaux-Mouches (food not included) is the **Batobus** (☎ 01-44-11-33-44), a kind of water taxi (no commentary) that stops at five major points of interest to visitors: Hôtel de Ville, Notre Dame, the Louvre, the Musée d'Orsay, and the Eiffel Tower.

➤ **Pay a Visit to *Le Mickey*.** Contrary to popular belief, **Disneyland Paris** (☎ 01-64-74-30-00) has been a fantastic success in terms of visitors. The theme park, a slightly Europeanized version of California's Disneyland with both familiar and new versions of rides and those contrived cultural areas, has been inundated with guests since the day it opened. It just ran into financial troubles when more people than expected stayed in Paris rather than in the Disney hotels. I find the place a little weird and out of place, but to homesick, museum-weary kids and lovers of kitsch it might prove a highlight of your trip to Paris. Admission varies with the season, and one day runs 150F to 195F ($25 to $32.50) for adults and 120F to 150F ($20 to $25) for ages 3 through 12. To get there, take the A line RER to Marne-la-Vallée/Chessy, which is within walking distance of the park. Fare is 75F ($15), and the trip takes about 45 minutes.

Get Outta Town: Day Trips & Excursions

Paris is a city where the day trips are as impressive as the in-town attractions. Among the many nearby destinations, I have chosen three that exhibit the France of old in its royal and religious splendor—the palaces at Versailles and Fontainebleau, and the marvelous cathedral at Chartres.

Nothing Succeeds Like Foppish Excess: The Palace at Versailles

Versailles, with its extravagant 17th-century palace and gardens, is Paris's best and easiest day trip. You can zip out there in half an hour on the **C RER line** (you want the C5 heading to Versailles–Rive Gauche station). The ride costs 35F ($5.80), but is free if you have a Eurail pass. It's a 15-minute stroll to the palace from the train station, or you can take a shuttle bus. Across avenue de Gal de Gaulle from the station and to the right a smidgen is a sunken shopping center with a branch of the **tourist information office** on the right-hand side (no. 10). The main tourist office (☎ 01-39-50-36-22) is a 5-minute walk to the right of the palace's main entrance at 7 rue des Réservoirs.

I was recently taking the "Everyday Life of Louis XIV" tour of the king's apartments at Versailles with a first-time visitor. As the guide took us through

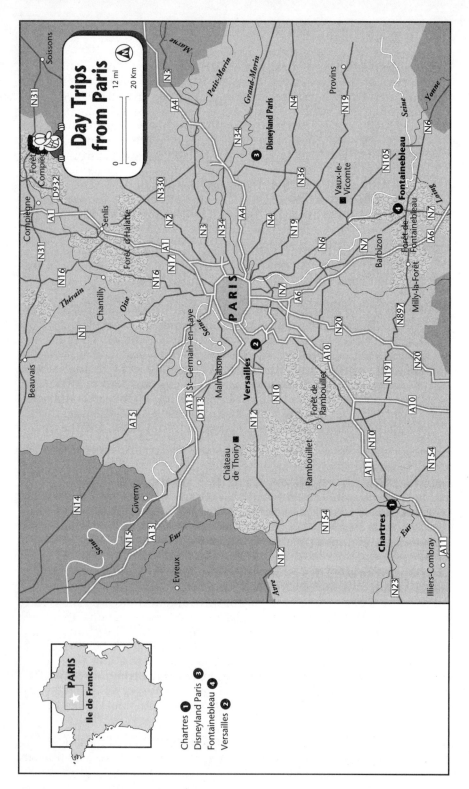

Day Trips from Paris

12 mi
20 Km

Chartres ❶
Disneyland Paris ❸
Fontainebleau ❹
Versailles ❷

PARIS
Ile de France

270

room after lavish room, my friend silently perused the gold-leafed cornices, the heavy rich fabrics sewn with gold and silver, the abundance of oil paintings, and finally pronounced "It's a bit busy." This stands as the best description I've heard yet for Europe's grandest palace, a sprawling, rambling, exhaustive display of the French monarchs' wealth and foppery in those last generations before the Revolution.

What started in 1624 as a hunting lodge for Louis XIII was turned by Louis XIV, the Sun King (and the man for whom Louisiana was named), into a palace of truly monumental proportions and appointments over his 72-year reign (1643–1715). The Sun King made himself into an absolute monarch, the likes of which hadn't been seen since the Caesars, and he created a palace befitting his stature. You can wander the State Apartments, Hall of Mirrors (where the Treaty of Versailles ending World War I was signed), and Royal Chapel on your own (or with an audio tour), but it's much more informative to take one of the guided tours, which get you into many parts of the palace not open to the casual visitor. These tours are popular and fill up fast, so your first order of business should be to head to the tour reservations office and sign up for one. There's a good chance that you'll have to wait an hour or more, so book an even later tour and use the intervening time to explore the magnificent gardens.

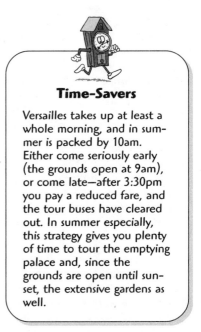

Time-Savers

Versailles takes up at least a whole morning, and in summer is packed by 10am. Either come seriously early (the grounds open at 9am), or come late—after 3:30pm you pay a reduced fare, and the tour buses have cleared out. In summer especially, this strategy gives you plenty of time to tour the emptying palace and, since the grounds are open until sunset, the extensive gardens as well.

Bet You Didn't Know

Louis XIV kept a court here of more than 3,000—with a support staff more than double that. Whatever his faults, he was a shrewd politician and realized that by keeping his entire court around him continually—allies and potential enemies alike—he could keep an eye on them all. One of his best techniques was turning daily tasks (such as eating breakfast or getting out of bed) into courtly events. Invitations to attend various parts of the king's day were handed out and revoked with seemingly capricious frequency. All the nobles and notables were then kept busy worrying about whether they were on the in or out list and devising ways to get in His Majesty's good graces. This way they were more likely to look straight to the king for alliances rather than to each other, and they were too busy to plot against him.

Louis XIV was not just smart when it came to courtiers (see sidebar), but also in placating the common folk. Anyone could visit the palace and gardens of Versailles, so long as they dressed neatly and in proper attire (for men, this meant a hat and sword—they'd equip you at the gate if you arrived without). The king himself wrote a guidebook to his gardens for public use. One of the commoners' favorite day trips was to head out to Versailles at mealtime, when they would be allowed to file past the royal dining table and watch the king and all those nobles eat lunch.

Of course, having every instant of your life open to public scrutiny on a daily basis—and having the "private" moments subject to noble inspection by invitation—would wear on anybody, which is why there are two sets of apartments for the king and the queen—the public ones and the private ones behind them, reached through little doors concealed in the fabric-covered walls. One of the more interesting tours you can take is of these private chambers, where the royals had liaisons with lovers, met with their most trusted confidants, put their feet up, and let their powdered wigs down.

Le Nôtre (who designed London's Greenwich Park and the Vatican Gardens in Rome) laid out the hundreds of acres of palace grounds in the most exacting 17th-century standards of decorative gardening. The highlights are the Grand Canal, $\frac{2}{3}$ of a mile long and once plied by a small warship and Venetian gondolas (you can rent a boat of your own here); The Grand Trianon, a sort of palace away from home for when the king wanted a break from the main château; and the Petit Trianon, a jewel of a mansion done in fine neoclassical style (built for Louis XV's mistress, but beloved by Marie Antoinette, wife of the Sun King's grandson, Louis XVI). Nearby is Marie Antoinette's fairy-tale Hameau, or hamlet, created so Her Majesty could enjoy a cleaned-up version of peasant life. Here the Queen fished, milked the occasional cow, and watched hired peasants lightly toil at the everyday tasks she imagined they did in the country—she even had a little "house in the faux country" built here, sort of a thatched mansion.

Versailles has complicated **hours** and admissions. The various palaces are only open Tuesday through Sunday; the park and gardens open daily (except during bad weather and the occasional official ceremony). **May 2 through September,** the Château is open 9am to 6:30pm, the Grand Trianon and Petit Trianon are open from 10am to 6:30pm. **October through April,** the Château is open 9am–5:30pm, and the Grand Trianon and Petit Trianon are open Tuesday through Friday 10am to 12:30pm and 2 to 5:30pm and Saturday and Sunday 10am to 5:30pm. The **gardens** are open year-round from 7am to sunset, which varies from 5:30pm to 9:30pm.

The basic **admission** to the **Château** is free with the Paris museum pass or is as follows: 45F ($7.50) adults, 35F ($5.80) ages 18 to 25, free under 18. After 3:30pm and all day Sunday, the cost is 35F ($5.80) for everyone over age 18. Use entrance A (A2 with the museum pass). The **audio guide** for the King's Chamber lasts one hour and costs 25F ($4.15) for adults and 17F ($2.80) for ages 7 through 17. Use entrance C. There are five to nine **guided visits** offered (a few are in French only and the tour of the garden's groves runs only in summer). Ninety-minute tours cost 37F ($6.15) for adults, 26F ($4.30) for ages 7 through 17; two-hour tours cost 50F ($8.30) for adults, 24F ($4) for ages 7 through 17. Use entrance D. The **Grand Trianon** is 25F ($4.15) for adults, 15F ($2.50) for ages 18 through 25, and free for children under 18. The **Petit Trianon** is 15F ($2.50) for adults, 10F ($1.65) for ages 18 through 25, and free for children under 18. A combined ticket to both is 30F ($5) for adults and 20F ($3.30) for ages 18 through 25.

Unhappily Ever After

The retreat into a fabricated reality—not just the Hameau, but the carousel of court life at Versailles itself—left the royals seriously out of touch with their real subjects. Louis XVI was an intelligent man, but he did not inherit his grandfather's keen political acumen. Despite all his book smarts, he didn't have the administrative savvy to maintain the absolute monarchy he inherited in 1774. He also inherited a growing popular resentment at the excesses of his two predecessors and the nobility in general. In 1789, the people rose in Revolution and quickly dispatched the upper class. Although the king had made weak attempts to ease taxation and force the nobility to carry their weight (this was, after all, the man who had helped finance the American Revolution with supplies, troops, and ships), he, too, was arrested. After three years in prison, Louis XVI and Marie Antoinette lost their heads to the guillotine in Paris, and the fairy-tale life of Versailles ended forever.

For the most part, the **Gardens** are free year-round. On Sundays in May through October, however, there is a weekly fountain water show accompanied by classical music that costs 23F ($3.80) to attend. Also in summer, there are special nighttime displays (usually Saturdays) of fireworks and illuminated fountains, for which tickets run from 70F to 185F ($11.65 to $30.80), depending on where you sit. Call **01-39-50-36-22** for more information on both summertime spectacles.

Royal Triumphs & Disgraces at Fontainebleau

Before French monarchs had Versailles to play with, they retreated to Fontainebleau. Here they could hunt in the vast forest and retreat from the dirty, crowded streets of Paris into a sumptuous mansion built, renovated, and extended into a rambling palace over 700 years of construction. You can see this place pretty easily in a day trip from Paris, but if you want to take your time, you might schedule two days here: one for the palace, the other to hike in the famed forest surrounding it. Some 10 **trains** daily head from Paris Gare de Lyon to Fontainebleau-Avon station, a ride that takes 35 to 60 minutes. From the station, a bus makes the two-mile run to the palace every

10 minutes or so. The **tourist office** (☎ **01-64-22-25-68**) is at 31 place Napoléon Bonaparte.

Although Fontainebleau enjoyed some vogue as a royal hunting lodge in the middle ages, its heyday didn't begin until François I's late Renaissance transformations in the 16th century. The Gallery of François I especially shows off the talents of Rosso Fiorentino and Primaticcio, the artists he hired to help decorate the place. François I's successor, Henry II, also had his ballroom here decorated in mannerist style, with interlocking H&D initials ("D" stood for Diane de Poitiers, Henry's mistress). Ever a politic fellow, Henry hedged his connubial bets by also emblazoning the decor with H&C—this time, the "C" was his lawful wife, Catherine d' Medici. Louis XIV was, of course, busy sprucing up Versailles in the 17th century, so he used Fontainebleau as a royal guest house, letting Queen Christina of Sweden set up housekeeping here after she abdicated her crown.

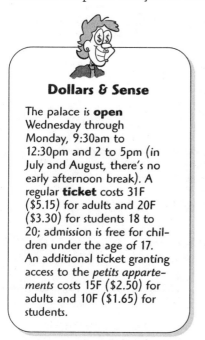

Dollars & Sense

The palace is **open** Wednesday through Monday, 9:30am to 12:30pm and 2 to 5pm (in July and August, there's no early afternoon break). A regular **ticket** costs 31F ($5.15) for adults and 20F ($3.30) for students 18 to 20; admission is free for children under the age of 17. An additional ticket granting access to the *petits appartements* costs 15F ($2.50) for adults and 10F ($1.65) for students.

When Napoléon got around to setting up court here in the early 19th century, he personalized things a little more subtly, scattering his symbol of the bee, rather than his initials, about the Napoleonic rooms. Most of these rooms are visitable only by guided tour and include the emperor's throne room, as well as the *grands appartements* of the emperor and the *petits appartements* of his wife, Josephine. Fontainebleau may have once been a palace to Napoléon, but by 1812 it had become his prison. It was here that the revolutionary citizen-turned-megalomaniacal emperor signed his abdication papers in 1814, bade farewell to his troops from the dramatic horseshoe staircase outside, and headed off for exile on the Italian island of Elba. (He was back in 1816, but he merely passed through on his way to ultimate defeat at Waterloo.)

Touring the palace may be tiring, but save some energy for exploring both the meticulously kept gardens and carp pond and the equally cared-for forest—which may appear wild, but seven centuries of land husbandry have kept France's second-largest forest in line with civilized notions of what a wilderness *should* be. Over 42,500 hectares of oak, birch, beech, and Scots pine in Fontainebleau forest are crisscrossed by old carriage roads and tangled with 190 miles of woodland paths. The tourist office can help you plan a good hike.

Le Caveau des Ducs (☎ **01-64-22-05-05**), 24 rue de Ferrare, can fix you up with simple French classic dishes in the evocative setting of a 17th-century storage cellar. The restaurant is in a château that's a 5-minute walk beyond the palace. Should you decide to stay the night, **Hôtel-Restaurant Legris et Parc** (☎ **01-64-22-24-24,** fax: 01-64-22-22-05), 36 rue Paul-Séramy, has 390F to 570F ($65 to $95) doubles in a building that comfortably mingles 17th-century and art nouveau styles.

Druids & Stained Glass: Chartres Cathedral

The French sculptor Rodin, after a dazed day sitting in the rain just staring at the sculptures on the facade of Chartres cathedral, dubbed the building "The Acropolis of France." "Chartres is no place for an atheist," declared Napoléon upon laying eyes on this greatest of High Gothic cathedrals (still the fourth largest church in the world). Perhaps the would-be emperor had been moved by the ethereal world of colored light that fills the cathedral on a sunny day, streaming through an awe-inspiring 3,000 square yards of 12th- and 13th-century stained glass, turning the church walls into quasi-mystical portals to heaven. All this beauty can be yours for the low price of just one local **train** ticket from Paris's Gare Montparnasse and less than an hour's ride. The **tourism office** (☎ **01-37-21-50-00**) is right on the place de la Cathédral.

The first cathedral here was built in the 4th century atop a Roman temple. Many historians hold that the site was religious even before the Romans invaded Gaul (Celtic France), and there's evidence that Druids worshiped in a sacred grove here centuries before Christ. You could spend hours, like Rodin, just scrutinizing the charismatic 12th-century sculptures adorning the main Royal Portal, and their 13th-century cousins around to the north and south sides of the church as well. That Royal Portal is part of the west facade, which, along with the base of the south tower, is the only part of the Romanesque church to survive an 1194 fire. The cathedral was quickly rebuilt in the 13th century, and the rest remains an inspiring tribute to High Gothic architecture. Tear your eyes from the stained glass inside for at least long enough to admire the 16th- to 18th-century choir screen whose niches are filled with 40 statuettes.

After the cathedral, make time to explore the cobbled medieval streets in the **Vieux Quartiers (old town)** and visit the 16th- to 19th-century paintings in the **Musée des Beaux-Arts de Chartres** (☎ **01-37-36-41-39**) at 29 Cloître Notre-Dame. When hunger strikes, head to the second floor of 10 rue au Lait for the tasty bistro food of **Le Buisson Ardent** (☎ **01-37-34-04-66**). If you decide to make a night of it, rest your weary head for 420F to 490F ($70 to $81.65) per double at the **Hôtel Châtlet** (☎ **01-37-21-78-00,** fax: 01-37-36-23-01), 6-8 Jehan-de-Beauce, where the rooms are filled with reproduction antiques; many of the rooms also have panoramic views of the cathedral.

Chapter 17

Amsterdam & the Best of the Netherlands

> **In This Chapter**
>
> ➤ Rooms with a view—of the canals
>
> ➤ Amsterdam's entire cultural spectrum, from Anne Frank and Rembrandt to the Red Light District
>
> ➤ High on life: There are coffee bars and then there are "coffee bars"
>
> ➤ Biking through the tulips and tilting at windmills: Dutch excursions

As far as great European cities go, Amsterdam is pretty young. Founded in 1200 as a fishing village at the mouth of the Amstel River, it rapidly grew to become the western world's trading powerhouse. The 17th century was the Dutch Golden Age, when a vast trade network and the American colony of Nieuw Amsterdam (later New York) filled its coffers while painters such as Rembrandt filled its cultural life.

After a bout with strict Protestant laws, Amsterdam became an exceedingly tolerant city in a continent of prejudice. It welcomed religious and other dissidents from across Europe, such as Jews and the English Puritan Pilgrims (a stuffy but devoted bunch who eventually set sail from here to Massachusetts). Wealthy,

Dollars & Sense

The Dutch unit of currency is the guilder (confusingly abbreviated Dfl because once upon a time they were called florins), which is divided into 100 cents. Conveniently, $1 equals roughly Dfl2; or Dfl1 equals 50¢. Dutch coins include 5, 10, and 25 cents and 1, 2.50, and 5 guilder. Bills come in denominations of 10, 25, 50, 100, and 250 guilder.

17th-century Amsterdam dug itself a slew of new canals, built stacks of town-houses, and welcomed in the artists.

Bet You Didn't Know

What's in a name? The Netherlands by any other name would be wrong. As far as the locals are concerned, their country is the *Nederland* (which means "Low Countries"), which makes them *Nederlanders*. All the other names are rooted in the misunderstandings of English–speakers. Americans call the people and their language Dutch because the Brits couldn't keep the *Nederlanders* straight from their neighbors, the Germans *(Deutsch)*. Americans also often refer to the nation by what is actually a name shared by two of its regions, North Holland and South Holland (this is like calling the entire United States "Carolina" or "Virginia").

These traditions of encouraging high art and tolerance and discouraging prudish morality laws have endowed the city with its greatest attractions. Amsterdam has some of the world's top museums; in addition to Rembrandt, the Dutch arts can claim native masters such as Frans Hals, Jan Vermeer, Jan Steen, Vincent van Gogh, and Piet Mondrian. Its cityscape is one of the most elegant and cohesive anywhere, with 250-year-old town houses lining well-planned and scrupulously well-kept canals. The Dutch leniency toward drugs and prostitution has produced a huge tourism industry that draws students and other mellow types to the city's "smoking coffeehouses" and visitors of all stripes who gawk at the houses of ill repute in the (in)famous Red Light District. Nazi occupation during World War II threw the light of Dutch tolerance into sharp, shadowed relief as, despite the efforts of many locals, thousands of Amsterdam Jews were tracked down and deported. Among them was Anne Frank, a teenager whose hiding place still stands and whose diary remains one of the most powerful and enduring pieces of Holocaust literature.

No other city has such a radical mix of sights, from the basest and most titillating of pleasures to the most somber reflections on human cruelty. Dutch strength in the fine arts spans from the Renaissance to the modern period, but just as many visitors come to shop for diamonds, drink Amsterdam beers such as Heineken and Amstel in brown cafes (so called because the best of them are stained a uniform pale brown from decades, if not from centuries, of smoke), or head out from the city for tulip fields and windmills. You can't really appreciate Amsterdam in less than two full days—for many, the museums alone will take at least that long.

Getting Your Bearings

Amsterdam, like Venice, is a city infiltrated by water. On a map, it looks kind of like a spiderweb, with the canals as the threads radiating out from the center in tight, concentric arcs. You don't think about addresses or directions in terms of streets here, but rather in terms of the canals and six major squares. There are just a very few street names you'll want to keep in your head, starting with the **Damrak.** Think of the Damrak as the backbone of the City Center. It runs from the Centraal Station at the north end of town straight down to **Dam Square,** the heart of the city and where the first dam across the Amstel River was built (hence the name *Amstelledamme*, later to become Amsterdam).

Time-Savers

Tourist offices in the Netherlands are indicated by VVV (usually in a blue-and-white triangle). Amsterdam's most complete VVV office is just outside the Centraal train station at Stationsplein 10. There's also a small desk in the station itself, a branch in the heart of town at Leidseplein 1, and another at the corner of Stadionplein and Van Tuyll van Serooskerkenweg. The only phone number to call is ☎ 06/3403-4066, which costs Dfl.75 (40¢) and will get you a recorded message (in Dutch). Hang on and you'll be able to speak with a live, English-speaking person (Monday to Friday 9am to 5pm). An information desk covering all of the Netherlands is in Schiphol Plaza, at the airport.

Out the other end of Dam Square, the main street changes names to **Rokin,** which curves down to the square and transportation hub of **Muntplein.** East of Muntplein, on the City Center's southeast corner, is **Waterlooplein,** home to one of the city's premier music halls and a flea market. Southwest of Muntplein, on the other side of the Canal Zone, lies **Leidseplein,** the bustling, throbbing center of Amsterdam's liveliest quarter of restaurants, nightclubs, and theaters. Farther south is **Museumplein,** ground zero for art lovers and museum hounds. Nearby is **P. C. Hoofstraat,** Amsterdam's most fashionable shopping drag.

Amsterdam's Neighborhoods in Brief

The **City Center** consists of a few straight canals and a tangle of medieval streets. It's bounded by the arc of the Singel Canal/Amstel River/Oude Schans canal and runs from the Centraal Station south to Muntplein, with Dam Square in the middle (this is where you'll find the **Red Light District**). **The Canal Zone** is next, wrapped around the City Center in a big arc. It's made up of a series of six concentric canals that are laid out with 17th-century regularity. The irregular canal Singelgracht bounds this neighborhood. To the south lies **The Museumplein,** where you'll find the city's greatest museums of art, finest shopping, and some of the best small hotels.

Further south is **Amsterdam South,** the most upscale residential district (of great interest to upwardly mobile Amsterdammers, but not to visitors). The **Jordaan,** a grid of small streets slung between two canals at the northeastern end of the Canal Zone, is an increasingly fashionable neighborhood with several good restaurants. **Amsterdam East,** east of the City Center, is the fairly pleasant and residential working-class and immigrant neighborhood, with attractions like the zoo and tropical museum.

Getting Into & Around Town

Trains arrive in Amsterdam at **Centraal Station,** built on an artificial island in the IJ River bounding the city's north edge. Amsterdam's spiderweb of canals and streets radiates out from this point. Regular trains connect this station with ultra-modern **Schiphol Airport** in about 20 minutes (or ask your hotel if they're part of the consortium serviced by the KLM shuttle bus, which will whisk you straight to your hotel—for three times the cost of the train). The square in front of the station has the city's main tourist office and tram terminal. Probably the easiest way to transport yourself and your luggage from the airport to your hotel is to take a taxi (see the "Taxi" entry in the "Amsterdam Fast Facts" section).

Ten of Amsterdam's 16 trolley, or **tram,** lines begin and end at Centraal Station. Other main tram connection points are Dam Square, Muntplein, and Museumplein. Most other chapters in this book explain how the transportation tickets work and what they cost in a little sidebar, but Amsterdam's system is a bit screwy and takes more explaining than fits in a box.

Amsterdam's **tickets** work differently from those of most cities. You can buy a **single trip** from the bus driver (board at the front), which will cost Dfl3 to 7.50 ($1.50 to $3.75), depending on how many zones you'll be passing through. It's more economical—if a bit more confusing—to buy a long, skinny Dfl11 ($5.50) *strippenkaart*, which has nothing to do with the Red Light District attractions. This multiple-use ticket has 15 strips on it, each good for one zone. You can get these from newsstands, post offices, or the GVB ticket booth outside Centraal Station.

When you board the bus, ask the driver how many zones to your stop (in central Amsterdam, usually only one or two), fold back that many "strips" plus one, and stamp it in the machine on the bus. It's the "plus one" rule that gets most visitors. In other words, if you're going three zones, skip the first three strips and fold back the ticket so that the fourth strip is at the end and then stamp that fourth strip; if you're going just one zone, stamp the second strip. You can transfer as often as you like for the next hour, provided you stay within the number of zones you've stamped.

If all this stripping drives you batty, and you plan to ride a lot, just buy a **day ticket** from the driver or any ticket dispenser. This ticket gives you unlimited travel all day for Dfl12 ($6). Two- to eight-day passes are also available. The doors on trams and buses don't open automatically; you have to punch the *deur open* button. All the lines operate as explained here, except lines 4 and 13, where you board the back of the bus and deal with the conductor, not the driver; and line 5, where you have to get a ticket from a machine ahead of time. If all else fails, keep in mind that Amsterdam, with all its canals, is a city made for walking.

Amsterdam Fast Facts

American Express   One branch of American Express, Damrak 66 (☎ 020/ 520-7777), boasts an ATM. The other office is at Van Baerlestraat 39 (☎ 020/671-4141). Both are open Monday to Friday 9am to 5pm and Saturday 9am to noon.

Consulates   The U.S. Consulate (☎ 020/664-5661) is at Museumplein 19.

Doctors/hospitals   For a list of doctors and dentists, call ☎ 06/3503-2042. For emergency care, try **Academisch Medisch Centrum,** Meibergdreef 9 (☎ 020/566-3333) or **Onze Lieve Vrouwe Gashuis,** Eerste Oosterparkstraat 179 1e (☎ 020/599-9111).

Emergency   To call an ambulance or report a fire, dial ☎ **0611.** For the police, call ☎ **622-2222.**

Pharmacies   An *apotheek* is a pharmacy that fills prescriptions; a *drogerji* sells toiletries. For a list of pharmacies that fill prescriptions at night or on weekends, call ☎ **06/3503-2042** or check the door of any apotheek; a sign will direct you to the nearest late-night pharmacy.

Safety   Violent crime is rare, but the Dutch tolerance of soft drugs invites drug-related crime. Beware of pickpockets in tourist areas; on public transportation; and around Damrak, Dam Square, and the Red Light District. The Red Light District, so titillating in the daylight, is less than savory after dark, particularly as the evening wears on and tourists have returned to their hotels. Late at night, I do not recommend that you call attention to yourself or wander the District alone.

Taxis   Amsterdam is best traveled on foot, by tram, or on bicycle, but getting you and your bags to and from the airport is easiest in a taxi. You'll find taxis at stands in front of most major hotels or at Leidseplein, Rembrandtplein, or Centraal Station. To call for a taxi, dial ☎ **020/6777-7777.** The initial charge is Dfl5.60 ($2.80) and Dfl2.80 ($1.40) for each additional kilometer.

Telephone   A local call in Amsterdam costs Dfl.50 (25¢) for three minutes. Almost all pay phones in the Netherlands accept only phone cards, which are sold at newsstands, post offices, tobacconists, and train stations for Dfl10 ($5), Dfl25 ($12.50), and Dfl50 ($25). Coin phones take Dfl.25, Dfl1, Dfl2.50, or Dfl5. On both coin and card phones, watch the digital reading: It tracks your decreasing deposit, so you'll know when to add more coins or another card. For directory assistance, call ☎ **06/8008.**

The country code for the Netherlands is **31.** Amsterdam's city code is **020,** but drop the initial zero if you're calling from outside the Netherlands. To call Amsterdam from the United States, dial **011-31-20,** then the number. To charge a call to your calling card, dial **AT&T** (☎ **06/022-9111**), **MCI** (☎ **06/022-9122**), or **Sprint** (☎ **06/022-9119**). To call the United States from the Netherlands direct, dial **001** followed by the area code and number.

Transit Info   For transportation information, call ☎ **06/9292.**

Not All Beds Charge by the Hour: Amsterdam's Hotel Scene

Amsterdam has plenty of beds (besides those in the Red Light District), but the hotel crunch can get tight in July and August—especially among budget places, which fill up with students eager to test Amsterdam's legendary lenient drug policy. Many of those picturesquely tall, gabled houses lining canals and historic streets have been converted into inns, but be warned: Dutch staircases give new meaning to the word "steep." The older the building, the harder it is for a hotel to get permission to install an elevator, so be sure to ask before booking if stairs present a problem. Rooms with canal views cost more, but they are often worth it for the atmosphere; plus, they're often better out-fitted and are sometimes larger than the viewless rooms. The half-dozen choices listed here are all in pleasant, safe neigh-borhoods.

Time-Savers

For help landing an accom-modation anywhere in the Netherlands, contact the free **Netherlands Reservations Centre** (☎ **070/320-2500;** fax 070/320-2611). The **VVV tourist office** will also reserve a room for you on the spot for a Dfl5 ($2.50) fee and a deposit.

Best Western Avenue
$$$. City Center.
The Avenue has all the bland, standardized charm of any international chain. But for solid, reliable comfort (if smallish rooms), American-style amenities at a great price, and a safe location very near the rail station, you can do no better. The full Dutch breakfast adds a bit of local color.

Nieuwezijds Voorburgwal 27 (1 street east of Spuistraat, just a few minutes from the Centraal Station). ☎ *020/623-8307.* **Fax:** *020/638-3946.* **Tram:** *1, 2, 5, 11, 13, 17.* **Rates:** *Dfl200–250 ($100–$125) double, including breakfast. AE, DC, MC, V.*

Hotel Acro
$. Near the Museumplein.
One of Amsterdam's (by no means secret) bargains, the Acro has bright, clean, and well-kept small rooms close to the city's major museums and P. C. Hooftstraat's shopping. With a shower in every room, a full Dutch breakfast included in the rates, and the hopping Leidseplein restaurant quarter just across a canal, what more could you ask for?

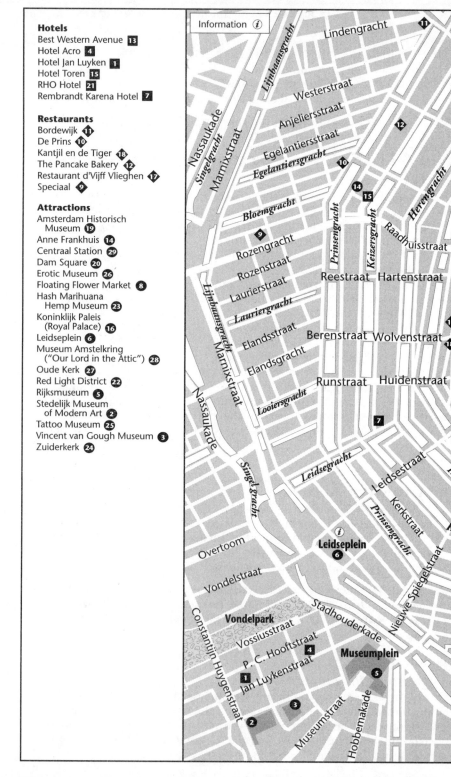

Hotels
Best Western Avenue **13**
Hotel Acro **4**
Hotel Jan Luyken **1**
Hotel Toren **15**
RHO Hotel **21**
Rembrandt Karena Hotel **7**

Restaurants
Bordewijk **11**
De Prins **10**
Kantjil en de Tiger **18**
The Pancake Bakery **12**
Restaurant d'Vijff Vlieghen **17**
Speciaal **9**

Attractions
Amsterdam Historisch
 Museum **19**
Anne Frankhuis **14**
Centraal Station **29**
Dam Square **20**
Erotic Museum **26**
Floating Flower Market **8**
Hash Marihuana
 Hemp Museum **23**
Koninklijk Paleis
 (Royal Palace) **16**
Leidseplein **6**
Museum Amstelkring
 ("Our Lord in the Attic") **28**
Oude Kerk **27**
Red Light District **22**
Rijksmuseum **5**
Stedelijk Museum
 of Modern Art **2**
Tattoo Museum **25**
Vincent van Gough Museum **3**
Zuiderkerk **24**

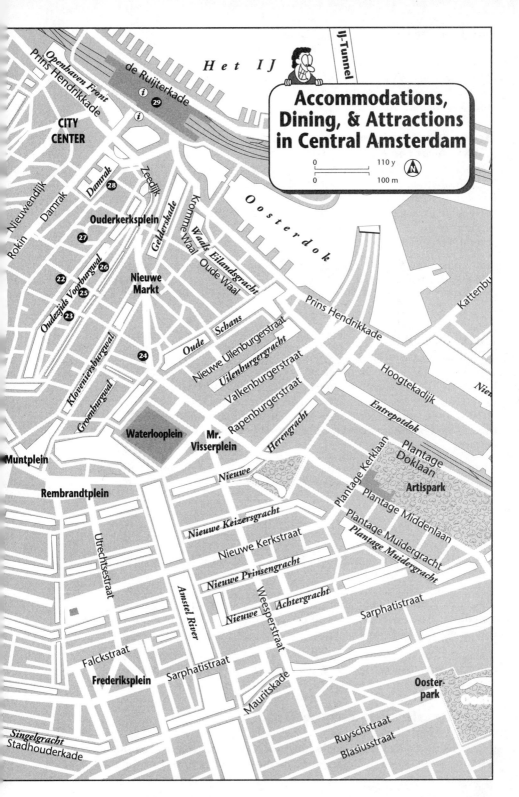

Jan Luykenstraat 44 (near the corner with Honthorststraat). ☎ **020/662-5538.**
Fax: *020/675-0811.* **Tram:** *2, 5, 6, 7, 10 to Rijksmuseum.* **Rates:** *Dfl90–180
($45–$90) double. AE, DC, MC, V.*

Hotel Jan Luyken
$$$$$. Near the Museumplein.
Set in a trio of 19th-century buildings between the city's top museums and
P. C. Hooftstraat's shops, this hotel of refined amenities and personalized service is a gracious splurge option. It offers the best of both an intimate inn—
with comfortably furnished bedrooms and complimentary afternoon tea in
the lounge—and a pricey hotel—with business services; modern baths; and
several bars, patios, and dining spaces to relax in.

Jan Luykenstraat 54-58 (between Va de Veldestraat and Van Baerlestraat). ☎ *020/
573-0730.* **Fax:** *020/676-3841.* **Tram:** *2, 5 to Van Baerlestraat.* **Rates:**
*Dfl330–435 ($165–$217.50) double, including breakfast. Children 4–12 half-
price. AE, DC, MC, V.*

Hotel Toren
$$$. Canal Zone.
One of the best values in canalside living, the Toren has medium-sized rooms
in two buildings on a posh stretch of canal. The furnishings are worn, but
the staff is very helpful, and there's even a cute (read: floral prints) little
guest house available for extra privacy. Insist on a room overlooking the
canal; some of the cramped rooms in the hotel's heart don't even have
windows.

*Keizersgracht 164 (near Raadhuisstraat, close to the Westerkerk and Anne Frank
house).* ☎ *020/622-6352.* **Fax:** *020/626-9705.* **Tram:** *13, 14, 17.* **Rates:**
Dfl150–245 ($75–$122.50) double. AE, DC, MC, V.

 RHO Hotel
$$. City Center.
This recently renovated hotel in a former gold company building is one of
the most conveniently located in Amsterdam. It's on a quiet side street off
Dam Square, with an Art Nouveau lobby that hints at its origins as a turn-of-
the-century theater. The rooms, unfortunately, are thoroughly modern and
functional. The hotel provides all the amenities and is an excellent price for
this level of comfort.

Nes 11-13 (just off the southeast corner of Dam Sq.). ☎ *020/620-7371.* **Fax:**
020/620-7826. **Tram:** *1, 2, 4, 5, 9, 14, 16, 24, 25 to Dam Sq.* **Rates:**
Dfl165–200 ($82.50–$100) double, including breakfast. AE, MC, V.

Rembrandt Karena Hotel
$$$$. Canal Zone.
In the heart of canal land, the Rembrandt Karena has many canalside rooms.
Whether you end up in the main 18th-century house or one of the small

16th-century homes lining the Singel out back, you have a very good chance of securing a canal view. The rooms are more modern than their settings: They have a full complement of amenities, almost all are of a generous size, and the odd wood beam or fireplace reminds you of the buildings' history.

Herengracht 255 (above Raadhuisstraat). ☎ *020/622-1727.* **Fax:** *020/624-0630.* **Tram:** *13, 14, 17 to Magna Plaza.* **Rates:** *Dfl295–350 ($147.50–$175) double. Children under 14 stay free in parents' room. AE, DC, MC, V.*

Going Dutch: Amsterdam's Restaurant Scene

Amsterdam, as the capital of a trading nation, has a well-rounded arsenal of restaurants boasting all sorts of cuisines, from Dutch to Indonesian. Traditional Dutch cuisine tends to be hearty and rather uninventive, but still good and filling. Specialties include **Hutspot** (beef rib stew) and **pannekoeken,** massive pancakes that can be eaten topped with sugar or fruit as a dessert or with meats and cheeses as a main course. Consider accompanying your meal with a Dutch beer such as Heineken, Grolsch, or Amstel (all light *pils* brews) or a dark Belgian beer.

Bet You Didn't Know

Amsterdam is famous for its excellent Indonesian restaurants. *The* dish to try in town is not Dutch, but rather the Indonesian feast called **rijsttafel.** This "rice table" smorgasbord of Southeast Asian specialties consists of 17 to 30 tiny dishes, offering you a taste of all the best food the former Dutch colony has to offer.

Bordewijk
$$$. Jordaan. FRENCH.
The setting may be starkly modern, but the food is richly textured and tastefully French, with modern accents and Italian and Asian twists. The service is attentive but not overbearing, and the menu changes constantly, but may include rib roast in a Bordelais sauce or red mullet with wild spinach. An outdoor terrace on the canal makes summertime meals here even more attractive.

Noordermarkt 7 (at the north end of Prinsengracht). ☎ *020/624-3899. Reservations very highly recommended.* **Tram:** *3, 10, 13, 14, 17.* **Main courses:** *3-course fixed-price dinner Dfl56 ($28). AE, MC, V.* **Open:** *Dinner Tues–Sun.*

Kids De Prins
$$. Canal Zone. DUTCH/FRENCH.
One of the best values in the city, this tiny neighborhood place is so popular for its inexpensive brown cafe-style food that the limited tables fill up fast, so call ahead. In a 17th-century canalside house, solid Dutch and French dishes are expertly prepared at remarkably low prices. This place is one of your best bets for rubbing elbows with the locals. It's also open late, until 1am during the week and until 2am on Friday and Saturday.

285

Prinsengracht 124 (near the Anne Frank House). ☎ *020/624-9382. Reservations not accepted.* ***Tram:*** *13, 14, 17.* ***Main courses:*** *Dfl19.80–27.50 ($9.90–$13.75). AE, DC, MC, V.* ***Open:*** *Lunch and dinner daily.*

Kantjil en de Tiger
$$$. Canal Zone. JAVANESE/INDONESIAN.

This large and popular restaurant features a good *rijsttafel* for two and a tasty *nasi goreng Kantjil* (fried rice with pork kebabs and stewed beef). Southeast Asian specialties like shrimp in coconut dressing round out the menu. Save room for the multilayered cinnamon cake.

Spuistraat 291 (below Raadhuisstraat). ☎ *020/620-0994. Reservations recommended.* ***Tram:*** *1, 2, 5, 11.* ***Main courses:*** *Dfl25–95 ($12.50–$47.50). AE, DC, MC, V.* ***Open:*** *Dinner daily.*

Kids The Pancake Bakery
$. Canal Zone. DUTCH/PANCAKES.

The name says it all: This canalside joint does one thing only—*pannekoeken*— and it does it great. Your meal may be one of these disks topped with Cajun chicken or curried turkey and pineapple; for dessert, fruit compotes, syrups, and ice cream are typical pancake stuffings. The decor is simple and slightly rustic, but in summer join the crowds (and the syrup-seeking bees) at the long outside tables with a canal view.

Prinsengracht 191 (1 block from the Anne Frank House). ☎ *020/625-1333. Reservations suggested.* ***Tram:*** *13, 14, 17.* ***Main courses:*** *Dfl8–19 ($4–$9.50). AE, MC, V.* ***Open:*** *Lunch and dinner daily.*

Restaurant d'Vijff Vlieghen
$$$$$. Canal Zone. DUTCH.

An Amsterdam institution for 350 years, "The Five Fliers" is set into a string of five canal-front buildings. It offers a variety of historic decors and an excellent cuisine prepared by a chef determined to prove that traditional recipes can be exquisite. Try the wild boar with stuffed apples or smoked turkey fillet with cranberry. Their list of Dutch gins offers more than 40 selections, and there's often outdoor seating in summer.

Spuistraat 294-302 (below Raadhuisstraat). ☎ *020/624-8369. Reservations recommended.* ***Tram:*** *1, 2, 5, 11.* ***Main courses:*** *Dfl72.50–300 ($36.25–$150). DC, MC, V.* ***Open:*** *Dinner daily.*

Speciaal
$$$$. Jordaan. INDONESIAN.

This crowded little place is one of Amsterdam's premier Indonesian restaurants and the best place to loosen your belt and dig into a full *rijsttafel,* including *rendang* (beef), *ayam* (chicken), *ikan* (fish), and *telor* (eggs). Also try the *spekkoek,* a rich layered cake that is the house specialty.

Nieuwe Leliestraat 140-142 (just above Bloemgracht). ☎ **020/624-9706.**
Reservations highly recommended. **Tram:** *3, 10.* **Main courses:** *Rijsttafel costs
Dfl45.50–60 ($22.75–$30). AE, MC, V.* **Open:** *Dinner daily.*

Quick Bites

Amsterdam's traditional snack consists of small sandwiches called *broodjes,*
available everywhere but best at the specialty *broodjeswinkel* **Eetsalon Van
Dobben,** at Korte Reguliersdwarsstraat 5-9 (off Rembrandtsplein), or **Broodje
van Kootje,** on the Leidseplein. For the unusual, try seafood on the go, fresh
from the counter of **Vishandel de Kreft** at Vijzelstraat 3, near the Muntplein.
You can buy ultra-fresh **picnic supplies** at the market on Albert Cuypstraat,
at the health–foody Boerenmarkt Farmer's Market at Noodermarkt, or in
Albert Heijn supermarkets (there's one at the corner of Leidstraat and
Koningsplein).

Sex, Drugs, & Vincent van Gogh: Amsterdam Sightseeing

For a quick overview of town, take a three-hour **bus tour** for about Dfl45
($22.50) from Key Tours (☎ **020/624-7304**), Dam 19; or **Holland Inter-
national Excursions** (☎ **020/551-2800**), Dam 6. Even better, take a
cruise on the canals (see "Other Fun Stuff to Do"). Amsterdam's most
innovative tour has to be the municipal **Museumboot** (☎ **020/622-2181**),
Stationsplein 8, a boat which stops near 16 of the city's museums, including
all of the ones mentioned in this chapter. The full-day fare—Dfl 22 ($11) for
adults, Dfl 18 ($9) under age 13—includes discounts on some museum
admissions. The 1½-hour tour costs Dfl 15 ($7.50).

Amsterdam Sights Not to Miss

Rijksmuseum

Though it doesn't get as much press as the Louvre or the Uffizi, Amsterdam's
Rijksmuseum is one of the top museums in Europe. Naturally, it has the
largest collection of Dutch masters in the world. Rembrandt is the star of the
show, weighing in with a couple of self-portraits, the gruesome *Anatomy
Lesson*, the racy *The Jewish Bride,* and his masterpiece, *The Night Watch,*
which is the defining work of Dutch painting's Golden Age. Frans Hals is
well-represented, with *The Merry Drinker* being one of his best portraits. There
are party scenes courtesy of Jan Steen, de Hooch's intimate interiors, still-lifes
by Bollengier, and four Vermeer paintings, including the famed *Woman
Reading a Letter* and *The Kitchen Maid.* One of my faves from among the less-
famous pieces is Avercamp's *Winter Landscape with Ice Skaters,* a scene that

sums up the Netherlands I had always pictured from storybooks growing up. You could easily spend all day here, and many art-lovers do, but if need be, you can get away with just a long morning.

Stadhouderskade 42 (at Museumplein). ☎ *020/673-2121.* ***Tram:*** *2, 5, 6, 7, 10.* ***Bus:*** *26, 65, 66.* ***Admission:*** *Dfl15 ($7.50) adults, Dfl7.50 ($3.75) kids 6–18.* ***Open:*** *Daily 10am–5pm.*

Anne Frankhuis (Anne Frank's House)

When 13-year-old Anne Frank began her diary in July 1942, she dealt with the usual problems of adolescence, including feelings about her family and the boy next door, as well as the defining fact of her life: she was Jewish and had just moved into a hidden attic apartment with seven other people, comprising two families, as the Nazis occupied Amsterdam. For two years Anne lived here, with only a crack in the window and some pictures of movie stars on the wall to remind her of the outside world. .

Eventually, the Franks and their companions were betrayed, and all were deported to concentration camps. Anne went first to Auschwitz, and then was moved to Bergen-Belsen as the Nazis retreated. She died of typhus just weeks before the camp was liberated. Of the eight people who lived in the attic, only her father, Otto, survived. His model of the rooms as it looked in those years of concealment and Anne's photos on the walls are all that adorn the little apartment hidden behind a swinging bookcase. Downstairs, a photograph display details the Holocaust in Amsterdam, and the bookshop carries copies of Anne's remarkable diary in dozens of languages. Half a million people come to pay their respects here every year, so expect crowds and arrive early.

Prinsengracht 263 (just below Westermarkt). ☎ *020/556-7100.* ***Tram:*** *13, 14, 17.* ***Admission:*** *Dfl10 ($5) adults, Dfl5 ($2.50) children 10–17.* ***Open:*** *June–Aug, Mon–Sat 9am–7pm, Sun and holidays 10am–7pm; Sept–May, Mon–Sat 9am–5pm, Sun and holidays 10am–5pm.*

Vincent van Gogh Museum

The Netherlands' most famous modern artist was an underappreciated, tormented genius who sold only one painting in his lifetime—to his brother. Bouts of depression led him at one point into an asylum and at another to hack off his own ear after an argument with the painter Gauguin. Yet even while the artistic establishment was virtually ignoring him, van Gogh managed to carry the freedom of impressionism to new heights, and he created an impressive, intensely expressive style all his own.

At this monument to the artist, you can follow a chronological progression of his works, 200 paintings and 500 drawings, alongside letters and personal effects (some of which feature in the paintings on display). A few of his more famous canvases here include *The Potato Eaters, Sunflowers, The Bedroom at Arles, Gauguin's Chair, Self Portrait with a Straw Hat,* and *The Garden of Daubigny.* At the exhibit's end hangs the powerful *Crows over the Cornfield,* one of the last paintings the troubled master completed in 1890 before committing suicide at the age of 37.

Paulus Potterstraat 7-11 (at Museumplein). ☎ *020/570-5200.* **Tram:** *2, 5, 16.* **Bus:** *26, 65, 66.* **Admission:** *Dfl12.50 ($6.25) adults, Dfl5 ($2.50) under 18.* **Open:** *Daily 10am–5pm.*

Extra! Extra!

To dig deeper into the history of Amsterdam's Jewish population, visit the **Joods Historisch Museum (☎ 020/626-9945)**, Jonas Dani'l Meijerplein 2-4. Located near Waterlooplein, which was the heart of the Jewish district, this vast museum chronicles the 350 years of Jewish history and culture in the city. It's open daily from 11am to 5pm with an admission of Dfl10 ($5) for adults and Dfl2 ($1) for ages 10 to 16. Ever a tolerant country, the Netherlands welcomed hundreds of mainly Sephardic Jews fleeing persecution in Spain and Portugal in the 15th and 16th centuries. The **Portuguese Synagogue** at Mr. Visserplein 3, built in 1665, is the only still-functioning temple to survive from that period. Although at first restricted to certain trades like diamond-cutting, by 1796 Jews in Amsterdam were granted full civil rights, unheard of in that era in Europe, a position they enjoyed until the Nazi occupation.

Stedelijk Museum of Modern Art

If you're into modern art from impressionism on, spend a morning at the Stedelijk. The permanent collections and regularly staged exhibitions highlight many movements and styles of the past century. Featured artists include Picasso, Chagall, Cézanne, Monet, Calder, Oldenburg, Warhol, Jasper Johns, and Man Ray. Of particular interest are Gerrit Rietveld's *Red Blue Chair* and paintings by Mondrian—two major forces in the Dutch abstract De Stijl movement, which prefaced the Bauhaus and modernist schools. This museum also has a large collection by the Russian Kazimir Malevich, who experimented with supersaturated color in a style he called Suprematism. The recently restored building itself is a stylish 1895 example of the northern neo-Renaissance.

Paulus Potterstraat 13 (at Museumplein). ☎ *020/573-2737.* **Tram:** *2, 5, 16.* **Bus:** *26, 65, 66.* **Admission:** *Dfl9 ($4.50) adults, Dfl4.50 ($2.25) kids 7–16.* **Open:** *Apr–Sept, daily 11am–7pm; Oct–Mar daily 11am–5pm.*

Red Light District

Dutch pragmatism mixed in with Dutch tolerance has led to the establishment of the best-known—and the safest and cleanest—prostitute zone of any Western city, one that has become one of Amsterdam's major sightseeing attractions for its sheer openness. Amsterdam never presumed to be able to stop the world's oldest profession, so it decided simply to regulate it and confine the licensed brothels to the old city streets surrounding the Oude Kirk (hey, it was closest to the docks). These houses of ill repute display their wares behind plate-glass windows. The storefronts of some of the prettiest 17th-century homes in Amsterdam are occupied by women half-naked or wrapped in leather, watching TV, darning socks, reading books, and otherwise occupying themselves until a customer comes along (at which point they either close the blinds or abandon the window for the privacy of an inner room).

The ladies pay their taxes, and the state ensures that they have regular medical check-ups and health coverage (this didn't stop 60 percent of them from contracting HIV in the days before the spread of the disease was understood). All very civilized, I guess; it's the streets and the clientele who wander them that feel less wholesome. The district is frequented by five types. Three are harmless: lots of tourists—giggling, blushing, gawking, considering, or shaking their heads in disbelief—as well as darty-eyed career guys in suits and age-old sailors. Two other types can be scary and tragic: unlicensed prostitutes strung out on heroin and trolling the streets and packs of shifty, seedy men who look like they indulge too heavily in both of Amsterdam's semi-illicit pleasures.

Bet You Didn't Know

The canals of Amsterdam, a city of 7,000 gables, are lined with elegant 17th-century row houses that often look impossibly tall and skinny. For years property was taxed on the width of the frontage, so everyone built as narrowly as possible. In order to get maximum square footage out of such skinny property, Amsterdammers extended their structures very high and very deep.

So come prepared to be provoked or saddened by the sight of scantily clad women behind glass, who manage to look bored and provocative at the same time—and be even more careful and aware than usual. Don't take any pictures if you don't want to risk having your Nikon pitched into a canal—these career gals don't want their faces recorded by anyone. I've always felt pretty safe here during the day, but by night I'd either steer clear entirely or stick only to the main streets and leave my valuables at the hotel.

The Red Light District fills the streets around the canals Oudezijds Achterburgwal and Oudezijds Voorburgwal. **Tram:** *4, 9, 16, 24, 25 to Dam Sq., and then duck behind the Grand Hotel Krasnapolsky.*

Museum Amstelkring ("Our Lord in the Attic")
Although the giant Gothic Oude Kirk (Old Church) is just down the block, this tiny, well-preserved baroque church is much more interesting. In the heart of the Red Light District, it's spread across the connected third floors of a trio of 17th-century homes. Although Amsterdam is famed for its tolerance,

it did go through a period in the 16th and 17th centuries when the practice of any religion save the official Dutch Reformed Calvinism was forbidden. In order to worship, Jews, Mennonites, Lutherans, and, in this instance, Catholics, had to go underground—or above ground, as the case may be— and hold services in secret. One of the houses below the church has been restored for visitors—it's the oldest Amsterdam house open to the public.

Oudezijds Voorburgwal 40 (about 3 blocks from Centraal Station, on the far side of the Damrak's canal). ☎ *020/624-6604.* ***Tram:*** *1, 2, 4, 5, 9, 11, 13, 16, 17, 24, 25 (any to Dam Sq.).* ***Admission:*** *Dfl7.50 ($3.75) adults, Dfl6 ($3) seniors, students, and children.* ***Open:*** *Mon–Sat 11am–5pm, Sun 1–5pm. Closed Jan 1.*

Other Fun Stuff to Do

➤ **Cruise the Canals.** Amsterdam has 160 canals spanned by more than 1,200 bridges, so no trip is complete without a canal cruise on a glass-roofed boat with multilingual commentary (recorded or live). There is no better way to get a feel for this city or to see its gabled houses, lithe bridges, busy harbor, and some unforgettable sights (such as the unlikely Cat Boat, home to about 150 of the furry felines who are *supposed* to detest being anywhere near water). Most tours last an hour and depart from the Damrak or near the Leisplein or Muntplein. They run every 15 to 30 minutes in summer (9am to 9:30pm), every 45 minutes in winter (10am to 4pm), and cost around Dfl10 to 15 ($5 to $7.50) adults, Dfl8 to 10 ($4 to $5) for ages 4 to 13.

Similar tours are operated by more companies than you could shake an oar at, so here are just a few contact numbers: **Amsterdam Canal Cruises** (☎ **020/626-5636**), **Holland International** (☎ **020/622-7788**), and **Meyers Rondvaarten** (☎ **020/623-4208**). For romantics, a two-hour **night cruise** with wine and cheese or a three-hour dinner cruise makes for a bit of light hedonism. The former run nightly year-round for Dfl45($22.50); the latter run nightly April through November, Tuesday and Friday only in winter for Dfl145 ($72.50). Reservations are required, so contact **Holland International** (☎ **020/622-7788**) or **Keytours** (☎ **020/624-7304**).

➤ **Diamonds Are Forever: Tour Amsterdam's Gem-Cutting Factories.** The massive Amsterdam diamond-cutting factories of the 1950s and 1960s, when rough gems still poured in from Dutch mines in South Africa, are these days reduced to salesrooms with a few polishers working in the back or upstairs. But gem-shaping is a Dutch craft that goes back to the 16th century, and tours of diamond-cutting shops and showrooms can still prove interesting. Just prepare yourself for the hard sell in the salesroom at the end.

Head to **Van Moppes Diamonds** (☎ **020/676-1242**), Albert Cuypstraat 2-6, to peer at the world's smallest cut diamond of 0.24 milligrams. At **Costers Diamonds** (☎ **020/676-2222**), established in 1840 at Paulus Potterstraat 2-6 near the Rijksmuseum, you can hear how they polished the 186-carat *Koh-i-Noor* down to the 108-carat

291

stone in the center of English Queen Victoria's crown (today in the Tower of London). The **Amsterdam Diamond Center** (☎ 020/ 624-5787), Rokin 1 off Dam Square, lays claim to having worked the biggest rough diamond in history, 3,106 carats, into nine cut gems, including a 530-carat whopper called Cullinan I.

➤ **Only in Amsterdam: Visit the Sex Museums.** These places are as squeaky clean as their subject matter allows and are full of tourists giggling, not dirty old men whispering. The **Amsterdam Sex Museum** (☎ 020/622-8376), Damrak 18, is the more carnival-like of the two, with a section of antique porn photographs that borders on being of historical interest and a room of everything you didn't want to know about deviant sex. (Open daily 10am–11:30pm.) More titillation can be had at the **Erotic Museum** (☎ 020/624-7303), Oudezijds Achterburgwal 54, which is a bit more clinical and adds in some mock-ups of an S&M "playroom" and a re-created alley from the Red Light District in the good old days. Hours are daily noon–midnight.

➤ **Drink Beer in a Brown Cafe, Gin in a *Proflokaal*.** When the Dutch want to go to the proverbial place where everybody knows their name, they head to the neighborhood brown cafe. There's no better place to sample Dutch beer, where glasses drawn extra frothy from the tap are beheaded by a knife-wielding bartender. The city has hundreds of these cafes, but a few of the best include the 1642 **Café Chris,** Bloemstraat 42, with opera music Sunday nights; **Gollem,** Raamsteeg 4, with over 200 beers to offer; **Hoppe,** Spuistraat 18-20, an always-crowded classic from 1670; **Reijnders,** with great people-watching on the Leidseplein at no. 6; and **De Vergulde Gaper,** Prinsengracht 30, another good people-watching place with coveted terrace tables and an atmospheric interior.

For a bit more kick, try the hard liquor the Dutch made famous. Visit a **gin-tasting house,** or *proflokaal,* similar in appearance to brown cafes, but usually owned by the distillery itself. It's customary to take the first sip no-hands style, slurping it from the brim-filled shot glass as you lean over the bar. Try **Brouwerij 't IJ,** Funenkade 7, in a defunct windmill near the harbor (good beers, too); **Café de Doktor,** Rozenboomsteeg near Spui Square, filled with antiques and tasty fruit brandies; or the 1679 **Wijnand Fockink,** Pijlsteeg 31, where they've already heard all the English jokes about their name and there's a series of liqueur bottles painted with portraits of all the city's mayors since 1591.

➤ **Is It Hot in Here? Spend an Afternoon in the Tropics.** Maybe because the winters here are so cold and icy, or maybe because the Dutch Empire once had footholds in many of the world's warmest climes, Amsterdam's ethnographic museum focuses on life in the tropical corners of the globe. The **Tropenmuseum** (☎ 020/568-8215) investigates the indigenous cultures of the country's former colonies in India, Indonesia, and the Caribbean. The best exhibits are set up as typical villages you can wander through. These exhibits are so realistic that you almost wonder where all the inhabitants went. This place may be a good bet when the kids' (or your own) interest in Dutch old masters starts flagging. It's in East Amsterdam on Linnaesstraat 2 at Mauritskade; take tram 9. It's open Monday through Friday 10am to 5pm, Saturday and Sunday noon to 5pm; Admission is Dfl10 ($5) for adults, Dfl5 ($2.50) for children 18 and under.

Tourist Traps

There's a special kind of "coffeehouse" in Amsterdam, where the drug of choice ain't caffeine. Under increasing pressure from the European Union, the Netherlands is cracking down on drugs both soft and hard, but the country is still pretty lenient when it comes to marijuana. Contrary to popular belief, marijuana *is* illegal here, though the police unofficially tolerate possession of a small amount for personal use—less than 5 grams (it used to be 30). These venerable establishments are allowed to sell you small amounts of grass and hash— they even have marijuana menus!—along with joints (rolled with tobacco) and various hash products, coffee, tea, and juice, but no food. The most famous smoking coffee shop is **Bulldog,** whose main branch is at Leidseplein 15 (☎ **020/627-1908**). Just remember: Anyone with presidential aspirations shouldn't inhale.

➤ **Toss Back a Few on the Heineken Brewery Tour.** At over 130 years old, Heineken is one of the world's favorite lagers. The Heineken reception center (☎ **020/523-9239**), down from the Rijksmuseum at Stadhouderskade 78, operated as the company's main brewery from 1868 to 1990. Although the operations have moved to a bigger, newer facility outside town, you can still tour this venerable suds factory Monday through Friday at 9:30am and 11am (in summer also at 1pm and 2:30pm). The short film covers 5,000 years of beermaking in about five minutes, which is probably as much history as a true brewhound can take in one sitting. The fermentation tanks in which the exhibits have been installed could hold a million glassfuls of beer, but you only get two with the tour. The best part is that the whole thing's free—if you don't count the expected 2Dfl ($1) donation to UNICEF.

➤ **Cycle around Amsterdam on Two Wheels.** The Dutch are some of the most avid bicyclists I've ever encountered, probably because their country is so flat and bikable. You'll quickly get used to streets being divided into lanes for cars, lanes for pedestrians, and lanes for bikes (each even has its own stoplights). **Renting a bike** is one of the best ways to explore Amsterdam away from the tram routes and major sights (quiet Sundays are best). The only hills you'll have to deal with are the humps of bridges over scenic canals. For rentals, try **Mac Bike Too** (☎ **020/626-6964**) at Marnixstraat 220, near the Leidseplein. Prices are about Dfl12.50 ($6.25) per day, Dfl60 ($30) per week.

Bet You Didn't Know

The Netherlands' mean elevation is 37 feet above sea level, and it is *flat*. Much of the country is below ocean levels and once lay under the North Sea. So how do you raise the land from under the water? Ring the coast with an ingenious series of dikes (mounds of earth) and use windmills to pump the water into drainage rivers (in case of leak, little Dutch boy with finger must be purchased separately).

Get Outta Town: Day Trips & Excursions

Several enticing destinations are within easy day-trip distance from Amsterdam—among them the tulip region near Haarlem, the traditional village of Zaanse Schans, and the Van Gogh museum in Hoge Veluwe national park.

Windmills, Tulips, & the Other Haarlem

Any of the three excursions described here could be an individual day trip from Amsterdam. However, you could also fit them comfortably into a two-day excursion by spending the night in Haarlem, whose art museums and 17th-century architecture make for a pleasant base. I'll cover the details under each mini-excursion as I go.

When the Dutch make way for progress, they also make sure to set aside space for preservation. As the countryside north of Amsterdam became industrialized over the first half of the 20th century, people realized that a way of life and mode of architecture was disappearing rapidly. In the late 1950s, dozens of local farms, houses, and windmills dating from that ever-popular 17th century were broken down, carted off, and reassembled into a kind of archetypal "traditional" village called **Zaanse Schans.**

Although Zaanse Schans is a little touristy, it's not just a sightseeing attraction—people live in most of the cottages and houses, doing their daily tasks in as much an early 18th-century way as possible. The grocery stores and the like truly are out of a different era, and a few of the buildings have been set up as museums for the public, including the four working windmills. Short cruises on the river Zaan are also popular. The visitable parts of the village are open April through October 10am to 5pm daily. Zaanse Schans is about 10 miles northwest of Amsterdam, just above the town of Zaandam. The Zaandam **tourist office** (☎ **075/616-8218**) has

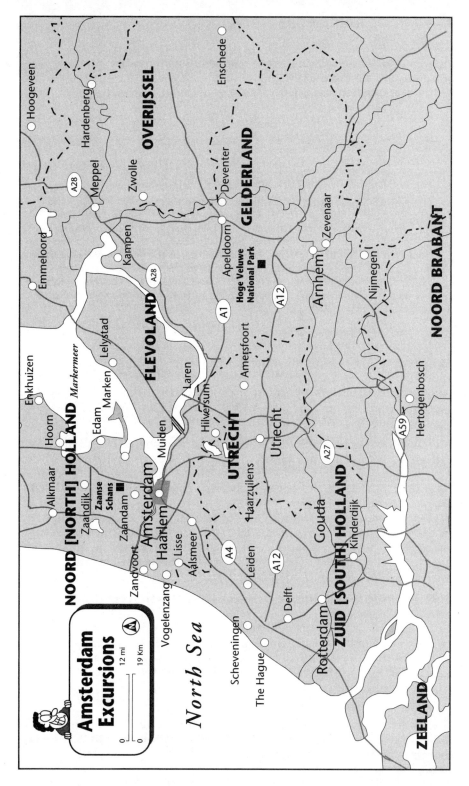

Amsterdam Excursions

12 mi
0

19 Km
0

North Sea

NOORD [NORTH] HOLLAND

ZUID [SOUTH] HOLLAND

UTRECHT

FLEVOLAND

OVERIJSSEL

GELDERLAND

NOORD BRABANT

ZEELAND

Markermeer

Hoogeveen

Hardenberg

Enschede

Meppel

Zwolle

Deventer

Zevenaar

A28

Emmeloord

Kampen

Apeldoorn

Hoge Veluwe
National Park

Arnhem

Nijmegen

A28

A1

A12

Enkhuizen

Lelystad

Marken

Laren

Amersfoort

Hoorn

Edam

Muiden

Hilversum

Alkmaar

Zaandijk

Zaanse
Schans

Zaandam

Amsterdam

Haarlem

Utrecht

A27

Hertogenbosch

A59

Zandvoort

Lisse

Aalsmeer

Haarzuilens

Gouda

Kinderdijk

Vogelenzang

A4

Leiden

A12

Delft

Rotterdam

Scheveningen

The Hague

295

information on the village; there are numerous daily **trains** from Amsterdam (a 12-minute ride).

Extra! Extra!

If the handful of windmills in Zaanse Schans aren't enough for you, head 66 miles south of Amsterdam to the **Kinderdijk** region (it's below Rotterdam). In this region, 19 working old-fashioned windmills built from 1722 to 1761 dot the landscape, turning their 42-foot-long sails slowly in the wind Saturdays from 2:30 to 5:30pm in July and August (the rest of the year, they just sit there looking picturesque). The visitor's mill is open to the public April through September, Monday through Saturday, 9:30am to 5:30pm. To get there, take the train from Amsterdam's Centraal Station to Rotterdam, then the metro to Zuidplein, then bus 154.

Haarlem makes perhaps the finest day trip from Amsterdam, offering a much more laid-back and less hectic version of a tidy Dutch city. It also has some great museums. Every half hour or so a **train** makes the 20-minute jaunt from Amsterdam. The local **VVV tourist office** (☎ 06/3202-4043) is just outside the station, on the right, at Stationplein 1.

The town's pretty central square, Grote Markt, is anchored by the late Gothic church St. Bavokerk, better known as the **Grote Kerk.** Inside are artist Frans Hals's tombstone, a cannonball embedded in the wall during the Spanish siege of 1572 to 1573, and one of the world's great organs, a 68-stop 5,068-pipe beauty built by Christian Müller in 1735 to 1738—both Handel and a 10-year-old Mozart once came to play it. Mid-May to mid-October there are free organ recitals Tuesdays from 8:15 to 9:15pm (also on Thursdays in July and August). Seventeenth-century shops and houses gather like barnacles on the church's south flank. These were built so rent could be charged to help with church upkeep.

Haarlem's biggest attraction is the **Frans Hals Museum** (☎ 023/516-4200), Groot Heiligeland 62, set up in the pensioner's home where the painter spent his last days in 1666. Frans Hals's works make up the bulk of the collections, but many Dutch painters from the 16th century to today are represented as well. It's all hung in 17th century-style rooms that often bear a striking resemblance to settings in the works themselves. It's open Monday through Saturday 11am to 5pm and Sunday from 1 to 5pm. Admission is Dfl8 ($4) adults and Dfl3.50 ($1.75) for ages 10 to 17.

The boisterous, tavern-like **Stadscafe** (☎ 023/532-5202) at Zijlstraat 57 has hearty Dutch food at great prices. The **Hotel Carillon** (☎ 023/531-0591) has clean Dfl130 ($65) doubles in the heart of town at Grote Markt 27.

Between Haarlem and Leiden stretches a 19-mile strip of land known as the **Bloembollenstreek,** Amsterdam's bulb belt, home of the **tulip.** These lowlands along the North Sea are carpeted with mile upon mile of fields of gladioli, hyacinths, lilies, narcissi, daffodils, crocuses, irises, dahlias, and the mighty tulip. The earliest blooms burst into color in January, and the floral show doesn't slow down until the late-blooming lilies make their exit near the end of May. Mid-April, though, is the Time of the Tulip. Buses running between Haarlem and Leiden service the region, and Haarlem is just a quick 15-minute ride by train from Amsterdam.

Just driving or biking through the countryside is rewarding, but there are a few stop-offs you'll want to make as well. The **Frans Roozen Nursery** (☎ 023/584-7245) in **Vogelenzang** is one of the first sights as you head south from Haarlem on the N206. Established in 1789, the nursery will give you an excellent introduction to the fine art of tulip husbandry on its free guided tours. If you're here from late March to mid-May, rush to the **Keukenhof Gardens** (☎ 0252/465-555), perhaps the top floral gardens on Earth, to see their 7,000,000-plus bulbs in full, blow-out bloom over 70 acres. It's open daily from 8am to 7:30pm, and there are cafeterias on-site so you don't have to tear your eyes away from the chromatic spectacle surrounding you.

Extra! Extra!

Tulips aren't even Dutch. They arrived from Turkey in the 1590s and quickly became popular. By 1620, tulip mania had taken hold and growers could not keep up with demand. By 1636, some rare bulbs were sold for their weight in gold. Soon after, though, the floral market bottomed out in the Great Tulip Crash. Bulbs have come down in price a wee bit since then, and the Netherlands remains one of the world's largest producers of flowers.

One of the bulbfield region's chief attractions is just six miles south of Amsterdam at the **flower auction in Aalsmeer** (☎ 0297/393-939). You can watch from the visitors gallery as 3.5 billion cut flowers and 400 million other plants are bid down in price at a breakneck pace (cut flowers especially are extremely perishable and must be moved quickly). Giant dials tick down rapidly from 100 to 1—as the numbers count down, the price drops—and the first bidder to buzz in on that lot stops the clock at that price and gets his bouquet (because there's only one bid, it's like a huge game of chicken). The auction runs Monday through Friday from 7:30 to 11am; bus 172 heads here from Amsterdam's Centraal train station.

Biking Hoge Veluwe & van Gogh-ing to the Kröller Müller Museum

Set in the middle of Hoge Veluwe, a 13,750-acre national park of heath, woods, and sand dunes, is the Kröller Müller Museum, one of the Netherlands' top modern art museums and Europe's largest sculpture garden. Loving art as I do, this is my favorite Dutch excursion and can easily be done as a day trip from Amsterdam. Twice hourly **trains** run from Amsterdam to Arnhem in 65 minutes. From Arnhem's station, hop on the no. 12 bus, which stops in the park both at the museum and at the **visitors' center/ cafeteria** (☎ **055/378-8100** or 0318/591-627), where you can pick up maps of the park.

Time-Savers

Before hopping on that bus in Arnhem, do some advance reconnoitering by popping into the city's VVV tourist office (☎ **026/ 442-6767**) at Stationsplein 45 outside the station to pick up park info and maps.

The primary form of transportation in Hoge Veluwe park is by bike; you can grab a free white bike by any entrance or at the visitors' center—just drop it off before you leave. Under the visitor's center lies the **Musenonder,** a series of displays and tunnels dedicated to underground ecology. In addition to **biking** through the calm greenery of the park, hoping to catch glimpses of red deer, foxes, wild boar, or badgers, visitors flock to the modern **Kröller Müller Museum** (☎ **0318/591-041**). Many of its rooms are hung with paintings from radically different artists and eras all side by side like wallpaper. There isn't enough wall space to display all 278 (!) van Gogh works, so they're rotated. Other artists featured include Picasso, Mondrian, Seurat, Monet, and Braque.

The 27-acre **sculpture garden** behind the museum is a great setting for works by Rodin, Oldenburg, Henry Moore, Barbara Hepworth, Mark di Suvero, and Lipchitz. My favorite is Jean Dubuffet's enormous *Jardin d'Emaille,* an interactive artscape of the sculptor's patented white-with-black-lines raised above ground level so you have to climb a set of stairs to wander around in it.

The museum is open Tuesday through Sunday 10am to 5pm. The park itself is open daily as follows: November through March 9am to 5pm, April 8am to 8pm, May 8am to 9pm, June through August 8am to 10pm, September 9am to 8pm, and October 9am to 7pm. Once you pay your admission to the park—Dfl8 ($4) for adults, Dfl4 ($2) for children ages 6 to 12—the museum is free. Call ☎ **0318/591-241** for museum admission information.

Chapter 18

Munich & Bavaria

In This Chapter

➤ Where the beers are: a guide to the top beer gardens and brew joints

➤ Beyond the beer: a guide to the city's royal palaces and fine art

➤ Bratwurst, anyone? The lowdown on German cuisine

➤ Romantic drives and a madman's castle: side trips in Bavaria

---

Munich is the gateway to the Bavarian Alps. It's also a German intellectual and industrial center, a lively European arts and culture hub, and the world capital of beer and BMW (but don't mix those last two). The city wears many hats—equally at ease as the capital of rustic, folklore-saturated Bavaria, a vibrant university town where the Nobel Prize-winning author Thomas Mann and Albert Einstein rank among the famed intelligentsia, and an economic powerhouse, with cutting-edge industry ringing its outskirts. Then again, for a few weeks each autumn, Munich becomes a place of sunshine, smiling faces, platters of sausages, huge mugs of tasty beer, oompah bands, and old-fashioned good times at the original

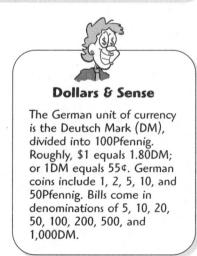

Dollars & Sense

The German unit of currency is the Deutsch Mark (DM), divided into 100Pfennig. Roughly, $1 equals 1.80DM; or 1DM equals 55¢. German coins include 1, 2, 5, 10, and 50Pfennig. Bills come in denominations of 5, 10, 20, 50, 100, 200, 500, and 1,000DM.

Oktoberfest. With museums galore and a thriving cultural and theater life, Munich's sights are sure to keep you busy for at least two or three days (you can do it in one, but you'll be giving the city short shrift).

Getting Your Bearings

Munich is one European city where the sights are not confined to its **Altstadt,** or old center—Munich's museums and cultural attractions are spread all across town. The Altstadt is a district of medieval streets tangled at the core of the city. Much of it was bombed during World War II, and then subsequently restored or replaced with modern structures, giving the city center a medieval-meets-contemporary look.

Time-Savers

Munich's main **tourist office** (☎ 089/233-03-00) is at Hauptbahnhof (the main train station) in a storefront to the left of the main entrance. The hours are Monday through Saturday, 9am to 9pm, and Sunday 11am to 7pm; the best times to reach someone on the phone are Monday through Thursday 9 am to 3pm, and Friday 9am to 12:30pm. There's also a tourist office branch at the airport and an office downtown in the Rathaus. The airport hours are Monday through Saturday 8:30am to 10pm, and Sunday 11am to 7pm.

The city's heart is **Marienplatz,** a bustling pedestrian square with a major light-rail juncture underneath. Running through Marienplatz is one of the city's main east-west arteries, **Neuhauserstrasse,** which begins at **Karlsplatz** (a few blocks east of **Hauptbahnhof station**). It changes names to **Kaufingerstrasse** and then beyond Marienplatz becomes **Im Tal** (the only non-pedestrianized bit); this street leads east into **Isartorplatz.** Isartorplatz is on the Altstadt's eastern edge, a few blocks from the **Isar River,** which runs along the city's eastern flank.

Munich's other main east-west drag is **Maximilianstrasse,** a wide street of art galleries and designer boutiques several blocks north of, and parallel to, Im Tal. Fashionable Maximilianstrasse runs from the Isar River west into the Altstadt, ending at **Max Joseph Platz**—another important square and the location of the Residenz royal palace—just a few blocks north of Marienplatz (see "Munich Sights Not to Miss"). **Residenzstrasse** runs from Max Joseph Platz to **Odeonsplatz.** Odeonsplatz is an elegant, if heavily trafficked, square surrounded by neo-Renaissance buildings that marks the Altstadt's northern edge.

From Odeonsplatz, the boulevard **Ludwigstrasse/Leopoldstrasse** heads due north toward the University district and **Schwabing,** a bohemian and trendy quarter from the first half of the 20th century (now gentrified but still fun) filled with restaurants and cafes. **Prinzregentenstrasse** runs east-west just north of the city center. It passes along the southern border of huge **Englischer Garten** park and is lined with several museums (including the Bavarian National Museum). More museums (including both the Neue and Alte Pinakotheks) are in a zone of neoclassical buildings off the northwest corner of the Altstadt. You can reach this area via **Briennerstrasse,** which heads west out of Odeonsplatz.

Getting Around Town

Trains to Munich arrive at the high-tech **Hauptbahnhof** station on the city's western edge. From here, light-rail lines (called S-Bahn) run into the center of town. Planes land at the ultra-modern **Franz Joseph Strauss Airport,** 18 miles northeast of the city. The S8 S-Bahn leaves the airport every 20 minutes for the 40-minute trip to Munich.

Munich was one of the first cities to pedestrianize many of the streets in its Altstadt, making getting around the inner city by **foot** both enjoyable and a necessity (not even trams spoil the car-free streets). There are, however, buses, trams, and two light-rail systems (the U-Bahn and S-Bahn) to help you get around Greater Munich.

Dollars & Sense

Buses, trams, S-Bahns, and U-Bahns all use the same **tickets,** which you buy at machines in S-Bahn/U-Bahn stations. The longer your trip, the more **zones** you'll cross, and the more you'll pay. One zone covers about two S-Bahn or U-Bahn stops or four bus or tram stops. *The S-Bahn is covered by Eurail, so if you have a rail pass, don't buy a separate ticket.*

The most expensive ride is a **single ticket.** Check the chart of stops posted on the machine and press the button for the number of zones it says you'll be riding. The average lowest cost this way is 3.30DM ($1.80). More economical is a ***Streifenkarte* (strip card),** which for 13DM ($7.20) gives you 10 strips, each worth one zone, to use over several rides. It's good for three hours and unlimited transfers, so long as you stay headed in the same direction (in other words, it doesn't cover your return). You can also use it for multiple passengers (for two people to ride two zones, simply stamp four strips).

An even better deal may be the **Tageskarte (Day Ticket),** which for 8DM ($4.45) gives you unlimited access within the central zone for a full day (double the price gives you access to all of Greater Munich—a 50-mile radius). For families, the **Day Partner Ticket** costs 12DM ($6.65) for two adults and up to three kids.

The difference between an **S-Bahn** and an **U-Bahn** is that the former is a state-run commuter train line that covers a wider area (and is often aboveground); the latter runs mostly underground as a city subway. In the center of Munich, they're both subways. The most important difference is that you can use your rail pass on the S-Bahn, but not on the U-Bahn. The major junctures of multiple lines are Hauptbahnhof, Karlsplatz, Marienplatz, Sendlingertor, and Odeonsplatz.

Almost all the **S-Bahn** lines discussed in this chapter (S1 through S8) run the same east-west route through the city, with stops at Hauptbahnhof,

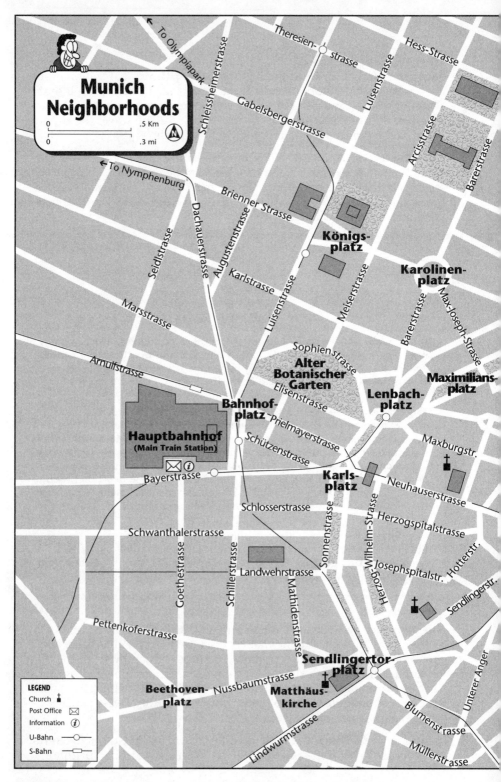

Munich Neighborhoods

0   .5 Km
0   .3 mi

← To Olympiapark

← To Nymphenburg

Schleissheimerstrasse

Theresienstrasse

Hess-Strasse

Luisenstrasse

Arcisstrasse

Barerstrasse

Gabelsbergerstrasse

Brienner Strasse

Königsplatz

Karolinenplatz

Max-Joseph-Strasse

Dachauerstrasse

Augustenstrasse

Karlstrasse

Luisenstrasse

Meiserstrasse

Barerstrasse

Seidlstrasse

Marsstrasse

Sophienstrasse

Alter Botanischer Garten

Maximiliansplatz

Arnulfstrasse

Elisenstrasse

Lenbachplatz

Bahnhofplatz

Prielmayerstrasse

Maxburgstr.

Hauptbahnhof
(Main Train Station)

Schützenstrasse

Bayerstrasse

Karlsplatz

Neuhauserstrasse

Schlosserstrasse

Herzogspitalstrasse

Schwanthalerstrasse

Sonnenstrasse

Herzog-Wilhelm-Strasse

Josephspitalstr.

Hotterstr.

Goethestrasse

Schillerstrasse

Landwehrstrasse

Mathildenstrasse

Sendlingerstr.

Pettenkoferstrasse

Sendlingertorplatz

Unterer Anger

Beethovenplatz

Nussbaumstrasse

Matthäuskirche

Blumenstrasse

Lindwurmstrasse

Müllerstrasse

LEGEND
Church ✝
Post Office ✉
Information ⓘ
U-Bahn ─○─
S-Bahn ─▭─

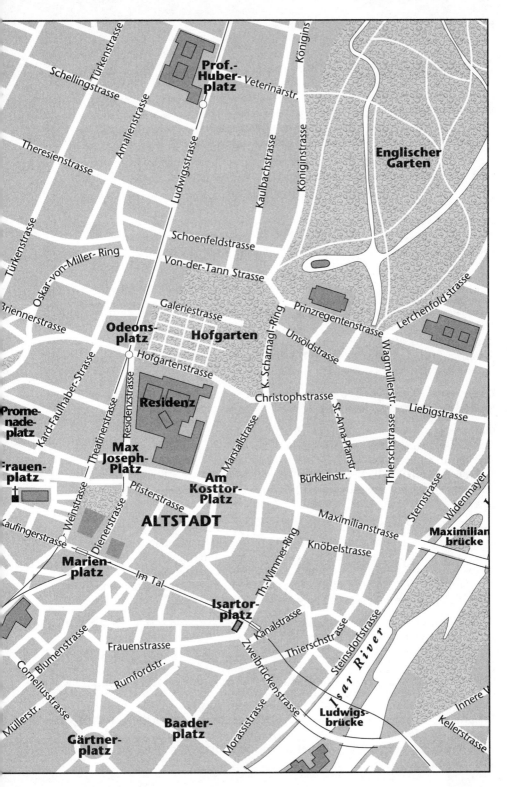

Karlsplatz, Marienplatz, and Isartorplatz. The most useful of the **U-Bahn** lines are U3 and U6, which run north-south through the city center, stopping at Sendlingertor, Marienplatz, and Odeonsplatz before continuing on into Schwabing.

Trams and buses don't service the center of the city very well, but they are handy for getting to a few areas within the Altstadt, and for traveling in Greater Munich. The 19 tram runs along Maximilianstrasse and the northern part of the Altstadt before heading to Hauptbahnhof. The 52 and 56 buses putter around the Altstadt's southeastern corner.

Munich Fast Facts

American Express   The American Express office at Promenadeplatz 6 (☎ 089/290-9000) is open Monday to Friday 9am to 5:30pm and Saturday 9:30am to noon.

Consulate   The U.S. Consulate is at Königstrasse 5 (☎ 089/28-880).

Doctors/hospitals   For a list of English-speaking physicians and dentists, contact the U.S. Consulate or ask an international pharmacy (*apotheke*) for recommendations. If you have a medical emergency during the weekend or evenings 8pm to 1am, call ☎ 089/551-771 for **Notfallpraxis,** Elisenstrasse 3, which staffs doctors of varied specialties.

Emergency   Dial ☎ 110 to call the police. For an ambulance, dial ☎ 089/557-755. Call ☎ 112 to report a fire.

Pharmacies   *Apotheke* in Munich rotate the duty of staying open nights and weekends. For the location of the nearest 24-hour pharmacy, check the sign in the window of any pharmacy or call ☎ 089/594-475. The **International Ludwigs-Apotheke,** Neuhauser Strasse 11 (☎ 089/260-3021), is open Monday to Friday 9am to 8pm and Saturday 9am to 4pm.

Safety   As a visitor to Munich, you're unlikely to fall victim to violent crime, but you may be targeted for petty crimes such as purse-snatching and pickpocketing. Be particularly careful in popular areas such as the Marienplatz and around the Hauptbahnhof (especially at night). If you shed your inhibitions (and your clothes) in the Englischer Garten, don't abandon your common sense as well. Keep your valuables in sight.

Taxis   Munich has such an efficient public transportation system that you shouldn't have to take a taxi—and at their steep prices, you probably won't want to. The initial charge is 5DM ($2.80) and 2.20DM ($1.20) for each additional kilometer. Luggage costs you an extra 1DM (55¢) per bag. You can call a taxi to pick you up by dialing ☎ 089/21-610 or 089/19-410, but you'll be charged 2DM ($1.10) more for the convenience.

Telephone   Germany's country code is **49**. The city code for Munich is **089**. If you're calling Munich from outside Germany, drop the city code's initial zero. In other words, to call Munich from the United States, dial **011-49-89** and the number.

A local call in Munich costs 30Pfennig (15¢) for the first three minutes. At a coin-operated phone just deposit more coins as needed. Some phones in Germany accept only phone cards, available in 12DM ($6.65) and 50DM ($27.80) denominations from newsstands. To charge your call to a calling card, dial **AT&T** (☎ **0130-0010**), **MCI** (☎ **0130-0012**), or **Sprint** (☎ **0130-0013**). To call the United States direct, dial **001** followed by the area code and phone number.

Transit Info   For public transportation information, call ☎ **089/238-030.** For S-Bahn information, call ☎ **089/557-575.**

Bavarian Bedrooms: Munich's Hotel Scene

As both a tourist and a commercial and industrial center, Munich has a healthy store of hotel rooms. Unfortunately, year-round demand keeps prices high. Rates in Munich bump up whenever a trade fair is in town, rise steadily through the summer tourist season, and spike as high as hoteliers can push them during Oktoberfest. If you don't book well in advance for the city's big keg party, you're going to find yourself either paying through the nose, stuck pretty far from the center, or both.

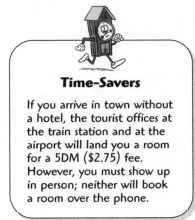

Time-Savers

If you arrive in town without a hotel, the tourist offices at the train station and at the airport will land you a room for a 5DM ($2.75) fee. However, you must show up in person; neither will book a room over the phone.

🌟 **An der Oper**
$$$. Near the Residenz.

One of the best all-around values in Munich, An der Oper is right in the pedestrian heart of town, near shopping, the theater, the major sights, and the Hofbräuhaus. Rooms are modern and basic, but pleasantly so, each a sort of budget minisuite with a sitting area. The restaurant serves Bavarian-meets-French cuisine.

Falkenturmstrasse 11 (just off Maximilianstrasse, near the Residenz end). ☎ *089/ 290-0270.* **Fax:** *089/2900-2729.* **Tram:** *19.* **Rates:** *250–280DM ($138.88– $155.55) double. AE, MC, V.*

Hotel Am Markt
$. Near Marienplatz.

Hidden down an alley near Munich's outdoor market is a perennial budget favorite, drawing regulars with a great location and low prices. The owner keeps the place spotless, welcoming all sort of visitors—"so long as they behave"—from families to students to stars of stage and opera. Rooms are spare but functional, small but comfortable; the price reflects the plumbing, not the season (remarkably, it doesn't raise prices for Oktoberfest).

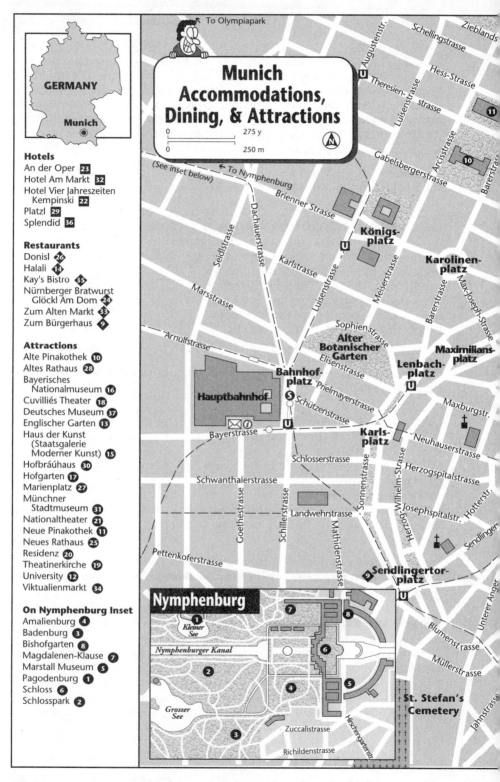

Munich Accommodations, Dining, & Attractions

0 — 275 y
0 — 250 m

Hotels
An der Oper 23
Hotel Am Markt 32
Hotel Vier Jahreszeiten Kempinski 22
Platzl 29
Splendid 36

Restaurants
Donisl 26
Halali 14
Kay's Bistro 35
Nürnberger Bratwurst Glöckl Am Dom 24
Zum Alten Markt 33
Zum Bürgerhaus 9

Attractions
Alte Pinakothek 10
Altes Rathaus 28
Bayerisches Nationalmuseum 16
Cuvilliés Theater 18
Deutsches Museum 37
Englischer Garten 13
Haus der Kunst (Staatsgalerie Moderner Kunst) 15
Hofbräuhaus 30
Hofgarten 17
Marienplatz 27
Münchner Stadtmuseum 31
Nationaltheater 21
Neue Pinakothek 11
Neues Rathaus 25
Residenz 20
Theatinerkirche 19
University 12
Viktualienmarkt 34

On Nymphenburg Inset
Amalienburg 4
Badenburg 3
Bishofgarten 8
Magdalenen-Klause 7
Marstall Museum 5
Pagodenburg 1
Schloss 6
Schlosspark 2

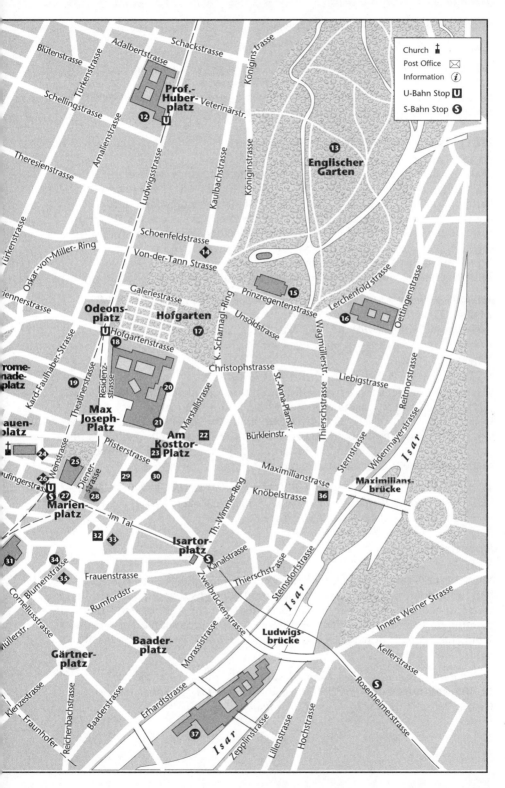

Heiliggeistrasse 6 (a tiny alley between the Tal and the Viktualienmarkt). ☎ *089/*
225-014. Fax: 089/224-017. **U-Bahn or S-Bahn:** *Marienplatz. Walk under*
the arches of the Altes Rathaus; the hotel is down the first right turn off the Tal.
Rates: *150–260DM ($83.33–$144.45) double. No credit cards.*

Hotel Vier Jahreszeiten Kempinski
$$$$$. Near the Residenz.
Munich's best splurge is one of Europe's grand old hotels, built in 1858 for
Maximilian II to accommodate the overflow of guests from his nearby
Residenz. Today's clientele includes heads of state, businessmen, and discern-
ing travelers who appreciate the superbly discreet service, constantly renovated rooms, rooftop pool, bevy of fine restaurants, boutique shops, posh
accommodations, and proximity of shopping, theater, and galleries. The least
expensive rooms are in the uninteresting 1972 wing; so as long as you're
splurging, go for the modern digs in the original building.

Maximilianstrasse 17 (3 blocks from the Residenz and hard to miss). ☎ *089/*
21-250. Fax: 089/2125-2000. **Tram:** *19.* **Rates:** *490–790DM*
($272.20–$438.90) double. AE, DC, MC, V.

Platzl
$$$$. Between Marienplatz and the Residenz.
Stay here to be steps away from all the sights of the Altstadt and steep yourself in everything Bavaria is supposed to be. Rooms are on the cozy side of
small and are outfitted in Bavarian rustic style. The hotel is owned by a brewery, and the legendary Hofbräuhaus is across the street—so it won't be a distant stumble home after a night of carousing. In a more sober mindset, you
might patronize the folk theater next door.

Sparkassenstrasse 10 (at the corner with Munzstrasse). ☎ *089/237-030. Fax:*
089/2370-3800. **U-Bahn:** *U3 or U6 to Marienplatz.* **Rates:** *290–410DM*
($161.10–$227.80) double. AE, DC, MC, V.

Splendid
$$$. Near the Isar.
Munich's best value in an Old World hotel has Oriental carpets, chande-
liers, and antiques in the public rooms and bedrooms that are outfitted in
Bavarian baroque country style. It's just outside of the Altstadt (with free
parking, no less), near the river, and close to several museums. The cheapest
rooms have a bath down the hall. You can take breakfast on the trellised
patio in summer.

Maximilianstrasse 54 (1 block before the Maximilian Bridge over the Isar).
☎ *089/296-606. Fax: 089/291-3176.* **U-Bahn:** *U4, U5.* **Tram:** *19, 20.*
Rates: *200–230DM ($111.11–$127.77) double. AE, DC, MC, V.*

The Best & "Wurst" of Munich's Restaurant Scene

Munich is not for the dieter. The primary food groups here are sausage, beer, salted white radishes, and pretzels. Sausages are called *wurstel* and come in so many shapes, sizes, and stuffings that it would take another book just to explain them all. The greatest hits include **bratwurst** (finger-sized seasoned pork), **frankfurter** (the forerunner of hot dogs, only more appetizing), **blütwurst** (blood sausage), **leberwurst** (liver), and, a specialty of Munich, **weisswurst** (veal, calf brains, and spleen, spiced to mild deliciousness and boiled; the proper way to eat it is to cut it in half, dip the cut end in mustard, and suck the filling out of the casing in one fell slurp). Any food ending in the word ***knödel*** is a dumpling, which may be made of *semmel* (bread), *leber* (liver), or *kartoffel* (potato). The best place to sample these specialties is the **beer hall tavern,** where people sit communally and amicably at big tables. Munich's other great contribution to the world of restaurant types is the outdoor **biergarten.** For more information on both, see "Other Fun Stuff to Do."

Now about that **beer.** Munich is deservedly one of the world's beer capitals, so celebrate that status with toast after toast of light beer (that's the color, folks, not the calories) that comes in a giant liter-sized mug called *ein Mass.* Outside of Oktoberfest tents, if you just order *ein Bier,* you'll usually get a more manageable half-liter; if you want that big boy, make sure to order it by name. Munich beer types include: *weissbier* (made with wheat); *pils* (ale); *dunklesbier, bock,* or *dopplebock* (all dark beers); and the beer-and-lemonade spritzer called *radlermass.* All beers are made under the strictest quality guidelines and almost never contain preservatives (Germans drink it so quickly, there's no need). *Helles* means light-colored beer; *dunkles* is dark beer.

The Beer Essentials

The average Bavarian drinks 280 liters (73 gallons) of beer a year. Bavaria is home to about one-fifth of the world's breweries, and Munich itself has over 400 beer halls and gardens. Brew rights have been fiercely debated through the ages, from the 16th-century Purity Laws, to the 19th-century riots protesting an ale tax, to the Beer Garden Revolution of 1995, when 20,000 Munichers gathered to defend their rights to drink in an open-air beer garden. So hoist a liter *mass* of frothy *bier* and say *Prost!* (cheers!) to perhaps the most beer-lovin' city on Earth.

Donisl
$. On Marienplatz. BAVARIAN/INTERNATIONAL.
Munich's oldest beer hall has summer tables right on the Marienplatz and rustic galleries inside. The menu's backbone of Bavarian cuisine features the traditional weisswurst; but the restaurant also serves specials that draw from many culinary traditions (when the chef offers duck, dive for it). It can be a bit hokey, but sometimes the accordion player makes it all feel that much more Bavarian.

Weinstrasse 1 (just above Marienplatz). ☎ *089/220-184. Reservations recommended.* **U-Bahn or S-Bahn:** *Marienplatz.* **Main courses:** *11.95DM ($6.65). AE, DC, MC, V.* **Open:** *Lunch and dinner daily.*

Halali
$$$$. North of the Residenz. FINE BAVARIAN.
Halali is refined, but very Bavarian: Picture an elegant candlelit dining room and throw in a few dozen trophy antlers. The kitchen takes Bavarian staples—blütwurst, venison, and other game—and treats them with a delicate touch, filling them with flavor and presenting them attractively. The genteel edge ensures that red wine, not beer, is the preferred beverage choice.

Schönfeldstrasse 22 (3 long blocks north of Odeonsplatz). ☎ *089/285-909. Reservations required.* **U-Bahn:** *Odeonsplatz.* **Main courses:** *27–39DM ($15–$21.65); fixed-price menu 85DM ($47.20). AE, MC, V.* **Open:** *Lunch and dinner Mon–Fri, dinner Sat.*

Kay's Bistro
$$$$$. Near Marienplatz. FRENCH/INTERNATIONAL.
A magazine columnist runs Munich's most sophisticated and perennially fashionable eatery, drawing a clientele of international trendies. Kay's alters its decor and menu regularly, so it's always a new place to visit. The kitchen turns out a French and international cuisine that's light and avant-garde, with the nearby market supplying fresh ingredients daily.

Utzschneiderstrasse 1 (across the boulevard Frauenstrasse from the Viktualienmarkt). ☎ *089/260-3584. Reservations required.* **U-Bahn or S-Bahn:** *Marienplatz.* **Main courses:** *38–45DM ($21.10–$25). AE, MC, V.* **Open:** *Dinner daily.*

Nürnberger Bratwurst Glöckl Am Dom
$$. Near Marienplatz. BAVARIAN.
This place is my choice for best traditional Munich beer-hall grub. Both the rustic setting of dark wood and carved chairs (sit downstairs if you can) and the tin plates piled high with tasty *wurstel* just scream Bavaria. Since 1893, this place has been serving up the finger-sized sausage specialty of nearby Nürnburg, which is best sampled alongside other wursts on the 19.80DM ($11) assortment platter. That, a pretzel, and a tankard of Augustiner Bollbier or Tucher Weissbier make the perfect meal.

Frauenplatz 9 (off the back end of the cathedral). ☎ *089/295-264. Reservations suggested.* ***U-Bahn or S-Bahn:*** *Marienplatz.* ***Main courses:*** *9.80–34.50DM ($5.45–$19.15). No credit cards.* ***Open:*** *Lunch and dinner daily.*

Zum Alten Markt

$$$$. Near Marienplatz. BAVARIAN/INTERNATIONAL.
This marketplace hole-in-the-wall offers finely observed Bavarian food in a 400-year-old decor lifted from a Tyrolean castle. The chef makes good use of the fresh ingredients available at his doorstep in such dishes as black truffle tortellini in a cream sauce, but the star here is *tafelspitz,* Bavaria's archetypal boiled beef dish that was the favorite of Emperor Franz Josef.

Am Viktualienmarkt, Dreifaltigkeitsplatz 3 (on the city market square). ☎ *089/ 299-995. Reservations recommended.* ***U-Bahn or S-Bahn:*** *Marienplatz.* ***Bus:*** *52.* ***Main courses:*** *30–40DM ($16.65–$22.20). No credit cards.* ***Open:*** *Lunch and dinner Mon–Sat.*

Zum Bürgerhaus

$$$. South of Hauptbahnhof. ALPINE.
This is one of the few antique Munich restaurants that survived World War II bombings intact. The original 1827 decor retains a cozy, countryside charm. The cuisine is uniquely pan-Alpine, with high-altitude specialties including venison in red wine, noodles in a herbed cream/mushroom sauce, lamb with rosemary, and *Burgerhaus Pfanne,* a pan-fried mix of turkey, veal, and pork.

Pettenkoferstrasse 1 (just outside the southwest edge of the Altstadt). ☎ *089/ 597-909. Reservations recommended.* ***U-Bahn or S-Bahn:*** *Sendlinger Tor Platz.* ***Bus:*** *18, 20, 21, 27, 31, 56.* ***Main courses:*** *24–32DM ($13.35–$17.80); lunch platter 16.50DM ($9.15); fixed-price menu 24DM ($13.35). AE, MC, V.* ***Open:*** *Lunch Mon–Fri, dinner Mon–Sat.*

Quick Bites

You can drop into any **beer hall tavern** and get a plate of sausages or just a mug of beer and a pretzel in 20 minutes or so, even if half the attraction is settling in for a while. **Butcher shops** offer slices of a beef-and-bacon meatloaf called *Leberkäs* (eaten with mustard and a roll). Summertime opens up countless **sidewalk stands** hawking sausages and sandwiches (*schinkensemmel* is a ham sandwich, *wurtzsemmel* features sliced sausages). But the best food value in town is the **Viktualienmarkt,** the old outdoor food market where you can put together a great **picnic** and stop for a brewski at the biergarten while you're at it.

Munich Sightseeing (What Do We Do Until the Beer Hall Opens?)

You've got two choices for orientation bus tours. The **Blue Bus** is a straight-forward affair—just hop on in front of Hauptbahnhof and buy your 15DM ($8.30) ticket onboard. The hour-long tour is conducted in German and English; departures are at 10am, 11:30am, and 2:30pm daily (November through February there's no 11:30am trip). A 2½-hour tour takes you through more of the city (into the Neue Pinakothek) and ensures that you hear the glockenspiel, all for 27DM ($15). This tour is available Tuesday to Saturday at 10am.

Panorama Tours (☎ 089/5502-8995), Arnulfstraase 8, also offers an hour-long city highlights bus tour for 17DM ($9.45). This tour is available daily at 10am and 2:30pm and, from May through October, also at 11:30am and 4pm. This tour company also offers 2½-hour, 30DM ($16.65) tours that, in addition to the city orientation tour, spend some time exploring a single site. One visits the Olympic Area to climb its 960-foot Olympic Tower; another spends time in the Residenz; and a third heads to the Schloss Nymphenburg.

Munich Sights Not to Miss

Marienplatz

The center of Munich is the lively, cafe-lined Marienplatz, home to street performers and the daily bustle of the city. This city square is bounded along its long north side by the pinnacles and tracery of the 19th-century **Neues Rathaus,** done in neo-gothic style. The clock on this town hall is equipped with a bilevel **glockenspiel,** the fourth largest in Europe, whose mechanical jousting show plays out daily at 11am and noon (and at 5pm in summer). Off the southeast corner of the square sits **St. Peter's** church, whose 300-foot tower you can climb (for a small fee) for excellent city views that on clear days reach the Alps.

Residenz Palace

The official residence of Bavarian royalty is a rambling palace whose long architectural history (started in 1385 and added on to until World War I) befits the political legacy of the Wittelsbach family (see "Bet You Didn't Know"). The parts of the palace to concern yourself with are the Residenz Museum, the Treasure House, and the Cuvilliés Theater. To see it all in detail, you have to take both a morning and an afternoon tour, but on your own you can drink in the ornate splendors in just a couple of hours.

Highlights of the **Residenz Museum,** 120 rooms of Wittlesbach history and furnishings, include the Ancestor's Gallery (1728 to 1730), a royal photo album of oil portraits set into the gilded stucco walls of a long hallway; and the huge Renaissance Hall of Antiquities, covered with 16th- and 17th-century frescoes. Don't miss Maximilian I's *Reiche Kappelle,* a closet-sized chapel dripping with marble inlay, gilding, and ivory carvings.

The Bavarian crown jewels, some dating back to A.D. 1000, are kept in the **Scatzkammer (Treasure House),** but the greatest treasure is the gold *St. George Slaying the Dragon* (1590). It's a wonder the saint, encumbered by all those diamonds, rubies, sapphires, and other gems, ever managed to slay the emerald beast.

You have to exit the Residenz, walk around the corner to Residenzstrasse 1, and re-enter the complex in order to get to the flamboyantly rococo **Cuvilliés Theater.** It was named after its architect, a former court jester who overcame 18th-century prejudices at his dwarfism, won the patronage of the Wittlesbachs, and went on to become one of southern Germany's most important architects. You can enjoy the setting, which premiered Mozart's *Idomeneo* in 1781, at frequent summer concerts and operas.

Max Joseph Platz 3. ☎ *089/290-671.* *U-Bahn:* *U3, U5, U6 to Odeonsplatz.* *Admission: Museum and Treasure House, 5DM ($2.75) adults, 3DM ($1.65) students and seniors; Cuvilliés Theater, 3DM ($1.65) adults, 2DM ($1.10) students and seniors. Kids under 15 are free at both. Open: Museum and Treasure House, Tues–Sun 10am–4:30pm; Cuvilliés-Theater, Mon–Sat 2–5pm, Sun 10–5pm (except when rehearsing or setting stage for a production).*

Bet You Didn't Know

The **Wittelsbachs** were medieval merchants who rose to control Bavaria in 1180. From 1316 to 1346, Wittelsbach Duke Ludwig IV even served as Holy Roman Emperor. Variously dubbed as counts, dukes, princes, and eventually kings, they didn't relinquish power until revolutionaries came banging at the Residenz front door in 1918—making them, by a long shot, Europe's longest-lasting dynasty.

Alte Pinakothek/Neue Pinakothek (Old & New Art Museums)

Until the renovations to the "Old Art Museum" (normally housed across the Theresienstrasse from this address) are finished, it shares space with the Neue Pinakothek. This cuts the work on display from both collections in half, but that's good news for those in a hurry—the museums have already boiled it down to just the masterpieces. Still, it takes a good two hours to just walk through the museum, three or four hours if you want to ponder all the art.

From the **Alte Pinakothek** (14th- to 19th-century works) come paintings by Italian Renaissance gurus Giotto, Fra Filippo Lippi, Botticelli, Perugino, Signorelli, Leonardo da Vinci (*Madonna and Child*), Raphael (*Holy Family* and a couple of *Madonna and Childs*), Titian (*Christ with the Crown of Thorns* is one of his most mature works), and Tintoretto. It also has several fleshy Rubens works and some Spanish pieces from El Greco, Ribera, and Murillo. The Dutch and Germans are very well-represented here; Roger van de Weyden weighs in with many works, including the huge *St. Colombia Altarpiece,* and Rembrandt has a number of canvases here as well. The

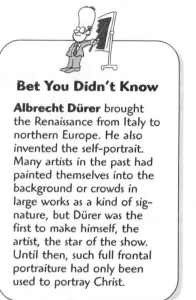

Bet You Didn't Know

Albrecht Dürer brought the Renaissance from Italy to northern Europe. He also invented the self-portrait. Many artists in the past had painted themselves into the background or crowds in large works as a kind of signature, but Dürer was the first to make himself, the artist, the star of the show. Until then, such full frontal portraiture had only been used to portray Christ.

gallery's greatest work is Albrecht Dürer's *Self Portrait* (1500). (See "Bet You Didn't Know.")

The **Neue Pinakothek** (covering the 19th and 20th centuries) features everyone from Gainsborough, Goya, Delacroix, and Manet to Monet, Degas, Cézanne, van Gogh, and more modern masters such as Gustav Klimt, Max Beckmann, and Edvard Munch. Although this is a fine collection, it doesn't hold a candle to the older set of paintings. As long as they're together, you might as well see both, but once the museums separate again (they're saying in 1998), I'd visit just the Alte Pinakothek if you're on a tight schedule.

Barerstrasse 27-29 (off Theresienstrasse, several long blocks northwest of city center). ☎ *089/238-05-215 or 089/238-05-195.* *U-Bahn: U2 to Königsplatz.* **Tram:** *27.* **Bus:** *53.* **Admission:** *7DM ($3.88) adults, 4DM ($2.22) students and seniors, 3DM ($1.66) for children under 15.* **Open:** *Wed and Fri–Sun 10am–5pm, Tues and Thurs 10am–8pm.*

Bayerisches Nationalmuseum (Bavarian National Museum)

One of this hodgepodge museum's main attractions is the impressive collection of medieval church art, including vibrant altarpieces, carved ivories (look for the A.D. 400 Munich Ivory showing the Lamentation and Christ ascending into Heaven), and especially statuary. No Bavarian sculptor was a greater master at his craft than Tilman Riemenschneider, who carved in the early 16th century and often managed to fashion the most eloquent expressive figures out of plain, unpainted wood.

You'll find armor from the 16th to 18th centuries, baroque porcelain confections, delicate stained-glass panels, and, in the basement, elaborate Christmas crèches from Germany, Austria, Italy, and Moravia. My favorite part, though, is the 15th-century Weaver's Guild Room, whose low, barrel-vaulted wooden ceiling is painted with stories from the Bible and the life of Alexander the Great.

Prinzregentenstrasse 3 (off the southeast corner of the Englischer Garten, northeast of the city center). ☎ *089/211-241.* *U-Bahn: U4, U5 to Lehel.* **Tram:** *20.* **Bus:** *53.* **Admission:** *3DM ($1.66) adults, 1.50DM (83¢) students and seniors.* **Open:** *Tues–Sun 10am–5pm.*

Schloss Nymphenburg

The Residenz may have been the official seat of the Wittelsbachs, but in summer they escaped to their more sophisticated countryside palace. It was named Schloss Nymphenburg, after the nymphs frescoed in its main **entrance hall** (concerts are presented here in summer). You wouldn't know it from the unified French baroque exterior, but this place started as a modest Italianate villa in 1664 and was changed radically over the following 150 years.

The palace is a network of pavilions. The most worthwhile is the south pavilion (the apartments of Queen Caroline) where you can see Ludwig I's **Gallery of Beauties**—filled with portraits commissioned by the king of the 36 most beautiful women in the realm. The **Mastrallmuseum** contains a collection of royal coaches including King Ludwig II's riotous wedding coach, entirely gilded and encrusted with a profusion of rococo stucco swirls.

Nymphenburg has a **park** to rival Versailles—over 500 acres of grassy lawns, English-style gardens, canals, and pavilions. Two pavilions to seek out are Electress Amalia's **Amalienburg,** extravagantly rococo inside; and the **Badenburg** on the lake, with its frescoed-ceilinged bath in the basement. Two of the park's other famed structures are the pseudo-Chinese **Pagoden-burg** and the built-to-look-like-a-ruin **Magdalenenklause,** a simple religious retreat for when the royals felt overdosed on the good life.

Schloss Nymphenburg 1 (3 miles west of the city center). ☎ *089/179-080. **U-Bahn:** U1 to Rotkreuzplatz, then tram 12 toward Amalienburgstrasse. **Bus:** 41. **Admission:** Full admission 8DM ($4.45) adults, 5DM ($2.75) students and seniors; limited admission (excluding Badenburg, Pagodenburg, and Magdalenenklause) 6DM ($3.30) adults, 4DM ($2.20) students and seniors. **Open:** Open hours are complicated, so give or take a half hour for the following: Apr–Sept, Tues–Sun 9am–12:30pm and 1:30–5pm (Oct–Mar, closes at 4pm).*

Kids Deutsches Museum (German Museum of Science & Technology)

This is a fantastic see-and-touch science museum, whose placards are in German and English, and whose rooms cover in incredible depth such diverse subjects as industrial machinery, the digging of tunnels, astronautics, computers and microelectronics, textiles, mining, and electricity. Definitely don't miss the High Voltage demonstrations (11am, 2pm, and 4pm daily) that actually produce lightning. Kids will have a blast. There's a hangar filled with historic aircraft and a collection of venerable cars, including the very first automobile (an 1886 Benz). Other firsts enshrined here include the diesel engine (1897), electric dynamo (1866), and the lab bench at which Hahn and Strassmann first split the atom (1938).

Museuminsel 1 (on an island in the Isar river). ☎ *089/21-791. **U-Bahn:** U1, U2 to Fraunhoferstrasse. **S-Bahn:** Isartorplatz **Tram:** 18. **Admission:** 10DM ($5.55) adults, 4DM ($2.22) students; 6DM ($3.30) seniors; kids under 6 free. **Open:** Daily 9am–5pm.*

Other Fun Stuff to Do

➤ **Eat Lunch at a Biergarten.** A biergarten is an outdoor space of picnic tables (occasionally with a few indoor tables) where you bring your own food, the servers provide the huge mugs of beer, and you can dine under the sun and shade trees. Beer gardens are generally open 10am to 10pm or midnight (balmy summer nights can be fantastic). Biergartens usually offer simple sandwiches as well, and as always, pretzels and other snacks are on hand for noshing. Some of Munich's best biergartens include the **Biergarten Chinesischer Turm** in the heart of the Englischer Garten Park under the shade of a Chinese pagoda; the venerable (est. 1328) **Augustiner-Keller** at Arnulfstrasse 52, several long blocks past Hauptbahnhof; and the **Hirschgarten,** in the middle of Nymphenburg Park, the world's largest beer garden (it can seat 8,000).

Time-Savers

The **Deutsches Museum** (German Museum of Science and Technology) is one of the few museums in Munich that is open on Monday.

➤ **Watch an Entire City Drink Itself into a Stupor at Oktoberfest.** Picture this: a city park filled with big-top tents, each of which can seat 6,000 people plus an oompah brass band. For 16 days, tens of thousands of people do nothing but party medieval-style, roasting whole oxen on spits and drinking more than five million liters of beer. This is **Oktoberfest,** the world's ultimate keg party. It started with the celebrations for Prince Ludwig's marriage to Princess Therese in 1810, and the locals enjoyed themselves so much they made it an annual event.

The name is a bit misleading, because the first weekend in October is the *end* of the festivities—the kick-off parade of some 6,000 people occurs about two weeks before the end of September. When they're tapping the 750,000th keg and you're starting to feel woozy, stumble off to one of the thoughtfully placed recovery tents to lie on cushions and chill out to zither music. Ground zero is the **Theresienwiese park fairgrounds,** southwest of Hauptbahnhof, but the whole city has a distinct party air (and beery smell). Reserve your hotel room months in advance; call the tourist office to determine the exact dates of this year's festival.

➤ **Just You and Your Brew: Make a Round of the Beer Halls.** If Munich is famous for anything, its the *bräuhaus,* that bar/dining room/communal meeting place/evening's entertainment that often consists of nothing more than long wooden tables, bustling waitresses, plates of sausages and baskets of pretzels, swirling cigarette smoke, and mug after liter-sized mug of frothy beer. The city is full of them. Besides the two listed as restaurants previously, check out the **Ratskeller** (under the town hall—a Bavarian tradition—at Marienplatz 8),

Weinhaus Neuner (Herzogspitalstrasse 8), **Augustinerkeller** (five blocks past the train station at Arnulfstrasse 52), and **Weisses Bräuhaus** (Tal 7).

The most famous beer hall of them all is the **Hofbräuhaus** (Am Platzl 9). The current building is only about 100 years old, but the Hofbräuhaus has been here since 1589. Though perpetually chock-ablock with out-of-towners these days, it's still fun. The Hofbräuhaus is state-run, can seat 4,500 people over three floors (there's dancing on the fourth), and provides the requisite oompah music from 11am on (the daily Bavarian folk evening show starts at 8pm). If you can't be in Munich for Oktoberfest, this place will give you a pretty good idea of what you're missing.

Tourist Traps

Beer Hall Etiquette: Like Norm's stool at *Cheers,* Munich beer halls have their regulars' private tables, called *stammtisch.* These unmarked but sacrosanct spots are usually near the doors and/or in the corners. Smile and catch someone's attention before trying to sit down so that others at the table can politely let you know whether you're inadvertently invading their private space. If they greet you by saying *Grüss Gott,* you're in.

➤ **Spend an Afternoon in the Englischer Garten.** Intrigued by the thought of a biergarten under the shadow of a faux 1790 Chinese pagoda? Looking for a spot to do some nude sunbathing? Perhaps you just want to walk under some shady trees to work off some of those beer calories? Munich's Englischer Garten (named after a British expat who first devised the park) stretches for three miles along the west bank of the Isar River. It's full of beer gardens, trees, grassy lawns, bicycle paths, and streams and lakes where you can go swimming. Around the **Eisbach,** people sunbathe in the nude, and near the park's southern entrance, just behind the Haus der Kunst on Prinzregentenstrasse, is a **Japanese teahouse** in the middle of a small lake (traditional Japanese tea service is available the second and fourth weekends of each month at 3pm, 4pm, and 5pm).

Get Outta Town: Day Trips & Excursions
Munich sits in the heart of the Bavarian Alps, a region of spectacular scenery; any trip out into the surrounding countryside is bound to be unforgetttable. In addition to the excursions mentioned here, Munich is just two to three hours away from **Innsbruck,** and 1½ to 2 hours from **Salzburg**

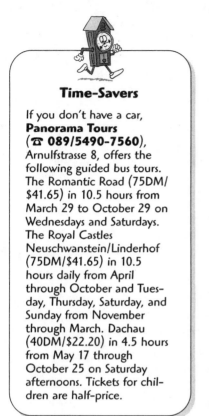

Time-Savers

If you don't have a car, **Panorama Tours** (☎ 089/5490-7560), Arnulfstrasse 8, offers the following guided bus tours. The Romantic Road (75DM/ $41.65) in 10.5 hours from March 29 to October 29 on Wednesdays and Saturdays. The Royal Castles Neuschwanstein/Linderhof (75DM/$41.65) in 10.5 hours daily from April through October and Tues-day, Thursday, Saturday, and Sunday from November through March. Dachau (40DM/$22.20) in 4.5 hours from May 17 through October 25 on Saturday afternoons. Tickets for chil-dren are half-price.

by train. Because both Salzburg and Innsbruck are in Austria, they're covered as excursions from Vienna in chapter 19.

A Longer Detour Into the Countryside: Driving the Romantic Road

From Würzburg to Füssen, a 180-mile road meanders through hamlets, medieval walled villages, and 2,000-year-old towns established by the Romans. It's called the Romantic Road and passes through the regions of Franconia, Swabia, and Bavaria to arrive in the foothills of the Alps. Along the way it wanders by much of what makes south-ern Germany attractive and fun: baroque churches, half-timbered, festive-colored houses, costumed locals, Renaissance palaces, cobblestone streets, carved wooden altarpieces, craft boutiques, and mile after mile of scenic countryside.

This area is dotted with picturesque vil-lages and castles, and most are well-prepared to receive visitors. Part of the fun of taking this trip is in exploring out-of-the-way places no guidebook covers, places where you'll have medieval Germany all to yourself for a few hours. With that in mind, I'll introduce you to the major, not-to-be-missed towns along the route, which together will already be more than enough to fill a two-day schedule.

Any good **map** will help **drivers** easily connect the dots between the towns mentioned here, and the classic route is fairly straightforward: just follow the green *Romantische Strasse* (Romantic Road) signs. Although officially the route runs from Würzburg to Füssen, Würzburg is a relative speck of a place; the real gateway to the northern end of the Romantic Road is Frankfurt-am-Main. For this reason, you'll see that in the "Suggested Itineraries" in chapter 1 I recommend starting this trip in Frankfurt, and taking the drive before arriving in Munich. From Frankfurt, you can zip to Würzburg on the Autobahn. Füssen, the southern terminus, is even tinier, so many people skip the last part of the trip and end their Romantic Road odyssey at Munich. To take the one-day trip from Frankfurt to Munich, hit just the main towns and do it very quickly. Abandon the *Romantishe Strasse* at Augsburg for the high-way east to Munich and let your Munich hotel know you'll be arriving late.

At a more leisurely pace, take two days to tour the whole road, spending the night in Rothenburg ob der Tauber. Another good plan is to drive all the way

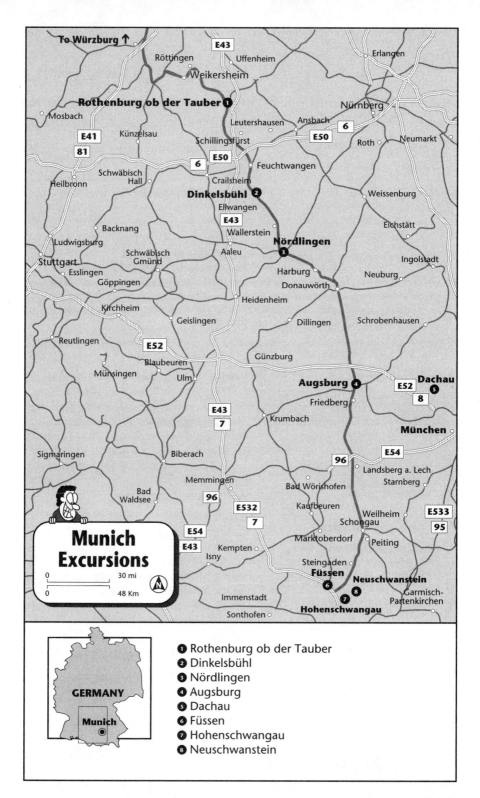

Munich Excursions

0 — 30 mi
0 — 48 Km

❶ Rothenburg ob der Tauber
❷ Dinkelsbühl
❸ Nördlingen
❹ Augsburg
❺ Dachau
❻ Füssen
❼ Hohenschwangau
❽ Neuschwanstein

GERMANY

Munich

to Füssen (much easier in two days, but doable in one) and spend the night there. The next morning, do the second excursion in this chapter (Mad King Ludwig's Fairy Tale Castle). You can then either return the car in Füssen and take the train to Munich or drive the car to Munich to drop it off.

Dollars & Sense

You can do the entire Romantic Road in a long (12½-hour) day on the **tour buses** of **Deutsche Touring Frankfurt** (☎ **069/790-3256** or 09851/ 90-271), which run April to October. The trip costs 126DM ($70), but only 10DM ($5.55) with a Eurail pass. Reserve in advance, especially in summer. If you want to stretch out your trip, you're welcome to abandon the bus at Rothenburg or any other stop and pick it up the next day, but be sure you let them know this when you reserve your ticket.

If you want to leave the driving to someone else take one of the popular and well-organized **bus tours** (see the "Time-Savers" sidebar on page 318). The official north endpoint is Frankfurt, from which buses leave at 8am. All buses let you get out and wander in Rothenburg (for 1½ to 2 hours) and in Dinkelsbühl (45 to 50 minutes). They also stop for 10 to 15 minutes in other scenic villages and spots—long enough to stretch and maybe pop into the local church or tiny museum.

Time-Savers

I'd choose either driving or taking the bus tour for this excursion. Trying to connect these villages by public transportation is a complicated and time-consuming juggling of bus and train schedules that wastes more of your time than it's worth.

In deference to the many travelers who intend to either start or end their Romantic Road journey in Munich, the bus company offers two south endpoints: Munich (arrive 7:50pm) or the traditional Füssen (arrive 8:40pm)—the two routes split off (southbound) or join up (northbound) at Dinklesbühl. If you want to do the Romantic Road in the other direction, northbound buses depart Füssen at 8am, Munich at 9am, and arrive in Frankfurt at 8:30pm.

Wine-Sotted Würzburg

Würzburg is a small, friendly university city and the capital of Franconia, a region renowned for its fine, dry white wines. Founded in the 4th or 5th century and converted to Christianity soon after, the city was ruled by princely bishops until the 20th century. Almost the entire town was flattened by an Allied bombing raid on March 16, 1945. The air raid's human toll was even worse—all but 5,000 of the city's 108,000 residents perished, and the city became known as *Grab am Main,* or "Grave on the Main." A few of Germany's greatest baroque buildings remained standing, however.

Atop a hill on the west end of town, across the Main River from the main part of Würzburg, is the **Festung Marienberg** (☎ **0931/43-016**). This fortress/residence of the city's bishops from 1253 to 1720 contains the tiny 8th-century Marien-kirche church and two small museums, one of winemaking and Riemenschneider sculptures; the other of typical Franconian household objects and clothing from past eras.

At the east end of town is Wurzburg's biggest draw, the huge baroque **Residenz** (☎ **0931/355-170**). It was built for the ruling bishops in 1720 and contains an elegant staircase (on the ceiling above it, the Italian master Tiepolo painted the world's largest fresco, at 6,4000 square feet). Also don't miss the fanciful and ornate Court Chapel, a festival of twisty columns and gilded stucco work.

Time-Savers

It takes a good two to three hours to see the major sights. In a hurry, head straight for the Residenz, and you can do Würzburg in an hour or so. The **tourist office** (☎ **0931/373-355**) is at Pavillon vor dem Hauptbahnhof across from the train station on the north end of town.

There's no finer place to sample Franconian wines than in the **Juliansspital Weinstuben** (☎ **0931/54-080**), Juliuspromenade 19, where the set-price lunches and inexpensive main courses are excellent. If you're ready to spend the night, try **St. Josef** (☎ and fax **0931/308-680**), Semmelstrasse 28, with 140 to 180DM ($77.75 to $100) doubles in the center of town. If you follow the traditional Romantic Road (and on southbound buses) to Rothenburg, you'll pass (a mile past Creglingen) the **Herrgottskapelle,** a church containing one of Riemenschneider's best carved wooden altarpieces.

Popular Rothenburg

Rothenburg ob der Tauber is undoubtedly the most heavily visited town on the Romantic Road. It's also one of the prettiest (it's full of gingerbread houses) and one the best-preserved medieval cities in Germany. It's a tangle of half-timbered houses, rambling city ramparts, gabled roofs, and cobbled streets. Even with the log jam of tourists in summer and the glut of gift shops stuffed with Bavarian souvenirs, it remains a picturesque sight and a highly recommended stop.

In the **Marktplatz,** you can get a city view from the tower of the Gothic/Renaissance **Rathaus** and watch the world's most boring mechanical clock show. A little door swings open in the clock face, a puppet pops out and drinks from a giant beer stein, and it's over. More interesting is the legend behind this display (see "Bet You Didn't Know").

Time-Savers

You can get away with just two or three hours here, but it's also a prime place to spend the night and break up your trip; it has enough sights to keep you occupied and plenty of hotels and restaurants and feels much more genuine after the day trippers leave. The **tourist office** (☎ **09861/ 40-492**) is in the Rathaus on Marktplatz.

The most photographed bit of Rothen-burg is the **Plönlein** a fork in the road at the south end of town where Spitalgasse, the main road, is split in two by a half-timbered house and both branches run under city gates just be-yond. Keep following the main branch of Spitalgasse to the left to reach Spitaltor, one of the towers in the city's very impressive **walls.** From many points on this medieval circuit surround-ing the city, you can climb up to its wooden ramparts and stroll around the city 30 feet up. From here you get views across nearby rooftops and can peer through arrow slits to the countryside beyond. The most popular and reward-ing walk along the walls starts at Spitaltor and winds counterclockwise all the way to Klingentor on the northern end of town (the walk takes a half-hour and about a half-dozen rolls of film). Halfway around you can climb up the eastern Rödertor for even better views.

Bet You Didn't Know

When a Catholic army threatened to level Rothenburg during the 17th–century 30 Years' War, a retired mayor named Nusch saved the day in true south German style. The army's General Tilly agreed to spare the town if any Rothenburger could drain a three-liter mug of wine in one gulp. To Tilly's sur-prise, Nusch was up to the challenge—although reportedly the hero *did* sleep straight through the next three days. The event is re-enacted live on the sec-ond weekend of September.

St. Jakobskirche has a wooden altar (1499 to 1505) carved by late Gothic master Tilman Riemenschneider. The **Reichsstadtmuseum** (☎ 09861/ **40-458**; Klosterhof 5), installed in a 13th-century convent, contains a mish-mash of artifacts from prehistory to the middle ages: paintings, furniture, objects from the city's old Jewish population, and one of those three-liter wine mugs. The **Kriminal Museum** (☎ 09861/5359), Burggasse 3, chroni-cles the laws of Germany from the 12th to 19th centuries and emphasizes the punishment aspect. There are plenty of iron shame masks, chastity belts, spiked chairs, iron maidens, finger-crushing neck violins, and other medieval party favors that were once inflicted upon criminals.

Although very busy and packed with visitors, the **Baumeisterhaus** (☎ **09861/94-700**), Obere Scmeidgasse 3 (just off the Marktplatz), is irresistible for a meal if only because of the setting—a 16th-century courtyard under a skylight ringed with ivy-trailing balconies. The Franconian grub is of the rib-sticking, meat-and-potatoes variety. Spend the night at **Hotel Reichs-Küchenmeister,** Kircheplatz 8, (☎ **09861/9700,** fax: 09861/86-965). It's centrally located, comfortable, and cheap at 140 to 250DM ($77.75–$138.90).

Dinky Dinkelsbühl

Dinkelsbühl has no particular sights other than its own half-timbered medieval self; it has been singled out as the one quaint little village to be sacrificed to the tour-bus schedule and is therefore perpetually crowded. Fortunately, this hasn't stopped it from staying charming in its simple way. The **tourist office** (☎ **09851/90-240**) is on Marktplatz and is open Monday through Saturday from April through October, Saturdays only from November through March.

If you're taking the tour bus, you'll have some time here; spend it in the 15th-century **Georgenkirche** and wandering the pretty streets lined with 16th-century gabled houses. Grab a bite at the **Deutsches Haus** (☎ **09851/6058,** fax: 09851/7911), Weinmarkt 3, where you can also stay the night for 165 to 210DM ($91.65 to $116.65) and enjoy the town once the crowds clear out.

Medieval Nördlingen

Nördlingen is a perfectly round town still encircled by its 14th- and 15th-century fortifications. It has a few more sights than Dinklesbühl, though nothing spectacular. Still, the odd history of the valley in which it sits—once thought to be an extinct volcano, but now known to be an enormous meteorite crater—has endowed the town with an interesting geological museum.

In many ways, Nördlingen feels more like a living extension of the Middle Ages than the other Romantic Road towns you'll

Time-Savers

Nördlingen makes a nice stop. You can see it in as little as 30 minutes or in an hour or two. The **tourist office** (☎ **09081/4380**) is at Marktplatz 2.

visit. Many townsfolk dress daily in something approaching traditional local costume, and the pace of life is slower, less modernized. They haven't, however, slowed down when it comes to the lively bustle of the food market on Gothic **Marktplatz,** the town's center. Poke your head into **St. Georgskirche,** a 15th-century German Hall Church with fan vaulting.

Check out the **Reiskrater-Museum** (☎ 09081/84-143), Hintere Gerbergasse, to learn about the meteorite that smashed into this spot 15 million years ago. It was half a mile across, traveled at 100,000 miles per hour, and destroyed all life within 100 miles, throwing debris as far away as Slovakia. Its imprint left the circular valley in which Nördlingen now sits, a landscape whose soil is exceedingly rich and yet eerie and rugged enough that *Apollo 14* and *Apollo 17* astronauts trained here for their trips to the moon. Before you leave, walk around the ramparts of the **city walls** (the best stretch is from Berger Tor to Reimlinger Tor).

The fertile valley provides **Meyer's Keller** (☎ 09081/4493), Marienhöhe 8, with fresh ingredients for its creative continental cuisine. To stay the night, try **Kaiser Hotel Sonne** (☎ 09081/5067, fax: 09081/23-999), Marktplatz 3, with 125 to 175DM ($69.45 to $97.20) doubles right on the main square.

Renaissance Augsburg

All that remains of the Roman era here is the city's name. Emperor Augustus's kinsmen established it as one of the first major stopping points on a Roman road (Via Claudia) after it crossed the Alps. Later, as a religious seat, it hosted Martin Luther in 1518 when he read the controversial "Confession" that laid out Protestantism. Its medieval wealth left the city with some of the finest Renaissance art and buildings in southern Germany.

Time-Savers

To many, Augsburg is the end of the Romantic Road, one last stopping point before turning east to Munich. Give it a good couple of hours. The **tourist office** (☎ 0821/502-070) is at Bahnhofstrasse 7.

In 1519, the Fuggers, one of Augsburg's wealthiest families, established a welfare housing complex for the poor that is still in operation today—and still charges the equivalent of just $1 in annual rent. The only requirement is that you must pray daily for the souls of its founders. This **Fuggerei** (☎ 0821/30-868) is a model of Renaissance planning, a self-contained city within the city at the end of Vorderer Lech. You can visit the simple interior of one of the units at Mittleregasse 13; next door at no. 14, an out-of-work mason named Franz Mozart once lived, great-grandfather of the famous composer.

The city's cathedral, **Dom St. Maria,** on Hoherweg, contains the world's oldest extant stained-glass windows (12th century), Romanesque relief panels in the bronze Virgin's Door, a gothic interior, and paintings by Hans Holbein the Elder on the side altars. Another pair of churches of note are **St. Ulrich** and **St. Afra,** next door to each other on Ulrichplatz. The latter has the more elaborate baroque interior, but the churches themselves are gothic. Their existence is a tribute to peaceful religious coexistence; they were built together in 1555, one Roman Catholic and the other Lutheran, to help seal the rift between the two faiths.

The Renaissance town hall, or **Rathaus,** Am Rathausplatz 2, was rebuilt after its destruction during World War II, and you can visit the restored magnificence of its "golden chamber." The city art gallery in the **Schaezlerpalais** (☎ 0821/324-2171), Maximilianstrasse 46, has a good collection of Renaissance and baroque works by German and Italian artists such as Holbein the Elder, Dürer, Rubens, Veronese, and Tiepolo. Don't miss the palace's rococo ballroom.

You can get cheap, filling food at **Fuggerei Stube** (☎ 0821/30-870), Jakoberstrasse 26, but more fun, if overly popular, is a medieval feast at **Weiser Kuche** (☎ 0821/33-930), Maximilianstrasse 83. You eat the three-hour meal with just your fingers and a knife here; the food is served by costumed "knaves and wenches," and the dishes are based on a 16th-century cookbook. Reserve ahead. To sleep off your feast, check into the **Dom Hotel** (☎ 0821/343-930, fax: 0821/3439-3200), Frauenorstrasse 8, which has a half-timbered facade and modernized doubles for 150 to 210DM ($83.30 to $116.65). Northbound buses between Füssen and Augsburg detour to stop at the **Wieskirche** (see "Mad King Ludwig's Fairy-tale Castle").

...and Finally, Füssen

Füssen is the southern terminus of the Romantic Road in the foothills of the Alps with a very picturesque setting on a river. It has few sights of its own, but it makes a great base for exploring the surrounding area, including Neuschwanstein (see "Mad King Ludwig's Fairy-tale Castle").

If you have time to kill here, stop by the 15th-century **Castle,** once used by the Augsburg prince-bishops as a summer home. The former **Benedictine Abbey** across the river is a nice assemblage of baroque architecture that's worth poking around.

Time-Savers

Skip Füssen if you're not interested in the next excursion. The **tourist office** (☎ 08362/93850) is at Kaiser-Maximilianplatz 1.

For a late dinner, head to **Zum Schwanen** (☎ 08362/6174), Brotmarkt 4, for filling portions of Bavarian and Swabian specialties. If you're too tired to head up to Munich from here, crash at the **Hotel-Schlossgasthof Zum Hechten** (☎ 08362/91-600, fax: 08362/916-099), a family-owned, modernized inn directly below the castle with doubles for 100 to 130DM ($55.55 to $72.20).

Mad King Ludwig's Fairy-tale Castle: Neuschwanstein

Ever wonder where Walt Disney got the idea for that precious Cinderella castle at his theme parks? He drew direct inspiration, and even some architectural blueprints, right from Bavaria's storybook castle, Neuschwanstein.

King Ludwig II—in many ways the epitome of a 19th-century romantic—built or renovated many a castle for himself. But in the end, he decided that the only thing that would completely satisfy him would be to create a castle that looked truly befitting of the knights of old, a fairy-tale edifice straight out of a story by the Brothers Grimm. Neuschwanstein was the result and is still a stunning, dreamlike sight, perched halfway up a forested mountain near a waterfall. It's all slender towers, ramparts, and pointy turrets done in pale gray. Sadly, the castle was never quite finished, and the king got to live in his half-completed fantasy for only 170 days before his death.

A strenuous 25-minute downhill walk (you can also take a bus) from Neuschwanstein is **Hohenschwangau,** the much more practical castle created by Ludwig II's father. Between these two fortresses and Munich, off a side road, hides the pilgrimage church of **Wieskirche,** one of the most over-the-top examples of the late baroque period in Germany (see the next "Extra! Extra!" sidebar).

Time-Savers

You can get information on the ever-popular Neuschwanstein at the tourist offices in Munich and Füssen. There's also a local **tourist office (☎ 08362/ 81-980)**, which is closed mid-November through mid-December, in the tiny village/parking lot of Schwangau.

It's best to get around by car for this trip, but you can swing it via public transportation from Munich. Take one of the nearly hourly **trains** to Füssen (a two-hour trip), from which hourly buses make the 10-minute trip to the castle parking lot. The sister castles of Neuschwanstein and Hoheschwangau are usually referred to collectively on road signs as *Königsschlösser* (king's castles).

Although you can do all this in a day, you may find it more relaxing to stay a night, basing yourself in Füssen (which is described as the last stop of the Romantic Road excursion). A good plan is to take a late train into Füssen and spend the night. That way, you can be up early and to Neuschwanstein with the first wave of crowds (it's as crowded early as at any other time, but at least the lines haven't backed up yet).

Of the many weird and theatrical details the tour of **Neuschwanstein** will show you, some of the most impressive include the king's bedroom—almost every inch covered in intricately carved wood—his near-finished neo–Byzantine-Romanesque Throne Room, and the huge Singers Hall, covered with paintings that refer to the work of composer Richard Wagner. The king was positively enthralled by Wagner's music; he supposedly convulsed and writhed in such bliss to the strains of the composer's operas that his aides feared he was having an epileptic fit. Ludwig fished Wagner out of hiding (his early career in shambles, the composer was hiding from creditors), bailed him out of his enormous debt, poured money into whatever project the composer desired, and generally went above and beyond the call of a patron's duty, often to the neglect of his state duties.

This was the sort of thing that earned Ludwig II the moniker "Mad King Ludwig," but the monarch probably wasn't certifiable. Although beloved by his subjects as a genial and well-meaning ruler, Ludwig's withdrawal into his fantasies caused him to lose touch with his court and the political machinations in Munich. In 1886, he was deposed *in absentia*, and a few days later his body was found drowned, under suspicious circumstances, in a few feet of water at the edge of a lake.

You can visit the interior of Neuschwanstein by guided tour only from April to September daily from 8:30am to 5:30pm, in winter daily from 10am to 4pm. Admission is 10DM($5.55) for adults, 7DM ($3.90) for students and those over age 65, free for those under 15. This is Bavaria's biggest tourist draw by a long shot. The crowds pack the place to the rafters by 9am, and they don't thin out until 4pm or so. You can wait hours just to take the requisite 35-minute tour (in English).

At the bottom of Neuschwanstein's hill is the tiny village/parking lot of Schwangau, which serves as a lunch stop for tour-bus crowds. Across its only road and on top of a much shorter hill is **Hohenschwangau (☎ 08362/ 81-127)**, a sandy-colored castle restored in neo-gothic style by Ludwig's father (Maximilian II). It's a much more businesslike, everyday fortress than its fanciful neighbor; although it doesn't have the same kind of excessive glamour, tours (usually in German, unless enough English speakers show up) can prove interesting. This was a real home of a castle, where Ludwig lived for 17 years (and hosted his buddy Wagner). You could almost picture yourself moving in here—though you might never use the dramatic Hall of the Swan Knight, with its dramatic wall paintings of the Germanic myths, unless it were a special occasion.

When driving into this castle complex, you'll have your choice of **parking** lots in Schwangau, that little tourist center by the lake. Park in lot D (first one on the left coming from Munich, just before the intersection) for the quickest, but steepest, walk up to Neuschwanstein (20 to 30 minutes). Go farther down the road to the big lot on the right if you want to take the long, but less steep, paved road up (30 to 45 minutes). It's a fairly strenuous hike either way. Costly horse-drawn carriages will take you as far as the ticket office, which is two-thirds of the way up.

The easiest route up is to take the shuttle bus that leaves from near that second parking lot, overshoots the castle, and stops at Marienbrücke, a bridge across the gorge above Neuschwanstein. This not only lets you walk (steeply) back downhill in 10 minutes to the castle, but also affords a great view, beloved by the local postcard industry, of the castle with Alpsee lake and its valley in the background.

Extra! Extra!

One of the masterpieces of the exceedingly flamboyant architectural period called rococo is Bavaria's **Wieskirche,** built in 1746 to 1754 by Dominikus Zimmerman and frescoed by his brother Johann Baptist. In the middle of an unassuming cow pasture in the Alpine foothills, they erected an enormous pilgrim's church whose stuccoed, frescoed interior is a sight to behold. It's light and airy, yet at the same time dense with decoration, with mathematically improbable geometric curves and a series of arches squeezed-together to form the high altar. The church is off a side road between routes 17 and 23, about 50 minutes north of Füssen. You can also take a bus from Füssen at 11:15am (1:05pm Sundays), returning on a 3:50pm bus.

The Nazi Concentration Camp at Dachau

In 1933, in a little town outside Munich called Dachau, SS leader Heinrich Himmler set up Nazi Germany's first concentration camp. Between 1933 and 1945, 206,000 prisoners were officially registered here, and countless thousands more were interned without record. To spend an hour or two here remembering the darkest days of modern history, take the S2 **S-Bahn** train from Marienplatz here in 20 minutes. From Dachau station, bus 722 takes you to the camp (☎ **08131/84-566**).

By the gate as you enter is inscribed the taunting Nazi slogan *Arbeit Macht Frei* (Work Brings Freedom)—as if working hard and being a model prisoner made a difference. Allied troops razed the 32 prisoners' barracks to the ground when they liberated the camp in 1945, but two have been reconstructed to illustrate the squalid living conditions. Each barrack was built to house 208 people; by 1936, they accommodated up to 1,600 each.

The former kitchen is now a museum whose photographs document the rise of the Nazis and the persecution of Jews, communists, gypsies, homosexuals, and other "undesirables." There's also a short documentary film (the English version usually shows at 11:30am and 3:30pm). At the back of the camp are the ovens of the crematorium and a gas chamber disguised as showers. No prisoners were gassed at Dachau (however, over 3,000 Dachau inmates were sent to an Austrian camp to be executed in this manner); this room was used for beatings and pointless cruel interrogations. Although Dachau, unlike other camps such as Auschwitz in Poland, was primarily for political prisoners and not expressly a death camp, over 32,000 people died here, and thousands more were executed. The camp is scattered with Jewish, Catholic, and Protestant memorials.

Chapter 19

Vienna & the Best of Austria

In This Chapter

➤ A cultural smorgasbord, from operas to choirs to waltzes

➤ Hapsburg haunts, horse dancing, and a Ferris wheel: sights to write home about

➤ Desserts to die for: the city's best cafes

➤ Reliving Olympic gold and the *Sound of Music:* excursions to Innsbruck and Salzburg

---

The city on the Danube, Vienna retains some of the splendor of the Austro-Hungarian Empire. Vienna's attitudes, architecture, and interior decor exude the stately elegance of the 18th and 19th centuries when its Hapsburg ruling dynasty controlled much of central and eastern Europe. It's a refined city of imperial palaces and art museums, of baroque churches and beer taverns, of ornate cafes and concert halls. As birthplace of the waltz and home to the likes of Mozart, Haydn, Beethoven, Schubert, the Strauss family, Brahms, Mahler, the Vienna Boys Choir (and, more recently, the late pop star Falco, of *Rock Me Amadeus* fame),

Dollars & Sense

The Austrian unit of currency is the schilling (AS), divided into 100 groschen. Roughly, $1 equals 12.5AS; or 10AS equals 80¢. Austrian coins include 2, 5, 10, and 50 groschen, and 1, 5, 10, and 20 schillings. Bills come in denominations of 20, 50, 100, 500, 1,000, and 5,000 schillings.

Vienna lays claim to one of Europe's strongest musical traditions. Give Vienna at least two or three days—not only for the sights, but also because it is one the best European capitals for just walking the streets and people-watching in the coffeehouses while munching on flaky *apfelstrudel.*

Getting Your Bearings

Vienna's **inner city** is the oldest part of town and home to the most spectacular sights and almost all the hotels and restaurants recommended in this chapter.

Vienna's Neighborhoods in Brief

The city's historic core is encircled by the **Ringstrasse,** or Ring Road, a wide, elegant, tree-shaded, tram-routed boulevard that follows the outline of the vanished medieval city walls. Along this road are strung many of the major palaces, churches, and museums. Although the Ring is one long curving street, its name changes often. A road is part of this boulevard if the name ends in *-ring,* such as Opernring or Kärntner Ring.

The **Danube Canal** forms the northeast edge of the old city. (The famed river itself, which doesn't appear to be *any* shade of blue, is farther to the northeast.) The shopping boulevard **Kärntnerstrasse,** which runs northward, begins where Kärntner Ring becomes Opernring at the Staatsoper opera house. This boulevard cuts through the middle of the inner city to **Stephansplatz,** the center of town and site of St. Stephan's cathedral.

Time-Savers

The main office of the **Vienna Tourist Board** is at Kärntnerstrasse 38 (☎ **0222/513-8892,** fax: 0222/216-8492), behind the Staatsoper. Here you can pick up a free copy of the events rag *Wien Monatsprogramm* as well as *Vienna A to Z,* a pocket guide to the city with sights keyed to a map; this guide costs 40AS ($3.20). Smaller branches of the tourist office are in Westbahnhof and Südbahnhof stations and at the airport.

The only part of Vienna outside the Ring where you might find yourself lies just south of the Staatsoper. To the opera's southeast is the elegant **Karlsplatz,** with its namesake church, history museum, and major U-Bahn (subway) junction. To the west of this area is the **Naschmarkt** fresh produce market and just beyond that stretches **Mariahilferstrasse,** a wide shopping street that runs from the Opernring to **Westbahnhof** train station.

Getting Into & Around Town

By train, you'll arrive in Vienna at **Westbahnhof** (trains from northern and central Europe) or **Südbahnhof** (southern and parts of central Europe). Some trains from Prague and Berlin arrive at the northerly **Franz-Josef Bahnhof,** and occasionally you'll end up at **Wien Mitte/Landstrasse** on the city's eastern edge (coming from Prague or the airport). The U-Bahn (subway) and tram system will run you between these stations and the center of town. **Wien Schwechat airport** is 12 miles southeast of the city. Every 20 minutes a bus leaves the airport for the 25-minute ride to Wien Mitte/Landstrasse; other buses run to Südbahnhof and Westbahnhof stations.

Although you can get around the inner city on foot, for longer hauls you'll need public transportation. The fastest way to get around is the **U-Bahn** (subway). The U3 heads from Westbahnhof station through the center of town, stopping at Stephansplatz, and then goes on to Wien Mitte/Landstrasse. The U1 bisects the center of town north-south, stopping at Karlsplatz, Stephansplatz, Swedenplatz (near the Danube Canal), and Praterstern/ Wien Nord (at the Prater city park). The U2 follows the curve of the western half of the Ring to Karlsplatz, where it ends, and U4 continues around the eastern half of the Ring before heading off north to the Friedensbrücke stop (the closest to Franz-Josef Bahnhof).

The **trams** are a more scenic way to get about town and include lines 18 (Süd-bahnhof to Westbahnhof), D (skirting much of the Ring before heading to Südbahnhof), and 1 and 2 (running circles along the Ring, stopping at the major sights). There are also **buses** that criss-cross the center of town (1A, 2A, and 3A) and lead out into the 'burbs.

Culture Shock

When reading a **Viennese address,** know that the building number comes *after* the street name. If there's a number before the name, especially a Roman numeral, it indicates the *bezirk* (city district) that address is in. (The inner city, contained by the Ring, is *bezirk* 1.)

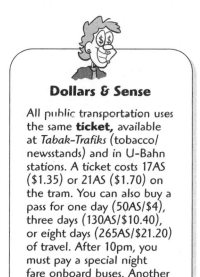

Dollars & Sense

All public transportation uses the same **ticket,** available at *Tabak-Trafiks* (tobacco/ newsstands) and in U-Bahn stations. A ticket costs 17AS ($1.35) or 21AS ($1.70) on the tram. You can also buy a pass for one day (50AS/$4), three days (130AS/$10.40), or eight days (265AS/$21.20) of travel. After 10pm, you must pay a special night fare onboard buses. Another option is the **Vienna Card,** described under "Sightseeing."

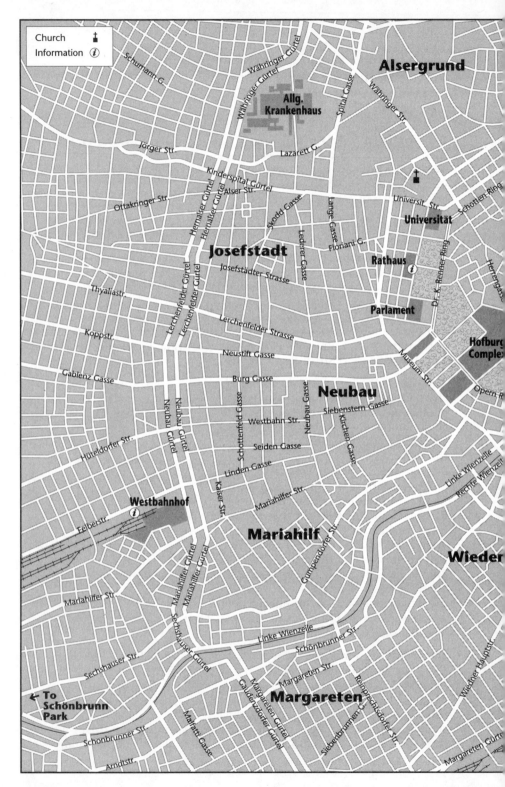

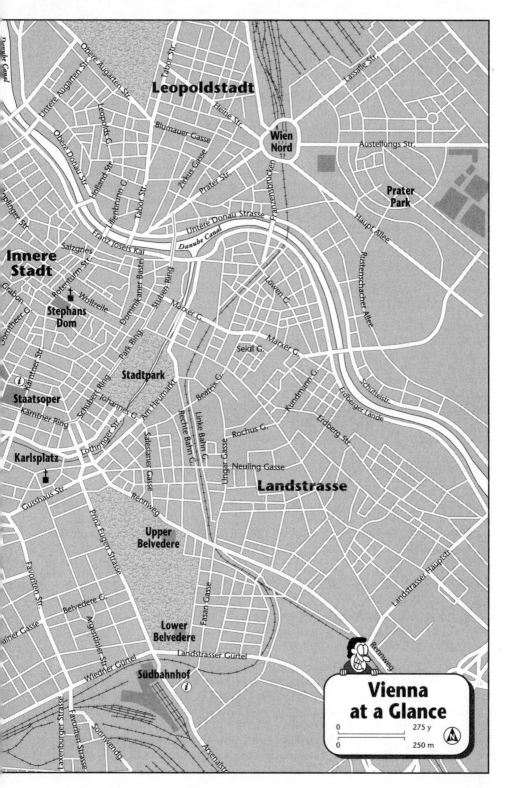

Vienna
at a Glance

Vienna Fast Facts

American Express   Vienna's American Express office is located at Kärntnerstrasse 21-23 (☎ **0222-515-40**) and is open Monday to Friday, 9am to 5:30pm and Saturday 9am to noon.

Consulate   The U.S. consulate is located at Gartenbaupromenade 2 in the Marriott Hotel (☎ **0222/31-339**).

Doctors/hospitals   If you have an emergency at night, call ☎ **141** (7pm to 7am daily) for a list of doctors. For a list of English-speaking physicians, call the **Doctor's Association** at ☎ **1771,** or try the **U.S. Embassy.** For emergency medical care, go to the **Neue Allgemeine Krankenhaus** at Währinger Gürtel 18-20 (☎ **0222/404-000**).

Embassy   The U.S. Embassy (☎ **0222/31-339**) is located at Boltzmanngasse 16.

Emergency   Dial ☎ **144** for an ambulance; call the police at ☎ **133;** or report a fire to ☎ **122.**

Pharmacies   Vienna's pharmacies are generally open Monday to Friday 8am to noon and 2 to 6pm, Saturday 8am to noon. A sign outside every pharmacy lists those drugstores open during the off hours, or call ☎ **1550.**

Safety   Vienna is home to its share of pickpockets and purse-snatchers. Be especially careful of these seedy characters in crowded areas frequented by tourists, particularly Kärntnerstrasse between Stephansplatz and Karlsplatz. Avoid opening your purse or pulling out your wallet in public areas—pitiable children begging for money are often accompanied by adult thieves who snatch your wallet and run. Karlsplatz is the only central area that becomes somewhat scary after dark when the heroin addicts come out.

Taxis   You'll reach most of Vienna's tourist sites easily on foot, but you may want a taxi for trips from the airport or train station to your hotel. You'll pay about 350AS ($28) for a taxi from the airport into town. Taxis do not cruise the streets of Vienna looking for fares. Instead, passengers hire taxis at stands located throughout the city, or call ☎ **31-300,** 60-160, 81-400, 91-091, or 40-100.

The initial charge for one passenger is 26AS ($2) and 12AS ($1) per kilometer. There is a 16AS ($1.30) surcharge for luggage. After 11pm and on Sundays and holidays, the basic fare is 27AS ($2.15) and 14AS ($1.10) per kilometer. You will be charged extra fees for additional passengers and for calling the taxi by phone. Rides to the airport cost an extra 110AS ($8.80).

Telephone   A local call in Vienna is just 2AS (15¢). You can use coins, or some phones work with a pre-paid phone card (wertkarte), available from post offices, newsstands, and tobacconists. Unused shillings are returned at the call's end. Post offices (most are open 24 hours a day) sell phone cards *(wertkarten),* available in denominations of 50AS ($4), 100AS ($8), and 200AS ($16). Post offices are also a good place from which to make direct-dial long-distance calls (see chapter 10, "Mastering Communication").

Austria's country code is **43**; Vienna has two city codes: **1** when calling from outside the country, **0222** when calling from within Austria. In other words, to call Vienna from the United States, dial **011-43-1** followed by the phone number; to call Vienna from another Austrian city, dial **0222** and then the number.

To charge your call to a calling card, insert 2AS (15¢) into the pay phone and dial ☎ **0222/903-011** for **AT&T,** ☎ **0222/903-012** for **MCI,** or ☎ **0222/903-014** for **Sprint.** To call the United States direct from Austria, dial **001** (**900** if you're calling from Vienna) and then the area code and phone number.

Phone Number Alert

Vienna's phone numbers are gradually being changed to seven digits, so numbers that appear in this chapter may soon become obsolete. To learn the new number, call **directory assistance** at ☎ **1611.**

Transit Info   For transportation information, call ☎ **711-01.**

Housing Fit for a Hapsburg: Vienna's Hotel Scene

If you're on a shoestring, there's a concentration of cheap, plain hotels around Westbahnhof, a short tram ride from the center of town. This area is usually safe at night, except as you near Karlsplatz, a pretty plaza that junkies claim after dark. Vienna's popularity booms in late spring and late summer, and rooms can get scarce, so reserve ahead or resign yourself to staying in the suburbs.

Hotel Astoria

$$$$$. Near the Staatsoper.
This turn-of-the-century bastion recaptures the dying days of the Austro-Hungarian Empire with a frayed but cared-for elegance. The prime location places you on the main shopping promenade between the opera house and the cathedral. Steer clear of the dark and cramped interior rooms in favor of those in the front. The *Jugendstil* (art nouveau) restaurant serves exquisite Austrian fare.

Time-Savers

The **tourist office** will find you a room in a hotel or private home and book it for a 40AS ($3.20) fee plus one night's deposit. **B&B Vienna** (Rielgasse 47b; ☎ **0222/885–219**) will match you up with a bed and breakfast or a private room.

Kärntnerstrasse 32-34 (between Krugerstrasse and Annagasse). ☎ *0222/515-770.* **Fax:** *0222/515-7782.* **U-Bahn:** *Stephansplatz.* **Rates:** *2,400AS ($192) double. AE, DC, MC, V.*

Hotels
Hotel Astoria **13**
Hotel Kärntnerhof **24**
Hotel Royal **18**
Hotel Schneider **1**
Hotel Wandl **17**
Pension Pertschy **16**

Restaurants
Augustinerkeller **15**
Drei Husaren **20**
Figimüller **23**
Firenze Enoteca **21**
Griechenbeisl **25**
Kardos **26**

Attractions
Augustinerkirche **11**
Die Burgkapelle
   (Vienna Boys' Choir) **7**
Freud Museum **4**
Gemäldegalerie Akademie
   der Bildenen Künste
   (Academy of Fine Arts) **2**
Hofburg Palace Complex **6**
Kaiserappartements
   (Imperial Apartments) **9**
Kaisergruft
   (Imperial Crypt) **14**
Kunsthistorisches Museum
   (Museum of Art History) **3**
Mozart-Wohnung Figarohaus
   (Mozart Memorial) **22**
Neue Burg **5**
Schatzhammer
   (Imperial Treasury) **8**
Spanische Reitschule
   (Spanish Riding School) **10**
Staatsoper (Opera House) **12**
Stephansdom
   (St. Stephen's Cathedral) **19**

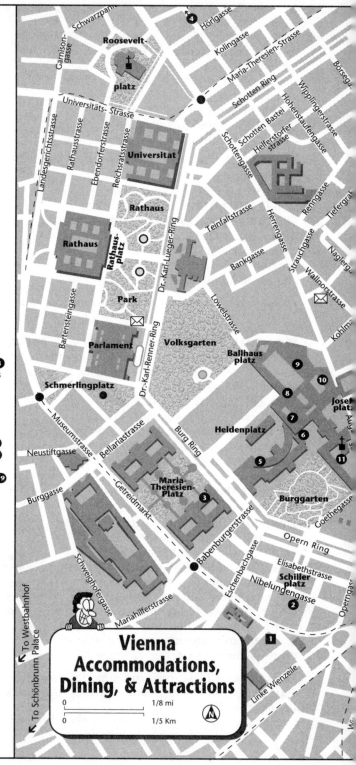

**Vienna
Accommodations,
Dining, & Attractions**

0 _____ 1/8 mi
0 _____ 1/5 Km

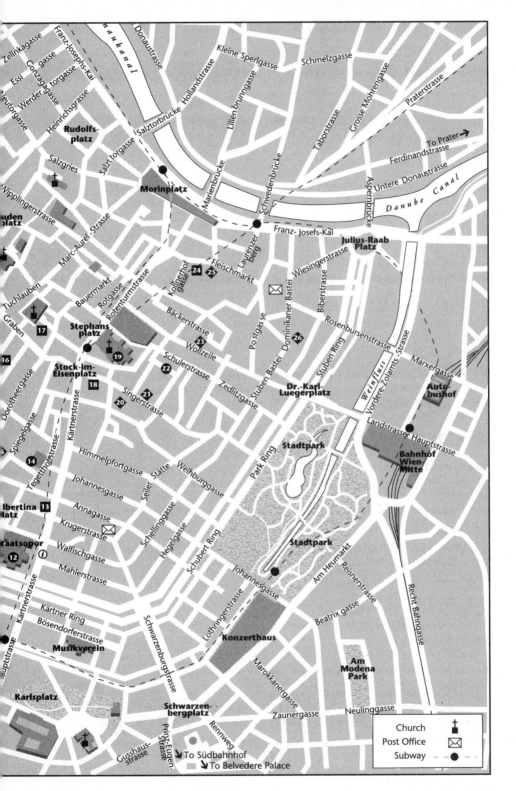

Church ✝
Post Office ✉
Subway - - - ●

337

Kids **Hotel Kärntnerhof**
$. North of Stephansdom.

A few minutes' walk north of the cathedral, this friendly, cozy, old-fashioned hotel is modest but not spare, and the price is right for any bracket (especially if you can get the cheapest rooms that share a bath). Accommodations tend to be near-modern, wood-floored, sparkling clean, and roomy enough for families.

Grashofgasse 4 (near the corner of Kollnerhof and Fleischmarkt). ☎ *0222/* **512-1923. Fax:** *0222/513-222-833.* **U-Bahn:** *Stephansplatz.* **Parking:** *180AS ($14.40).* **Rates:** *900–1,680AS ($72–$134.40) double. AE, DC, MC, V.*

Hotel Royal
$$$$. Near the Staatsoper.

At the intersection of two prestigious streets and just a block from the cathedral, the modern Royal offers good value in the city's heart. There's a piano in the lobby that was once owned by Wagner, and some antiques in the rooms, but don't come here for history; it was built in 1960. The best accommodations are the corner rooms with spacious foyers and the ones whose balconies have views of Stephansdom.

Singerstrasse 3 (at the corner with Kärntnerstrasse). ☎ *0222/51-568.* **Fax:** *0222/513-9698.* **U-Bahn:** *Stephansplatz.* **Rates:** *1,600–2,200AS ($128–$176) double. AE, DC, MC, V.*

Kids **Hotel Schneider**
$$$$. Just southeast of the Ringstrasse.

This entertainers' fave is a modern building fitted with 19th-century antiques. Families appreciate that half of the comfortable rooms feature kitchenettes (there's a produce market nearby). Although outside the Ringstrasse, it's an excellent location for art lovers; it's behind the Academy of Fine Arts and near the Kunsthistoriches Museum.

Getreidemarkt 5. ☎ *0222/588-380.* **Fax:** *0222/5883-8212.* **Parking:** *250AS ($20).* **U-Bahn:** *Karlsplatz.* **Rates:** *1,600–2,160AS ($128–$172.80) double. AE, DC, MC, V.*

Kids **Hotel Wandl**
$$$. Near Stephansdom.

Run by the same family for generations, this good-value inn sits right on the cathedral square. Rooms are a decent size, but they are boringly furnished with functional pieces. Be sure to request a room with a view of St. Stephen's Cathedral.

Petersplatz 9. ☎ *0222/534-550.* **Fax:** *0222/534-5577.* **U-Bahn:** *Stephansplatz.* **Parking:** *300–400AS ($24–$32).* **Rates:** *1,450–1,750AS ($116–$140) double. AE, DC, MC, V.*

Pension Pertschy
$$. Near Stephansdom.
About as central in town as you can get, this baroque palace (built in 1725) has been a family-run hotel for over 30 years. Rooms are done in old-fashioned Biedermeir style, including chandeliers; a few even have 200-year-old ceramic heaters. This is one of the most atmospheric hotels in town and is a bargain to boot.

Habsburgergasse 5 (just off the Graben). ☎ *0222/534-490.* **Fax:** *0222/ 534-4949.* **U-Bahn:** *Stephansplatz.* **Rates:** *1,080–1,260AS ($86.40–$100.80) double. DC, MC, V.*

Vienna's Restaurant Scene (or, Schniztel, Schniztel Everywhere)

With influences culled from neighboring Germany, Switzerland, and Italy, as well as the eastern-tinged cuisines of Turkey, Hungary, and the Balkans, Viennese cooking is varied and palate-pleasing. Far and away, Vienna's most famous contribution to the world's table is **wiener schnitzel,** a simple and steam-roller-flat cutlet of pork or veal breaded and fried (most tradition-ally in lard), served either overwhelming a plate or tucked into a roll as a sandwich. **Tafelspitz,** boiled beef, is another dyed-in-the-wool Viennese specialty—Emperor Franz Joseph ate it every day. Hungary, that other half of the Austro-Hungarian Empire, has likewise left its influence on the local pantry, and paprika seeps into many dishes and is best in the spicy beef or pork stew called **gulasch.**

When the Ottoman Turks repeatedly besieged the city in the 16th and 17th centuries, they left behind what was to become one of Vienna's passions, a taste for the exotic drink called **kaffee (coffee).** (For some of the best cafes in town, see "Other Fun Stuff to Do.") With your kaffee, you'll want to order one—make that several—of Vienna's world-renowned **pastries.** *Strudel* comes with many more fillings other than that of the redoubtable master, the apple (**apfelstrudel**). Other must-try sweets include the cream-filled **gugelhupf** horn and the cakes **rehrucken** (chocolate cake set with almonds) and especially **Sachertorte** (see "Bet You Didn't Know").

Austria's top **beers** are the lighter Gold Fassl, Kaiser, and Weizengold (a wheat beer); richer brews include Gösser Spezial and Eggenberger Urbock, the latter dating back to the 17th century and considered one of the world's most powerful beers. The best Austrian **wines** are white, tops being the fruity Grüner Veltiner. Many of the dry Rieslings are also renowned, and the Austrians make good Chardonnays and Pinot Blanc as well. One specialty is the dessert wine **Eiswein,** so called because the grapes are left on the vine to ripen and sweeten until frost hits, freezing the water in the grapes and con-centrating their taste and alcohol level. Austrians also distill juniper, rowan berries, apricots, or quinces, and call the product **schnapps.**

Bet You Didn't Know

Sachertorte is the original death by chocolate with a twist of apricot jam. The Hotel Sacher (Philharmonikerstrasse 4; ☎ **0222/51–456**) invented this dense dessert in 1832, but had to engage in a lengthy legal battle with Café Demel in the 1960s over the right to call their confection "Original Sachertorte." The Hotel Sacher won, but my taste buds are hard-pressed to tell the difference. Either place can overload a chocolate lover's palate to ecstasy.

Augustinerkeller
$. Near the Staatsoper. AUSTRIAN.

Since 1857, this vaulted brick cellar filled with long communal tables under the Hofburg palace has been serving simple fare such as schnitzel, spit-roasted chicken, and tafelspitz, accompanied by Viennese beer and wine. The location and wandering accordion players have driven away many a local, but it's still fun, and the food is ample and good.

Augustinerstrasse 1 (a little ways off Albertinaplatz, across from Augustinia church). ☎ *0222/533-1026. Reservations not necessary.* **U-Bahn:** *Stephansplatz.* **Main courses:** *110–170AS ($8.80–$13.60); glasses of wine 28–32AS ($2.25–$2.55). AE, DC, MC, V.* **Open:** *Lunch and dinner daily.*

Drei Husaren
$$$$. Near Stephansdom. VIENNESE/INTERNATIONAL.

Vienna's top restaurant since World War I, Drei Husaren is decorated with Gobelin tapestries and antiques. The chef decorates your table with the finest of both traditional and inventive Viennese cuisine, including an hors d'oeuvres table laden with over 35 goodies, *kalbsbrücken Metternich* (the chef's specialty veal dish), and cheese-filled crêpes topped with chocolate sauce.

Weihburggasse 4 (2 blocks south of Stephansplatz, Weihburggasse branches off to the left/east; the restaurant is just past the intersection with Liliengasse). ☎ *0222/ 512-1092. Reservations required.* **U-Bahn:** *Stephansplatz.* **Main courses:** *255–395AS ($20.40–$31.60); tastings menu 880AS ($70.40); fixed-price lunch 390AS ($31.20). AE, DC, MC, V.* **Open:** *Lunch and dinner daily. Closed mid-July to mid-Aug.*

Figimüller
$$. Near Stephansdom. VIENNESE.

This archetypal Viennese *beisel* (tavern) is always crowded and famous for its enormous wiener schnitzel, which is larger than the plate it comes on. The dining room is over 500 years old, aged by the patina of the thousands who've enjoyed their sausages, tafelspitz, salads, and glass after glass of excellent wines.

Wollzelle 5 (go 1 block north on Rotenturmstrasse from Stephansplatz and turn right; it's a block and a half down on the left). ☎ *0222/512-6177. Reservations recommended.* **U-Bahn:** *Stephansplatz.* **Main courses:** *90–198AS ($7.20–$15.85). No credit cards.* **Open:** *Lunch and dinner daily. Closed Aug.*

Firenze Enoteca
$$$. Near Stephansdom. TUSCAN/ITALIAN.
Vienna's premier Italian restaurant can be a welcome break from an overdose of schnitzel. The Renaissance decor includes reproduction frescoes, and the food includes such central Italian delicacies as penne with salmon, spaghetti with seafood, and veal cutlets. Forget the beer for a while and order a bottle of Chianti with your meal.

Singerstrasse 3 (1 short block south of Stephansplatz, Singerstrasse branches off to the left/east; the restaurant is 2½ blocks down). ☎ *0222/513-4374. Reservations recommended.* **U-Bahn:** *Stephansplatz.* **Main courses:** *100–350AS ($8–$28). AE, DC, MC, V.* **Open:** *Lunch and dinner daily.*

Griechenbeisl
$$$$$. North of Stephansdom. AUSTRIAN.
This 550-year-old restaurant of low vaulted ceilings and iron chandeliers has been pleasing taste buds long enough to count Beethoven and Mark Twain among its patrons. The hearty cookery includes such mouth-watering foods as Hungarian goulash and venison steak. Accordion and zither music liven things up at dinner.

Quick Bites

You'll never want for food on the run in Vienna, which offers everything from sidewalk schnitzel to pastry *objets d'art* in 19th-century **konditoreien** (pastry bakeries, often doubling as cafes). Generally, you'll get excellent light meals at any of Vienna's numerous and often grand **cafes** (see "Other Fun Stuff to Do"), but to get the quickest bite, just saunter up to a sidewalk **würstelstand** and order the most appetizing-looking sausage *mit senf* (with mustard; usually served with a roll) and a beer or soda. Less mobile meals can be had at **Buffet Trzesniewski** (☎ 0222/512-3291), Dorotheergasse 1, which was neighbor Franz Kafka's favorite spot for a wide selection of scrumptious finger sandwiches and beer. **Picnic** pickings are best at the **Naschmarkt,** an open-air produce and food market stretching south (away from the Ring) from Karlsplatz. (On Saturdays, the operation expands to add flea market stalls; the market is closed Saturday afternoon and Sunday.)

Fleischmarkt 11 (From Swedenplatz, take Laurenzerberg away from the Canalto Fleischmarkt and turn right). ☎ **0222/533-1977** *or 0222/533-1947. Reservations required.* **U-Bahn:** *Swedenplatz.* **Tram:** *N, Z.* **Main courses:** *270–445AS ($21.60–$35.60). AE, DC, MC, V.* **Open:** *Lunch and dinner daily.*

Kardos

$$$. East of Stephansdom. HUNGARIAN/BALKAN.

A cellar restaurant of Gypsy-rustic accents, Kardos serves dishes that stem from the days when Austria's empire extended much farther eastward. Tasty morsels include *grammel* rolls stuffed with minced pork and spices, Balkan fish soup, and grilled meats. Start with the Hungarian apricot aperitif *barack.*

Dominikaner Bastei 8 (Take Wollzeile several long blocks east of Stephansdom and turn left up Stuben Bastei, which becomes Dominikaner Bastei). ☎ *0222/ 512-6949. Reservations recommended.* **U-Bahn:** *Schwedenplatz.* **Main courses:** *100–220AS ($8–$17.60). AE, MC, V.* **Open:** *Lunch and dinner Tues–Sat.*

Waltzing Through Vienna's Sights

There are plenty of city orientation tours, but why pay $20 when a tram ticket gets you the same thing minus the stilted commentary? Armed with a good map, the cheapest and most fun tour is **self-guided.** Buy an all-day ticket, step onto the #1 or #2 tram, and ride it all the way around the Ring, hopping on and off at sights where you want to spend time. The whole ride only takes half an hour if you don't get off. After you're oriented, you can abandon the tram to visit the sights off the Ring, such as the Hofburg Palace and Stephansdom. The tourist office has a brochure called *Walks in Vienna* that can fill you in on other, more organized guided tours.

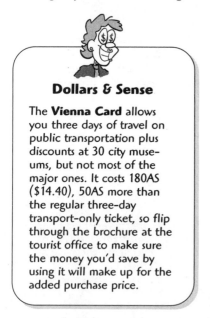

Dollars & Sense

The **Vienna Card** allows you three days of travel on public transportation plus discounts at 30 city museums, but not most of the major ones. It costs 180AS ($14.40), 50AS more than the regular three-day transport-only ticket, so flip through the brochure at the tourist office to make sure the money you'd save by using it will make up for the added purchase price.

Vienna Sights Not to Miss

Stephansdom (St. Stephan's Cathedral)

Vienna's epicenter is this 12th- to 14th-century church, which has been a visual and cultural landmark for centuries (Mozart's pauper funeral was held here in 1791). Inside are some fanciful tombs, a nifty 15th-century carved wooden altar, and a crypt filled with urns containing the entrails of the Hapsburgs. Climb the 450-foot, 343-stepped **Steffl** (south tower) for a panorama of Vienna and a close-up view of the distinctive roof with its colorful pattern of mosaic-like tiling. The unfinished north tower offers a less impressive view, but you can see the Danube from there.

Stephansplatz. ☎ *0222/51-552.* **U-Bahn:** *Stephansplatz.* **Open:** *church, daily 6am–10pm; north tower, daily 9am–6pm; south tower, daily 9am–5:30pm; catacomb tours, Mon–Sat at 10, 11, and 11:30am and daily at 2, 2:30, 3:30, 4, and 4:30pm.* **Admission:** *The church is free, but the south tower costs 25AS ($2) for adults, 15AS ($1.20) for students, 5AS (40¢) for kids under 15. The catacombs and the north tower each cost 40AS ($3.20) for adults, 15AS ($1.20) for children under 15.*

Hofburg Palace

Spread over many blocks with multiple entrances is the jumbled complex of Hofburg, started in 1279 and added on to more or less continuously until 1913. The main entrance on Michaelerplatz leads into the grand courtyard of In der Burg. From here, you can enter the **Kaiserappartments** or **Imperial Apartments** (☎ 0222/533-7570). The Hofburg was the Hapsburgs' winter home, and the private apartments of the imperial family are decorated in the lavish style you'd expect from monarchs who considered themselves gods, and who had been in power since the 13th century. Next door is the **Silberkammer,** with silver and porcelain collected from 18th- and 19th-century Hapsburg table settings.

Bet You Didn't Know

The remains of the former imperial family are spread around Vienna. The Hapsburg entrails are in Stephansdom, their hearts are in the Augustinerkirche, and the bodies—at least what's left of them—are in the Kapuziner Church.

The other top attraction at the Hofburg is the **Schatzkammer** Imperial Treasury (☎ 0222/533-7931), which you enter through the Swiss Court (off the left of the In der Burg courtyard). This is Europe's greatest treasury, a collection of historic jewelry and gems that impresses even the most jaded of visitors. From a heavy, jewel-encrusted crown first worn in A.D. 962 to sets of extravagant imperial robes dating back to the 12th century, this museum glitters like few others.

A third section of the vast palace worth taking in is the **Neue Burg,** or New Castle (☎ 0222/521-770), built in the early 20th century with a stately curving facade. The several museums inside are all on the same ticket and house collections of, in descending order of interest: historical musical instruments (many used by famous composers); arms and armor (great stuff, from crossbows to pistols); classical statues

Extra! Extra!

The audio tour of Neue Burg's musical instrument collection may be in German, but it's worth lugging along because it treats you to snippets of period music featuring the instruments.

(mainly from the Greco-Turkish site of Ephesus); and ethnography (featuring the only intact Aztec feather headdresses in the world).

The palace takes up many square city blocks, but the main entrance is on Michaelerplatz. Each section has its own phone number, which is listed in the previous description. **U-Bahn:** Herrengasse or Stephansplatz (walk down Graben, then left onto Kohlmarkt). **Tram:** 1, 2, D, J. **Open:** Kaiserappartments/Silberkammer, Mon–Sat 8:30am–4:30pm, Sun 8:30am–1pm; Schatzkammer and Neue Burg, Wed–Mon 10am–6pm. **Admission:** Kaiserappartments/Silberkammer by tour only (and in German, to boot) for 70AS ($5.60); Schatzkammer, for 60AS ($4.80) adults, 30AS ($2.40) for students, children, and seniors; Neue Burg, 30AS ($2.40) for adults, 15AS ($1.20) for children.

Staatsoper (State Opera House)

One of the most important opera houses in the world, Vienna's opulent Staatsoper opened in 1869 with a performance of Mozart's *Don Giovanni* and has counted Mahler and Richard Strauss among its musical directors. You can tour it during the day, but it's even better to attend a performance there at night (see "Other Fun Stuff to Do").

Opernring 2. ☎ *0222/514-442-959. U-Bahn: Oper or Karlsplatz. Tram: 1, 2, D, J, 62, 65. Open: The ever-changing schedule of tours (2–5 daily) is posted at the entrance. Admission: Tours cost 40AS ($3.20) for adults, 25AS ($2) for students.*

Kunsthistoriches Museum

This excellent art collection is one of Vienna's must-sees; it's 100 rooms filled with paintings and sculpture from the Renaissance on, along with ancient Egyptian and Greek art. From the Flemish, Dutch, and German schools come works by Memling, van Dyck, Rembrandt, and especially Breughel the Elder—over half of his known works are here. Also don't miss Dürer's *Blue Madonna;* Vermeer's *The Artist's Studio;* and works by Italian masters Titian, Raphael, Veronese, Caravaggio, and Giorgione. Of the ancient works, the tops are the *Gemma Augustea,* which is a Roman cameo carved from onyx, and the museum's mascot, a pudgy little blue hippopotamus from 2000 B.C. Egypt.

The museum is in a massive 19th-century building on Maria Theresien Platz (across the Burgring from the Neue Burg). ☎ *0222/521-770. U-Bahn: Babenburgerstrasse. Tram: 1, 2, D, J. Open: Tues–Sun 10am–6pm. Admission: 95AS ($7.60) adults, 60AS ($4.80) students and seniors, free for children under 11.*

Akademie der Bildenden Kunste (Academy of Fine Arts)

If you have time, try to squeeze in this gallery's small but choice collection of paintings spanning the 15th to 17th centuries. It features a 1504 *Last Judgment* by Hieronymus Bosch (a precursor of the surrealists), as well as a teenage *Self Portrait* by Van Dyck; passels of Rubens; Guardi's Venice scenes; and works by Rembrandt, Botticelli, and Cranach the Elder.

Schillerplatz 3 (just south of the Staatsoper). ☎ *0222/58-816.* **U-Bahn:**
Karlsplatz. **Tram:** *1, 2, D, J, 62, 65.* **Open:** *Tues, Thurs, and Fri 10am–1pm,*
Wed 10am–1pm and 3–6pm, Sat–Sun 9am–1pm. **Admission:** *30AS ($2.40).*

Bet You Didn't Know

One of the most idiosyncratic artists of the late Renaissance mannerist movement was the Milan-born **Archimboldo,** whose paintings are an ingenious
hybrid of portraiture and still life. He took thematically similar everyday objects
and cobbled them together to look like a face from afar. For example,
Summer has a rosy peach for a cheek, a pear chin, a grape eyeball, a corncob
ear, teeth of peas, and a fat cucumber of a nose. They are ostensibly allegories
of the elements and seasons, but more than one bears a suspicious resemblance
to caricatures of contemporary monarchs and other notables—craggy, wooden-
faced *Winter* is really Francis I of France and flame-haired *Fire* just may be
Emperor Maximillian II himself. All these works are on display at the
Kunsthistoriches Museum.

Scloss Schönbrunn

Vienna's last great sight lies four miles outside town. This rococo playground
of Empress Maria Theresa was the Hapsburgs' summer palace after its mid-
18th century completion. The palace sprawls, but only 40 of its 1,441 rooms
are open to the public. There are two audio tours of the gold-leafed, stuccoed, and chandeliered state apartments.
The basic "Imperial Tour" costs 80AS
($6.40), but for only 30AS ($2.40) more,
the "Grand Tour" walks you through
almost twice as many rooms. If you show
up at the right time, you can join a guided
tour as well. (Call ahead for tour costs and
times; in summer they can leave as frequently as every half-hour.) Make sure you
poke around the grandiose baroque gardens, complete with 18th-century "Roman
ruins." If you're into imperial coaches, pop
into the Wagenburg carriage museum.

Bet You Didn't Know

Child prodigy Mozart once
played for the bemused
court at Schloss Schönbrunn.
After Maria Theresa
expressed her approval of
the lad's performance,
the six-year-old genius
shocked the decorum police
(and probably his atten-
dant father as well) by
brazenly hopping into the
Empress's lap.

Schönbrunner Schlossstrasse. ☎ *0222/*
81-113. **U-Bahn:** *U4.* **Open:** *Palace,*
daily Apr–Oct 8:30am–5pm, Nov–Mar
9am–4:30pm; Gardens, daily until sunset.
Admission: *95AS ($7.60) adults, 40AS*
($3.20) for kids 6–15; tours extra.

Other Fun Stuff to Do

➤ **Spend a Night at the Opera.** Vienna's **Staatsoper** is one of the world's finest theaters, and its performances are not to be missed, even if you aren't an opera fan. The season runs September to June, and you can get tickets at the box office one month in advance by calling ☎ **0222/514-440** or six days in advance by calling ☎ **0222/513-1513** or stopping at the Bundestheaterkasse at Goethegasse 1.

Dollars & Sense

Standing room *Praterrestehplatz* tickets at the Staastoper are sold for a mere 30AS ($2.40) on the day of the performance. Show up three hours early to wait in line and bring a scarf or something to tie around the railing at your standing spot. This scarf will save your place so you can wander through gilded rooms and mingle with the black–tie crowd until the performance begins.

➤ **Drink Java, Eat Strudel, and People-watch at a Kaffeehaus.** By legend, Vienna's first **coffeehouse** was established in 1683, and coffeehouses have been going strong ever since. One of the grandest is Freud's old hangout, the chandeliered Café Landtmann at Dr. Karl Lueger Ring 4 (☎ **0222/532-0621**). The granddaddy of all Viennese cafes is Café Demel (☎ **0222/533-5516**), which moved to Kohlmarkt 14 in 1888; the ornate decor really hasn't changed since. You can order your *kaffee* many ways, the most popular being *schwarzer* (black), *melange* (mixed with hot milk), or *mit schlagobers* (topped with whipped cream).

➤ **Get Down with the Vienna Boys Choir.** The world's most popular religious warblers have been a Viennese institution since 1498, training such talents as Joseph Hayden and Franz Schubert. The lyrical lads sing Mass on Sundays and religious holidays (September to June only) at 9:15am in the Hofburg's Burgkapelle, accompanied by members of the Staatsoper chorus and orchestra. You can pick up tickets at the box office the preceding Friday from 5 to 6pm (line up early; this is one of the few times you'll find people shelling out $6 to $27 to go to church; standing room is free, but you still need a ticket). You can also reserve tickets eight weeks in advance by writing to: Verwaltung der Hofmusikkapelle, Hofburg, A-1010 Vienna, Austria.

➤ **Take a Spin on the *Riesenrad* in Prater Park.** A former imperial hunting ground on the Danube Canal, Prater Park witnessed the birth of the waltz in 1820, courtesy of Johann Strauss, Sr. Besides the requisite greenery, the park is home to both a year-round fair-like amusement park with plenty of restaurants, food stands, a beer garden, and the **Riesenrad**—at 220 feet and 100 years, one of the world's oldest (and slowest) operating Ferris wheels.

➤ **See the Horse Ballet at the Spanish Riding School.** You don't have to attend a show to see the world-famous **Lippizaner horses** strut their stuff at the Hofburg's Spanish Riding School in a tradition dating to the 16th century. The complicated baroque choreography of the stallions' shows, based on ancient battle maneuvers, needs to be practiced regularly (usually mornings 10am to noon). Tickets for these training sessions are available from travel agencies or at the door for about $10 without music, $23 with music. If only the full show will do (mornings March through June and September through December), reserve a ticket as far in advance as possible by faxing ☎ **0222/ 535-0186;** tickets run $18 to $76.

➤ **Take a *Heuriger* crawl in Grinzig.** *Heurige* is the name of both Viennese new wines and the rustic taverns that serve them. Most **heuriger** cluster around the fringes of the famous Vienna Woods, a 15-minute ride northwest of the city center. The tradition's capital is the former village, now suburb, of Grinzing, home to around 20 taverns (take tram 38 to get there). It's become very popular, but at least the influx of visitors will guarantee that the village stays looking medieval. Stroll down Cobenzigasse, stopping in one heurige after another. Sample each one's local wine while you listen to atmospheric accordion and zither music.

Get Outta Town: Excursions from Vienna

Though the two side trips I recommend here, Salzburg and Innsbruck, are technically in Austria, it is faster and more convenient to travel to each of them from Munich, Germany (covered in the previous chapter). Directions from both Munich and Vienna are provided in the following sections.

The Hills Are Alive with the Sound of Salzburg

Salzburg is a musical city, birthplace of Mozart and original home of the real-life singing von Trapp family, who warbled their way out of Nazi clutches in *The Sound of Music.* The church-filled old city is hemmed in on one side by the Salzach river and on the other by a curling set of cliffs and a glowering medieval fortress. You can do this pretty baroque burg in a day, but it takes two if you plan on the *Sound of Music* tour. Half-hourly **trains** from Vienna (3½ hours) and 10 daily trains from Munich (1½ to 2 hours) arrive at Hauptbahnhof, a 20-minute walk (or five-minute ride on bus 1, 5, 6, or 51) from

Dollars & Sense

The **Salzburg Card** gets you free travel on all public transportation, along with discounts or free admission to all of the city's sights, even the top ones. It's available at the tourist offices and costs 180AS ($14.40) for 24 hours, 260AS ($20.80) for two days, and 350AS ($28) for three days.

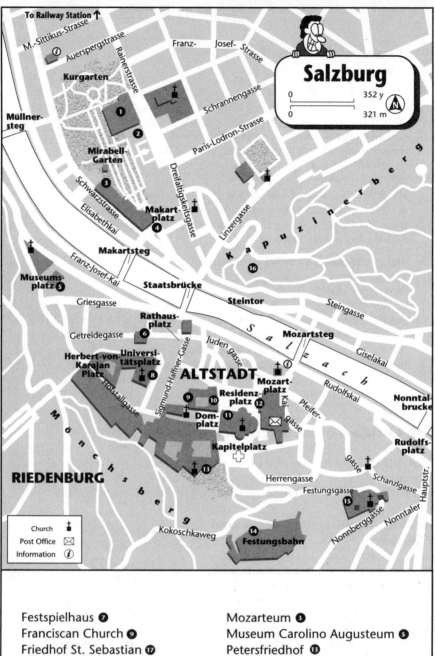

Salzburg

0 — 352 y
0 — 321 m

To Railway Station ↑

M.-Sittikus-Strasse
Auerspergstrasse
Rainerstrasse
Franz- Josef- Strasse
Schrannengasse
Kurgarten
Paris-Lodron-Strasse
Mirabell-Garten
Dreifaltigkeitsgasse
Linzergasse
Schwarzstrasse
Makart-platz
Elisabethkai
Makartsteg
Museums-platz
Franz-Josef-Kai
Staatsbrücke
Kapuzinerberg
Griesgasse
Steintor
Steingasse
Rathaus-platz
Mozartsteg
Getreidegasse
Juden Gasse
Giselakai
Salzach
Herbert-von-Karajan Platz
Universi-tätsplatz
ALTSTADT
Mozart-platz
Rudolfskai
Nonntal-brucke
Hofstallgasse
Sigmund-Haffner-Gasse
Residenz-platz
Pfeifer-gasse
Dom-platz
Kai Gasse
Rudolfs-platz
Kapitelplatz
Schanzlgasse
Hauptstr.
RIEDENBURG
Mönchsberg
Herrengasse
Festungsgasse
Nonntaler
Kokoschkaweg
Festungsbahn
Nonnbergasse
Nonntaler

Church ✝
Post Office ✉
Information ⓘ

Festspielhaus ❼
Franciscan Church ❾
Friedhof St. Sebastian ⑰
Glockenspiel ⑫
Hohensalzburg Fortress ⑭
Kapunzinerkloster ⑯
Kollegienkirche ❽
Mozart Geburtshaus ❻
Mozart Wohnhaus ❹

Mozarteum ❸
Museum Carolino Augusteum ❺
Petersfriedhof ⑬
Residenz ❿
Salzburg Cathedral ⑪
Salzburger Barockmuseum ❷
Schloss Mirabell ❶
Stift Nonnberg ⑮
St. Peter's Cemetery ⑬

348

the center of town. There's a **tourist information** booth in the station at track 2A; the main office is on Mozartplatz (☎ **0662/847-568**) in the town center.

The city center seems more a series of interconnected squares than a grid of streets, giving the city a very cozy, homey feel. The Domplatz square is anchored by Salzburg's fine **Cathedral,** one of the finest Italianate buildings north of the Alps; Mozart was baptized here and once served as organist. Speaking of the young musical prodigy, one of the city's top sights is the **Mozart Geburtshaus,** or birth house, (☎ **0662/844-313**) at Getreidegasse 9. The third-floor apartment is just stuffed with musical mementos from letters and sheet music to portraits (the unfinished one by his brother is thought to be the truest to life of any Mozart likeness) and the varied instruments on which the young master honed his talents.

Tourist Traps

A requisite Salzburg experience is the half-day *Sound of Music* tour—as cheesy as it sounds, but fun. For about 350AS ($28), you get a quick once-over of the city and the buildings featured in the film, and then it's off to the terribly scenic hills, alive with the sounds of singing tourists. The best outfits are **Salzburg Panorama Tours** (☎ **0662/883-2110**) on Mirabellplatz and **Bob's Special Tours** (☎ **0662/849-5110**) at Kaigasse 19.

The hauntingly beautiful **St. Peter's Cemetery** is shoehorned up against, and in some parts dug into, the cliffs behind the south side of the cathedral. Nearby on Festungsgasse, a funicular (cable car) takes you up the cliffside to **Hohensalzburg Fortress** (☎ **0662/8424-3011**). The castle tour grants you access to the apartments, torture chambers, and arms museum of the largest completely preserved fortress in Central Europe. Built from the 11th to the 17th centuries, this was once the safe house of Salzburg's ruling archbishops.

The thoroughly Austrian **Krimpelstätter** (☎ **0662/432-274**), at Müllner Haptstrasse 31, has been satisfying Salzburger appetites for 450 years with würstel and wild game dishes, washed down with tankards of beer. The **Hotel Blaue Gans,** (☎ **0662/841-317,** fax: 0662/841-3179) at Getreidegasse 43, has small but comfortable rooms in a 700-year-old building near Mozart's birthplace. Doubles run 650 to 1,700AS ($52 to $136). If this hotel is full, the tourist office will **book rooms** for you for a deposit and a 30AS ($2.40) fee.

Out & About in Innsbruck

Innsbruck, imperial home away from home and occasional host to the Winter Olympics, is a sleepy little gem of a town, nestled amid a ring of stupendous Alps on a milky white river. This city-sized village is also a base for some of the best skiing, hiking, and scenic drives around. Ten daily trains arrive at **Hauptbahnhof** from Vienna (5 hours away), passing through Salzburg (2 hours away). The nearby German city of Munich sends 14 trains daily (1½ to 2 hours away).

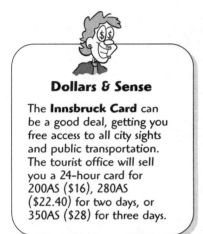

Dollars & Sense

The **Innsbruck Card** can be a good deal, getting you free access to all city sights and public transportation. The tourist office will sell you a 24-hour card for 200AS ($16), 280AS ($22.40) for two days, or 350AS ($28) for three days.

The **tourist office** (☎ 0512/59-850) is at no. 3 Burggraben, which rings the Altstadt at the end of Maria Theresien Strasse. This street ducks under a triumphal arch to become the rustic, souvenir shop-lined **Herzog Friedrich Strasse.** Near the end of this street is the **Stadtturm** tower, offering views over the rooftops to the surrounding Alps. The street ends in a wide spot overlooked by the **Goldenes Dachl,** an overblown imperial balcony erected and gilded for Emperor Maximillian I in the 16th century as a box seat for the festivities on the square below.

Turn right on Universitätsstrasse then left on Rennweg for a half-hour tour of the exuberant, curving, rococo stylings of Maria Theresa's **Hofburg** palace (☎ 0512/587-186). Next door is the equally rococo **Dom** (cathedral), its altar decorated by Cranach the Elder's *Maria Hilf*. Across from the Hofburg on Universitätsstrasse is the **Hofkirche,** containing a massive, statue-ridden monument to Maximillian I. Next door is the **Tiroler Volkskunst-Museum** (☎ 0512/584-302), a folk museum celebrating everyday life in the history of the Tyrol district.

Extra! Extra!

The zoo sits at the base of the **Hungerburg plateau,** which offers magnificent city views. From here, the Nordkette cable rail rides into the mountain wilderness to Hafelekar, a 7,655-foot vista and trail base for Alpine hikes. Check with Innsbruck's tourist office about year-round **glacier ski packages** that include both lift tickets and rentals for as low as 550AS ($44).

Outside the Alstadt is the **Alpenzoo** (☎ **0512/292-323**) at Weiherburggasse 37, all but clinging to the side of an Alp and featuring animals indigenous to the region. From the center, cross the Inn river, turn right, and follow the signs a long way; you can also take bus C, D, or E or tram 1 or 6 to Hungerburg, where you catch the funicular up to the zoo.

Quell your hunger pangs at the inexpensive **Restaurant Ottoburg** (☎ **0512/574-652**) at Herzog Friedrich Strasse 1, an Austrian tradition since 1745. The **City-Hotel Goldene Krone** (☎ **0512/586-160,** fax: 0512/ 580-1896) at Maria Theresien Strasse 46, offers modern comforts in a baroque house just outside the Altstadt. Doubles run 880 to 1,320AS ($70.40 to $105.60).

Chapter 20

Bern & the
Swiss Alps

In This Chapter

➤ Picturesque lakeside villages perfect for strolling

➤ Alps adventures that take you to new heights

➤ The lowdown on skiing, both cross-country and alpine

➤ Artful excursions to Zurich and Basel

I'm handling this chapter a little differently than the others. Although the Swiss capital of Bern is a fine place to visit—and, unlike Switzerland's larger cities, still has an almost medieval, Swiss village feel—the real attractions of this country are those mighty, snow-covered Swiss Alps. Half of the sights, hotels, and restaurants I'll recommend will be in Bern; the rest will be south of the city in the Bernese Oberland region that encompasses the legendary peak Jungfrau, Queen of the Alps.

Dollars & Sense

The Swiss unit of currency is the Swiss franc (SFr), divided into 100 centimes. Roughly, $1 equals 1.5SFr; or 1SFr equals 66¢. Swiss coins include 5, 10, 20, and 50 centimes and 1, 2, and 5 francs. Bills come in denominations of 10, 20, 50, 100, 500, and 1,000 francs.

The gateway to the Bernese Oberland is **Interlaken,** a bustling resort town in the foothills of the Alps that is flanked by a pair of lakes and is just a one-hour train ride from Bern. Interlaken itself doesn't have too much to hold your interest, but it makes an optimal base—and a requisite stop—for forays into the Bernese Oberland. The Alps are scattered with tiny villages and quaint resort towns. One of the most visitor-friendly of these is **Mürren,** where you'll notice I've recommended a few restaurants and hotels. Although I think the region deserves at least three or four days, especially for hikers, on the tightest of schedules you could take an overnight train to Interlaken, switch for a train up to Jungfraujoch to spend the day, and make it back to Interlaken by evening for another overnight train out—but that's pushing it.

Getting Your Bearings

The **Bern Tourist Office** (☎ 031/311-6611) is in the bahnhof (train station). For information on the Bernese Oberland and the Alps, the **Tourism Organization Interlaken** (☎ 036/222-121) is the unofficial central information bureau, with maps and advice on getting around the region. It's in the Hotel Metropole at Höheweg 37, near Westbahnhof station.

Bern's Basic Layout

Bern's most interesting section, the pedestrianized **Altstadt** (Old City), is very small and easily navigable on foot. Tucked into a sharp, U-shaped bend of the **Aare River,** it's basically made up of five long, arcaded streets whose names change at every block. Imagine this bend of the Aare as a sideways "U." At the open (western) end of the U is the **Hauptbahnhof** train station. From here, follow the Spitalgasse east into the heart of the Altstadt (old city). The street's name soon changes to **Marktgasse,** the main road of the old city. Just south of the Altstadt, across the Aare, are several museums and the embassy district (take the Kirchenfeldbrücke Bridge to get there).

Interlaken & Getting Around the Bernese Oberland

There are hourly **trains between Bern and Interlaken** (a 50- to 60-minute ride). Get off at Interlaken's Westbahnhof station to go to the city itself and at Ostbahnhof station to transfer to trains into the Jungfrau region. **Interlaken** lies on a brief stretch of the Aare River (yes, the same river that runs through Bern) that connects two lakes, Lake Thun and Lake Brienz—hence the city's name, which means "between the lakes." Its busiest tourist area stretches between the two train stations along the Aare. The road that connects the stations is Bahnhof Strasse, which becomes the park-like Höheweg.

Now about those **Alps.** The Bernese Oberland is large, but this chapter stays with the western half—it's the most popular and the easiest to reach from Interlaken. Imagine you're standing in Interlaken and looking south toward the **Alps.** There are low mountains directly in front of you. Behind them, to the east, is a trio of enormous peaks called Eiger, Mönch, and, the most famous, **Jungfrau.**

Tourist Traps

Switzerland is a linguistic potpourri. There are four official languages: Italian in the southernmost corner; French in the west; Romansch in a small zone of the east; and, mainly, Schwyzerdütsch, a German dialect that even most Germans can't understand. You'll get by fine with High German, however, and with so many local languages already in their arsenal, most citizens have found it easy to tack English on as a fourth or fifth tongue.

Farther off to the west is the slightly more modest peak of the **Schilthorn.** Running south from Interlaken between the Jungfrau and Schilthorn is a wide valley called the **Lauterbrunnen;** this is where the area's main train line leads to various Alpine destinations (halfway up the valley in the town of Lauterbrunnen is a station where you'll find yourself transferring trains frequently). Between Interlaken and Lauterbrunnen town, the Alpine foothills are interrupted by a valley that branches off to the east from Lauterbrunnen Valley. Train tracks lead through here to the village of **Grindelwald.** Scattered throughout this area are many other small resorts and alpine towns, such as **Mürren** (at the base of the Schilthorn).

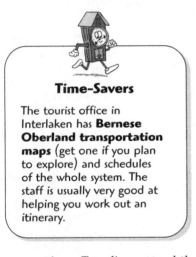

Time-Savers

The tourist office in Interlaken has **Bernese Oberland transportation maps** (get one if you plan to explore) and schedules of the whole system. The staff is usually very good at helping you work out an itinerary.

Unfortunately, the various scenic and private **rail lines**—not to mention funiculars, ski lifts, and cable cars—that connect the peaks and towns are ridiculously expensive. Rail passes such as Swissrail or Eurail only get you a 25% discount at most. Always ask about discounts for children, seniors, students, and so on. For each of the sights in this chapter, I've given specific directions and some idea of the frequency of trains and connections. Traveling around the Bernese Oberland means plenty of train changes, but this usually turns out to be kind of fun (if pricey). The wait between connections is usually kept to 5 to 10 minutes. Because the schedule is consistent, and trains tend to run hourly, it's fairly easy to hop off at any station, go see whatever town you've stopped in, and pick up the transfer an hour or two later.

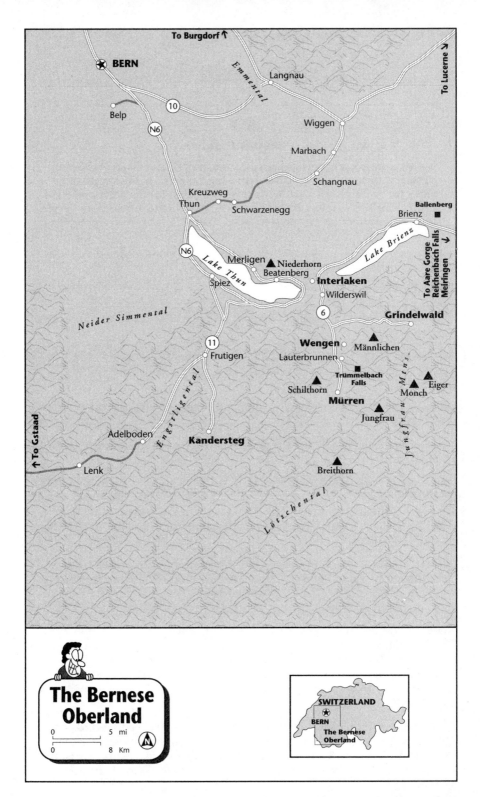

To Burgdorf ↑

BERN

To Lucerne ↘

Langnau

Emmental

Belp

10

N6

Wiggen

Marbach

Schangnau

Kreuzweg

Thun

Schwarzenegg

Ballenberg

Brienz

N6

Lake Thun

Merligen

Niederhorn

Beatenberg

Spiez

Lake Brienz

To Aare Gorge
Reichenbach Falls
Meiringen ↘

Interlaken

Wilderswil

Grindelwald

6

Neider Simmental

11

Frutigen

Wengen

Lauterbrunnen

Männlichen

Jungfrau Mtns.

Engstligental

Schilthorn

Trümmelbach
Falls

Mönch

Eiger

↑ To Gstaad

Adelboden

Mürren

Jungfrau

Kandersteg

Lenk

Breithorn

Lötschental

**The Bernese
Oberland**

0   5 mi

0   8 Km

SWITZERLAND

★
BERN

The Bernese
Oberland

Dollars & Sense

There is a **Bernese Oberland pass** for 185SFr ($123.35) adults, 93SFr ($62) children 6 to 16, but it only works on some train lines, so don't invest in it unless you're sure it will pay off. More likely to work to your advantage is the **Family Card.** For around 20SFr ($13.35), this card lets children under 16 ride free and unmarried young adults between 16 and 25 get half off the regular price.

Bern Fast Facts

American Express   Bern's American Express office at Bubenbergplatz 11 (☎ 031/311-9401) is open Monday to Friday 8:30am to 6pm and Saturday 9am to noon.

Doctors/hospitals   For a list of doctors and dentists, dial ☎ 031/311-2211. For emergency care, go to **Insel Hospital,** Freiburgstrasse (☎ 031/632-2111).

Embassy   The U.S. Embassy is located at Jubiläumsstr 93 (☎ 031/357-7011).

Emergency   Dial ☎ 117 for the police, ☎ 144 for an ambulance, or ☎ 118 to report a fire. For help when your car breaks down, call ☎ 140.

Pharmacies   **Central-Apotheke Volz & Co.,** Zeitglockenlaub 2 (☎ 031/311-1094), has English-speaking attendants. Located near the Clock Tower, it's open Monday 9am to 6:30pm, Tuesday to Friday 7:45am to 6:30pm, and Saturday 7:45am to 4pm. For information about 24-hour pharmacies, dial ☎ 031/311-2211.

Safety   With the exception of the park surrounding Parliament (where heroin addicts roam after dark), you'll feel comfortable on the streets of central Bern day or night. Don't let your sense of safety lull you into carelessness, however; take the usual precautions to protect yourself against crime.

Taxis   If you're restricting your sightseeing to the tiny Altstadt, you'll do fine on foot. If, however, you plan to venture far beyond the old city, you can find a cab at a taxi rank (stand), or call ☎ 031/311-1818 or 031/301-5353. The initial charge is 6.50SFr ($4.30) and 2.70SFr ($1.80) for each kilometer thereafter. On Sunday and at night, the per-kilometer charge rises to 3SFr ($2).

Telephone   A local call in Bern costs 70 centimes (45¢). Phonecards, available at post offices and train stations, come in denominations of 10SFr ($6.65) and 20SFr ($13.35). Dial ☎ 111 for directory assistance. Switzerland's country code is **41.** Bern's city code is **031.** If you're calling Bern from beyond Switzerland's borders, drop the city code's initial zero. To call Bern from the United States, dial **011-41-31** followed by the phone number.

To charge your call to a calling card, dial the appropriate number: **AT&T** (☎ 0800/890-011), **MCI** (☎ 0800/890-222), or **Sprint** (☎ 0800/155-9777). To dial the United States directly from Bern, dial **001** followed by the area code and phone number.

Transit Info　Call ☎ **031/157-3333** for rail information. For bus information, call ☎ **031/386-6565**.

Hotels with Altitude: The Bern & Bernese Oberland's Hotel Scene

Bern is small for a national capital, and conventions and international meetings overbook it regularly. For this reason, I've chosen some of town's larger hotels to try to maximize your chances of finding a room. Make reservations far in advance no matter what the time of year, or pay the folks at the tourist office 3SFr ($2) to book you a room.

When to Go?

Bern has no real **high season.** Interlaken has high season in the summer (the rates go way up at most hotels, but not at the ones I've listed in this section). Once you get up into the Alps, high season runs all year *except* during a brief period in mid-summer, when ski conditions are pretty sad.

Interlaken certainly doesn't lack hotels, but it also doesn't lack visitors to fill them. If you're having trouble locating a room, there's a hotel billboard with a phone outside each train station, or visit the tourist office, which will book you a room for free (heck, the office is even located in the town's most modern hotel). The tourist offices of **Mürren** and other Bernese Oberlander towns will help you find rooms as well, but these burgs are so small that you can do just as well following one of the many hotel signs as you exit the station.

Hotel Bern
$$$$. Bern, Altstadt.
Behind an Art Deco facade, this massive hotel is popular with diplomats and business travelers drawn to its comfortably furnished modern rooms and plethora of in-house restaurants. The best rooms open onto a garden courtyard.

Zeughausgasse 9 (between Kornhausplatz and Waisenhausplatz). ☎ *031/*
312-1021. Fax: 031/312-1147. Tram: 9. Rates: 230SFr ($153.35) double.
AE, DC, MC, V.

De la Paix
$$. Interlaken.
This hotel near the train station is managed by the friendly Etterli family.
Within the Gothic fairy tale of a building (complete with gabled roof) are
simple, comfortable rooms. This hotel is a good, central value.

Bernastrasse 24 (1 block from Interlaken West station). ☎ *036/227-044. Fax:*
036/228-728. Parking: Free. Rates: 108–160SFr ($72–$106.65) double.
AE, DC, MC, V. Closed Nov 10–Apr 10.

Hospiz Zur Heimat
$. Bern, Altstadt.
This hotel is about as good a deal as you're going to get in Bern. The building
dates from the 1700s, which seems to be the last time any staff member
cracked a smile. But the simple rooms are clean, you can get rock-bottom
rates if you choose a hall bath, and it's smack in the center of town.

Gerechtigkeitsgasse 50 (tucked into the river bend near Nydeggbrücke Bridge).
☎ *031/311-0436. Fax: 031/312-3386. Tram: 12. Parking: Free at night,*
8SFr ($5.30) during the day. Rates: 96–124SFr ($64–$82.65) double. AE, DC,
MC, V.

Hotel Ambassador
$$$. Bern, Altstadt.
A mile from the station and the town center, this inn offers standard
comforts and smallish rooms at good prices. The indoor pool and sauna are
a bonus, as are the good—if oddly out of place—Japanese garden and
restaurant.

Seftigenstrasse 99. ☎ *031/371-4111. Fax: 031/371-4117. Tram: 9. Parking:*
Free. Rates: 170–190SFr ($113.35–$126.65) double. AE, DC, MC, V.

Hotel Palace
$$$$$. Mürren.
This comfy if boring resort hotel, established early in the 20th century, has
recently received a much needed refurbishment (a boost to the pretty Alpine
architecture). Rooms have balconies, and the restaurant is passable. It's nothing special, though cheap by Mürren standards. Try not to get stuck in the
modern annex.

Mürren. ☎ *036/552-424. Fax: 036/552-417. Rates: 220–270SFr ($146.65–*
$180) for a double in summer, 270–330SFr ($180–$220) for a double in winter.
AE, DC, MC, V.

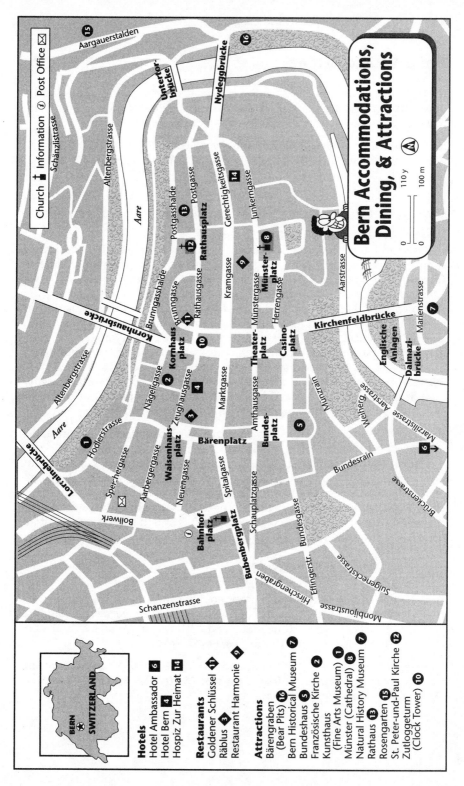

Hotel Weisses Kreuz

$$$$. Interlaken.

On the classiest drag in town, which is basically a city park, this all-year hotel has functionally spartan rooms. But the comfort is good, the price is right, and the people-watching from its terrace is unparalleled.

Höheweg (at the corner with Jungfraustrasse). ☎ *036/225-951.* **Fax:** *036/ 233-555.* **Parking:** *Free.* **Rates:** *210–230SFr ($140–$153.35) double. AE, DC, MC, V.*

Cheese, Chocolates, & Then Some: The Bernese Oberland's Restaurant Scene

Switzerland has taken culinary influences from the surrounding countries of Germany, France, and Italy, giving Swiss cooking a very international flavor. **Cheese** is, of course, a holey Swiss ingredient—and there are about 100 varieties besides the sour, hole-riddled Emmentaler we generically refer to as "Swiss cheese." Emmentaler and Gruyère, along with white wine, garlic, and lemon, often get thrown together in a melting crock, carried to your table, and called **fondue,** one of the country's specialties. (Everyone at your table gets a long spearing fork for dunking chunks of bread into the communal fondue pot.) Another national specialty is **raclette,** created when half a wheel of cheese is held over an open fire; when the exposed surface begins to melt, it is rushed over to you, and a melted layer is scraped off on your plate. This dish, too, is meant to be eaten with hunks of brown bread.

To go with your cheese, the Swiss offer the omnipresent **rösti** (a sort of delicious hash brown), lake fish, or **sausages.** Another typical Bernese dish is the **Bernerplatte,** a plate of sauerkraut or beans, piled with sausages, ham, pig's feet, bacon, or pork chops. Can't you just hear your arteries clogging? An excellent way to wash it all down is with one of Switzerland's fine white or light red wines or a hand-crafted local beer. Swiss **chocolates** are some of the world's finest (Nestlé is a Swiss company). Though some locals eat it at breakfast, many Americans find that a bit too rich so early in the morning.

Goldener Schlüssel

$$. Bern, Altstadt. SWISS.

You can tuck into hearty Swiss peasant cooking such as *schweinbratwurst mit zweibelsauce* (fried sausage in an onion sauce) and *mignon d'agneau* (lamb tenderloin) in this converted stone and wood 13th-century stable. Upstairs are 29 cozy doubles for rent for 105 to 128SFr ($70 to $85.35).

Rathausgasse 72 (in the center of town). ☎ *031/311-0216.* **Reservations** *recommended.* **Tram:** *9.* **Bus:** *12.* **Main courses:** *16.50–29.50SFr ($11–$19.65).* **Open:** *Lunch and dinner Tues–Sat.*

Il Bellini
$$$$$. Interlaken. ITALIAN.
One of the best Italian restaurants in Switzerland, this 19th-century styled place is a bit fancy, but well worth it. After an appetizer of prosciutto and melon, try the tasty minestrone and then a Florentine steak or veal *saltimbocca.*

Höheweg 37 (in the Hotel Metropol at the center of town). ☎ **036/212-151.** *Reservations recommended.* **Main courses:** *20–50SFr ($13.35–$33.35). AE, DC, MC, V.* **Open:** *Lunch and dinner daily.*

Räblus
$$$$$. Bern, Altstadt. FRENCH.
A 200-year-old building near the Clock Tower is the setting for the Swiss-accented French cuisine popular with Bern foodies. Pernod-flavored seafood potpourri, tournedos Rossini, and citrus-flavored veal are among the chef's specialties.

Zeugausgasse 3 (between Kornhausplatz and Waisenhausplatz). ☎ **031/ 311-5908.** *Reservations required.* **Tram:** *3, 9.* **Main courses:** *26–44SFr ($17.35–$29.35); fixed-price menu 44SFr ($29.35). AE, DC, MC, V.* **Open:** *Lunch and dinner Mon–Sat. Closed July 18–Aug 16.*

⭐Kids Restaurant Harmonie
$$$. Bern, Altstadt. SWISS/BERNESE.
This family-run spot dishes up lovely Bernese home-cooked meals. Sausages with rösti, tripe with tomatoes, and traditional cheese fondues top the list. If the ivy-shaded sidewalk tables are occupied, then hole up in the Art Nouveau interior.

Hotelgasse 3 (at the corner of Münstergasse). ☎ **031/311-3840.** *Reservations recommended.* **Tram:** *9.* **Main courses:** *15–35SFr ($10–$23.35). No credit cards.* **Open:** *Lunch Tues–Sat, dinner Mon–Fri. Closed mid-July to mid-Aug.*

Restaurant im Gruebi
$$$$. Mürren. SWISS.
Located in the Hotel Jungfrau, this restaurant excels in both mountain views (from its outdoor terrace or the glassed-in hexagonal dining room) and local cuisine, from herb-flavored rack of lamb for two to fondue bourguignonne.

In the Hotel Jungfrau (follow signs from the station). ☎ **036/552-824.** *Reservations recommended.* **Main courses:** *25–42SFr ($16.65–$28); fixed-price lunch 19SFr ($12.65). AE, DC, MC, V.* **Open:** *Lunch and dinner daily.*

Restaurant Piz Gloria
$$$$. Schilthorn. SWISS.
To cap off an idyllic trip to the Swiss Alps, dine in Europe's most stratospheric restaurant—it slowly rotates on a dramatic perch atop a 9,804-foot mountain. If you can tear your eyes away from the view for a moment,

sample the hearty Hungarian goulash or sirloin steak. This place is also a good place to have a high-altitude breakfast if you catch the first cable car up.

Atop Schilthorn mountain, above Mürren. ☎ ***036/552-142.*** *Reservations suggested, but not required.* ***Cable car:*** *Cars depart from Mürren twice per hour starting around 7:30am (8am in winter); the trip takes 20 minutes and costs 53SFr ($35.35); the last car down leaves at 6pm (5pm in winter).* ***Main courses:*** *20–42SFr ($13.35–$28). AE, DC, MC, V.* ***Open:*** *Daily from the first cable car's arrival until the last one's departure. Closed Nov 15–Dec 15, 1 week in May, and during blizzards.*

Quick Bites

Your best bet for good, fast eats in **Bern** is the **Bärenplatz,** home to a fruit and veggies market (May through October) and lined with inexpensive cafes and pastry shops. One of the best, **Gfeller am Bärenplatz,** has a tea room, a reasonable Swiss restaurant, and a self-service cafeteria upstairs overlooking the lively square. **Mazot,** at no. 5, serves cheap fondues and rösti. Arcaded streets are also filled with kiosks selling *Gschnätzltes,* a Bern specialty of fried veal, beef, or pork (order *sur chabis* sauerkraut to go with it). The **Migros** supermarket at Marktgasse 46 can provide **picnic** ingredients (and has a cafeteria). There's a Migros in **Interlaken,** too, just to the right of Westbahnhof. It's a good place to fill your daypack for hikes.

Bern Sights Not to Miss

Bern's historic center is comfortably scenic and walkable with low-key sights such as the **Zutgloggeturm (Clock Tower),** which has treated Bern to a mechanical puppet show four minutes before every hour for over 460 years (on Kramgasse at the corner with Bärenplatz). Münsterplatz boasts both a **16th-century Moses fountain** and the **Münster (cathedral),** a Gothic structure from 1421. An elaborate *Last Judgment* is carved over the main door and enormous stained-glass windows await inside. The biggest draw of the cathedral, though, is its 300-foot belfry. Anyone who can handle the 270 steps is rewarded with a great panorama across Bern and its river with the Alps in the distance.

Of Bern's museums, the best is the **Kunsthaus,** or **Fine Arts Museum** (☎ **031/311-0944**) at Hodlerstrasse 12, a little ways north of the train station on the banks of the Aare. It's particularly strong in late 19th- and early 20th-century art, from the impressionists and surrealists to Kadinsky, Modigliani, Matisse, and Picasso; it also has the world's largest collection of Paul Klee works. Bern's most unique sight, though, has to be the

Bärengraben Bear Pits, just across Nydeggbrücke Bridge from the Altstadt. Since 1420, this place has been full of live, very well-fed examples of Bern's furry civic symbol. Beyond it stretches the **Rosengarten,** a fragrant flower garden that has killer views of medieval Bern.

Bet You Didn't Know

The Duke of Zähringen founded Bern on the Aare River in 1191. Because the new city had no name, he reputedly promised to call it after the first animal slain by his hunters in the surrounding woods. When they killed themselves a *Bär* (bear), he dutifully christened the town "Bärn," or Bern. I've always wondered if he would have stuck to his word had they returned with a chipmunk.

Getting High on the Alps: Exploring the Bernese Oberland

The Jungfrau region is dominated by the triple peaks of the Eiger (13,025 feet), Mönch (13,450 feet), and Jungfrau (13,642 feet). A trip through the area can be a thrilling, scenic ride on trains that hug (or punch through) cliffsides and ski-lift gondolas that dangle high above mountain glaciers.

The Queen Peak at Jungfraujoch

The most spectacular and rewarding excursion is to **Jungfraujoch,** where at 11,333 feet—the highest rail station in Europe—your breath is quickened both by the stupendous views and the extremely thin air. Switzerland's most famous thrill ride doesn't come cheap, and you'll be shelling out 146SFr ($97.35) for a round-trip, second-class ticket (thankfully, kids under 16 ride for free). Leave from Interlaken's Estbahnhof (trains every half hour or so), change once in Lauterbrunnen, and again in Kleine Scheidegg. This popular route runs like a machine well-oiled with tourist money, so the transfers are smooth, but the slow trip takes 2 hours, 20 minutes. For the last leg of the trip, four of the six miles of track are through tunnels, but the train pauses a few times to let you peer out through windows in the rock at the glaciated surroundings.

Time-Savers

Check **weather conditions** and forecasts with Interlaken's tourist office or by calling ☎ **036/225-252** before you set off into the mountains. An overcast day can make an excursion to the panoramic terraces of Jungfrau or Schilthorn a moot point, and the occasional avalanche warning might crimp your plans for that hike from Grindelwald.

An elevator takes you up from the station to the even higher **Sphinx Terrace** viewpoint to look out over Europe's longest glacier, the 14-mile Aletch. (Melt-off from this behemoth eventually makes its way into the Mediterranean.) The view seems to go on forever—on a clear day, you can even catch a glimpse of Germany's Black Forest. One of the main attractions up here is the **Eispalast (Ice Palace),** a maze of tunnels carved into a living glacier—this one moves rather slowly—and filled with whimsical ice sculptures, including a life-sized car. There are several restaurants around the station in case you didn't pack a lunch. On your way back down, you can hop off at Kleine Scheidegg station and take a different train to detour west through the village of Grindelwald (see "Hike the Hills from Grindelwald").

Tourist Traps

Make sure you prepare for the unique climate of the skyscraping Alps before you get on that train to the top of the world. A warm, sunny day in Interlaken may still be sunny atop the Jungfrau, but the wind can make you feel chilly, so bring a jacket. The sun reflects strongly off all that snow, so consider wearing shades and sunscreen. The highest peaks poke into a very thin atmosphere, so don't overexert yourself into dizziness and hyperventilation.

A Bit of Bond History atop the Schilthorn

One of my favorite excursions is to take a ride from **Mürren**—home to a fabulous **Sportzentrum** sports complex, with an indoor pool, outdoor skating rink, squash, tennis, curling facilities, and more—up the dizzying cable car to the 9,804-foot peak of the **Schilthorn.** The trip takes you across the Lauterbrunnen Valley with views of the Big Three peaks, so you get a great panorama of the Alps' poster children. The summit shares its scenic terrace with the Piz Gloria restaurant (recommended previously). From Interlaken's Estbahnhof (east train station), ride one of the half-hourly trains to Lauterbrunnen (30 to 45 minutes). From here switch to the funicular to Grütschalp, where you transfer again to the narrow-gauge rail up to Mürren (the last two legs of the trip total 25 to 35 minutes). From Mürren, half-hourly cable cars take off for the 20-minute thrill ride up to Schilthorn. You have to buy each ticket separately (they're all private railways), and the whole shebang should run you about 83SFr ($55.35) round-trip.

Alpine Skiing & Other Outdoorsy Stuff

If you came to Switzerland hoping to log a few miles of Alpine skiing, there's no better base for it than **Wengen,** a resort under the looming Jungfrau trio and near the Lauterbrunnen Valley. The tourist office (☎ **036/551-414**) can help you make sense of the multitude of trails, some 20 lifts (both cable car and chair), and over seven miles of cross-country terrain. They can also point you toward rental outfitters and the local branch of the famous Swiss Ski School (☎ **036/855-2022**). Less intrepid sports enthusiasts can skate or curl in town.

Bet You Didn't Know

When the financiers building the restaurant atop the Schilthorn went over budget, James Bond came to the rescue. A film company used the half-finished structure to play the role of "Piz Gloria," headquarters of evil SPECTRE leader Telly Savalas in *On Her Majesty's Secret Service*. Agent 007 (here, George Lazenby, filling in as Bond between Sean Connery's and Roger Moore's gigs) got a *real* view to a kill as he fought bad guys while hanging from the cable car lines (and on skis and in a bobsled). After shooting wrapped, the film company helped pay for the building's completion, and because the movie provided such great advance publicity, the restaurant decided to adopt its stage name.

When snow's sparse, take the hourly postal bus or walk 45 minutes to **Trümmelbach Falls.** The falls are five stairstepped waterfalls in one, which translates into a whole lot of water thundering down a gorge. For a different view, get behind the waterfall and ride an elevator up the inside of the cliff to see the falls cascade from the other side. This is not the driest experience, so bring a raincoat. This sneak peek behind the falls is available April to October for 10SFr ($6.65) for adults and 4SFr ($2.65) for children 6 to 16. You can do more cascade viewing at **Staubbach Falls,** a 1,000-foot ribbon of water plunging straight down the valley's cliffside at the edge of Lauterbrunnen town. Wegen is just a 15-minute train ride from Lauterbrunnen (there are one or two trains per hour), which in turn is half an hour from Interlaken (trains run half-hourly).

Hike the Hills from Grindelwald

Cars can reach **Grindelwald,** so this resorty village in the eastern alpine foothills gets more crowded than its less accessible neighbors. However, it is also one of the best bases for hiking. The tourist office has trail maps covering everything from easy scenic rambles to rock climbing up the sheer eastern face of Mount Eiger. **Bergsteigerzentrum** (☎ **036/535-200**) can organize guided hikes of all degrees of difficulty, from glacier-climbing lessons to an easy, three-hour guided romp along the foot of Mount Eiger. On your own, an hour's hike up to **Milchbach** brings you to the base of the Obere Gletscher glacier, whose milky white runoff gives the spot its name. If you continue 45 minutes up the side of the glacier, you're treated to the **Blue Ice Grotto.** Glacial ice turns a deep, resonant blue as you get down into it, and you can walk inside a slowly creeping glacier here for 18SFr ($12) from June to October. A postal bus can run you back down to town in 15 minutes.

Castles & Caves: Around Interlaken's Lakes

When you tire of the heights, you can explore the mild weather and resorty feel of Interlaken's lakes. **Lake Thun** is the more popular of the two. Its main town is sensibly called **Thun** and lies at the opposite end of the lake from Interlaken, centered on an island. Thun has long since overgrown its island; on the Aare's right bank lies the town's main drag, Hauptgasse, that has a walkway above arcaded shops. From the 17th-century town hall on Rathausplatz, you can climb a long stairway up to **Castle Kyburg** (☎ 033/232-001), a fortress from the 1100s turned into a museum with historical military collections, archeological finds, and a Gobelin tapestry (open April to October). A four-hour boat tour of the lake from Interlaken, stopping in Thun, (April through October) costs 29.90SFr ($19.95).

Bet You Didn't Know

The Lake Thun boat also stops at **Beatushöhlen** (☎ 036/411–663), where instead of going up you go down for once—3,300 feet down into a cavern system. It's said to have been the 6th-century lair of a dragon until the Irish St. Beatus slew it and moved in himself. The 30-minute tour, run in April through October, shows you the saint's cell and reconstructed prehistoric settlements and costs 10SFr ($6.65) for adults, 5SFr ($3.35) for kids.

You can also tour **Lake Brienz** out the other end of Interlaken for 22SFr ($14.65). The round trip takes a little under three hours and stops at the cute lakeside village of Iseltwald and at Geissbach, whose magnificent waterfalls you can reach via a funicular from the boat's final stop, Brienz. Near Brienz, outside the village of Ballenberg (there's a bus), is the **Swiss Open-Air Museum of Rural Dwellings and Lifestyles** (☎ 036/511-123). The name says it all: A Colonial Williamsburg type of place with some 2,000 acres of regional architecture laid out as a Switzerland in miniature. Rather than eat in the cafeteria at the entrance, save your hunger for the freshly made breads, cheeses, and sausages sold at the various working farmhouses and "settlements" that make up the park. This odd but enjoyable museum/park is open April 15 through October, 10am to 5pm, and costs 12SFr ($8) for adults, 6SFr ($4) for children. You can also take a train from Interlaken to Brienz town.

Get Outta Town: Day Trips & Excursions

Since we've spent this chapter in the countryside, the excursions I recommend are more urban—the banking captial of Zurich, and Basel, a college town with an amazing repository of art.

Zurich: Swiss Counterculture Meets High Finance

Switzerland's largest city and banking capital, Zurich is the prettiest of the country's big cities. Its oldest quarter is spread over the steep banks on either side of the swan-filled Limmat River as it flows out of the Zürichsee (Lake Zurich). I would spend a relaxing 48 hours in Zurich, but you still can get a surprisingly good feel for the city in just a day. Zurich is well connected with Europe's major cities and is only 75 to 120 minutes **from Bern by train** (50 daily). Trains arrive at **Hauptbahnhof** (main train station) on the riverbank at the north end of town. The **tourist office** (☎ 01/211-4000) is at the station, Bahnhofplatz 15.

From the station, the tree-shaded shopping street of Bahnhofstrasse runs south, paralleling the Limmat a few blocks away, all the way to the shores of the Zürichsee. Running off to the left of this street are a series of medieval alleys that lead down to the river. Several bridges cross the river to the wide Limmatquai Street. Narrow side streets lined with shops lead to the other half of the old city.

The 13th-century **St. Peter's Church** at St. Petershofstaat 6 has the largest clock face in Europe—28.5 feet across with a 12-foot minute hand. Nearby is one of Zurich's top sights, the Gothic **Fraumünster** church, with five 1970 stained-glass windows by artist Marc Chagall (they're best in the morning light). From here, cross the Münsterbrücke over the Limmat River to reach Zurich's cathedral, the twin-towered **Grossmünster.** Founded on a site said to be chosen by Charlemagne's horse (he bowed his head on the spot where a trio of 3rd-century martyrs were buried), its construction ran from 1090 through the 14th century. The stained glass was designed by Swiss artist Alberto Giacometti in 1933. Climb the tower (2SFr/$1.35) from May to October for a great city view.

> ### Time-Savers
>
> Although you can easily navigate most of central Zurich by foot, you'll need to hop a tram or bus for some of the outlying sights and hotels. The cost is 1.90SFr ($1.25) for rides up to five stops, 3.20SFr ($2.10) for longer trips, and 6.40SFr ($4.25) for a *Tageskarte* 24-hour ticket.

A long walk up Kirchgasse from the church and a left on Seiler Granben/Zeltweg takes you to Heimplatz and the **Kunsthaus** (☎ 01/218-6511), Zurich's fine arts museum. The main collection starts with the impressionists of the late 19th century and runs to contemporary times, featuring works by Monet, Degas, Cézanne, Chagall, Rodin, Picasso, Mondrian, Marini, and especially the Swiss-born Giacometti. Admission is

4SFr ($2.65) for adults, 3SFr ($2) for children, and it's closed Monday (you can also take tram 3 here).

Bet You Didn't Know

Zurich has always been a hotbed of radicalism and liberal thought. The Swiss Protestant Reformation started here in the 16th century, and the 20th century has drawn the likes of Carl Jung, Lenin (who spent World War I here, planning his revolution), Thomas Mann, and James Joyce, who worked on *Ulysses* in Zurich and returned a month before his death in 1941. Joyce's grave in Friedhof Fluntern cemetery (take tram 2) is near those of Nobelist Elias Canetti and *Heidi* author Joanna Spyri.

Zurich's cheapest sight is the park lining the mouth of the Zürichsee. You can join Swiss joggers and romantic couples **strolling the west bank of the lake** up and down the General Guisan quai (at the end of Bahnhofstrasse), which leads to an arboretum. Also at the base of Bahnhofstrasse are the piers from which dozens of steamers embark for **tours of the lake.** Most boat trips fall into two categories. The four-hour journey all the way to the opposite end of the lake and back (add in more time to get off and explore en route) runs about 26SFr ($17.35). A 90-minute jaunt just around the northern end of the lake should cost about 10SFr ($6.65). Before boarding the train out of town, pop into the free **Landesmuseum (Swiss National Museum)** just behind the station at Museumstrasse 2 (☎ 01/218-6511). The well-laid out collections trace Swiss civilization from prehistory to the 19th century.

Zur Oepfelchammer (☎ 01/251-2336), Rindermarkt 12 (just off the Limmat), serves up reasonably priced Swiss and French cuisine in a friendly, atmospheric ambiance. Although a bit pricey at 360 to 430SFr ($240 to $286.65) a double, the romantic **Hotel Zum Storchen** (☎ 01/211-5510), Am Weinplatz 2, is the best bet in town—an 640-year-old inn right on the river in the center of Zurich's Altstadt. The tourist office can find you cheaper digs or other rooms if this place is full.

Three, Three, Three Countries in One! A Visit to Basel

The Swiss answer to Four Corners, USA, Basel is a university city that has a place where you can walk in a circle on a pylon on the Rhine River and move from Switzerland into Germany, then France, and back into Switzerland (the spot's called **Dreiländereck**). Basel's sheer number of museums (27) makes it an art capital of Switzerland, and it claims Hans Holbein the Younger (along with thinker Friedrich Nietzche) among its famous past residents. Non-art lovers needn't bother coming, but if you have

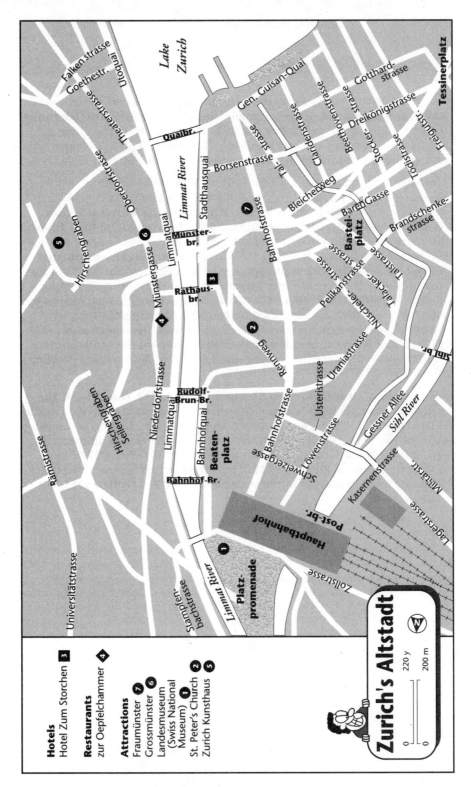

Zurich's Altstadt

W

220 y
0 _____
0 _____
200 m

Hotels
Hotel Zum Storchen 3

Restaurants
zur Oepfelchammer 4

Attractions
Fraumünster 7
Grossmünster 6
Landesmuseum
(Swiss National
Museum) 1
St. Peter's Church 2
Zurich Kunsthaus 5

a thing for paintings, give the city at least a day—two if you're a fan of modern and contemporary art.

Half-hourly trains make the 60 to 75 minute trip from **Bern** and arrive at **SBB Hauptbahnhof.** There's a small branch of the **tourist office** in the train station, but the main office (☎ 061/261-5050) is on the Rhine at Schifflände 5 just past the Mittlere Bridge (take tram 1). Basel's compact, historic center lies mainly on the south bank of the Rhine River.

Although it has an impressive 14th-century **Münster** (cathedral), whose elaborately carved facade is the pride of Basel, this city is really about museums. Top honors go to the eclectic collections of the **Kunstmuseum** (☎ 061/271-0828), at St. Alban Graben 16. It has everything from Holbein the Younger and Konrad Witz to Van Gogh, Picasso, Klee, Chagall, Rodin, and Alexander Calder. Nearby are the **Museum für Gegenwartskunst** (☎ 061/272-8183), with contemporary art ranging from the 1960s to the present day by the likes of Bruce Nauman, Joseph Beuys, and Donald Judd; and the **Kunsthalle** (☎ 061/272-4833), whose changing installations by contemporary artists are advertised on banners throughout town. Most museums are closed on Monday. There's also a world-renowned **zoo** (☎ 061/295-3535), at Binningerstrasse 40, a seven-minute stroll from the train station, with 600 species represented and a famous breeding program for endangered animals.

The restaurant **Zum Goldenen Sternen** (☎ 061/272-1666), St. Alban-rheinweg 70 (at the Rhine's edge), has served up a good, inexpensive medley of French-accented Swiss and continental dishes since 1421. Art aficionados with shallow pockets will want to stay just across the river from the main part of town at the **Hotel Krafft am Rhein** (☎ 061/961-8877), overlooking the Rhine at Rheingasse 12. The setting is 19th century, and the rooms are modern and comfy. Rates are 150 to 320SFr ($100 to $213.35) for doubles.

Chapter 21

Prague & Environs

In This Chapter

➤ Medieval castles and fanciful bridges: discovering the joys of the city

➤ Musical interludes, from street performers to Mozart's opera

➤ Retracing history in Prague's Jewish quarter

➤ Where to find the best beer halls

If you think of Eastern Europe as dreary and somehow monochromatic, as if reality were filmed in black and white, then visit Prague. It's one of the most beautiful cities in the world. Medieval cobbled streets weave past baroque palaces, lively beer halls, glowering castles, and light-infused cathedrals. Street musicians play on elegant bridges that span a swan-filled river.

I'm not alone in my infatuation. In 1989, a group of activist writers and artists (led by the current president, Vaclav Havel) spurred what was then Czechoslovakia to make a peaceful transition from communism to democracy (dubbed the "Velvet Revolution"). Seemingly overnight, Prague became the hot new destination, a "Paris of the '90s" for earnest Gen Xers desperate to do the Hemingway expat thing. The inevitable backlash ensued, and many claimed the city's magic had been tainted by the attendant influx of Western culture (McDonald's and the like).

Dollars & Sense

The Czech unit of currency is called the koruna (Kč) and is divided into 100 hellers. Roughly, $1 equals 35Kč, or 10Kč equals 30¢. Czech coins include 10, 20, and 50 hellers and 1, 2, 5, 10, 20, and 50 koruna. Bills come in denominations of 20, 50, 100, 200, 500, 1,000, and 5,000 koruna.

Prague has finally come into its own, little the worse for wear. Sure, in summer, the backpackers descend, drawn to the low prices and the romantic setting—you're likely to hear more English than Czech spoken on the street. Come fall and winter, though, the crowds clear out, and Prague is all yours; prepare to be enchanted. I'd devote a good two or three days of your trip here to fully capture the city's dreamy flavor. With a skyline defined by dozens of spires, steeples, and towers, Prague becomes a hazy, fairy-tale place at sunrise and sunset.

Getting Your Bearings

Central Prague is divided into four main neighborhoods straddling both sides of the **Vltava River,** which flows through the city from the south and then curves off to the east. **Staré Město (Old Town)** is tucked into this bend of the river (on the east bank), bounded by the Vltava on the west and north and by the continuous arc of streets **Národní/Října/Na příkopé/ Revolučni** on the south and east.

Prague's Neighborhoods in Brief

Staré Město is Prague's center, a combination of meandering streets dating back to the Middle Ages cut across by wide boulevards from more recent centuries. You'll probably spend most of your time in this pedestrian-friendly zone of restaurants, cafes, and gorgeous Gothic and baroque architecture. Within Staré Město is Josefov, the famed old Jewish quarter. The focal point of the Old Town is Staroměstské náměstí, or Old Town Square.

Time-Savers

Prague doesn't have an official tourist information office. Although the following private travel agencies will try to sell you tours and tickets in the process, they will also dispense free city information (maps, pamphlets, and so on). **Čedok** (☎ **02/2419-7111,** fax: 02/232-1656) was once the state-run visitors bureau and has offices at Na Příkopě 18 and Václavské Náměstí 24. **Prague Information Service** (☎ **187** or 02/264-022), Na Příkopě 20, is the second largest tourism office in town. PIS also has a branch in the main train station. The best office for information is **AVE Ltd.** (☎ **02/2422-3226** or 02/ 2422-3521, fax: 02/549-743), found in either train station. Some travelers find the best info by waltzing into the priciest hotel they see, acting for all the world as if they're a registered guest, and asking the concierge for information. Newsstands carry an English-language weekly newspaper, the *Prague Post,* and a monthly magazine, *Velvet,* both of which have useful information.

Surrounding the Old Town on all but the riverside is the Nové Město (New Town). Not nearly as interesting as the Old City or Malá Strana districts, it is as modern as its name implies, filled primarily with boring office and apartment buildings. The National Theater is among the few attractions found here, along with hotels that are generally less expensive than those in Old Town.

Nové Město's nucleus is Václavské náměstí (Wenceslas Square), a four-block-long divided boulevard sloping gradually up (southward) to the dramatic neo-Renaissance mass of the National Museum. The pedestrian zone down the middle is lined on both sides with sausage stands and neoclassical and art nouveau buildings. (This area has been called New Town since its 1348 founding; it's just a coincidence that much of that medieval neighborhood was replaced in the 19th and 20th centuries by an even newer New Town.)

Crossing the famous, statue-lined Karlův most (Charles Bridge) from the Old Town brings you into the Malá Strana, the "Little Quarter" on the west bank of the Vltava River. Settled by Germans in 1257, this slope leading up to Prague Castle became very fashionable a few centuries ago—a status that has left the area filled with Renaissance and baroque palaces. Above the Malá Strana is the small Hradčany, the "Castle District," occupied almost entirely by the city's dominating edifice and major sight, Prague Castle. Over the centuries, many palaces (several now housing museums) and monasteries have gathered around this traditional seat of government.

Those are Prague's four traditional neighborhoods, but of course the city has sprawled outward in every direction since its founding. Of these outlying districts, the main one dealt with in this chapter borders the eastern edge of New Town. Vinohrady was named after the vineyards (owned by the king) that once filled this upscale residential zone. If Prague has a modern trendy district, Vinohrady is it—clean, full of shops and restaurants, and just a short hop from the city center on the Metro line A.

Getting Into & Around Town

Trains arrive in Prague either at the Hlavní Nádraží (**Main Station**) on the east edge of Nové Město; or, from Berlin and other northerly points, at the smaller Nádraží Holešovice (**Holešovice Station**) across the river to the north of the city center. Metro line C connects both stations.

From Prague's small **airport,** 12 miles west of the city center, a shuttle bus runs in 30 minutes to Dejvická, the northern terminus of the Metro line A, for 15Kč (40¢). You can take it all the way into náměstí Republiky, which straddles the Old

Tourist Traps

Both train stations, especially the main one, are seedy and chaotic. Perhaps the most annoying feature is the dozens of touts who practically assault you the instant you step off the train, trying to sell you a hotel room. Just ignore them and push on ahead. If you want a reputable accommodations agency in the station, see the introduction to hotels.

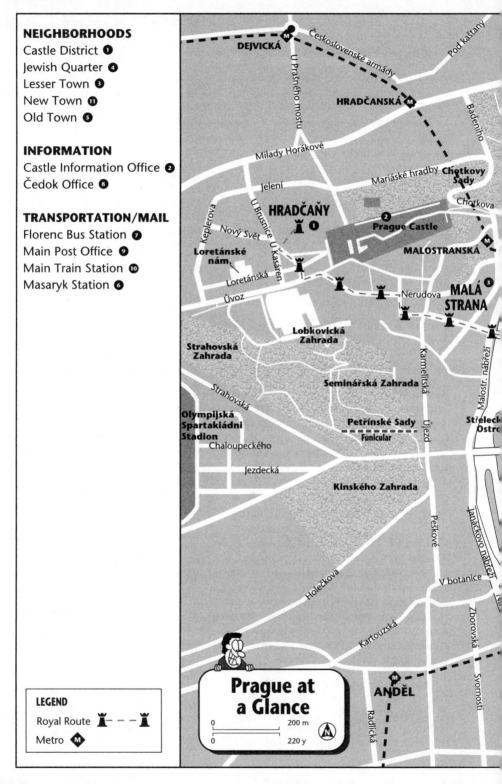

NEIGHBORHOODS
Castle District ❶
Jewish Quarter ❹
Lesser Town ❸
New Town ⓫
Old Town ❺

INFORMATION
Castle Information Office ❷
Čedok Office ❽

TRANSPORTATION/MAIL
Florenc Bus Station ❼
Main Post Office ❾
Main Train Station ❿
Masaryk Station ❻

DEJVICKÁ

Československé armády

Pod kaštany

U Prašného mostu

HRADČANSKÁ

Badeniho

Milady Horákové

Mariáské hradby · Chotkovy Sady

Jeleni

Chotkova

HRADČANY ❶

Prague Castle ❷

Keplerova

Nový Svět

U Brusnice

U Kasáren

MALOSTRANSKÁ

Loretánské nám.

Loretánská

Nerudova

MALÁ STRANA ❸

Úvoz

Lobkovická Zahrada

Karmelitská

Malostr. nábřeží

Strahovská Zahrada

Seminářská Zahrada

Strahovská

Olympijská Spartakiádni Stadion

Petřínské Sady

Funicular

Újezd

Střelec Ostro

Chaloupeckého

Jezdecká

Kinského Zahrada

Peškové

Janáčkovo nábřeží

Holečkova

V botanice

Zborovská

Kartouzská

LEGEND
Royal Route ♜ – – – ♜
Metro Ⓜ

Prague at a Glance

ANDĚL

Radlická

Svornosti

0 ———— 200 m
0 ———— 220 y

374

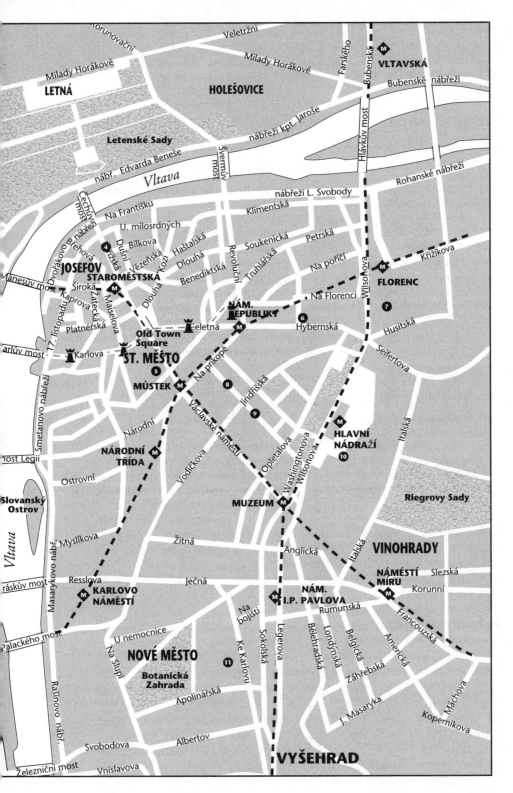

and New Towns and has a Metro line B stop, for an extra 15Kč (40¢). City bus 119 will carry you from the airport to the Dejvická Metro stop in 40 minutes.

Prague's **Metro (subway)** system does a pretty good job of covering the center with only three lines: A, B, and C. Lines intersect once in the Nové Město: A and B at Můstek (north end of Václavské náměstí), A and C at Muzeum (south end of Václavské náměstí), B and C at Florenc.

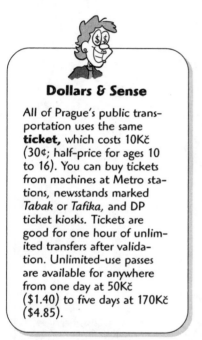

Dollars & Sense

All of Prague's public transportation uses the same **ticket,** which costs 10Kč (30¢; half-price for ages 10 to 16). You can buy tickets from machines at Metro stations, newsstands marked *Tabak* or *Tafika*, and DP ticket kiosks. Tickets are good for one hour of unlimited transfers after validation. Unlimited-use passes are available for anywhere from one day at 50Kč ($1.40) to five days at 170Kč ($4.85).

The **tram** system, supplemented by **buses,** is a more complete network that effectively covers much of central Prague. In winter, the tram seats are heated. Tram 22 has been dubbed the "pickpocket tram," because it is frequented by visitors (and the pickpockets who want to take advantage of them). The line passes by the National Theater and heads through the Malá Strana up to Prague Castle. Staré Město has little public transportation, just a few trams and buses following its boundary roads. Several lines skirt the riverbank (especially tram 17) to hit Staroměstské naměstí, which also has a Metro line A station.

Although a few trams and buses are getting computerized ticket canceling machines, most still have the old manual boxes. The simple versions have a black lever you pull to do the trick. Then there are those older boxes with a slot for your ticket but no apparent way to operate the stamping feature. I took a good half-dozen unintentionally free rides my first time in Prague before I finally saw someone place their ticket in the slot and then push the entire little box down from the top, which punctured the ticket with two holes, Dracula-style.

Prague Fast Facts

American Express   Prague's American Express office, Václavské nám (Wenceslas Square) 56, Praha 1 (☎ **02/2421-9992**), is open daily 9am to 7pm.

Doctors/hospitals   In a medical emergency, call or go to the **Foreigner's Medical Clinic,** Na Homolce Hospital, Praha 5 (☎ **02/5292-2146** or 02/5292-2191). If your condition is not life-threatening, go to the **First Medical Clinic of Prague, Ltd.,** Vyšehradská 35, Praha 2 (☎ **02/292-286**). The clinic offers emergency care, house calls, and referrals to specialists. It's open Monday to Saturday, 7am to 7pm.

Embassy   The U.S. Embassy is located at Tržiště 15, or you can call it by dialing ☎ **02/5732-0663.**

Emergency   Dial ☎ **158** to call the police or report a fire. For an ambulance, call ☎ **155.**

Pharmacies   A Czech pharmacy is called a *lékárna*. Several pharmacies remain open 24 hours a day. Try the ones at Belgická 37 (☎ **02/258-189** or 02/2423-7207) or Štefánikova 6 (☎ **02/2451-1112**).

Safety   Walking or taking the Metro or trams alone at night is safe, but always be on the lookout for pickpockets, especially on Charles Bridge, around parts of Old Town, and on public transportation. A little seedy during the day, Wenceslas Square at night is traveled mainly by prostitutes.

Taxis   Unless your hotel is some distance from Prague's center, avoid taking a taxi. Prague's taxi drivers are notorious for ripping off unsuspecting tourists. If you *must* take a taxi, pick one up at a taxi stand (in front of tourist sites, large hotels, and transportation centers), or in a pinch, hail one on the street—but be especially careful using this method, because you have a better chance of flagging down an unlicensed mafia cab this way ("mafia" may sound dangerous, but the only mortal danger here is to your wallet).

No matter where you get the cab, always keep an eagle eye on the meter. The display window on the left shows your fare; the window on the right, which should read 1, 2, 3, or 4, shows the rate you're being charged (the higher the number, the higher the rate). Unless you venture far out from the center of town, the window on the right shouldn't read anything but 1. The initial charge should be 10Kč (30¢) and then 12Kč per kilometer. If the rate is increasing by more than that, question it.

Tourist Traps

Do not let a taxi driver cover the meter's displays or surreptitiously change the rate as he changes gears (it should *always* read 1, unless you're heading way into the outskirts). Make a show of copying down the taxi number and any other identifying info as you get into the cab and sit in the front seat to keep an eye on the driver.

Your chances of being ripped off are considerably less if you call a radio cab company. Because the trip is logged in an office, it's more difficult for the driver to inflate the fare. Companies with English-speaking dispatchers include **AAA Taxi** (☎ **02/2432-2432** or 1080 locally), **RONY Taxi** (☎ **02/692-1958** or 02/430-403), or **ProfiTaxi** (☎ **02/6131-4111** or 1035 locally).

Telephone A local call in Prague costs at least 2Kč (5¢). Pay phones accept either coins or phone cards, sold at post offices or newsstands in denominations ranging from 50 to 500Kč ($1.40 to $14.30). Coin-operated phones do not make change, so insert money as needed, but use smaller coins. To avoid confusion: A Czech dial tone sounds similar to a busy signal in the United States; Czech busy signals sound like U.S. dial tones.

The country code for the Czech Republic is **420.** Prague's city code is **02;** drop the initial zero if you're calling from outside the country. In other words, to call Prague from the United States, dial **011-420-2** followed by the number. To charge a call to your calling card, dial **AT&T** (☎ **00-4200-0101**), **MCI** (☎ **00-4200-0112**), or **Sprint** (☎ **00-4208-7187**). To call the United States direct from Prague, dial **001** followed by the area code and number.

Transit Info Call or visit **Čedok,** Na príkopě 18 or Václavské námě̆stí 24, Praha 1 (☎ **02/2419-7111**), for transportation information.

Czeching In: Prague's Hotel Scene

Prague is the most expensive city in eastern Europe. Although prices have soared in the years since it came out from under communist rule, things have cooled off of late. Prices have stabilized and, in some cases, have even gone down as the forces of competition temper runaway inflation and development. In other words, Prague may not be as cheap as you'd hoped, but it won't be as expensive as you may fear. The priciest rooms are in the most desirable neighborhoods: Staré Město and Mála Strana.

Dollars & Sense

Prague is full of agencies that will help you track down a hotel room, pension, or even a full apartment (for a fee, of course). Among the more reputable ones are **AVE Ltd.** and **Čedok,** both mentioned as tourism offices previously; and **Prague Accommodations Service,** Haštalské nám (☎ **02/231-0202,** fax: 02/231-6640).

The rapid capitalist invasion has also led to more than a fair share of shysters and dubious business practices. Many hotels charge one price for Czechs and another for foreign tourists. It's annoying, but unavoidable. Try not to pay in dollars; hotels convert the koruna prices to greenbacks at extremely unfavorable rates. Remember: You'll be accosted by an army of name tag–wearing, notebook-toting, usually unscrupulous touts at the train station offering you, in broken English, rooms that seem too cheap to be true. *They almost always are.* They're either located way out from the center of town and much more of a dump than the "creative" photos suggest, or they're full of hidden extras that pump the price way up. Avoid these guys and visit a more legitimate accommodations agency (see the sidebar).

Hotel Evropa
$$. Nové Město.
The remarkable, statue-topped art nouveau facade and classy sidewalk cafe of Prague's prettiest hotel will definitely suck you in. Unfortunately, the rooms seem to belong to a different hotel entirely. They vary widely in size and decor. Most are merely adequate, and some verge on dingy. But the better rooms on the high-ceilinged first two floors make for quite an enjoyable stay.

Václavské náměstí 25. ☎ *02/2422-8117. Fax: 02/2422-4544. Metro: Můstek. Rates: 2,160–2,800Kč ($65–$80) double. AE, MC, V.*

Hotel Harmony
$$$$. Nové Město.
Close to the edge of Old Town, the Harmony offers one of Prague's best values in a contemporary, clean, relatively spacious hotel. With functional furnishings and modern amenities, it's one of the most reliable, if uninteresting, hotels in town.

Na poříčí 31 (at the corner of Zlatnická, 1 long block east of náměstí Republiky). ☎ *02/232-0016 or 232-0720. Fax: 02/231-0009. Metro: náměstí Republiky or Florenc. Rates: 3,510Kč ($106) double; 12% discount for stays over 1 night. AE, MC, V.*

Hotel Kampa
$$$. Malá Strana.
The Kampa inhabits a 17th-century armory on a quiet side street across the river, about a five-minute walk from the Charles Bridge. The simple, whitewashed, large-ish rooms are fitted with plain-Jane dark wood furnishings; try to get one overlooking the river or nearby park.

Všehrdova 16 (just off Újezd). ☎ *02/5732-0404. Fax: 02/5732-0262. Metro: Malostranská. Rates: 3,550Kč ($107) double. AE, MC, V.*

Pension Unitas
$. Staré Město.
You can't get much more bare bones than Unitas, but you can't get much more central, either. It was a prison of the communist-era secret police and is now run by nuns, which should give you some idea about the glamour of the rooms. They are clean and bright, though. The biggest drawback to this place is a 1am curfew.

Bartolomějská 9 (1 block north of, and parallel to, Národní and the Old Town's southern edge). ☎ *02/232-7700. Fax: 02/232-7709. Metro: Staroměstská. Rates: 1,200Kč ($34.30) double. No credit cards.*

Prague Renaissance Hotel
$$$$$. Nové Město.
Bland but reliably comfortable, the cushiest of my selections for Prague is favored by the business community and those seeking the standard hotel features and amenities they're used to finding in Western Europe. "King" rooms

Hotels
Hotel Evropa **24**
Hotel Harmony **21**
Hotel Kampa **8**
Pension Unitas **12**
Prague Renaissance Hotel **22**

Restaurants
La Provance **18**
Parnas **11**
Quido **25**
U Radnice **16**
Vinárna U Maltézských Rytíru
(Knights of Malta) **7**

Attractions
Charles Bridge
(Karlův most) **9**
Charles Square
(Karlovo náměstí) **10**
Church of St. Nicholas
(at Old Town Square) **14**
Estateś Theater **20**
Havel's Market **19**
New Jewish Cemetery **26**
Old Jewish Cemetery **13**
Old-New Synagogue **13**
Old Town Hall
& Astronomical Clock **15**
Old Town Square
(Staromestské námestí) **17**
Prague Castle **4**
Royal Garden **2**
St. George's Convent
at Prague Castle **6**
St. Vitus Cathedral **5**
Šternberk Palace
Art Museum **3**
Strahov Monastery
and Library **1**
Church of Our Lady
Before Týn **17**
Wenceslas Square
(Václavské námestí) **23**

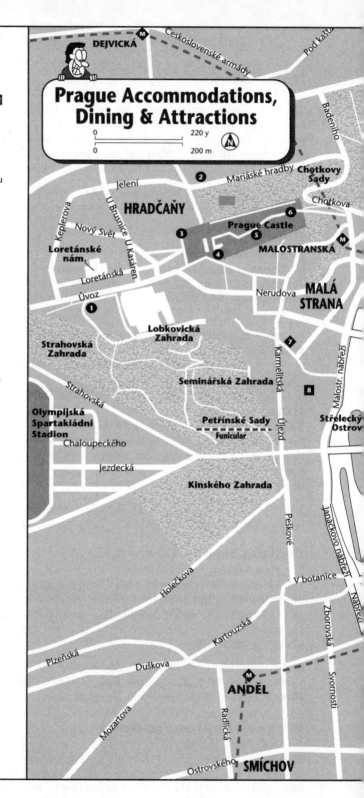

Prague Accommodations, Dining & Attractions

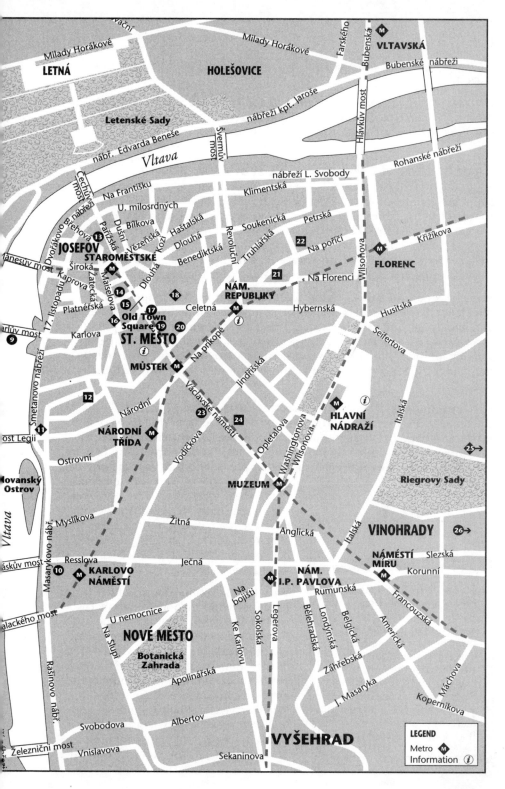

are usually the same price as smaller standard ones, and the corner rooms are biggest.

V Celnici 7 (just off náměstí Republiky). ☎ *02/2182-1111.* **Fax:** *02/2182-2200.* **Metro:** *náměstí Republiky.* **Rates:** *6,800Kč ($206) double. Children under 16 stay free in parents' room. AE, CB, DC, MC, V.*

Czech, Please! Prague's Restaurant Scene

Traditional Czech cuisine tends to be hearty in a simple, rib-sticking way. Soups are garlicky or meaty—the best is **hovězí polévka s játrovými knedlíčky** (liver dumplings in beef stock). Praguers are fond of their dumplings, called **knedlíčky,** which are usually made of *bramborové* (potatoes) or *houskové* (bread) and sliced into discs. Dumplings are side dishes to such favorites as **svíčková na smetaně,** a beef pot roast sliced and served with a creamy and rich vegetable sauce and a sour cranberry chutney.

Also check out **pečená kachna,** roast duck with bacon dumplings and sauerkraut. **Game,** such as *zvěřina* (venison), *zajíc* (hare), *bažant* (pheasant), and *hus* (goose), are usually roasted. Popular **freshwater fish** are *pstruh* (trout) and *kapr* (carp). Hungarian **guláš** (beef goulash) is a good, cheap standby for quick lunches. The best desserts are **ovocné knedlíky** (fruit dumplings), *vdolek* (jam tart), and chocolate- and/or fruit-filled **palačinky** (crêpes).

Czech **pivo (beer)** is among the best unsung brew on the planet. This is the home of **Pilsner Urquell,** the country's famed lager (the brewery also makes a smooth, for-local-consumption-only beer, **Gambrinus**). Also try **Staropramen** (the most common Prague suds), **Velkopopovický** (a wonderful dark beer), **Kozel** (a spicy, nonbitter brew), and **Budvar,** the original Budweiser—though they will tell you that to be associated with what they call the watery, mass-produced American beverage is an affront to their name (see "Bet You Didn't Know"). Light-colored beer is *světlé* (svyet-lay); dark beer is *černé* (cher-nay).

Bet You Didn't Know

Budvar, the original Czech brewery, and Anheuser-Busch (makers of Budweiser) have been at it for years over the right to the beer name. Their provisional settlement over the issue explains why you won't find Budweiser in some European markets such as Germany and why you can't get Budvar in the United States.

With the exception of some of the better restaurants and the tourist-trap places nearest the sights, meals in Prague can be very inexpensive. One of the trade-offs is remarkably **poor service,** a relic of the Communist era, when restaurant patrons received their meals only at the extreme convenience of the server. When service is haughty, ignore it and don't tip; when service is scarce, just sit back and chalk it all up to economic growing pains. As investors start up finer and finer restaurants, their attention to service and food presentation should trickle down through the rest of the industry.

Tourist Traps

There are a few **restaurant rip-offs** to be on the alert for. Every item brought to your table may be charged to your bill, including bread, bowls of nuts, and so on. Often these small items turn out to be ridiculously expensive. Make sure you know the price of *everything* before you eat it. Examine your bill closely at the end of the meal to make sure it isn't padded with items you didn't order. Also, some restaurants doctor the amount written on a credit card slip, so it pays to write the total, in letters, somewhere on the slip. You needn't let these few bad apples ruin your *jablkový* (apple) strudel; just be wary.

La Provance

$$$. Staré Město. FRENCH.

La Provance is one of Prague's more successful eateries. The Provençal-inspired cooking may be uneven (though coq au vin and roasted duck are both winners), but the convivial-leaning-to-noisy atmosphere is guaranteed. It's set below one of the city's trendier bars, so plenty of people come here to have a good time.

Štupartská 9 (1 long block off the east side of Staroměstské náměstí). ☎ *02/232-4801. Reservations recommended.* **Metro:** *náměstí Republiky.* **Main courses:** *250–480Kč ($7.57–$14.54). AE, MC, V.* **Open:** *Lunch and dinner daily.*

Bellevue (formerly Parnas)

$$$$$. Staré Město. INTERNATIONAL.

Surrounded by live music and, if you scam a window seat, a view of Prague Castle, you can dine on some of the city's best food at one of its finest restaurants. The international menu varies from spinach tagliatelle in a salmon cream sauce to braised rabbit, always well prepared and presented. Steer clear of the unimaginative veggie dishes. Sunday brunch features live jazz. This was once the location of the famed restaurant Parnas; though owned by the same company, Parnas has moved down the street by the National Theater. Stick with Bellevue; the food's far better.

Smetanovo nábřeží 2 (at the foot of most Legli). ☎ *02/2422-7614. Reservations highly recommended.* **Metro:** *Staroměstská.* **Main courses:** *360–690Kč ($10.90–$20.90); fixed-price menu 790–990Kč ($23.93–30). AE, DC, MC, V.* **Open:** *Lunch and dinner daily.*

Quido
$$. Vinohrady. CZECH.

This rustic-wood spot is the best in Prague for traditional Czech food well beyond goulash. They trot out large portions of the best of Bohemian cookery here: blue cheese–stuffed hunter's steak; garlic, meat, and potato soup; and pig's knee with mustard and rye bread, considered a delicacy.

Kubelíkova 22 (about 5 blocks east of the main train station, off Slavíkova). ☎ *02/270-950. Reservations highly recommended.* **Metro:** *Jiřího z Poděbrad.* **Main courses:** *130-250Kč ($3.70–$7.15). AE, MC, V.* **Open:** *Lunch and dinner Mon–Sat.*

U Radnice
$. Staré Město. CZECH.

Little separates the appearance of this place from that of the area's countless touristy joints, but this one is the original. If you want quality, traditional working-class goulash, come to this steadfast holdout in the heart of the old city. U Radnice also has a pub and bar; the laid-back, beer-and-pretzels atmosphere rubs off on the dining room.

U Radnice 10 (1 block behind the west side of Staroměstské náměstí). ☎ *02/ 2422-8136. Reservations not accepted.* **Metro:** *Staroměstská.* **Main courses:** *70–150Kč ($2–$4.30). No credit cards.* **Open:** *Lunch and dinner daily.*

Vinárna U Maltézských Rytírů (Knights of Malta)
$$$. Malá Strana. CZECH.

On the hill rising toward the Castle perches one of Prague's most beloved eateries, a bastion of Czech food, good flavors, and warm welcomes. Seating is limited, so reserve ahead to enjoy turkey breast stuffed with asparagus, a lamb cutlet, or vegetables au gratin. The apple strudel is a must for dessert.

Quick Bites

There's a great Czech deli at **Obchod Čerstvých Uzenin** (Václavské náměstí 36) that has goulash and other stand-up hot foods available at the back. Tasty, tiny, open-faced sandwiches called *chelbíčky* are all the rage at **U Bakaláře** (Celetná 12). Sidewalk stands hawk *klobásy* (grilled sausages) and *párky* (boiled frankfurters) served with bread and *hořčice* (mustard). You can put together a **picnic** from the pickings in the basement grocery department of the **Krone** department store (Wenceslas Square) and the **fruit and vegetable market** at the corner of Havelská and Melantrichova.

Prokopská 10 (off Karmelitská). ☎ *02/536-357. Reservations highly recommended.* **Metro:** *Malostranská.* **Main courses:** *165–380Kč ($5.00–$11.52). AE, MC, V.* **Open:** *Lunch and dinner daily.*

Czech It Out: Prague Sightseeing

Welcome Touristic (☎ 02/231-7598), at náměstí Republiky, offers a 3½-hour guided bus "Grand City Tour." It costs 590Kč ($16.85) for adults, 390Kč ($11.15) for kids and leaves at 9:30am year-round, with an additional 2:30pm run April through October. The two-hour version costs 340Kč ($9.70) for adults, 280Kč ($8) for kids, and departs at 11am, 1:30pm, and 3:30pm in summer, 1:30pm only in winter. **Wittman Tours** (☎ 02/251-235) offers excellent English-language guided walks Sunday through Friday at 10:30am. They last 2½ hours and include all sight admissions for 480Kč ($13.70) for adults.

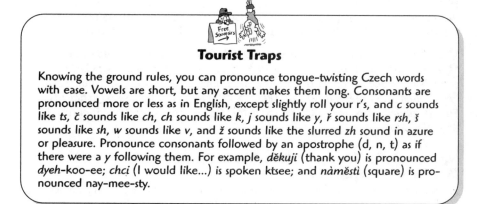

Tourist Traps

Knowing the ground rules, you can pronounce tongue-twisting Czech words with ease. Vowels are short, but any accent makes them long. Consonants are pronounced more or less as in English, except slightly roll your r's, and *c* sounds like *ts*, *č* sounds like *ch*, *ch* sounds like *k*, *j* sounds like *y*, *ř* sounds like *rsh*, *š* sounds like *sh*, *w* sounds like *v*, and *ž* sounds like the slurred *zh* sound in azure or pleasure. Pronounce consonants followed by an apostrophe (d, n, t) as if there were a *y* following them. For example, *děkuji* (thank you) is pronounced *dyeh*-koo-ee; *chci* (I would like...) is spoken ktsee; and *nàměsti* (square) is pronounced nay-mee-sty.

Prague Sights Not to Miss

Prague Castle (Pražský Hrad)

Work on Prague's fortress, which dominates the Malá Strana side of the river and sternly overlooks the entire city, began in the 9th century and, considering the continual renovations, has never really stopped. It is its own tiny city, enclosed by massive fortifications and spilling over with churches, palaces, buildings, shops, and alleys that together take a full day to explore properly (or a *quick* run-though in maybe two to three hours). This is Prague's only truly must-see sight, especially for its massive cathedral, one of Europe's grandest Gothic churches.

Construction on **St. Vitus Cathedral,** the castle's centerpiece, began under Emperor Charles IV in 1344. After a long interruption, it was finished in the 19th and 20th centuries in a neo-Gothic style that tried to follow closely the original plans (with a few flourishes for good measure). The mosaic over the door dates from 1370. The light-filled interior of the cathedral contains, about midway along the right side, the sumptuously decorated **Chapel of St. Wenceslas** (built in the 14th to 16th centuries). The sarcophagi of Bohemian kings are stored in the crypt.

The **Royal Palace** was the home to those same kings from the 9th century on. Inside, the vaulted Vladislav Hall is still used for state occasions such as the inauguration of the Czech president, but the Czechs don't quite celebrate like they used to. In the Middle Ages, knights on horseback rode in via the funky, sloping Rider's Staircase for indoor jousting competitions.

St. George's Basilica was built in the 10th century and is the oldest Romanesque structure in Prague. Its adjacent **convent** houses a museum of Gothic and baroque Bohemian art. The row of tiny houses clinging to the inside base of the castle ramparts was known as **Golden Lane,** because they were once home to goldsmiths and shopkeepers; today it's home to souvenir stands and cafes. Franz Kafka worked, and perhaps lived, for a time at no. 22. Whether alchemists practiced their craft of trying to turn lead into gold on *this* "golden" lane is a point of debate (some say yes, but others point to a similar lane off the left flank of St. Vitus Cathedral as alchemy central).

Main entrance at Hradčanské náměstí. ☎ *02/3337-3368 or 02/2437-3368. **Metro:** A to Malostranská or Hradčanská. **Tram:** 22. **Admission:** Castle grounds are free. Combined ticket (good for 3 days) to St. Vitus Cathedral, Royal Palace, and St. George's Basilica, 100Kč ($3.03) adults, 50Kč ($1.51) students. English guided tours are 40Kč ($1.15) extra. **Open:** Tues–Sun 9am–5pm (until 4pm Nov–Mar).*

National Gallery at Sternberk Palace (Sternberskýpalác)

Prague's main art gallery is housed in a gorgeous late 17th-century palace near the Castle. Its works span the 15th to 20th centuries, including works by Rembrandt, Brueghel the Elder, Klee, and Munch. The finest piece is Dürer's huge *Feast of the Rosary,* painted in 1506. Across the entry courtyard from the main collections are the galleries dedicated to impressionists and post-impressionists. Look here for the creations of Delacroix, Rodin, Gauguin, Monet, Seurat, Rousseau, Cézanne, van Gogh, and a whole bunch of cubist paintings by Picasso and Braque.

Hradčanské náměstí 15 (across from the main entrance to Prague Castle). ☎ *02/ 2051-4599. **Metro:** A to Malostranská or Hradčanská. **Tram:** 22. **Admission:** 70Kč ($2.12) adults, 40Kč ($1.21) students and children. **Open:** Tues–Sun 10am–6pm.*

Charles Bridge (Karlův most)

You won't find a more lovely or lively span anywhere in Europe. The statue-lined Charles Bridge is bustling with people throughout the day and evening—not just pedestrians, but dozens of musicians, street performers, caricature artists, and crafts peddlers. The 1,700-foot span was constructed in the 14th century, but the majority of statues date from the early 18th century (most of the originals have been moved inside for protection from the weather; these are copies). Two of the earliest include the 1629 crucifix near the Old Town end (great effects during sunrise or sunset) and, halfway across, the haloed statue of St. John Nepomuk (1683), which honors the holy man who King Wenceslas IV tortured to death then tossed off this bridge. A bronze plaque under the statue describes the event; rubbing the shiny, worn figure of the saint is supposed to bring good luck.

Look Out Below!

Praguers have a disturbing history of throwing people they don't like out windows. The First Defenestration, utilizing a third-story window of the New Town Hall, occurred in 1419 as a result of an argument between early pro-reform Protestants and status quo Catholics. The Second Defenestration saw the bodies of three pro-Hapsburg Czechs come flying out the windows of the Royal Palace's Ludwig Wing in 1618. The result of a quarrel between Protestants and Catholics, this event helped spark the bloody 30 Years' War that raged across Europe. The most recent defenestration was in 1996, when Tom Cruise came hurtling out of a seafood restaurant's glassed-in storefront in *Mission Impossible*, followed by a tidal wave of aquarium water (being a highly paid hero, of course, Cruise survived).

Old Town Square (Staroměstské náměstí)

The crossroads of Prague and its most gorgeous baroque square, Staroměstské is centered on a massive memorial to the 15th-century religious reformer and martyr Jan Hus. Some of Prague's prettiest buildings surround the square, which is perpetually crowded with street performers, tourists, and the general bustle of the city. Take time out to sit at an outdoor cafe table and soak it all in.

The **Old Town Hall** (☎ 02/2422-8456) has a steep tower to climb for views across the rooftops, but its most popular feature is the **Astronomical Clock.** Rather than tell the hour, this 15th-century timepiece keeps track of moon phases, equinoxes, and various Christian holidays tied to them. On every hour from 8am to 8pm, it puts on a glockenspiel-style show of marching apostles and dancing embodiments of Evil—skeletal Death and haughty Vanity are straightforward enough, but on a politically incorrect note, Corruption is played by a Turk, and until after World War II, the character now called Greed had horns, a beard, and was known as the moneybag-gripping Jew.

Bet You Didn't Know

The architect of the Astronomical Clock, Master Hanuš, did such a good job that the city council feared he might one day build a better one elsewhere. To ensure that their clock remained superior, they had him blinded. Legend has it that, in despair and revenge, Master Hanuš threw his body into the clock's mechanism, crushing himself but also throwing the works off-kilter for a century.

The **Church of Our Lady Before Týn** stands out with its twin multisteepled towers. It's mainly Gothic, dating from 1380, and is the seat of Prague's Protestant congregation.

Staroměstské náměstí. **Metro:** *A to Staroměstská.* **Tram:** *17, 18, 51, 54.* **Bus:** *135, 207.* **Admission:** *Old Town Hall tower 30Kč (90¢) adults, 20Kč (60¢) students and children.* **Open:** *Old Town Hall, May–Oct, Tues–Sun 9am–6pm, Mon 11am–6pm; Nov–Apr, Tues–Sun 9am–5pm, Mon 11am–5pm.*

Jewish Prague (Josefov)

On the north end of the Old Town lies the Jewish ghetto. Jews were living in Prague before the 10th century, but by the 12th century, they were confined to their own small part of town (at the time, walled off). Ironically, even though 88,000 of the country's 118,000 Jews died during the Holocaust, Nazi occupiers spared this center of Jewish culture. Hilter had been collecting the riches of Judaism as he systematically exterminated their people across Europe, and he planned to put all the scrolls, torahs, and other artifacts on display in Prague, turning Josefov into a "museum to a vanished race." Most of those seized items were returned in 1994 to the diaspora from which they had been taken. It's possible to see Josefov's highlights in maybe 45 minutes to an hour, but I'd spend a full morning here.

The official center for Josefov is the **Maisel Synagogue,** which contains exhibits of Jewish objects. Escorted tours to all of the area's buildings begin here. The **Old-New Synagogue,** at červaná 2, was built in 1270. It's small but beautiful inside with high ceilings crisscrossed with five-ribbed fan vaulting. (Gothic church vaulting uses four ribs, but because these ribs represent the cross, the Jews decided five would be a bit more appropriate.)

Off U Starého hřbitova, behind a high wall, is the **Old Jewish Cemetery,** one of Prague's most evocative sights. It's one of the oldest Jewish burial grounds in Europe, dating back to the 15th century—a time when Jews couldn't bury their dead outside of the ghetto. Within this one-block plot, they had to find final resting places for some 20,000 to 80,000 deceased (the exact number is unknown). Consequently, they stacked the bodies 12 deep in some places. The shady, overgrown, undulating ground is blanketed with some 12,000 time-worn tombstones lurching and tilting in varying degrees of disrepair. The air is melancholy yet serene. If you have time for only one sight in Jewish Prague, make it this one. The relatively elaborate sarcophagus of the venerated holy man Rabbi Loew (he died in 1609; see sidebar) stands out.

Josefov's most moving sight, however, is the **Pinkas Synagogue,** built in the flamboyant high Gothic style of the 16th century. From 1950 to 1958, Holocaust survivors painted the names of 77,297 Czech Jews who died under the Nazi regime on the inside walls. The communist regime closed the synagogue and, claiming dampness was leading to the deterioration of the walls, had the place replastered. As soon as communism ended and the synagogue was reopened, the Jews got out the paintbrushes and started the meticulous task of inscribing every last one of those names back on the walls. They don't expect to be finished any time soon.

The Maisel Synagogue is on Maiselova St. (the northern extension of U Radnice). ☎ *02/2481-0099. Metro: A to Staroměstská. Tram: 17. Bus: 135, 207. Admission: Guided tours to all of Prague's major Jewish sights (a group of at least 10 must gather before they'll do a tour) costs 270Kč ($7.70) for adults, 170Kč ($4.85) for ages 8–15. Open: Tours leave hourly May–Oct.*

Extra! Extra!

Jewish Prague's mythology boasts one of the first Frankenstein-type monsters. In the 15th century, it is said, Rabbi Loew scraped clay from the riverbed and fashioned it into a giant he called Golem. Loew placed a prayer scroll in the Golem's mouth, and the figure came to life, charged with protecting the Jews from persecution. Eventually, as in all good monster stories, the creature ran amok, and it took all of Rabbi Loew's power to subdue the Golem. As the magical life seeped out of his creation, the rabbi dragged the disintegrating clay body up to the loft of the Old-New Synagogue, where a lifeless mound of clay supposedly remains to this day.

Strahov Monastery (Strahovskýklášter)

Founded in 1140 by the Premonstratensian monks (an order that still lives here), this monastery was rebuilt in the Gothic style of the 13th century. It's renowned for its libraries, both the collections—over 125,000 volumes, many of them priceless illuminated manuscripts—and for the long baroque hall that houses the philosophy and theology books. Crowning the hall is a ceiling fresco of the *Struggle of Mankind to Know Real Wisdom.* Also check out the baroque Church of Our Lady.

Strahovské nádvoří. ☎ *02/5732-0828. Tram: 22. Admission: 20Kč (60¢) for adults, 5Kč for (15¢) students. Open: Tues–Sun 9am–noon and 1–5pm.*

Other Fun Stuff to Do

➤ **Go Concert-hopping.** As my first visit to Prague ended, I seriously considered abandoning the planned next leg of my journey to stay here. Not because I hadn't seen all the sights, but because I had fallen in love with the dozens of classical concerts offered every evening throughout town—in churches and concert halls, in intimate private chambers and large public halls, under street arches and in the squares. I came across 14-year-old virtuosos who could hold their own in any professional orchestra playing their violins in the alleys of Prague Castle for handouts. Many estimate that there are more musicians per capita in the Czech Republic than anywhere else.

In the city that gave the world the composers Smetana and Dvořák, and where Mozart wrote *Don Giovanni* and found greater acclaim than in his native Austria, you'll have a smorgasbord of offerings to choose from: an organ concert in the Týn Church, a chamber ensemble in a defunct monastery, or the Czech Philharmonic in the 19th-century Rudolfinum (☎ 02/2489-3352). The *Prague Post* and *Velvet* both list most events around town, or you can just wander the Old City, especially around Staroměstské square, where you'll find the highest concentration of posters proclaiming this week's concerts and venues. If it's playing, attend Mozart's *Don Giovanni* in the venue where it premiered, the restored 1783 Estateś Theater (Stavovské divadio; ☎ 02/2421-5001). This theater is the only baroque performance space preserved just as it appeared in Mozart's day.

➤ **Make Friends in a Beer Hall.** "Wherever beer is brewed, all is well. Whenever beer is drunk, life is good." So goes the Czech proverb. Praguers love their *pivo* (beer)—to the tune of 320 pints per year per Czech—and they love their local *hospoda* (pub or beer hall). **Beer halls** serve as gathering places for friends, intellectuals, trendies, and glitterati. The different types of Czech beer were introduced in the dining section, but here's a quick lesson in beer-hall etiquette. Share tables. *Always* ask *Je tu volno* (Is this spot taken?). Put a coaster in front of you if you want beer and never wave down the waiter (he'll ignore you entirely). When a waiter approaches, nod and hold up your fingers for how many beers you want. He'll leave a marked slip of paper at your table with the drinks. The waiter visits you only two times, tops, so when he comes around again, order all the beer you'll want for the rest of your stay. When he brings that, pay him (otherwise, you may wait for hours).

Some of the better beer halls to try include the most famous, **U Fleků** (☎ 02/2491-5118), Křemencova 11, a brewery from 1459 (check out the brass band in the courtyard garden). Go to **U Medviku** (no phone), na Pertýn at Narodní tridaù, for real Budvar on tap and good Czech pub grub. For a real, albeit famous, Praguer's bar, hit **U Zlatého tygra** (☎ 02/2422-9020), Husova 17, a smoky haunt of writers and politicians.

➤ **Visit a Park along the River. Letná Park** (Letenské sady) is a wide, flat swath of greenery and trees on the western bank of the Vltava River, north of Malá Strana. There are plenty of quiet picnic spots, a beer garden in summer on the park's north side, and lots of paths winding through the trees and along the river. Walk along the river tossing bread to, and making friends with, Prague's famed mute swans. Take tram 1, 8, 25, or 26 to get there.

➤ **Rent a Paddle Boat for a Cheesy Photo Op.** The Vltava's such a pretty river, full of graceful swans and spanned by dramatic bridges, that sometimes you're compelled to just be a part of it—but because of the pollution, swimming's out of the question. March to September you can rent paddle boats (30Kč/85¢ per hour) and rowboats (20Kč/ $60¢ per hour) from **Půjčovna Romana Holana** at the docks of Slovanskýostrov, an island two blocks south of the National Theater. Next door, **Rent-A-Boat** costs twice as much, but it also offers the unique opportunity to rent a rowboat with a lantern at the bow in the evenings (until 11pm) and row around the river under the romantic moonlight and floodlit spires of the city. This boat will cost you 80Kč ($2.30) per hour. Rent-A-Boat also stays open until October (November if the weather holds).

Get Outta Town: Day Trips & Excursions

Several fascinating destinations lie just a short bus or train ride from the city center. Among them are a 14th-century castle, a church adorned with human bones, and a "model" Nazi internment camp that was designed to mask Hitler's true, diabolical motives.

Medieval Karlštejn Castle

Prague's most popular day trip (tour companies love it and over 350,000 people visit annually) is to this highly picturesque 14th-century castle perched scenically above the river. **Trains** out here take 45 minutes and leave from Prague's Smíchov Station (take Metro line B to Smichovské nádraží).

The walk up to the **castle** from the train station is a rigorous uphill mile. (Unfortunately, no buses are available for those who can't manage the walk.) Charles IV built the fortress (between 1348 and 1357) to protect the crown jewels, which are no longer in residence. A 19th-century restoration stripped the place of later additions and rebuilt it in line with how folks from the Romantic Era thought a medieval castle should look (close to the original, but a bit fanciful in places). You can get inside only by guided tour,

Time-Savers

It takes only a few hours to get here, see the castle, and return to Prague, but sticking around for lunch to enjoy Karlštejn's small-town setting is one of the attractions (though it's usually quite crowded). This is a one-trick town, so there's no tourism office; just hike up to the castle and its admissions office for information.

which takes you through parts of the South Palace to see the Audience Hall and Imperial Bedroom—both impressive in an austere, medieval way.

Sadly, vandalism as well as the environmental impact of all those visitors has closed the castle's most spectacular rooms, including the famed Holy Rood Chapel with its ceiling of glass "stars." The view from the castle across the fertile river valley, though, makes the climb worth it. The tour costs 90Kč ($2.60) for adults, 45Kč ($1.30) for children. It's open daily from 9am to noon and 12:30 to 4pm (closing at 7pm in July and August; 6pm May, June, and September).

The main road leading up to the castle is padded with many souvenir shops and restaurants. The best eats are at **Restaurace Blanky z Valois,** a cozy place serving good Czech food with a French twist.

Skeletons & Silver Memories in Kutná Hora

There's silver under that thar village! The cry went something like that in the 14th century when the small mining community of Kutná Hora started hauling up bucketfuls of the precious metal. The king, knowing a good thing when he saw it, promptly took control of the mines and started drawing six tons of pure silver a year out of the ground, building Kutná Hora into Bohemia's second city. The fortune made the Czech monarchs the richest rulers in Europe for a century or so, and the *groschen* coins minted here became one of the continent's foremost currencies.

The silver began to peter out in the 16th century. By the 1700s, it was gone entirely, and the little city was left to collect dust. The communists showed little interest in modernizing the town, so it still looks very much like it did centuries ago. It's a popular destination for its fabulously ornate Gothic cathedral, creepy Bone Church (see "Holy Scapula! The Bone Church" sidebar below), and well-preserved late medieval center. **Buses** here from Prague (leaving from either Želivkého metro station or Florenc bus depot) take about 90 minutes.

Time-Savers

The sights in Kutná Hora are easy enough to see in a day. On Paláckého náměstí, the town's main square, is both a **tourist information kiosk** and a Čedok office (☎ **0327/2534**), at no. 330.

On the southwest end of town, down the statue-lined Barborská Street, is Kutná Hora's most spectacular sight, the 14th-century **St. Barbara's Cathedral—** named after the patron saint of miners. Started in 1380, it took 200 years to complete in an extravagant Bohemian Gothic style, with three wide steeples rising like mountain peaks above an orderly forest of minispires and flying buttresses. Under the vaulted ceiling inside, the walls are richly decorated with religious scenes full of references to mining and minting. Admission is 40Kč ($1.21) for adults, 20Kč (60¢) for kids. It's open Tuesday through Sunday 9am to noon and 1 to 5pm.

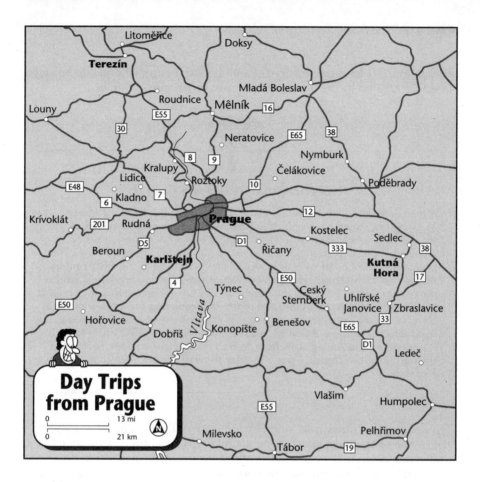

Day Trips
from Prague

0 ___ 13 mi
0 ___ 21 km

In the **Hrádek,** a 15th-century castle at the opposite end of Barborská Street, is the **District Museum of Mining (Okresní Muzeum),** which takes you down into the former mine shafts for a guided half-hour tour around the town's former font of wealth (because all tours are in Czech, ask for an English-language explanation sheet when you arrive). It's open Tuesday through Sunday, 9am to noon and 1 to 5pm; admission is 50Kč ($1.51) for adults, 25Kč (76¢) for kids. In the 13th-century **Italian Court,** a former mint named for the Florentine master coiners who were imported to make *groschen,* you can ogle monies from the 14th to 18th centuries as you pass by several ornate chapels. There's a killer view of the cathedral from the south terrace.

For a quick meal, stop by **Restaurace Harmonica,** on Komenského náměstí (near the Italian Court). **Ú Morového Sloupu,** Šultyšova 3, offers more substantial Czech fare.

The Nazi Trick at Terezín

The Nazi camp at Terezín—a town that had been built as a city/fortress in the 19th century—was not a death camp or concentration lager. It served mainly as a transfer station in the despicable traffic of human cargo—Jews, homosexuals, gypsies, and political dissidents—on to other, more deadly

destinations. At least half of the 140,000 human beings who passed through
Terezín ended up in the death mills of Auschwitz and Treblinka.

Holy Scapula! The Bone Church

A mile down the road in the hamlet of Sedlec (take the local bus from
Masaryokova Street) sits the Gothic **Kostnice,** known more familiarly as
the **Bone Church.** Here you'll find ranks of human skulls and finger bones
arranged in pretty patterns, and shoulder blades serving as angel's wings. The
church was surrounded by mass graves filled with victims of the 14th-century
plague and 15th-century Hussite Wars. When the area was developed, workers
plowed up human bones by the hundreds. The local monks decided to respect
these disturbed dead in a curious manner—by decorating the interior of the
church with the bones in mosaic patterns. It's a bit macabre and gruesome, but
fascinating nonetheless. Admission is 25Kč (76¢) for adults, 10Kč (30¢) for kids.
It's open July and August daily from 9am to noon and 1 to 5pm. September
through June, the church is open Tuesday through Sunday, 9am to noon and
1 to 4pm.

Terezín, an hour's **bus** ride from Florenc station, lives on in infamy as the
site of one of the most effective public relations deceptions perpetrated by SS
leader Himmler. In 1944, the Nazis allowed three Red Cross workers to visit
the camp to see if the horrible rumors about SS methods were true. Instead,
they found a model guarded community, a self-governed modern ghetto
with children studying at school, stores
stocked with goods, internees apparently
healthy, and none of the overcrowding
they had suspected.

Time-Savers

Budget a full morning to
fully explore Terezín. There's
an **information office**
(☎ **0416/92-227**) on
the town's main square,
Náměstičs 179.

What the Red Cross didn't know was
that it was all elaborately staged. The
"schools" had been quickly set up for the
observers' benefit, and just as quickly
dismantled the moment they left. The
stores were fake, with goods shipped in
from Prague for the occasion, and the
prisoners had been forced to feign happiness and pretend they governed themselves. The apparent health and lack of
overcrowding of prisoners was due to the fact that 7,500 of the camp's sick
and elderly were sent to the gas chambers at Auschwitz just before the Red
Cross arrived.

The **Main Fortress** (Hlavní Pevnsot) houses a **Museum of the Ghetto,** detailing life in this camp and the rise of Nazism. In the **Minor Fortress,** a 10-minute walk away, are the prison barracks, execution grounds, and isolation cells. Out in front is the **National Cemetery,** where bodies exhumed from Nazi mass graves were properly reburied. Admission to the Main Fortress is 50Kč ($1.52) for adults, 25Kč for (76¢) children. A combined ticket to both Major and Minor Fortresses is 100Kč ($3.03) for adults, 50Kč ($1.52) for children. The fortresses are open daily from 9am to 6pm.

Part 5

Mediterranean Europe

Ah, the sunny Mediterranean. A region of crinkly coastal drives and long, late dinners, of jewel-like islands and midafternoon siestas, of olives and fine wine. The Mediterranean pace of life is slower and more laid back than that of northern and central Europe. These are the cultures that gave us what Spain calls the paseo and Italy the passeggiata—the see-and-be-seen pre-dinner stroll along the main drag in town.

The Mediterranean is also the cradle of Western civilization, where you think in terms of millennia instead of just centuries. Come with me and explore the ruins and treasures of ancient Greece and Rome: the Colosseum, Pantheon, and Forum in Rome; the Parthenon in Athens; the Oracle at Delphi. But a few dusty rocks and broken columns do not a Western civilization make; Italy, especially, has been a center of art through the ages and was the birthplace of the Renaissance. I'll guide you through the museums and churches of Rome, Florence, and Venice, filled with masterpieces by Michelangelo, Raphael, Donatello, da Vinci, Botticelli, and many, many others.

Don't stop there. Madrid's Prado museum, with its Velázquez and Goya masterpieces, matches up against the Louvre any day. In Barcelona, we'll wander the Gothic old town and puzzle over the funky buildings by the visionary architect Gaudí. But perhaps by now you're saying, enough of all this culture! If so, I'll whisk you away to the warm, whitewashed simplicity and sunshine of Santoríni in the Greek islands. There, we'll laze the day away with nary a toga, temple, or artistic treasure in sight.

Chapter 22

Rome & the Best of Southern Italy

In This Chapter

➤ The lowdown on ancient Rome, from the ruins to the statues to those wacky emperors

➤ Tips for touring the Vatican and seeing the many masterpieces

➤ In the shadow of history: hotels with a view

➤ The best cafes and trattorias

➤ The night the lights went out in Pompeii and other excursions

---

Dollars & Sense

The Italian units of currency are called lire (L). Roughly, $1 equals 1,667L; or 1,000L equals 60¢. Italian coins include 50, 100, 200, and 500 lire. It's easy to get confused—there are two different 50 lire coins, and three types of 100-lire pieces. Old 10-lire and 20-lire coins still turn up (though they're completely worthless), as do *gettoni*, old grooved phone tokens—but those are worth 200L. Keep in mind the government will soon release a 1,000L coin. Bills come in denominations of 1,000, 2,000, 5,000, 10,000, 50,000, and 100,000 lire.

Rome is the Eternal City, the seat of two great empires, one Roman and one Christian. Ancient Rome's 2,000-year-old ruins are strewn about the city—major sights such as the Colosseum, Pantheon, and Roman Forum. The era of Caesars and togas also cranked out tens of thousands of sculptures; you can find the cream of this crop in the Vatican and Capitoline museums.

Not to be outdone, the early Christians left behind well over 900 churches. Many of these aren't so much houses of worship as they are marble-clad museums where you'll find centuries' worth of art from the masters of the Renaissance and baroque eras. Works by such artists as Michelangelo, Raphael, Bernini, Borromini, Botticelli, and Caravaggio abound. One church rises way above the rest, however. As the capital of Christendom, Rome is home to the huge basilica of St. Peter's. Right next door is the pope's home, Vatican City. The Vatican's museums are vast, but what draws the crowds here is Michelangelo's masterpiece, the ceiling of the Sistine Chapel.

Though history is everywhere, Rome is not a city that lives in the past. I hope that between the ruins and the museums, you'll find time to sip a morning cappuccino in a local bar as motorscooters buzz down medieval cobblestone streets. I encourage you to take evening strolls past Renaissance palaces and fountains before sitting down to a long, leisurely dinner over-looking one of the city's many *piazze* (squares). Or maybe you'll just window-shop in the city's posh retail districts, where the best of Italian fashion is on display.

Someone once said it would take a lifetime to see all of Rome; I'd wager 100 lifetimes wouldn't be enough (after all, it wasn't built in a day, now was it?). You can't reasonably expect to see it in one day either, but you can get at least a healthy taste of it in three or four. Just be sure, before you leave, to toss a coin into the Trevi Fountain—legend has it that if you do, you are guaranteed to return someday.

Tourist Traps

Rome's throwing a party, and the whole world's invited. The year 2000 has been designated the Holy Year, or Papal Jubilee, and will be a time of pilgrim-ages, special masses, art and history exhibits, popular events, and music and theater festivals galore. The crowds promise to be tremendous—40 to 50 mil-lion people are expected to descend upon the city over the course of those 365 days. Officials are trying desperately to prepare the city as the 1990s draw to a close, so you may find more monuments than usual closed for renovations or wrapped in scaffolding for a good cleaning. If you're planning your trip for the year 2000, reserve everything *well* in advance, and be prepared for a tourist crush like you've never imagined.

Getting Your Bearings

Rome stretches along an S-shaped bend of the **Tevere (Tiber River).** The bulk of the *centro storico* (historic center) lies east of the Tevere. The city is divided into official administrative districts, but Romans themselves refer to an address as being near this piazza (square) or that major monument, so I'll do the same. That said, there are a *lot* of these piazze and monuments; they effectively divide the city into a few dozen little neighborhoods, which, coupled with the dozen or so major streets, makes orienting yourself in Rome a bit tricky. Using the map in this chapter, along with the following brief synopsis, will give you a good handle on the layout.

Time-Savers

There's a dinky **tourist information** office inside Termini train station, which is usually crowded and sparse of information. This office is most useful on Sundays when the main office (☎ **06/4889-9253;** fax: 06/4889-9228) at Via Parigi 5 (about a five-minute walk from the station) is closed. There's another desk at Fiumicino airport. Rome has three helpful **information kiosks** around town, linked into a computer database. You'll find them at Largo Goldoni (across from where Via dei Condotti spills into Via del Corso), on Via Nazionale (near the Palazzo degli Esposizioni), and on Largo Corrado Ricci (across Via dei Fori Imperiali from the main entrance to the Roman Forum). From any newsstand, pick up *Roma C'è,* an Italian-language events magazine, or buy the Thursday copy of *La Reppublica* newspaper, which has a pullout section called *Trovaroma.* For events information in English, buy the monthly *Wanted in Rome.*

Rome's Neighborhoods in Brief

The first neighborhood you'll likely see lies to the east of the city center in the grid of 19th-century streets surrounding the **Termini,** or main train station. Aside from some churches and other sights, this part of town is pretty boring. Although it has a glut of cheap hotels, it's not the nicest of areas.

At the north end of the city center is the oval **Piazza del Popolo.** Three major roads radiate south from here: Via del Babuino, Via del Corso, and Via di Ripetta. **Via del Corso** (usually just called the **Corso**) divides the heart of the city in half.

To the east of the Corso lie the **Spanish Steps** and **Trevi Fountain.** Surrounding these monuments are most of Rome's priciest hotels, as well as its most stylish shopping streets—including the boutique-lined **Via dei Condotti,** which runs straight from the Spanish Steps to the Corso.

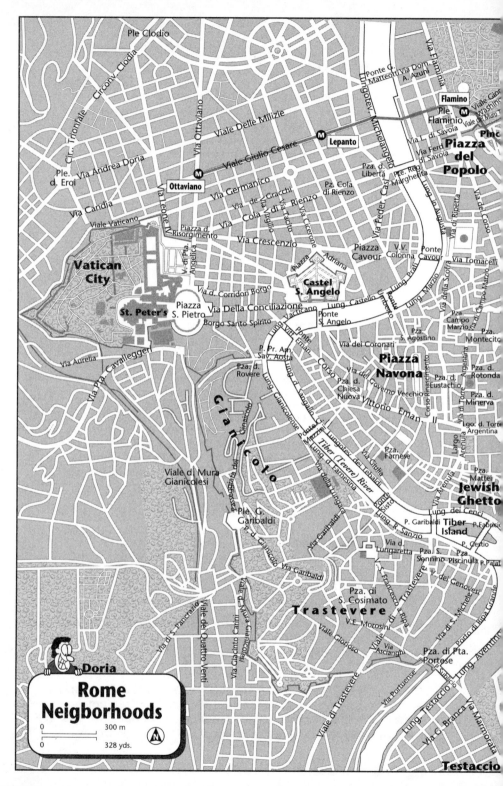

Rome
Neigborhoods

0 ——————— 300 m
0 ——————— 328 yds.

Doria

Vatican
City

St. Peter's

Piazza
S. Pietro

Gianicolo

Viale di Mura
Gianicolesi

Ple. G.
Garibaldi

Ple Clodio

Circonv. Clodia

Cir. Trionfale

Via Andrea Doria

Ple.
d. Eroi

Via Candia

Viale Vaticano

Via Leone IV

Via di Pta. Angelica

V. di Pta. Angelica

Piazza d.
Risorgimento

Viale Delle Milizie

Via Ottaviano

Viale Giulio Cesare

Via Germanico

Via de' Gracchi

Via Cola di Virginio

Via Cola di Rienzo

Via Crescenzio

Via Tacito

Via Cicerone

Lepanto

Ottaviano

Pza. Cola
di Rienzo

Piazza
Cavour

V.V.
Colonna

Ponte
Cavour

Via Tomacelli

Via della Scrofa

Via di Ripetta

Via del Corso

Viale Gior.
Washingt

Flamino

Ple.
Flaminio

Via di Muro

Piazza
del
Popolo

Pin

Via L. di Savoia

Via Ferd.
di Savoia

Pza. d.
Libertà

Pte. Reg.
Margherita

Lungotev. Michelangelo

Ponte G.
Matteotti Via Dom.
A. Azuni

Via Flaminia

Via Flaminia

Via Feder. Cesi

Lung. d'Augusta

Castel
S. Angelo

Piazza
Adriana

Via d. Corridori Borgo

Via Della Conciliazione

Borgo Santo Spirito

Via Aurelia

Via Pta Cavalleggeri

Lung. Vaticano

Ponte
S. Angelo

Lung. Castello

Lung. Tor di Nona

Ponte Umberto I

P. Pr. Am.
Sav. Aosta

Pza. d.
Rovere

Lung. Gianicolense

Ponte d. Sangallo

Via Vitt. Eman.

Ponte V. Eman.

Lung. dei Fiorentini

Lung. d. Sangallo

Corso Vittorio Emanuele

Via del Governo Vecchio

Pza. d.
Chiesa
Nuova

Corso Vittorio Eman. II

Piazza
Navona

Via dei Coronari

Pza.
S. Agostino

Piazza
Campo
Marzio

Pza.
Campo
Marzio

Pza.
Montecito

Pza. d.
Rotonda

Pza. d.
Minerva

Via della Torretta

Campo Marzio

Corso Rinascimento

Pza. d.
Eustachio

Lgo. d. Torre
Argentina

Largo Arenula

Pza.
Argentina

Via Arenula

Jewish
Ghetto

Pza.
Mattei

Lung. dei Cenci

P. Fabricio

Tiber
Island

P. Garibaldi

P. R. Sanzio

Via d.
Lungaretta

Pza. S.
Sonnino

Piscinula P. Palat

P. Cestio

Pza.
Pza. di
S. Cosimato

Trastevere

V.E. Morosini

Via di Trastevere

V. dei Genovesi

Via di S. Michele

V. S. Francesco a Ripa

Via
Ascianghi

Viale Glorioso

Viale Trastevere

Pza. di Pta.
Portese

Porto di Ripa Grande

Via di Trastevere

Via Portuense

Lung. Testaccio

Lung. Aventino

Via Marmorata

Via G. Branca

Testaccio

Ponte
Sisto

Lung. d. Farnesina

Via della Lungara

Lung. d. Tebaldi

Lungotev. dei Tebaldi

Via Giulia

Tiber (Tevere) River

Ponte Garibaldi

Via Garibaldi

Via Garibaldi

Via di Gianicolo

P. di Gianicolo

Via di Porta S. Pancrazio

Via di S. Pancrazio

Viale di Quattro Venti

Via Giacinto Carini

Via Dandolo

Via di Mura Gianicolensi

Passeggiata del Gianicolo

Pza.
Farnese

402

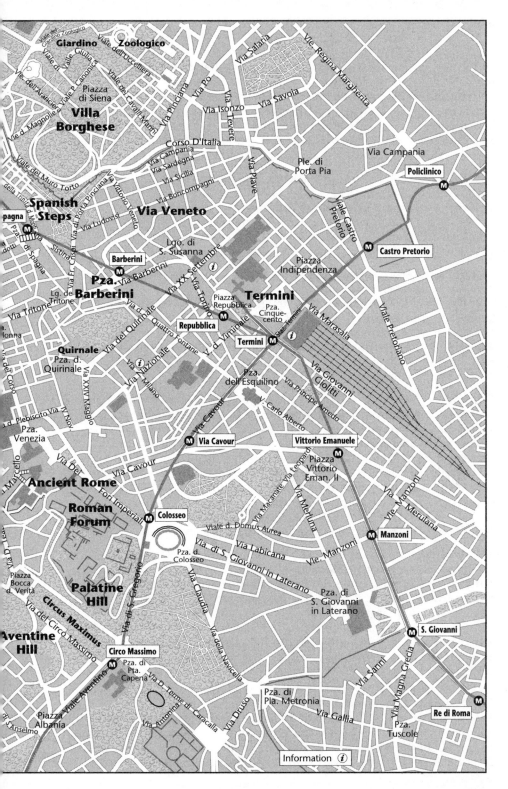

To the west of the Corso spreads the medieval **Tiber Bend area,** one of the most sight-filled zones in Rome. It contains landmarks such as the long, bustling **Piazza Navona,** the **Pantheon,** the market square of **Campo dei Fiori,** and the medieval **Jewish Ghetto,** still home to Europe's oldest Jewish population, countless churches, and a few small museums. The Tiber Bend area has some of Rome's best restaurants and much of it is pedestrian-only. It's great for wandering and people-watching.

The Corso ends roughly at Rome's center, the **Piazza Venezia.** This major traffic circle and bus juncture is marked by the enormous, garish, white **Vittorio Emanuele Monument** (nicknamed the Wedding Cake or Giant Typewriter). Leading west from Piazza Venezia is Via Plebescito, which turns into **Corso Vittorio Emanuele II,** a wide street that bisects the Tiber Bend area as it heads toward the river and the Vatican.

Back at Piazza Venezia, you'll see stairs leading up to **Capitoline Hill,** Rome's seat of government since before the Empire. From the piazza, the wide **Via dei Fori Imperiali** goes straight to the **Colosseum,** passing the famous **Roman Forum** on the right and the **Imperial Forums** on the left. The monuments in this area are often referred to collectively as **Ancient Rome.** South of the Forum and Colosseum rises the residential **Aventine Hill,** beyond which is another hill, the old-working-class-now-trendy restaurant and nightclub quarter called **Testaccio.**

Those are the areas of Rome where you'll spend most of your time, though a few other areas of the city warrant mention. To the northwest of the train station (east of the Spanish Steps area) is a neighborhood where many of the embassies are located; the main drag here is a lazy S-curve called **Via Veneto.** In the 1950s, this street was the center of *La Dolce Vita* ("the sweet life"), made famous by the 1960 Federico Fellini film of the same name. Via Veneto still has the cafes of its decadent heyday, though today they're overpriced and frequented almost exclusively by tourists. Via Veneto ends at the southern flank of the giant **Villa Borghese** park, located northeast of the *centro storico;* this park is also accessible from Piazza del Popolo.

Across the river are two major neighborhoods you'll be interested in. Mussolini razed a medieval district to lay down the wide **Via della Conciliazione,** which links the Ponte Vittorio Emanuele bridge with **Vatican City and St. Peter's.** The area surrounding the Vatican is usually crowded with tour groups and the restaurants and businesses that cater to them, but also many modestly priced (if boringly modern) hotels. South of here, past the long, parklike **Gianicolo** hill, lies the now-fashionable medieval district of **Trastevere,** with lots of authentically Roman restaurants and little shops.

Getting Into & Around Town

Almost all trains to Rome pull into **Termini.** From the station, a special train shuttles passengers on the half-hour trip to and from **Fiumicino** (also known as **Leonardo da Vinci**) **airport.** This is Rome's main international airport, but some charter flights land at **Ciampino airport;** from there, take the blue ACOTRAL city bus to the Metro line A terminus, where you can catch the subway to Termini. Taxi rides average 70,000L ($42) from Fiumicino airport into the center of town; from Ciampino plan on paying 40,000–50,000L ($24–$30) to get into town.

Dollars & Sense

All city transportation uses the same **ticket.** A regular *biglietto* gives you 75 minutes in which you can transfer buses (but not bus-to-metro) as often as you'd like; just stamp it once on the first bus, and again when you board the final bus. There are also daily (6,000L/$3.60) and weekly (24,000L/$14.40) passes. You can buy tickets and passes at *tabacchi* (tobacconist shops marked by a brown-and-white T sign), newsstands, Metro stations, and machines at major bus stops. Hold on to your ticket until you're off the bus or out of the station to avoid paying a fine.

Rome has a **Metro (subway),** but it isn't very extensive; every time workers try to dig new tunnels, they run across ancient ruins and have to stop so archaeologists can putter about. The two lines, the orange A line and the blue B line, make a rough X pattern with Termini at the intersection. Line A runs from Ottaviano (a dozen blocks from the Vatican) through such stops as Flaminia (near Piazza del Popolo), Spagna (Spanish Steps), Termini, and San Giovanni (Rome's cathedral). The B line is most useful for shuttling you quickly from Termini to stops for the Colosseo (Colosseum) and Circo Massimo (the Circus Maximus). Plans are underway to dig a third, C line that will link Termini directly to the Vatican.

The **bus and tram** system is much more extensive, and you usually don't have to walk far for a connection. The tourist office hands out a free bus route map. The most useful lines are the 64, which runs from Termini to the Vatican (known as the Pickpocket Express because con artists take this route to prey on travelers—be careful), and the 116 and 117, two teensy electric buses that trundle through the streets of the *centro storico*. Many buses start their routes at the large Piazza dei Cinquecento in front of Termini. Otherwise, there are three major squares in the *centro storico* where multiple bus lines converge for easy transfers: Largo di Tritone (east of the Trevi Fountain), Largo di Torre Argentina (south of the Pantheon), and Piazza San Silvestro (just off the Corso, between the Spanish Steps and Trevi Fountain).

Rome Fast Facts

American Express   Rome's American Express office is next to the Spanish Steps at Piazza di Spagna 38 (☎ **06/67-641**). The financial and mail services are open Monday to Friday 9am to 5pm and Saturday 9am to noon. The travel and tour desks are open Monday to Friday 9am to 5:30pm and Saturday 9am to 12:30pm. From May to October, the tour desk is also open Saturday 2 to 2:30pm.

Doctors/hospitals First aid is available 24 hours a day in the emergency rooms *(pronto soccorso)* of major hospitals. Try the **International Medical Center** at Via Giovanni Amendola 7 (☎ **06/488-2371**). Call the **U.S. Embassy** (☎ **06/46-741**) for a list of English-speaking doctors, or in an emergency, English-speaking doctors are always on duty at the **Rome American Hospital,** Via Emilio Longoni 69 (☎ **06/22-551**), and at the privately run **Salvator Mundi International Hospital,** Viale delle Mura Gianicolensi 67 (☎ **06/586-041**).

Embassy The U.S. Embassy (☎ **06/46-741**) is located at Via Veneto 121.

Emergency Dial ☎ **113** for any sort of emergency. You can reach the *carabinieri* (police) at ☎ **112,** call an ambulance at ☎ **118,** and report a fire by dialing ☎ **115.** If your car breaks down, call ☎ **116** for roadside assistance.

Pharmacies *Farmacie* follow a rotation schedule so that several remain open at night and on Sundays. (The schedule is posted outside each pharmacy.) The **Farmacia Internazionale** at Piazza Barberini 49 (☎ **06/679-4680**) is open 24 hours.

Time-Savers

Almost all Italian shops, and most churches and museums, observe a siesta-like midafternoon shutdown called *riposo*, which lasts roughly from noon or 1pm to 3 or 4pm. It's a good idea to figure out the few sights in town that remain open during *riposo* so you can schedule them and a leisurely lunch for this time.

Safety Random violent crime is extremely rare in Rome, but pickpockets—especially Gypsy children (see "Tourist Traps")—target tourists. Thieves favor buses that run between Termini and the major tourist sites (particularly bus 64 to the Vatican). Keep a close eye on your wallet when you're in the Termini, near the Forums and Colosseum, in Piazza del Popolo, and around the Vatican in particular.

Taxis Although you can reach most of Rome's sights easily by bus, trips from the airport or train station to your hotel may be more comfortable in a taxi. Taxi stands are located at major piazze, including Piazza Venezia, Largo Argentina, at the Pantheon, and in front of Termini. You can also call a taxi at ☎ **3570** or ☎ **4994,** but the meter begins running when the driver picks up your call. The initial charge is 6,400 lire ($3.85) and increases 300 lire (20¢) per kilometer. There are additional charges for luggage and travel at night or on Sundays.

Telephone A local call within Italy costs 200L (10¢). Pay phones accept coins or phone cards *(carta telefonica),* available in increments of 5,000L ($3), 10,000L ($6), and 15,000L ($9) from many newsstands and all *tabbachi* (tobacconist shops). Break off the corner of the phone card before you insert it. A digital display keeps track of how much money is left on the card. For **directory assistance,** call ☎ **12** (though keep in mind, it's unlikely the operators will speak English).

Tourist Traps

Some gypsies prefer the direct approach to pickpocketing. They surround you, distract you with cries for money or by waving cardboard, and then go for your pockets (if you're near a wall, they'll try to pin you to it with the cardboard). Should you be surrounded by aggressive children, shout "*Va via!*" (Go away!) and threaten to call the police *(polizia)*. Although not physically dangerous, Gypsy kids are extemely adept pickpockets; don't let them get close enough to touch you or your valuables will be gone. If need be, shove them away violently—don't hold back because they're children. Some gypsies ply their trade wherever tourists gather.

Italy's country code is 39; Rome's city code is 06. Drop the zero before the city code if calling from outisde Italy. In other words, to call Rome from the United States, dial **011-39-6,** followed by the number. To charge your calls to a calling card, insert 200L (you'll get it back), and call **AT&T** at ☎ **172-1011, MCI** at ☎ **172-1022,** or **Sprint** at ☎ **172-1877.** You can also call these numbers to place a collect call or dial the **Italcable** operator at ☎ **170** (free). If you must dial the United States directly from Italy, dial **001** followed by the area code and phone number.

Transit Info   For information about city buses, call **ATAC** at ☎ **06/4695-4444.** For information about suburban buses, call **COTRAL** at ☎ **06/591-5551.**

Shacking Up with Caesar—Rome's Hotel Scene

Rome has enough good accommodations in the historic center that you needn't relegate yourself to the hotel-glutted, dingy, boring grid of streets that surround the train station at the edge of town. Of course, if you're in a bind or on a severe budget, you may have to settle for the station neighborhood. If so, head for the hotels south of Termini; the area north of the station is kind of seedy (the area has been improving, but I still wouldn't spend too much time there after dark).

You'll also find moderately priced hotels with standardized comforts across the river near the Vatican and in the Via Veneto area; this area is where most tour groups stay and where many package tour operators will book you. The Via Veneto neighborhood is famous as the stomping grounds for the hedonistic jet-set of *La Dolce Vita*—a movie that chronicled Rome's upper-class

Time-Savers

The private outfit **Enjoy Rome** at Via Varese 39 (☎ **06/445-1843**) dispenses good Rome information and will find a room to suit your budget. It's located three blocks northwest of Termini.

decadence in the 1950s. These days, the neighborhood is not the happening place it once was, and I find it boring and removed from most of the sights.

Hotel-wise, the real heart of the city is tucked into the Tiber Bend and just across the Corso along those shop-lined streets surrounding the Spanish Steps and Trevi Fountain. That's where you'll find *pensioni* converted from antique palaces and where most of the hotel choices I describe are. Although the *centro storico* hotels tend to be on the pricey side, there are plenty of good values—and even frugal finds—right in the heart of things.

Albergo Abruzzi
$. Near Piazza Navona.
In a number of rooms in the Abruzzi, you open your window and look out to the Pantheon. When you can do this for well under $100, you've found something special. Of course, it's hard to keep something this good a secret; you'll need to book ahead (and send an international money order as a deposit) to snag a room with a view away from the students and budget travelers who covet them. Though not every room is blessed with the vista, they all are large, utterly basic, and clean. Bathrooms are down the hall, and the rooms do catch noise from the piazza—but with this location and that view, who cares?

*Piazza della Rotunda 69. ☎ 06/679-2021. No fax. **Bus:** 116 (or one of the many to Largo Argentina and walk 4 blocks north). **Rates:** 100,000–120,000L ($60–$72) double. No credit cards.*

Albergo Cesàri
$$$. Near Piazza Navona.
You couldn't ask for a better location—just off the Corso, halfway between the Pantheon and the Trevi Fountain, the Spanish Steps and the Roman Forum. Over the course of the Cesàri's 200 years, it has hosted the likes of Stendhal (the French author) and Italian statesman Giuseppe Garibaldi. These days, most of the comfortable rooms are outfitted in a modern style, with the occasional antique. To get the cheapest prices, you'll have to share a bath.

*Via di Pietra 89A (just off the Corso, a block south of Piazza Colonna). ☎ 06/ 679-2386. **Fax:** 06/679-0882. **Bus:** 56, 60, 62, 81, 85, 96, 116, 117, 160, 175, 492, 628, 850. **Rates:** 100,000–260,000L ($60–$156) double. AE, DC, MC, V.*

Hotel Campo de' Fiori
$$. Near Campo de' Fiori.

Rooms vary greatly at this centrally located budget gem. Some are modern and carpeted; others have brick arches and rustic wood-beam ceilings. Most are sizable, although the few smaller rooms aren't much larger than the beds. Room No. 602 (a long walk up—there's no elevator) is still the choicest room for its view across the city's rooftops and domes, a vista beat only by that of the roof terrace. The shared baths are clean. The hotel also rents four apartments in nearby buildings.

Via del Biscione, 6 (just off the northeast corner of Campo de' Fiori). ☎ *06/ 687-4886 or 06/6880-6865.* **Fax:** *06/687-6003.* **Bus:** *46, 62, 64, 116.* **Rates:** *130,000–190,000L ($78–$114) double. MC, V.*

Hotel Columbus
$$$$. Near the Vatican.

This 15th-century palazzo was once owned by Michelangelo's patron, Pope Julius II; indeed, the tapestry- and oil painting-lined public rooms seem straight out of a Renaissance castle. Although a few bedrooms retain fresco bits and decorated ceilings, most are very simple, with comfortable but purely functional furnishings.

Via della Conciliazione 33 (on the wide boulevard leading to St. Peter's). ☎ *06/ 686-5435.* **Fax:** *06/686-4874.* **Bus:** *23, 34, 62, 64, 982.* **Rates:** *250,000–320,000L ($150–$192) double. AE, DC, MC, V.*

Hotel Raphael
$$$$$. Near Piazza Navona.

Located in a tangle of medieval streets near the elegant Piazza Navona, the Raphael is a fairly plush choice, with well-appointed contemporary bedrooms and a terrific view from the roof terrace. It has amenities and facilities galore (including a fitness room), but be warned: A few of the rooms are quite small.

Largo Febo 2 (just off the northwest corner of Piazza Navona). ☎ *06/682-831.* **Fax:** *06/687-8993.* **Bus:** *70, 81, 87, 115, 116, 186, 492, 628.* **Rates:** *475,000–655,000L ($285–$393) double. AE, DC, MC, V.*

Scalinata di Spagna
$$$$. Near the Spanish Steps.

Atop the Spanish Steps sits one of Rome's most consistently popular inns, a "budget" steal (so to speak) surrounded by some of the city's priciest hotels. Some rooms are boringly average, but many have low wood ceilings and antique furnishings. Breakfast is served on the roof terrace, where the views are spectacular. Reserve well in advance.

Piazza Trinità dei Monti 17 (at the top of the Spanish Steps). ☎ *06/679-3006 or 06/6994-0896.* **Fax:** *06/6994-0598.* **Metro:** *Spagna.* **Bus:** *117, 590.* **Rates:** *200,000–420,000L ($120–$252) double. AE, MC, V.*

409

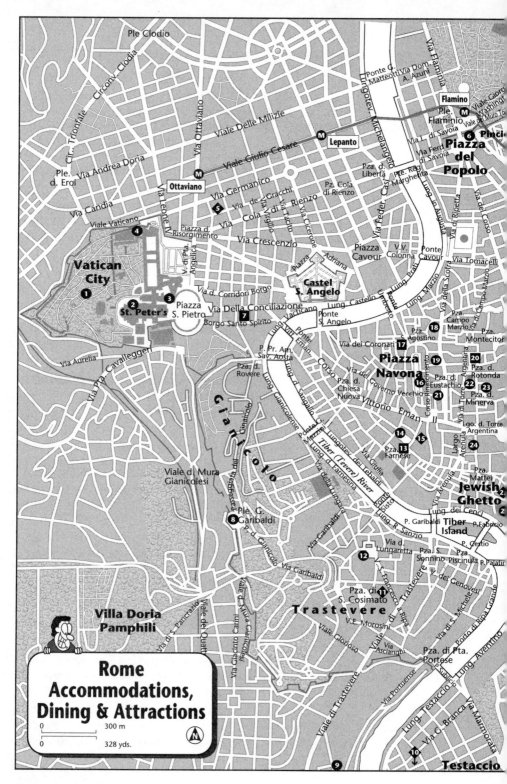

Rome
Accommodations, Dining & Attractions

0   300 m

0   328 yds.

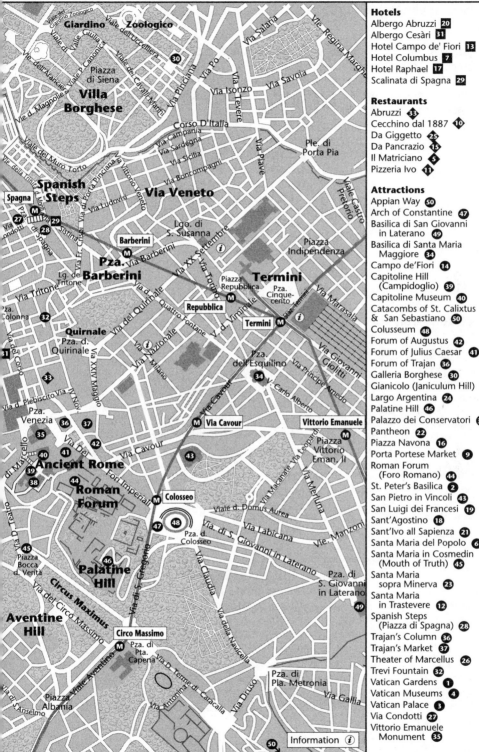

Hotels

Albergo Abruzzi **20**
Albergo Cesàri **31**
Hotel Campo de' Fiori **13**
Hotel Columbus **7**
Hotel Raphael **17**
Scalinata di Spagna **29**

Restaurants

Abruzzi **33**
Cecchino dal 1887 **10**
Da Giggetto **25**
Da Pancrazio **15**
Il Matriciano **5**
Pizzeria Ivo **11**

Attractions

Appian Way **50**
Arch of Constantine **47**
Basilica di San Giovanni
  in Laterano **49**
Basilica di Santa Maria
  Maggiore **34**
Campo de'Fiori **14**
Capitoline Hill
  (Campidoglio) **39**
Capitoline Museum **40**
Catacombs of St. Calixtus
  & San Sebastiano **50**
Colosseum **48**
Forum of Augustus **42**
Forum of Julius Caesar **41**
Forum of Trajan **36**
Galleria Borghese **30**
Gianicolo (Janiculum Hill) **8**
Largo Argentina **24**
Palatine Hill **46**
Palazzo dei Conservatori **38**
Pantheon **22**
Piazza Navona **16**
Porta Portese Market **9**
Roman Forum
  (Foro Romano) **44**
St. Peter's Basilica **2**
San Pietro in Vincoli **43**
San Luigi dei Francesi **19**
Sant'Agostino **18**
Sant'Ivo all Sapienza **21**
Santa Maria del Popolo **6**
Santa Maria in Cosmedin
  (Mouth of Truth) **45**
Santa Maria
  sopra Minerva **23**
Santa Maria
  in Trastevere **12**
Spanish Steps
  (Piazza di Spagna) **28**
Trajan's Column **36**
Trajan's Market **37**
Theater of Marcellus **26**
Trevi Fountain **32**
Vatican Gardens **1**
Vatican Museums **4**
Vatican Palace **3**
Via Condotti **27**
Vittorio Emanuele
  Monument **35**

411

Trattoria Talk: Rome's Restaurant Scene

The typical Roman evening meal is often huge and lasts for hours. Some suspect that this conga line of courses is just a scam to get tourists to order more, but Italians often do actually eat such gargantuan meals (though admittedly, in today's fast-paced world they eat them less frequently than they once did). When dining out, you're expected to order at least two courses, and it helps when you stretch out dinner with good wine and lively conversation. If you're not up to a monster meal, however, just ask for a *mezza portion* (half portion), which usually consists of an appetizer and a pasta.

You start off with an appetizer, the Roman best being simple **bruschetta** (peasant bread grilled, rubbed with garlic, drizzled with olive oil, and sprinkled with salt; *al pomodoro* adds a pile of cubed tomatoes on top). One of the city's greatest specialties is **carciofi** (artichokes), done *alla giudea* (lightly fried in olive oil) or otherwise. This dish is especially popular in restaurants around the Jewish Ghetto.

Bet You Didn't Know

Although not quite the ice-cream mecca Florence is, Rome's **gelato** is still heavenly. *The* parlor for enjoying the sweetly sinful snack is the 19th-century **Giolitti** (☎ **06/699-1234**), a few long blocks north of the Pantheon at Via Uffici del Vicario 40. Other ice-cream parlors around town are good, too; just look for a sign proclaiming *produzione propria* (homemade).

After the appetizer, your first course (called the *primo*) could be a soup—try **stracciatella,** egg-drop and parmesan in broth—or a pasta: **spaghetti all'Amatriciana** (in a spicy tomato sauce studded with *pancetta* bacon), **alla carbonara** (with eggs, *pancetta*, and cracked pepper), or **al pomodoro** (in a plain tomato sauce); **penne all'arrabbiata** ("hopping mad" pasta quills in a spicy tomato sauce); or **gnocchi** (potato-based pasta dumplings).

Romans excel at these first courses, a fact you'll appreciate even more when you get to the main course *(secondo)*. This is the part of the meal where you may encounter "traditional local cuisine"—travel writer-speak for the bits of the animal you never thought were edible. Some of the more eyebrow-raising, but still delicious, dishes are **coda alla vaccinara** (braised oxtail with tomatoes) and **pajata** (made of calves' intestines still clotted with mother's milk). If you shy away from such culinary adventure, other main courses could include **pollo** (chicken), **scallopine** (veal cutlets, cooked in a variety of ways), **involtini** (veal rolled with veggies and stewed in its own juices), or **bocconcini di vitello** (veal nuggets, usually stewed with potatoes and sage). One of the best Roman *secondi* is **saltimbocca,** which means "jumps-in-the-mouth;" it's a tender veal cutlet cooked in white wine with sage leaves and a slice of prosciutto ham draped over it.

Finish off dinner with **tartufo** (a fudge center surrounded by vanilla ice-cream and chocolate ice-cream and dusted with cocoa) or **tiramisù** (espresso-soaked ladyfingers layered with sweetened, creamy *mascarpone* cheese and dusted with cocoa).

If you order a table wine in Rome, you will most likely get a light, fruity white from the hills south of the city, either a **Frascati** or a **Castelli Romane.** Another excellent white wine from an Umbrian town north of Rome is **Orvieto Classico.** The capital's restaurants are also usually equipped with a cellar that draws on the best wines from throughout Italy.

Abruzzi
$$. Near Ancient Rome. ABRUZZESE.
This friendly and busy trattoria specializes in the foods of mountainous Abruzzi, which is east of Rome. The bounty of cold antipasti attracts hordes of budget diners, as do the hearty, simple dishes such as *saltimbocca* and *stracciatella.*

Via del Vaccaro 1 (off the northern end of the long, skinny Piazza SS. Apostoli, just northeast of Piazza Venezia). ☎ **06/679-3897.** *Reservations recommended.* **Bus:** *57, 64, 65, 70, 75, 170.* **Main courses:** *14,000–18,000L ($8.40–$10.80).* **Open:** *Lunch and dinner Sun–Fri. Closed 2 weeks in Aug.*

Dollars & Sense

Italian restaurants have an unavoidable "bread and cover" charge (*pane e coperto*) of anything from 1,500L to 10,000L (90¢ to $6) added on to your bill. Although dining in Italy is relatively inexpensive, remember that the cost of your meal will include much more than just a first and second course. This *coperto* plus water and wine, an appetizer, coffee, dessert, and a *digestivo* (after-dinner drink) can add up quickly on your check.

Cecchino dal 1887
$$$$. In Testaccio (south of Ancient Rome). ROMAN.
Rome's temple of traditional cuisine was a working-class wine shop over 100 years ago. Such tasty dishes as *pajata* and *coda alla vaccinara* evolved because back then, the only ingredients available to slaughterhouse workers were the undesirable tails, feet, and other offal. Cecchino offers plenty of less adventurous foods as well. While here, visit the wine cellars carved into the "hill" (really just an ancient pile of discarded jars).

Via di Monte Testaccio 30 (in trendy Testaccio, just south of the Aventine Hill). ☎ **06/574-3816.** *Reservations very highly recommended.* **Bus:** *27.* **Main** *courses:* *13,000–28,000L ($7.80–$16.80).* **Open:** *Lunch Tues–Sun, dinner Tues–Sat. Closed Aug, 1 week around Christmas, and Sun June–Sept.*

Da Giggetto
$$$. Near Campo de' Fiori. ROMAN JEWISH.

One of the Jewish Ghetto's top purveyors of Roman Jewish cookery, Da Giggetto serves the house specialty *carciofi alla giudia* (lightly fried artichokes) in the shadow of some still-standing columns from an ancient temple. Other great dishes at this refined restaurant include *fiori di zucca* (stuffed zucchini flowers), *fettucine all'amatriciana,* and *saltimbocca.*

Via de Portico d'Ottavia 21-22 (1 block up from Lungotevere d. Cenci). ☎ *06/ 686-1105. Reservations recommended.* **Bus:** *23, 717, 774, 780.* **Main courses:** *18,000–24,000L ($10.80–$14.40). AE, DC, MC, V.* **Open:** *Lunch Tues–Sun, dinner Tues–Sat. Closed Aug 1–15.*

Da Pancrazio
$$$$$. Near Campo de' Fiori. ROMAN/ITALIAN.

Dining doesn't get more atmospheric than this—a restaurant whose basement rooms are set into the restored arcades of Pompey's 55 B.C. theater. It's like dining in a museum. Although the historic downstairs rooms are often booked up by tour groups, try your darndest to get a seat there. Dig into spaghetti alla carbonara or a seafood-studded risotto alla pescatora, and follow up with involtini or roast abbacchio (lamb).

Piazza del Biscione 92 (just off the northeast corner of Campo de' Fiori). ☎ *06/ 686-1246. Reservations recommended.* **Bus:** *46, 62, 64, 116.* **Pasta:** *12,000–18,000L ($7.20–$10.80).* **Main courses:** *16,000–32,000L ($9.60–$19.20); fixed-price menu 43,000L ($25.80).* **Open:** *Lunch and dinner Thurs–Tues.*

Il Matriciano
$$$. Near the Vatican. ROMAN.

A family restaurant with solid, country-style fare, Il Matriciano has outdoor tables in summer. The classic *primo* is the pasta after which the restaurant is named: *bucatini* (thick, hollow spaghetti) *all'amatriciana.* This restaurant offers plenty of typical Roman dishes, including *abbacchio* (succulent roasted lamb) and *trippa* (tripe).

Via dei Gracchi 55 (from the north side of Piazza del Risorgimento, head up Via Ottaviano and turn right onto Via dei Gracchi). ☎ *06/321-2327. Reservations required, especially for dinner.* **Metro:** *Ottaviano.* **Bus or tram:** *19, 51, 81, 492, 907, 982, 991.* **Main courses:** *14,000–24,000L ($8.40–$14.40). AE, DC, MC, V.* **Open:** *Lunch and dinner daily. Closed Aug 5–25, Wed Nov–Apr, and Sat May–Oct.*

Pizzeria Ivo

$. In Trastevere. PIZZA/ROMAN.

Trastevere's huge, famed pizza parlor is always packed with locals as well as visitors, but the hordes haven't led it to compromise taste or prices. Pizzeria Ivo remains an excellent place to introduce yourself to genuine, wood-oven Italian pizza. My favorite is the "plain" *margherita* (tomato sauce, mozzarella, and basil), but *al prosciutto* and the *capricciosa* (at the whim of the chef, but likely to include anchovies, prosciutto, olives, and a fried egg) are also good.

Via San Francesco a Ripa 158 (from Viale di Trastevere, take a right onto Via Fratte di Trastevere, then left on Via San Francesco a Ripa). ☎ *06/581-7082. Reservations not usually necessary.* **Bus:** *44, 75, 170, 181, 280, 710, 717, 719, 774, 780.* **Pasta and pizza:** *8,000–16,000L ($4.80–$9.60).* **Main courses:** *9,500–15,000L ($5.70–$9). DC, MC, V.* **Open:** *Lunch and dinner Wed–Mon.*

Quick Bites

Italy offers great take-out at any **tavola calda** or **rosticceria,** where you can get pre-prepared hot dishes sold by weight. Any **bar** can supply you with inexpensive *panini* (sandwiches) or *tramezzini* (giant tea sandwiches with the crusts cut off), both stuffed with fresh mozzarella and *pomodori* (tomatoes), prosciutto and provalone, or perhaps *tonno* (tuna). Rome's best food-on-the-go, though, is **pizza rustica** or *pizza a taglio,* sold in tiny shops where they cut the pizza of your choice from big, steaming sheets. It's priced by weight; 4,000L ($2.40) worth is usually plenty for one (3,000L will leave you room for gelato afterward). Some varieties to try: *margherita* (tomato sauce, cheese, and basil), *patate* (with julienned potatoes, but no sauce), and *napolitana* (with anchovies). Or go minimalist with *rosso* (just the sauce) or *bianca* (just the dough, brushed with olive oil and salt, sometimes with rosemary). For **picnic supplies,** visit a succession of *alimentari* (small grocery stores), *forno* (bakery), and *fruttivendolo* (fruit and vegetable stand), or head to the basement supermarket of a **Standa** department store (Viale Trastevere 60 or Via Cola di Rienzo 173, near the Vatican).

When in Rome, Your Feet Will Get Sore: Sightseeing

What kind of guided **bus tour** you get in Rome depends on how much you spend. For 15,000L ($9), the city-run **ATAC bus 110** (☎ 06/4695-4444) runs a three-hour circuit on an old-fashioned bus, but your only "guide" is an information leaflet. It leaves from outside Termini at 3:30pm daily, 2:30pm in winter. **Panorama Tour** (☎ 06/487-861) gives you an audio guide in the language of your choice for its hop-on, hop-off bus tour; cost is 30,000L ($18) for a day ticket (10am to 3pm). If you want live commentary, you'll have to cough up 53,000 to 60,000L ($31.80 to $36) to **American Express** (☎ **06/6764-2413**), Piazza di Spagna 38, for its four-hour introductory tours, which depart at 9:30am and/or 2:30pm daily, depending on the season. One tour gives a general overview of all Rome and the Vatican; another focuses mainly on ancient Rome.

Rome Sights Not to Miss
St. Peter's Basilica (Basilica di San Pietro)
St. Peter's is the pulpit for a parish priest known as the pope, is one of the grandest creations of Rome's Renaissance and baroque eras, and is the largest church in Europe. The church itself takes at least an hour to see—not because there are too many specific sights, it just takes that long to walk down to one end of it and back. A more complete visit will take two to three hours, including climbing Michelangelo's **dome** (an outstanding view); descending to the **crypt** to see the papal tombs; and visiting the **treasury** with its embroidered robes, silver chalices, and bits of statuary.

Tourist Traps

St. Peter's has a strict dress code: no shorts, no skirts above the knee, and no bare shoulders. *You won't be allowed in* if you do not come dressed appropriately. In a pinch, guys and gals alike can buy a big, cheap scarf from a nearby souvenir stand and wrap it around their legs as a long skirt or throw it over their shoulders as a shawl.

St. Peter's is absolutely enormous, longer than two football fields, but because every part of it is oversized (including the cherubs), it doesn't appear nearly that large—until you look down to the opposite end and see that the people walking about look *really* tiny. You approach the church through Bernini's oval colonnade, a series of columns that encloses the **Piazza San Pietro.** To the right as you enter is the greatest single sight, **Michelangelo's *Pietà*,** which was carved when he was in his early 20s. It has been behind protective glass since the 1970s, when a hammer-wielding lunatic attacked it. Under the dome is Bernini's twisty-columned ***baldacchino,*** a fancy altar canopy that was constructed with bronze taken from the Pantheon.

Piazza San Pietro (there's an information office/bookshop on the the square near the steps up to the church). ☎ *06/6988-4466. Bus: 23, 62, 64, 982; or 19, 51, 81, 492, 907, 991 to the end of their lines at Piazza del Risorgimento.*
Admission: *The church, sacristy, and crypt are free; the dome is 5,000L ($3) adults, 1,000L (60¢) students, or 6,000L ($3.60) to take the elevator most of the*

way. A guided tour of the subcrypt around St. Peter's tomb costs 10,000L ($6); ask about this tour at the information office. **Open:** *All parts are open daily year-round. Church: Apr–Aug 7am–7pm, Sept–Mar 7am–6pm. Crypt: Apr–Sept 7am–6pm, Oct–Mar 7am–5pm. Dome: Mar–Sept 8am–6pm, Oct–Feb 8am–4:30pm.*

Extra! Extra!

Want to spend some quality time with his Holiness? When his travel schedule allows him time at home, the pope holds a public audience every Wednesday at 11am (sometimes 10am). Tickets are free, but you must get them ahead of time (before Tuesday would be wise). Apply in person at the Prefecture of the Papal Household (☎ **06/69-82**) through the bronze door where the colonnade to the right of the church begins on Piazza San Pietro. It's open Monday through Saturday from 9am to 1pm. Less of a hassle is the brief blessing the pope tosses out his office window to the people thronging Piazza San Pietro at noon on Sundays. From mid-July to mid-September, his Holiness is cooling his heels at his summer estate, so there are no audiences at the Vatican.

Vatican Museums

The Vatican harbors one of the world's greatest museum complexes, a series of some 12 collections and apartments whose highlights include the Sistine Chapel and the Raphael Rooms. There are four color-coded itineraries you can follow, depending on your interests and amount of time. Plan A takes about 90 minutes (it shuttles you through the Raphael Rooms to the Sistine); plan D takes five hours. Add 30 to 45 minutes to all of the tours to account for waiting in lines. Here's my suggestion for the best short visit (2½ hours): Before you hop on to plan A, head to the right when you first get in and move quickly (spend 20 to 30 minutes) through the Picture Gallery, which isn't included on the short itinerary but should be.

The **Pinacoteca (Picture Gallery)** shelters Giotto's *Stefaneschi Triptych,* Leonardo da Vinci's unfinished *St. Jerome,* and Caravaggio's *Deposition from the Cross.* The most famous work here is undoubtedly Raphael's masterpiece, the huge study in colors and light called the *Transfiguration,* which was almost finished when the artist died suddenly at the age of 37.

That young Renaissance genius is also the star of the **Stanze di Raffaello (Raphael Rooms).** His assistants handled much of the painting in the first and last rooms, but in the Stanza d'Eliodoro and Stanza della Segnatura, the master wielded the brush himself. The latter room contains one of his most famous works, the *School of Athens.* This fictional "gathering of the philosophers" features Greece's greatest thinkers sporting the faces of the

Renaissance's greatest artists. In the center and pointing to the heavens is Leonardo da Vinci with a flowing beard as Plato; the architect of St. Peter's (and Raphael's mentor), Bramante, is portrayed as Euclid drawing on a chalkboard; Raphael himself looks out at you from the right-hand corner; and at the bottom center, brooding on the stairs in his stonecutter's boots, sits Michelangelo as Heracleitus. This picture is an embodiment of the Renaissance, an age of art and reason to rival that of ancient Greece.

Time-Savers

I suggest getting up extra early and being at the museum entrance before it opens (30 minutes before in summer). If you don't, be prepared to wait behind a dozen busloads of tour groups. After the museums, you can make your way around to see St. Peter's, which is so big it can handle tens of thousands of people with no problem (legend holds that a general once lost his small army in there—turns out they were just worshipping in one of the transepts).

The pinnacle of Renaissance painting covers the ceiling and end wall of the **Sistine Chapel.** Pope Julius II had hired Michelangelo to craft a grand tomb for him, but then pulled the sculptor off the job and asked him instead to decorate the chapel ceiling. Michelangelo complained that he was a sculptor, not a frescoist, but he just couldn't say no to the pope. Grumbling and irritable, he spent 1508 to 1512 daubing at the ceiling, craning his neck, and arching his back, with paint dripping in his eyes and an impatient pope looking over his shoulder.

When the frescoes were unveiled, everyone knew it had been worth the wait. Michelangelo had turned a barrel-vaulted ceiling into a veritable blueprint for the further development of Renaissance art, inventing new ways to depict the human body, new designs for arranging frescoes, and new uses of light and color that would be embraced by a generation of painters. He covered the Sistine ceiling with nine scenes from Genesis (the fingers-almost-touching *God Creating Adam* is but the most famous) and ringed these with figures of the ancient prophets and sybils and with nudes in various contorted positions that show off their musculature.

Lining the walls are frescoes by other earlier Renaissance greats—Botticelli, Signorelli, Perugino, Pinturicchio, Ghirlandaio—that would command all of your attention were they anywhere but under this magnificent ceiling. In 1545, at the age of 60, Michelangelo was called in to paint the entire end wall with a *Last Judgment*—a masterwork of color, despair, and psychology.

The **Pio-Clementino Museum** is perhaps the best of the rest in the Vatican, housing ancient Greek and Roman sculpture. Look here for the famed *Laocoön* group (1st century B.C.), the *Apollo Belvedere* (ancient Roman copy of a 4th century B.C. Greek original), and the muscular *Belvedere Torso,* a 1st century B.C. fragment of a Hercules statue that Renaissance artists such as Michelangelo studied to learn how ancient artists so perfectly captured the human physique.

The Vatican has many more museums; it would take months to go through them all. Among them are an **Egyptian** collection, another of **Etruscan** artifacts, a **Modern Religious Art** gallery featuring robes by Matisse, an **Ethnological Museum** covering 3,000 years of history across all continents (the Chinese stuff is particularly good), an outstanding **Library,** and a museum devoted to the **History of the Vatican.**

Viale Vaticano (on the north side of the Vatican City walls, between where Via Santamaura and the Via Tunisi staircase hit Viale Vaticano; about a 5–10 minute walk around the walls from St. Peter's). ☎ *06/ 6988-3333.* **Bus:** *49 stops in front; or 19, 23, 51, 81, 492, 907, 982, 991 to Piazza del Risorgimento.* **Admission:** *15,000L ($9) adults, 12,000L ($7.20) students, 10,000L ($6) children. Free the last Sun of each month (and crowded like you wouldn't believe).* **Open:** *June 16–Aug and Nov–Mar Mon–Sat 8:45am–1:45pm; Apr–June 15 and Sept–Oct, Mon–Fri 8:45am–4:45pm, Sat 8:45am–1:45pm. Also open the last Sun of each month. Last admission is 45 min. before closing.*

Bet You Didn't Know

Rome's greatest museum is technically not even in Italy. The Vatican is the world's smallest independent state, a theocracy ruled by the pope with about 1,000 residents, some 400 of whom are Vatican citizens. It's been that way ever since the 1929 Lateran pacts. But don't worry; your lire are still good here (though the Vatican post office, which is much more efficient than the Italian one, does use different stamps).

Roman Forum & Palatine Hill

Slung between the Palatine and Capitoline Hills, the Forum was the cradle of the Roman Republic, a low spot whose buildings and streets became the epicenter of the ancient world. The Palatine Hill was where Rome began as a tiny Latin village in the 8th century B.C. You need a healthy imagination to turn what are now dusty chunks of pediment, crumbling arches, and a few shakily re-erected columns into the glory of Ancient Rome, but this archaeological zone is fun to explore nonetheless. You could wander through in an hour or two, but many people spend four or five hours and pack a picnic lunch to eat on Palatine Hill. It gets hot and dusty in August here, so if you explore the ruins during that time, visit in the cool morning, wear a brimmed hat, and bring bottled water.

419

The Rise & Fall of the Roman Empire in a Nutshell

A tiny Latin kingdom is founded by the legendary Romulus (ca. 753 B.C.), and then ruled by Sabine and Etruscan kings (715 to 509 B.C.). The monarchy is deposed, and a republic, which is controlled by an aristocratic senate and powerful men called consuls (509 to 45 B.C.), is set up. Rome conquers the known world from Scotland to Egypt and Spain to Armenia. Powerful general Julius Caesar becomes dictator for life (45 B.C.), but is murdered in 44 B.C. (*"Et tu, Brute?"*). His heir Augustus becomes the first Roman emperor (27 B.C. to A.D. 14). The dangers of royal inbreeding are revealed through a string of often lunatic emperors such as Tiberius, Caligula, and Nero, along with some good seeds such as Hadrian and Marcus Aurelius (A.D. 14 to 476). Emperor Constantine has a vision of a cross, wins a battle, and declares Christianity legal (313). Barbarians (Visigoths, Vandals, Ostrogoths) take a liking to Rome's riches and repeatedly sack the city (411 to 568). Rome declines. In 476, German king Odoacer deposes the last emperor, ironically named Romulus. Rome falls.

The early Etruscan kings drained this swampy lowland, and under republican rule it became the heart of the city, a public "forum" of temples, administrative halls, podiums for speakers, markets, and law courts. There are standing ranks of columns here and there, marking the sites of once-important temples and buildings. Their names mean little if you're not an ancient history buff, so I'll just highlight a few of the more visually spectacular sights.

On the eastern end (where you first enter) is the triumphal **Arch of Septimius Severus** (A.D. 203), whose time-worn reliefs display the emperor's victories in what are today Iran and Iraq. During the Middle Ages, Rome became a provincial backwater town, and frequent flooding of the nearby river rapidly helped bury most of the Forum. This former center of the empire became, of all things, a cow pasture. Some bits of it did still stick out above ground, including the top half of this arch, which was used to shelter a barbershop! Not until the 19th century did people become interested in excavating these ancient ruins to envision what Rome in its glory must have been like.

As you meander east among the ruins, head back against the south side of the grounds to find the partially reconstructed **House of the Vestal Virgins** (3rd to 4th centuries). This was home to the consecrated young women who once tended the sacred flame in the nearby Temple of Vesta. The overgrown rectangle of gardens has lily-strewn goldfish ponds and is lined with broken, worn statues of senior Vestal virgins on pedestals (and, when the guards aren't looking, several visitors posing as Vestal virgins on the empty pedestals).

Back on the Forum's north side are the massive brick remains and coffered ceilings of the **Basilica of Constantine and Maxentius** (4th century), which were once the public law courts. (Early Christians adopted this architectural style for their houses of worship, which is why so many ancient churches are called *basilicas*.) Zigzag back south and east, and you'll find another triumphal arch, the **Arch of Titus** (81 A.D.); one relief on the arch depicts the carrying off of treasures from Jerusalem's temple. The war this arch glorifies ended with the expulsion of Jews from the colonized Judea and the beginning of the Jewish diaspora throughout Europe.

Bet You Didn't Know

The cult of the goddess Vesta was quite serious about the virgin part of the job description. If any of Vesta's earthly servants were found to have misplaced their virginity, the miscreant Vestal was sentenced to death and buried alive. (Her amorous accomplice was merely flogged to death.)

From here you climb the **Palatine Hill,** home to that original Latin village and later to the palaces of patrician families and the early emperors. It's an overgrown, tree-shaded hilltop with gardens and fragments of ancient villas, and for some reason, most visitors don't bother climbing it. As such, it can make for a romantic, scenic escape from the crowds; you can wander across the floors and peer down the gated-off passageways that were once the homes of ancient Rome's rich and famous. From Palatine Hill's southern flank, you can look out over the long grassy oval that was the **Circus Maximus,** where Ben Hur-types used to race chariots (it's now mainly used by joggers).

Via dei Fori Imperiali (Forum entrance across from where Via Cavour ends). ☎ *06/ 699-0110.* **Bus:** *27, 85, 87, 115, 117, 175, 186, 850.* **Admission:** *12,000L ($7.20) for Forum only (not the Palatine Hill), free on Sun.* **Open:** *Winter Mon–Sat 9am–3pm, Sun 9am–1pm; summer Mon–Sat 9am–6pm, Sun 9am–1pm.*

Tourist Traps

At the western foot of the Palatine Hill, on Piazza della Bocca della Verità, sit two small **temples** from the 2nd century B.C. and the church **Santa Maria in Cosmedin,** with its early 12th-century bell tower and marble inlay floors. Crowds flock to the front porch of this church to stick their hands inside the **Mouth of Truth,** a 4th-century B.C. sewer cover with a gaping maw. Medieval legend says that if you stick in your hand and tell a lie, the Mouth will clamp down on your fingers (apparently, a priest once added some sting to this belief by hiding behind the Mouth with a scorpion, dispensing justice as he saw fit).

Colosseum

This wide, majestic oval with the broken-toothed profile is the world's most famous sports arena—even though it's been well over 1,500 years since gladiators fought each other and exotic wild beasts while emperors debated whether the loser got the thumbs up signal to live or thumbs down to be finished off. Started in 70 A.D., this grand amphitheater served up blood and gore to entertain 50,000 folks at a time. The inaugural contest in 80 A.D. lasted 100 days and killed off 5,000 beasts and countless gladiators.

The Colosseum fell into disuse as the empire waned; earthquakes caused considerable damage, and later generations used its stones and marble cladding as a source of pre-cut building materials. The interior is a bit disappointing. The seats are all gone, as is the wooden floor, so it looks like a series of nested broken eggshells. The maze of walls in the center was once under the floor (the walls mark the corridors and holding pens for the animals, equipment, and gladiators). The place is littered with lazy cats. The most impressive aspect of the Colosseum is viewing it from afar and admiring that unmistakable silhouette—a symbol of Rome itself—as you walk up the grand boulevard Via dei Fori Imperiali from the Roman and Imperial Forums. Next to the Colosseum is the triumphal Arch of Constantine.

Colosseo. ☎ *06/700-4261.* **Metro:** *B to Colosseo.* **Bus:** *13, 27, 30B, 81, 85, 87, 117, 175, 186, 673, 810, 850.* **Admission:** *10,000L ($6).* **Open:** *Winter Mon–Tues and Thurs–Sat 9am–3pm, Wed and Sun 9am–1pm; summer Mon–Tues and Thurs–Sat 9am–7pm, Wed and Sun 9am–1pm.*

Bet You Didn't Know

No, Christians were not thrown to the lions at the Colosseum, but prisoners were tossed into the arena to fight to the death with wild animals. Since Christianity was sometimes outlawed, worshippers of Christ were probably among those unfortunates on occasion. But it's unlikely anyone screamed for Christian blood by name.

Musei Capitolini (Capitoline Museums)

On the Piazza del Campidoglio, behind Piazza Venezia's Vittorio Emanuele monument, are a copy of the 2nd-century A.D. bronze statue of Marcus Aurelius, his outstretched hand seeming to bless the city of Rome, and two of Rome's top museums. On the left is the **Palazzo Nuovo,** filled with ancient sculpture such as the *Dying Gaul,* busts of ancient philosophers, and the *Mosaic of the Doves.* You'll also find the original Marcus Aurelius statue. (The regilded bronze equestrian statue had been tossed into the Tiber. When

Christians later fished it out, they mistakenly thought it was Constantine the Great, the first Christian emperor—a misinterpretation that saved it from being hacked to pieces.)

Bet You Didn't Know

According to legend, Rome was founded by twin brothers, Romulus and Remus, who had been abandoned in the woods and raised by a she-wolf. Romulus later quarreled with and killed Remus á la Cain and Abel, which is why you're visiting Rome and not Reme. The heroic she-wolf with the motherly instincts became the most famous of the trio and since ancient times has been the symbol of Rome and all it stands for.

If you only have time for one museum, though, make it the one on the right, the **Palazzo dei Conservatori.** The entrance is to the left of a courtyard filled with the oversized marble head, hands, foot, arm, and kneecap of what was once a 40-foot-high colossal statue of Constantine II. The collections have their share of antique statuary, including the 1st-century A.D. *Spinario,* a little bronze boy picking a thorn out of his foot, and the Etruscan bronze *She-Wolf,* crafted in the late 6th century B.C. (the suckling toddlers were added in the 16th century; see the preceding "Bet You Didn't Know"). But the collection excels with its paintings. The upstairs galleries house works by Guercino, Veronese, Titian, Rubens, Pietro da Cortona, and two by Caravaggio: the *Gypsy Fortune Teller* and the scandalously erotic *St. John the Baptist,* where the young, nubile saint twists to embrace a ram and looks out at you coquettishly.

Piazza del Campidoglio. ☎ *06/6710-2071. Bus: 44, 46, 57, 75, 81, 95, 160, 170, 181, 628, 710, 716, 719, 810. **Admission:** Both museums are on the same 10,000L ($6) ticket; they're free (and crowded) the last Sun of the month. **Open:** Tues–Sun 9am–7pm.*

Pantheon

"Simple, erect, severe, austere, sublime…" That's the poet Byron groping to capture the magic and power of Rome's best-preserved ancient building. This may sound a little strange, but it's the empty space inside that makes the architectural achievement so awe-inspiring. The emperor Hadrian built it in the 2nd century A.D., and his engineering skill allowed him to create a mathematically exacting and gravity-defying space inside.

The bronze entrance doors—1,800-year-old originals—weigh 20 tons each. The interior is circular and the entire coffered ceiling is a perfect half-sphere of a dome, with an 18-foot oculus, or hole, in the center that lets sunlight and rain stream in. The dome is exactly 140 feet across, and the building is 140 feet high. Such an engineering marvel remained unduplicated until the Renaissance, and it was only relatively recently that scholars finally figured out all of Hadrian's secrets. For one thing, the roof is made of poured concrete (a Roman invention) composed of light pumice stone, and the weight of it is distributed by brick arches embedded sideways into the walls and channeled into a ring of tension around the lip of that oculus. It also helps that the walls are 25 feet thick.

Sightseeing Tips

If you walk around the right side of the Piazza del Campidoglio's central building, you'll come to a terrace that offers the best panorama of the Roman Forum, with the Palatine Hill and the Colosseum in the background. Returning to the square, walk around the left side of the building, and you'll find a stairway that winds down past the Forum wall, passing close by the Arch of Septimius Severus, and then out around to the Forum's main entrance; it's a nifty little shortcut.

The decoration is spare, but includes the tombs of Italy's short-lived 19th-century monarchy (three kings total, only two of which are here) and the painter Raphael. The Pantheon has survived the ages because it was left alone by the barbarians, who recognized its beauty, and by zealous, temple-destroying Christians, who turned it into a church in 609. Later Christians weren't as charitable. Pope Urban VIII, a prince of the Barberini family, removed the bronze tiles from the portico and melted them down to make 80 cannons and the baldacchino (altar canopy) in St. Peter's.

Piazza della Rotunda. ☎ *06/6830-0230.* **Bus:** *116 stops here, or take 44, 46, 56, 60, 62, 64, 65, 70, 75, 81, 87, 115, 170, 186, 492, or 710 to Largo Argentina, then walk north for 3 long blocks.* **Admission:** *Free.* **Open:** *Mon–Sat 9am–6:30pm, Sun 9am–1pm.*

Galleria Borghese

This newly restored and recently reopened collection is my favorite small museum in the world. In a frescoed early 17th-century villa, you can spend 45 to 90 minutes walking around some of the finest marble sculptures of the baroque period. These masterpieces are courtesy of the era's greatest genius, Gianlorenzo Bernini, and all were sculpted before the master turned 28. On the ground floor are his *Aeneas and Anchises* (which he completed at the age of 15), *Hades and Persephone, Apollo and Daphne,* and the vibrant *David*—a resounding baroque answer to Michelangelo's Renaissance take on the same subject. The Renaissance *David* was pensive, all about proportion and philosophy. This baroque *David* is a man of action, twisting his body as he is about to let the stone fly from his sling. Bernini modeled this *David's* face on his own mug. Also on the ground floor is a room with six Caravaggio paintings. The second floor contains the rest of the painting collection, starring works by Andrea del Sarto, Titian, Corregio, and a large masterpiece by a young Raphael, *The Deposition.*

In the northeast corner of Villa Borghese Park, off Via Pinciana. ☎ *06/ 8424-1607 for ticket reservations, 06/854-8577 for the main desk.* **Bus:** *95, 490, 495 to the middle of the park; or 52, 53, 910 to Via Pinciana.* **Admission:** *10,000L ($6). You have to call ahead and reserve an entry time and ticket; book at least a day beforehand to ensure you get the entry time you want.* **Open:** *Tues–Sat 9am–5pm, Sun 9am–1pm.*

It's Hip to Be (in a) Square

Rome is as much about its squares and fountains as it is about museums and monuments. Take the time to visit the lively, oval **Piazza Navona,** the focus of which is Bernini's masterful *Fountain of the Four Rivers* (see "Other Fun Stuff to Do"). Hit the morning flower and veggie market on **Campo de' Fiori,** Rome's public execution ground in the Middle Ages. The center of **Largo Argentina** sits a good 15 feet below street level (to what was ground level in ancient Roman times). Trees shade the remains of three small temples and (along the west edge) a bit of Pompey's Curia, the building Julius Caesar was leaving when he was assassinated.

The off-center, yet graceful curves of the **Spanish Steps** are covered with bright azaleas in spring and are teeming with visitors year round; they're capped by the twin-towered Trinità dei Monti church and at the bottom by the beloved "Ugly Boat" fountain. A few blocks to the south sits an even more famous set of waterworks, the huge baroque confection called the **Trevi Fountain,** presided over by a muscular Neptune. Legend (and a host of silly American movies) holds that if you toss a coin into this fountain, you will one day return to Rome. Some say you should toss it backward over your shoulder. Others insist you use three coins for it to work. City authorities don't want you throwing any coins, because they rust at the bottom and do irreparable damage to the fountain. The original tradition was to drink the fountain's water, but unless you like chlorine, I suggest you stick with tossing cash.

Bet You Didn't Know

One of the Galleria Borghese's most famous pieces is Canova's scandalous sculpture of Pauline Bonaparte, Napoleon's sister. When asked whether she was uncomfortable posing half-naked, she reportedly responded, "Oh, no—the room was quite warm."

The Via Appia Antica & the Catacombs

The Via Appia Antica, built in 312 B.C. and still one of Rome's major roads, is lined with ancient tombs of Roman families and, beneath the surface, miles of tunnels hewn out of the soft tufa stone. These "catacombs" were where early Christians buried their dead. If subterranean cemeteries float your boat, a few of them are open to the public. You can wander through mile after mile of musty-smelling tunnels whose soft walls are gouged out with tens of thousands of burial niches, long shelves made for two to three bodies each. Most of these are still walled up with tombstones, but many are open, and bones and skulls abound—macabre, but rather interesting. The requisite guided tours, hosted by priests and monks, feature a smidgen of Christian-centric history and a large helping of sermonizing. Unless you have all day (visits take one to two hours, depending on how long you have to wait for an English-language tour to fill up), you'll have to choose between the two most frequently open catacombs.

Tourist Traps

Beware the literal "tourist trap." Some visitors to the catacombs don't heed the guides' warning to stay with the group. At best, you get a little lost and then extremely embarrassed as you call out for the guide to come rescue you. On rare occasions, people have taken the late tour, strayed from the group, gotten lost, and been locked in the catacombs overnight. I don't know about you, but I can't think of a less fun Roman experience than being trapped in damp, dark tunnels surrounded by thousands of dead early Christians. Stick with the group.

The **San Sebastiano** catacombs, about seven miles long (no, you don't walk them all), once held the remains of Sts. Peter and Paul (now, reputedly, they're resting under the Vatican) along with almost 175,000 other dead.

There are some interesting graffiti and mosaics of animals you get to see along this tour. I'd recommend, though, the catacombs of **St. Callisto,** which are the oldest, largest (12 miles of tunnels on four levels, housing the remains of 500,000), and the final resting place of 16 early popes. On this tour, you also get to ogle some of the oldest Christian art—frescoes, carvings, and drawings scratched into the rock depicting ancient Christian symbols such as the fish, the anchor, the dove, and images that tell some of the earliest popular Bible stories.

Via Appia Antica 110 (San Callisto) and 136 (San Sebastiano). ☎ *06/513-6725 (San Callisto) or* **06/788-7035** *(San Sebastiano).* **Bus:** *Metro A to San Giovanni, then bus 218 down to the church of Domine Quo Vadis, where you change to the 660 that heads down the Via Appia Antica; tell the driver which catacomb you want to be left off at.* **Admission:** *Both catacombs charge 8,000L ($4.80) adults, 4,000L ($2.40) ages 6–15.* **Open:** *Thurs–Tues 8:30am–noon and 2:30–5pm, to 5:30pm in summer (San Callisto); Wed–Mon 9am–noon and 2:30–5:30pm (San Sebastiano). Both close for a full month sometime between Nov and Feb.*

Other Fun Stuff to Do

➤ **Commandeer a Cafe Table in Piazza Navona.** Of all Rome's squares, the oblong and vivacious Piazza Navona is the best one to hang out in for a while. The cafes that ring the square are indeed overpriced, especially if you order from the outdoor tables. But don't think of it as buying a $6 cappuccino—it's an admission price for a front row seat to the piazza's living carnival of splashing fountains, musicians, hack artists hawking watercolors and caricatures, Roman teens posing stylishly on their scooters, kids playing soccer, tourists snapping pictures, couples smooching, and just general lively Italian chaos. As an added treat, make **Tre Scalini** (☎ **06/687-9148**) at no. 30, your cafe of choice and sample its renowned, rich *tartufo* ice cream balls.

➤ **Do the Shopping Strut around the Spanish Steps.** Not all Italian art is confined to museums and the Renaissance. Like Paris, Italy is a world fashion capital, and although most of the major houses and designers are based in Milan and Florence, they all have boutiques in Rome. The most famous shops concentrate in the triangle of streets between Piazza del Popolo, the Spanish Steps, and the Corso. On **Via de' Condotti** you'll find: fashion from **Gucci** (no. 8), **Valentino** (no. 13), and **Benetton** (no. 18-19); shoes from **Fragiacomo** (no. 35), and **Ferragamo** (no. 73-74); jewelry and silver from **Bulgari** (no. 10) and

Dollars & Sense

The big fashion names aren't much cheaper in Rome's boutiques than in the States, so do your wallet a favor: If you plan to shop, get an idea of prices back home before you leave so you'll know when you find a true discount overseas. For many, the price isn't even an issue—it's just the cachet of buying your Ferragamo shoes direct from Italy.

Buccellati (no. 31); and some of the finest men's shirts in the world at **Battistoni** (no. 61A).

Via Frattina is home to **Max Mara** fashions (no. 48), fine lingerie at **Brighenti** (no. 7-8) and the French **Princesse Tam-Tam** (no. 72), and antique and modern silver at **Anatriello del Regalo** (no. 123) and **Fornari** (no. 133). **Via Borgognona** boasts fashions from **Givenchy** (no. 21), **Fendi** (no. 36A-39), and **Gianfranco Ferré** (no. 42B). **Via del Babuino** offers the relatively affordable "Emporio" division of fashion giant **Armani** (no. 119), sportswear at **Oliver** (no. 61), historic prints at **Olivi** (no. 136), and paintings of Italian scenes—no Renaissance masterpieces, but good prices and fine quality control—at **Alberto di Castro** (no. 71) and **Fava** (no. 180). A bit farther south, where Via Tritone hits the Corso at no. 189, is **La Rinascente,** Rome's biggest and finest upscale department store.

➤ **Walk into Every Church You Pass.** This is one of my favorite Roman pastimes. Because there are approximately 914 churches in Rome, this could keep you busy for quite a while. Some of the top Roman churches include the following (Keep in mind that St. Peter's, as part of the Vatican, is technically in a different country):

Though Rome's massive cathedral **San Giovanni in Laterano** was first built in the 4th century, it has been sacked and redone so many times that very little of the original structure remains. The huge pilgrimage church of **Santa Maria Maggiore** is famous for its glittering mosaics, some of which date back to the 5th century. **San Luigi dei Francesi** houses three paintings by Caravaggio (his St. Matthew cycle). **Sant'Agostino** (which is near to San Luigi dei Francesi) also has a Caravaggio *(Adoration of the Shepherds)*. You'll find Michelangelo's muscular *Christ* and frescoes by Filippo Lippi in **Santa Maria Sopra Minerva,** Rome's only Gothic church. **Santa Maria del Popolo** has frescoes by Pinturicchio, two of Caravaggio's most famous paintings *(The Conversion of St. Paul* and *The Crucifixion of St. Peter)*, and a chapel designed by Raphael. Crowds flock to **San Pietro in Vincoli** to see Michelangelo's *Moses* statue. **Santa Maria in Trastevere** is one of the prettiest neighborhood medieval churches in the city. It's over 1,000 years old and has an intricate floor of 12th-century marble inlay.

➤ **Spend an Evening in Trastevere.** Trastevere has a strange mix of working-class roots and a modern trendiness that has led many American and British expats to settle here. It's chockablock with places to eat, both refined restaurants and laid-back trattorie, and its tangle of narrow medieval cobbled streets and pretty little piazze are packed with funky shops, galleries, bars, clubs, and even an English-language movie house (the **Pasquino**, just off Piazza Santa Maria in Trastevere).

Wander through the neighborhood's narrow streets in the evening, dodging the drops from dripping laundry stretched between medieval buildings, and seek out that perfect little trattoria. After your fill of homemade pasta and table wine from the Roman hills, stop by a late-night bakery for a chocolate-stuffed *cornetto* (croissant) or pop into a bar for a nightcap, and then walk off your meal by climbing the Gianicolo Hill from the back side. Join the lip-locked lovers stationed along Gianicolo's wall and stare out at the sweeping moonlit panorama of Rome across the river.

➤ **Bike the Borghese or the Via Appia Antica.** Biking through the Villa Borghese park any day is a joy because it's full of fountains, monuments, a modest zoo, groomed gardens, and three museums (the Galleria Borghese, mentioned previously, plus the city's modern art gallery and a huge museum of Etruscan antiquities called the **Villa Giulia**). On Sundays, the whole city is yours. Traffic is light everywhere, and several roads are closed to cars for the day. The two best biking roads are Via de Fori Imperiali, which runs to the Colosseum past the Roman and Imperial Forums, and the Via Appia Antica, lined with ancient tombs, picnicking families, and early Christian catacombs.

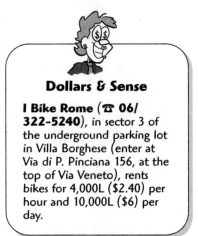

Dollars & Sense

I Bike Rome (☎ **06/322-5240**), in sector 3 of the underground parking lot in Villa Borghese (enter at Via di P. Pinciana 156, at the top of Via Veneto), rents bikes for 4,000L ($2.40) per hour and 10,000L ($6) per day.

➤ **Roam Rome's Porta Portese Flea Market.** The quiet, wide streets in Trastevere's southwest corner burst to life from 7am to 1pm every Sunday with Rome's biggest, most chaotic flea market, Porta Portese. What started as a black market following World War II has grown into a colorful, noisy, crowded bargain fest with stalls selling second-hand home appliances, bootleg pop music, piles of slightly used clothing, antiques and reproduction furniture, paintings, car parts, underwear, grilled corn cobs, birds, religious icons, and comic books. Take the 170 or 280 bus, get off with the crowd halfway down Viale Trastevere, and beware of pickpockets.

Get Outta Town: Day Trips & Excursions

If you don't care to handle the logistics of these suggested day trips yourself, and especially if you want to be sure you get to Pompeii and back in a day, take a **guided bus tour. American Express** (☎ **06/6764-2413**), Piazza di Spagna 38, has a five-hour tour of Tivoli for 63,000L ($37.80) and one to Naples, Pompeii, and Sorrento for 132,000L ($79.20), lunch included, that leaves around 7am and doesn't get back until 9 or 10pm.

The Good Life: The Villas of Roman Emperors, Princes, & Popes at Tivoli

The ancient town of Tivoli, 19 miles east of Rome, has been a retreat for the wealthy since Rome was founded. The enlightened 2nd-century emperor Hadrian indulged in his passion for architecture by building a vacation home here; a Renaissance cardinal and 19th-century pope followed suit. Take Rome's **Metro** line B to Rebibbia, the end of the line, and there catch a COTRAL (suburban line) bus for the 30-minute ride to Tivoli (the bus runs 2–3 times an hour).

Time-Savers

The best way to see Tivoli is to take a picnic, spend the day, and return to Rome in time for dinner. Tivoli's **tourist office** (☎ **0774/ 311–249** or 0774/21-249) is on Largo Garibaldi.

As a general, and later as Emperor of Rome, Hadrian traveled far and saw much. As the talented amateur architect of **Hadrian's Villa** (☎ **0774/530-203**), he was able to re-create his favorite structures from across Egypt, Greece, and Asia Minor. Among the replicas spread over 300 acres (much of it's still being excavated): the *Canopus*, a sacred Egyptian canal 225 feet long and ringed with statues; the *Maritime Theatre* (a pool with an island retreat in the middle); several baths; and the *Lyceum* (the ancient school where Aristotle taught). Spend two to four hours exploring the site and take a picnic amid the olive and cypress trees and broken bits of ancient columns littering the grasses. It's open daily 9am to sunset (around 6:30pm from April to October, 4pm November to March). Admission is 8,000L ($4.80) for adults; it's free for those under 17 and over 60.

Time-Savers

The **Villa d'Este's foun- tains** are at their most spec- tacular, obviously, when the villa lets the plumbing go full force and the jets are at their zenith. It pays to call ahead before making the trek out here to be sure the fountains will be full blast (they usually are on sunny weekend days).

Cardinal Ippolito d'Este, son of the noto- rious Lucrezia Borgia, transformed a 13th-century convent into the sumptu- ous **Villa d'Este** in the 16th century. The real draw of his estate is the fanciful gardens, spread over a vast slope and studded with 100 fountains—wide pools, stair-stepping cascades, spurting jets, wall fonts covered with mossy gargoyles, and one that once even played an organ with its water jets. The villa is open daily 9am to sunset. Admission is 5,000L ($3) for adults when there's only a trickle from the fountains; admission is 8,000L ($4.80) for adults when the waterworks are at their best. For those under 17 and over 60, admission is always free.

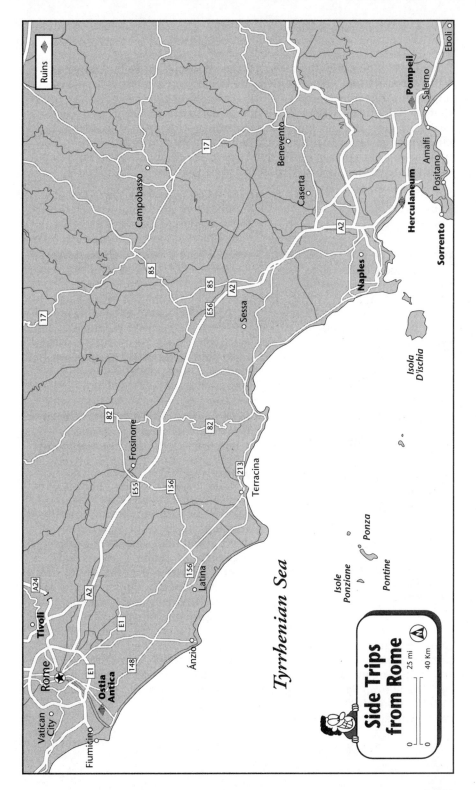

Side Trips
from Rome

Tyrrhenian Sea

Ruins

Rome
Vatican City
Tivoli
Ostia Antica
Fiumicino
Ánzio
Latina
Frosinone
Terracina
Sessa
Campobasso
Benevento
Caserta
Naples
Herculaneum
Pompeii
Salerno
Amalfi
Positano
Sorrento
Eboli

Isola D'ischia

Isole Ponziane
Ponza
Pontine

25 mi
40 Km

A24
A2
E1
148
E55
156
82
213
E56
85
A2
17

A better bet when the Villa d'Este's fountains aren't on is the 19th-century **Villa Gregoriana,** whose gardens are much more sedate. This villa has the largest, most charming water-staircase in Tivoli; it's a slow-motion waterfall that leaps gently down the long slope of the gardens. The views out over the valley are nice, and there are some inviting grottoes off to the sides as well. One warning: Following the waterfall to the bottom is easy; climbing back up is more arduous than you might expect. It's open daily 9am until one hour before sunset, and admission is 2,500L ($1.50).

Since the 1950s, **Le Cinque Statue** (☎ **0774/335-366**), Via Quintillio Varo 1, has been pleasing the palates of Tivoli visitors with honest home cooking, Roman style.

No Time for Pompeii? Ostia Antica's Just a Metro Ride Away

Rome's Tevere (Tiber) River was too shallow to ever serve as a trading artery, so the ancient republic built Ostia, a port at the Tiber's mouth. A city of 100,000, it flourished in trade and commerce until the 4th century A.D., when the river mouth began to silt up and the shoreline began creeping away. As the empire fell, malaria set in, driving out all the inhabitants, and Ostia was quickly buried in the marshy land. It wasn't uncovered until the early 20th century and has remained a relatively unknown but marvelously evocative sight ever since. Best of all, it's an easy ride on public transportation from the city center. Take the **Metro** line B to Magliana station and transfer to the Lido train (you'll need another Metro ticket) and ride it 20 minutes to the Ostia Antica stop.

Time-Savers

I'd come to Ostia first thing in the morning, spend about two to three hours at the site, and head back to Rome for lunch (or bring a picnic to eat amid the ruins). There's no **tourist office,** so just head to the site's entrance (☎ **06/565-0022**) for a map and information.

You can often wander this ghost city virtually alone, striding down stone streets where grass grows through the cracks and passing lines of roofless brick buildings that once housed grocers and money lenders and clothing shops. Sit on a bench in the restored theater and imagine a Greek tragedy unfolding on the stage below, or wander among the columns of a raised temple now seemingly dedicated to the gods of sky and sunshine. Enjoy a picnic in the grass in the company of a solitary, armless, nameless statue, or examine up close the crumbling mosaic floor of a former patrician's residence. Ostia Antica is open daily from 9am to 6pm April through September and from 9am to 5pm October through March. Admission is 8,000L ($4.80) for adults and free for those who are under 17 or over 60.

Naples, Gateway to Pompeii

If you go to visit Pompeii (see next excursion), make time to pop into the Archeological Museum in **Naples**, because the best artifacts from the buried city are kept in this collection. Naples also gives you a glimpse into the bright, chaotic life of southern Italy, still primarily an economically depressed agricultural society where the people tend to be vibrant and emotional, quick to anger, and just as quick to break out into smiles. Naples is 2 to 2¾ hours by frequent **train** (two to four times hourly) from Termini station in Rome. Pompeii is 30 to 45 minutes from Naples.

Time-Savers

Naples has a **tourist office** (☎ **081/268-779**) in Stazione Centrale, and another at Piazza del Gesù Nuovo 7 (☎ **081/ 552-3328**).

The **Museo Archeologico Nazionale** (☎ **081/440-166**), Piazza Museo 18-19, in Naples has one of the greatest and most valuable collections of antiquities in Europe. Besides important statuary works such as the *Farnese Bull,* an ancient Roman copy of a 3rd-century B.C. original, this museum houses the mosaics taken from Pompeii and Herculaneum for safe-keeping. The grandest is the complex *Alexander Fighting the Persians*. This museum, a requisite preamble to visiting Pompeii, should take you about one to two hours to visit. From June through August, it's open Tuesday through Saturday 9am to 7pm and Sunday 9am to 1pm. From September to May, it's open Tuesday through Saturday 9am to 2pm, Sunday 9am to 1pm. Admission is 12,000L ($7.20) for adults; there's no charge for those under 18 and over 60. To get there, take the Metro to Piazza Cavour.

Tourist Traps

Naples isn't the safest of places. Pickpockets and camera- and purse-snatchers are more prevalent here than in most European cities. Be especially careful with your valuables, and do not hang around the train station more than you need to—it and the piazza outside it are notorious for petty crime. It's also not a good idea to bring a car into town; it will most likely be broken into and may even be stolen.

Full of musty baroque churches and a pulsing street life, Naples is the sort of city that just invites exploration. Make time for the **Museo e Galleria Nazionale di Capodimonte** (☎ **081/744-1307**), in the Parco di Capodimonte, Via Milano 1. The works here cover early masters such as Simone Martini and Masaccio through Renaissance greats such as Signorelli,

Perugino, Raphael, Mantegna, and Bellini. From July to September, this museum is open Tuesday through Saturday 9am to 7:30pm, Sunday 9am to 1pm. From October to June, it's open Tuesday through Saturday 9am to 2pm, Sunday 9am to 1pm. Admission is 8,000L ($4.80) for adults and free for those under 18 and over 60. Take bus 110 or 127 to get there.

Naples invented pizza, and there's no better place to sample it than at the parlor that created *pizza margherita* (tomatoes, mozzarella, and basil), **Brandi** (☎ 081/741-0455) at Via Miano 27-29. If pizza isn't your style, sample Naples's famed seafood at **Ristorante la Fazenda** (☎ 081/575-7420), Via Marechiaro 58A. Although location-wise it's a good base, Naples is not the most scenic place to spend the night. However, you'll be safe and comfy in the upscale Santa Lucia neighborhood at the modern **Hotel Royal** (☎ 081/764-4800,** fax: 081/764-5707), Via Partenope 38, for 230,000 to 340,000L ($138–$203.95) per double.

If Naples feels just too unsafe for you, consider staying in nearby **Sorrento.** This middle-class resort town is an hour's train ride across Naples's crescent-shaped bay from the city and a jumping-off point for ferries to Capri and SITA buses down the Amalfi Coast. Eat hearty Neapolitan fare here at **La Favorita-O'Parrucciano** (☎ 081/878-1231), Corso Italia 71, and stay in a room with a sea view for 150,000L ($90) per double at **Hotel Regina** (☎ 081/878-2722,** fax: 081/878-2721), Via Marina Grande 10.

Pompeii & Herculaneum: Ghost Town of the Roman Empire

In A.D. 79, Mount Vesuvius blew its top and buried the cities around its base—an upscale Roman beach and trading city called Pompeii and the more patrician residential community of Herculaneum—under thundering rivers of hot mud and lava and clouds of ash and pumice. Pompeii lay hidden under layers of ash and pumice until the 18th century, when excavations began to unearth a Roman city preserved for the ages almost exactly as it was on that final day. Nearby Herculaneum is less visited but every bit as interesting.

Time-Savers

You could leave Rome early in the morning, see Pompeii, and be back before bed-time, but I wouldn't push it. Spend at least one night in this area, and you'll have time to see Pompeii and Herculaneum as well as some of Naples.

The *Circumvesuviana* Railway leaves Naples every half-hour for the 30- to 45-minute trip to **Pompeii** (☎ 081/850-7255). (Get off the train at Pompeii-Villa dei Misteri.) Many Pompeii survivors, those who prudently left town at the first rumblings, returned to dig some of their valuables out from the cooling ash and cart it away. Treasure hounds of the 17th and 19th centuries did the same. Still, much of the city remains perfectly preserved, and you can walk the wheel-rutted stone streets, wander through the abandoned houses, shops, and villas, and visit the baths, public buildings, and theaters of a once thriving ancient metropolis.

Pompeii and its artifacts have taught scholars more about the Roman world and daily way of life than any other site. You can see bakers' shops with wheels to grind the grain out back, frescoes and mosaics decorating the richest of homes, and a *Cave Canem* ("Beware of the Dog") sign in mosaic as a house's welcome mat. There's even a two-story brothel where little bas relief plaques at each room picture what sexual specialty awaited inside (until just a few decades ago, this building was off-limits to female visitors).

Bet You Didn't Know

How do we know so much about that final day? The writers Pliny the Elder and Pliny the Younger both witnessed the event from the opposite side of the bay. The elder Pliny sailed to a community at the mountain's foot to rescue some friends, dictating his observations as the boat raced across the waters, but he was overcome by fumes at the scene and died. His nephew, the younger Pliny, passed his own harrowing night under the ashfall, but survived to write about it on behalf of the historian Tacitus.

The most moving exhibits, though, are the plaster casts of the victims. The end came so suddenly, and in the middle of the night, that some 2,000 people didn't make it out and died in their beds or in the street, choking to death on the falling ash and vapors. Their bodies decomposed, but the pumice and ash had packed around them so tightly that human-shaped pockets were left within the hardened ash. Excavators searched for these pockets and filled them with plaster from above before digging. The resulting casts are often so detailed that you can see the agonized facial expressions—a more eloquent statement than any passage from Pliny.

Most people spend an entire day exploring the ruins, and I heartily recommend the same. You can do a quick tour in about three hours. The site is open daily 9:30am to one hour before sunset (about 4pm in winter, 8pm in summer). Admission is

Tourist Traps

Pompeii can be brutally hot and dusty under the August sun, and the most popular areas are crowded with tour groups. But even at its busiest, the back streets and empty houses of Pompeii offer one of the ancient world's most evocative sights. Bring a brimmed hat, bottled water, and wear comfortable, flat-soled walking shoes (the ancient stone streets are hard and uneven).

12,000L ($7.20), but you may have also to tip the custodians within the site a few thousand lire to open a few frescoed rooms for you (technically, this isn't allowed, but such time-honored Italian traditions die hard). Either pack a picnic lunch, or dine on great regional cuisine in the modern town of Pompeii (near the ruins) at the acclaimed **Il Principe** (☎ **081/850-5566**), Piazza B. Longo 8.

Herculaneum (☎ **081/739-0963**) is Pompeii's sister city, smaller and only partially excavated (difficult because it was buried under a much harder mix of hot mud and lava rather than the relatively easy to dig ash and pumice of Pompeii). But happily for you, this means it's much less crowded.

Ercolano was a more regular and planned city than Pompeii, and it preserves some impressive luxury villas and baths patronized by the upper classes who lived here. Make sure you see "The House of the Wooden Partition," "The House of the Wooden Cabinet," the elegant and statue-filled "House of the Stags," and the mosaic-filled "House of Poseidon and Amphitrite." Herculaneum takes a good four to five hours to explore. It's closer to Naples than Pompeii and is on the same rail line, the *Circumvesuviana* (20 minutes from Naples; get off at the *Ercolano* stop). The site is open daily 9am to one hour before sunset. Admission is 12,000L ($7.20) plus those tips to the guides.

Chapter 23

Florence & the Best of Tuscany

In This Chapter

➤ All about the Renaissance: where to see the best by Michelangelo and the rest

➤ Getting good deals on leather goods

➤ I scream, you scream, we all scream for gelato

➤ Day trips in Tuscany: the Leaning Tower, Siena, and more

Dollars & Sense

The Italian units of currency are called lire (L). Roughly, $1 equals 1,667L; or 1,000L equals 60¢. Italian coins include 50, 100, 200, and 500 lire. It's easy to get confused—there are two different 50 lire coins and three types of 100 lire coins. Old 10 and 20 lire coins still turn up (though they're completely worthless), as do *gettoni*, old grooved phone tokens—but those are worth 200L. The government will soon release a 1,000L coin. Bills come in denominations of 1,000, 2,000, 5,000, 10,000, 50,000, and 100,000 lire.

If you want a taste of the Renaissance, you've come to the right place. From the late 14th through late 16th centuries in Florence, a creative boom resounded throughout Europe that came to be called the Renaissance. It rang the death knell of the Middle Ages, signifying the "rebirth" of culture, thought, art, and music. An era of humanist thought and classical ideals, the

Renaissance began in Florence, coinciding with the ascendancy of a powerful ruling family called the Medicis—who also happened to be great lovers of art. To begin your Renaissance adventure, you can start with Michelangelo's *David*, and then move on to Giotto's frescoes in Santa Croce or maybe Brunelleschi's massive, ingenious cathedral dome. Don't forget the Uffizi Galleries, the world's mightiest congregation of Renaissance paintings, with highlights such as Botticelli's *Birth of Venus*.

But by no means is Florence a one-note town. When you're art- and museum-weary, treat yourself to a Tuscan feast with copious quantities of Chianti wine from the hills around Florence. Or delve into the medieval heart of the city, home to Dante and Boccaccio, two of Europe's great early poets. Shop 'til you drop on high fashion and fine leather in the city that brought the world Gucci, Pucci, Ferragamo, and Beltrami. Pisa and its Leaning Tower and Tuscany's hill towns, such as Siena and San Gimignano, all lie within easy day trip distance. Better yet, just relax in the Boboli Gardens and let the green hills and lazy sunshine inspire you to write your own poetry or paint your own masterwork. Spend at least two days here, three if you can swing it, a lifetime if you can.

Getting Your Bearings: Florence's Old Town

Because Florence's *centro storico* (old center) is too small to divide into neighborhoods, I've decribed the location of the hotels and restaurants in this chapter in relation to the nearest sightseeing landmarks. Florence's *centro storico* has at its very core two focal points: a religious one around the cathedral at **Piazza San Giovanni/Piazza del Duomo** and a civic one several blocks to the south around the irregularly shaped **Piazza della Signoria.**

Time-Savers

There is a small **tourist office** inside the train station and another small branch near the Uffizi at Chiasso Baroncelli 17–19r. The largest, most central, and most helpful branch is 1½ blocks up from the Duomo at Via Cavour 1r (☎ 055/290-832).

Piazza della Signoria is a lively, statue-studded square lined with cafes; it's home to the imposing, fortresslike Palazzo Vecchio, off of which stretches the "U" of the Uffizi Galleries, Florence's great art museum. The wide, pedestrian-choked promenade **Via Calzaiuoli** connects these two piazzas, and between them lies a thicket of cobblestone streets that makes up the medieval heart of Florence.

West of this core and centered on **Via Roma** is Florence's main shopping district, the 19th-century **Piazza della Repubblica,** and the main artery of Florence's high fashion industry, **Via de' Tournabuoni.** Via Roma changes names as it moves south, becoming **Via Calimata,** and then **Via Por Santa Maria.** As you continue walking south, you step onto a bridge, the famous **Ponte Vecchio,** at the end of Via Por Santa Maria. On both sides of the bridge are an army of goldsmith and silversmith shops that make it seem as though the street just continues. There's a small piazza in the bridge's center where you can look up and down the Arno River. From the Ponte Vecchio, **Via Guicciardini** leads straight up to **Piazza Pitti** and the Pitti Palace.

Northwest of Piazza del Duomo is **Piazza Santa Maria Novella,** fronting a church of the same name. This spot is in the western edge of the visitor's city. Just north of the church is the **train station,** whose surrounding streets are packed with cheap hotels. Between the station and the Duomo lie **Piazza San Lorenzo** and **Piazza del Mercato Centrale.** These two squares, and the streets around them, are filled with the stalls of Florence's outdoor leather market.

Tourist Traps

Florence has two separate numbering systems for addresses. Shops, businesses, and restaurants have plaques numbered in red, while homes, offices, and hotels have plaques numbered *independently* in black (and sometimes blue). Red addresses show an "r" after the number; black ones may have a "b," but more often have nothing after the number. The two systems overlap, but don't affect each other. Unfortunately, this means that a street with a row of buildings designated shop, restaurant, hotel, shop, and home could have address plaques that read, in order, "1r, 3r, 1, 5r, 3..." So if something doesn't appear to be at the address you've written down, try looking for a plaque with the same number but in a different color.

Back at Piazza del Duomo, three main streets run north. **Via de' Martelli/ Via Cavour** leads straight up to **Piazza San Marco,** bus junction and home to the San Marco monastery. **Via Ricasoli** heads to the Accademia, home to Michelangelo's *David.* **Via de' Servi** runs into the exceedingly pretty **Piazza SS. Annunziata,** surrounded on three sides by Brunelleschi-designed and inspired porticoes. **Borgo de' Greci** meanders east from Piazza della Signoria to **Piazza Santa Croce,** home to a major church and the eastern edge of the visitor's city. This neighborhood is home to many of Florence's finest restaurants.

The **Arno River** flows across the southern end of the city. The bulk of Florence lies north of the Arno. The artisan's quarter, called the **Oltrarno,** sits across the river. In this quarter you'll find some excellent restaurants and shopping. The Oltrarno's center is **Piazza Santo Spirito,** which contains a fine early Renaissance church interior courtesy of Brunelleschi.

Getting Into & Around Town

Trains to Florence pull into Stazione Santa Maria Novella. Bus 62 shuttles passengers every 20 minutes between the station and **Amerigo Vespucci**

Dollars & Sense

There are two regular **bus tickets,** one (1,400L/85¢) good for unlimited transfers within 60 minutes of its cancellation, the other (1,900L/$1.15) good for unlimited transfers within 120 minutes of its cancellation. A 24-hour ticket costs 5,000L ($3). All are available from newsstands and *tabacchi* (tobacconists).

Airport, 3.1 miles northwest of town. Mainly national and a few continental flights land at Florence's airport. Most flights from elsewhere in Europe land at Pisa's **Galileo Galilei Airport,** 60 miles and an hour's shuttle train ride from Florence.

Florence's *centro storico* is much smaller than that of most of the cities I've mentioned, and the bulk of it is pedestrian-only, so it's supremely easy to get about **on foot.** It only takes about a half-hour to stroll from one end of the city to the other. To get your bags from the station to your hotel, or to visit the most outlying attractions, however, the **bus** system can prove useful. Almost all buses begin, end, or stop at the train station, and many also pass through Piazza San Marco (near the Accademia and its *David*). After three or four stops, you're already out of Florence on your way to the hills. The historic center itself, though, is not very well-serviced by buses, so if your hotel is in this part of town, you and your luggage would

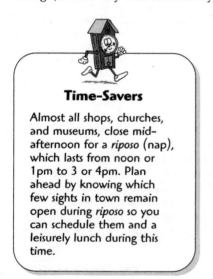

Time-Savers

Almost all shops, churches, and museums, close mid-afternoon for a *riposo* (nap), which lasts from noon or 1pm to 3 or 4pm. Plan ahead by knowing which few sights in town remain open during *riposo* so you can schedule them and a leisurely lunch during this time.

be wise to take a taxi from the train station. Since the train station is in the *centro storico*, the taxi ride is bound to be short, and shouldn't cost more than 15,000L ($9).

Florence Fast Facts

American Express   The central office (☎ **055/50-981**) is at Via Dante Alghieri 22r and is open Monday to Friday 9am to 5:30pm and Saturday 9am to 12:30pm. There's another office across the river at Via Giucciardini 49r that's open Monday to Friday 9am to 5pm.

Doctors   **Dr. Scappini's** walk-in clinic (☎ **055/483-363** or 0330/774-731) is open Monday, Tuesday, and Thursday 5:30 to 6:30pm or by appointment at Via Bonifacio Lupi 32. Monday, Wednesday, and Friday go to Via Guasti 2 from 3pm to 4pm (north of Fortezza del Basso).

There's a **Tourist Medical Service** (☎ **055/475-411**) open 24 hours at Via Lorenzo il Magnifico 59. You can walk into most Italian hospitals with a minor ailment, and they'll give you a prescription and send you on your way (hurrah for socialized medicine). The most central are the **Ospedale di**

Santa Maria Nuova (☎ 055/27-581), a block from the Duomo on Piazza Santa Maria Nuova, and the **Misericordia Ambulance Service** (☎ 055/212-222 for ambulance) on Piazza del Duomo. For a free translator to aid in medical issues, call the volunteers at **A.V.O.** (☎ 055/425-0126 or 055/234-4567).

Emergency   Dial ☎ **113** for an emergency of any kind. You can also call the carabinieri (police) at ☎ **112,** dial an ambulance at ☎ **118,** and report a fire at ☎ **115.** For car breakdowns, call ACI at ☎ **116.**

Pharmacies   For pharmacy information, dial ☎ **110.** All Italian *farmacie* (drug stores) have a poster by the entrance listing the pharmacies in town that are open on Sundays and holidays. There are 24-hour pharmacies in the Santa Maria Novella train station (☎ 055/289-435), at Piazza San Giovanni 20r and the corner of Borgo San Lorenzo (☎ 055/211-343), and at Via Cazzaiuoli 7r, just off Piazza della Signoria (☎ 055/289-490).

Safety   Central Italy is an exceedingly safe area with practically no random violent crime. As in any city, there are plenty of pickpockets (especially gypsy children) who hang out near tourist sights (between the train station and the church Santa Maria Novella is their hot turf in Florence). Steer clear of the Cascine Park and the mudflats below the Arno embankments after dark; these areas become somewhat seedy after sunset, and you run the risk of being mugged.

Taxis   Taxis are most useful for getting you and your bags between the train station and your hotel in the virtually busless *centro storico*. The standard rate is 1,350L (81¢) per kilometer with a 6,000L ($3.60) minimum. There is a taxi stand outside the train station; otherwise, you have to call for a **Radio Taxi** at ☎ **4242,** 4798, or 4390. Keep in mind that if you call a taxi, the meter starts running as soon as the car is sent to pick you up.

Telephone   A local call in Italy costs 200L (12¢). The phones accept coins and/or phone cards *(carta telefonica),* which are available in increments of 5,000L, 10,000L, and 15,000L from many newsstands and all *tabbachi* (tobacco shops). Break off the corner of the card before you insert it and make your call. A digital display keeps track of how much money is left on the card; don't forget to take it with you when you leave. For international directory assistance dial ☎ **176** (1,200L/72¢); for national Italian directory assistance, call ☎ **12** (this is a free call).

Italy's country code is **39;** Florence's city code is **055.** Omit the city code's initial zero when calling from outside Italy. To call Florence from the United States, dial **011-39-55** followed by the number. To charge your calls to a calling card, insert 200L (you get it back), and dial one of the following numbers for an American operator: **AT&T** ☎ **172-1011; MCI** ☎ **172-1022; Sprint** ☎ **172-1877.** You can also call these numbers to place a collect call or dial the Italcable operator at 170 (free). To call the United States direct, dial **001** and then the area code and number.

Transit Info   ☎ 055/565-0222.

Finding That Room with a View: The Florence Hotel Scene

Florentine hotels run the gamut from institutionally antiseptic crash pads for the shallowest pockets to restored Renaissance palaces for those with big bucks. Florence is so small that bunking down anywhere in the *centro storico* will put you within easy walking distance of most every sight. That said, the area around the train station (especially to the east) is a thoroughly uninteresting part of town. Although it's packed to the gills with hotels, these places tend to be the cramped budget joints favored by students. As a last resort, you're almost assured of finding a bed just by walking up Via Faenza (the area's main hotel drag) and trying every inn.

Time-Savers

If you're having trouble tracking down a room, the tourist office in the train station will book a space for you for a modest fee (3,000 to 10,000L/$1.80 to $6) tied to the price range of the hotel.

Albergo Firenze
$. Between the Duomo and Palazzo Vecchio.
This establishment is as bare-bones as you're going to get. It's well-worn like a college dorm, but clean and right in the pedestrian center of town on a quiet piazza. You can overlook the spartan blandness when, at rock-bottom rates, you get breakfast included and are mere steps away from Florence's major sights.

Piazza Donati 4 (off Via del Corso). ☎ *055/214-203 or 055/266-301.* **Fax:** *055/212-370.* **Bus:** *14, 23, 71.* **Rates:** *100,000–120,000L ($60–$72) double. No credit cards.*

Grand Hotel Cavour
$$$$. Near the Bargello.
Created out of a medieval palazzo in the 1860s, this plush central hotel is outfitted with modern conveniences and standard comforts, all in contemporary good taste. The roof terrace has a spectacular view of Florentine landmarks, and the windows of rooms on the front and side look out to the Bargello and Badia towers. The refined hotel restaurant serves excellent traditional cuisine.

Via del Proconsolo 3 (next to the Badia). ☎ *055/282-461.* **Fax:** *055/218-955.* **Bus:** *14, 23, 71.* **Rates:** *255,000L ($152.95) double. AE, DC, MC, V.*

Hotel Bellettini
$$. Just northwest of the Duomo.
Run with enthusiasm by a pair of congenial sisters, the Bellettini lies on a quiet street between the Duomo and the outdoor leather market. The

comfortable rooms are mainly modern, with a few antique pieces interspersed. The breakfast spread is abundant. A large repeat clientele keeps the place busy year-round.

Via de' Conti 7 (just off Via dei Cerretani). ☎ **055/213-561.** *Fax: 055/283-551.* **Bus:** *36, 37.* **Rates:** *140,000–170,000L ($84–$102) double. AE, DC, MC, V.*

Hotel Monna Lisa
$$$$$. North of Santa Croce.
Florence has its share of standardized opulent hotels, but because the city conjures up images of Merchant/Ivory Old World elegance, the eclectic Monna Lisa is my splurge choice. Set up like the villa of a wealthy Florentine family, it's filled with oil paintings and sculptures, lush potted plants, and room decor that varies widely, in keeping with the private home atmosphere. You may find a coffered painted wood ceiling, antique furnishings, or the odd Jacuzzi tub gracing your room.

Borgo Pinti 27. ☎ **055/247-9751.** *Fax: 055/247-9755.* **Bus:** *B, 14, 23, 71.* **Rates:** *300,000–450,000L ($180–$270) double. AE, DC, MC, V.*

Hotel Hermitage
$$$$. Very near the Ponte Vecchio and Uffizi.
Hidden on a tiny piazza just off the foot of the Ponte Vecchio, the antiques-filled Hotel Hermitage boasts rooms that look over the Arno and its famous old bridge. The best view, though, is from the flower-bedecked roof terrace; from here, you can see the nearby Palazzo Vecchio. The friendly management serves a filling breakfast in a sunny room, and a 1997 renovation made sure most rooms now come equipped with Jacuzzis and wood floors.

Vicolo Marzio 1/Piazza del Pesce (left of the Ponte Vecchio). ☎ **055/287-216.** *Fax: 055/212-208.* **Bus:** *23, 71.* **Rates:** *210,000–290,000L ($126–$174) double. MC, V.*

Hotel Pensione Pendini
$$$. Between the Duomo and Palazzo Vecchio.
This classic Italian pension offers turn-of-the-century comfort updated to modern standards. It's been a favorite of travelers for over 100 years, and the devoted roster of regulars appreciates the mix of antiques and conveniences in the usually spacious rooms. The hotel rises above the storefronts and cafes of Piazza della Repubblica, is near the major sights, and is smack in the middle of Florence's best shopping zone.

Via Strozzi 2 (just through grand arch of Piazza della Repubblica on the right). ☎ **055/211-170.** *Fax: 055/281-807.* **Bus:** *22, 36, 37.* **Rates:** *180,000–220,000L ($108–$132) double. AE, DC, MC, V.*

443

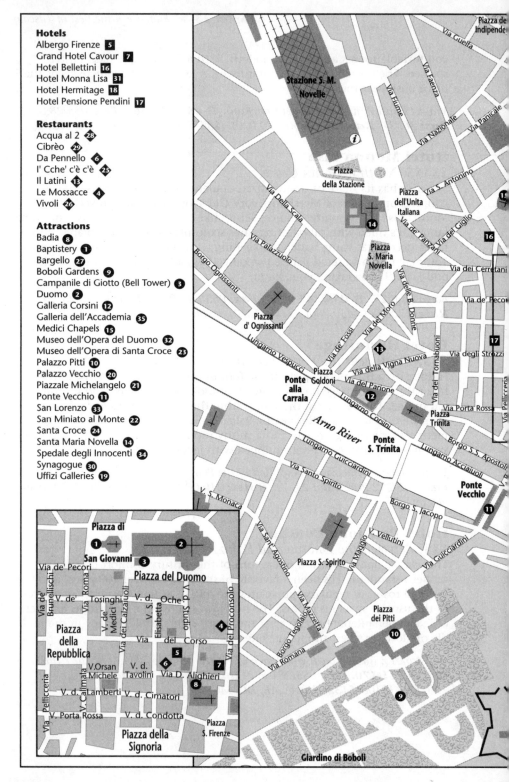

Hotels
Albergo Firenze **5**
Grand Hotel Cavour **7**
Hotel Bellettini **16**
Hotel Monna Lisa **31**
Hotel Hermitage **18**
Hotel Pensione Pendini **17**

Restaurants
Acqua al 2 **28**
Cibrèo **29**
Da Pennello **6**
I' Cche' c'è c'è **25**
Il Latini **13**
Le Mossacce **4**
Vivoli **26**

Attractions
Badia **8**
Baptistery **1**
Bargello **27**
Boboli Gardens **9**
Campanile di Giotto (Bell Tower) **3**
Duomo **2**
Galleria Corsini **12**
Galleria dell'Accademia **35**
Medici Chapels **15**
Museo dell'Opera del Duomo **32**
Museo dell'Opera di Santa Croce **23**
Palazzo Pitti **10**
Palazzo Vecchio **20**
Piazzale Michelangelo **21**
Ponte Vecchio **11**
San Lorenzo **33**
San Miniato al Monte **22**
Santa Croce **24**
Santa Maria Novella **14**
Spedale degli Innocenti **34**
Synagogue **30**
Uffizi Galleries **19**

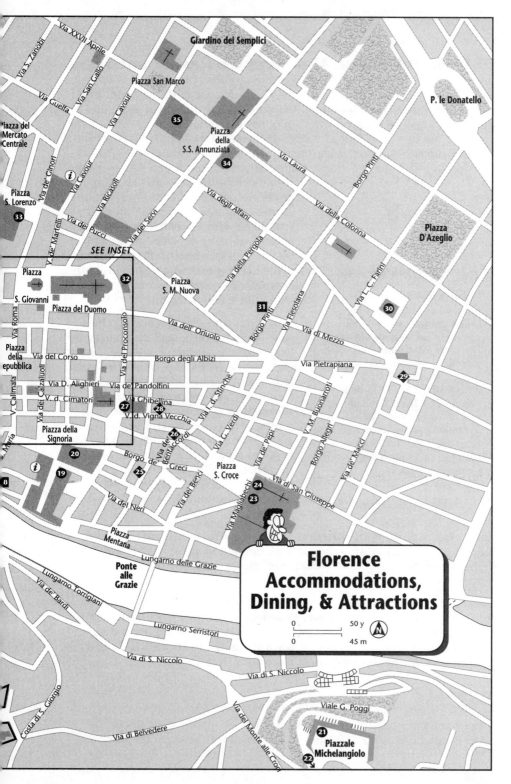

Florence
Accommodations,
Dining, & Attractions

0   50 y
0   45 m

Giardino dei Semplici

Piazza San Marco

Via XXVII Aprile

Via S. Zanobi

Via San Gallo

Via Guelfa

Via Cavour

Piazza del
Mercato
Centrale

P. le Donatello

Piazza
della
S.S. Annunziata

Via de' Ginori

Via Cavour

Via Ricasoli

Via Laura

Borgo Pinti

Piazza
S. Lorenzo

Via de' Martelli

Via dei Pucci

Via dei Servi

Via degli Alfani

Via della Colonna

Piazza
D'Azeglio

SEE INSET

Piazza

S. Giovanni

Piazza del Duomo

Via Roma

Via del Proconsolo

Piazza
S. M. Nuova

Via della Pergola

Borgo Pinti

Via Fiesolana

Via L. C. Farini

Via dell' Oriuolo

Via di Mezzo

Piazza
della
Repubblica

Via del Corso

Via del Calzaiuoli

Borgo degli Albizi

Via Pietrapiana

V. Calimala

Via D. Alighieri

Via de' Pandolfini

V. d. Cimatori

Via Ghibellina

V. d. Vigna Vecchia

Piazza della
Signoria

Via de' Benci

Via l.d. Stinche

Via G. Verdi

Via de' Pepi

V. M. Buonarroti

Borgo Allegri

Via de' Macci

Via S. Maria

Borgo de' Greci

Borgo de' Greci

Piazza
S. Croce

Via di San Giuseppe

Via del Neri

Via dei Benci

Via Magliabechi

Piazza
Mentana

Lungarno delle Grazie

Ponte
alle
Grazie

Lungarno Torrigiani

Via de' Bardi

Lungarno Serristori

Via di S. Niccolo

Costa di S. Giorgio

Via di S. Niccolo

Via del Monte alle Croci

Viale G. Poggi

Via di Belvedere

Piazzale
Michelangiolo

Of Steak & Chianti: The Florence Restaurant Scene

The typical Florentine meal has many courses, and it can take a few hours to work your way through them properly. The multitude of dishes is not just a scam to get tourists to order more; traditionally, Italians do eat such full meals, accompanied by good wine and lively conversation. It starts with an appetizer, the two most Tuscan being *affettati misti* (assorted salami) and *crostini misti* (rounds of toast topped with liver pâté, mushrooms, tomatoes, and so on). Your first course (called the *primo*) could be a soup—try the stew-like **ribollita** (vegetables, cannellini beans, and bread). You may get one of these pastas as your primo instead: *spaghetti alla carrettiera* (in a spicy tomato sauce) or *al pomodoro* (in a plain tomato sauce); *papardelle al cinghiale* (wide noodles in a wild boar sauce); or *crespelle Fiorentine* (pasta layered with cheese and béchamel sauce).

Bet You Didn't Know

Florence makes some of the world's best ice cream, called **gelato,** and no visit is complete without indulging. The city's most renowned temple of the cool, creamy snack is **Vivoli** (☎ **055/ 292-334**) at Via Isole delle Stinche 7r, off Via Ghibellina east of Santa Croce. Other ice cream parlors around town are good, too; just look for a sign proclaiming *produzione propria* (homemade).

Your main course *(secondo)* could be a *pollo* (chicken) dish, *scallopine* (veal cutlets, cooked in a variety of ways), *lombatina di vitello* (veal chop), *involtini* (veal rolled with veggies and stewed in its own juices), or the mighty **bistecca Fiorentina** (a huge steak grilled and brushed with olive oil and pepper). You are expected to order a side dish (a *contorno*) to go with this main dish and *fagioli,* white Tuscan cannellini beans (sometimes served *all'uccelleto,* stewed with sage and tomatoes), are the tastiest choice.

Finish your meal off with *cantucci con vin santo,* which are tiny, hard almond cookies (the original biscotti) for dipping in sweet dessert wine or a *tiramisù,* which is espresso-soaked lady fingers layered with sweetened, creamy mascarpone cheese and dusted with cocoa.

The countryside surrounding Florence is world-renowned for its **wines**—especially the famous red **Chianti Classico,** which will most likely be the table wine in a Florentine restaurant. Also try the more complex and expensive reds from southern Tuscany: **Vino Nobile di Montepulciano** and **Brunello di Montalcino** (perfect to go with steak).

Acqua al 2
$$. Just behind the Bargello. TUSCAN/ITALIAN.
If you want a sampling of some of Florence's best pastas, duck under the barrel-vaulted ceilings of this popular trattoria for its *assaggio dei primi*, a

tasting platter of five flavorful first courses. If you have any room left over for a main course, try the poor Tuscan's steak: a giant portobello mushroom grilled to perfection.

Via della Vigna Vecchia 40r. ☎ *055/ 284-170. Reservations highly recommended.* **Bus:** *14.* **Pasta:** *9,000–10,000L ($5.40–$6).* **Main courses:** *10,000– 20,000L ($6–$12). AE, MC, V.* **Open:** *Dinner daily.*

Dollars & Sense

There's an unavoidable "bread and cover" charge (*pane e coperto*) of about 1,500L to 10,000L (90¢ to $6) added onto your bill at all Florentine restaurants.

Cibrèo

$$$$$ ($$ for the trattoria). North of Santa Croce. REFINED FLORENTINE.
Cibrèo is two restaurants in one: a famous, rustically elegant *ristorante* on one side of the kitchen and a less expensive basic *trattoria* on the other (with a limited selection of the same dishes). The menu at this well-known haven for foodies changes daily, with dishes based on whatever was most fresh that morning at the market next door. There are no typically Tuscan pastas or grilled meat offered, but the kitchen's superb creations are still based on antique Florentine recipes, with the occasional modern touch, of course.

Via A. del Verrocchio 8r (at San Ambrogio Market, off Via de' Macchi). ☎ *055/ 234-1100. Reservations required for the restaurant (although you'll still have to wait); reservations not accepted at the trattoria (come early).* **Bus:** *B, 14.* **Pasta:** *15,000L ($9) at restaurant, 7,000L ($4.20) at trattoria.* **Main courses:** *45,000L ($27, includes side dish) at restaurant; 15,000L ($9, without 5,000L/$3 side dish) at trattoria. AE, DC, MC, V.* **Open:** *Lunch and dinner Tues–Sat. Closed July 17–Sept 4.*

Da Pennello

$$. Between the Duomo and Palazzo Vecchio. FLORENTINE.
This classic Florentine restaurant is descended from a 16th-century osteria. One of the keys to Da Pennello's success is its famed antipasto table, a buffet of vegetables, fish, and other delicacies. The rest of the meal here is good, too, with spaghetti in a spicy tomato sauce, grilled sea bass, and the Florentine sponge-cake-and-mousse *zucotto* dessert heading up the list.

Via Dante Alghieri, 4r. ☎ *055/294-848. Reservations recommended.* **Bus:** *14.* **Pasta:** *7,000–10,000L ($4.20–$6).* **Main courses:** *10,000–20,000L ($6–$12); fixed-price menu 28,000 ($16.80). AE, MC, V.* **Open:** *Lunch Tues–Sun, dinner Tues–Sat.*

I' Cche' c'è c'è

$$$. Between the Palazzo Vecchio and Santa Croce. TUSCAN.
In Florentine dialect, the name of this restaurant means "What you see is what you get," and what you get is quality Tuscan cooking in a simple

trattoria setting. Although you can reserve one of the private tables along the walls, I opt for a seat at the long, central communal table. Here you'll rub elbows with locals and travelers who come to fill up on ravioli in a creamy tomato sauce, tagliatelle with mushrooms, and beef rolls stewed in Chianti.

Via Magalotti 11r (just off Via Proconsolo). ☎ *055/216-589. Reservations recommended, but not available for the lunch set menu.* **Bus:** *23, 71.* **Pasta:** *6,000-14,000L ($3.60–$8.40).* **Main courses:** *13,000-30,000L ($7.80–$18); fixed-price menu 19,000L ($11.40); tasting menus 45,000-50,000L ($27–$30). AE, MC, V.* **Open:** *Lunch and dinner Tues–Sun.*

Il Latini

$$$. Near Santa Maria Novella. TUSCAN.

Although now a bit touristy, this down-home trattoria has stayed genuine in the most important aspect: the food. Join the crowd at the door at 7:30 and wait to be seated at sturdy communal tables under wood beams that support ranks of hanging prosciuttos. There is a menu, but most everybody opts for the unofficial set meal, where 50,000L ($30) buys you a primo (soup or pasta), a helping from a heaping platter of roasted meats for your main course, dessert, and all the house wine you can drink.

Via del Palchetti 6r (off Via d. Vigna Nuova). ☎ *055/210-916. Reservations highly recommended (but still show up early).* **Bus:** *C, 6, 11, 36, 37, 68.* **Pasta:** *10,000–12,000L ($6–$7.20).* **Main courses:** *14,000–25,000L ($8.40–$15); fixed-priced meal 50,000L ($30). AE, MC, V.* **Open:** *Lunch and dinner Tues–Sun. Closed 15 days in Aug and Dec 24–Jan 6.*

Quick Bites

Italy offers great take-out at any **tavola calda** or **rosticceria,** where you can get delicious, pre-prepared hot dishes sold by weight. Try **Giuliano's** (☎ 055/ **238-2723**) at Via dei Neri 74. One of Florence's best quick lunches can be had at **I Fratellini,** Via dei Cimatori 38r (just off Via Calzaiuoli), a hole-in-the-wall where a glass of wine and a sandwich cost 6,000L ($3.60) and you eat standing on the street. For a true Florentine experience, try the boiled **tripe sandwich** called *lampredotto* at the street stand in front of the American Express office on Piazza de' Cimatori. Don't get pizza slices in Florence; you'll get the wrong impression of Italian pizza, which is only worth eating if it comes from Rome or southernmost Italy. For **picnic supplies,** visit any succession of *alimentari* (grocery stores), *forno* (bakeries), and *fruttivendolo* (fruit and veg-etable stand).

Le Mossacce
$. Near the Bargello. FLORENTINE.
The best Italian meals are usually had in a simple, tiny trattoria such as this one, where there's a line out the door of businessmen, farmers, and a few knowledgeable tourists all waiting for their turn at the hearty Tuscan dishes. Its *ribollita* soup is bested only by the *crespelle*, and its *involtini* are exquisite.

Via del Proconsolo 55r (near the Bargello). ☎ *055/294-361. Reservations recommended (but there's always a line anyway).* **Bus:** *14, 23, 71.* **Pasta:** *7,000–8,000L ($4.20–$4.80).* **Main courses:** *9,000–11,000L ($5.40–$6.60). AE, MC, V.* **Open:** *Lunch and dinner Mon–Fri. Closed Aug.*

Sightseeing in Florence, a Real Renaissance Town
There's not much difference between the orientation **bus tours** offered by **American Express** (☎ 055/50-981) and **SitaSightseeing** (☎ 055/214-721). Both have morning tours of the top sights, and afternoon tours of the secondary sights. Each tour costs 50,000L ($30), with museum admissions included.

Florence Sights Not to Miss

The Uffizi Galleries
The Uffizi Galleries are a visual primer of the development of the Renaissance from the 13th to the 18th centuries. Although only a fraction of the size of such galleries as the Louvre or the Vatican, the Uffizi still ranks in the world's top echelon of museums. What it lacks in quantity, it more than makes up for in quality, with room after room of unequivocal masterpieces. It can be downright exhausting. You can easily spend all day here, but the super-fast visit will take about three hours.

Time-Savers

The Uffizi's open late, and most of Florence's other sights are best seen in the morning, so it's wise to save the Uffizi for an afternoon. In summer, the line waiting to get in to the Uffizi can last for two hours—no joke. You'll have less of a wait early in the morning and again around 1:30pm when most people are either already inside or are out having lunch. The museum has also been testing a reservations system of late that may let you call the day before to reserve a time slot. Give the museum a ring when you get to town to see if this great time-saver is still offered.

You get off to a roaring start with the trio of giant *Maestà* paintings in the first room. Together, these paintings show how painting quickly moved from the rigid, Byzantine style of Cimabue's version, through some Gothic elements courtesy of the Sienese great Duccio, to the groundbreaking work by Giotto, who broke painting out of its static mold and infused it with life, movement, depth, and emotion. Move on through rooms featuring the work of early Sienese greats such as Pietro Lorenzetti and Simone Martini and then continue on to Florentine and other Tuscan masters such as Fra Angelico, Masaccio, Piero della Francesca, Paolo Uccello, and Filippo Lippi.

Now you come to a vast room dedicated to Botticelli and focused on his two most famous works, *The Birth of Venus* (that blonde-on-the-half-shell rising out of the sea) and *The Allegory of Spring.* Crowds tend to camp in front of these for 20 minutes at a time, so you may have to wait for a good look. Meanwhile, you can entertain yourself with the lesser-known works by Boticelli and his contemporary Ghirlandaio (who first taught a young Michelangelo how to fresco). Beyond this, you've got Signorelli, Perugino, and a young Leonardo da Vinci's *Annunciation.* What follow are rooms filled with northern European art from the pre- and early-Renaissance eras (Dürer, Cranach, Hans Holbein the Younger) and Venetian masters such as Correggio, Bellini, and Giorgione.

Move on around to the second corridor to marvel at Michelangelo's bright and colorful *Holy Family,* signaling your entry into the High Renaissance. The startling colors and attention to the musculature of twisting bodies that Michelangelo used influenced a whole generation of artists called mannerists; you'll see them (Rosso Fiorentino, Pontormo, Andrea del Sarto, and Parmigianino) in the next few rooms. These works are interspersed with paintings by some big guns such as Raphael, Titian, and Caravaggio.

Piazzale degli Uffizi 6 (off Piazza della Signoria). ☎ **055/23-885** *or 055/ 238-8651.* **Bus:** *23, 71.* **Admission:** *12,000L ($7.20), free for those under 18 and over 60.* **Open:** *Tues–Sat 8:30am–6:50pm, Sat 8:30am–1:50pm. Ticket window closes 45 minutes before museum does.*

Extra! Extra!

In 1993, a car bomb went off after hours under the Uffizi's second wing, killing five people and damaging several paintings and the fabric of the building itself. You needn't worry about terrorist attacks (as far as police can tell, the bomb was a political hit against the museum's director), but the catastrophe has kept many rooms in the last half of the museum closed for restoration. Most of the major works are now on display, but you still may find a few rooms off-limits.

Galleria dell'Accademia (Michelangelo's *David*)

Many visitors come to Florence and don't care about the Uffizi or the Duomo (cathedral). They just have one question on their lips: "Which way to the *David*?" The Accademia contains many paintings (by Perugino, Botticelli, Pontormo, and such) and Giambologna's plaster study for the *Rape of the Sabines,* but most people come here for one thing only.

In 1501 Michelangelo took an enormous piece of marble that a previous sculptor had chipped at before declaring it unworkable and by 1504 turned it into a Goliath-sized *David,* a masterpiece of the male nude. The sculpture is so realistic, so classically lifelike—the weight shifted onto one leg, the sling held nonchalantly on the shoulder—that it completely changed the way in which people thought about sculpting the human body. *David* was for a long time in front of the Palazzo Vecchio (a replica stands there now); stuck inside this room it looks a little over-large, giving it an oafish air.

Time-Savers

The Accademia lines start early and can stretch for blocks in the height of summer. If you show up at opening time and don't have a long wait, you can pop in and admire *David* in about 20 minutes, although it takes at least 45 to wander through the rest of the Accademia's collections.

The hall leading to the *David* is lined with Michelangelo's *nonfiniti* (unfinished) *Slaves.* To many people, these statues are more interesting than the *David*. These *Slaves* are in varying degrees of completion and give a critical insight into how Michelangelo approached his craft—chipping away first at the abdomen and fully realizing that part before moving on to rough out limbs and faces. Their title, *Slaves,* is rather appropriate; these muscular, primordial figures do seem to be struggling to emerge from their stony prisons.

Via Ricasoli 60. ☎ *055/238-8609. Bus: 1, 6, 7, 11, 17, 33, 67, 68.* **Admission:** *12,000L ($7.20).* **Open:** *Tues–Sat 8:30am–6:50pm, Sun 8:30am–1:50pm.*

The Duomo (Cathedral), Baptistery, & Giotto's Bell Tower

The **Duomo** of Florence is clad in festive white, green, and pink marble, with a flamboyant neo-Gothic facade from the 18th century, all capped by a massive brick-red dome that juts nobly above the city skyline. The cathedral is joined on its lively square by the Baptistery, Giotto's Bell Tower, and a museum, a group of buildings that together will gobble up about one to three hours of your time.

Florence's cathedral appears to be inside out—prettily decorated on the outside but rather barren within. It's best to enjoy it from the little piazza out in front, where visitors congregate, street musicians and artists ply their trades, and students strum guitars. When you do go inside, there are some interesting early Renaissance frescoes (see "Bet You Didn't Know"). In the crypt, you can see the remains of an earlier church on this site. The frescoes inside the dome are colorful, but not terribly good. Make your way to the back left corner of the cathedral to admire the bronze doors (by Luca della Robbia) and wood inlay of the New Sacristy.

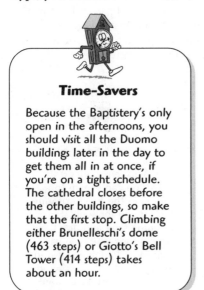

Time-Savers

Because the Baptistery's only open in the afternoons, you should visit all the Duomo buildings later in the day to get them all in at once, if you're on a tight schedule. The cathedral closes before the other buildings, so make that the first stop. Climbing either Brunelleschi's dome (463 steps) or Giotto's Bell Tower (414 steps) takes about an hour.

Climb the 348-foot-high **dome** both for its panoramic views across the city and to see Brunelleschi's architectural marvel up close and personal. All the experts of his day said he'd never be able to erect a dome that big without using scaffolding and supports that would be too costly to build. Brunelleschi proved them wrong by unlocking the secrets of Rome's Pantheon (ribs to distribute the weight and using two shells that thinned as they approached each other and the center).

To the right of the cathedral facade is what's known as **Giotto's Bell Tower,** even though that early Renaissance painter only designed and built the first two levels of it. Several architects (and styles) later, it emerged as "The Lily of Florence," a 277-foot-high pillar of marble pierced with slender windows. If climbing the Duomo's dome wasn't enough, you can scale this baby, too—and without the crowds found at the Dome. The view's not quite so sweeping, but you get a great close-up of Brunelleschi's dome.

Bet You Didn't Know

On the Duomo's left aisle is a greenish fresco of a man on horseback. It's the mercenary leader Giovanni Acuto (born John Hawkwood in England), hired by Florence to help them conquer much of Tuscany. He was promised a bronze equestrian statue as a memorial, but after he died the city figured that it would save a buck by hiring artist Paolo Uccello to paint this realistic-looking "statue" instead.

The **Baptistery,** across from the Duomo, is the oldest building of the whole ensemble, dating back to somewhere between the 4th and 7th centuries. Its bronze doors covered with relief panels are all famous, but the grandest are those facing the Duomo, which were cast by Ghiberti from 1425 to 1453. Replaced now by gleaming replicas, these large panels display a remarkable skill in using perspective and composition to tell complicated stories. Michelangleo once called them "The Gates of Paradise," and the name stuck. The Baptistery's interior is swathed in glittering 13th-century mosaics, with a cone-shaped ceiling covered in an incredibly detailed *Last Judgment* scene presided over by an enormous, ape-toed Christ.

The **Museo dell'Opera Del Duomo (Museum of Cathedral Works)** is directly behind the cathedral at Piazza del Duomo 9. All the statues removed from the facade of the cathedral (and taken out of the elements) in order to preserve them are kept here. The museum rooms are filled with early works by Andrea Pisano, Arnolfo di Cambio, Luca della Robbia, and especially the expressive and emotional statues of Donatello, including a wooden *Mary Magdalen* and the leering bald prophet *Habbakuk* that locals call "Pumpkinhead." The original relief panels from Ghiberti's *Gates of Paradise* are slowly being put on display as they're cleaned. On the landing between the first and second floors sits Michelangelo's *Pietà* group—the figure of Nicodemus at the back is a self-portrait.

Piazza del Duomo/Piazza San Giovanni. ☎ *055/230-2885. Bus: B, 14, 23, 71, 36, 37.* **Admissions:** *Cathedral: The church itself is free; Santa Reparata excavations are 3,000L ($1.80); the dome is 8,000L ($4.80), children under 6 get in free. Baptistery: 3,000L ($1.80), under 6 free. Giotto's Bell Tower: 8,000L ($4.80). Museo dell'Opera: 8,000L ($4.80).* **Open:** *Cathedral: Mon–Fri 10am–5pm; first Sat of month 10am–3:30pm, other Sat 10am–4:45pm; Sun 1–5pm. Free tours every 40 minutes daily, 10:30am–noon and 3–4:20pm. Baptistery: Daily 1:30–6:30pm; holidays 8:30am–1:30pm. Giotto's Bell Tower: Daily Apr 1–Sept 30 8:30am–6:50pm; Oct 9am–5:20pm; Nov 1–Mar 31 9am–6:20pm. Museo dell'Opera: Mon–Sat 9am–7pm.*

Palazzo Pitti (Pitti Palace)

This massive palace across the Arno river was once home to the Medici Grand Dukes; it now houses a plethora of museums and one heck of a painting gallery that makes the Uffizi look like a preamble. You'd be hard pressed to visit all six of its museums *and* the Boboli Gardens in a single day, but 1½ to 2 hours will suffice for a run through the main paintings collection, the **Galleria Palatina.** These richly decorated rooms are set up to look very much the way they did in the 18th century, with masterworks by late-Renaissance and baroque geniuses such as Caravaggio, Rubens, Perugino, Giorgione, Guido Reni, Fra Bartolomeo, Tintoretto, Botticelli...the list goes on and on. It's especially strong in works by Raphael, Titian, and Andrea del Sarto. Admission is 12,000L ($7.20), and it's open Tuesday to Saturday from 8:30am to 6:50pm and on Mondays from 8:30am to 1:50pm.

If you only see two parts of the Pitti Palace, make them the Galleria Palatina and the **Boboli Gardens,** one of the finest Renaissance parks anywhere. This statue-filled park, which was laid out between 1549 and 1656, features fountains, grottoes, a rococo kaffehaus for stylish refreshment in summer, and some pleasant wooded areas to wander in. Admission is 4,000L ($2.40) for adults and free for those under 18 and over 60. The park is open daily from 9am to sunset (it's closed the first and last Monday of each month).

The Pitti Palace itself housed the Italian royal family when Florence was briefly capital of a newly unified Italy in the 1870s. The **Apartamenti**

Reali (Royal Apartments), although they don't hold a candle to those at Versailles or other northern European palaces, are still a sight to behold with their rich fabrics, frescoes, and oil paintings. January through May, you can only get in on a guided tour, which runs Tuesday and Saturday (and sometimes Thursday) hourly from 9 to 11am and 3 to 5pm. Reserve ahead.

Bet You Didn't Know

In 1589, the Medici held a wedding reception in the Boboli Gardens and for the occasion commissioned musical entertainment from Jacopo Peri and Ottavio Rinuccini. The composers came up with the novel idea of setting a classical story to music and having actors sing the whole thing. Thus was opera born. The team later collaborated on *Erudice* (1600), which also premiered in Florence and whose score has survived as the oldest opera.

As for the rest of the Pitti Palace, the **Galleria d'Arte Moderna** (Modern Art gallery) has some good works by the *Macchiaioli* school, which is the Tuscan variant on impressionism. The **Galleria del Costume (Costume Gallery)** has some fabulous dresses that date back to the 1500s. The **Museo degli Argenti (Silver Museum)** is a decorative arts collection that seems to show off nothing more than the Grand Duke's relentless bad taste, but it does have kitsch value. Admission for these museums ranges from 4,000 to 8,000L ($2.40 to $4.80), and they're open Tuesday to Saturday 9am to 2pm.

Piazza Pitti (cross the Ponte Vecchio and follow Via Guicciardini). ☎ *055/ 238-8614.* **Bus:** *B, C.* **Admission:** *See preceding sections.* **Open:** *See preceding sections.*

Bargello (Sculpture Gallery)

What the Uffizi is to painting, the Bargello is to Renaissance sculpture. You could spend 45 minutes or two hours here, depending on how engrossed you become in the works. Among the early works of Michelangelo are a wonderfully tipsy *Bacchus,* the *Madonna of the Stairs,* and a *Bust of Brutus* that may be a semi self-portrait. Be sure to check out the pieces by Donatello, the first truly great sculptor of the Renaissance (one of his students would later teach Michelangelo how to sculpt). A huge room on the second floor contains some of his masterpieces, including a mischievous bronze *Cupid* and two versions of a *David*—the first an early work in marble, the second a remarkable bronze that depicts the Biblical hero as a prepubescent young boy.

Via del Proconsolo 4. ☎ *055/238-8606.* **Bus:** *14.* **Admission:** *8,000L ($4.80).* **Open:** *Tues–Sat 8:30am–1:50pm. Also open 2nd and 4th Sun and 1st, 3rd, and 5th Mon of every month.*

Santa Croce

This big barn of a Franciscan church on Florence's western edge has some great Giotto frescoes and is also the Westminster Abbey of the Renaissance. You'll find the tombs of Michelangelo, composer Rossini (*Barber of Seville* and the *William Tell Overture,* also known as the *Lone Ranger Theme),* political thinker/writer Machiavelli, and scientist Galileo (the guy who dropped balls of differing weights off the Leaning Tower of Pisa and proceeded to get excommunicated for claiming that Earth orbited the sun).

Head to the right transept to see two chapels covered by the frescoes of Giotto, a former shepherd who became the forefather of the Renaissance in the early 14th century. Off the right transept, a corridor leads through the gift shop to the famed leather school (pricey, but very high quality).

Piazza Santa Croce. ☎ *055/244-619.* **Bus:** *23, 71, B, 13.* **Admission:** *Church: free. Museum: 3,000L ($1.80).* **Open:** *Church: Summer Mon–Sat 8am–6:30pm, Sun 3–6pm; winter Mon–Sat 8am–12:30pm and 3–6:30pm, Sun 3–6pm. Museum: Summer Thurs–Tues 10am–12:30pm and 2:30–6:30pm; winter Thurs–Tues 10am–12:30pm and 3–5pm.*

Other Fun Stuff to Do

➤ **Bargain at the Outdoor Leather Market.** Break out your haggling skills—the **streets around San Lorenzo church** are packed with stalls peddling knock-off Gucci scarves, souvenir T-shirts, marbleized paper products, jewelry, wallets, and especially leather. Many stalls are just outposts for the stores behind them, and every owner seems to speak English better than you, so be ready for the hard sell. Be firm, be patient, and you should be able to get the goods at a price you're willing to pay. If nothing else, it's a carnival of colors and noise, and as long as you watch out for pickpockets, it can be a welcome, earthy break from all that art. The stalls stay open from 8am to 8pm (later if business is booming) daily in March to October and Tuesday to Saturday from November to February.

➤ **Drop by Dante's Florence.** The tangle of narrow, cobbled streets between the Duomo and Piazza della Signoria still looks much the way it did in the 13th century when statesman and poet Dante Alghieri called the neighborhood home. **Dante's house,** located appropriately on Via Dante Alghieri, is a typical home of the era (actually, no one's sure which building Dante lived in, so "his" house is most likely that of one of his neighbors). Inside is a museum (☎ **055/219-416**) that chronicles the poet's life and times. Around the corner at the **Badia** church, Dante first laid eyes on Beatrice, the woman whom he loved from afar and who inspired his greatest poetry. The museum is open Monday and Wednesday to Saturday from 10am to 4pm and Sunday from 10am to 2pm. Admission is 5,000L ($3.35), 3,000L ($2) for children.

➤ **Shop for High Fashion on Via de' Tornabuoni.** Alongside Milan, Florence ranks as Italy's co-capital of high fashion. Pucci, Gucci,

Beltrami, and Ferragamo all established themselves here, and their flag-ship stores make for some exciting browsing even if you didn't bring your gold card. Florence has a plethora of shopping streets and areas, but the best concentration lies along **Via de' Tournabuoni,** Florence's Fifth Avenue, and its tributary side streets. On Via de' Tournabuoni itself you can stroll past **Ferragamo** (16r), **Beltrami** (48r), and **Gucci** (73r). **Buccellati** (71r) specializes in jewelry and sil-ver. On **Via della Vigna Nuova,** you'll find styles from Italy's fashion guru **Armani** (51r) and Tuscan **Enrico Coveri** (27r), as well as stylish threads for women at **Alex** (19r). Italy excels in industrial design, and **Controluce** (89r) has some of the best examples of the craft in light fixtures.

➤ **Catch a Bird's-Eye View from Piazzale Michelangiolo.** Bus nos. 12 and 13 wind up the hills of the Oltrarno to **Piazzale Michelangiolo,** a plateau packed with tour buses and lined with visi-tors snapping shots at the panorama of Florence spread below their feet. Just up the road a bit is **San Miniato,** a Romanesque church with some good medieval art inside and a lovely, geometrically precise facade. (This facade, by the way, was the object of the original view out the hotel window in E. M. Forster's *A Room with a View.*)

➤ **Spend an Afternoon in Hilltop Fiesole.** You can experience a bit of the Tuscan village good life with a **ride on Florence's no. 7 bus.** Older than Florence and overlooking it from on high, the Etruscan vil-lage of **Fiesole** has a few sights, cafes on the main square, and best of all, a cool mountain breeze even on the hottest August days. There's a tourist office (☎ **055/598-720**), Piazza Mino 37, to the right as you step off the bus. Pop into the 11th-century **cathedral,** which contains some delicate Mino da Fiesole carvings, and make your way up (and I do mean *up*) Via San Francesco to the **panoramic gardens;** they overlook a postcard view of Florence down in the valley. Perhaps the biggest sight is the ruins of the **Roman theater and baths (☎ 055/ 59-477**), an excavated complex that has a 4th century B.C. temple, a 1st-century B.C. theater (which hosts summertime concerts under the stars), and a few arches remaining from some A.D. 1st century baths.

Get Outta Town: Day Trips & Excursions

If you like your excursions fast and easy, take a **guided bus trip.** **American Express (☎ 055/50-981**) and **SitaSightseeing (☎ 055/ 214-721**) both run afternoon jaunts to Pisa (50,000L/$30) and to the wine-growing Chianti region south of Florence (54,000L/$32.40), as well as an all-day excursion that includes both Siena and San Gimignano (73,000L/$43.80).

The Leaning Tower & Other Pisan Miracles

When Pisa was a world trading power riding high on its maritime empire from the 11th to 13th centuries, it used its wealth to commission a new

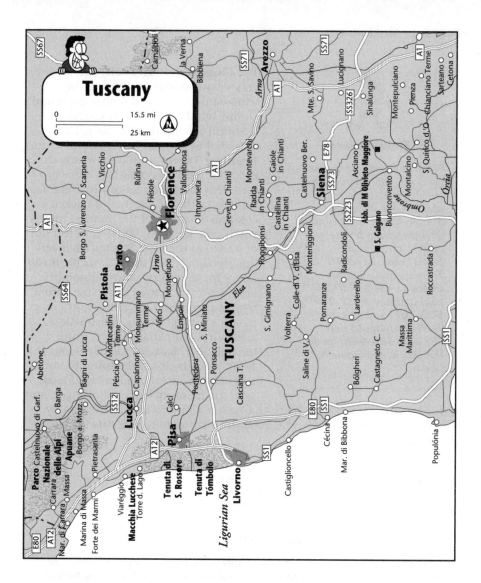

religious core for the city. This Campo dei Miracoli, or "Field of Miracles," is a collection of marble-clad buildings beautiful in their simplicity and crafted in a eastern-influenced style that became known as the Pisan Romanesque. The fact that the *campanile,* or bell tower, of this group is a little off-kilter attracts hordes of the curious to Pisa each year to pose for snapshots of them holding up the **Leaning Tower.** Half-hourly **trains** from Florence make the trip in 60 to 75 minutes. From the train station, bus 1 (or a 15-minute walk) will take you to the Piazza del Duomo (also known as Campo dei Miracoli).

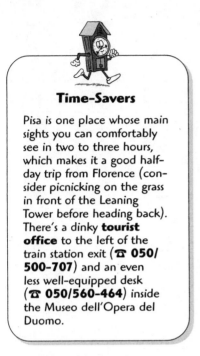

Time-Savers

Pisa is one place whose main sights you can comfortably see in two to three hours, which makes it a good half-day trip from Florence (consider picnicking on the grass in front of the Leaning Tower before heading back). There's a dinky **tourist office** to the left of the train station exit (☎ **050/ 500-707**) and an even less well-equipped desk (☎ **050/560-464**) inside the Museo dell'Opera del Duomo.

The **Campo dei Miracoli,** a huge grassy lawn studded with gleaming white-and-gray striped Romanesque and Gothic buildings, is one of the most beautiful squares in all of Italy. The cathedral bell tower, better known as the **Leaning Tower,** would draw crowds even if it didn't have such horrible posture. This long cylinder of white marble threaded with lithe arches of stacked colonnades is one of the prettiest towers you'll ever see (well, OK, it *is* 15 feet out of plumb at the top). The big engineering problem is that all that marble is too heavy for the shifty, sandy subsoil of Pisa; the tower started tilting right from the get-go in the 12th century. Attempts to correct its tilt during construction gave it a slight banana curve. Unfortunately, the slant got too dangerous in 1990; officials closed the tower to visitors, wrapped steel bands around it to keep the masonry from falling apart, and stacked unattractive lead weights on one side to try to reverse the lean by a few feet. Sometime after the year 2000, they figure to have it safe for you to climb again.

Bet You Didn't Know

Pisan scientist Galileo Galilei spent the 16th century observing the motions of pendulums, asserting the Earth revolved around the sun, and dropping balls of differing weights off the Leaning Tower to prove they would hit the ground at the same time. Many people at the time thought he was kooky, and the church even excommunicated (and nearly executed) him for the blasphemy of suggesting that the Earth wasn't the center of the universe. Today, we know Galileo as the man who gave a name to gravity and one of the fathers of modern physics.

Pisa's **Duomo (cathedral)** (☎ **050/560-547**) is a massive Romanesque structure with blind arcades running down the side and a facade of stacked colonnades. Make sure you check out the medieval bronze doors on the back side of the right transept, facing the Leaning Tower (the only set to survive a

1595 fire). The interior was rebuilt after the fire, but a few details remain from its earlier era, including Cimabue's 1302 mosaic of *Christ Pancrator* filling the apse and in the aisle one of Giovanni Pisano's greatest carved pulpits (1302 to 1311), whose panels are a masterpiece of Gothic sculpture. Admission is 2,000L ($1.20) after 10am from April to September; otherwise, it's free. The cathedral is open from April to September daily 8am to 8pm; in March and October it's open daily from 9am to 6pm; November through February, the cathedral is open Monday to Saturday 7:45am to 1pm and 3 to 5pm, Sunday 7:45am to 1pm and 3 to 6pm.

If you liked the Pisano pulpit, check out the one his dad Nicola Pisano sculpted in 1255 to 1260 in the **Baptistery.** This massive drum-like building has a Romanesque base, but Nicola and Giovanni Pisano finished it off with a Gothic skullcap of a roof, which is all minispires and statuettes. Get the guard to warble a few notes at the baptistery's center so you can hear the brilliant acoustics bounce around (when a choir sings, you can hear it for miles).

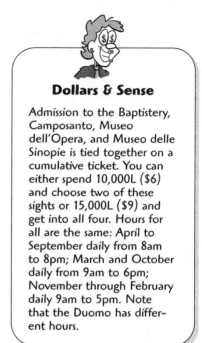

Dollars & Sense

Admission to the Baptistery, Camposanto, Museo dell'Opera, and Museo delle Sinopie is tied together on a cumulative ticket. You can either spend 10,000L ($6) and choose two of these sights or 15,000L ($9) and get into all four. Hours for all are the same: April to September daily from 8am to 8pm; March and October daily from 9am to 6pm; November through February daily 9am to 5pm. Note that the Duomo has different hours.

The north end of the square is bounded by a long wall of Gothic marble that quietly heralds the **Camposanto,** a kind of cloister/mausoleum whose halls are stuffed with ancient sarcophagi and Renaissance tombs, separated from the grassy central courtyard by delicate Gothic three-light windows. Allied firebombs in World War II destroyed most of the dazzling medieval frescoes that once covered the walls, but the few that were salvaged—including the macabre *Triumph of Death*—are on display in a side room. Across the square from the Camposanto, hidden behind souvenir stands, is the **Museo delle Sinopie,** which contains the *sinopie,* or preparatory drawings, of the destroyed frescoes.

Behind the Leaning Tower is the **Museo dell'Opera del Duomo** (☎ 050/561-820), which houses many of the statues and other works removed from the exterior of the Duomo group for safekeeping. Among them is an 11th-century Islamic bronze griffin (a beast with the head and wings of an eagle and the body of a lion). On the second floor are etchings of the Camposanto frescoes that were destroyed.

When hunger strikes, head just north of the city walls to **Da Bruno** (☎ 050/560-818), Via Luigi Bianchi, for excellent traditional Pisan cuisine in a trattoria setting. The **Villa Kinzica** (☎ 050/560-419, fax: 050/551-204), Piazza Arcivescovado 2, may not be much to look at, but it's just a few yards from the Campo dei Miracoli and has doubles for 155,000L ($93). Ask for a room with a view of the Leaning Tower.

Siena, Home of the Gothic

Siena is a city of the Gothic Middle Ages rather than the Renaissance. Here, you'll find brick-and-marble palaces rather than an overdose of museums, cafes rather than fashion boutiques. It's really just a medieval hill town that's overgrown to city size. It has its own proud artistic tradition, one that pitted emotion, elegance of line, and richness of colors against Florence's precise, formula-driven, exacting classical painting. Siena's heavily decorated cathedral is an artistic jewel box of gargantuan proportions. Sometimes, though, Siena is just about lying back on the sloping brick scallop of the Campo square with a bottle of Chianti and a good book by your side or taking a nap under the Tuscan sun.

There are 18 daily **trains** making the 90 to 135 minute trip from Florence, but Siena's station is two miles from town (take bus C to Piazza Gramsci at the north end of town or a taxi). On a day trip, you'll save time and hassle by taking a Tra.in express **bus** (19 daily; 75-minute trip) or even the slower bus (18 daily, 1½ to 2 hours) directly from Florence's SITA bus depot (Via Santa Caterina 17, just west of the train station) to Piazza San Domenico in Siena, a five-minute stroll from the main square.

Time-Savers

Many people come to Siena just for half a day, but I'd give it at least one overnight so you have a good day and a half to drink in its scattered sights and medieval ambiance. There's a **tourist office** (☎ 0577/280-551) at Piazza del Campo 56, which is sometimes closed in winter (and on abbreviated hours even when it's open), so you may have to visit the administrative office at Via di Città 43 nearby.

Siena's center is **Il Campo,** a beautiful fan-shaped square of herringbone brick sloping down to the **Palazzo Pubblico** (1297 to 1310). You can climb the 503 steps of its 14th-century bell tower, the **Torre di Mangia,** for 5,000L ($3) to get an unforgettable view across the burnt sienna rooftops of the cityscape to the surrounding green countryside. Inside the palazzo is the **Museo Civico** (☎ 0577/292-226), the top art museum in town. It's most renowned for several works that were painted specifically for this town hall. Simone Martini's 1315 *Maestà*—a Mary in majesty surrounded by her court of saints under a tentlike canopy—was the artist's first work, and his masterpiece at that. He later frescoed across the room *Guidoriccio da Foligno,* a gracious knight on horseback with a fabulously checkered cloak.

In the room next door is preserved the greatest secular fresco to survive from medieval Europe, the *Allegory of Good and Bad Government and Its Effect on the Town and Countryside.* This 1338 Ambrogio Lorenzetti masterpiece is as long as its name implies, wrapping around three walls and chronicling the medieval ideal of civic life. On one wall (badly damaged), bad government ruins the town, sends the citizens into hiding, burns the fields, crumbles the buildings, and populates the streets with thieves and armed patrols. On the good government side, teachers lecture to students, tradesmen sell their wares, women dance in the streets, nobles ride on horseback and go out to hunt, and farmers tend their fields or bring the pig to market. I keep a post-card of one detail, workmen on a scaffold repairing a building, taped to my computer to remind me that, in Italy, the more things change, the more they remain the same. The Museo Civico charges admission of 6,000L ($3.60) adults, 3,000L ($1.80) students and over 65, and is open January 6 through February and November through Dec 24 daily from 9:30am to 1:30pm. In March and October, it's open Monday to Saturday 9:30am to 6pm, Sunday 9:30am to 1:30pm; in April and September, it's open Monday to Saturday 9:30am to 6:30pm, Sunday 9:30am to 1:30pm; in May to June, it's open Monday to Saturday 9am to 7pm, Sunday 9:30am to 1:30pm; in July through August, it's open Monday to Saturday from 9am to 7:30pm, Sunday 9:30am to 1:30pm. The ticket window closes 45 minutes before the museum does.

Dollars & Sense

For 8,500L ($5.10), you can purchase a **combined ticket** that gets you into the Museo dell'Opera Metropolitana, the Baptistery, and the Duomo's Libreria Piccolomini.

Siena's other grand sight is the **Duomo (Cathedral),** a massive, zebra-striped Gothic endeavor with a facade by Giovanni Pisano and an interior whose floor is a jubilation of inlaid, carved, or mosaicked marble panels (1372 to 1547). The panels in the nave are usually visible, but most of the ones that lie under the transept are protected by cardboard (except August 7 through 22). At the right transept is the **Chigi Chapel,** designed by that Roman master of the baroque, Bernini. At the start of the left transept is Nicola Pisano's greatest pulpit. The intricately carved Gothic panels (which his son Giovanni helped with) depict the life of Christ in vibrant, tumultuous detail; the columns sup-porting the pulpit rest on the backs of lions.

Off the left aisle is the entrance to the **Libreria Piccolomini,** which was entirely frescoed by Umbrian master Pinturicchio with scenes from the life of Pope Pius II. Just outside this room is a large marble altar against the wall whose niches hold statuettes of Sts. Peter, Paul, and Gregory carved by a 26-year-old Michelangelo. Admission to the cathedral is free, but the Libreria

Piccolomini costs 2,000L ($1.20). The cathedral is open March 16 through October daily from 9am to 7:30pm, November to March 15 daily from 10am to 1pm and 2:30 to 5pm.

Extra! Extra!

Walk around the Duomo's right side down the steep stairs and at the bottom do an about-face. You'll see the Duomo's second facade, this one prefacing the **Baptistery**, which was built under the cathedral. Inside is a font with bronze panels by some of the early Renaissance's greatest sculptors: Donatello, Ghiberti, and Siena's Jacopo della Quercia. The walls and ceiling are covered with imaginative 15th-century frescoes (look for the alligator). The Baptistery keeps similar hours to the Duomo, and admission is 3,000L ($1.80).

Siena at one point planned to expand its cathedral massively, turning the present Duomo into a mere transept of the grand new structure. Construction only got so far as building one thick nave wall and the beginning of the new facade wall before the Black Death hit in 1348 and wiped out three-fourths of the town's population. The interior of these walls (enter across from the back right corner of the Duomo's exterior) are now filled with the **Museo dell'Opera Metropolitana** (☎ **0577/283-048**). This museum was set up to house the sculptures removed from the Duomo for preservation.

Upstairs is Siena's most venerated work of art, Duccio's *Maestà*, a double-sided altarpiece whose style and use of color in a multitude of little panels virtually created the Sienese school of painting. It has been generally accepted as one of Europe's finest medieval masterpieces ever since the day it was unveiled in 1311 and paraded through the streets in a ceremony that every single Sienese turned out for. Next to it is Pietro Lorenzetti's *Birth of the Virgin*, another remarkable work by the brother of the man who brought you the *Allegory of Good and Bad Government*. Admission is 6,000L ($3.60), and the museum is open November though Mar 15 daily from 9am to 1:30pm, March 16 through September daily from 9am to 7:30pm, October daily from 9am to 6pm.

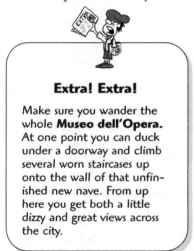

Extra! Extra!

Make sure you wander the whole **Museo dell'Opera.** At one point you can duck under a doorway and climb several worn staircases up onto the wall of that unfinished new nave. From up here you get both a little dizzy and great views across the city.

Take a break from art and history at the **Enoteca Italiana Permanente** (☎ **0577/288-497**), Italy's official wine tasting bar (774 labels in stock). It takes up the echoing brick halls and cellars of the 16th-century *Fortezza Medicea* fortress in the northwest corner of town. Glasses range from 2,500 to 5,000L ($1.50 to $3), and it's open Monday noon to 8pm and Tuesday to Saturday noon to 1am.

Antica Trattoria Papei (☎ **0577/280-894**), Piazza del Mercato 6, serves good, solid Sienese fare on a piazza behind the Palazzo Pubblico. **Cannon d'Oro** (☎ **0577/44-321;** fax: 0577/280-868), Via Montanini 28 (a northerly continuation of Via Banchi di Spora), is only a few minutes from the Campo on the main street in town. Rooms are far from fancy, but they're large and only 80,00 to 100,000L ($48 to $60) per double.

San Gimignano: The Medieval Manhattan

San Gimignano, perhaps the most famous of Tuscany's hill towns, bristles with 14 medieval towers, a remnant of the days when tiny city-states such as this one were full of feuding families who occasionally turned the cobblestone streets of town into a civil war zone. No other Italian city has preserved so many of its towers (to give you an idea of what's been lost, San Gimignano sported at least 70 towers in its 13th- to 14th-century heyday). Though this little burg is frequently packed with day trippers, no other spot can give you such a profound taste of the Middle Ages.

The only way to get here is by **bus,** and you must almost always transfer in the village of Poggibonsi. From Florence, SITA (Via Santa Caterina 17, just west of the train station) runs 26 buses daily to Poggibonsi in 50 to 90 minutes, 13 of which meet right up with the connection to San Gimignano. There is also a direct bus from Florence (80 minutes) at 8:30am Monday through Friday. From Siena, Tra.in (Piazza San Domenico) runs about 33 daily buses to Poggibonsi in 35 to 45 minutes. From Poggibonsi, 19 buses make the 20-minute run to San Gimignano Monday through Saturday, but only two buses run on Sunday (at 7:20am and 12:55pm).

Time-Savers

You can see San Gimignano in two to three hours or so, but savvy travelers bank on the fact that dusk sends all the day trippers scattering for their tour buses, leaving wonderful medieval towns like this virtually untouched. Those who stay the night can drink in the ancient village atmosphere and get to know the locals. The **tourist office** (☎ **0577/940-008**) is at Piazza del Duomo 1.

A pair of interlocked triangular squares makes up the tiny town center, with a 13th-century well in the center of the first and the Collegiata (main church) taking up one end of the second. If you're just dying to scale one of those looming towers, head directly to the **Museo Civico/Torre Grossa.** After you check out paintings by the likes of Pinturicchio, Gozzoli, and Lippo Memmi in the gallery section (and, in an anteroom, secular 14th-century frescoes that show a racy medieval courtship), you can clamber up the tallest remaining tower in town. It provides a 178-foot-high, 360° vista across the tiny town and the rolling green countryside just outside its walls. The place is open March through October daily from 9:30am to 7:30pm. November through February, it's open Tuesday to Sunday 9:30am to 1:30pm and 2:30 to 4:30pm. See sidebar for admission prices.

Dollars & Sense

Admission to the Museo Civico is weird. For the museum only, it's 7,000L ($4.65) for adults and 5,000L ($3.35) for children under 18 and students. Admission to the tower only is 8,000L ($5.35) for adults and 6,000L ($4) for children under 18 and students. A combined ticket to both is 12,000L ($7.20) for adults and 9,000L ($5.40) for children under 18 and students, but it's only valid as follows: April to September 12:30 to 3pm and 6 to 7:30pm; October and March 12:30 to 2:30pm. *Another* combination ticket gets you into most sights in town for 16,000L ($9.60) adults, 12,000L ($7.20) students, but it is only a savings if you visit, in addition to the sights described here, one of San Gimignano's other minuscule museums (not worth it on a tight schedule).

Although the **Collegiata** has no bishop's seat and therefore technically is not a duomo (cathedral) anymore, it certainly is decorated to look like one. Every last inch of the interior walls is covered with a colorful collage of 14th- and 15th-century frescoes. Those down the left wall tell Old Testament stories; the right wall features the New Testament. Against the entrance wall is a *St. Sebastian* thick with arrows, and near the entrance, high on the interior nave wall, spreads a gruesome *Last Judgment* scene where the agonies of hell unfold in inventive medieval Technicolor.

Off the right aisle is the tiny **Chapel of St. Fina,** which Ghirlandaio frescoed with a pair of scenes from the young saint's brief life (she fasted to death, praying the whole time, whereupon flowers sprouted everywhere in town and angels made the church bells ring). Bring lots of 500L pieces to feed the lightboxes and illuminate this fresco wonderland. The church is open daily 9:30am to 12:30pm and 3 to 5:30pm, and although admission to the church is free (not counting those lightbox coins), the Chapel of St. Fina costs 3,000L ($1.80) for adults and 2,000L ($1.20) for those under 18 and students.

La Mangiatoia (☎ **0577/941-528**), Via Mainardi 5, has a cozy atmosphere and a hearty Tuscan menu (it excels at its more imaginative dishes). **La Cisterna** (☎ **0577/940-328,** fax: 0577/922-080), Piazza della Cisterna 23-24, occupies the remains of two towers in the center of town, with 115,000 to 155,000L ($69–$93) doubles and one of the best restaurants in town.

Venice & Environs

Dollars & Sense

The Italian units of currency are called lire (L). Roughly, $1 equals 1,667L; or 1,000L equals 60¢. Italian coins include 50, 100, 200, and 500 lire. It's easy to get confused because there are two different 50 lire coins, and three types of 100 lire coins. Old 10 lire and 20 lire coins still turn up (though they're completely worthless), as do *gettoni*, old grooved phone tokens—but those are worth 200L. Keep in mind that the government will soon release a 1,000L coin. Bills come in denominations of 1,000, 2,000, 5,000, 10,000, 50,000 and 100,000 lire.

Venice is a city of stone built on the water, or at least on the marshy mud-flats of a lagoon—a feat of engineering and determination if ever there were one. Its main "streets" are the canals that meander through town, and its chief form of transportation is by boat (you've no doubt heard of the gondolas). This lifestyle hints at the city's seafaring past.

As barbarians overran the Italian peninsula in the 5th century, some locals in the Veneto region fled to where no barbarian in his right mind would come looking for them (or their loot): in the middle of the water. Fishing communities had taken over other islands in the Venetian lagoon, but young Venice quickly established itself as a commercial seafaring power. By the 16th century, this trading republic had become the Queen of the Adriatic, a mercantile powerhouse that exercised its control over the entire Mediterranean. Venice's tremendous wealth and centuries of stable rule allowed it to enrich the urban and cultural landscape with hundreds of churches (such as the Basilica de San Marco). Venice was also home to some of the great late-Renaissance artists such as Titian and Tintoretto, masters of color and mood.

In modern-day Venice, armies of another sort have begun to invade. Each year, the city's 70,000 residents are outnumbered by the hordes of visitors to their small lagoon. Up to 1.5 million people visit Venice annually, at times making the town called *La Serenissima* (the Most Serene) anything but calm. At peak season in June, July, and September, the crowds can be staggering, and hotels are booked solid. Venice gets more attention than it wants; the city government is debating the passage of quota laws to stem the tide of tourists. Venice may soon become the first European city that you'll need a ticket to enter.

Time-Savers

The two main **tourist information offices** you'll be dealing with are the one inside the train station (☎ **041/529-8727**) and the one off the southeast corner of Piazza San Marco, wedged in between the Giardini Reali and Harry's Bar (☎ **041/522-6356**). The administrative APT office (☎ **041/529-8711**) is at Castello 4421, a jog around the left side of the Basilica di San Marco and across the Rio di Palazzo.

Many people leave Venice enchanted, but just as many hurry away feeling as though they've spent two days in tour bus hell, being taken for a ride in some kind of canalside Disneyland. Don't believe it; Venice can be wonderful—you just have to learn how to avoid the crowds and know when to cut loose from your sightseeing agenda. Stick with me and I'll show you the real Venice: long lines, souvenir stands, and all.

Getting Your Bearings

There's no two ways about it: Venice has one of the most confusing, frustrating, and unfathomable layouts of any city. On the surface, it looks simple: a few big islands wrapped around the sweeping backward-S curve of the breathtaking, palace-lined *Canale Grande* **(Grand Canal),** with lots of smaller canals worming their way through those islands. The reality is much more complicated. So buy the best map you can find, take a deep breath, and prepare to get lost repeatedly.

Tourist Traps

Venice doesn't use the same labels for its streets and squares as the rest of Italy does. A *calle, ruga,* or *ramo* is a street; a *rio terrà* is a street made from a filled-in canal; and a *fondamenta* or *riva* is a sidewalk along the edge of a canal. A *campo* or *campiello* is a square (Piazza San Marco, Piazzetta San Marco, and Piazzale Roma being the exceptions). A *canale* or *rio* is a canal.

Venice's Neighborhoods in Brief

Venice has two infrastructures, one of narrow streets and the other of canals. These networks sometimes work together, and sometimes interfere with each other. The impossibly twisty, narrow alleyways of the city often dead-end abruptly at a blank wall, or run you in circles, or suddenly turn into steps that disappear into a canal. Constant backtracking is inevitable. Occasionally, the alleyways will get you from one place to another, or spill unexpectedly into a large campo (square), or lead over one of the thousands of tiny arched marble bridges straddling the canals (the most magnificent is the **Rialto Bridge** over the Grand Canal) and dump you into another crazy tangle of streets on the other side.

Little signs with arrows pointing the way to one major sight or another are scattered along the main routes; if you're sharp-eyed, you can follow these along the convoluted path all the way from, say, the train station to Piazza San Marco (in about 30 to 45 minutes). Plan on any journey taking three times as long as you imagine, and don't fret about being late. Setting out from your hotel door in Venice is always an adventure—as long as you treat it as such, you'll have fun getting lost.

Venice's chaos is divided into six *sestieri,* or districts. (That doesn't include the some 168 outlying islands.) The center of Venice is the **San Marco** district, much of which is crowded with visitors these days. In this district, you'll find the gorgeous **Piazza San Marco** (St. Mark's Square) with its

Venice Neighborhoods

0 ————— .5 mi

0 ————— .8 km

cathedral and Palazzo Ducale (Doge's Palace). The extension of Piazza San Marco that runs along the Palazzo Ducale to the Grand Canal is called **Piazzetta San Marco.** The San Marco district is home to hundreds of souvenir shops, the priciest hotels, the world-renowned (and recently burned down, but being rebuilt) **La Scala** opera house, and many (generally expensive) restaurants. East of San Marco lies the large **Castello** neighborhood, which features a classy stretch of lagoon-front property called **Riva degli Schiavoni,** home to a bunch of upscale hotels. Castello is focused upon the Arsenale, the old ship-building sector of the city. This sector is still a navy yard and is therefore mostly closed to the public.

The first neighborhood you'll see when you enter Venice, whether taking the train or driving in, is the **Canareggio** on the very north end of the city, above the top curve of the Grand Canal's backward "S". Canareggio also has the dubious honor of incorporating Europe's first Jewish Ghetto (see sidebar). There is, as usual, cheap lodging right around the train station, but it's mainly a residential neighborhood; unless you're coming up here to see specific sights, you probably won't hang around too long.

Bet You Didn't Know

In the early 1500s, Venice forced its Jewish residents to move into a sector of the city where they lived in partial self-governed isolation, cut off from opportunities and much movement within the rest of Venice. It was called the Jewish Ghetto. In an age of intolerance, other closed-minded cities thought this was a capital idea, and the practice spread rapidly throughout Europe.

San Polo (or San Paolo) fills up much of the area on the west side of the Grand Canal. It's a commercial district with lots of moderately priced hotels, shops, and trattorie, as well as some big churches that beckon the sightseer. To its north is the *sestiere* of **Santa Croce,** half industrial and half filled with sleepy old palazzi along the Grand Canal—and all very untouristed.

Across the Grand Canal from San Marco is the southern district of **Dorsoduro.** It's the trendiest quarter in a city that, despite its reputation for a Carnival to rival the one in New Orleans, doesn't seem to have heard of nightlife. The area is sparsely populated and has a smattering of bars and cafes, some good trattorie and cheap hotels, and Venice's two great art museums, the Accademia and the Peggy Guggenheim.

Tourist Traps

Each street or campo name can be used only once within a Venetian neighborhood, but there's no rule against the next sestiere over using the same label. As a result, the most popular names (such as *Calle della Madonna*) pop up three or four times on the map, but refer to streets miles apart from one another. For this reson, it's crucial that you know the sestiere along with any address. By the way, the street-numbering system in Venice is completely without any logic whatsoever.

Getting Into & Around Town

The **train** station in Venice itself is Stazione Santa Lucia. If your ticket is to "Venezia-Mestre," never fear. Mestre is merely the landlubbing industrial suburb of Venice, and every few minutes shuttle trains leave for the 10-minute, five-mile ride halfway across the lagoon into Venice proper. Venice's **Marco Polo Airport** is also in Mestre. From here, you can catch a *motoscafo* boat direct to Piazza San Marco (it stops once en route at the Lido, Venice's resorty beach island). Another (cheaper) option is the half-hour bus ride to Piazzale Roma, the parking lot next to Stazione Santa Lucia. (Incidentally, no cars are allowed in Venice proper. You'll have to park in a lot at Piazzale Roma.) It's also possible to take a water taxi (*Taxi acquei*) from the train station; this method may be easier when you've got luggage to schlep, but that convenience comes at a price—roughly 80,000L ($48) to get to Piazza San Marco.

As for getting around town, Venice is a walking city. With the exception of taking the **vaporetto** (**water bus;** details to follow) between the train station and Piazza San Marco, on long hauls, or to outlying islands—or shelling out big bucks for a private *taxi acquei* (**water taxi;** see "Fast Facts")—you'll be walking everywhere in Venice. There is no other way to get around.

Dollars & Sense

Because a vaporetto *biglietto* **(ticket)** is priced according to how far you go, it's best to buy them from the kiosk at the dock when you go to take the trip. The average fare for puttering about central Venice is a steep 4,500L ($2.70). Unless you're going to use the vaporetti a lot, the *biglietto turistico* all-day pass isn't worth the 15,000L ($9). There's also a three-day pass for 30,000L ($18).

The **vaporetto** is a public ferry service that is for all intents and purposes the bus network of Venice. You'll find a route plan on the back of the map the tourist office hands out. The most useful vaporetto is line 82, which chugs regularly from the train station down the Grand Canal, stopping five times (including at the Rialto Bridge and the Accademia) en route to the San Marco stop, which is just off Piazzetta San Marco in the Giardinetti Reali. Line 1 is a commuter line that follows a similar route but takes longer and makes more stops. In summer, lines 3 and 4 also run from the station to S. Zaccaraia, which is just past the Doge's Palace off the other side of Piazzetta San Marco. Line 52 makes the same trip the long way around the Dorsoduro (not along the Grand Canal).

Venice Fast Facts

American Express   Venice's American Express office is at San Marco 1471, on Salizzada San Moisé (☎ 041/520-0844), just out the west end of Piazza di San Marco. May to October, the currency exchange desk is open Monday to Saturday, 8am to 8pm (the other services are open 9am to 5:30pm). In the winter, it's open Monday to Friday 9am to 5:30pm and Saturday 9am to 12:30pm.

Consulate   The nearest U.S. Consulate is in Milan at Via Príncipe Amadeo 2 (☎ 02/290-351).

Doctors/hospitals   Call the American Express office (☎ 041/520-0844) for a list of English-speaking doctors and dentists in Venice. For emergency care, call or go to the **Civili Riuniti di Venezia** (☎ 041/260-711), Campo Santi Giovanni e Paolo.

471

Tourist Traps

Long, sleek, black, and slightly crooked, it looks like a cross between a canoe and a coffin. Its single oar is worked by a professional *gondoliere*. That's the **gondola**—the primary form of transportation in Venice from the 12th century until speedboats roared into the canals in the late 20th century. Your visit to Venice isn't complete until you take one of these time-honored water taxis for a spin. The average ride lasts just under an hour. Make absolutely sure you agree upon the price and the duration of the trip before you step into the boat, write it down, and time the ride by *your* watch (strangely, the gondoliers' watches often run fast).

The official rates if you're using a gondola as a taxi are 120,000L ($72) for the first 50 minutes (for up to six people) and then 60,000L ($36) for each 25 minutes after that (it's more after 8pm). The guidelines for a 45-minute *carovana* ride (a circular route decided upon by the gondolier) are 100,000 to 120,000L ($60 to $72). However, if you come across a *gondoliere* that sticks even remotely by those official rates, get his name and write me about it, because a reasonably priced gondola ride is a Venetian rarity I've just got to see.

Emergency   Call ☎ **113** for the police, dial ☎ **523-0000** for an ambulance, and report a fire to ☎ **522-2222**.

Time-Savers

Almost all Italian shops, and most churches and museums, observe a midafternoon shutdown called *riposo*, which lasts roughly from noon or 1pm to 3 or 4pm. It's a good idea to figure out the few sights in town that remain open during *riposo* so you can schedule them (and a leisurely lunch) for this time.

Pharmacies   *Farmacie* in Venice rotate the duty of staying open nights and Sundays. Check the schedule posted in the window of each pharmacy or call ☎ **192** for information.

Safety   The worst criminal you'll encounter in Venice is the occasional pickpocket. Watch your wallet on crowded streets, near popular tourist sites, and on the vaporetti. One other tip: Don't even think of swimming in the canals. These things are used as sewers.

Taxis   *Taxi acquei* provide an excellent (if expensive) way to get you and your luggage down the canal without the headache of crowds on public vaporetti. You may not be the only passenger, because captains take on as many travelers as can fit. They also charge a steep fare—at least 80,000L ($48) to get from Piazzale Roma to Piazza San Marco. The basic rate, good for the first seven minutes, is a whopping 27,000L ($16.20), going up in 500L (30¢) increments every 15 seconds thereafter. Call **Cooperative San Marco (☎ 041/522-2303)** or have a porter take you down to one of the piers.

Telephone Local calls cost 200L (12¢). Phones accept either coins, a phone card (*carta telefonica*), or both. You can buy phone cards in 5,000L ($3), 10,000L ($6), or 15,000L ($9) denominations at newsstands and *tabbachi* (tobacco shops). Break off the corner of the card, insert it, and dial. A digital display tracks the amount of money left on the card. For **directory assistance,** dial ☎ **12.**

Italy's country code is **39.** Venice's city code is **041,** but drop the zero if you're calling Venice from outside Italy. To call Venice from the United States, dial **011-39-41** and then the number. To charge your call to a calling card, dial **AT&T (☎172-1011), MCI (☎172-1022),** or **Sprint (☎172-1877).** To call the United States direct from Italy, dial **001,** followed by the area code and phone number.

Transit Info For flight information, call ☎ **041/541-5491.** For rail information, call ☎ **041/715-555.** For vaporetto information, call ☎ **041/ 528-7886.**

Water Beds: The Venice Hotel Scene

Break out your credit cards: Venice is a bank-breaking city in just about every respect, especially when it comes to lodging. As an island, Venice holds a captive audience, and hotel owners can charge whatever they please. Prices in summer often soar astronomically, and the hotel situation can be pretty grim if you haven't reserved well in advance. Some people find it easiest and cheapest to stay a half-hour's train ride away in Padova instead (see "Get Outta Town: Day Trips & Excursions"). As always in Italy, it doesn't hurt to try bargaining for a discount in the winter low season (don't hope for more than 10 to 15%, though).

A shoestring budget may land you in a cramped, dingy room, but at least you can still find such accommodations in the heart of the city. Many wallet-watching visitors, however, head away from the San Marco tourist core into the more residential, and in many ways more genuine, neighborhoods of Castello or Dorsoduro. For a few lire more, you can get into a

Time-Savers

If you don't want to hotel hunt on your own, visit an **AVA hotel association reservations booth.** There's one at the train station, in the parking garage at Piazzale Rome, or at the information booth on the mainland where the highway ends (☎ **041/522-8640**). You must put down a deposit of 20,000 to 75,000L ($12 to $45; depending on the price of the room), which is credited to your hotel bill.

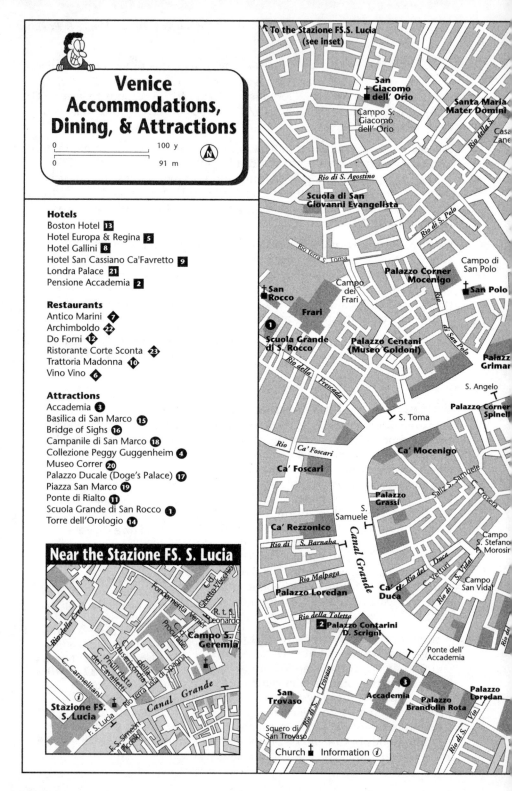

Venice
Accommodations,
Dining, & Attractions

0   100 y

0   91 m

Hotels
Boston Hotel **13**
Hotel Europa & Regina **5**
Hotel Gallini **8**
Hotel San Cassiano Ca'Favretto **9**
Londra Palace **21**
Pensione Accademia **2**

Restaurants
Antico Marini **7**
Archimboldo **22**
Do Forni **12**
Ristorante Corte Sconta **23**
Trattoria Madonna **10**
Vino Vino **6**

Attractions
Accademia **3**
Basilica di San Marco **15**
Bridge of Sighs **16**
Campanile di San Marco **18**
Collezione Peggy Guggenheim **4**
Museo Correr **20**
Palazzo Ducale (Doge's Palace) **17**
Piazza San Marco **19**
Ponte di Rialto **11**
Scuola Grande di San Rocco **1**
Torre dell'Orologio **14**

Near the Stazione FS. S. Lucia

To the Stazione FS.S. Lucia
(see inset)

San
† Giacomo
■ dell' Orio

Campo S.
Giacomo
dell' Orio

Santa Maria
Mater Domini

Rio della S.

Casa
Zane

Rio di S. Agostino

Scuola di San
Giovanni Evangelista

Rio di S. Polo

Rio Terrà S. Toma

Campo di
San Polo

Palazzo Corner
Mocenigo

†San
■Rocco

Campo
dei
Frari

† San Polo

Rio di San Polo

Frari

1

Scuola Grande
di S. Rocco

Palazzo Centani
(Museo Goldoni)

Palazz
Grimar

Rio della Frescada

S. Angelo

Palazzo Corner
Spinell

↳ S. Toma

Rio | Ca' Foscari

Ca' Mocenigo

Ca' Foscari

Saliz S. Samuele

Crosera

Palazzo
Grassi

S.
Samuele

Campo
S. Stefano
P. Morosin

Ca' Rezzonico

Rio di | S. Barnaba

Canal Grande

Rio del | Duca

Rio Malpaga

C. Vetturi

C. S. Vidal

Campo
San Vidal

Palazzo Loredan

Ca' d'
Duca

Rio di

Rio della Toletta

Rio di

2 Palazzo Contarini
D. Scrigni

Ponte dell'
Accademia

3

San
Trovaso

Accademia

Palazzo
Brandolin Rota

Palazzo
Loredan

Rio di S.

Squero di
San Trovaso

Church ■   Information ⓘ

Near the Stazione FS. S. Lucia

C. d'
Ghetto Vecchio

Fondamenta Venie

C. d.
Procuratie

R. t. d.
Leonardo

Museo

della
dei Cavalletti

C. Prulid della

Campo S.
Geremia

Rio di della Cret

C. Carmeliani

Rio Terrà Lista di Spagna

Stazione FS.
S. Lucia

†

Canal Grande

F. S. Simeon
Piccolo

F. S. Lucia

474

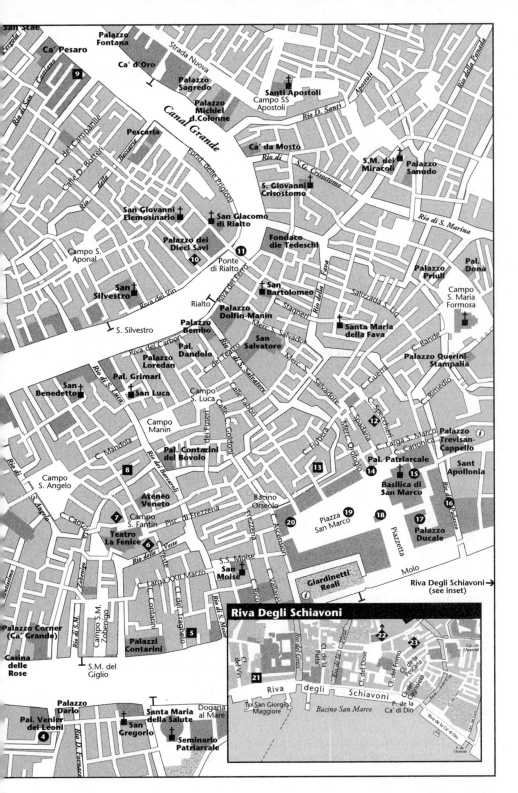

pleasant little hotel, sometimes very centrally located and maybe even get a canal view.

Boston Hotel
$. San Marco.
A perennial frugal favorite, the Boston offers cozy rooms fitted with a hodge-podge of antiques and modern pieces, all just steps away from Piazza San Marco. The best accommodations have little balconies over a canal, and you can get a TV upon request.

Ponte de Dai (halfway down the north colonnade of Piazza San Marco, a street leads north across a canal; the hotel is just over the bridge on the right). ☎ *041/ 528-7665. Fax: 041/522-6628. Vaporetto: San Marco. Rates: 110,000– 240,00L ($66–$144) double. AE, DC, MC, V. Closed Nov–Feb.*

Hotel Europa & Regina
$$$$$. San Marco.
One of Venice's venerable Grand Canal bastions was recently overhauled to rank it back among the city's top hotels. Hidden down a tiny side alley just two minutes from Piazza San Marco, this ITT Sheraton hotel's Tiepolo and Regina wings sport eclectic turn-of-the-century European furnishings and modern fabrics. The Europa wing is decorated in traditional Venetian style. There's a cozy bar with tables right on the Grand Canal, and the new open-kitchen restaurant has been getting good reviews.

Off Via XXII Marzo (head west out of the southwest corner of Piazza San Marco down Saliz San Mose; cross the bridge to continue straight on Calle Larga XXII Marzo; you'll see hotel signs directing you down the alleyways to the left). ☎ *041/ 520-0477. Fax: 041/523-1533. Vaporetto: San Marco. Rates: 360,000– 536,800L ($216–$322) double. AE, DC, MC, V.*

Hotel Gallini
$$. San Marco.
If the Boston is booked, try this reliable bargain bet. A family-run institution in Venice, the immaculate Gallini has big, modern rooms with marble and parquet floors and friendly service. The cheapest rooms lack baths and are on the back side of the hotel; the more expensive ones look over the tiny Rio della Verona canal.

Calle della Verona (from La Fenice opera house on Campo San Fantin, head up the main street going north, over a bridge, and the hotel is on the right). ☎ *041/ 520-4515. Fax: 041/520-9103. Vaporetto: Sant'Angelo. Rates: 120,000– 180,000L ($72–$108) double. AE, MC, V.*

Hotel San Cassiano Ca'Favretto
$$$. San Polo.
Call this place a moderate splurge choice. About half the rooms here look across the Grand Canal to the gorgeous Ca d'Oro; most of the others open

onto a side canal. Built into a 14th-century palace and steeped in dusty Old World elegance, the rooms are outfitted with antiques and reproductions. There's a dining room porch overlooking the Grand Canal.

Calle della Rosa (stepping off the vaporetto, turn left to cross in front of the church, take the bridge over the side canal and turn right. Then turn left, cross another canal and turn right, then left again. Cross yet another canal and turn right, then immediately left and then left again toward the Grand Canal and the hotel). ☎ *041/524-1768. Fax: 041/721-033. Vaporetto: San Stae. Rates: 170,000–327,000L ($102–$196.15) double. AE, DC, MC, V.*

Londra Palace
$$$$. Castello.
This 19th-century neo-Gothic palace is one of the best values on the prime real estate of the Riva degli Schiavoni. Tchaikovsky wrote his 4th Symphony in room 108. Accommodations are cushy, with lacquered furniture, and attic rooms are most romantic. With 100 windows overlooking the San Marco basin, you can enjoy watching people strolling below, as well as distant vistas of the lagoon. Quieter, cheaper rooms look out to the inner courtyard. Its restaurant, Do Leoni, is one of the best hotel dining rooms in town.

Riva degli Schiavoni (on the canal right at the San Zaccaria vaporetto stop). ☎ *041/520-0533. Fax: 041/522-5032. Vaporetto: San Zaccaria. Rates: 280,000–616,000L ($168–$369.60) double. AE, DC, MC, V.*

Pensione Accademia
$$$. Dorsoduro.
This pension is beloved by Venice regulars. You'll have to reserve far in advance to get any room here, let alone one overlooking the breakfast garden, which is snuggled into the confluence of two canals. The 17th-century villa is fitted with period antiques, and the atmosphere is decidedly old-fashioned and elegant (Katherine Hepburn's character lived here in the movie *Summertime*).

Fondamenta Bollani (step off the vaporetto, and turn right down Calle Gambara, which doglegs first left and then right. It becomes Calle Corfu, which ends at a side canal; walk left for a few feet to cross over the bridge, then head to the right back up toward the Grand Canal and the hotel). ☎ *041/523-7846. Fax: 041/523-9152. Vaporetto: Accademia. Rates: 225,000L ($135) double. AE, DC, MC, V.*

Dollars & Sense

Anyone age 14 to 29 should pick up a **Rolling Venice Card,** which is good for discounts on selected hotels (mostly hostel-type setups), restaurants, sights, and public transportation. The pass, good for a year, is 5,000L ($3), 10,000L ($6) if you include the special guide geared toward younger visitors. You can buy it at the Assessorato alla Gioventù (☎ **041/274-7651**) at Corte Contarina, just west of Piazza San Marco.

Something's Fishy: Venice's Restaurant Scene

A Venetian meal has many courses, and it can take a few hours to work your way through them all. This abundance is not just a scam played on tourists; Italians actually eat such full meals and accompany them with good wine and lively conversation. Start with an appetizer, which in Venice means a seafood dish. *Frutti di mare* are "fruits of the sea" and include a plethora of shellfish, crustaceans, and tentacled sea critters. Another archetypal dish is *sarde in saor,* sardines prepared with a sweet-and-sour sauce and often served with grilled slices of *polenta,* a wetter, more dense cousin to corn-bread. For the first course (called the *primo*), try the *zuppa di cozze* (mussels soup). If a rice dish is what you're after, *risotto alle seppie,* stained with squid ink, is popular, but it's beat out by *risi e bisi,* a creamy blend of rice and fresh peas, sometimes with bacon. Of the pastas, *spaghetti alle vongole* (with clams) or *al pomodoro* (in a plain tomato sauce) is the most common.

For the main course *(secondo)*, take advantage of the coastal setting and try some **fish.** Most seafood entrees are priced by weight, grilled or otherwise simply prepared, and served on a bed of bitter red radicchio lettuce. Other popular secondi include *anguille in umido* (eels stewed with tomatoes, garlic, and white wine) and the staple *fegato alla Veneziana* (tender calf's liver cooked with onions). Finish your meal off with a selection of *formaggi* (cheeses) or *tiramisù* (espresso-soaked lady fingers layered with sweetened, creamy mascarpone cheese and dusted with cocoa).

Italy is famed for its wines, and the Veneto region around Venice produces some great ones, including the white **Soave,** and reds **Bardolino** and **Valpolicello.** The best table wines tend to be whites.

Dollars & Sense

Although dining in Italy is relatively inexpensive, remember that the cost of your meal will include much more than just a first and second course. Italian restaurants add an unavoid-able "bread and cover" charge *(pane e coperto)* of about 1,500L to 10,000L (90¢ to $6) to your bill. This *coperto* plus water and wine, an appetizer, coffee, dessert, and a digestivo can quickly add up.

Antico Marini

*$$$$$. San Marco.
VENETIAN/INTERNATIONAL.*
One of Venice's top restaurants started out in the 18th century as a cafe, and the airy, clubby atmosphere remains to a degree, especially at the outdoor tables in summertime. Venetian specialties such as *risotto di frutti di mare* and *fegato alla Veneziana* are prepared perfectly here, but the food, reputation, and location across from the opera house all come at a stiff price.

Campo San Fantin (on the edge of the square occupied by La Fenice opera house).
☎ *041/522-4121. Reservations required.*
Vaporetto: *San Marco or Santa Maria del Giglio.* ***Main courses:*** *32,000–50,000L*

*($19.20–$30); fixed-price menu 40,000–55,0000L ($24–$33) at lunch, 75,000–98,000L ($45–$58.80) at dinner. AE, DC, MC, V. **Open:** Lunch Thurs–Mon, dinner Wed–Mon.*

Archimboldo
$$$$. Castello. VENETIAN/ITALIAN.

Archimboldo is always popular and is fast becoming one of Venice's leading restaurants. In summer, it's a crime not to snag one of the outdoor tables overlooking the canal. This restaurant serves up meticulously prepared Venetian cuisine, but if you're tired of seafood and liver, cuisines from the rest of Italy are also represented. The ingredients are bought fresh daily, and the wines are heavenly.

*Calle dei Furlani (a little street leading east from San Giorgio degli Schiavoni; when you reserve, ask about their boat service from San Marco). ☎ 041/528-6569. Reservations recommended. **Vaporetto:** Arsenale or San Zaccaria. **Main courses:** 22,000–38,000L ($13.20–$22.80); fixed-price lunch 40,000L ($24). AE, DC, MC, V. **Open:** Dinner Wed–Mon.*

Do Forni
$$$$. San Marco. VENETIAN/INTERNATIONAL.

The dining rooms in this place have a split personality: one is decorated country style and the other doing its best to imitate an *Orient Express* car. The food is purely Venetian, with a huge menu that promises all the bounty of the sea, along with select specialties from world cooking. It's not cheap, though. Do Forni keeps busy, and the bustling sometimes detracts from the posh atmosphere.

*Calle dei Specchieri (on the street leading north from Piazzetta dei Leoncini, which is around on the left flank of San Marco basilica). ☎ 041/523-2148. Reservations required. **Vaporetto:** San Marco. **Main courses:** 20,000–36,000L ($12–$21.60). AE, DC, MC, V. **Open:** Lunch and dinner daily.*

Ristorante Corte Sconta
$$$. Castello. VENETIAN SEAFOOD.

The bare, simple decor doesn't hint at the trendiness of this out-of-the-way trattoria, nor at the high quality of its heavy-on-the-fish food. The emphasis is on freshness here; they put the shrimp live on the grill. A tender beef fillet will satisfy landlubbers, but fans of seafood will want to make reservations here for their very first night to hang with the foodies, artists, and writers at this hidden gem.

*Calle del Pestrin (from San Marco, walk east along Riva degli Schiavoni a ways; you'll pass the church of La Pietà then over a canal named for it; just after this is a left turn onto Calle del Dose, which leads into Campo Bandiera e Moro; turn right to exit this square on Calle dei Preti; where this road turns right, Calle del Pestrin branches to the left). ☎ 041/522-7024. Reservations required. **Vaporetto:** Arsenale. **Main courses:** 20,000–30,000L ($12–$18); fixed-price menu 70,000L ($42). AE, DC, MC, V. **Open:** Lunch and dinner Tues–Sat. Closed Jan 7–Feb 7 and July 15–Aug 15.*

479

Trattoria Madonna
$$. San Paolo. VENETIAN.

This seafood mecca verges on the chaotic; service is friendly, but waiters can often be brusque in their hurry to satisfy everyone. People don't linger over their meals here, so if you just want a fast dinner of good, traditional food, it's the ideal spot. If they're offering a mixed fish fry, go for it. Otherwise, dig into Venetian specialties surrounded by local families, Italian businessmen, and other travelers.

Calle della Madonna (cross the Rialto Bridge and immediately turn left to walk down the Grand Canal's embankment; turn right down the second side street and the restaurant is 100 yards down on the left). ☎ **041/522-3824.** *Reservations recommended but not always accepted.* **Vaporetto:** *Rialto.* **Pasta:** *8,000–14,000L ($4.80–$8.40).* **Main courses:** *5,000–20,000L ($3–$12). AE, MC, V.* **Open:** *Lunch and dinner Thurs–Tues. Closed Jan 7–Feb 7 and Aug 1–15.*

Vino Vino
$. San Marco. VENETIAN/WINE BAR.

The owner of the exclusive, pricey Antico Martini restaurant opened this relaxed, affordable little joint, which provides solidly excellent dishes alongside an impressive list of wines both Italian and foreign. Order at the counter, and then go find a free seat at the simple tables in one of two cramped rooms. Your meal will be brought out to you, and you can sit back and treat yourself to a self-guided wine tasting.

Ponte della Veste (head west out of the southwest corner of Piazza San Marco down Saliz San Mose. Cross the bridge to continue straight on Calle Larga XXII Marzo, from which you'll turn right up Calle delle Veste. The restaurant is at the opposite end of a short bridge, just before La Fenice opera house). ☎ **041/523-7027.** *Reservations suggested.* **Vaporetto:** *San Marco.* **Pasta:** *8,000L ($4.80).* **Main courses:** *15,000L ($9). No credit cards.* **Open:** *Lunch and dinner Wed–Mon.*

Quick Bites

Italy offers great take-out at any **tavola calda** or **rosticceria,** where you can get pre-prepared hot dishes sold by weight. Most **bars** sell *tramezzini,* which are like giant tea sandwiches with the crusts cut off and are filled with tuna, ham, tomatoes, mozzarella, and so on. Don't get pizza slices to take away in Venice; you'll get the wrong impression of Italian pizza, which is only worth eating from Rome or the region south of Rome. For **picnic supplies,** visit any succession of *alimentari* (grocery stores), *forno* (bakeries), and *fruttivendolo* (fruit and vegetable stands).

Churches, Canals, & Towers, Oh My! Venice Sightseeing

Because **American Express** (☎ 041/520-0844) can't run buses in Venice, it is forced to offer guided orientation tours the old-fashioned way—on foot. It offers a morning tour of the major Piazza San Marco sights and an afternoon one of palaces and churches in the San Marco and San Polo districts. Both cost about 35,000L ($21). After dark, you can go on one of its "Evening Serenade" gondola tours for 50,000L ($30).

Venice Sights Not to Miss

Piazza San Marco (St. Mark's Square)

Piazza San Marco is Venice's living room, a year-round carnival of milling visitors, kids feeding swarms of pigeons, locals relaxing at outdoor cafe tables, and couples dancing on the cobblestones to the strains of live piano music. The epicenter of the city, San Marco is flanked on three sides by a 16th-century arcade and anchored by Italy's most mosaic-covered cathedral (see following entry). It's mobbed at midday, but late at night or at dawn it's virtually deserted, and this emptiness animates it with a Venetian magic all its own.

Tourist Traps

Although they're creating mechanical dams to prevent this, every season the tides bring the Adriatic Sea rushing into Venice's lagoon and the lagoon rushing into the streets. These *acqua alte,* or high waters, raise the water levels in town up to three feet for brief periods (one to five hours). When the *acque alte* strike, usually between October and March, low-lying Piazza San Marco is the first area to flood. As the waters rise, you may find yourself having the peculiarly Venetian experience of walking about the inundated city atop long lifelines of jerry-rigged wooden planks.

On July 14, 1902, the over-tall **Campanile,** or bell tower (☎ 041/522-4064), crumbled within seconds into a pile of debris. Because no city in Italy is worth its salt without a dome, tower, or some other high edifice that requires a laborious, wheezing climb, Venice quickly built a new campanile. It looked just like the old one, but with two major differences: it's now more architecturally sound, and even better, it now has an elevator. From up here, you can the multiple domes and spires of the cathedral's rooftop, along with a glorious sweep across the city and the Grand Canal. Admission is 6,000L ($3.60) for adults and 3,000L ($1.80) for kids; the tower is open daily from 9:30am to 4pm.

The north side of the square is enlivened by the **Torre dell'Orolorgio,** a late 15th-century clock tower whose bells chime the hours with the help of two hammer-wielding statues called the Moors of Venice. (They're actually European shepherds, but centuries of outdoor life have darkened the bronze figures to the point where the locals decided they looked more Moorish.)

The core collections of the **Museo Civico Correr** (☎ 041/522-5625), in the square's southwest corner, trace Venetian painting from the 14th to 16th centuries, including Tintoretto, Veronese, Carpaccio, and the Bellini family (Jacopo and sons Gentile and, the greatest of the three, Giovanni). But some of its strongest works are by non-Venetians such as Antonello da Messina and Cosmé Tura. Admission is cumulative with a ticket to the Palazzo Ducale, and it's open the same hours (see the Palazzo Ducale section).

Piazza San Marco. **Vaporetto:** *San Marco or San Zaccaria.*

Basilica di San Marco (St. Mark's Basilica)

No church in Europe is more lavishly decorated, more exquisitely mosaicked, more glittering with gold than Venice's San Marco. Built in the 11th century, its guiding principle in architecture and decoration is Byzantine, but more than six centuries of expansion and decoration have left behind Romanesque and Gothic touches as well.

The atrium, ceilings, walls, and multiple domes are all encrusted with over 40,000 square feet of gold-backed mosaics crafted between the 12th and 17th centuries. The oldest were created by eastern masters, and later ones were based on cartoons by Tintoretto, Veronese, and Titian. The floor is a reflection of the mosaic craft in marble, an undulating wonderland of color and pattern. The church's most disappointing aspect is that it's so popular, visitors are shuffled through like sightseeing cattle and kept moving so the next batch of tourists can cram in. Still, your 20 to 60 minutes inside (depending on how many of the church's side attractions you visit) will be unforgettable.

Tourist Traps

A few **Basilica di San Marco** ground rules: 1) Dress appropriately—no bare shoulders or knees (no shorts, short skirts, or tank tops). 2) Keep silent. 3) No photography is permitted.

Don't miss popping into the baptistery alcove, with a font carved by Sansovino, or checking out the presbytery with its *Pala d'Oro*, a gem-studded golden trophy from Constantinople. Above the church proper and entered through the atrium is the **Marciano Museum** (also known as *Logia dei Cavalli*), which affords you a close-up look at some of those mosaics. It also houses the original *Triumphal Quadriga* of four horses, replicas of which stride across the facade's roof. These life-size bronze equines are one of Venice's treasures. Taken in 1204 from Constantinople during the crusades, their exact origin is unclear, but they're at least ancient (2nd century A.D. is the best guess) and either Roman or Hellenistic. The cathedral runs free guided tours in summer, usually around 10:30am Monday to Saturday (check in the atrium for specifics).

Piazza San Marco. ☎ **041/522-5205. Vaporetto:** *San Marco or San Zaccaria.* **Admission:** *Basilica free; treasury 4,000L ($2.40); presbytery 3,000L ($1.80); Marciano Museum 3,000L ($1.80).* **Open:** *Basilica and presbytery: Apr–Sept Mon–Sat 9:30am–5:30pm, Sun 2–5:30pm; Oct–Mar Mon–Sat 9:30am–5:30pm, Sun 1:20–4:30pm. Treasury: Mon–Sat 9:30am–5pm, Sun 2–5pm. Marciano Museum: Apr–Sept Mon–Sat 10am–5:30pm, Sun 2–4:30pm; Oct–Mar Mon–Sat 10am–4:45pm, Sun 2–4:40pm.*

Palazzo Ducale (Doge's Palace)

One of Italy's grandest and most history-saturated town halls is this massive Gothic-Renaissance confection (raised in 1309, and rebuilt after a 1577 fire). Its public halls are heavily decorated with canvases and frescoes by Venice's greatest artists; works by Veronese and Tintoretto are abundant. The sign-posted route walks you through the palace in about 45 to 100 minutes.

Even with an informative audio guide and the English placards describing the artworks and the civic purpose of each room, I find wandering the public halls leaves me a bit cold. The real governing of the Venetian republic was not done here in plain sight. True power was wielded in a network of low-ceilinged, wooden-plank corridors and tiny offices wrapped around this public palace like a clandestine cocoon; the entrances were hidden behind secret doors set into all those fancy oil paintings and carved woodwork in the public rooms.

Here, private secretaries kept records and compiled accusations made against people both lowly and high-placed (see "Bet You Didn't Know"). The only way to see this inner sanctum, and to get a great primer on Venetian politics and intrigue, is to take the 90-minute **Secret Itineraries** tour. This tour will show you where the dreaded Council of Ten met to decide the fate of the republic and the people who crossed it. Also on the tour are the inquisition room and the "leads," the prison cells in the roof rafters where your guide will recount the tale of Casanova's famous escape. After the tour, you can visit the public palace on your own.

Off the back of the palace, you cross over the famous, enclosed **Bridge of Sighs (Ponte dei Sospiri)**, named by romantic-era writers who imagined condemned prisoners letting out a lament as they crossed it and got their final glimpse of Venice and its lagoon through tiny windows in the center. The cells on the other side preserve the scrawls and graffiti of ancient prisoners.

Piazzetta San Marco, San Marco. ☎ **041/522-5625. Vaporetto:** *San Marco or San Zaccaria.* **Admission:** *14,000L ($8.40) for adults, 8,000L ($4.80) for ages 7 to 29; the ticket also gets you into the Museo Civico Correr (see description under Piazza San Marco). Secret Itineraries tour is 8,000L ($4.80) for adults, 6,000L ($3.60) for students and those under 18.* **Open:** *Nov–Mar daily 9am–5pm,*

Apr–Oct daily 9am–7pm (ticket office closes 1 hour before museum). "Secret Itineraries" tour is usually Thurs–Tues at 10am and noon.

Bet You Didn't Know

Any Venetian citizen could accuse someone of misdeeds by writing the denunciation down and slipping it through specially placed "Lion's Mouth" slots in the Palazzo Ducale's walls. Although this activity sounds like prime breeding ground for backstabbing, it was a highly regulated procedure. All accusations had to be signed and witnessed, and if they proved merely to be slanderous, the would–be denouncer was in serious legal trouble of his own.

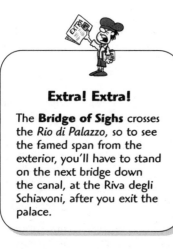

Extra! Extra!

The **Bridge of Sighs** crosses the *Rio di Palazzo*, so to see the famed span from the exterior, you'll have to stand on the next bridge down the canal, at the Riva degli Schiavoni, after you exit the palace.

Accademia

If you only make time for one museum in Venice, make it the Accademia. It'll take you a good 1½ to 3 hours to peruse the vast collections of masterpieces by those color-obsessed Venetian artists. The museum covers the giants of Venetian painting, from Paolo Veneziano's 14th-century *Coronation of the Virgin* altarpiece to Giorgione's weirdly lighted *The Tempest* and Giovanni Bellini's many *Madonna and Child*s. Also on display are Carpaccio's intricate *Cycle of St. Ursula*, Titian's late *Pietà*, and Tintoretto's *The Stealing of St. Mark*, commemorating the Venetian merchants who, in 828, spirited the body of the saint away from Alexandria during an era when acquiring bona fide saints was *de rigueur* for relic hunters.

Campo della Carità, Dorsoduro. ☎ *041/522-2247.* **Vaporetto:** *Accademia.* **Admission:** *12,000L ($7.20).* **Open:** *Tues–Sat 9am–7pm, Sun–Mon 9am–2pm.*

Collezione Peggy Guggenheim

One of the world's top modern art museums sits in Peggy Guggenheim's former residence in Venice, the uncompleted (only the first floor was built) 18th-century *Palazzo Venier dei Leoni*, right on the Grand Canal. Based around the late, great artistic patron's personal collection, it is one of the most complete surveys of avant-garde art from the early and mid-20th century. There are works by her short-lived hubby Max Ernst and her discovery Jackson Pollock, as well as pieces by some of her favorites: Picasso (his 1911 *The Poet* is notable), Miró, Mondrian, Brancusi, Duchamp, Kadinsky,

Chagall, Dalí, and Giacometti. A racy version of Tuscan sculptor Marino Marini's patented man-on-horseback bronzes cools its spurs in the small garden.

Calle San Cristoforo, San Gregorio 701, Dorsoduro. ☎ ***041/520-6288.*** ***Vaporetto:*** *Accademia.* ***Admission:*** *12,000L ($7.20) adults, 8,000L ($4.80) students and children.* ***Open:*** *Wed–Mon 11am–6pm.*

Extra! Extra!

When Paolo Veronese unveiled his *Last Supper,* now in the Accademia, the puritanical leaders of the Inquisition nearly had a conniption. They threatened him with charges of blasphemy for portraying this holiest of moments as a rousing, drunken banquet that resembled the paintings of Roman orgies. Veronese quickly retitled it *Feast in the House of Levi,* a more safely secular subject, and the mollified censors let it pass.

Scuola Grande di San Rocco

A *scuola* was a lay fraternity whose members dedicated their time and money to a charitable cause. It was also a venue for these private gentleman's clubs to show off; to that end, many *scuole* commissioned artists to decorate their home bases. When the Scuola di San Rocco held an art competition in 1564, Renaissance master Tintoretto pulled a fast one on his rivals. Instead of preparing a sketch for the judges like everyone else, he went ahead and finished a painting, secretly installing it in the ceiling of the Sala dell'Albero off the second-floor hall. The judges were suitably impressed, and Tintoretto got the job. Over the next 23 years, the artist filled the scuola's two floors with dozens of works. The *Rest on the Flight into Egypt* on the ground floor is superb, but his masterpiece hangs in that tiny Sala dell'Ablergo, a huge *Crucifixion* that ranks among the greatest and most moving works in the history of Venetian art.

Campo San Rocco, San Polo. ☎ ***041/523-4864.*** ***Vaporetto:*** *San Tomà.* ***Admission:*** *8,000L ($4.80) adults, 6,000L ($3.60) students and children.* ***Open:*** *Daily 10am–4pm.*

Other Fun Stuff to Do

➤ **Get Lost.** Pick up a good map of Venice. OK, now put it in your daypack and use it as a bookmark or something—you're not going to need it. Because it's so darn easy to get lost in Venice, you might as well make a day of it. Those signposted routes leading between major sights are always teeming with travelers. Stray from the route just a block or so and plunge into the private side of Venice, where the only sounds are church bells, kids playing soccer, and the lapping of water against canal embankments. Set aside a few hours of your day to practice the art of Zen walking—turning left when you feel like it and avoiding at all costs the major calle and campi. Stop for a meal in an osteria populated by locals, or pick up picnic supplies from little shops before choosing a scenic tiny campo or canalside *riva* to have your meal in. When you're ready to rejoin the world, just wander until you inevitably pop out onto a major square or street, get out that unused map, and navigate your way back to the well-known side of Venice.

➤ **Cruise the Grand Canal.** The Grand Canal is the watery Champs-Elysées of Venice, plied by hundreds of ferries, gondolas, garbage scows, speedboats, and small commercial craft daily. It's lined with the most gorgeous of Venetian *palazzi* (palaces), called home at times by a legion of expats such as Wagner, Byron, Robert Browning, Hemingway, Proust, Henry James, Ruskin, and James Fenimore Cooper. The buildings and palaces fronting the Grand Canal range in style from early Byzantine-Romanesque—where pale green, creamy yellow, or blood-red plaster walls are hung with marble sills sporting pointy, eastern style windows—to proportionately precise Renaissance palaces and neo-classical temple-like mansions.

Just sit back on the no. 1 or 82 vaporetto line and take an excursion in observation. Don't worry about which palazzo is which, rather open your eyes and your camera lens to search for the telling details—an old woman swathed in black leaning out her window; workmen replacing water-rotted wooden mooring piles by pounding in fresh-cut trunks; cats sleeping precariously on open windowsills; churches whose entrances lead up out of the canal, as if only the faithful with boats can attend; and private docks whose algae-covered ancient marble stairs disappear under the murky water.

➤ **Shop for Fine Glass, Lace, and Carnevale Masks.** You'll find examples of this triumvirate of Venetian craft specialties plastered everywhere about town, in every little hole-in-the-wall shop and big, crowded boutique (it's estimated that there are over 1,000 glass shops in the San Marco district alone). Quality varies tremendously, and many of the items are machine-produced or crafted anywhere from Eastern Europe to Taiwan, but the best rule of thumb is to buy it if you like it and to blazes with its provenance. If you're looking for the real thing or are buying with a collector's eye, however, you'll have to shell out big bucks to ensure quality.

Here are some of the top emporia for each art, where every piece on display is guaranteed hand-crafted by Venetian artisans. For **glass,** visit **Venini,** Piazzetta dei Leoncini (off the left flank of Basilica di San Marco); **Pauly & Co,** Ponte Consorzi (just behind the Doge's Palace, although they also have boutique shops on Piazza San Marco); or **Salviati,** on Piazza San Marco. For **lace,** go to **Jesurum,** on Mercerie del Capitello. At Carnevale time, don papier-mâché or leather **masks** made by the **Laboratorio Artigiano Maschere,** at Barbaria delle Tole, in the Castello district. Incidentally, the most traditional craftsmen of Venetian glass are located on the island of Murano, and the ladies who tat the best lace are on the island of Burano, both described under "The Islands of the Venetian Lagoon."

Get Outta Town: Day Trips & Excursions

If Venice's crowds get too much for you, consider leaving the city for a day in search of quieter pleasures. Just a quick boat ride from town you'll find the low-key islands of the Venetian Lagoon (there's great shopping here). And a mere half-hour train ride brings you to Padova, a college town with stunning art and architecture galore.

The Islands of the Venetian Lagoon

Ever wonder what Venice looked like before all the tourists or even before the fancy *palazzi* and art-stuffed museums? Well the answer is just a 1½-mile vaporetto ride away on the fishing village islands of the northern Venetian lagoon: Murano with its glass-blowing factories; sleepy, colorful Burano where little old ladies still tat old-fashioned lace; and swampy, half-deserted Torcello, with its remarkable medieval church and where Hemingway was fond of tramping about.

Most **vaporetto ferries** to the islands leave from Fondamenta Nuova in Venice, which is way up on the north side of the Castello district. However, you can catch line 52 to Fondamenta Nuova from San Zaccharia (on Riva degli Schiavoni near Piazzetta San Marco). If you're lucky, it will be the 52 that veers off at Fondamenta Nuova to chug up to Murano. Otherwise, from Fondamenta Nuova take line 12 or 13 to Murano. Line 12 will move you from Murano to Burano, and both 12 and 14 go from Burano to Torcello. From Torcello, return to Venice on line 12 (to Fondamenta Nuova, where you can catch the 52 back) or via a much longer way around on line 14 (to San Zaccharia).

> **Extra! Extra!**
>
> For a simple shopping stroll along one of Venice's premier (and priciest) avenues, head out of Piazza San Marco at the clock tower onto **Le Mercerie.** This route, lined with fancy boutiques and souvenir shops, is a series of streets whose names change constantly—but are always prefaced with the word "mercerie"—and that together thread all the way to the Rialto Bridge.

The island of **Murano** is the biggest of the trio, bustling with fishermen unloading the day's catch and heated by the furnaces of its many glass factories, an age-old tradition of this island and a craft that has long since spread to Venice itself. Shoppers can head directly to the outlet stores (most stores on Murano take quality seriously) where you never pay the sticker price (bargain down to at least two-thirds of the asking price). Even better, in many of the workshops glassblowers will create items, especially trinkets, for you on the spot. If you like your artisan craft with a bit of history, head to the

Museo Vetraio di Murano (☎ 041/739-586), where you can examine a large collection of glass objects from ancient Roman times through the 19th century as well as see displays on the history and practice of the craft itself.

Time-Savers

Get up early in the morning because visiting all three islands takes a good five to seven hours. The time you spend on Burano and Torcello is in hour increments (ferries leave hourly), and one hour is enough for each. Add in 35 minutes for the ride from Venice to Murano, 20 minutes from Murano to Burano, 5 minutes from Burano to Torcello, and 50 minutes from Torcello to Venice. If you leave by 9 or 10am, you can be back in Venice by late afternoon.

To get away from the glass, visit the church of **San Pietro Martire,** filled with the unexpected riches of oil paintings by Tintoretto, Veronese, and Giovanni Bellini. It costs 1,000L (60¢) in change for the light boxes to illuminate each side of the nave and another 3,000L ($1.80) to see the carved paneling in the sacristy. The truly ancient church of **Santa Maria e Donato** turns the gorgeous exterior of its apse to the canal so you can admire the stacked colonnades, dog-tooth molding, and inlaid Byzantine designs. The current structure was rebuilt in the 12th century, but it uses Corinthian columns that date from Roman times to the 6th century, a 6th-century pulpit, a patterned floor from 1141 that rivals that of San Marco, and some 15th-century frescoes.

Tourist Traps

Note that Murano has five vaporetto docks. You usually land at *Colonna* or *Museo,* but you should continue on to Burano from *Faro.*

The name of the game on tiny **Burano** is lacemaking, an antique art that can still fetch high prices in Venetian shops. Prices can be a bit more reasonable here; you can get an edged hankie for about 5,000L ($3). You can learn a bit about the history of lacemaking at the **Scuola di Merletti** (☎ 041/730-761), but its main purpose is to keep the tradition alive, and on the second floor women are diligently at work learning this excruciatingly delicate craft. Admission is 5,000L ($3), and it's usually open Wednesday to Monday from 10am to 4pm (in winter, it often closes if no tourists appear). The island has as Tiepolo *Crucifixion* in the parish church of **San Martino,** but Burano's best attraction is itself, a village whose houses are all painted in bright primaries and pastels, with a leisurely pace of life tied to the rhythms of the tides and the coming and going of fishing boats.

The Venetian Islands

0 ____ 100 y
0 ____ 161 m

Litorale di Lido

Airport ✈
Ferry Route - - -

Grassy, semi-deserted **Torcello** is a one-trick pony. From the ferry dock, follow the solitary long canal on a 10-minute stroll to the 11th-century Byzantine **cathedral,** whose west wall is covered with a remarkable 11th-century mosaic of the *Last Judgment,* echoed by a massive *Madonna* mosaic in the apse. Admission is 1,500L (90¢), and it's open daily from 10am to 12:30pm and 2:30 to 6:30pm (from November through March, it closes at 5pm). Across the square is the dinky **Museo dell'Estuario,** a collection split between archaeological fragments and the remains of some 10 other churches that once sprinkled Torcello's landscape. Admission is 3,000L ($1.80) and it's open Tuesday through Sunday 10am to 12:30pm and 2 to 4pm (sometimes it closes in winter).

Bet You Didn't Know

Torcello's marshy badlands give you the best feeling for what Venice looked like when people first started settling there. Torcello predates Venice, and it was a thriving center of some 20,000 souls from the 7th to 11th centuries. Then malaria and competition from *La Serenissima* set in and quickly depopulated the isle. It now runs on a skeleton crew of 75 inhabitants.

As far as lunch goes, you can either pack a picnic in from Venice (Torcello is prime for picnicking) or sit down for a good meal at the trattorie **Al Corallo** (☎ **041/739-080**), Fondamenta dei Vetrai 73 in Murano, or **Trattoria da Romano** (☎ **041/730-030**), at Via Baldassare Galuppi 223 in Burano. Or go all out and splurge on Hemingway's old favorite **Locanda Cipriani** (☎ **041/730-150**), a refined restaurant in the middle of nowhere on Torcello.

Poking Around Padova

A city of scholars and saints, arcaded piazze and Giotto frescoes, Padova (Padua) is my choice for the best day trip into the Veneto region. It's only 32 minutes by half-hourly **train** from Venice (a fact that leads many savvy travelers to stay in Padova during peak tourist season and day trip into crowded, expensive Venice).

Padova's biggest sight by far is on the very north edge of town (take bus 3, 8, 12, or 18) at the Piazza Eremitani off Corso Garibaldi. The **Cappella degli Scrovegni (Arena Chapel)** (☎ **049/650-845**) was entirely frescoed from 1303 to 1306 by Giotto, a genius artist whose use of emotion, foreshortening, modeled figures, saturated colors, and narrative space revolutionized the concept of art and kicked off the modern era in painting. The chapel as a whole is breathtaking, depicting scenes from the life of Mary and Jesus in 38 panels.

Although many people's attention is drawn to the *Last Judgment* covering the entrance wall, my favorite panels are three emotion-packed scenes. In the *Meeting of Joachim and Ann at the Gate,* the soon-to-be parents of Mary greet each other touchingly after a long separation. In the *Arrest of Christ,* a yellow-cloaked Judas locks eyes with Jesus as he betrays his Christ with a kiss (the signal Judas used to identify Jesus for the waiting soldiers), and the two men form a chillingly quiet, still center to the martial commotion that swirls around them. The woe-filled *Lamentation of Christ* speaks for itself. Admission, which also gets you into the Musei Civici di Eremitani, is 10,000L ($6) for adults and 7,000L ($4.20) for ages 6 to 17. The church is open February to October daily from 9am to 7pm, November to January daily from 9am to 6pm.

The nearby **Musei Civici di Eremitani** (☎ **049/875-1153**), Piazza Eremitani 8, houses an archaeological collection on the ground floor and a Giotto *Crucifix* and minor works by major Venetian painters (Giorgione,

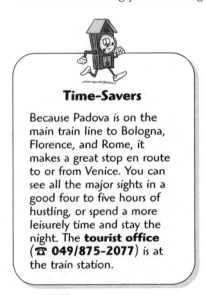

Time-Savers

Because Padova is on the main train line to Bologna, Florence, and Rome, it makes a great stop en route to or from Venice. You can see all the major sights in a good four to five hours of hustling, or spend a more leisurely time and stay the night. The **tourist office** (☎ **049/875-2077**) is at the train station.

Jacopo Bellini, Veronese, Tintoretto) from the 14th century on upstairs. Admission is combined with the Scrovegni Chapel; the museum is also open the same hours.

Padova's other great sight is the eastern-looking **Basilica di Sant'Antonio** (☎ **049/663-944**), Piazza del Santo 11. It's all domes and mini-minarets from the outside, with Donatello bronzes on the high altar inside. In the north transept is the tomb of St. Anthony, in the south transept is a 14th-century fresco of the *Crucifixion*. On the piazza in front of the church sits a bronze man on horseback called *Gattamelata,* by Donatello, who revived the lost art of the equestrian statue in the 15th century.

Extra! Extra!

For one of Italy's most elegant cafe experiences, head to the extravagantly neoclassical **Caffé Pedrocchi** (☎ **049/876-2576**), Piazzetta Pedrocchi 15. Drinks are pricey, but the colorful 19th-century setting and whimsical references to ancient Rome and Egypt are worth the trip. In summer, sit out on the stone patio to watch the ebb and flow of Paduan life on the pedestrian piazza outside.

Il Dotto (☎ **049/875-1490**), Via Squarcione 23 (off Via Roma), gets my nod for best value in a set-priced menu—50,000L ($30) buys you some of the most inventive Paduan cuisine in town. One of the best central values in Paduan hotels is the **Leon Bianco** (☎ **049/875-0814**), Piazzetta Pedrocchi 12 (at Via Cavour), where contemporary doubles in a 100-year-old palazzo run 156,000L ($93.60).

Chapter 25

Madrid & Environs

In This Chapter

➤ A guide to the very best of Madrid's art-packed museums

➤ Feeding the need on tapas delicacies and monstrous paellas

➤ Pinching pesetas while living in comfort at Madrid's best value hotels

➤ Olé! Where and when to see a bullfight

➤ El Greco's Toledo, King Felipe II's monastery, and Segovia's Roman ruins

---

The capital city and center of all Spain, Madrid is a museum lover's paradise. This is where you'll find Picasso's *Guernica*, Velázquez's *Las Meninas*, and works by Goya, El Greco, and hundreds of other European artists lining the halls of the Prado Museum. But Madrid is not just about art. It's also the capital of the evening pre-dinner stroll, called the *paseo* (or if you pause in countless little bars that serve the bite-sized morsels called *tapas*, it's called a *tapeo)*.

Madrid is also the place to party, because it's a round-the-clock town. You can spend the morning at the royal palace, the afternoon in an 18th-century art gallery, and late afternoon at the bull-fights. Come nightfall, the evening kicks off with a fashionably late dinner, per-haps followed by a flamenco show, or dancing until dawn at one of the city's

Dollars & Sense

The Spanish unit of currency is the peseta (ptas.). Roughly, $1 equals 150ptas.; or 10ptas. equals 6.6¢. Spanish coins include 1, 5, 25, 50, 100, 200, and 500 pesetas. Bills come in denominations of 500, 1,000, 5,000, and 10,000 pesetas.

clubs. If you're an art fan, spend four to five days in Madrid. If not, give it at least two days, with another two thrown in for day trips to Toledo and Segovia (see "Get Out of Town").

Getting Your Bearings

Mastering Madrid's layout is relatively easy, thanks to the many major *plazas* (squares) and the grand boulevards linking them. The map in this chapter points out all the main ones, but I will describe some of the most important.

Plaza del Sol is the absolute center of Madrid (and of Spain, for that matter; there's a 0 kilometer mark in the southwest corner of the plaza from which all Spanish distances are measured). More scenic is the nearby **Plaza Mayor,** flanked by cafes and colonnades, with an equestrian statue of Felipe III (done by Italian mannerist Giambologna and his student Pietro Tacca) in the center. These two plazas are the heart of Old Madrid, a quarter full of authentic restaurants and nightlife action. South of Plaza del Sol is Madrid's 17th-century district, and to the north of it are pedestrian shopping streets.

Time-Savers

Madrid's **tourist office** (☎ **91/541-2325**) is on the ground floor of the Torre de Madrid skyscraper on Plaza de España. There are also small offices in Chamartín train station and at the airport. The office's free *Enjoy Madrid,* a monthly English–language magazine, has some good information, but its *En Madrid* events guide isn't nearly as complete as the *Guia del Ocio* you can pick up cheaply at newsstands.

The wide, modern **Plaza de España** marks the city's northwest corner. Running south from there is **Calle de Bailén,** which borders the Palacio Real (royal palace) and delineates the city's western edge. **Gran Vía,** Madrid's main boulevard, zigzags from Plaza de España across the northern Old City. It's lined with department stores, cafes, cinemas, and corporate headquarters. North of it are the rundown **Malasana** and **Chueca** districts—not the sort of place you'd want to raise your kids, but a trendy nightlife zone nonetheless.

The eastern flank of Old Madrid is bounded by the tree-planted **Paseo del Prado,** running north-south from Plaza de la Cibeles through Plaza C. del Castillo to the square in front of the Atocha train station. It's lined with hotels, cafes, and the big museums. On the east side of the Paseo lies the vast **Retiro Park,** center of the up-and-coming **Retiro** neighborhood.

Getting Into & Around Town

By **train,** you'll most certainly arrive at **Chamartín,** the main station, which services the east of Spain and the French border (where international lines come through). In the northern suburbs, Chamartín is right on Metro line 8, so it's a quick hop downtown from the station. Madrid has two other train stations. **Atocha** runs trains to southwest Spain and Portugal (there are

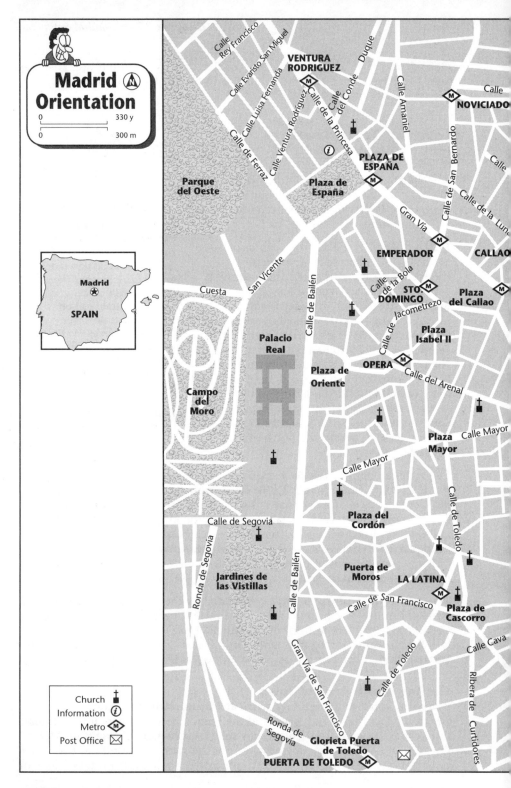

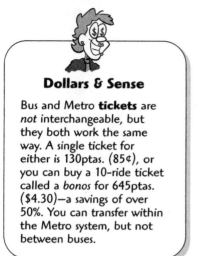

Dollars & Sense

Bus and Metro **tickets** are *not* interchangeable, but they both work the same way. A single ticket for either is 130ptas. (85¢), or you can buy a 10-ride ticket called a *bonos* for 645ptas. ($4.30)—a savings of over 50%. You can transfer within the Metro system, but not between buses.

two metro stops called Atocha; the station is the one marked Atocha RENFE). **Norte,** or **Príncipe Pío,** services northwest Spain. **Barajas,** Madrid's **airport,** is about 10 miles outside town. Regular buses shuttle you to Plaza de Colón in the city center.

The **Metro** system has 11 lines, with major junctures at Puerta del Sol, Alonso Martinez, ópera, and Avienda de América. It's very fast and efficient (slower and much more crowded at rush hour) and helps you navigate the great distances between Madrid's widely dispersed sights.

Madrid is less appealing to walk about than other European cities; its wide boulevards are fine for getting somewhere, but most are rather devoid of character. With a few exceptions, such as Plaza Mayor, this is one city where you won't miss much by tunneling around on the Metro. The **bus** network is pretty straightforward and even more efficient than in most cities; buses travel in their own special lanes, rather than fighting traffic.

Madrid Fast Facts

American Express   There are two branches of American Express in Madrid. One (☎ 91/322-5500) is on Plaza de las Cortés, 2, across from the Palace Hotel. The other is at Calle Francisco Gervás, 10 (☎ 91/572-0320). Both are open Monday to Friday 9am to 5:30pm and Saturday 9am to noon.

Doctors/hospitals   The U.S. Embassy (☎ 91/587-2200) will provide a list of English-speaking doctors and dentists, or you can call 061 for this information. For emergency care, go to the **Hospital La Paz,** Castellana 261 (☎ 91/734-2600), or the **Hospital 12 de Octubre,** Carretera de Andalucía (☎ 91/390-8000).

Embassy   The U.S. Embassy is located at Calle Serrano 75; the telephone number is ☎ 91/587-2200.

Emergency   Call ☎ 091 for the police. For an ambulance, dial ☎ 734-2554. Report a fire to ☎ 080.

Pharmacies   If you need a late-night pharmacy, finding one won't be difficult. Every pharmacy posts a list of nearby *farmacias* that stay open late. You can also call ☎ 098 or look in the newspaper for the *Farmacias de Guardia*.

Safety   Purse-snatchers and pickpockets are probably the worst criminals you'll encounter in Madrid, but these crooks are slick; thieves often work in groups to relieve you of your wallet, and even a locked car is no deterrent to a determined purse-snatcher. Carry only the cash you need for that day and be cautious when using the Metro.

Taxis   Madrid's taxis cruise the streets looking for passengers, but make sure you hail a legitimate taxi (they are black with horizontal red bands or white with diagonal red bands) rather than a gypsy cab, which is unmetered and may charge higher fares.

The initial charge is 170 pesetas ($1.10) plus 50 or 75 pesetas (30¢ or 50¢) for each additional kilometer. Travel at night or on Sundays and holidays incurs a surcharge of 150 pesetas ($1). A trip to the airport costs 325 pesetas ($2.15) more, and a ride from a railway station costs 160 ($1.05) pesetas more. If you travel beyond the city limits, the driver is permitted to charge twice the fare shown on the meter. To call a taxi, dial ☎ **91/445-9008** or 91/447-5180.

Telephone   A local call in Madrid costs at least 15 pesetas (10¢). At a coin-operated phone, place coins in the rack at the top of the phone, and they'll roll in as needed to pay for the call. Other phones accept only phone cards, called *tarjeta telefónica,* which are sold at tobacco shops and post offices in 1,000 pesetas ($6.65) and 2,000 pesetas ($13.30) denominations.

Spain's country code is **34.** The city code for Madrid is **91;** use this code if you're calling Madrid from another city within Spain. If you're calling from outside the country, drop the 9. (Yes, this is different from most other countries, where the initial digit is a 0.) To call Madrid from the United States, dial **011-34-1** followed by the number. To charge your call to a calling card, dial **AT&T** (☎ **900/990-011**), **MCI** (☎ **900/990-014**), or **Sprint** (☎ **900-99-0013**). To call the United States direct from Spain, dial **07,** wait for the dial tone, then dial **1,** the area code, and phone number.

Transit Info   ☎ 91/552-4900.

Mi Casa Es Su Casa: Madrid's Hotel Scene

There are three main **types of accommodation** in Madrid: regular hotels, which range from turn-of-the-century deluxe establishments to moderate modern inns; *hostals,* usually good-value bare-bones places; and *pensiones,* even cheaper and simpler boarding houses, often requiring half or full board. Many accommodations are scattered up the Gran Vía, which can get a little rough after dark, and near Atocha Station. There's also a good selection of accommodations in the Old City around Madrid's central squares, such as Plaza Mayor and Puerta del Sol. As prime real estate for travelers, these areas have

Time-Savers

The offices of Viajes Brújula will **book you a room** for a fee of 300ptas. ($2). You must go in person to the main office (☎ **91/ 559-9704**) on the 6th floor of the Torre de Madrid on Plaza de España or to one of their branches, either in Atocha station (AVE terminal), Chamartín station, or at the airport bus terminal on Plaza de Colón.

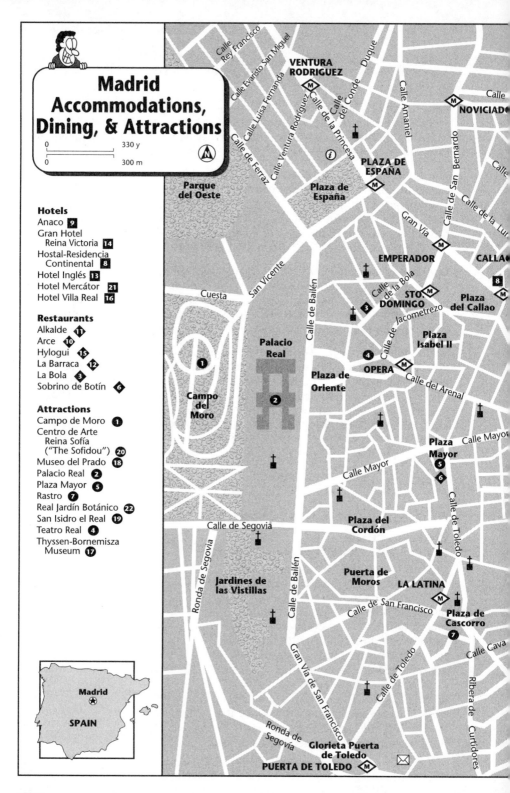

Madrid Accommodations, Dining, & Attractions

0   330 y
0   300 m

Hotels
Anaco **9**
Gran Hotel
  Reina Victoria **14**
Hostal-Residencia
  Continental **8**
Hotel Inglés **13**
Hotel Mercátor **21**
Hotel Villa Real **16**

Restaurants
Alkalde **11**
Arce **10**
Hylogui **15**
La Barraca **12**
La Bola **3**
Sobrino de Botín **6**

Attractions
Campo de Moro **1**
Centro de Arte
  Reina Sofía
  ("The Sofidou") **20**
Museo del Prado **18**
Palacio Real **2**
Plaza Mayor **5**
Rastro **7**
Real Jardín Botánico **22**
San Isidro el Real **19**
Teatro Real **4**
Thyssen-Bornemisza
  Museum **17**

Madrid ★
SPAIN

498

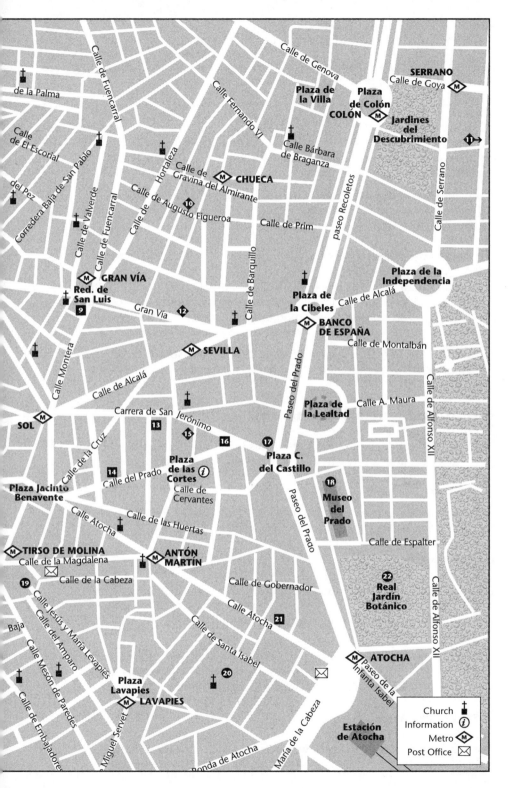

their share of pickpockets, but they're also some of the more exciting places to be because they're near plenty of restaurants and sightseeing.

Anaco
$$. Near the Gran Vía.
This budget choice on a tree-shaded plaza at a Madrid crossroads has clean, contemporary rooms with built-in furnishings. The top floor has the choicest, largest rooms with terraces.

Tres Cruces 3 (just down from the Metro stop). ☎ **91/522-4604. Fax:** *91/531-6484.* **Metro:** *Gran Vía.* **Rates:** *9,000–9,500ptas. ($60–$63.35) double. AE, DC, MC, V.*

Gran Hotel Reina Victoria
$$$$. Near the Puerta del Sol.
This historic monument is one of Madrid's top hotels, a favorite of bullfighting stars and discriminating travelers. There's plenty of early 20th-century ambiance to go around, and even though the neighborhood's busy, the rooms are soundproofed. There's even a private plaza for relaxing.

Plaza Santa Ana 14 (on the Calle del Prado). ☎ **91/531-4500. Fax:** *91/522-037.* **Metro:** *Tirso de Molina or Puerta del Sol.* **Rates:** *From 21,900ptas. ($146) double. AE, DC, MC, V.*

Hostal-Residencia Continental
$. On the Gran Vía.
In a building stuffed with cheap hotels, this is the finest (in terms of being clean, updated, and comfy—basic is still the key word at these prices). To save even more, stay at any of the cheaper, less tidy hostels and pensions at this address.

Gran Vía 44 (just up from the Metro stop). ☎ **91/521-4640. Fax:** *91/521-4649.* **Metro:** *Callao.* **Rates:** *5,000ptas. ($33.35) double. AE, DC, MC, V.*

Hotel Inglés
$$. Near the Puerta del Sol.
You won't want for food or fun here; the street is lined with music bars and *tascas* (bars). The lobby's usually taken over by soccer fans glued to the TV, and although rooms are boringly modern, many have sitting areas and all are well-maintained.

Calle Echegaray 8 (between Carrera de San Jerónimo and Calle del Prado). ☎ **91/429-6551. Fax:** *91/420-2423.* **Metro:** *Puerta del Sol or Sevilla.* **Parking:** *1,200ptas. ($8).* **Rates:** *10,000ptas. ($66.65) double. AE, DC, MC, V.*

Hotel Mercátor
$$$. Near Atocha Station.
This area is ground zero for art lovers becuse it's within easy walking distance of both the Prado and Reina Sofía museums. Ask to see several

accommodations, because the modernly furnished rooms vary widely (the best come with desks and armchairs). In summer, reserve ahead if you want air-conditioning.

Calle Atocha 123 (1½ blocks up from Atocha station). ☎ *91/429-0500. Fax: 91/369-1252. Metro: Atocha or Antón Martín. Rates: 11,350ptas. ($75.65) double. AE, DC, MC, V.*

Hotel Villa Real
$$$$$. On Plaza de las Cortés.
Going on its 10th birthday, this is one of Madrid's most posh hotels, an odd mix of neoclassical, modern, and Aztec with scads of amenities, such as satellite TV with videos and leather-upholstered room furnishings. The central location is excellent, the staff accommodating, and the aura comfortably plush.

Plaza del las Cortés 10 (where the Carrera de San Jerónimo meets Calle del Prado, very near the Paseo del Prado). ☎ *91/420-3767. Fax: 91/420-2547. Metro: Antón Martín. Rates: 34,400. ptas ($229.35) double. AE, DC, MC, V.*

Roast Pork & Paella: Madrid's Restaurant Scene
The best and most innovative Spanish cooking, hands down, is that of the **Basque** country in the north. It is extremely sophisticated and always changing, particularly the Basque codfish dishes and exquisite preparations of baby eel. Madrid's restaurant roster celebrates the cooking of all Spain's regions, however, including local Madrileños and Castillian cuisine. The most Spanish of dishes is **paella,** a Mediterranean medley of seafood and rice traditionally eaten at lunch. **Roast meats** are popular, especially *cordero* (lamb) and *cochinillo* (suckling pig), and you certainly won't want for pork here, what with everyone constantly pushing **chorizo** sausage and salty **jamón serrano** ham on you. Madrid's king of meaty pleasures is the hearty stew of **cocido madrileño,** which is a mix of beef, chicken, pig's feet, sausage, garbanzo beans, veggies, pasta, and bread dumplings all cooked together for a long time.

Madrid maintains a lifeline of trucks and airplanes to keep the landlocked capital in constant supply of excellent fresh **fish.** Even so, one of the most popular seafoods is **bacalao,** dried salt cod softened and served by itself or *al ajoarriero* (flaked and stewed with tomatoes, potatoes, garlic, and peppers). After dinner, dip your spoon into the omnipresent **flan,** which many rank even above its French cousin crème caramel. Spanish table **wine** is usually quite excellent, especially Castillian **Valdepeñas** and **Rioja.** My favorite drink is **sangria,** a sort of wine punch filled with ice and fruit chunks. The sweet, powerful wine from Jerez (Americans call it **sherry**) is one of Europe's greatest alcoholic treats.

Culture Shock

Tapas is Spanish for "lid," because pieces of bread or slices of ham were once used as wineglass covers to guard against flies. These morsels evolved into an array of snacks eaten in tiny portions at bars called *tascas*. Today, thousands of Spaniards turn out in the afternoons and evenings to *tapeo*, which means walking from *tasca* to *tasca*, drinking, and chatting and gobbling up those delicious tapas. (I'll point you to some of the better *tascas* and describe some typical tapas under "Other Fun Stuff to Do.")

I get cavities just thinking about a traditional Spanish **breakfast,** which consists of thick, soupy hot chocolate and **churros.** *Churros* are a bready batter pulled into long, star-shaped sticks, deep fried until the chewy insides are coated with a crisp crust, and served piping hot, dripping with oil and crusted with sugar. Although *churros* are truly one of nature's divine foods (if a wee bit terrible for your health) and should be tried at least once (a day), you may want to stick to coffee or tea and rolls for breakfast.

Speaking of breakfast, Madrileños keep somewhat different **dining hours** from the rest of Europe. They've fared better than their neighbors at resisting the frantically paced daily schedule of the modern, Americanized world, and many still manage to have their biggest meal in the middle of the day, between 1 and 4pm. Around 5pm, after a siesta, they go out to *paseo*—kind of an evening constitutional stroll to see and be seen and, most importantly, to eat tapas (see sidebar). This *tascas* hopping is important because it tides your hunger over until dinnertime at 10pm. Some restaurants catering to travelers will serve dinner as early as 8pm, but no self-respecting Spaniard would be caught dead having a meal that early. Most restaurants, certainly the better and more authentic ones, don't even open their doors until 9 or 9:30pm. This late supper is usually a light affair. After all, you don't want to be weighed down for the dancing until dawn, now, do you?

Alkalde
$$$$. In Retiro. BASQUE/INTERNATIONAL.
With ham hocks hanging from wood-beamed ceilings upstairs and stony cellar dining rooms, this place feels more like a Basque country inn than the fine big-city restaurant it is. You can't beat the combination of incredible cookery and great atmosphere. Don't miss the *cigalas* (crayfish) and trout Alkalde.

Jorge Juan 10 (behind the archaeological museum, off Calle de Serrano). ☎ *91/ 576-3359. Reservations required.* **Metro:** *Retiro or Serrano.* **Main courses:** *1,550–5,600ptas. ($10.35–$37.35); fixed-price menus from 4,750ptas. ($31.65). AE, DC, MC, V.* **Open:** *Lunch and dinner daily. Closed Sat and Sun July–Aug.*

Arce
$$$$$. Near the Gran Vía. BASQUE.

Arce has some of the best, most inventive Basque cuisine in the city. The chefs/owners stick to basic combinations of fresh ingredients to ensure the highest quality of their creations. Settle in to the comfy dining room and try the casserole of boletus mushrooms or pheasant with seasonal spices.

Augusteo Figueroa 32 (between Calle de Pelayo and Calle de Barbieri). ☎ **91/522-5913.** *Reservations recommended.* **Metro:** *Colón.* **Main courses:** *2,500–3,500ptas. ($16.65–$23.35). AE, DC, MC, V.* **Open:** *Lunch Mon–Fri, dinner Mon–Sat. Closed a week before Easter and Aug 15–31.*

Hylogui
$. Near the Puerta del Sol. SPANISH.

If simplicity and goodness are what you look for in a restaurant, head here. Hylogui's huge dining rooms are a Madrid legend for serving up hearty, tasty, home-style cooking at great prices. Save room for the flan; it gets particularly high marks.

Ventura de la Vega (just off Carrera de San Jerónimo). ☎ **91/429-7357.** *Reservations recommended.* **Metro:** *Sevilla.* **Main courses:** *1,000–2,200ptas. ($6.65–$14.65); fixed-price menus 1,400–1,700ptas. ($9.35–$11.35). AE, DC, MC, V.* **Open:** *Lunch daily, dinner Mon–Sat.*

La Barraca
$$$. Near the Gran Vía. VALENCIAN.

Step off the bustling Gran Vía and into a Valencian country inn, with two floors of dining rooms brimming with paintings, ceramics, lanterns, and other Spanish bric-a-brac. Among the savory specialties are *paella à la Barraca* (made here with pork and chicken) and brochette of angler fish and prawns.

Reina 29-31 (just off the Gran Vía between Calle de Alcalá and Calle Clavel). ☎ **91/532-7154.** *Reservations recommended.* **Metro:** *Gran Vía or Sevilla.* **Main courses:** *1,800–3,000ptas. ($12–$20); fixed-price menu 3,500ptas. ($2.35). AE, DC, MC, V.* **Open:** *Lunch and dinner daily.*

La Bola
$$. Between Ópera and Plaza de España. MADRILEÑA.

Escape to old Madrid in this 1870's tavern—nothing has changed behind this crimson facade since the days when Ava Gardner (complete with a bullfighter entourage) and Hemingway were regulars. You can start with a lobster cocktail, but the real thing to do here is order the Madrid specialty, *cocido madrileño.*

Calle del la Bola (just north of the Ópera). ☎ **91/547-6930.** *Reservations required.* **Metro:** *Santo Dominigo or Ópera.* **Main courses:** *1,400–2,200ptas. ($9.35–$14.65); fixed-price menu 2,125ptas. ($14.15). No credit cards.* **Open:** *Lunch and dinner Mon–Sat.*

Sobrino de Botín

$$. Near Plaza Mayor. SEGOVIAN/SPANISH.
Botín doesn't seem to have changed a whit since it opened in 1725; it has an open kitchen, hanging copper pots, and an 18th-century tile oven. You can still get the house specialty, roast suckling pig, that Hemingway's heroes ate in the closing scene of *The Sun Also Rises*. Be prepared for a crowd—a restaurant doesn't stay in business almost 275 years without being *very* popular.

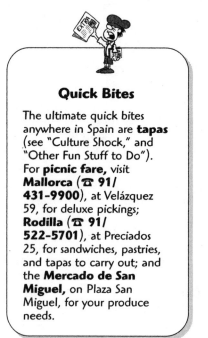

Quick Bites

The ultimate quick bites anywhere in Spain are **tapas** (see "Culture Shock," and "Other Fun Stuff to Do"). For **picnic fare**, visit **Mallorca** (☎ 91/431-9900), at Velázquez 59, for deluxe pickings; **Rodilla** (☎ 91/522-5701), at Preciados 25, for sandwiches, pastries, and tapas to carry out; and the **Mercado de San Miguel**, on Plaza San Miguel, for your produce needs.

Calle de Cuchilleros 17 (a few steps down from Plaza Mayor, off Calle de Toledo). ☎ *91/366-4217. Reservations required.* **Metro:** *La Latina or ópera.* **Main courses:** *800–3,000ptas. ($5.35–$20); fixed-price menu 3,700ptas. ($24.65). AE, DC, MC, V.* **Open:** *Lunch and dinner daily.*

Sightseeing in the Madrid of Many Museums

Pullmantours (☎ 91/541-1807), Plaza de Orienta 8, organizes half-day **guided bus tours** of the city. The artistic tour whips you through a few top museums for 4,950ptas. ($33), admission included; the panoramic tour swings past the exteriors of all the sights for 2,750ptas. ($18.30). A cheaper alternative is the **Madrid Vision Bus** run by **Trapse Tours** (☎ 91/542-6666), whose panoramic sweep only takes half an hour and 600ptas. ($4) if you don't get off the bus. You also can shell out 1,200ptas. ($8) for a hop-on, hop-off day ticket.

Madrid Sights Not to Miss

Museo del Prado

Despite the fact that the Prado is often considered to be the second best art museum in Europe (after the Louvre), it is relatively unknown to the majority of travelers. More than 7,000 works are on display, so I wouldn't advise trying to see them all at once. The list of masterpieces ranges from Fra' Angelico's *Annucniation* (1430) and El Greco's eerily lit *Adoration of the Shepherds* (1614) to José de Ribera's Caravaggesque *The Martyrdom of St. Philip* (1630) and Rubens' fleshy *Three Graces* (1739). The walls overflow with many more works by Italian, Dutch, Flemish, French, and, of course, Spanish painters. Break up your visit by spending most of one day here and at least half of another. Even if you're in Spain just for a day, spend at least three hours inside.

No single picture represents the Prado more than the supreme masterpiece of Spanish painting, Velázquez's *Las Meninas* (*The Ladies-in-Waiting*)—a large, courtly oil perfectly hung in a room that seems to have been built just for it. It depicts the king (Felipe IV) and queen having their picture painted—not the portrait itself, but rather the *act* of painting it. In other words, you are the royals looking at Velázquez who's painting your portrait. The king and queen are reflected in the mirror in the background, and Velázquez's mastery of space and perspective is so perfect you get the eerie feeling that their Royal Highnesses must be standing right next to you, so real is the scene and so intense are the gazes of the figures in it. Joining the artist is the Infanta Margherita, surrounded by her handmaidens (after whom the painting is named) and a sleepy dog.

Extra! Extra!

Another of the Prado's masterworks is the triptych ***The Garden of Earthly Delights,*** painted in 1516 by **Hieronymus Bosch** (he's called El Bosco here). It's a weird landscape of tiny nude figures, some half human/half bug, engaging in the oddest of activities. It's an early surrealist vision of heaven and hell. Certainly it rivals anything dreamed up by Salvador Dalí or William Burroughs.

Goya, after designing tapestries for a few years, started painting playful, joyful scenes such as *Blind Man's Bluff*. By 1800, he was pushing the acceptable limits of nudity in art at that time by painting both a *Naked Maja* and a *Clothed Maja*, and he ended his long career in a very dark, somber state of mind with an expressionistic series called *The Black Paintings,* the most disturbing and famous of which is *Saturn Devouring One of His Sons* (1823).

Paseo del Prado. ☎ *91/420-2836.* **Metro:** *Banco de España or Atocha.* **Bus:** *10, 14, 27, 34, 37, 45.* **Admission:** *450ptas. ($3).* **Open:** *Tues–Sat 9am–7pm, Sun 9am–2pm.*

Centro de Arte Reina Sofía

Madrid's modern art museum is packed with the works of Spain's 20th-century greats such as Picasso, Miró, Dalí, and Gris, but these are all overshadowed by the most famous, moving work in the collection. *Guernica* (1937) is Picasso's eloquent and massive black-and-white commentary on the horrors of war (see sidebar). The painting is surrounded by studies Picasso made before undertaking the main work. *Guernica* demands contemplation, so give the gallery a solid hour or two in your schedule.

Calle de Santa Isabel 52 (parallel to Calle Atocha, 3 blocks from the station). ☎ *91/467-5062.* **Metro:** *Atocha.* **Bus:** *6, 14, 26, 27, 32, 45, 57, C.* **Admission:** *450ptas. ($3).* **Open:** *Mon and Wed–Sat 10am–9pm, Sun 10am–2:30pm.*

Bet You Didn't Know

Picasso's *Guernica* was inspired by a tragic event in Spanish history. Spain's bloody Civil War (1936 to 1939) left half a million dead and the fascist dictator Francisco Franco in power from 1939 to 1975. During the war, German Luftwaffe bombers working for Franco's forces tested the new technique of saturation bombing on the town of Guernica, a Basque religious center. Guernica was flattened, and 1,645 civilians were killed.

Thyssen-Bornemisza Museum

The newest addition to Madrid's art scene is directly across from the Prado. Its unique survey of European art from the 13th century up to the 1960s contains works by (deep breath now) Ghirlandaio, Caravaggio, Tintoretto, Memling, Rembrandt, El Greco, Dürer, Velázquez, Goya, Manet, Monet, Degas, Picasso, Hopper, Dalí, Mondrian, and de Kooning. It opened here in late 1992 to house a considerable collection that had outgrown its original Swiss home. Spain beat out several other interests, including England, West Germany, and even Disney World, in the bidding to acquire the collection. You could spend from one to three hours here.

Paseo del Prado 8. ☎ *91/369-0151.* **Metro:** *Banco de España.* **Bus:** *1, 2, 5, 9, 10, 14, 15, 20, 27, 34, 45, 51, 52, 53, 74, 146, 150.* **Admission:** *650ptas. ($4.35).* **Open:** *Tues–Sun 10am–7pm.*

Palacio Real (Royal Palace)

Although the reinstated royal family now lives outside town, the Royal Palace is still used for state occasions, so not all of its 2,000 rooms are open to the public tours. Construction began on this palace after Madrid's Alcazar fortress-palace burned to the ground in 1734. It's outfitted in the baroque and rococo styles preferred by the Bourbon monarchs (especially Carlos II and IV). Rich marbles, sumptuous tapestries, guilded stuccoes, frescoes, and chandeliers hang in an opulent ambiance of muted dark blues, burgundies, shiny gold, and gleaming brass. The free tours last 50 minutes plus a 10 to 20 minute wait; you can breeze through on your own in half an hour.

The Porcelain Room is aptly named; its walls are sheathed in green-and-white ceramics from the royal Buen Retiro factory. Imagine what it took to entertain in the elegant Dining Room and to kneel before the king and queen in the mirrored Throne Room. The tour will take you through the neoclassical Hall of Columns and into the historical Pharmacy. The Museo de las Carruajes (Carriage Museum) gives you some idea of what the big shots drove before Mercedes and BMWs were invented.

Plaza de Oriente, Calle de Bailén 2. ☎ *91/*
542-0059. **Metro:** *ópera or Plaza de*
España. **Admission:** *Palace 900ptas. ($6);*
Carriage Museum 200 ptas ($1.30). **Open:**
Mon–Sat 9am–6pm, Sun 9am–3pm.

Museo Lázaro Galdiano

Ranking at the top of Madrid's second tier
of important art museums, this one is the
most atmospheric in town, still set up as a
private gallery in the 19th-century mansion of its founder. Señor Lázaro Galdiano
was quite a prodigious collector, focusing
both on decorative and fine arts. Of the
former, there are crystal and enamels from
Limoges, royal daggers and swords (and
pocket watches—check out Carlos V's
cross-shaped timepiece), medieval armor,
and ancient Roman bronzes. The paintings

Extra! Extra!

When even palatial back-
ground art gets to me after
a while (a syndrome I like to
call Museum Overload), I
like to relax by wandering
the long, green slope of the
palace's Campo del Moro
gardens, with its fountains,
gravelly paths, and ponds
stocked with white and
black swans.

include works by El Greco, Velázquez, Goya, Bosch, and Ribera thrown in
with Brits such as Constable, Reynolds, and Gainsborough and the Italian
rococo master Tiepolo. It's worth a good 60 to 90 minutes of your time.

Serrano 122. ☎ *91/561-6084.* **Metro:** *Avienda de América.* **Bus:** *9, 16, 19, 51,*
89. **Admission:** *300ptas. ($2).* **Open:** *Tues–Sun 10am–2pm. Closed Aug.*

Bet You Didn't Know

Columbus may have been Italian, but it was the Spanish Queen Isabella and
her husband, Ferdinand, who bankrolled his little excursion to find a sea passage to India (the deluded navigator died convinced the Caribbean isles were
merely some offshore islands of Japan). When the Spaniards learned there was
gold, silver, and lots of free land and cheap labor (Indian slaves) to be had
over in Columbus' New World, explorers, conquistadors, and settlers went over
in droves. Claiming the land for God and for Spain—protests of the native
inhabitants notwithstanding—they quickly conquered and colonized most of
Central and South America (not to mention Florida, Texas, and what is today
the American Southwest and California).

Museo de América (Museum of the Americas)

From Spain's colonial conquests in the New World (see sidebar), treasures
untold poured into the royal coffers and private collections. Some of what
wasn't melted down to make gold bricks and bouillon is preserved here. It's
one of the world's most remarkable collections of Native American artifacts,

treasures, textiles, parchments, inscriptions, and jewelry from prehistoric times to the present. Everything's organized by cultural theme: religion, communication, social interaction, and so on. Spend an hour or two learning more about the ancient cultures of your own home continent (and to think, you came all the way to Europe for this). The collections bring themselves up to date with contemporary folk craft and art from countries that were once Spanish colonies.

Avienda de los Reyes Catolicos 6. ☎ *91/549-2641.* **Metro:** *Moncloa.* **Admission:** *400ptas. ($2.65) adults, 200ptas. ($1.30) children.* **Open:** *Tues–Sat 10am–3pm, Sun 10am–2:30pm.*

Other Fun Stuff to Do

➤ **Pick Through the Everyday Treasures of El Rastro's Flea Market.** Madrid's frenetic El Rastro flea market is one of Europe's most colorful and one of the largest. It's a mishmash of antiques, used car parts, paintings, assorted junk, secondhand clothes, and yes, even the kitchen sink. Stalls open Tuesday through Sunday from 9:30am to 1:30pm and 5 to 8pm (the best action is in the mornings, especially Sundays). Take the Metro to La Latina; the market fills the streets around Ribera de Curtidores and Plaza Cascorro. Beware of pickpockets, and be ready to bargain.

➤ **Olé! Witness the Bloody Spectacle of the Bullfight.** It's barbaric, it's ballet, it's bloody, it's breathtaking, it's brutally cruel, but above all it's beloved by the Spanish people. Viewed as something between sport and art form, the bullring draws the best and brightest young men (and a few women) from all corners of Spain who dream of becoming the Spanish equivalent of a movie star or sports hero, and their fame can be just as fleeting. One misstep, one misjudgment, one falter into the bull's charge, and they quite literally get the bull by the horns—in their gut. This risk helps explain the deadly seriousness the *matador* takes into the bullring. The bullfight is a dance with death that's meticulously choreographed and yet entirely unpredictable. If it sickens you, by all means stay away, but an afternoon at the bullring offers a slice of life and death that is truly and uniquely Spanish.

Bullfights in Spanish are *corridas,* and the main season lasts from early spring to mid-October. **Plaza Monumental de Toros de las Ventas** (☎ **91/356-2200;** Metro: Ventas) is Madrid's (not to mention Spain's) primary bullring, where *corridas* are performed on Sundays and holidays. Seats range widely from 400 to 15,000ptas. ($2.65 to $100), with the cheapest seats being up high and in the sun (which for many people is as close to the gore as they want to get anyway). Fights start a few hours before sundown, which means at 7pm in summer and around 5pm in fall and spring.

➤ *Tapeo:* **Sample Wines and Snacks in a Tapas Crawl Across Town.** From 5 to 8pm, you can strut your stuff during the evening *paseo,* fortifying yourself until your 10pm dinner reservations by dropping by a succession of tapas bars and filling up on specialties such as *chorizo* (sausage), *jamón serrano* (salty ham), *tortilla española* (onion and potato omelet wedges), *albondigas* (tender meatballs), *calamares fritos* (fried squid), *gambas al la plancha* (grilled shrimp), and *queso manchego* (sheep's cheese). Sitting at the bar is cheaper than sitting at a table. At the 1827 **Casa Alberto** (☎ **91/429-9356**), Huertas 18, you can snack surrounded by bullfighting mementos in the house where the Spanish author Cervantes once lived. **Antonio Sanchez** (☎ **91/ 539-7826**), Mesón de Parades 13, is another *tascas* (tapas bar) rife with bullring memories. **Cervecerîa Alemania** (☎ **91/429-7033**), Plaza de Santa Ana 6, is a former Hemingway haunt on a lively little square.

➤ **Thrill to the Rhythm of Flamenco.** It's the music of rhythm, of suffering, of eroticism, of secret joy. Flamenco was born out of the murky histories of Spain's unwanted classes of Jews and Moors in the Middle Ages, interpreted through the gypsy culture of Andalusia. The best flamenco erupts spontaneously in bars in the wee hours of the morning, when guitars strum, hands clap furiously, castanets clatter, voices call out, and men and women begin moving to the rhythm with statuesque fluidity and a haughty, earthy grace. But even the set shows at flamenco clubs can be a spectacle; the best ones are no less authentic merely because they're put on for the out-of-towners. Shows run from 10:30 or 11pm until 2 or 3am, but many clubs open around 9pm to serve dinner beforehand (I'd opt for a regular restaurant instead and just show up for the performance). Two of the more consistently reliable are **Café de Cinitas** (☎ **91/559-5135**) at Torija 7, which costs about $30 for just the show and a drink, and the tad more authentic **Casa Patas** (☎ **91/369-0496**) at Calle Cañizares 10, which runs 1,800 to 2,400 ptas. ($12 to $16) per show.

➤ **Dance the Night Away—Literally.** Madrid is a town that parties until sunrise. After your evening tapeo, you hit a club to dance from about 6 to 9pm. Then you have dinner and head back out to the clubs around 11pm or midnight. Somewhere between 1 and 2am, they really start hopping, and people don't start clearing out until the dawn's early light. At most, you'll have to pay an admission of around $10, which includes the first drink. The hottest nightclubs and discos come and go with ephemeral ease, but some of the current biggies include **Aqualung,** on Paseo de la Ermita del Santo, with live music and an indoor waterpark; the massive, sprawling, anything-goes, cross-cultural (and occasionally cross-sexual) **Kapital,** Calle Atocha 125; and perennial favorites the Art Deco **Archy,** Calle Marqués de Riscal, and stylish **Joy Eslava,** Arenal 1.

Get Outta Town: Day Trips & Excursions

It seems strange to say, but one of the best things you can do when you're visiting Madrid is to leave town and check out the surrounding sights. Among them are Toledo, the one-time capital of Spain and home of the painter El Greco; El Escorial, an imposing, austere 16th-century palace/ monastery; and Segovia, with its fairy-tale castle and incredible cathedral.

Time-Savers

For **guided bus tours** to the excursions listed here, contact Pullmantours (☎ **91/541-1807**). This company runs both half-day (5,000ptas./$33.30) and full-day (7,650ptas./$51) jaunts to Toledo; an all-day tour that stops briefly in Toledo before hurrying on to El Escorial and the Valley of the Fallen (a memorial to Spain's Civil War dead) and costs 10,700ptas. ($71.30); and an all-day tour to Segovia for 6,200 ptas ($41.30; it costs more with lunch).

Holy Toledo!

Toledo as a whole is designated as a national landmark, and it's by far the most rewarding day trip from Madrid. It was the capital of Castile until the 1500s, home to the painter El Greco, and has always been the religious seat of Spain—both the Primate of Spain and one-time host to a thriving Jewish community. Visit it for its Gothic cathedral, renaissance paintings, and the views of the city made famous by many a painter. There are **trains** every other hour that make the journey from Madrid's Atocha station to Toledo in 72 to 82 minutes. In Toledo, bus no. 5 takes you from the station outside town to Plaza de Zocodover in the heart of the old city (where there's a visitors' information kiosk).

Time-Savers

If you hustle, you can tour Toledo in just a few hours, making it a long half-day excursion from Madrid, or spend the whole day and get back to Madrid late. Spending the night is preferable—it allows you to explore Toledo at leisure after the day-tripping crowd has cleared out. Don't visit on a Monday, when half the sights are closed. The **tourist office** (☎ **925/220-843**) is at Puerta de Bisagra, on the north end of town (turn right out of the station, go over the bridge, and walk along the city walls).

At Toledo's center is the Gothic **Cathedral** (☎ **925/222-241**) on Arcos de Palacio, built from 1226 to 1493. Inside are paintings by El Greco and Goya, a humongous carved and painted wooden reredos (screen) on the high altar,

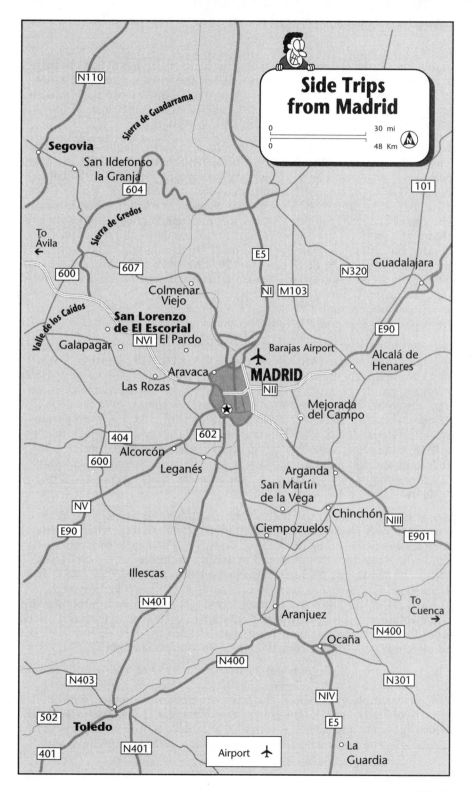

Side Trips from Madrid

N110

Sierra de Guadarrama

Segovia

San Ildefonso
la Granja
604

Sierra de Gredos

To
Ávila

600   607

E5

N320   Guadalajara

101

Colmenar
Viejo

NI   M103

San Lorenzo
de El Escorial

Valle de los Caídos

Galapagar   NVI   El Pardo

E90

Aravaca

Las Rozas

Barajas Airport

Alcalá de
Henares

MADRID

NII

404   602

Alcorcón

600

Leganés

Mejorada
del Campo

NV

E90

Arganda
San Martín
de la Vega

Ciempozuelos

Chinchón   NIII

E901

Illescas

N401

To
Cuenca

Aranjuez

N400

Ocaña

N400

N301

N403

NIV

502

401   N401

Toledo

Airport   ✈

E5

La
Guardia

and behind it the alabaster and marble baroque Transparente altar, lit by a skylight. Admission to the church is free, but the treasury, with its 10-foot-high, 500-pound gilded 16th-century monstrance (made with gold brought back by Columbus), costs 500ptas. ($3.30). The cathedral is open daily 10:30am to 1pm and 3:30 to 7pm (to 6pm in winter).

For El Greco fans, the more important church in town is **Iglesia de Santo Tomé** (☎ 925/210-209), Plaza del Conde 2, Via Santo Tomé, where a tiny chapel is overpowered by the Greek painter's masterpiece, the turbulent *Burial of Count Orgaz* (1586). Admission is 150ptas. ($1), and it's open daily 10am to 1:45pm and 3:30 to 6:45pm (to 5:45pm in winter). If you can't get enough of El Greco, you can visit his Toledo home. (Actually, his house and studio was probably the one next door to this residence in the old Jewish quarter, but this is the place set up as an El Greco museum.) The works in the **Casa y Museo de El Greco** (☎ 925/224-046), Calle Samuel Leví, admittedly aren't his greatest, consisting mainly of small portrait-style paintings of Christ and the apostles, along with one of his famous *View of Toledo* paintings. Admission is 400ptas. ($2.65), and it's open Tuesday to Saturday from 10am to 2pm and 4 to 6pm and Sunday 10am to 2pm.

Some visitors feel that the Renaissance entranceway and stairs of the 16th-century hospice-turned-**Museo de Santa Cruz** (☎ 925/22-1036), Miguel de Cervantes 3, are more impressive than the works inside—great arstists, but mediocre paintings. Amid 15th-century Flemish and Spanish tapestries, jewelry, Visigothic artifacts, and swords and armor fashioned of the famed Toledo damascene steel (blackened and traced with gold wire), you'll find works by Goya, Ribera, and the omnipresent El Greco, who's represented by a 1613 *Assumption,* one of his last paintings. Admission is 200ptas. ($1.30) for adults and free for children. The museum is open Tuesday to Saturday 10am to 6:30pm, Sunday 10am to 2pm, Monday 10am to 2pm and 4 to 6:30pm.

A synagogue named for the Virgin Mary? Such is what happens when a thriving Jewish community is crushed by the Catholic Inquisition and its temples are overtaken by the local diocese. Now restored to its Hebrew origins, which was heavily influenced by Islamic architectural principles and styles, the **Sínagoga de Santa María La Blanca** (☎ 925/227-257) at Calle Reyes Católicos 2 is the oldest remaining of Toledo's eight synagogues. It was built in the 1100s and features Moorish horseshoe arches topping the squat columns of the spare interior. Admission is 150ptas. ($1), and it's open April through September daily from 10am to 2pm and 3:30 to 7pm; October to March, it's open daily from 10am to 2pm and 3:30 to 6pm.

The 14th-century **Sínagoga del Tránsito** (☎ 925/223-665), Calle Samuel Leví, also melds Gothic, Islamic, and traditional Hebrew motifs to create an evocative, simple space, sporting a frieze inscribed with Hebrew script and set with a coffered ceiling. Connected to the synagogue is the **Museo Sefardí,** which preserves ancient Hebrew tombs, manuscripts, and sacred objects of Toledo's Sephardic (Spanish Jewish) community. Admission (temple and museum together) is 400ptas. ($2.65), and it's open Tuesday to Saturday 10am to 1:45pm and 4 to 5:45pm, Sunday 10am to 1:45pm.

Towering over the town, the rebuilt **Alcázar** (☎ 925/223-038), Calle General Moscardó 4, is not too much to look at in its 20th-century form, but this fortress has withstood many a siege. Its most famous defense was in 1936, when it held out for 70 days of bombardment during the Civil War. A museum inside recalls with photographs, models, and a walking tour those days of fierce pride and horror. Admission is 125ptas. (80¢) for adults and free for those under 10. It's open Tuesday to Saturday 10am to 1:30pm and 4 to 6:30pm (to 5:30pm in winter).

The **Hostal del Cardenal** (☎ 925/220-862), Paseo de Recaredo 24, serves great Spanish cuisine such as roast suckling pig at reasonable rates, and it also rents 10,800ptas. ($72) doubles. Otherwise, stay at **Hotel Maria Cristina** (☎ 925/213-202, fax: 925/212-650), Marqués de Mendigorría 1, with modern 10,800ptas. ($72) doubles in a historic setting.

A Monastery Fit for a King: El Escorial

When zealous Felipe II decided to build a new royal residence, rather than erect a palace like most of his European peers, he built himself a live-in monastery—but what a monastery. It's a frescoed and tapestried complex of royal apartments, a huge basilica, great art gallery, lavish library, and Spain's pantheon of royal tombs, all encased by fortress-thick walls.

Buses to El Escorial leave from Madrid's Moncha Metro station (there's a kiosk where you can buy tickets) and drop you off right in front of the monastery after an hour's ride. Some 25 **trains** daily depart Madrid's Atocha station for the hour-long ride. Buses meet incoming trains to shuttle you the remaining mile to Plaza Virgen de Gracia, a block east of the monastery.

The late 16th-century monastery/fortress of **San Lorenzo de El Escorial** (☎ 91/890-5902) was built for the devout Felipe II, and his apartments are appropriately as austere and monastic as you'd ever imagine a king could get. This guy was so fanatically Christian that he had his bedroom built overlooking the high altar of the impressive basilica, with its four organs, Cellini Crucifix, and dome (which was based on Michelangelo's plans for St. Peter's in Rome). Under the basilica's altar is the **Royal Pantheon,** a mausoleum housing the bones of every king from Charles I to Alfonso XII. More lavish

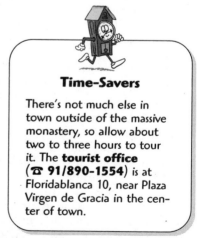

Time-Savers

There's not much else in town outside of the massive monastery, so allow about two to three hours to tour it. The **tourist office** (☎ 91/890-1554) is at Floridablanca 10, near Plaza Virgen de Gracia in the center of town.

and in keeping with the tastes of most monarchs are the tapestried apartments of the Bourbon kings, Carlos III and IV. The **New Museum** is popular for paintings such as Titian's *Last Supper,* Velázquez's *The Tunic of Joseph,* El Greco's *Martyrdom of St. Maurice,* and works by Dürer, van Dyck, Tintoretto, and Rubens. The Royal Library houses more than 40,000 precious antique volumes under a barrel-vaulted ceiling frescoed by Tibaldi in the 16th century. From April to September, El Escorial is open Tuesday through Sunday from 10am to 6pm; from October to March it's open Tuesday through Sunday from 10am to 5pm. Admission is 850ptas. ($5.65) adults, 350ptas. ($2.35) children.

El Escorial is an easy half-day trip, but you'll be ready for lunch before you leave to return to Madrid, so try the sublime Castillian grub at the cavelike **Mesón la Cueva** (☎ 91/890-1516), San Antón 4.

Segovia: Spain's Time Capsule

Segovia is like a survey of Spain's history—still standing are a Roman aqueduct, a Moorish Alcazar, and a Gothic cathedral. Its medieval streets, Romanesque churches, and 15th-century palaces make it an enjoyable place to stroll and soak up Castillian small city life. **Trains** leave Madrid every other hour for the two-hour trip to Segovia (they depart Madrid from Atocha station, but also pause at Charmartín station en route). From Segovia's train station, bus no. 3 runs to Plaza Mayor in the center of town.

Time-Savers

You can easily do Segovia in three to four hours, but it also makes a nice place to hang around for an over-night escape from the big city. The **tourist office** (☎ 921/460-334) is at Plaza Mayor 10.

Running a majestic 895 yards along the Plaza del Azoguejo out the east end of town is the **Roman aqueduct,** built in the 1st century A.D. using cut stone blocks with no mortar. The stretch, much of it two tiers high, is made up of 118 arches and is 96 feet at its highest. It constituted a major water supply for the city all the way until the 19th century.

Smack in the center of town is the last great Gothic **cathedral** (☎ 921/435-325) built in Spain (1515 to 1558), and it's all pinnacles and buttresses. Isabella I (of Ferdinand and Isabella fame) was proclaimed queen on this spot in 1474. The cathedral has some lovely stained-glass windows, which light the carved choir stalls, the 16th- and 17th-century paintings, and the grille-fronted chapels inside. The attached cloisters date from an earlier church on this spot. Admission to the church is free, but entry to the cloisters, chapel room, and tiny museum (paintings by Ribera, 16th- and 17th-century Flemish tapestries, jewelry, and manuscripts) costs 250ptas. ($1.65) for adults and 50ptas. (50¢) for kids. It's open in spring and summer daily 9am to 7pm, fall and winter daily 9:30am to 1pm and 3 to 6pm.

Segovia's commanding **Alcázar** (☎ 921/430-176), anchoring the west end of town, was raised between the 12th and 15th centuries, but had to be

514

largely rebuilt after a disastrous 1862 fire that destroyed many of its Moorish embellishments. The formidable exterior hides some sumptuous rooms inside, from the Gothic King's Room to the stuccoes in the Throne Room. Clamber up the Torre de Juan II, built as a dungeon, for panoramic views. Admission is 375ptas. ($2.50) for adults and 175ptas. ($1.15) for kids 8 to14; it's open daily from 10am to 7pm (to 6pm from October to March).

The tavern-like **El Bernardino** (☎ **921/433-225**), Cervantes 2, serves up a huge paella and other hearty Castillian specialties. You can get a double room for 8,000ptas. ($53.30) in the modern **Gran Hotel la Sirenas** (☎ **921/434-011,** fax: 921/430-633), Juan Bravo 30, on one of Segovia's prettiest plazas.

Chapter 26

Barcelona &
Environs

> **In This Chapter**
>
> ➤ Budget hotels in historic villas
> ➤ The best Barcelona eats, from tapas bars to market restaurants
> ➤ Exploring the Gothic Quarter and Gaudí's Modernisme buildings
> ➤ Barcelona nightlife, from flamenco to disco
> ➤ Day tripping to a mile-high monastery and a Roman amphitheater by the sea

Barcelona is the capital of the proudly independent region of Catalonia, a Mediterranean city that used the 1992 Olympics to come roaring out of a Franco-induced stupor. In the process, it has transformed itself into a vibrant new capital of European commerce and tourism.

It's also a city of the arts. Home to Gaudí's whimsical *Modernisme* style of Art Nouveau architecture, Catalonia also gave birth to painters Salvador Dalí and Joan Miró. Picasso trained in Barcelona, and the city's Picasso Museum is the best outside Paris, offering unique insight into the earliest works of one of the 20th century's greatest artists.

Dollars & Sense

The Spanish unit of currency is the peseta (pta.). Roughly, $1 equals 150ptas.; or 10ptas. equals 6.6¢. Spanish coins include 1, 5, 25, 50, 100, 200, and 500 pesetas. Bills come in denominations of 500, 1,000, 5,000, and 10,000 pesetas.

So take a stroll down the shady Les Rambles promenade, explore the Gothic Quarter around the cathedral, haggle over fruit at the Boquería market, and ride the funicular up to the park on Montjuïc hill, with its museums and re-created Spanish village. Or perhaps you simply want to relax with a drink in a tapas bar. Barcelona is a great town for just hanging out—the perfect place to schedule extra time to relax without all the usual sightseeing pressures. If you're just passing through, I'd give it at least two full days.

Getting Your Bearings

Barcelona is another of those burgs with a split personality. The **Ciutat Vella** (Old City) is a hexagon of narrow streets nudged up against the harbor. The massive street grid that makes up the new city surrounds the old one.

Time-Savers

The main **tourist information offices** are at Gran Vía de las Corts Catalanes 658 (☎ 93/301-7443) northeast of Plaça de Catalunya; Plaça Països Catalanes; Estació Sants; and the airport. Strategically placed throughout the tourist areas are map-dispensing **information booths** and (in summer) 100 multilingual **youths in red-and-white jackets,** all offering help and travel tips. You can pick up the local events calendar *Guía del Ocio* at newsstands.

Barcelona Neighborhoods in Brief

The famed **Les Rambles** (Las Ramblas in Castilian; see "Bet You Didn't Know") bisects the Ciutat Vella, running from the harbor north to **Plaça Catalunya.** Les Rambles is a wide, tree-shaded boulevard taken over by street entertainers, flower stalls, cafes, and the bustle of the city. (It runs northwest, but all city maps are oriented with this street pointing straight up and down.) The street degenerated a bit during the fascist Franco era earlier in this century, as did much of old Barcelona, but has slowly regained its footing and respectability as new businesses revive the Ciutat Vella.

To the east of Les Rambles lies the **Barri Gòtic,** the medieval heart of town around the cathedral. This area was the site of the original Roman city, and it's the most fun area for wandering. Its narrow lanes and old buildings are filled with shops, museums, and restaurants. The Barri Gòtic's eastern edge is **Via Laietana,** and from this wide street over to the Passeig de Picasso stretches the **Barri del la Ribera.** Formerly fallen on bad times as well, the Barri del la Ribera is now an up-and-coming district of art galleries, bars and clubs, and grand old mansions. South of these two districts is the scenic, lake-spotted **Parc de la Ciutadella.** Just south of that, on a triangular

517

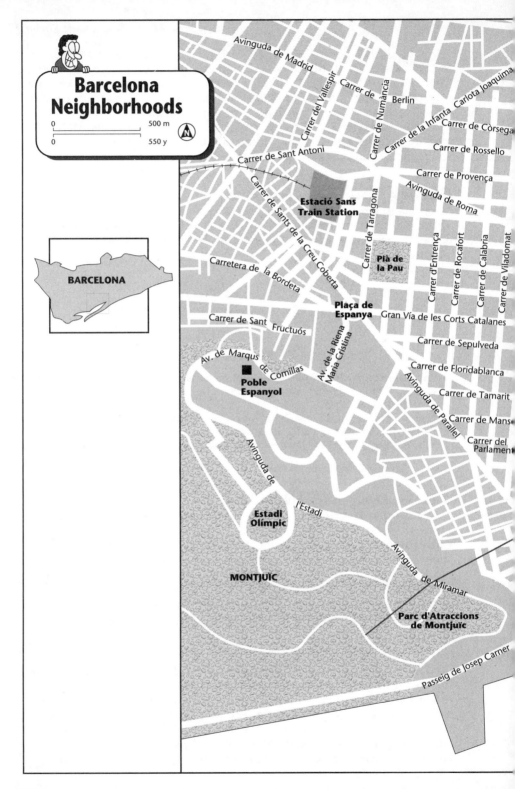

Barcelona Neighborhoods

0 _____ 500 m
0 _____ 550 y

BARCELONA

Avinguda de Madrid
Carrer del Vallespir
Carrer de
Carrer de Numància
Berlin
Carrer de la Infanta Carlota Joaquima
Carrer de Còrsega
Carrer de Rossello
Carrer de Sant Antoni
Carrer de Provença
Carrer de Sants de la Creu Coberta
Avinguda de Roma
Estació Sans Train Station
Carrer de Tarragona
Plà de la Pau
Carrer d'Entrença
Carrer de Rocafort
Carrer de Calabria
Carrer de Viladomat
Carretera de la Bordeta
Carrer de Sant Fructuós
Plaça de Espanya
Gran Vía de les Corts Catalanes
Av. de Marqus de Comillas
Av. de la Riena Maria Cristina
Carrer de Sepulveda
Carrer de Floridablanca
Poble Espanyol
Carrer de Tamarit
Avinguda de Parallel
Carrer de Mans
Carrer del Parlamen
Avinguda de l'Estadi
Estadi Olímpic
Avinguda de Miramar
MONTJUÏC
Parc d'Atraccions de Montjuïc
Passeig de Josep Carner

518

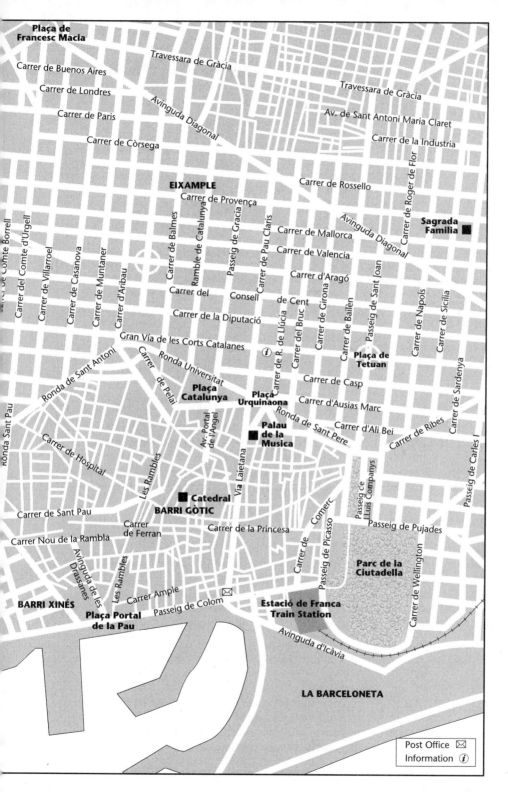

Plaça de
Francesc Macia

Carrer de Buenos Aires

Travessara de Gràcia

Carrer de Londres

Travessara de Gràcia

Avinguda Diagonal

Carrer de Paris

Av. de Sant Antoni Maria Claret

Carrer de Còrsega

Carrer de la Industria

Carrer de Rossello

EIXAMPLE

Carrer de Provença

Carrer de Roger de Flor

Avinguda Diagonal

Sagrada
Familia

Carrer de Balmes

Ramble de Catalunya

Passeig de Gracia

Carrer de Pau Claris

Carrer de Mallorca

Carrer de Valencia

Carrer d'Aragó

Carrer de Napols

Carrer de Sicilia

Carrer del Comte d'Urgell

Carrer del Comte d'Urgell

Carrer de Villarroel

Carrer de Casanova

Carrer de Muntaner

Carrer d'Aribau

Carrer del

Consell

de Cent

Carrer de R. de Llúcia

Carrer del Bruc

Carrer de Girona

Carrer de Bailén

Passeig de Sant Joan

Carrer de la Diputació

Gran Vía de les Corts Catalanes

Ronda Universitat

Plaça de
Tetuan

Carrer de Sardenya

Ronda de Sant Antoni

Carrer de Pelai

Plaça
Catalunya

Plaça
Urquinaona

Carrer de Casp

Carrer d'Ausias Marc

Ronda de Sant Pere

Carrer d'Ali Bei

Carrer de Ribes

Passeig de Carles I

Ronda de Sant Pau

Ronda de Sant Pau

Carrer de Hospital

Av. Portal
de l'Angel

Palau
de la
Musica

Via Laietana

Passeig de Lluis Companys

Carrer de Sant Pau

Catedral

BARRI GÒTIC

Carrer
de Ferran

Carrer de la Princesa

Passeig de Pujades

Carrer Nou de la Rambla

Carrer de Comerc

Passeig de Picasso

Carrer de

Parc de la
Ciutadella

Carrer de Wellington

Avinguda de les Drassanes

Les Rambles

Carrer Ample

BARRI XINÉS

Plaça Portal
de la Pau

Passeig de Colom

Estació de Franca
Train Station

Avinguda d'Icàvia

LA BARCELONETA

| Post Office | ✉ |
| Information | ⓘ |

519

peninsula jutting into the harbor, the former fishing village of **Barceloneta** teems with activity, seafood restaurants, and tapas bars.

Bet You Didn't Know

You may notice that Spanish is spoken a little differently in Barcelona. That's because it isn't Spanish—it's **Catalán.** As an autonomous region of Spain, Catalonia is slowly reasserting the native traditions that were squashed during Spain's Franco years, including reverting to their native language, a romance tongue related closely to that of France's Provençe. Evidence of Catalán's comeback coup came during the 1992 Olympics, when all the signs and official news reports were printed in Catalán first and Castilian Spanish second.

To the west of Les Rambles, down near the harbor front, is the **Barri Xinés,** a historically seedy neighborhood of prostitutes, beggars, and thieves. It's improved marginally and makes an intriguing walk by day, but I wouldn't venture there after dark. Well beyond this, to the city's west, rises the hill of **Montjuïc,** site of the World's Fair and Olympic parks.

The **Plaça de Catalunya** at Les Rambles' north end is the center of Barcelona, dividing the old city from the new. The grid of streets spreading north from this plaza is known as the **Eixample,** and its grandest avenue is the uninventively named **Avinguda Diagonal,** which cuts diagonally across the grid. Beyond this, the thoroughly Catalán neighborhood of **Gràcia** expands to the north, where Castilian truly is a foreign language and plenty of colorful local nightspots liven things up.

Getting Into & Around Town

Most trains to Barcelona arrive either at the **Estació Sants** on the western edge of the Eixample or the **Estació de Franca,** near the harbor at the base of the Ciutadella park. Both stations are hooked into the Metro network. Trains from Barcelona's **airport** run very regularly to Estació Sants, or you can take a frequent Aerobús to Plaça de Catalunya.

Barcelona's **Metro** system covers the city pretty well. Line 3 runs down Les Rambles (and to the Sants-Estació train station), and line 4 follows Via Laietana, bordering the eastern edge of the Ciutat Vella. Plaça de Catalunya is one of the main Metro junctions, with nearby Passeig de Gràcia as another main transfer station. You can hoof it from most Metro stations to wherever you're headed, but occasionally you may find it expedient to take a **bus.** **Funiculars** run up some of the hills around the city, such as Montjuïc; other slopes are fitted with **outdoor escalators** to ease your way.

Dollars & Sense

Tickets for the bus and Metro cost 135ptas. (90¢). On Sundays, the buses charge 150ptas. ($1). The 700ptas. ($4.65) **T1 pass** gets you 10 rides on *any* city transport, including bus, Metro, and funicular and is a better buy than the 680ptas. ($4.50) T2 pass, which doesn't include the bus. If you plan to ride the bus and/or Metro more than four times in a day, the 500ptas. ($3.30) *abono temporales* (one-day pass) is worthwhile.

Barcelona Fast Facts

American Express   Barcelona's American Express office is at Passeig de Gràcia 101 (☎ **93/217-0070**). It's open Monday to Friday 9:30am to 6pm and Saturday 10am to noon.

Consulate   The U.S. Consulate is at Passeig Reina Elisenda 23 (☎ **93/280-2227**).

Doctors/hospitals   Dial ☎ **061** to find a doctor. The U.S. Consulate will provide a list of English-speaking physicians, as will many hotel concierges. If you need a hospital, try the *urgencias* at **Hospital Clínic i Provincial,** Casanova 143 (☎ **93/454-6000**); **Hospital Creu Roja de Barcelona,** Dos de Maig 301 (☎ **93/433-1551**); or **Hospital Sant,** Sant Antoni Maria Claret 167 (☎ **93/347-3133**).

Emergency   Dial ☎ **092** for the **police.** For a medical emergency, call ☎ **061.** To report a fire, call ☎ **080.**

Pharmacies   *Farmàcias* rotate the duty of staying open late. The *farmàcias de guardia* (night pharmacies) are listed in daily newspapers and on the doors of all drug stores.

Safety   Petty thieves and pickpockets target tourists, so be particularly alert in the old city, in shopping areas, and around popular sights. Be aware of thieves who work in groups: One jostles you while another helps you recover—and helps himself to your wallet. Also, the Barri Xinés, while interestingly seedy by day, is not an area to loiter in after dark. For help reporting a theft and obtaining new documents, call **Tourist Attention** (☎ **93/301-9060**) 24 hours a day. This organization is staffed by the municipal police and has English-speaking attendants.

Taxis   Thanks to the 1992 Olympics, Barcelona's public transportation system has been fully updated, so you probably won't need a taxi except perhaps for travel to and from the airport (though trains and buses run out there frequently). In addition to the numerous taxi stands located throughout the city, cabs cruise the streets looking for fares. Available cars advertise

521

with signs reading "Libre" or "Lliure" or with an illuminated green sign. If you'd like to call a taxi, try ☎ **93/357-7755,** 93/358-1111, or 93/300-3811. The initial charge is 285ptas. ($1.90) and 95ptas. (60¢) for each additional kilometer. After 10pm and on weekends and holidays, the per-kilometer charge is slightly higher. You will be charged an extra 400ptas. ($2.65) for rides to and from the airport plus 300ptas. ($2) per suitcase.

Telephone Pay phones accept coins and phone cards (sold in *estancos* or at the post office) worth 1,000 or 2,000ptas. ($6.65 or $13.35). To make a local call, place at least 25 pesetas' worth of coins in the rack at the top of the phone; the coins will roll in as needed to pay for the call.

Spain's country code is **34**; Barcelona's city code is **93**. Drop the 9 if you're calling from outside Spain, but within the country dial 93. To call Barcelona from the United States, dial **011-34-3** and the number. To charge your calls to a calling card, call **AT&T** (☎ **900/990-011**), **MCI** (☎ **900/990-014**), or **Sprint** (☎ **900/990-013**). To call the United States direct from Barcelona, dial **07,** wait for the dial tone, then dial **1,** the area code, and the phone number.

Transit Info ☎ **93/412-0000.**

Barcelona Bedrooms: The Hotel Scene

Barcelona's hotels are relatively inexpensive for a big European city. (Guide-books that disagree with this statement are just expressing sour grapes because the city was dirt cheap until the 1992 Olympics, and now it's merely on the low end of moderate.) The only real concern in Barcelona is safety, for although it's not a seriously dangerous town, pickpockets and other thieves do work the night a bit more brazenly here than in comparable European cities.

Although rapidly improving, much of the Ciutat Vella still has a slightly unsavory tinge it picked up earlier in this century. In looking for a room, def-initely steer clear of the Barri Xinés and anywhere near it. Most of the Barri Gòtic is pretty safe now, so long as you're careful about pickpockets, and the part of the Ciutat Vella to the west of Les Rambles up near the Plaça de Catalunya is just fine (and, indeed, is full of hotels). I find the grid of the Eixample a bit boring, but it's certainly a safe neighborhood in which to base yourself, and often you'll find rooms are cheaper there than in the old city.

Hotel Astoria

$$. Sur Diagonal.

Behind an art deco facade lies a budget hotel of good service and very well-kept rooms. The high ceilings and geometric designs in the common areas evoke a Moorish feel. Older accommodations are done in exposed cedar; more recently renovated ones sport louvered closets and whitewashed walls.

Carrer de París 203 (4 long blocks down the Diagonal from Plaça de Francesc Macià, 2 blocks up the Diagonal from the Diagonal Metro stop). ☎ *93/209-8311.*

Fax: 93/202-3008. *Metro:* Diagonal. *Rates:* 8,000–16,200ptas. ($53.35–$108) double. AE, DC, MC, V.

Hotel Condes de Barcelona
$$$$. Eixample.
This late-19th century villa is one of Barcelona's finest Old World hotels and is set within one of Barcelona's architectural wonderlands—the *Modernisme* buildings of the Passeig de Gràcia. The facade is neo-medieval, and the interior is a mix of high-tech and traditional opulence. Rooms come with all the standard amenities, plus marble baths and reproduction Spanish paintings. The art deco piano bar off the lobby is a lovely place to wind down with a drink.

Passeig de Gràcia 73-75 (between Carrer de Mallorca and Carrer de Provença). ☎ *93/488-2200. Fax:* 93/488-0614. *Metro:* Passeig de Gràcia. *Rates:* 19,000ptas. ($126.65) double. AE, DC, MC, V.

Hotel Regencia Colón
$$$. Barri Gòtic.
On the edge of the Barri Gòtic and just a few steps from the cathedral, the Regencia Colón is one of Barcelona's great central values. The rooms are bland but comfortably worn, and most are plenty large. The only drawback is that the hotel is sometimes crowded with tour groups.

Carrer Sagristans 13-17 (just north of the cathedral). ☎ *93/318-9858. Fax:* 93/317-2822. *Metro:* Jaume 1 or Urquinaona. *Rates:* 15,500ptas. ($103.35) double. AE, DC, MC, V.

Le Meridien Barcelona
$$$$$. On Les Rambles.
This Modernisme structure is Barcelona's top hotel, a thoroughly contemporary affair spilling over with amenities, such as heated bathroom floors and in-room VCRs. The location is superb, but even the double glazing can't keep out all the noise of Les Rambles below. You don't often get such posh comfort so (relatively) cheap.

Rambles 111. ☎ *800/543-4300 in the United States, 93/318-6200 in Spain. Fax:* 93/301-7776. *Metro:* Liceu or Plaça de Catalunya. *Rates:* 29,000–38,000ptas. ($193.35–$253.35) double. AE, DC, MC, V.

Mesón Castilla
$. Ciutat Vella.
A clean budget hotel of simple amenities and a huge breakfast buffet, the Mesón Castilla has a perfect location, near Les Rambles and on the border between the new and old cities. Rooms are reliably comfortable, with interesting, ornate headboards; request one of the rooms with a large terrace.

Valldoncella 5 (a few blocks west of Plaça de Catalunya). ☎ *93/318-2182. Fax:* 93/412-4020. *Metro:* Plaça de Catalunya or Plaça Universitat. *Rates:* 9,500ptas. ($63.35) double. AE, DC, MC, V.

523

BARCELONA

Hotels
Hotel Astoria **4**
Hotel Condes
  de Barcelona **7**
Hotel Regencia
  Colón **17**
Le Meridien
  Barcelona **14**
Mesón Castilla **12**
Montecarlo **13**

Restaurants
Beltxenea **8**
Els Quatre Gats **15**
Garduña **18**
Los Caracoles **23**
Pitarra **22**
Pollo Rico **19**

Attractions
Casa Amatller **10**
Casa Batlló **9**
Casa Lleó Morera **11**
Casa Milà **5**
Catedral **20**
Fundació Joan Miró **3**
Museu Nacional
  d'Art de Catalunya **2**
Museu Picasso **24**
Palau de la Musica **16**
Palau Güell **21**
Parc de la
  Ciutadella **25**
Poble Espanyol **1**
Sagrada Familia **6**

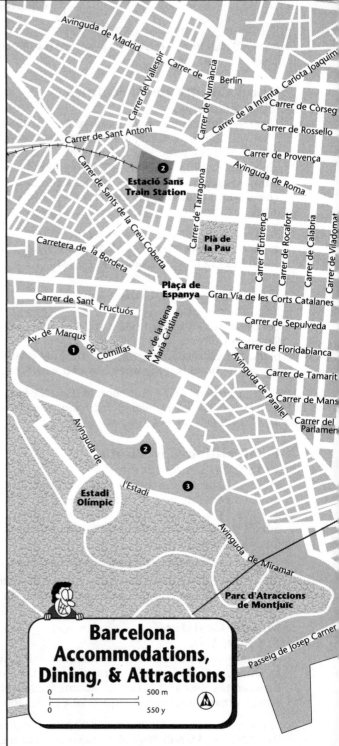

Avinguda de Madrid

Carrer del Vallespir

Carrer de Numància

Carrer de Berlin

Carrer de la Infanta Carlota Joaquim

Carrer de Còrseg

Carrer de Rossello

Carrer de Sant Antoni

Carrer de Provença

Avinguda de Roma

Estació Sans Train Station **2**

Carrer de Sants de la Creu Coberta

Carrer de Tarragona

Carrer d'Entrença

Carrer de Rocafort

Carrer de Calabria

Carrer de Viladomat

Carretera de la Bordeta

Plà de la Pau

Carrer de Sant Fructuós

Plaça de Espanya

Gran Vía de les Corts Catalanes

Carrer de Sepulveda

Av. de Marqus de Comillas

Av. de la Riena Maria Cristina

Carrer de Floridablanca

Carrer de Tamarit

Avinguda de Parallel

Carrer de Mans

Carrer de Parlamen

1

Avinguda de l'Estadi

2

3

Estadi Olímpic

Avinguda de Miramar

Parc d'Atraccions de Montjuïc

Barcelona Accommodations, Dining, & Attractions

0   500 m
0   550 y

N

Passeig de Josep Carner

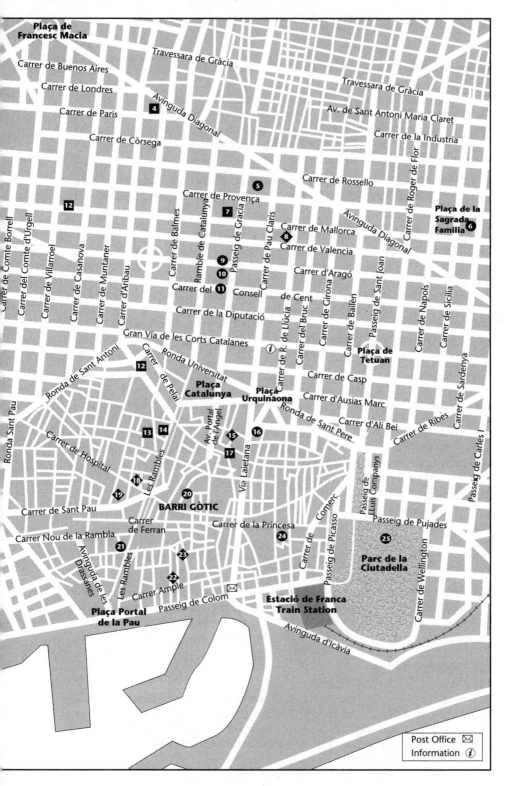

Plaça de Francesc Macia

Carrer de Buenos Aires

Travessara de Gràcia

Carrer de Londres

Travessara de Gràcia

Avinguda Diagonal

Carrer de Paris

4

Av. de Sant Antoni Maria Claret

Carrer de la Industria

Carrer de Còrsega

Carrer de Rossello

Carrer de Roger de Flor

Carrer de Provença

5

Plaça de la Sagrada Familia

12

Carrer de Balmes

Ramble de Catalunya

7

Passeig de Gracia

Avinguda Diagonal

6

Carrer de Mallorca

Carrer de Comte Borrell

Carrer del Comte d'Urgell

Carrer de Villarroel

Carrer de Casanova

Carrer de Muntaner

Carrer d'Aribau

8

Carrer de Pau Claris

Carrer de Valencia

9

10

Carrer d'Aragó

Passeig de Sant Joan

Carrer de Napols

Carrer de Sicilia

Carrer del

11

Consell

de Cent

Carrer de Girona

Carrer de Bailen

Carrer de R. de Llúcia

Carrer del Bruc

Carrer de la Diputació

Gran Vía de les Corts Catalanes

Ronda Universitat

i

Plaça de Tetuan

Carrer de Sardenya

Passeig de Carles

Ronda de Sant Antoni

Carrer de Pelai

12

Plaça Catalunya

Plaça Urquinaona

Carrer de Casp

Carrer d'Ausias Marc

Ronda de Sant Pere

Carrer d'Ali Bei

Carrer de Ribes

Ronda Sant Pau

Carrer de Hospital

13 **14**

Av. Portal de l'Angel

15

16

17

Via Laietana

Les Rambles

18

19

20

BARRI GÒTIC

Carrer de Sant Pau

Carrer de Ferran

Carrer de la Princesa

Passeig de Lluis Companys

Passeig de Pujades

Carrer Nou de la Rambla

21

Les Rambles

23

24

Passeig de Picasso

Carrer de Comerc

25

Parc de la Ciutadella

Carrer de Wellington

Avinguda de les Drassanes

22

Carrer Ample

Passeig de Colom

Estació de Franca Train Station

Plaça Portal de la Pau

Avinguda d'Icàvia

Post Office	⊠
Information	*i*

525

Montecarlo
$$. On Les Rambles.
This is my frugal choice for a hotel at the heart of the action. Although the rooms are functionally modern, the public areas still have the chandeliers, fireplaces, and carved doors that harken back to the private mansion it was 120 years ago. You're right on Les Rambles here, which is wonderful location-wise, but a bit noisy.

Rambla dels Estudis 124. ☎ *93/412-0404.* ***Fax:*** *93/318-7323.* ***Metro:*** *Plaça de Catalunya.* ***Rates:*** *10,000–12,000ptas. ($66.65–$80) double. AE, DC, MC, V.*

Catalán Cuisine: Barcelona's Restaurant Scene
As the capital of Catalonia, Barcelona has plenty of traditional local restaurants that make the excellent casseroles this region is famous for. As a port city, Barcelona has incredible seafood. Make sure you try some of the interesting surf-n-turf combinations, such as the traditional **llagosta i pollastre** (chicken and lobster in a tomato-hazelnut sauce). **Suquet** is made of shellfish stewed with tomatoes, potatoes, saffron, and wine. Unattractive but tasty is **butifarra negra amb mongetes,** a fat black sausage (pork bellies, blood, and spices) in a plate of white beans.

Nearby Valencia contributes to Barcelona's tables the mighty **paella,** saffrontinged rice simmered with a medley of seafood, chicken, tomatoes, peppers, beans, pork, hare, and so on. Don't leave Spain without sampling some **Basque cuisine**—although Catalonians are no slouches in the kitchen, supremacy for invention and refinement goes to the Basque (see the introduction to Madrid dining in Chapter 25). Spend at least one evening doing a **tapeo,** or tapas bar crawl (see "Other Fun Stuff to Do").

Beltxenea
$$$$$. Eixample. BASQUE.
Some of Barcelona's finest Basque chefs hold court in this converted *Modernisme* apartment building. Splurge for a special occasion here and sample succulent Basque cooking in dishes such as hake garnished with clams or grilled rabbit. In summer, you can dine in the formal garden.

Carrer Mallorca 275 (between Carrer de Roger de Llúria and Carrer de Pau Claris). ☎ *93/215-3024. Reservations recommended.* ***Metro:*** *Passeig de Gràcia.* ***Main courses:*** *2,500–5,500ptas. ($16.65–$36.65); tasting menu 6,900ptas. ($46). AE, DC, MC, V.* ***Open:*** *Lunch Mon–Fri, dinner Mon–Sat. Closed 2 weeks in Aug.*

Els Quatre Gats
$$$. Barri Gòtic. CATALÁN.
This turn-of-the-century cafe/restaurant was the legendary gathering place of Barcelona's bohemians and Modernisme intellectuals, a place where Picasso once displayed his works. The set-price menu is one of the city's best values, with dishes based on whatever is most fresh at the market that day. There's live music some evenings.

Carrer Montsió 3 (just off Av. Portal de l'Angel). ☎ ***93/302-4140.*** *Reservations required Sat–Sun.* **Metro:** *Plaça de Catalunya.* **Main courses:** *1,200–2,800ptas. ($8–$18.65); fixed-price menu 1,800ptas. ($12). AE, MC, V.* **Open:** *Lunch and dinner Mon–Sat (cafe open daily).*

Garduña
$$$. Ciutat Vella. CATALÁN.

The cooks at this popular workaday restaurant can practically reach out the window to do their shopping—it's inside Barcelona's covered produce market. At crowded tables, dig into paella, veal brochettes, or a *zarzuela* stew of spicy fishes.

Carrer Morera 17-19 (in the Boquería market off Les Rambles, between Carrer de l'Hospital and Carrer del Carme). ☎ ***93/302-4323.*** *Reservations recommended.* **Metro:** *Liceu.* **Main courses:** *1,200–2,800ptas. ($8–$18.65). AE, MC, V.* **Open:** *Lunch daily, dinner Mon–Sat.*

Los Caracoles
$$$$. Barri Gòtic. CATALÁN/SPANISH.

This colorful Barcelona institution of good, solid cooking patronized both by artist Salvador Dalí *and* John Wayne lies near the port. Try the snails (its namesake) or the spit-roasted chicken. Its fame does draw the crowds, but the quality remains uncompromised.

Carrer dels Escudellers 14 (turn east off Les Rambles at Plaça del Teatre and just follow the curving street). ☎ ***93/302-3185.*** *Reservations required.* **Metro:** *Drassanes.* **Main courses:** *1,500–3,600ptas. ($10–$24). AE, DC, MC, V.* **Open:** *Lunch and dinner daily.*

Pitarra
$$. Barri Gòtic. CATALÁN.

Named after the famous Catalán poet/playwright who once lived here, Pitarra has, since 1890, stuck to the staples—traditional dishes cooked just like Mama used to do. The Valencian paella is good, as is the grilled squid, but in winter go for a hearty game dish, such as hare with wild mushrooms.

Carrer de Avinyó 56 (off Carrer de Ferran). ☎ ***93/301-1647.*** *Reservations required.* **Metro:** *Liceu.* **Main courses:** *950–2,000ptas. ($6.35–$13.35); fixed-price lunch 1,100ptas. ($7.35). AE, DC, MC, V.* **Open:** *Lunch and dinner Mon–Sat.*

Pollo Rico
$. Ciutat Vella. SPANISH.

Most frugal travelers eventually find their way to Pollo Rico, where you can eat rich with a poor man's purse. On the ground floor, there's scrumptious spit-roasted chicken and *tortillas* (omelettes); you can carry out or sit at the scruffy tables. The comfortable upstairs dining room offers simple fixed-price menus.

527

Carrer Sant Pau 31 (2 blocks west of Les Rambles). ☎ **93/441-3184.** *Reservations suggested.* **Metro:** *Liceu.* **Main courses:** *475–1,750ptas. ($3.15–$11.65); fixed-price menu 900 ptas ($6). No credit cards.* **Open:** *Lunch and dinner Thurs–Tues.*

Quick Bites

In Barcelona as in Madrid, the quintessential Spanish food on the go is **tapas,** available at *tascas* (bars) all over town (for specific recommendations, see "Other Fun Stuff to Do"). In addition, the take-out at **Pollo Rico** (see preceding paragraph) can make for an excellent hot meal. **L. Simo,** at Passeig de Gràcia 46, makes good sandwiches and salads, and **Las Campanas,** at Mercè 21, specializes in spicy chorizo sandwiches, best washed down with ample beer and wine. The best **picnic** pickings by far are at the excellent **La Boquería market,** off Les Rambles—it's loaded with produce, meats, fish, and cheeses.

Sightseeing in Barcelona: A Little Gothic, a Little Picasso, & Some *Very* Unusual Buildings

Pullmantur (☎ 93/317-1297), Gran Via de les Corts Catalanes 635, offers a morning **guided bus tour** of the old city and Montjuïc and an afternoon tour of Eixample architectural sights, including Sagrada Familia, the Park Güell, and the Picasso Museum. **Juliatours** (☎ 93/317-6454), Ronda Universitat 5, has an afternoon tour of artistic Barcelona that also hits Gaudí's buildings and either the Picasso or Modern Art Museum. All these tours run around 4,200 ptas ($28). Juliatours also has a nighttime tour for 7,950ptas. ($53) that drives you past all the illuminated monuments of the city and ends with a flamenco performance.

Barcelona Sights Not to Miss

Cathedral

Behind an elaborate neo-Gothic facade and spire from the 19th century lies Madrid's massive Gothic cathedral, a dark, echoey space built between 1298 and 1450. There's not much to see inside besides the marvelously carved 15th-century choir stalls and ranks of glowing votive candles, but it'll take a good 45 minutes to move through and visit the shady cloisters. This tranquil oasis in the midst of the old city is surrounded by magnolias and palm trees and ponds swimming with geese. The little museum adjacent to the cathedral is stuffed with medieval Catalonian art. The Plaça de San Jaume, in front of the cathedral, is a pleasant place to spend time people-watching; at noon on Sundays a troupe performs the complicated folk dance *sardana* here.

Plaça de la Seu. ☎ *93/315-1554. Metro: Jaume I. Admission: Church is free; the museum costs 100ptas. (65¢). Open: Church daily 8am–1:30pm and 4–7:30pm; museum daily 10am–1pm.*

Museu Picasso

Although born in Andalusia, Picasso moved to Barcelona at age 14, and it was here, in the academy where his father taught, that he learned his craft. Barcelona was lucky enough when opening this museum to secure from the master himself many of his earliest works, which his sister had preserved. The very first room disproves the tongue-in-cheek myth that Picasso invented cubism merely because he couldn't draw properly, for here you'll see remarkable drawings and paintings executed with a high degree of realism—all when Picasso was barely a teenager. Of the other 3,000 works in this collection, seek out his *Las Meninas* paintings and drawings, a series of cubist studies made of Velázquez's masterpiece in Madrid's Prado museum (see that entry in Chapter 25). The curious can run through in half an hour; Picasso fans will want to spend one to two hours.

Montcada 15-19. ☎ *93/319-6310. Metro: Jaume I. Admission: 500ptas. ($3.30) adults, 250ptas. ($1.65) students, free for those under 17. Open: Tues–Sat 10am–8pm, Sun 10am–3pm.*

Sagrada Familia

The Sagrada Familia kind of looks as though a giant race of people decided to build a drippy sand castle-like cathedral. It's certainly the weirdest-looking church in Europe, an ongoing project that represents the architect Gaudí's creativity at its whimsical, feverish best. Only eight of what will be 13 spires and the two lesser facades are finished. The Civil War interrupted construction, but it's been picked up again as a slow trickle of donated funds allows work to continue on the nave, remaining towers, and main facade.

Bet You Didn't Know

Gaudí got the Sagrada Familia commission in 1883, and it consumed him. He poured every peseta he had into the project and went begging door to door when that dough ran out. He even lived on the site for 16 years. Gaudí died in 1926, after being run over by a trolley, but left behind no master plan for the church. Workers inch toward finishing his masterpiece, but it's unclear exactly *what* kind of building he ultimately intended. Many (often vocal) critics believe the church should remain unfinished. You can be sure Gaudí's keeping a sharp (albeit posthumous) eye on the proceedings—he is buried in the church crypt.

The architectural details are almost Gothic in their intricacy, but with a modern, fluid twist—rosy brown and gray stone is flecked with the colors of Gaudí's signature tile-chip mosaics. You can climb conch-shell spiral staircases (or take elevators) up several of the spires to look through the glassless rose windows, admire the rounded-off grid of the Eixample around you, and examine up close the funky gargoyles—over here is the Virgin Mary, there a snail creeps up the building's side, and around the corner pops up a stone cypress tree sprouting from a spire and fluttering with white doves. In the crypt is a museum that details the ongoing construction and shows through models and drawings what Gaudí's original plans were and how the finished building will appear.

Gaudí or Gaudy? The Birth of Modernisme Architecture

Around the turn of this century, Art Nouveau arrived in Barcelona in the form of Modernisme, a particularly fluid and idiosyncratic Catalán version of a larger architectural revolution. The high priest of Modernisme, Antoni Gaudí, apprenticed as a blacksmith before taking up architecture. Creative wrought-iron patterns became just one of the many signature details Gaudí incorporated into his flowing, organic structures; he was especially fond of creating colorful mosaics out of chips of ceramic and mirror.

If you see only a handful of Modernisme buildings, make them Gaudí's most famous trio: the **Sagrada Familia** (see listing); the colorful **Casa Battló** (Passeig de Gràcia 43) with a roof shaped like a dragon's back and theater-mask balconies; and **Casa Milà** (Passeig de Gràcia 92), often called *La Pedrera* (the quarry) for its undulating rocky shape. Here, especially, Gaudí seemed to avoid straight lines at all costs—the place looks like it's melting. There's an exhibition space on Gaudí and Modernisme inside; and for the 500 ptas ($3.35) admission you can also tour the architectural fun park and swirly, ice-cream chimneys. It's open Tuesday to Saturday 10am to 8pm, and Sunday 10am to 3pm (☎ **93/484-5980** or 487-3613).

Two other Modernisme architects of note were Domènech i Montaner and Puig i Cadafalch. To compare them to each other, and to master Gaudí, take a walk down the Illa de la Discòrdia (the block of discord) on Passeig de Gràcia between Carrer del Consell de Cent and Carrer d'Arago. Here, their interpretations of Modernisme compete in the form of apartment buildings. At no. 35 is Montaner's **Casa Lleo Morera,** at no. 41 is Cadafalch's **Casa Amatller,** and at no. 43 is Gaudí's Casa Battló. Montaner also designed the gorgeous venue **Palau de la Música Catalana,** Carrer de Sant Francesc de Paula 2, now a UNESCO World Heritage Site (go inside to see the sky-lit stained glass of the inverse dome in the auditorium). One of Cadafalch's other major works is **Els Quatre Gats,** which I recommended as a restaurant.

Carrer de Majorca 401. ☎ **93/455-0247. Metro:** *Sagrada Familia.* **Admission:** *750ptas. ($5) for entry, plus 200ptas. ($1.30) for the elevator to the top.* **Open:** *It's open daily: Nov–Feb 9am–6pm; Mar–Apr and Oct 9am–7pm; May and Sept 9am–8pm; June–Aug 9am–9pm.*

Museu Nacional d'Art de Catalunya

In an enormous 1929 palace atop Montjuïc hill is one of the world's biggest and best collections of Romanesque art, centered around a series of gorgeous 12th-century frescoes removed from Catalonian churches in the Pyrenees. There's also a good store of Spanish Gothic art and sculpture. Outside the palace is a network of stair-stepping fountains that feature in a sound and light show on summer nights (Thursday through Sunday).

Palau Nacional, Parc de Montjuïc. ☎ **93/423-7199. Metro:** *Espanya.* **Admission:** *Depends on exhibit, usually 500ptas. ($1.30).* **Open:** *Tues–Wed and Fri–Sat 10am–7pm, Thurs 10am–9pm, Sun 10am–2:30pm.*

Park Güell/Casa-Museu Gaudí

In the northern reaches of the Gràcia district, north of the Eixample, rises one of Gaudí's most colorful creations. It was intended to be an unusual little residential community, but only two houses were built. The city bought the property in 1926 and turned it into a public park with colonnades of crooked columns (they look like tree trunks), narrow gardens, small fountains, and whimsical animals. One sitting area is dominated by a large, spectacular curving bench brightened by a patterned mosaic of tile and mirror; from this spot, you get great views of the city. The entrance is flanked by two mosaicked pavilions designed by Gaudí, but the **Casa-Museu Gaudí** (☎ **93/284-6446**), where the master lived from 1906–26, was built by Ramón Berenguer. It's filled with Gaudí's models, furnishings, and drawings.

Carrer d'Olot. ☎ **93/424-3809. Bus:** *24, 25, 31, 74.* **Admission:** *The park is free; the museum costs 150ptas. ($1).* **Open:** *May–Sept daily 10am–9pm, Oct–Apr daily 9am–6pm (the museum is closed 2–4pm and on Sat).*

Other Fun Stuff to Do

➤ **Tour Spain in a Nutshell at the Poble Espanyol.** For the 1929 World's Fair, Barcelona created a simulated Spanish village high atop Montjuïc, where 115 houses and structures reproduce Spanish monuments and buildings from over the last 1,000 years. Many of the replicas are crafts and souvenir shops, but over a dozen have been converted into restaurants that serve cuisines from Spain's various regions. With others housing discos, bars, and a flamenco club, the Poble Espanyol (☎ **93/325-7866**) is an entertaining spot for an evening out. Take the Metro to Espanya then the free red double-decker bus. Admission is 950ptas. ($6.30), and it's open Monday from 9am to 8pm, Tuesday to Thursday 9am to 2am, Fri and Saturday 9am to 3am, Sunday 9am to midnight.

➤ **Enjoy a *Tapeo*.** When in Spain, do like the Spanish—indulge in an early-evening *tapeo* (tapas bar crawl). For more details on this most Spanish of activities (tapas rank somewhere between a snack and a passion), see Madrid's dining section in Chapter 25. One of Barcelona's best *tascas* (tapas bars) is **Casa Tejada** at Tenor Viñas 3, offering the widest selection in town. Mercè Street in Barceloneta is also renowned for its many *tascas*. Try **Bodega la Plata** (no. 28), specializing in deep-fried sardines, and **La Jarra** (no. 9)—short on refined atmosphere but stupendous in its flavors and authenticity.

➤ **Break out the Castanets, It's Time for Flamenco.** Inspired by the medieval tribulations of Spain's Jews and Moors, and influenced by gypsy rhythms and style, the exotically fluid dance known as **flamenco** heats up the night in two of Barcelona's bars. Admittedly, these shows are put on for the tourists—you'll have to head to Madrid or even Andalusia, the birthplace of flamenco, for more authentic versions. But if Barcelona is your only chance to experience the hand-clapping, guitar-strumming lifebeat of this folk art, try the **Tablao Flamenco Cordobés** (☎ 93/317-6653), at Les Rambles 35, or **El Tablao de Carmen** (☎ 93/325-6895) in the Poble Espanyol. Call to confirm show times and prices, but there's usually a dinner performance around 8:30 or 9:30pm for 7,500ptas. ($50), and a late show with just drinks around 11pm for 4,000ptas. ($26.65).

➤ **Disco 'Til Dawn with Barcelona's Throbbing Nightlife.** Like most of Spain, Barcelona loves its late night action, be it bar-hopping, dancing, or just general partying until the wee hours. The most traditional evening can be had in the Modernisme architectural triumph of the **Palau de la Musica Catalán** (☎ 93/268-1000), San Francest de Paula 2, which features year-round classical, jazz, and pop concerts as well as recitals. You can stay passive in your after-dark pleasures at a flamenco bar like those listed previously or dance your own socks off at clubs **Estudio 54** (☎ 93/329-5454), Avinguda del Parallel 64, or **Up and Down** (☎ 93/280-2922), Numancia Diagonal 179. The best bar action is at trendy **Nick Havanna** (☎ 93/237-5405), Roselló 208, or minimalist havens **Zig-Zag Bar** (☎ 93/201-6207), Platón 13, and the massive **Otto Zutz Club** (☎ 93/238-0722), Carrer Lincoln 15.

Get Outta Town: Day Trips & Excursions

Leave cosmopolitan Barcelona behind to venture out into the Catalan countryside, and you'll find several enticing destinations—among them the monastery at Montserrat and the old Roman settlement of Tarragona.

Montserrat's Mountain Monastery

One of Spain's holiest pilgrimage sites is nestled halfway up a 4,000-foot mountain at the base of the jagged, thin spine of rock that gives the area the name "serrated mountain." A monastery has perched here since the 9th century, drawing the pious and the curious to worship the fabled La Moreneta, or "Black Virgin." Montserrat also harbors a good little art museum and some stunning views of the surrounding area. **Trains** leave hourly from the Plaça d'Espanya station in Barcelona; the ride takes about 90 minutes. Try to take an odd-hour train; the ones on even hours require a transfer at Martorell-Enllaç. Get off at the Aeri de Montserrat stop to catch the funicular (included in the ticket price) the rest of the way up to town.

The **monastery** itself, enlarged in the 11th century and rebuilt in 1844, sports a neo-renaissance entry courtyard and 16th-century basilica. Enter the church through the right-hand door to pay your respects to the Black Virgin (see "Bet You Didn't Know"). She hides behind a sheet of glass, but sticks her gilded arm out so pilgrims can rub the orb in her hand for a blessing and good luck. Try to be here at 1pm, when the **Escolania boy's choir** sings hymns in honor of the Virgin and her monastery. The basilica is open daily 8am to 10:30am and noon to 6:30pm.

Time-Savers

It only takes a few hours to see the monastery and surrounding sights, but budget all day for the trip, returning to Barcelona in time for a *tapeo* and dinner. *Stay away on Sunday*—that's when the faithful come in droves. The **tourist information center** (☎ 93/835-0251) is in town at Plaça de la Creu.

On Plaça de Santa María is the **Museu de Montserrat** (☎ 93/835-0251), housing prehistoric remains (anyone for a 2,000-year-old crocodile mummy?) alongside canvases from a diverse group that includes El Greco, Caravaggio, Picasso, Monet, Dalí, and Degas. Admission is 400ptas. ($2.65), and it's open daily 10:30am to 2pm and 3 to 6pm.

Other short funicular rides from Plaça de la Creu will take you either down to the 17th-century grotto of the **Santa Cova,** where the paths are lined with Modernisme shrines by Gaudí and Puig i Cadafalch, or up to the 4,119-foot peak of **Sant Jeroni,** where the views can extend both across the Pyrenees Mountains and over the Mediterranean to the islands of Mallorca and Ibiza. **Abat Cisneros** (☎ 93/835-0201), on Plaça de Monestir, offers inexpensive set-price meals of unpretentious Catalonian fare.

Bet You Didn't Know

According to legend, St. Luke himself carved La Moreneta, and the venerated image arrived in Barcelona around 50 A.D. Carbon dating, however, suggests that the time-blackened statue was most likely crafted in the 12th century.

Tarragona's Roman Ruins

Tarragona was the Roman Empire's base of operations during its conquest of the Iberian peninsula, beginning in 218 B.C.—Julius Caesar himself even bivouacked here for a while. Though it boasts Spain's best Roman ruins, including a crumbling seaside amphitheater, Tarragona is still an underrated destination. Best of all for you, it's a mere hour's **train** ride from Barcelona on the main line to Madrid (trains leave Barcelona from the Sants station, but many call at Franca and/or Passeig de Gràcia stations first). When you're in Tarragona, Bus 1 runs you past all the major sights in town.

Time-Savers

You can see the top sights in two to three hours, take a leisurely stroll along the ancient walls, and then enjoy a picnic in their shadow—and call it all a half-day excursion. The regional **tourist office** (☎ 977/233–415) is at Carrer Fortuny 4, off Rambla Nova in the newer part of town; there's also a city office at Carrer Major 39, just off Civaderia Merceria near the cathedral.

Near the modern harbor, a stretch of the Mediterranean shore has been converted into a park to commemorate the ruins of the 2nd century A.D. **Amfiteatre Romà (Roman Amphitheater),** carved directly out of the beachside cliff. Admission is 400ptas. ($2.65). April to September, it's open Tuesday to Saturday 9am to 8pm, Sunday 9am to 3pm. October to March, it's open Tuesday to Saturday 9am to 5:30pm, Sunday 9am to 3pm.

The Museu Nacional Arquològic (Archaeological Museum) (☎ 977/ 236-209), Plaça del Rei 5, contains Catalonia's biggest collection of Roman sculpture, frescoes, bronzes, and mosaics, including a *Head of Medusa*. Admission is 300ptas. ($2). From June 16 to October 15, it's open Tuesday to Saturday 10am to 2pm and 4 to 7pm, Sunday 10am to 2pm. From October 16 to June 15, it's open Tuesday to Sunday 10am to 1pm and 4:30 to 8pm, Sunday 10am to 2pm.

Tarragona is a modern industrial center, but this port city's origins are ancient, as evidenced by the 5th century B.C. walls that curl around the city's eastern edge. The Romans built their own fortifications atop this protective belt, medieval Catalonians further reinforced them, and the Brits topped it off with new ramparts in the 17th century. The cypress-shaded **Passeig Arqueológic,** or architectural path (☎ 977/245-796), around the walls makes a nice half-mile walk. Admission is 420ptas. ($2.80). From October to May, it's open Monday to Saturday 10am to 1pm and 3 to 7pm, Sunday 10am to 2pm; from June to September, it's open Monday to Saturday 9am to 8pm, Sunday 10am to 2pm.

The walls encircle the oldest part of town, built around the 12th-century **cathedral** (977/238-685). Stained-glass windows illuminate the interior, which sports an alabaster altarpiece (1430) honoring St. Thecla. The beautiful, orange tree-shaded cloisters, like the rest of the cathedral, show how seemlessly the architecture of this church slipped from its romanesque beginnings into a vaulted, Gothic finale. Off of the cloisters is a small museum of tapestries and medieval sculpture. Admission to the church is free; admission to the museum is 300ptas. ($2). Both are open daily: from March 16 to June, the hours are 10am to 12:30pm and 4 to 6:45pm; from July to October 15, the hours are 10am to 7pm; from October 16 to November 15, the hours are 10am to 12:30pm and 3 to 6pm; from November 16 to March 15, the hours are 10am to 1:45pm.

On the western edge of town, beyond the remains of the **Roman Forum** at Carrer Cervantes, lies a 3rd- to 6th-century **Necropolis** (☎ 977/211-175), whose little museum houses ancient Christian tombstones and sarcophagi—many of them recycled from even older pagan tombs.

If hunger hits you, check out **Barquet** (☎ 977/240-023), at Gasometro 16, for excellent Catalán seafood and a 1,100ptas. ($7.30) fixed-price menu. Should you choose to spend the night, the **Hotel Lauria** (☎ 977/236-712, fax: 977/236-700), Rambla Nova 20, rents modern doubles for 9,500 to 10,000ptas. ($63.30 to $66.65) in the heart of town, just off the seafront promenade.

Chapter 27

Athens & the Best of Greek Island-Hopping

In This Chapter

➤ Hotels that won't drain your drachma

➤ The best gyros on the go and the finest tavernas for genuine Greek cuisine

➤ Majestic temples, ancient myths, and wild folk dancing

➤ Exploring Delphi's temples and soaking up the Santoríni sun

Athens built a mighty metropolis; organized one of the world's first successful democracies; and founded schools of art, architecture, literature, drama, and philosophy that continue to be the touchstones of today's western civilization—all this by the 5th century B.C., when folks in the rest of the western world were still in their proverbial diapers. Modern Athens preserves three magnificent sights: the Acropolis Hill, whose Parthenon to Athena is the world's most famous ancient temple; a massive archeological museum; and the Ancient Agora, the civic laboratory in which modern democratic ideas were first developed and tested.

Dollars & Sense

The Greek unit of currency is the drachma (Dr). Roughly, $1 equals 280Dr, or 10Dr equals 3.5¢. Greek coins include 5, 10, 20, 50, and 100 drachmas. Bills come in denominations of 50, 100, 1,000, and 5,000 drachmas (the 50Dr and 100Dr notes are in circulation, but being phased out, and a 10,000Dr bill is being introduced).

Athens carries one of Europe's most sacred cultural heritages, but honestly, I'd see those greatest hits quickly and then move on to the rest of Greece. The rest of the city, it must be said, leaves much to be desired; it's a tangled mess of overdevelopment, traffic, and pollution. Also, Athens is much farther from the heart of Europe than most people realize. On a first-time or whirlwind trip, I'd give serious consideration as to whether you want to invest the time it takes to visit Greece. Either budget for a plane ticket here from a more central European city or be prepared to spend a full six days of sheer travel by train and ferry just to get from Rome to Athens and back. I'm not trying to talk you out of Greece by any means. Just heed my advice: If you try to squeeze it in, you might be sorely disappointed.

If, however, you plan to stay a while and explore this country and its ancient culture, by all means make the trip. Athens may be crowded and polluted, but Greece itself is a magical, beautiful, complex, and history-ridden land. With enough time and a willingness to delve deeply into the history, culture, and mythology, you'll no doubt find Greece an unforgettable part of your journey.

Getting Your Bearings

Athens isn't so much a city as it is a land-hungry force of human nature—a slapdash construction zone that has engulfed miles of the surrounding countryside and rapidly swelled to a metropolis. Still, its core preserves the Acropolis and many other ancient ruins scattered among Byzantine churches, Turkish buildings, 19th-century boulevards, and 20th-century gridlock.

Time-Savers

The **Greek Tourist Organization (EOT)** has an information desk (☎ 01/ 322-2545) on Sýntagma Square next to the National Bank and a desk at the airport. Another very handy Athens resource is the **tourist police** (☎ 171), who offer 24-hour visitor support in English and are the ones to turn to in case you run into any problems. The weekly *Athenscope* magazine, available at news kiosks, lists cultural events in English.

Athens Neighborhoods in Brief

The one place you have to remember in Athens is **Sýntagma Square,** the political, geographical, traveler's, and traffic center of the city. Southwest of

First Aid Station **2**
EOT (Greek Tourist
  Organization) **7**
Omónia Square **3**
OTE (Telecommunications)
  Office at Omónia
  Square **4**
OTE (Telecommunications)
  Office at Sýntagma
  Square **6**
Peloponnese Train Station **1**
Sýntagma Square **8**
Theseum Station **5**

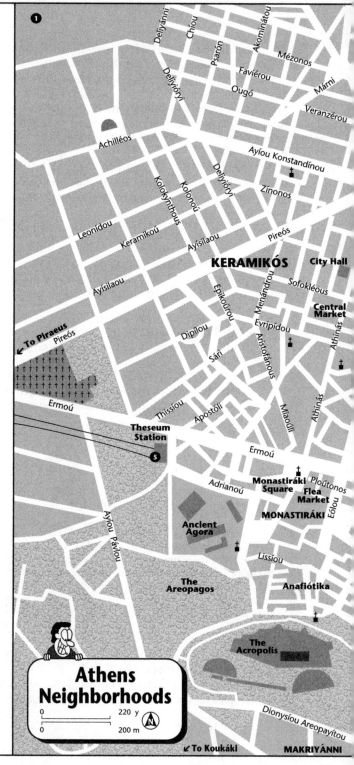

KERAMIKÓS

City Hall

Sofokléous

Central Market

Theseum Station **5**

Monastiráki Square

Flea Market

MONASTIRÁKI

Ancient Agora

Lissíou

The Areopagos

Anafiótika

The Acropolis

Athens Neighborhoods

| 0 | 220 y |
| 0 | 200 m |

To Koukáki

MAKRIYÁNNI

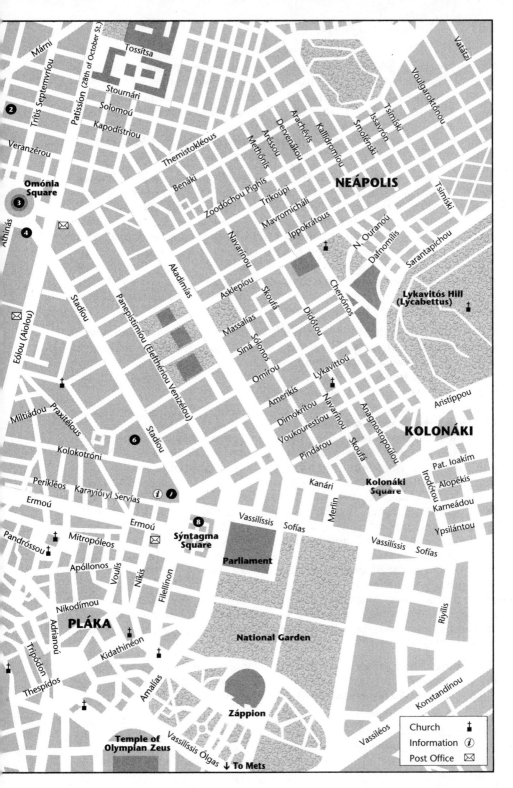

it stretches the largely pedestrianized quarter called the **Pláka**—thoroughly tourist-oriented, but also one of the most colorful old sections of town where you'll spend the bulk of your visit. The Pláka's southwest corner is bounded by the **Acropolis Hill,** a beacon to all visitors with its majestic Parthenon temple and other famed ruins from Athens' ancient prime. North of the Acropolis and west of the Pláka, the tangled neighborhood of **Monastiráki,** with its shop-lined streets and flea market, abuts the Ancient Agora.

To the north of the Pláka and Sýntagma Square, you'll notice that all roads lead to **Omónia Square,** center of a district that was once the commercial and hotel heart of the city. The neighborhood has recently fallen on bad times, however, and has become somewhat rundown. It's useful as a transportation hub, but I wouldn't hang out here. Northeast of Sýntagma Square lies the fashionable shopping and residential zone of **Kolonáki,** no longer the hottest glamour spot in town (newer suburbs have stolen that title) but still a chic, happening area. Due south of Sýntagma Square is the residential and trendy intellectual quarter called **Mets,** named after a literati's cafe— how much more Euro-trendy can you get?

South of the Acropolis is the moderately upscale and relatively undiscovered neighborhood of **Makriyánni,** which is full of good hotels, restaurants, and shopping. Southwest of this neighborhood is the even less-discovered residential zone of **Koukáki,** with great inexpensive hotels and a modest, thoroughly Athenian restaurant scene.

Getting Into & Around Town

With the hordes of visitors taking the **ferry from Italy** to Greece, you'd think fares and schedules would be standardized. You'd be wrong. The most popular route is from Brindisi (on the heel of Italy's "boot," seven hours by train from Rome) to Greece's port of Patras. This crossing takes 18 to 20 hours; ferries usually leave around 10pm from Brindisi (be on board *at least* two hours early). Prices, ranging anywhere from $30 for a deck chair and an uncomfortable night outside to $230 for the best cabins, are highest from late June through August, and Eurailpass holders get up to 30% off. From Patras, you can catch a train to Athens or a bus to Delphi. Make your connections as quickly as possible, because the last train/bus of the day tends to leave quickly after the ferry pulls in, leaving many stranded in uninspiring Patras for the night. To get from Rome to Athens this way takes about three full days. Many people find flying into Athens to be the easiest and overall cheapest alternative (especially once you factor in all the rail, ferry, meal, and accommodation costs).

Trains into Athens from Patras arrive at Peloponnese Station (Stathmós Peloponníssou) about a mile northwest of Omónia Square. Across the tracks is Athens' main **Larissa Station** (trains from the north). From this station, trolley no. 1 runs to Sýntagma Square.

Regional buses pull into either Terminal A or B. Terminal A (buses from Patras, northern, southern, and western Greece, and the Peloponnese) is at 100 Kifíssiou St.; city bus. no 51 runs to a terminal near Omónia Square.

Terminal B (buses from central Greece, including Delphi, Thebes, and Meteóra) is at 260 Liossíon St.; city bus no. 24 runs to Amalías Avenues and the National Garden, one block from Sýntagma Square.

Hellenikon International Airport is seven miles south of the city center. A taxi downtown should cost about 2,500Dr ($8.90) and take 30 to 90 minutes (depending on traffic). Or you can take city bus no. 090, or the slower no. 133, to Sýntagma Square. From the airport's West Terminal (Olympic Airways), the Olympic Airways bus leaves half-hourly to shuttle passengers to Sýntagma Square and costs 190Dr (70¢), to be paid on the bus (exact change only). Express bus no. 19 runs from the airport to the ferry port town of Piraeus.

Traffic Alert!

Athens has the worst traffic of any European city. It beats out even Rome and Naples for the horn-honking, lane-ignoring, fender-bending, pollution-spewing, high-speed traffic snarl that daily fills the streets. Drivers regularly make left turns from the far right lane of a six-lane boulevard, or use a string of empty parking spaces as a temporary passing lane. I'd *definitely* vote against trying to drive here.

Athens' **metro (subway)** system is clean and efficient, but not nearly finished. There is currently only one line, which connects Omónia and Monasteráki (nearest the Pláka) and runs all the way to the docks at Piraeus (where you catch boats to the islands). Many more stations that will eventually service two other lines are under construction, but the completion date keeps being postponed. Athens is simply too archeologically rich. The crews are digging some 67 feet below the surface, but they still keep running into ancient ruins that need to be excavated before construction can resume.

There are several overlapping **bus and bus-trolley** networks. Most useful are the yellow trolley-buses, which cover the core of Athens; many of these pass through the Pláka and/or Sýntagma Square. Blue-and-white buses form the suburban commuter network. Because they make but a few stops in town before heading out into Greater Athens, you won't be hopping on them regularly, except for the few lines that stop at major points of interest. An affiliated system of red minibuses does cover the city center, and you will find them handy. Green buses run regularly from downtown Athens to the main port of Piraeus. I only wish I could share with you which of these lines are most useful, but alas, Athens revamps its bus system and reassigns route numbers on an

Dollars & Sense

Although **tickets** for single rides on both the metro and bus/trolley system cost 75Dr (25¢), they are not interchangeable. For the bus, buy tickets at the kiosks you'll see all over town. For the metro, tickets are sold at machines or booths inside the stations. Some longer metro rides cost 100Dr (35¢).

annoyingly regular basis. Chances are that any specific info I impart to you here will have changed by the time this book reaches the shelves.

In general, I find my feet and the occasional **taxi** to be the best way to move about town. Athens taxis (as described in "Fast Facts") are the cheapest of any major European city, so long as you keep your wits about you and pay close attention to avoid getting scammed on the rates. They remain the simplest way to get door-to-door service in Athens and the occasional white-knuckle thrill ride guided by the most aggressive of Athens's maniac drivers (see "Traffic Alert!"). Except for a few excursions out into the city at large to visit museums, you'll probably spend most of your time in and around the pedestrianized Pláka.

Athens Fast Facts

American Express   American Express is at 2 Ermoú St. (☎ **01/324-4975**) above McDonald's in Sýntagma Square. It's open Monday to Friday 8:30am to 4pm. On Saturday, the travel and mail desks *only* are open 8:30am to 1:30pm.

Doctors/hospitals   For a list of English-speaking doctors, call **SOS Doctor** at ☎ **01/331-0310** or ask as the **U.S. Embassy** (☎ **01/721-2951**). The **Tourist Police** (☎ **171**) will give you the location of the nearest hospital, but admittance is usually gained through a physician. If you need a doctor between 2pm and 7am, call ☎ **105.**

Embassy   The U.S. Embassy (☎ **721-2951**) is at 91 Vassilíssis Sophías Avenue. For emergency assistance when the embassy is closed, call the embassy receptionist at ☎ **01/722-3652** or the duty officer at ☎ **01/729-4301.**

Emergency   Dial ☎ **100** for the police, call an ambulance at ☎ **166,** and report a fire to ☎ **199.** If your car breaks down, call ELPA Road Assistance at ☎ **104;** it's free for light repairs. If you have a run-in with a difficult taxi driver, hotel, restaurant, or shop owner, call the **Tourist Police** at ☎ **171.**

Pharmacies   *Pharmakia* are identified by green crosses and are usually open 8am to 2pm. For a list of pharmacies open 24 hours a day, check the sign that all pharmacies hang on their doors, pick up a copy of the *Athens News*, or call ☎ **107.**

Safety   Greece has the lowest crime rate in Europe, and Athens is the continent's safest big city. Aside from dodging the maniac traffic, there are only two minor worries. Women, especially single women, will often get hassled and rudely propositioned by lecherous shopkeepers (especially in the Pláka). Unscrupulous bar owners sometimes run a scam on single men, distracting them with beautiful women while the barkeep pours drink after ludicrously expensive drink. The astronomical bill comes without any prior warning of the prices, and the hapless visitor is forced to pay through the nose.

Taxis   Travel by taxi is relatively cheap in Athens. The initial charge is 200Dr (70¢), plus 60Dr (20¢) per kilometer. If you go out of the city, the per-kilometer charge may rise. There is a luggage fee of 55Dr (20¢) and a surcharge of 160Dr (55¢) for stops at the port of Piraeus or rail or bus station; the surcharge is 300Dr ($1.05) for stops at the airport.

Always use a metered taxi, never a gypsy cab or unmetered car. Make sure the meter rate reads "1"—it should only read "2" if you're going well outside the central city, which you probably are not. Don't be surprised if your driver picks up additional passengers during your ride. A taxi may carry others to destinations that are on the way, but everyone pays separately; check the amount on the meter when you climb in, and pay the difference when you get out. You can hail a taxi on the street or call a radio taxi company: **Express** (☎ **01/993-4812**), **Kosmos** (☎ **01/801-9000**), or **Parthenon** (☎ **01/581-4711**). There is a 200Dr (70¢) surcharge for calling a taxi; the surcharge is 300Dr ($1.05) if you call a taxi for an appointed time.

Telephone   A local call in Athens costs 20Dr (5¢). Most of the pay phones take only phone cards, which are sold at newsstands and OTE (the national telephone company) offices for 1,300Dr ($4.65). At other phones, you pay for what the meter records.

Greece's country code is **30;** Athens's city code is **01.** Use the zero before the city code only when calling Athens from within Greece; when calling from outside Greece, drop the zero. To call Athens from the United States, dial **011-30-1** and the number. To use a calling card or to call collect, dial **AT&T** (☎ **00-800-1311**), **MCI** (☎ **00-800-1211**), or **Sprint** (☎ **00-800-1411**). To call the United States direct from Greece, dial **001,** the area code, and telephone number.

Transit Info   Call the **Tourist Police** at ☎ **171.**

Athenian Accommodations: The Hotel Scene

Athens hotels are almost uniformly simple and basic. Many of the cheapest can get pretty scruffy, but there are plenty of clean options if you look around. For maximum sightseeing and nightlife action, stay in the Pláka or Monasteráki. There are also lots of good, clean places in the residential zones of Koukáki and Makriyánni, which are cheaper than staying in the city center. The only area to steer clear of is the downtrodden Omónia Square zone—once a haven for budget inns, it's now too seedy for most people's tastes. For stays of fewer than three nights, hotels can legally slap a 10% surcharge onto their regular rates. In low season, by all means bargain.

Time-Savers

The **Hellenic Chamber of Hotels** (☎ **01/323-7193**), at a desk inside Sýntagma Square's National Bank of Greece, can help you book a hotel anywhere in Greece.

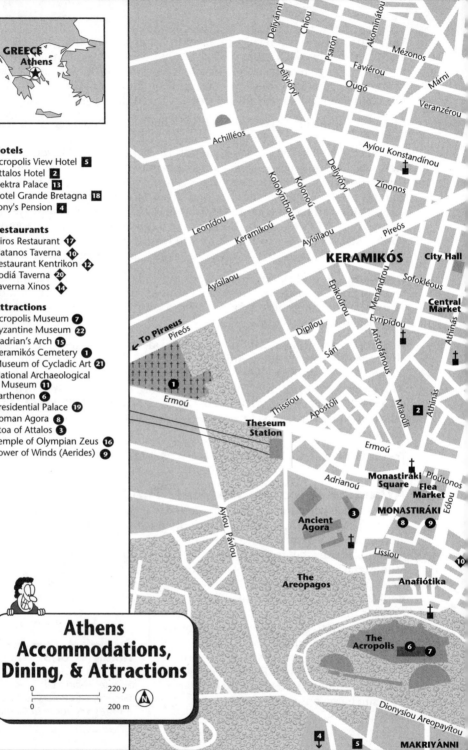

GREECE
Athens

Hotels
Acropolis View Hotel **5**
Attalos Hotel **2**
Elektra Palace **13**
Hotel Grande Bretagna **18**
Tony's Pension **4**

Restaurants
Diros Restaurant **17**
Platanos Taverna **10**
Restaurant Kentrikon **12**
Rodiá Taverna **20**
Taverna Xinos **14**

Attractions
Acropolis Museum **7**
Byzantine Museum **22**
Hadrian's Arch **15**
Keramikós Cemetery **1**
Museum of Cycladic Art **21**
National Archaeological
   Museum **11**
Parthenon **6**
Presidential Palace **19**
Roman Agora **8**
Stoa of Attalos **3**
Temple of Olympian Zeus **16**
Tower of Winds (Aerides) **9**

**Athens
Accommodations,
Dining, & Attractions**

0   220 y
0   200 m

N

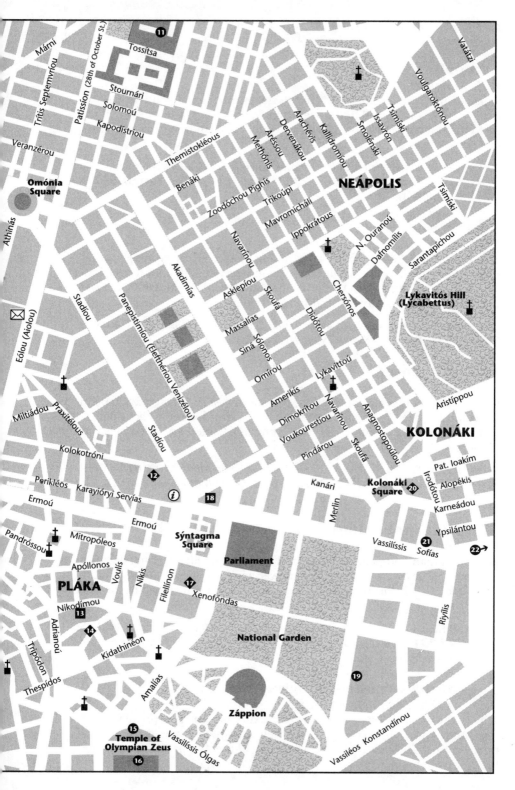

Acropolis View Hotel

$$$. Makriyánni.

Snuggled into a quiet side street on the slopes of Philopáppou Hill, the Acropolis View has small but modern renovated rooms, a few of which live up to the hotel's name. The roof terrace offers outstanding Acropolis views, especially at sunset.

10 Webster St. (off Rovértou Gálli, 2 blocks down from its intersection with Dionysíou Aeropayítou). ☎ *01/921-7303.* **Fax:** *01/923-0705.* **Rates:** *20,000Dr ($71.40) double. AE, MC, V.*

Attalos Hotel

$. Monasteráki.

The Attalos maintains its popularity among budgeteers by keeping squeaky clean (if yawningly spare) rooms and friendly service. The roof terrace has a view across the city to the Acropolis. Air-conditioning costs 2,000Dr ($7.15) extra, which is definitely worth it in summer.

29 Athinás St. (1.5 blocks from Monasteráki Square). ☎ *01/321-2801.* **Fax:** *01/324-3124.* **Rates:** *9,500Dr ($33.90) double. V.*

Elektra Palace

$$$$. Pláka.

For the price, this is a great location, just southwest of Sýntagma Square in the colorful Pláka. The clean, contemporarily furnished rooms get smaller as you go up, but the balconies get proportionately larger. An added plus is the rooftop pool.

18 Nikodímou St. (on the Pláka's main drag, near Adrianoú St.). ☎ *01/ 324-1401.* **Fax:** *01/324-1875.* **Rates:** *26,500Dr ($94.65) double. AE, DC, MC, V.*

Hotel Acropolis House

$$$. Pláka.

You'll find many original moldings and other classic architectural details in this restored, 150-year-old villa. The newer wing is not as charming, but it has modern, tiled bathrooms. Continental breakfast is included in the price of the room.

6–8 Odós Kodroú St. (3 blocks from Hadrian's Arch, at the south end of Voulís St.). ☎ *01/322-2344.* **Fax:** *01/324-4143.* **Rates:** *15,000–16,800 Dr ($53.57–$60) double. No credit cards.*

Hotel Grande Bretagna

$$$$$. Sýntagma Square.

This Beaux Arts bastion of 19th-century luxury has an appropriately neoclassical lobby and 12-foot ceilings in the well-appointed rooms. Accommodations on the busy square have a view (some of the Acropolis), but those on the courtyard are quieter.

105 Sýntagma Square. ☎ *01/323-0251.* **Fax:** *01/322-8034.* **Rates:** *63,000–125,650Dr ($225–$448.75) double. AE, DC, MC, V.*

![Kids] Tony's Pension
$$. Koukáki.

This budget standard was once a hostel, but since it redecorated and up-graded, it has attracted a varied clientele of value-seekers. It's still utterly basic, but it's run by a very amicable couple, and half the accommodations are studios with kitchenettes.

26 Zacharítsa. (2 blocks over from Moussón St., between Lazéon and Dikéou sts.). ☎ *01/923-6370.* **Fax:** *01/923-5761.* **Rates:** *9,000–12,000Dr ($32.15–$42.85) double or studio apartment. MC.*

Food of the Gods: The Athens Restaurant Scene

Greeks concentrate their culinary energies on the quality of the cooking and freshness of the food, not the decor of the restaurant. Athens is one place where the old travel truism holds—seek out the place crowded with local families having a good time. It'll probably look like a dive, but the food will be straight from the gods on Mt. Olympus. Dinner starts late, anywhere from 9 to 11pm., so be sure to drop by a taverna in the early evening to stoke your engines.

An integral part of the Greek diet are *mezédes,* appetizer portions served before the meal or on their own (similar to Spain's concept of *tapas*). *Mezédes* accompany wine at a laid-back taverna or ouzo at an ouzerie. The best are **tzatzíki** (a yogurt dip with cucumber, garlic, and mint), **taramosaláta** (mullet roe and potatoes pureed into a dip), **melitzanosaláta** (eggplant salad), grilled **kalamarákia** (squid), **oktapódi** (octopus), or **loukánika** (sausage).

Also excellent and served either as *mezédes* or as main courses are **dolmádes** (grape leaves stuffed with rice, pine nuts, and currants), **souvlaki** (shishke-bab of pork or lamb), **keftédes** (coriander– and cumin-spiced fried meat-balls), **spanokópita** (spinach and feta pie), **moussaká** (a casserole of egg-plant, potatoes, and minced meat topped with a melted cheese crust), along with other preparations of *arní* (lamb), *kotópoulo* (chicken), or *choirinó* (pork).

The Greeks make the richest, creamiest, tastiest **giaoúrti** (yogurt) I've ever tasted. My favorite meal is to dip apple slices in thick gobs of plain yogurt. The ancient Greeks called **méli** (honey), along with nectar, *ambrosia,* the "food of the gods." After drizzling some over your yogurt for dessert, you just might agree. **Baklavá** is flaky phyllo dough layered with nuts and soaked in honey. **Sýka Mavrodáfni** are figs baked in red wine and served in a sauce spiked with spices, orange-water, and honey.

Seafood isn't always as good as you'd expect in Athens; over-fishing and the preventative laws the practice has provoked lead to high prices and questions over freshness. The best seafood restaurants of the capital are in the attached port city of Piraeus.

The Greeks may very well have invented **wine,** and although **retsína**— flavored with pine resin and tasting of turpentine—may be the most famous, you may find un-resined **krasí** more palatable. Most Greeks prefer whisky these days, but the national alcoholic drink is the clear, anise-flavored **ouzo,** which turns milky white when you add water. Personally, I find it disgusting.

Dionysos-Zonar's
$$$$$. Kolonáki. CONTINENTAL.
Take the funicular at Kolonáki Square to get to this lovely restaurant atop the highest hill in Athens. The city is spread out before you, which makes for a lovely view—especially at sunset. The international menu is a tad pricey for dinner, so if you're counting drachmas, come instead for a salad or sandwich at lunch.

Atop Lykavittós Hill. ☎ **01/722-6374.** *Reservations recommended.* **Main courses:** *2,500–7,200Dr ($8.90–$25.70). AE, DC, MC, V.* **Open:** *Lunch and dinner daily. Closed Jan 31–Feb 28.*

⭐Kids Diros Restaurant
$$. Near Sýntagma Square. GREEK.
It's cheap, it's right off Sýntagma Square, there's air-conditioning inside and tables on the sidewalk, and the food couldn't be more satisfying. This family-friendly joint also serves tamer, western-style dishes such as spaghetti and roast chicken with french fries if the little ones tire of Greek food.

10 Xenofóndos St. (1 block south of Sýntagma Square). ☎ **01/323-2392.** *Reservations suggested.* **Main courses:** *1,400–2,500Dr ($5–$8.90). AE, DC, V.* **Open:** *Lunch and dinner daily.*

Platanos Taverna
$$$. Pláka. GREEK.
Platanos is a dyed-in-the-wool taverna. On a sycamore-shaded bend of a residential street, it serves hearty staples of Greek cuisine cooked simply but with rigorous attention to freshness and quality. The interior is a hodgepodge of paintings, photos, and simple old-fashioned Greek ambiance.

4 Dioyénous St. (near the intersection of Adrianoú and Eólou). ☎ **01/322-0666.** *Reservations suggested.* **Main courses:** *1,500–2,500Dr ($5.35–$8.90). No credit cards.* **Open:** *Lunch and dinner Mon–Sat.*

Restaurant Kentrikon
$$$$$. Near Sýntagma Square. INTERNATIONAL.
Despite the (relatively) high prices, locals feel the excellent food at this huge, air-conditioned 1960s restaurant is worth it. The lamb ragoût with spinach, chicken with okra, and their special macaroni top the list of best eats. Although everything is quite informal, the service here is some of the best in town.

3 Kolokotróni St. (1 block up from Stadíou). ☎ *01/323-2482. Reservations suggested.* **Main courses:** *1,600–4,000Dr ($5.70–$14.30). No credit cards.* **Open:** *Lunch Sun–Fri.*

Kids **Rodiá Taverna**
$. Kolonáki. GREEK.

It's cheap, and one of the most atmospheric joints you'll come across, with a decor of lacy curtains, dark wood paneling, wine kegs, and a vine-arbored garden out back. The food is superb; try octopus in mustard sauce, light *bourékis* (veggie-filled pastries), or lemon-tinged beef.

44 Aristípou St. (off Kolonáki Square). ☎ *01/722-9883. Reservations suggested.* **Main courses:** *600–2,500Dr ($2.15–$8.90). No credit cards.* **Open:** *Dinner Mon–Sat.*

Taverna Xinos
$$$$. Pláka. GREEK.

The atmosphere may be low-key and informal, with live music and folksy murals, but this is one of Athens' best restaurants. Try to make reservations after 9pm—that's when the locals and connoisseurs arrive—and sit back, relax, and dine late and long. The dolmádes, moussaká, and lamb fricassee are all scrumptious.

4 Angélou Yéronda (in the heart of the Pláka between Kidathinéon and Iperídou Sts.). ☎ *01/322-1065. Reservations recommended.* **Main courses:** *2,000–2,800Dr ($7.15–$10). No credit cards.* **Open:** *Dinner Mon–Fri. Closed July.*

Quick Bites

You can get **souvlaki** on the go accompanied by a hunk of bread—the best is from **Thanasis** (☎ **01/324-4705**) at 69 Metropóleon St. Or gobble up a **gyro,** a pita pocket stuffed with strips carved from a rotating hunk of roasting spiced meat on a vertical spit. A good gyro stand in the heart of the Pláka is **Grill House Pláka** (☎ **01/324-6229**) at 28 Kidathinéon St. Otherwise, you can pop into any taverna for a nourishing round of mezédes.

It's All Greek to Me: Athens Sightseeing

There's little difference between the **guided bus tours** of the city offered by **GO Tours** (☎ **01/322-5951**), 31-33 Voulís St., 5th floor; **CHAT (Hermes en Grece) Tours** (☎ **01/322-3137**), 4 Stadíou; and **Key Tours** (☎ **01/923-3166**), 4 Kallirois St. Most leave around 9am and return between noon or 1pm, taking in sights like the Acropolis and the major museums. All cost around 8,400Dr ($30).

549

Athens Sights Not to Miss

The Acropolis & the Parthenon

The Acropolis Hill is the heart of Athens, the spot where the gods Athena and Poseidon held a contest to see who could best provide for the local citizens and thus become the city's patron (Poseidon produced a salty spring of water from the ground; Athena invented the versatile olive tree and won). The Acropolis is the symbol of Greece itself, focused on the mighty Parthenon. The temple rears nobly above the metropolis, reminding the modern city of its ancient lineage. Allow a good two to three hours to pick over the Acropolis and its museum.

You climb stairs to enter through the **Beulé Gate,** built by the Roman Emperor Valerian in A.D. 267. On your right as you climb perches the cute little Ionic **Temple of Athena Nike** (built 424 B.C., rebuilt 1940 A.D.). The stairs end in the dramatic entryway called the **Propylaia,** which since the 5th century B.C. has served as the pilgrims' antechamber to the Acropolis proper.

The **Parthenon** is not the largest, nor the best preserved, of the ancient world's shrines, but it has nonetheless become the poster child of Greek temples. The Athenians spared no expense in raising this primary temple to their patron between 447 and 438 B.C.. Made entirely of marble, it once housed a 40-foot statue of Athena (there's a small Roman copy of it in the Archeological Museum). The temple is exquisitely proportioned; the ratio of 9 to 4 pops up in measurements everywhere, and architectural tricks make it appear perfect to the naked eye. To combat natural optical illusions, the flat surfaces are bowed slightly up in the middle to seem straight, the columns lean inward to appear parallel, and each is fatter in the middle so they look perfectly cylindrical.

The Parthenon survived the ages virtually intact, becoming an Orthodox church in the 6th century, a Catholic church during the Crusades, and an Islamic mosque under the Turkish occupation, but it wasn't so lucky when the Venetians laid siege to the Turkish city in 1687. The Turks were using the venerable temple as a munitions dump, and when a Venetian cannonball hit the stockpile, it set off the armaments and blew the place sky-high. From the remains, British Lord Elgin gathered up almost all the sculpted friezes and pediment pieces, destroying many in the process, and shipped them home to England from 1801 to 1811, where they have remained in the British Museum despite repeated requests by the Greek government to repatriate them. Although the temple was once covered almost entirely with carved friezes and sculptures, only a few crumbs of sculpture remain on the Parthenon itself.

Less famous but more complex than the Parthenon is the temple called the **Erechtheum,** built from 421 to 406 B.C. Named for a mythical king of Athens, it was the place of worship for the city's most ancient cults. It's a cobbled together Ionic structure of small temples and porches, one side supported by a half-dozen caryatids (columns disguised as female figures). These caryatids are all copies; the originals are in the **Acropolis Museum,** a low structure at the back of the site. Also housed here are the remains of the Parthenon friezes that have remained in Athens and a 6th-century kouros (stylized male figure) carrying a calf across his shoulders.

The Acropolis entrance is on the west end of the site, reached from a path off Dioskoúon and Theorías Sts. ☎ *01/321-0219.* **Admission:** *2,000Dr ($7.15) adults, 1,000Dr ($3.55) students.* **Open:** *Summer hours are Mon–Fri 8am–7pm, Sat–Sun 8:30am–7pm. Winter hours vary widely, but are usually much shorter, and the Acropolis is occasionally closed in the early afternoon. Call the tourist office for details and precise hours for this year.*

Extra! Extra!

Looking down the south side of the Acropolis, you'll see the half-moons of two theaters. The enormous, mostly ruined one on the east end is the **Theater of Dionysos,** built in 330 B.C. (entrance on Dionyssíou Aeropayítou; admission 500Dr/$1.80). Near the Acropolis entrance lies the **Odeum of Heródes Átticus,** built in A.D. 174 and restored in recent centuries to host concerts during the Athens Festival from June to October (call the festival office at ☎ **01/322-1459** or the Odeum at ☎ **01/323-2771** for details).

The Ancient Agora (Market)

The Acropolis was in reality just a religious seat; the *real* daily life of Athens revolved around the Agora, or marketplace. Like the Forum in Rome, little remains today beyond a dusty bowl filled with scrubby trees, crumbling pediments among the grass, and the outlines of former temples and buildings marked by stubby rows of broken column bases. Still, it will take you a good two hours to pick over the rubble and reconstructed bits—longer for real antiquities buffs. The two most impressive remains are the **Hephaisteion,** built between 449 and 444 B.C. (it's one of the best preserved Greek Doric temples in the world), and the reconstructed **Stoa of Attalos.**

The monumental **Stoa of Attalos** was first raised in the 2nd century B.C. and rebuilt in the 1950s to house the Agora's intriguing museum, whose most fascinating relics document some of the systems used by the ancients to implement their

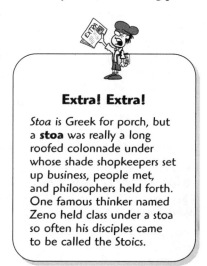

Extra! Extra!

Stoa is Greek for porch, but a **stoa** was really a long roofed colonnade under whose shade shopkeepers set up business, people met, and philosophers held forth. One famous thinker named Zeno held class under a stoa so often his disciples came to be called the Stoics.

551

famous democratic process. There are bronze ballots for jury votes; jurors cast a solid bronze axle if they felt the man on trial was innocent; they cast an empty one if they found the defendant's story as hollow as the rod. A marble allotment machine with a crank and colored balls bears a remarkable resemblance to modern Lotto machines and once determined who would serve jury duty for the year. There's also a fine collection of broken pottery shards called *óstraka,* on which once a year Athenians scribbled the name of any man thought to be growing too powerful and hence a threat to the democracy. If any person gained a majority of *óstraka* with his name on it, he would be *ostracized,* or banished, from Athens for 10 years.

At the northwestern foot of the Acropolis Hill, just southwest of Monasteráki Square. ☎ *01/321-0185.* **Admission:** *1,200Dr ($4.30) adults, 600Dr ($2.15) students.* **Open:** *Daily 8:30am–3:45pm.*

Archeological Museum

This museum is one of the world's truly great archeological museums, a testament to the glory of Greece and the beauty of its art and culture hundreds of years before the rise of Rome and thousands of years before Columbus set sail for America. I'd buy a catalog guide when you enter because the collections are hard to wrap your mind around without some guidance and plenty of background info. Allow yourself three hours for even a cursory run-through. Aspiring archeologists will want to stay most of the day and perhaps come back for seconds the next day.

Many of the most striking works are life-sized and oversized bronzes from Athens's Golden Age in the 400s B.C.—Poseidon on the verge of throwing his (now missing) trident, a galloping horse mounted by a tiny child jockey, the "Marathon Boy" striking a disco pose. Most of these bronzes were preserved at the bottom of the sea in shipwrecks and rediscovered by divers in the late 19th and 20th centuries.

From even earlier centuries are fluidly simplistic Cycladic figures from 3,000 B.C. (look for the tiny harp player), Minoan frescoes from Santoríni, and Mycenean gold hordes from 1600 to 1100 B.C. (the incorrectly named "Mask of Agamemnon" is among these treasures). From the 7th and 6th centuries B.C. is a collection of kouros—attractive young men with cornrow hair, their arms rigidly at their sides as they take one step forward. These highly stylized figures were adapted from Egyptian models and set the standard in Greek art until the more anatomically correct and naturalistic Classical period came in full swing. Among the later Roman sculpture is a 1st-century A.D. bronze equestrian statue of Emperor Augustus, also fished out of the sea.

44 Patissíon (October 28 Avenue; several long blocks north of Omónia Square). ☎ *01/821-7717.* **Bus/trolley:** *2, 4, 5, 9, 11, 12, 15, 18.* **Admission:** *2,000Dr ($7.15) adults, 1,000Dr ($3.55) students.* **Open:** *Mon 11am–5pm, Tues–Fri 9am–5pm, Sat–Sun 8:30am–3pm.*

Greek History in a Nutshell

Civilization in Greece starts with the Bronze Age (around 3,000 B.C.) and on the islands. This 3rd millennium B.C. is dominated by the Cycladic culture, the source of all those minimalist statuettes. The first half of the 2nd millennium B.C. sees the Minoan trading empire controlling the Aegean Sea from bases such as Crete and Santoríni. But Mycean warriors are already taking control by 1600 B.C., and the volcanic eruption of Santoríni in 1525 B.C. sounds the death knell of the Minoans. Mycenean rule ends with a bang around 1250 to 1200 B.C. with King Agamemnon's destruction of Troy (starring Achilles, Hector, the Trojan Horse, and Helen).

In the 8th and 7th centuries B.C., Greece sees the rise of city-states such as Athens. These powers form Magna Graecia, or Greater Greece, taking control of most of the coastline of the Aegean and Black Seas, along with bits of northern Africa and southern Italy. By the 5th century, allied Athens and Sparta trounce the rival Persians and kick off the Classical era of democracy, art and architecture (the Parthenon, for example), philosophy (Socrates and Plato), and trade. Athens rises to be the main city of Greece by 478 B.C. This time is considered the Golden Age.

The Macedonians under King Philip II come nipping at Greece's heels in 338 B.C. Philip's son Alexander (the Great) conquers everything from Greece to Egypt to India and inaugurates an ancient sort of multiculturalism, where eastern and western ideas and styles merge to form a new basis for western culture. The Romans come a-conquerin' in the 2nd century B.C., holding sway for about 600 years until their empire divides in 395 A.D., and Greece becomes a capital of the Byzantine empire. Ottoman Turks conquer the area in the 14th century and quarrel over control of Greece with the Venetians for a few centuries. Greece gets tired of both of them and boots them out in the 19th century, after which a series of kings, democracies, dictators, and even theocracies keep taking over the state. Things have been fairly stable since 1974, but the current democratic government has only been in place since 1990, so stay tuned.

Goulandris Museum of Cycladic and Ancient Greek Art

Of all the other museums in town, the Goulandris is best if you have another hour or two to spare. The collections celebrate the art and hauntingly simple sculpture of the Cycladic tradition, which dates back to 3,000 B.C. If the style of these sculptures seems familiarly modern, it's because famed 20th-century artists such as Brancusi, Henry Moore, Modigliani, and Picasso were all inspired by these forms, which minimalize the figure to a very basic set of lines and shapes that manages both to capture fundamental humanity and to imbue it with an ethereal timelessness and spirituality. The second floor of the museum houses ancient Greek pieces, many from the 5th-century B.C. Golden Age.

4 Neophýtou Douká Kolonáki. ☎ *01/722-8321.* **Admission:** *400Dr ($1.40).* **Open:** *Mon, Wed, Fri 10am–4pm, Sat 10am–3pm.*

Other Fun Stuff to Do

➤ **Wander the city in search of less touristy ruins.** Everyone rushes to the Acropolis, and most make their way to the Agora and the Archeological Museum too, but then the vast majority of visitors take off for the islands, leaving the rest of Athens's rich archeological heritage to the few who stay an extra day and explore a bit. The best of the rest includes **Hadrian's Arch** (on Amalías Avenue, between Vasilissis Olgas and Dionissiou Streets), through which the Roman emperor marched in A.D. 132 to inaugurate the humongous **Temple of the Olympian Zeus.** Built on and off between 515 B.C. and A.D. 132, the temple measures 360 by 143 feet. Fifteen of the original 104 columns remain, each a towering 56 feet high.

Bet You Didn't Know

Note the small stream running through Athens' ancient cemetery. Thousands of years ago, this was a modest river whose banks gave up the clay that made the reputation of early Athenian potters. Their craft was named after this area: Keramikós (or, if you prefer, ceramics).

The octagonal **Tower of the Wind** (where Eolou Avenue ends at Pelopída Street), was built in the 1st century B.C. and once held a water clock. In the 18th century, it was a religious stage where whirling dervishes did their spinning dance. The **Keramikós** (500 yards from the Agora on Ermoú Street), an ancient cemetery, was outside the ancient city walls—some of which can still be seen here along with the important ancient city gates. The archeological site contains roads lined with tombs and a section of the Sacred Way.

➤ **Witness the Changing of the Guard.** The Athens version of this spectator march is much more entertaining than its London counterpart. The guards have pompom-toed shoes and a truly comical stifflegged marching style that's executed with all the due solemnity of Monty Python's "Silly Walks" skit. They stand at attention in front of the Parliament building and march back and forth in front of the Tomb of the Unknown Soldier (both are on Sýntagma Square), and every Sunday at 11am the duty rotates in a parading ceremony.

➤ **Soak up Some Traditional Music and Dancing.** Clap your hands, feel the music, dance like crazy. All across Athens, **Bouzoúki clubs**—named after the mandolin-like instrument so often played there—will introduce you to traditional folk music and dancing, be it the *rebétika* tunes of the urban underclass or foot-tapping *dimotiká* country folk music. Check before smashing plates, though; many clubs no longer allow you to express your appreciation in the traditional Greek manner (the places that still do will charge you by the plate or let you buy them before the show by the dozen). Most clubs these days are tourist-oriented, but they are still a lot of fun; the waiters will show you the steps to some simple dances. Things really start hopping around 11pm, but get there early to get a good seat (of course, it helps to be properly liqoured up). The further you go from the the Pláka neighborhood, the more authentically Greek these places get.

For good *rebétika* action, try **Rebétiki Istorís** (☎ **01/642-4937**), 181 Ippókratous St.; **Dias** (☎ **01/832-6888**), 25 Ionías and Ayíou Melétiou; or **Fantastiko** (☎ **01/922-8902**), 140 Syngroú Ave. One of the best *dimotiká* clubs is **Taverna Mostroú** (☎ **01/324-2441**), 22 Mnissikléos St. *Athenscope* magazine will point you toward more. For the most authentic, artistic folk dancing, check out a show put on by the troupe of the **Dora Stratou Folk Dance Theater** (☎ **01/ 924-4395**) nightly at 10:30pm on Philopáppou Hill.

Get Outta Town: Day Trips & Excursions

Most folks come to Greece for two reasons: to dig into an ancient culture and/or to kick back and chill out on a sun-bleached island. Archeology-wise, it's hard to beat the site at Delphi, both for its interesting artifacts and the sheer beauty of its mountain setting. It's a welcome respite after the relentless traffic and noise of Athens. But perhaps you're itching to island-hop—and with the country's more than 6,000 islands (though fewer than 200 are inhabited), that's a lot of hopping. For my island escape, I've picked Santoríni (also called Thira). Though geographically the farthest from Athens, it has an established tourist infrastructure that makes the island quite accessible for the first-time visitor. Santoríni offers several fascinating ancient sites, as well as quaint seaside towns, a thriving nightlife, and oh yeah, truly excellent beaches.

Consulting the Oracle at Delphi

If I had to choose between Athens and Delphi as the only archeological site to visit in Greece, Delphi would win hands down. The ancients considered this place the center of the world, and they couldn't have picked a prettier spot for it. Delphi sits halfway up a mountainside, with the impressively craggy Mount Parnassos surrounding the site and a lush, narrow valley of olive trees stretching below it down to the azure Gulf of Corinth. Six buses make the three-hour trip daily from Athens, but if you're arriving in Greece by ferry, I'd suggest taking the bus here from the ferry terminal in Patras, spending the day and night in Delphi, and continuing on to Athens the next morning.

Modern Delphi clings to the valley edge, a two-road town with little streets snaking between the two. The bus lets you off at the west end, and the archeological site is just under a mile's stroll from the east end. Many visitors start at the museum, which you pass along the way to the ruins, but I advise that you rush straight to the outdoor archeological area early in the morning to beat the crowds and the heat. The ruins are also extremely evocative and will get you in the right frame of mind for appreciating the more intellectual experience of perusing the museum's statues and treasures.

Time-Savers

Although you can conceivably do Delphi as a single long day trip from Athens (the site and museum take at least three to four hours), it makes more sense, and is much more fun, to stay the night. Delphi is a lovely, sleepy town removed from the hectic pace of the city. The **tourist office (☎ 0265/ 89-920)** is at 44 Odós Frideríkis.

The **Sanctuary of Apollo (☎ 0265/82-313)**, the main ruins complex, clings to and extends up the lower slopes of Mount Parnassos. Your visit follows the **Sacred Way,** lined with the ruined treasuries of Greek city-states who vied with each other to offer the greatest riches to the sanctuary; just after the first bend in the Sacred Way, the **Athenian Treasury** is a remarkably well-preserved example. The vast plateau ringed with column stumps was once the inner sanctum of this holy site, the Doric **Temple of Apollo.** It was here that pilgrims came from all over the western world to consult the oracle (see "Bet You Didn't Know"). Earthquakes, pillaging, and landslides have all but destroyed the temple's partially underground chambers, where the business of sacrificing and producing cryptic predictions was conducted. The only sounds you'll hear today are the chirps of birds, the babble of tourists, and the prophecy of the winds.

At the top of the site is the 4th-century B.C. **theater,** the best-preserved of its kind in Greece (the Romans helped by rebuilding it about 2,000 years ago). It was here that musicians and performers vied for honors in the Pythian Games, second only to the Olympic Games (but because they were in honor of Apollo—god of poets and inventor of the lyre—the games were more cultural than physical). The view overlooking the site from up here is fantastic, but you can climb even further up to the long, tree-rimmed **stadium,** begun in the 6th century B.C. and site of the Pythian Games' athletic contests.

Exit the Sanctuary of Apollo site and continue down the main road around the bend. Below you rest the most beautiful ruins at Delphi, occupying the **Marmaria**—so named because later Greeks used its gymnasium and temples as a marble quarry. The most striking sight is the remains of the small round temple called **tholos,** built in 380 B.C. in an elongated Doric style. In the 1930s, three of an original 20 columns that made up the outer shell of this rotund temple were re-erected and a section of the lintel replaced on top. The effect of the sun setting behind it is superb. Admission to the ruins as a whole is 1,200Dr ($4.30) for adults, 900Dr ($3.20) for seniors, and 600Dr ($2.15) for students. The ruins are open Monday to Friday 7:30am to 6:30pm (5:30pm in winter), Saturday and Sunday 8:30am to 3pm.

Bet You Didn't Know

Kings and peasants traveled hundreds of miles to Delphi to have their fortunes told by the preeminent soothsayer of the Mediterranean world. A 50-year-old woman named Pythia was the Oracle of Delphi—in high season, three Pythias would work in shifts. Pythia's job was to chew on bay leaves, sit on a tripod over a fissure in a rock, breathe in the fumes rising from beneath, and then speak the wisdom of Apollo in tongues. A priest was on hand to interpret this message for the pilgrim, who'd spent the morning sacrificing animals at the altar and inscribing his question on a tablet. The Delphic oracle was consulted before any major undertaking. Although she was widely known to be the most truthful and accurate of all the seers, her answers were patently cryptic or vague, leaving wide room for interpretation. King Croesus came here just before launching war on Persia, and Pythia's priest dutifully reported that if the king went ahead with his plans, he'd "destroy a great empire." The oracle didn't bother to mention that it was Croesus's own empire that would crumble.

Delphi's **Archeological Museum** (☎ **0265/82-312**) is second only to the one in Athens. Among its treasures are 7th century B.C. kouri (those stylized statues of youths) and gifts that once comprised the Sacred Way's treasuries; among items once offered by those competing city-states are statues of ivory and a wooden bull sheathed in hammered silver and gold. Don't miss the winged sphinx of the Naxians, and the museum's pride, a bronze charioteer from 474 B.C., who still grips a few of the reins that once controlled a mighty statue group of horses. Also here is the Omphalós, or "Navel Stone," a nub of rock that once marked the very center of the world, under the Temple to Apollo (see "Extra! Extra!"). Admission rates are the same as for the ruin sites; the museum is open Monday 11am to 5:30pm, Tuesday to Friday 7:30am to 6:30pm, and Saturday and Sunday 8:30am to 3pm.

The **Taverna Vackchos** (☎ **0265/82-448**) at 31 Odós Apóllonos near the bus stop, is an utterly simple but delicious and inexpensive restaurant with great views. Stay the night at the revamped **Hotel Hermes** (☎ **0265/ 82-318,** fax: 0265/82-639), 27 Odós Frideríkis, where modern doubles run 11,000Dr ($39.30).

Extra! Extra!

How did the Greeks determine that the world's bellybutton was to be found at Delphi? Myths describe how Zeus, in a cartographic mood, let loose two eagles at opposite ends of the Earth (which, of course, was flat back in those days). Because the birds flew directly toward each other at an identical speed, where they bonked heads and fell to the ground marked the world's central point.

Sunning on Santoríni

Santoríni (Thíra in Greek) lies in the Cyclades, a long string of islands strewn with ruins and populated by fishermen and sun-worshippers. The last island in the chain, far out in the Aegean Sea, it beckons with a siren call of sunny beaches and the indulgent good life. Santoríni is a volcanic crescent—a sheer black cliff slashed with red stone and curving protectively around a caldera of green water where newer volcanic cones still hiss and smoke. This sliver of land is spotted with black-sand beaches, vineyards, whitewashed villages, and the excavations of ancient cities.

Santoríni's charms have not gone unnoticed—it is one of the most heavily visited of all the Greek islands. In July and August, it can get brutally crowded and seem like one big disco, a latter day homage to Dionysian hedonism. But in spring and fall, when the visiting hordes ebb, Santoríni still shines with that fishing village magic; it becomes the prototypical "island in the sun."

Bet You Didn't Know

Santoríni was a circular island volcano until an eruption in the 1600s B.C. blew half the island into the air, creating massive tidal waves, ashfall, and earthquakes that swept the Aegean—an event thought by many to have helped destroy the Minoan civilization, which was centered on Crete. Akrotíri, a rich Minoan city, was here on Santoríni, and some theorists are convinced that it was this city's volcanic destruction, on the brink of recorded history, that served as the source of the mythology surrounding a "lost continent." In other words, welcome to Atlantis.

Several daily **flights** from Athens make the trip in an easy 50 minutes. Most **ferry** companies offer two daily boats from Athens's Piraeus port; that trip takes 10 to 12 hours, often stopping at other Cycladic islands along the way. Buses on the island take you from the airport or ferry port to the main town of **Firá.**

Most visitors flock to Santoríni with just one thing in mind—the beach. The island's best is the 4½ miles of black pebbles and sand called **Kamári Beach** on the southeast shore of the island (horribly crowded in July and August). Other non-historical diversions include shopping at the island's overabundance of boutiques and sampling the fine wine produced from the rich volcanic soil, but try to fit in an excursion to Santoríni's two most impressive archeological sites.

On the island's southern tip lie the ruins of the wealthy Minoan city of **Akrotíri.** Covered excavations of the streets, shops, and houses in this 4,000-year-old city have been going on since the 1930s, so you can wander this emerging ghost town, which was already dead and gone 1,000 years before Athens's heyday. Buses run here regularly and admission is 1,250Dr

($4.45). The site is open daily from 8:30am to 3pm; your best bet is to visit in the early morning to beat the crowds and the heat. The nearby **Red Beach** is good for lunch and a swim afterwards.

Time-Savers

By plane, many people make Santoríni a day trip from Athens, which I suppose is possible if you simply cannot do without a Greek island but *only* have 24 hours. As packed as the island gets, these day trippers (and those who call here for an afternoon cruise break) make high noon the most crowded time. If you stay the night you can get a friendlier, less crowded take on Santoríni. I'd give the island two to four days if you can. There's no official **tourist office,** but the private agency Kamari Tours (☎ **0286/22-666**), two blocks south of the main square in Firá, has lots of good information. They can help you find a hotel or arrange guided visits to the island's sights.

Ancient Thíra, 1,200 feet above Kamári Beach, was the capital of the island under its second incarnation starting around 900 B.C. The ruins here are out in the open, so considerably less is left standing than at Akrotíri. But here you can cap off an exploration of the buildings (300 to 145 B.C.) with a picnic overlooking the sea and shaded by scrubby trees or an ancient portico still supported by Doric columns. This site is free to enter, but you'll have to arrange some way to visit because it's off any beaten path. Take the bus to Kamári, which lets you off at the bottom of a rather steep and trying 2½-mile hike up to the site. At the bus stop, mule drivers offer to take you up and around on a half-day tour for 4,000Dr ($14.30). The other alternative is to pay for a round-trip excursion from Firá by taxi, which should run you about 12,000Dr ($42.85). The site is open Tuesday to Saturday 9am to 2:30pm and Sunday 9am to 1pm.

Dollars & Sense

Santoríni is an unabashed traveler's mecca. The summertime feeding frenzy of the local tourism industry often drives unscrupulous types to take advantage of visitors dazzled by the sun glinting off all those whitewashed houses. Have fun, but play it safe. Scrutinize every restaurant menu and especially the bill for hidden charges, examine all purchases carefully before putting money down, and make sure all the hotel charges are agreed upon before you take a room.

The main town of Firá also has a small but exquisite **archeological museum** (☎ 0286/22-217), with finds from the island's digs as well as some early Cycladic figurines. Admission is 800Dr ($2.85) for adults, 600Dr ($2.15) for seniors, and 400Dr ($1.40) students; it's open Tuesday to Sunday from 8:30am to 3pm.

You can dine lightly in Firá at **Kástro** (☎ 0286/22-503); the location across from the cable car terminus draws hordes of day trippers, but the snacks and sandwiches and stellar views of the volcanic crater are worth it. For a more romantic evening, hit **Aris Restaurant** (☎ 0286/22-480), Odós Ayíou Miná; this converted winery serves amazing *mezédes* and moussáka. Beach snacks in Kamári can be had at **Alexis Grille** (no phone) in a pine grove at the beach's north end. For more refined international food, try **Camille Stephani** (☎ 0286/31-716), just 500 yards from the bus stop.

Firá is a bit noisy and touristy, but it has by far the highest concentration of hotels. (If you want to get under the skin of Santoríni, stay in one of the smaller villages.) Try to score a room with a view of the caldera, which is just what you'll get with the 30,000Dr ($107.15) doubles at **Loucas Hotel** (☎ 0286/22-480, fax: 0286/24-882). To stay on the beach at Kamári, try the aptly named **Kamári Beach Hotel** (☎ 0286/31-216, fax: 0286/31-243), a resorty place whose 30,000Dr ($107.15) doubles all have balconies for taking in the view of the beach and the sea. Many hotels on the island, including these two, are only open April 15 to October 15. In the off-season, the hotel demand doesn't quite fill up the supply that's left, plus you can easily negotiate for a private room (see "Dollars & Sense").

Dollars & Sense

As on most Greek islands, your boat will be met by touts who want to rent you a private room. In Greece, this is often a pretty good bet, so long as you ask questions before setting off with them and don't agree to *anything* until you see the room. Private rooms are often the only recourse if you arrive in July or August without reservations. Most rooms run from 6,000Dr ($21.40) in low season to as high as 15,000Dr ($53.55) in summer.

National Tourist Boards

The official Web site of the European Travel Commission is
www.visiteurope.com.

Austrian National Tourist Office

> **In the United States:** P.O. Box 1142, New York, NY 10108-1142
> (☎ **212/944-6880**); 500 N. Michigan Ave., Suite 1950, Chicago, IL
> 60611 (☎ **312/644-8029**); P.O. Box 491938, Los Angeles, CA 90049
> (☎ **310/477-3332**).

> **In Canada:** 1010 Sherbrooke St. W., Suite 1410, Montréal, PQ H3A
> 2R7 (☎ **514/849-3709**); 2 Bloor St. E., Suite 3330, Toronto, ON M4W
> 1A8 (☎ **416/967-3381**); Suite 1380, Granville Square, 200 Granville
> St., Vancouver, BC V6C 1S4 (☎ **604/683-5808**).

> **In the United Kingdom:** 30 St. George St., London W1R 0AL
> (☎ **0171/629-0461**).

> **E-mail:** None.

> **Web site:** www.anto.com

Belgian Tourist Office

> **In the United States:** 780 Third Ave., New York, NY 10017 (☎ **212/
> 758-8130**).

> **In Canada:** P.O. Box 760 NDG, Montréal, PQ H4A 3S2 (☎ **514/
> 489-8965**).

> **In the United Kingdom:** 29 Prince St., London W1R 7RG (☎ **0171/
> 629-3777**).

> **E-mail:** belinfo@nyxfer.blythe.org

> **Web site:** www.visitbelgium.com

British Tourist Authority

> **In the United States:** 551 Fifth Ave., Suite 701, New York, NY 10176
> (☎ **800/462-2748** or 212/986-2200); 625 N. Michigan Ave., Suite
> 1510, Chicago, IL 60611 (☎ **312/787-0464**).

In Canada: 111 Avenue Rd., Suite 450, Toronto, ON M5R 3J8 (☎ 416/961-8124).

In Australia: Level 16, Gateway, 1 Macquarie Place, Sydney, NSW 2000 (☎ 02/9377-4400).

In New Zealand: Suite 305, Dilworth Bldg., Customs and Queen streets, Auckland 1 (☎ 09/303-1446).

E-mail: travelinfo@bta.org.uk

Web site: www.vistibritain.com

Czech Tourist Authority

In the United States: 1109 Madison Ave., New York, NY 10028 (☎ 212/288-0830).

In Canada: P.O. Box 198, Exchange Tower, 130 King St. W, Suite 715, Toronto, ON M5X 1A6 (☎ 416/367-3432).

In the United Kingdom: 95 Great Portland St., London W1M 5RA (☎ 0171/291-9920).

E-mail: nycenter@ny.czech.cz

Web site: wwwczech.cz/new_york

French Government Tourist Office

In the United States: 444 Madison Ave., 16th Floor, New York, NY 10022 (☎ 212/838-7800); 676 N. Michigan Ave., Suite 3360, Chicago, IL 60611 (☎ 312/751-7800); 9454 Wilshire Blvd., Suite 715, Beverly Hills, CA 90212 (☎ 310/271-6665). To request information at any of these offices, call the **France on Call hotline** at ☎ 900/990-0040 (50¢ per minute).

In Canada: Maison de la France/French Government Tourist Office, 1981 av. McGill College, Suite 490, Montréal, PQ H3A 2W9 (☎ 514/288-4264).

In the United Kingdom: Maison de la France/French Government Tourist Office, 178 Piccadilly, London, W1V 0AL (☎ 0891/244-123).

In Australia: French Tourist Bureau, 25 Bligh St., Sydney, NSW 2000 (☎ 02/9231-5244).

E-mail: info@francetourism.com

Web site: www.fgtousa.org or www.francetourism.com

German National Tourist Office

In the United States: 122 E. 42nd St., 52nd Floor, New York, NY 10168 (☎ 212/661-7200); 11766 Wilshire Blvd., Suite 750, Los Angeles, CA 90025 (☎ 310/575-9799).

In Canada: 175 Bloor St. E., North Tower, 6th Floor, Toronto, ON M4W 3R8 (☎ 416/968-1570).

In the United Kingdom: Nightingale House, 65 Curzon St., London, W1Y 8NE (☎ 0171/495-0081).

In Australia: Lufthansa House, 143 Macquarie St., 12th Floor, Sydney, NSW 2000 (☎ 02/9367-3890).

E-mail: gntony@aol.com

Web site: www.germany-tourism.de

Greek National Tourist Organization

In the United States: 645 Fifth Ave., 5th Floor, New York, NY 10022 (☎ 212/421-5777); 168 N. Michigan Ave., Suite 600, Chicago, IL 60601 (☎ 312/782-1084); 611 W. 6th St., Suite 2198, Los Angeles, CA 90017 (☎ 213/626-6696).

In Canada: 1300 Bay St., Upper Level, Toronto, ON M5R 3KB (☎ 416/968-2220); 1233 rue de la Montagne, Suite 101, Montréal, PQ H3G 1Z2 (☎ 514/871-1535).

In the United Kingdom: 4 Conduit St., London W1R D0J (☎ 0171/734-5997).

In Australia: 51-57 Pitt St., Sydney, NWS 2000 (☎ 02/9241-1663).

E-mail: None.

Web site: www.hellas.de or www.greektourism.com

Hungarian National Tourist Office

In the United States: 150 E. 58th St., New York, NY 10155 (☎ 212/355-0240).

In the United Kingdom: c/o Embassy of the Republic of Hungary, Trade Commission, 46 Eaton Place, London, SW1 X8AL (☎ 0171/823-1032).

E-mail: huntour@idt.net

Web site: www.hungarytourism.hu

Irish Tourist Board

In the United States: 345 Park Ave., New York, NY 10154 (☎ 800/223-6470 or 212/418-0800).

In Canada: 160 Bloor St. E., Suite 1150, Toronto, ON M4W 1B9 (☎ 416/929-2777).

In the United Kingdom: 150 New Bond St., London W1Y OAQ (☎ 0171/493-3201).

In Australia: 36 Carrington St., 5th Level, Sydney, NSW 2000 (☎ 02/9299-6177).

E-mail: info@irishtouristboard.com

Web site: www.ireland.travel.ie

Italian Government Tourist Board

In the United States: 630 Fifth Ave., Suite 1565, New York, NY 10111 (☎ **212/245-4822**); 401 N. Michigan Ave., Suite 3030, Chicago, IL 60611 (☎ **312/644-0990**); 12400 Wilshire Blvd., Suite 550, Beverly Hills, CA 90025 (☎ **310/820-0098**).

In Canada: 1 place Ville-Marie, Suite 1914, Montréal, PQ H3B 2C3 (☎ **514/866-7667**).

In the United Kingdom: 1 Princes St., London W1R 8AY (☎ **0171/408-1254**).

E-mail: None.

Web site: None.

Monaco Government Tourist Office

In the United States: 565 Fifth Ave., New York, NY 10017 (☎ **800/753-9696** or 212/286-3330); 542 S. Dearborn St., Suite 550, Chicago, IL 60605 (☎ **312/939-7836**).

In the United Kingdom: 3-8 Chelsea Garden Market, Chelsea Harbour, London, SW10 0XE (☎ **0171/352-9962**).

E-mail: mgto@monaco1.org

Web site: www.monaco.mc/usa

Netherlands Board of Tourism

In the United States: 355 Lexington Ave., 21st Floor, New York, NY 10017 (☎ **212/370-7360**); 225 N. Michigan Ave., Suite 1854, Chicago, IL 60601 (☎ **312/819-0300**).

In Canada: 25 Adelaide St. E., Suite 710, Toronto, ON M5C 1Y2 (☎ **416/363-1577**).

In the United Kingdom: 18 Buckingham Gate, London, SW1E 6LB (☎ **0171/828-7900**).

E-mail: go2holland@aol.com

Web site: www.goholland.com

Portuguese National Tourist Office

In the United States: 590 Fifth Ave., New York, NY 10036 (☎ **800/PORTUGAL** or 212/354-4403).

In Canada: 600 Bloor St. W., Suite 1005, Toronto, ON M4W 3B8 (☎ **416/921-7376**).

In the United Kingdom: 1-5 New Bond St., London, W1Y 0NP (☎ **0171/493-3873**).

E-mail: aavila@portugal.org

Web site: www.portugal.org

Scandinavian Tourist Boards

In the United States: P.O. Box 4649, Grand Central Station, New York, NY 10163 (☎ **212/949-2333** or 212/885-9700); 8929 Wilshire Blvd., Beverly Hills, CA 90211 (☎ **213/854-1549**).

In the United Kingdom: The **Danish Tourist Board,** 55 Sloane St., London SW1X 95Y (☎ **0171/259-5959**); the **Swedish Travel and Tourism Council,** 73 Welbeck St., London W1M 8AN (☎ **0171/724-5869**).

E-mail: info@gosweden.org

Web sites: www.visitdenmark.com or www.gosweden.org

Switzerland Tourism

In the United States: 608 Fifth Ave., New York, NY 10020 (☎ **212/757-5944**); 150 N. Michigan Ave., Suite 2930, Chicago, IL 60601 (☎ **312/630-5840**); 222 N. Sepulveda Blvd., Suite 1570, El Segundo, CA 90245 (☎ **310/335-5980**).

In Canada: 154 University Ave., Suite 610, Toronto, ON M5H 3Y9 (☎ **416/971-9734**).

In the United Kingdom: Swiss Centre, Swiss Court, London, W1V 8EE (☎ **0171/734-1921**).

E-mail: stnewyork@switzerlandtourism.com

Web site: www.switzerlandtourism.com

Tourist Office of Spain

In the United States: ☎ **888/OK-SPAIN.** 666 Fifth Ave., 35th Floor, New York, NY 10103 (☎ **212/265-8822**); 845 N. Michigan Ave., Suite 915E, Chicago, IL 60611 (☎ **312/642-1992**); 8383 Wilshire Blvd., Suite 960, Beverly Hills, CA 90211 (☎ **213/658-7188**); 1221 Brickell Ave., Suite 1850, Miami, FL 33131 (☎ **305/358-1992**).

In Canada: 2 Bloor St. W., 34th Floor, Toronto, ON M4W 3E2 (☎ **416/961-3131**).

In the United Kingdom: 57 St. James's St., London SW1 (☎ **0171/499-0901**).

In Australia: 203 Castlereagh St., Suite 21A (P.O. Box 675), Sydney, NSW 2000 (☎ **02/9264-7966**).

E-mail: oetny@here-i.com

Web site: www.okspain.org

Airlines & Rental Car Companies

Major North American Carriers

For the latest on airline Web sites, check **http://airline-online.com** or **http://www.itn.com**.

Air Canada ☎ **800/776-3000** in the United States, 800/555-1212 in Canada for local number; www.aircanada.ca

American Airlines ☎ **800/433-7300**; www.americanair.com

Canadian Airlines ☎ **800/426-7000** in United States, 800/665-1177 in Canada; www.cdnair.ca

Continental Airlines ☎ **800/231-0856**; www.flycontinental.com

Delta Airlines ☎ **800/241-4141**; www.delta-air.com

Northwest Airlines ☎ **800/447-4747**; www.nwa.com

Tower Air ☎ **800/221-2500**; www.towerair.com

TWA ☎ **800/892-4141**; www.twa.com

US Airways ☎ **800/622-1015**; www.usairways.com

European Carriers (National & Country-Affiliated Airlines)

Aer Lingus (Ireland) ☎ **800/223-6537**; www.aerlingus.ie

Aeroflot (Russia and the former Soviet Union) ☎ **888/340-6400**; www.aeroflot.ru

Air France ☎ **800/237-2747**; www.airfrance.com

Alitalia (Italy) ☎ **800/223-5730**; www.alitalia.it

Austrian Airlines ☎ **800/843-0002**; www.aua.com

British Airways ☎ **800/247-9297**; www.british-airways.com

Finnair (Finland) ☎ **800/950-5000**; www.us.finair.com

Iberia (Spain) ☎ **800/772-4642;** www.iberia.com

Icelandair (Iceland) ☎ **800/223-5500;** www.centrum.is/icelandair/front.html

KLM (Royal Dutch Airlines) ☎ **800/374-7747;** www.klm.nl

Lufthansa (Germany) ☎ **800/645-3880;** www.lufthansa.com

Olympic Airways (Greece) ☎ **800/223-1226;** agn.hol.gr/info/olympic1.htm

SAS (Scandinavian Airlines) ☎ **800/221-2350;** www.flysas.com

Swissair ☎ **800/221-4750;** www.swissair.com

TAP Air Portugal ☎ **800/221-7370;** www.TAP-AirPortugal.pt

Virgin Atlantic Airways (British) ☎ **800/862-8621;** www.fly.virgin.com

Major Car Rental Agencies

Avis ☎ **800/331-1212;** www.avis.com

Budget ☎ **800/527-0700;** www.budgetrentacar.com

Dollar (Europcar) ☎ **800/800-6000;** www.dollarcar.com

Hertz ☎ **800/654-3131;** www.hertz.com

National ☎ **800/227-7368;** www.nationalcar.com

The following companies specialize in Europe:

Auto-Europe ☎ **800/223-5555;** www.autoeurope.com

Europe by Car ☎ **800/223-1516,** 800/252-9401 in California, 212/581-3040 in New York City; www.europebycar.com

Kemwell ☎ **800/678-0678;** www.kemwell.com

Art & Architecture
Glossary of Terms

apse   The niche, often shaped as a half-cylinder, behind the altar of a church.

Art Deco   A 1920s to 1930s descendant of Art Nouveau in decorative arts and architecture that uses more expensive materials but simpler, somewhat more rectilinear and severe shapes and lines (still kitschy, though).

Art Nouveau   A 1880s to 1914 style in architecture, design, and decorative arts characterized by organic asymmetry, inventiveness, and flowing curving lines. It went by a different alias in every country, including Jugendstil (Germany), Liberty Style (Italy), and Modernisme (Spain's Catalan region).

baroque   A broad term describing the overwrought art style widely practiced from 1580 to the 1750s; the next big thing after the Renaissance and its mannerist offshoot. It's florid and self-indulgent, using curving, broken lines in architecture and a proliferation of colors, materials, illusory techniques, and large, complex compositions. It concentrated much more strongly than the Renaissance on unified ensembles of painting, architecture, sculpture, decorative arts, and design. Schlocky, but it lent itself well to the era of exceedingly flamboyant palace building.

Byzantine   The eastern-style, iconographic, and ethereal art and architecture of the Byzantine empire (headquartered in Constantinople, which is today Istanbul). Glittering gold mosaics and icons of the Madonna and Child were two influences seen in Western Europe, but it was ultimately supplanted by the Romanesque and later Gothic movements in Europe between the 900s and 1200s. The Byzantine style lasted from the 400s to 1453.

capital (of columns)   The top of a column. There are three "orders" of classical architecture based primarily on what the **capitals** look like. The simplest is **Doric,** with just a plain, square capital and often no base (the column runs straight into the floor). Next comes **Ionic,** whose capitals have a pair of big scrolls sticking out each end like Princess Leia's hair buns. Finally, there's **Corinthian,** whose capital is carved to look leafy.

caryatid   A column or pillar shaped like a woman.

classical   A general term applied to the art and especially sculpture and architecture of ancient Greece (especially the 5th century B.C. Golden Age) and ancient Rome.

cloister   An inner courtyard of a church, monastery, or convent; a spot for quiet reflection, often planted with small gardens and often ringed on all four sides by an open colonnade.

colonnade   Any row of columns supporting an entablature, roof, or series of arches (in which case it's usually called an *arcade*). Colonnades often form the open, outer side of a covered walkway.

Corinthian   See *capital (of columns)*.

cubism   Perhaps the 20th century's most important artistic experiment (from 1907 to 1930s), whereby Picasso, Braque, and followers tried to show that objects could be examined from all sides at once, not just from one perspective. Rather than try to create the illusion of depth on the flat plane of a canvas, the artists visually flattened and connected all the planes of an object on a single flat surface. In other words, cubism shows more than just the side of the object that's facing the artist. The cubists were heavily influenced by Cézanne's theories and African tribal art. The practical upshot? It's better than it looks.

Doric   See *capital (of columns)*.

flying buttress   A buttress is a structural support, often a stone pillar built in a ramp-like slope out from the side of a building to help support the weight of the walls. A flying buttress was a hallmark of Gothic architecture, a graceful span of arch connecting the outer, upper walls of a building and a vertical pillar beside it.

fresco   The technique of painting on wet plaster so the colors sink below the surface and bond with the wall; also the term for such a painting. A very popular way to decorate surfaces from ancient Greek and Roman times through the Renaissance and baroque periods (until the baroque artists started the popularity of oil on canvas).

frieze   The long horizontal portion of a Classical building that's being supported by all those columns is called an **entablature.** It's made up of three parts: the **architrave** (the bit that runs right across the tops of the column capitals), the **frieze** (the wide band in the middle, often decorated with a pattern or a series of carved reliefs), and the **cornice** (the thin strip at the top, usually projecting out a bit).

Georgian   An understated, elegant 18th-century neoclassical architectural style practiced throughout the British Isles during the reigns of Georges I, II, and III (1714 to 1820).

Gothic   A general term describing everything between the Romanesque and Renaissance eras (from the 1000s to the 1500s). More specifically, a late Medieval era in architecture and sculpture. In architecture, that meant churches with lots of stained glass, pointed arches, flying buttresses, and ribbed vaulting. In sculpture, it employed naturalistic figures of flowing lines and expressive faces. In painting, it was called "International Gothic," and it broke away from the stylized rigidity of the Byzantine school with a more naturalistic approach, which paved the way for the Renaissance. From the late Renaissance on, most people looked back on this era and found it coarse, crass, and barbaric, and they labeled it all after the name of one of the barbaric peoples who overran the Roman empire, the Goths (even though it was more accurately descended from the styles practiced by the Franks and Gauls of modern-day France).

Hellenistic   From *hellas,* the Greek word for Greece. A more flamboyant, experimental, and sometimes uninventive or ludicrous version of classicism's main guiding principles, and the homogenized artistic mainstay of the Mediterranean world from the end of Greece's classical Golden Age until Rome took over (330 to 27 B.C.). It started when Alexander the Great conquered just about everything and then melded eastern style and sensibility with traditional western Greek classicism. This style was prevalent from 5th century B.C. to 330 B.C.

impressionism   The original avant garde art, whereby artists such as Monet, Renoir, and Degas thumbed their painterly noses at realistic art of the establishment and began creating more expressive art with visible brushwork and a concentration on the effect light has on color and mood, instead of the more formal and traditional artistic preoccupations with form and line. Also see the box in Chapter 16. This movement lasted from 1872 to the 1890s.

Ionic   See *capital (of columns).*

Jugendstil   The somewhat restrained German variant on Art Nouveau.

Kouros   A Greek statue of a boy (though there were also female versions) from the 7th to 6th centuries B.C. Very stylized and rigid and heavily influenced by Egyptian models.

Liberty Style   The Italian version of Art Nouveau.

Mannerism   A 16th-century offshoot of the High Renaissance, an artistic movement that used increasingly garish colors (in painting), twisting poses (in painting and sculpture), and exaggerations of classicism (in architecture) to stretch Michelangelo's experiments with color, posing, and Renaissance ideals to their logical limits (1530-1600).

Modernisme   Catalán version of Art Nouveau; Gaudí was its most prolific and innovative perpetrator in Barcelona.

Moorish   Anything pertaining to the Moors, a Muslim people of Arabic origins who lived in and controlled most of Spain and Portugal (along with the Middle East and North Africa) from A.D. 711 to 1492.

nave   The main aisle of a church, usually containing the main doors, main pews, choir, and/or apse. The altar is usually either at one end of the nave or at the intersection of the nave and transept.

571

neoclassical   An 18th century resurgence of interest in the sculpture and architecture of the classical world, brought on by a backlash against the excesses of the baroque and rococo styles and by the fledgling discipline of archeology, which was uncovering ancient sites of Greece and Rome. It was more a romanticized rather than scrupulously accurate version of classical forms, sometimes overemphasizing the mathematical rigidity and austere simplicity of the ancient orders and sometimes softening it up for contemporary tastes. This movement lasted from the 1750s to the early/mid-19th century.

neogothic   Also called Gothic Revival, this late-medieval style came back into vogue (albeit with some revisions) mainly in England and the United States (whole buildings) and Italy (mostly church facades) at the same time other tastes were exploring the neoclassical style. This style lasted from the mid-18th to the mid-19th centuries.

pediment   The triangle of space below the roof and above the frieze on the end walls of many classical temples. It's often filled with sculptural groups in low or high relief.

Renaissance   A French word meaning "rebirth," it refers to the period that started in Florence in the 15th century when humanist philosophy and a study of classical models led art and architecture to free themselves from static medieval traditions and explore both the emotional and scientific sides of art. The phenomenon of the Renaissance spread to literature and other arts and from Italy throughout all of Europe by the 17th century. This period lasted from 1401 through the 1750s.

rococo   If baroque was considered over the top, then rococo was garishly, ludicrously lavish. It remains one of the most wildly overdone and exceedingly flamboyant decorative styles ever perpetrated, kicked off by the court of Louis XV in France. Good taste was thrown to the wind. Rococo spaces were encrusted with expensive marbles, dripping with stuccoes, and otherwise impenetrably packed with excessive decoration. The artistic community quickly got aesthetic indigestion and retreated to the antacid simplicity of the neoclassical. This style lasted from the 1710s to the 1760s.

Romanesque   An early medieval form of architecture (decorated with stylized sculpture, charmingly crude vernacular frescoes, or Byzantine mosaics) marked by a heavy construction of thick walls and piers with tiny windows, all supported by low, rounded arches. In England, they called it the Norman style. This style lasted from A.D. 700s to the 1100s.

surrealism   Before virtual reality, artists such as Dalí and Magritte would use a very realistic painting style to create scenes that looked genuine but were physically impossible (elephants with long, jointed insects' legs, melting clocks, women with drawers instead of breasts, and so on). This style (which lasted from 1924 to the 1950s) was rich with symbolic imagery (Freudian, usually), and spread to sculpture, photography, and film as well.

transept   In Latin-cross (crucifix-shaped) churches, it's the shorter cross-arm of the floor plan. In Greek-cross (plus sign-shaped) churches, it's the cross arm of the floor plan that runs perpendicular to the nave.

Trompe l'oeil   French for "trick the eye," it's a particularly successful illusory painting technique—painting on a flat wall what appears to be a niche with a statue in it or making the ceiling of a church appear to open up into the heavens through a sky filled with angels and cherubs, for example.

Dictionary of Words & Phrases

English	French	Italian	German	Spanish
Thank you	Merci (mair-*see*)	Grazie (*grat*-tzee-yay)	Danke (*dahn*-kah)	Gracias (*grah*-thee-yahs)
Please	S'il vous plaît (seel-vou-*play*)	Per favore (pair fa-*vohr*-ray)	Bitte (*bih*-tuh)	Por favor (por fah-*bohr*)
Yes	Oui (wee)	Si (see)	Ja (yah)	Sí (see)
No	Non	No	No	No
Do you speak English?	Parlez-vous anglais? (par-lay-*vou* on-*glay*)	Parla Inglese? (par-la een-*glay*-zay)	Sprenchen Sie Englisch? (*zprek*-can zee *een*-glish)	Habla usted inglés? (*ah*-blah oo-*sted* een-*glais*)
I don't understand	Je ne comprende pas (zhuh nuh *cohm*-prohnd *pah*)	Non capisco (non ka-*peesk*-koh)	Ich verstehe night (eek fair-*shtay*-yuh neecht)	No comprendo (nohn cohm-*pren* doh)
I'm sorry	Je suis desolée (zhuh swee day-zoh-*lay*)	Mi dispiace (mee dees-pee-*yat*-chay)	Es tut mir leid (ehs toot meer lyd)	Lo siento (lo see-*yen*-toh)
How much is it?	Combien coûte? (coam-bee-*yehn* koot)	Quanto costa? (*kwan*-toh *coast*-ah)	Wieviel kostet es? (*vee*-feel *koh*-steht es)	Cuánto cuesta? (*kwan*-toh *kway*-stah)

574

English	French	Italian	German	Spanish
That's too much	C'est trop (say troh)	É troppo (ay *troh*-po)	Das ist zu teuer (dahs ihst tsoo *toy*-yer)	Eso es es demasiado caro (*ays*-oh day-mahs-*syah*-doh *kah*-roh)
Good day	Bonjour (bohn-*szourh*)	Buon giorno (bwohn *jour*-noh)	Guten tag (*goo*-tehn tahg)	Buenos días (*bway*-nohs *dee*-hs)
Good evening	Bon soir (bohn *swah*)	Buona sera (*bwoh*-nah *sair*-rah)	Guten Abend (*goo*-tehn *ah*-bnd)	Buenos tardes (*bway*-nohs *tar*-days)
Good night	Bon nuit (bohn *nwee*)	Buona notte (*bwoh*-nah *note*-tay)	Gute nacht (*goo*-teh nahckt)	Buenas noches (*bway*-nohs *noh*-chays)
Goodbye	Aurevoir (oh-ruh-*vwah*)	Arrivederci (ah-ree-vah-*dair*-chee)	Auf wiedersehen (owf *vee*-dair-zay-yen)	Adiós (ah-dee-*yohs*)
Excuse me (to get attention)	Excusez-moi (eh-skooze-ay-*mwa*)	Scusi (*skoo*-zee)	Entschuldigung, bitte (ent-*shool*-dee-gung *hih*-tuh)	Perdóneme? (pair-*dohn*-eh-meh)
Excuse me (to get past someone)	Pardon (pah-*rdohn*)	Permesso (pair-*meh*-so)	Gestatten Sie (ge-*shta*-ten zee)	Perdóneme (pair-*dohn*-eh-meh)
Where is?	Où est? (ou *eh*)	Dov'é (doh-*vay*)	Wo ist? (voh eest)	Dónde está? (*dohn*-day eh-*stah*)
...the bathroom	la toilette (lah twah-*let*)	il bagno (eel *bahn*-yoh)	die toilette (dee toy-*leht*-tah)	el servicio (el sair-*bee*-thee-yo)/ el baño (el *bahn*-yoh)

English	French	Italian	German	Spanish
...train station	la gare (lah gahr)	la stazione (lah stat-zee-*o*-nay)	der bahnhof (dair *bahn*-howf)	la estación (lah es-tah-thee-*yon*)
to the right	à droite (ah *dwa*)	a destra (ah *deh*-strah)	rechts (rekts)	a la derecha (ah lah deh-*ray*-chah)
to the left	à gauche (ah *goh*-sh)	a sinistra (ah see-*neest*-trah)	links (leenx)	a la (ah lah izquierda eeth-*kyair*-dah)
straight ahead	en avant (ahn ah-*vohn*) tout droit (too dwah)	avanti (ah-*vant*-tee) diritto (dee-*ree*-toh)	geradeaus (gair-*raad*-eh-ohws)	siga dere cho (*see*-gah deh-*ray*-cho)
ticket	un billet (uh bee-*yay*)	un biglietto (bee-*lyet*-toh)	eine fahrkarte (*eye*-nuh *faar*-kar-tuh)	un billete (oon beel-*yay*-tay)
first class	premiére classe (pruh-mee-*yair* klahs)	prima classe (*pree*-mah *clah*-say)	erste klasse (*air*-stuh klah-suh)	primera classe (pree-*mair*-ah *klah*-say)
second class	deuxiéme classe (duhz-zee-*yem* klahs)	seconda classe (say-*cohn*-dah *clah*-say)	zweite Klasse (*tsvy*-tuh klah-suh)	segunda classe (seh-*goon*-dah *klah*-say)
one way	aller (ah-*lay*)	solo andata (so-low ahn-*daht*-tah)	einfach (*ayn*-fahk)	ida (*ee*-dah)
round trip	aller-retour (ah-*lay*-ray-*tour*)	andata ritorno (ahn-*daht*-tah e ay ree-*tour*-noh)	hin und zurück (hin oont tzu-*ruwk*)	ida y vuelta (*ee*-dah ee *bwehl*-tah)
Just the supplement	Seulment le supplément (suhl-*mahn* luh sou-play-*mahn*)	Soltanto il supplemento (soal-tahn-toh eel sou-play-*men*- toh)	Nur der zuschlag (noor dair *tzu*-shlahg)	Sólo el suplemento (*soh*-loh el soo-play-*meyn*-toh)

English	French	Italian	German	Spanish
Just a seat reservation	Seulment une réservation (suhl-*mahn* oun ray- sair- vaht-tzsee-yon)	Soltanto una preno-tazione (soal-tahn-toh oo-nah pray-no-tah-tsee-*yohn*-nay)	Nur eine reservierung (noor *ai*-nuh rez-air *feer*-oong)	sólo una reserva (*soh*-loh *oo*-nah ree-*sair*-bah)
I have a Eurailpass	J'ai le Eurailpass (szhay luh you-rail *pahs*)	Ho il rail Eurailpass (oh eel *yoo*-pahs)	Ich habe eine Eurailpass (eek *ha*-buh *ai*-nuh *yoo*-rail-pas)	Yo tengo el Eurailpass (yo *tain*-go hel *yoo*-rail-pahs)
sleeping couchette	couchette (kou-*shet*)	una cucetta (*oo*-nah koo-*chet*-tah)	einen platz im schlafwagen (*eye* -nen plahtz eem *schlahf*-vah-gehn)	una litera (*oon*-ah lee-*tair*-ah)
berth in a sleeping car	une place wagon-lit (oou-n plahs en ahn vah goh-*lee*)	un posto nel vagone letto (oon *poh*-sto nell vah-*goan*-nay *let*-toh)	einen Platz im Liegewagen (*eye*-nen plahtz eem *lee*-guh-vah-gehn)	una litera en el coche cama (*oon*-ah lee-*tair*-ah en el *coh*-chay *kah*-mah)
track	quai (kay)	binario (been-*ar*-ree-yoh)	Gleis (glice)	el andén (el ahn-*dayn*)
hotel	un hôtel (ehn oh-*tel*)	un albergo (oon al-*bear*-goh)	ein hotel (eye'n hoh-*tehl*)	un hotel (oon oh-*tel*)
single room	une chambre pour une personne (oou-n *shaum*-bra pour oou-n pair-*sohn*)	uno singolo (*oo*-noh *seen*-go-loh)	ein Einzelzimmer (eye'n *eye'n*-tzehl-tzim-merr)	una habitación sencilla (*oo*- nah ah-bee-ta-thee-*yon* sen-*theey*-yah)

English	French	Italian	German	Spanish
double room with two beds	une chambre pour deux (oou-n *shaum*-bra pour douh)	una doppia con due letti (*oo*-nah *dope*-pee-ya cone *doo*-way *let*-tee)	ein mit Doppelzimmer zwei Einzelbetten (eye'n *doh*-pel-tzim-merr mitt tsvy *eyen*-tsell-beht-tehn)	una habitación doble con dos camas (*oo*-nah ah-bee-ta-thee-*yon* *doh*-blay kohn dohs *cah*-mas)
double room with one bed	une chambre avec un grand lit (oou-n *shaum*-bra ah-*vehk* ehn grawn lee)	una doppia col letto matrimoniale (*oo*-nah *dope*-pee-ya coal *let*-toh mat-tree-moan-nee-*yaal*-lay)	ein Doppelzimmer mit einem Doppelbett (eye'n *doh*-pel-tzim-merr mitt *eye*-nem *doh*-pell-bett)	una habitación doble con una cama matrimo-nial (*oo*-nah ah-bee-ta-thee-*yon* *doh*-blay kohn *oo*-nah *cah*-mah mah-tree-maon-*yaal*)
for two nights	pour deux soirs (pour douh swa)	per due notte (pair *doo*-way *noh*-tay)	für zwei nachts (fear tsvy nahkts)	por dos noches (poar dohs *noh*-chays)
with/without bath	avec (ah-*vek*)/sans (sahn) bain (baahn)	con (coan)/ senza (*sen*-zah) bagno (*bahn*-yoh)	mit (miht)/ ohne(*oh*-nuh) Bad (baad)	con (cohn)/ sin (seen) baño (*bah*-nyoh)
Is breakfast included?	C'est compris le petit déjeu-ner? (say coam-*pree* luh p'*tee* day-zhuh-*nay*)	é incluso la prima colazione? (ay in-*cloo*-soh lah *pree*-mah coal-laht-zee-*yoan*-nay)	Ist Früh-stück inbegrif-fen? (ihst *froo*-shtook *in*-beh-grih-fen)	Está incluido el desayuno? (eh-*stah* een-kloo-*wee*-doh el des-ah-*yoo*-noh)

English	French	Italian	German	Spanish
May I see the room?	Puis-je voir la chambre? (*pwee*-zhuh vwah lah *shawm*-bra)	Posso la camera? (*poh*-soh vedere veh-*dair*-eh lah *cah*-mair-rah)	Kann ich Zimmer das sehen? (kahn eek *tsih*-merr dahs *zay*-en)	Se puede ver la habitación? (say pweh-day bear lah ah-bee-tah-thee- *yohn*)
restaurant	un restaurant (uhn ray-stah-*rahn*)	un ristorante (oon rees-toh-*rahn*-tay)	ein restaurant (eye'n reh-stow-*rahn*)	un restaurante (oon res-tau-*rahn*-tay)
casual restaurant	un bistro (uhn bee-*stro*) / une brasserie (oon bra-sair-*rhee*)	una trattoria (oo-nah trah-toar-*rhee*-yah) / un'osteria (oon ohst-air-*ee*-yah)	bierhalle (*beer*-hall-uh)/ weinstube (*vine*-shtoo-buh)/ beisel (*bye*-zell)	una hosteria (*oo*-nah ohs-tair-*ee*-yah) / una posada (*oo*-nah poh-*sah*-dah)
table for two	un table pour deux (uhn *tah*-bluh pour douh)	una tavola per due (oo-nah *tah*-voal-lah pair *doo*-way)	einen tisch für zwei (*eye*-nen tish fyour tsvy)	una mesa para dos (*oo*-nah *meh*-sah *pa*-rah dohs)
I would like	Je voudrais (zhuh vou-*dray*)	Vorrei (voar-*ray*)	Ich möchte (eek *mowk*-tah)	Quisiera (kee-see-*yair*-ah)
...some (of)	un peu (de) (uhn puh (duh))	un po' (di) (oon poh (dee))	ein biß -chen (von) (eye'n *bih*-shen (fawn))	unos (de) (*oo*-nos (day))
...this/ that	ce (suh)/ ça (sah)	questo (*kway*-sto)/ quello (*kwel*-loh)	dieses (*dee*-zes)/ das (dahs)	éste (*eh*-stay)/ ése (*eh*-seh)
and	et (ay)	e (ay)	und (oond)	y (ee)

579

English	French	Italian	German	Spanish
...a glass of	une verre de (oun vair duh)	un bicchiere di (oon bee-key-*yair*-eh)	ein Glas von (eye'n glahs fohn)	un vaso de (oon *bah*-soh day)
...fizzy/ still water	eau gazeuse (oh gah-*zuhz*)/ non gazeuse (no gah-*zuhz*)	acqua gassata (*ah*-kwah gah-*saht*-tah)/non gassata (noan gah-*saht*-tah)	Mineralwasser mit Kohlensäure (*meen*-air-ahl-vah-sair mitt *koh*-len-zow-r)/ wasser (*vah*-sair)	agua mineral (*ah*-wah mee-nay-*rahl*)/ agua (*ah*-wah)
...red/white wine	vin rouge (vah roozhuh)/ blanc (blahn)	vino rosso (*vee*-noh *roh*-so)/ bianco (bee-*yahn*-koh)	Rotwein (*roht*-vine)/ Weisswein (*vice*-vine)	vino tinto (*bee*-noh *teen*-toh)/ blanco (*blahn*-coh)
...beer	biére (bee-*yair*)	birra (*beer*-a)	bier (beer)	una cerveza (*oo*-nah thair-*bay*-thah)
Check, please	La conte, s'il vous plaît (lah kohnt seel-vou-*play*)	Il conto, per favore (eel *coan*-toh pair fah-*voar*-ah)	Die Rechnung, bitte (dee *rek*-noong *bit*-tuh)	La cuenta por favor (lah *kwain*-tah fah-*bohr*)
Is service included?	Le service est-il compris? (luh sair-*vees* eh-*teal* coam-*pree*)	é incluso il servizio? (ay een-*clou*-so eel sair-*veet*-zee-yo)	Ist die Bedienung inbegriffen? (ihst dee beh-*dee*-nung *in*-beh-grih-fen)	Está el servicio incluido? (*eh*-stah el sair-bee-thee-yo een-clu-wee-doh)
When is it open?	Quand est-il ouvert? (coan eh-*teal* oo-*vair*)	Quando é aperto? (*kwan*-doh ay ah-*pair*-toh)	Welches sind die Öffnungszeiten? (vel-kehs zint dee *euf*-noongs-tsai-ten)	Cuándo abren? (*kwahn*-do *ah*-bren)
When does it close?	Quand est l'heure de fermeture? (coan eh lure duh fair-mah-*tour*)	Quando si chiude? (*kwan*-doh see key-*you*-day)	Wann schliesst es? (vahn shleest es)	Cuándo se cierra? (*kwahn*-do say *thee*-yair-rah)

English	French	Italian	German	Spanish
Yesterday	Hier (ee-*yair*)	Ieri (ee-*yair*-ee)	Gestern (geh-*stairn*)	Ayer (ah-*yair*)
Today	Aujoud'hui (ow-zhuhr-*dwee*)	Oggi (*oh*-jee)	Heute (*hoy*-tuh)	Hoy (oy)
Tomorrow	Demain (duh-*mehn*)	Domani (doh-*mahn*-nee)	Morgen (*mohr*-gen)	Mañana (mah-*nyah*-nah)
Monday	Lundi (luhn-*dee*)	Luned (loo-nay-*dee*)	Montag (*mohn*-taag)	Lunes (*loo*-nays)
Tuesday	Mardi (mahr-*dee*)	Marted (mar-tay-*dee*)	Dienstag (*deens*-taag)	Martes (*mahr*-tays)
Wednesday	Mercredi (mair-dray-*dee*)	Mercoled (mair-coh-lay-*dee*)	Mittwoch (*mitt*-voak)	Miércoles (*myair*-coh-lays)
Thursday	Jeudi (zhuh-*dee*)	Gioved (jo-vay-*dee*)	Donnerstag (*dohn*-ners-taag)	Jueves (*kway*-bays)
Friday	Vendredi (vawn-cruh-*dee*)	Venerdì (ven-nair-*dee*)	Freitag (*fry*-taag)	viernes (*byair*-nays)
Saturday	Samedi (saam-*dee*)	Sabato (*sah*-baa-toh)	Samstag (*zahmz*-taag)	Sábado (*sah*-bah-doh)
Sunday	Dimanche (*dee*-maansh)	Domenica (doh-*men*-nee-ka)	Sonntag (*zohn*-taag)	Domingo (doh-*meen*-goh)
1	un (uhn)	uno (*oo*-no)	eins (eye'nz)	uno (*oo*-noh)
2	deux (douh)	due (*doo*-way)	zwei (zv'eye)	dos (dohs)
3	trois (twah)	tre (tray)	drei (dr'eye)	tres (trays)
4	quatre (*kah*-truh)	quattro (*kwah*-troh)	vier (feer)	cuatro (*kwah*-troh)
5	cinq (sahnk)	cinque (*cheen*-kway)	fünf (foonf)	cinco (*theen*-koh)
6	six (sees)	sei (say)	sechs (zeks)	seis (says)
7	sept (sehp)	sette (*set*-tay)	sieben (*zee*-ben)	siete (see-*yay*-tah)
8	huit (hwhee)	otto (*oh*-toh)	acht (ahkt)	ocho (*oh*-choh)
9	neuf (nuhf)	nove (*no*-vay)	neun (noyn)	nueve (*nway*-beh)

English	French	Italian	German	Spanish
10	dix (dees)	dieci (dee-*yay*-chee)	zehn (tsain)	diez (*dee*-yaath)
11	onze (ownz)	undici (*oon*-dee-chee)	elf (elf)	once (*ohn*-thay)
12	douze (dooz)	dodici (*doh*-dee-chee)	zwölf (zvelf)	doce (*doh*-thay)
13	treize (trehz)	tredici (*tray*-dee-chee)	dreizehn (*dry*-tsain)	trece (*tray*-thay)
20	vingt (vahn)	venti (*vent*-tee)	zwanzig (*tzvahn*-tsig)	veinte (*bain*-tay)
30	trente (truhnt)	trenta (*trayn*-tah)	dreissig (*drys*-sig)	treinta (*train*-tah)
40	quarante (kah-*rant*)	quaranta (kwa-*rahn*-tah)	vierzig (*feer*-tsig)	cuarenta (kwa-*rayn*-tah)
50	cinquante (sahn-*kant*)	cinquanta (cheen-*kwahn*-tah)	fünfzig (*foonf*-tsig)	cincuenta (theen-*kwain*-tah)
60	soixante (swa-*sahnt*)	sessanta (say-*sahn*-tah)	sechzig (*zehk*-tsig)	sesenta (say-*sayn*-tah)
70	soixante-dix (swa-sahnt-*dees*)	settanta (seh-*tahn*-tah)	siebzig (*seeb*-tsig)	setenta (say-*tain*-tah)
80	quatre-vents (kat-tra-*vahnt*)	ottanta (oh-*tahn*-tah)	achtzig (*ahkt*-tsig)	ochenta (oh-*chain*-tah)
90	quatre-vents-dix (kat-tra-vahnt-*dees*)	novanta (no-*vahn*-tah)	neunzig (*noin*-tsig)	noventa (noh-*bain* tah)
100	cent (sant)	cento (*chen*-toh)	hundert (*hoon*-dairt)	ciento (thee-*yen*-toh)
1,000	mille (meel)	mille (*meel*-lay)	tausend (*tau*-zend)	mil (meel)
5,000	cinq mille (sank meel)	cinque milla (*cheen*-kway *meel*-lah)	fünftausend (*foonf*-tau-zend)	cinco mil (*theen*-koh meel)
10,000	dix mille (dees meel)	dieci milla (dee-*yay*-chee *meel*-lah)	zehntausend (*tsayn*-tau-send)	diez mil (*dee*-yaath meel)

Index

A

Aalsmeer (Netherlands), 297

Aare River (Switzerland), 10, 353, 363

Abbey Theatre (Dublin), 236

Academy of Fine Arts (Vienna), 336 (map), 344–45

Accademia (Florence), 444 (map), 451

Accademia (Venice), 474 (map), 484–85

Accommodations, 107–18
  Amsterdam, 281, 282–83 (map), 284–85
  Athens, 543, 544–45 (map), 546–47
  Barcelona, 522–23, 524–25 (map), 526
  bathrooms, 108–10
  without baths, 80, 109, 112
  Bern, 357–58, 359 (map)
  booking services, 112–14
  Dublin, 226–27, 228–29 (map), 230
  Edinburgh, 203, 204–5 (map), 206–7
  about European hotels, 107–8
  Florence, 442–43, 444–45 (map)
  hunting strategies, 110
  London, 177–81, 178–79 (map)

Madrid, 497, 498–99 (map), 500–501
  money-saving tips, 80–71, 111–12
  Munich, 305, 306–7 (map), 308
  Paris, 253–57, 254–55 (map)
  Prague, 378–79, 380–81 (map), 382
  prices, 110–12
  rating systems, 114
  reservations, 110
  Rome, 407–9, 410–11 (map)
  scams, 149
  showers, 109
  during special events, 31
  toilets, 109–10
  types of, 115–18
  using travel agents, 41–42
  Venice, 473, 474–75 (map), 476–77
  Vienna, 335, 336–37 (map), 338–39

Acropolis (Athens), 544 (map), 550

Acropolis Hill (Athens), 540, 544 (map), 550–51

Acropolis Museum (Athens), 550–51

Acuto, Giovanni, 452

Agora (Athens), 544 (map), 551–52

Airports, 48–49. *See also specific airports*

Air travel, 46–51
  airfares, 46–48

airlines, 45, 47, 55
  Web sites and telephone numbers, 567–68
  within Europe, 54–55
  jet lag, 50–51
  open-jaw tickets, 49
  package tours, 45
  seat reservations, 49
  tips on, 49–51
  worksheets, 51–53

Akademie der Bildenden Kunste (Vienna), 336 (map), 344–45

Akrotíri (Santoríni, Greece), 559–60

Alcázar (Segovia, Spain), 514–15

Alcázar (Toledo, Spain), 513

Alcoholic beverages. *See* Beer; Wine

Allegory of Spring (Botticelli), 450

Alpenzoo (Austria), 351

Alps, 6
  Austrian, 350–51
  Bavarian, 299, 317–27
  Swiss, 352–70
  gondolas, 12, 363

Alte Pinakothek (Munich), 306 (map), 313–14

Altstadt (Munich), 300–01, 303 (map), 308

Amalienburg (Munich), 315

American Express, 84, 86, 143, 151

Americas, Museum of the (Madrid), 498 (map), 507–8

583

585